50p

CHAMBERS

WORD
FILE

CHAMBERS
WORD
FILE

ROGER PREBBLE & MICK GRITTITHS
Introduction by FRANK MUIR

CHANCELLOR
PRESS

Chambers Word File
First published in 1986 in Great Britain
by Keesing International (Publishers and Printers Ltd)

Second edition 1987

This edition published in 1995 by Chancellor Press
an imprint of Reed Consumer Books Ltd
Michelin House, 81 Fulham Road, London SW3 6RB
and Auckland, Melbourne, Singapore and Toronto
© Keesing International
For sale in all countries except USA

ISBN 1 85152 853 9

A CIP catalogue record for this book is available from the British Library

Printed and bound in Great Britain by Cox & Wyman Ltd

CONTENTS

INTRODUCTION

I call nobody's bluff when I say that the English language may be – indeed, *is* – a thing of beauty and a joy for ever for many of us, but it is also, particularly for those unfortunate beings trying to speak English when it does not come naturally to them, e.g., parrots, foreigners, Radio One disc-jockeys, fraught with problems and perils.

So bizarre and irrational is our English vocabulary that a knowledge of other languages, even Latin and Greek, is not much help in trying to find out the meaning of a great many English words, even to somebody like myself who speaks English fluently, well up to O-level standard. For instance, I wonder how many readers, however deeply British, knew the meanings of more than two or three of the following useful and everyday words (well, they were useful and everyday once)?

> Bonze:*The Portuguese word for a Japanese clergyman.*
> Vives: *An equine disease of the submaxillary glands.*
> Muckluck: *An Eskimo's boot.*
> Jettatura: *The spell of the evil eye.*
> Zwanziger: *An old Austrian silver coin.*
> Bearleap: *A Tudor housewife's large shopping-basket.*
> Wapentake: *An early administrative division of Yorkshire.*

There are probably as many word fanciers like us as there are bird fanciers, yet *we* have no Royal Society for the Protection of Words, or Word Sanctuaries (affiliated to the Wildvowel Trust), and so lovely old words like those above fall by the wayside and drop out of the language. But, and it's a big but, we who love the language and enjoy messing about with it now have something immediately helpful, a guide to living English, a book, *Word File*, to nourish and sustain us in playing our little but obsessional word-games. Stuck for a 13-letter word, hyphenated, a tree, beginning TOO. . .? Page 286. There it is: TOOTHACHE-TREE. Win your Scrabble® game if there is such a thing as an 8-letter word beginning with Z? There is. Page 135, ZASTRUGA. Geographical.

You can look words up from whatever starting-point you wish – number of letters in word, subject-matter, alphabetical order. . .

So if you are reading this Preface in a bookshop, act now. Take this book over to the till immediately, pay for it, and pop it proudly into your bearleap. It's all of a Yorkshire division to an Eskimo's boot that you'll never regret it.

Frank Muir

HOW TO USE THIS BOOK

Word File is really very simple to use. In most word puzzling, both the number of letters and subject of the required word are known. For this reason, the book has been categorised systematically into main headings, most of which divide into several sub-sections. In each section all the relevant words are arranged alphabetically within lists of three to fifteen letters. So, you just check the particular subject you need in the Index, turn straight to the relevant page and zone in to the required word-length for the instant solution.

Notes

(a) Whereas standard 's' plurals are not listed, common irregular plurals (eg, FUNGI) have been included.

(b) Where any one word has two accepted spellings, both have been listed.

(c) Where abbreviated forms of words such as SAINT occur (eg, ST BERNARD), they appear strictly alphabetically.

(d) If you are looking for a particular kind of person, you must refer to PEOPLE, as they are not listed under any other heading (eg, FARMER is not in AGRICULTURE, but may be found under PEOPLE, sub-heading WORKERS).

(e) If a word is not in one list where you think it should be, it may well appear in another more specialised list (eg, RIFLE is not to be found in MILITARY TERMS, but is in WEAPONRY).

(f) Words have been duplicated in certain lists where there is an obvious overlap (eg, BAROMETER is in INSTRUMENTS & GAUGES as well as METEOROLOGY).

"Words are, of course, the most powerful drug used by mankind."

RUDYARD KIPLING
(Speech, February 14th, 1923)

AGRICULTURE

3

BED
CRU
CUB
DIP
ERF
FAN
HAY
HOE
HUT
LEA
LEY
LOY
MOW
PEG
PEN
PIT
POT
RUN
RUT
SET
SOD
STY
WAD

4

BAIL
BALE
BARN
BOMA
BRAN
BYRE
CART
COCK
COOP
CRIB
CROP
DIKE
DRAG
DUFF
DUNG
DYKE
FARM
FEED
FOLD
FORK
FRIT
GATE
HACK

HERD
HOOK
JUBE
KERF
LAND
LAWN
LOAM
LOCK
LOFT
MARL
OATS
OXER
PALE
PECK
PEST
PLOT
POST
RACK
RAKE
RICK
ROSE
ROVE
SAIL
SEAR
SEED
SEPT
SILO
SOCK
SOIL
SPAN
SPIT
SPUD
TILL
TRIP
TURF
WAIF
WAIN
WISP
YARD
YOKE

5

BAULK
BENCH
BOWER
BRAKE
BRAND
BRASH
BREED

CAVIE
CHAFF
CHUTE
CLAMP
CROFT
CRUSH
DITCH
DRAIL
DRILL
EARTH
FENCE
FIELD
FLAIL
FLOAT
FLOOR
FRAME
GLEAN
GRAFT
GRASS
GUANO
HEDGE
HUMUS
HUTCH
LEVEL
MOULD
MOWER
MULCH
NURSE
OASIS
PADDY
PLANT
PLASH
POUND
RAKER
RANCH
RANGE
REGUR
RIDGE
ROGUE
ROOST
SCRAW
SHARE
SHEAF
SHEAR
SHOCK
SHOOK
SNATH
SOLUM
SPADE
STACK
STAGE
STALL

STEAD
STILE
STOCK
STOOK
STORE
STRAW
SWARD
SWILL
TILTH
TIMBÓ
TRUSS
VERGE
YIELD

6

ANBURY
ANNUAL
APIARY
ARBOUR
BARTON
BINDER
BLIGHT
BORDER
BOTTLE
BOWERY
CLOCHE
CORRAL
CRATCH
DERRIS
DIBBER
DIBBLE
DOLLOP
EATAGE
EDDISH
EDGING
FALLOW
FANNER
FODDER
FORAGE
FURROW
GARDEN
GARNER
GO-DOWN
GROUND
HARROW
HAYING
HAYSEL
HEN-RUN
HOBBLE
HOG-PEN

HOPPER
HOTBED
HUSKER
HYBRID
INNING
KENNEL
KHARIF
LEA-RIG
LISTER
MANGER
MANURE
MARKET
MEADOW
MILKER
MOTHER
MOWING
OXGANG
OXLAND
PADANG
PALING
PARING
PEELER
PIG-BED
PIG-STY
PIPING
PLOUGH
PODSOL
POTTLE
RADDLE
RATOON
REAPER
RENNET
RICKER
RIDDLE
ROLLER
ROSERY
SCREEN
SCYTHE
SEEDER
SHEARS
SHEWEL
SHORTS
SICKLE
SILAGE
SLEDGE
SOWING
STABLE
STIRPS
TAN-BED
TAR-BOX
TEDDER
TETHER

THRASH
THRESH
TRENCH
TROUGH
TROWEL
VINERY
WEEDER
WINNOW

7

ALVEARY
BATTERY
BEDDING
BEEHIVE
BOULTER
CHANNEL
COMBINE
COMPOST
CORN-BIN
COULTER
COW-BELL
COW-SHED
CRIBBLE
CROPPER
CULTURE
CUTTING
DOVECOT
EARMARK
FARMING
FEED-LOT
FENCING
GOOSERY
GRANARY
GRAPERY
GRAZING
HARVEST
HAYBAND
HAYCOCK
HAYFORK
HAYLOFT
HAYRICK
HAYSEED
HAYWIRE
HEDGING
HEN-COOP
HENNERY
HERBARY
HOLDING
HOPPING
HOPPLES

1

AGRICULTURE

HOP-POLE
HOP-YARD
HOT WALL
HUMOGEN
HUSKING
KAINITE
KOLKHOZ
KRILIUM
LAZY-BED
LEADING
LINDANE
MARL-PIT
MILKING
MORAINE
MULTURE
NITRATE
NURSERY
NUTTING
OATCAKE
OLITORY
ORCHARD
OX-FENCE
PADDOCK
PASTURE
PENFOLD
PEONAGE
PEONISM
PERGOLA
PIGGERY
PINETUM
PINFOLD
PISCINA
PITCHER
PLANTER
PRODUCE
PRUNING
REAPING
ROCKERY
ROOTAGE
ROUND-UP
SAIL-ARM
SCUFFLE
SEED-BED
SEED-BOX
SEEDLIP
SHACKLE
SITTING
SKIMMER
SPANCEL
STADDLE
STUBBLE
SUBSOIL

SWINERY
TILLAGE
TILLING
TOPIARY
TOP-SOIL
TRACTOR
TRAILER
TRELLIS
TURFING
VENDAGE
VINTAGE
WAINAGE
WATERER
WEEDING
WINDROW

8

AGROLOGY
AGRONOMY
APHICIDE
BARN-DOOR
BARNYARD
BEANPOLE
BEE-HOUSE
BIENNIAL
BIRDBATH
BONE-DUST
BONE-MEAL
BRAN-MASH
BROODING
BULL-RING
CARUCATE
CHINAMPA
CHURNING
COMPOUND
CORNLAND
CORNLOFT
COWHOUSE
CROFTING
CROPPING
CROSSING
DRAINAGE
DOVECOTE
DUNG-CART
DUNG-FORK
DUNG-HEAP
DUNGHILL
DUNGMERE
DUTCH HOE
ELEVATOR

ENSILAGE
ESPALIER
ESTANCIA
FARMYARD
FAT-STOCK
FISH-POND
GLEANING
GRAFTING
HATCHERY
HAYFIELD
HAY KNIFE
HAYSTACK
HEADROPE
HEDGEROW
HEN-HOUSE
HOME-FARM
HORSE HOE
HOSEPIPE
HOSE-REEL
HOTHOUSE
LAND-HERD
LAND-ROLL
LEAF-CURL
LOOSE-BOX
MANURING
MÉTAIRIE
MÉTAYAGE
MUCK-RAKE
NOSE-RING
ORANGERY
OSIER BED
OUTFIELD
PALISADE
PARAQUAT
PARTERRE
PEA-STRAW
PEDIGREE
PENSTOCK
PIG'S-WASH
PIG-SWILL
PLANTING
PLANT-POT
PLASHING
PLATBAND
POMOLOGY
POT-PLANT
PRONG-HOE
RABBITRY
RANCHING
RICKYARD
ROCK-WORK
ROOT-CROP

ROSARIUM
ROTATION
ROTENONE
ROUGHAGE
RYE-STRAW
SCUFFLER
SEED-CORN
SEED-PLOT
SEED-TIME
SEPIMENT
SHEARING
SHEEP-DIP
SHEEP-PEN
SHEEP-RUN
SKIMMING
SPRAY-GUN
SPRAYING
SPREADER
STABLING
STACKING
STAMPEDE
STEADING
STOCKADE
STRICKLE
SWANNERY
SWILL-TUB
SWINE-STY
THRASHER
THRESHER
THUMBPOT
TRUSSING
VIGNERON
VINEYARD
VITICIDE
WINDFALL

9

ACARICIDE
AFTER-CROP
AFTERINGS
AFTERMATH
ALLOTMENT
APPLE-CART
ARBORETUM
BARLEYMOW
BASIC SLAG
BEESTINGS
BELL-GLASS
BIRD-TABLE
BRANDRETH

BROADCAST
COCOONERY
COLD-FRAME
COLDHOUSE
COLE-GARTH
COLUMBARY
COOL-HOUSE
CORN-BRAKE
CORNFIELD
COVER CROP
DAIRY-FARM
DEER-FENCE
DEFOLIANT
DOG-KENNEL
DROP-DRILL
DUTCH BARN
ENCLOSURE
FIELDWORK
FISH-GUANO
FLOWER-BED
FLOWERPOT
FUNGICIDE
GAMMEXANE
HARVESTER
HERBICIDE
HOP-GARDEN
HORSE-POND
HORSE RAKE
HOVEL-POST
HUSBANDRY
INCUBATOR
INTERCROP
IRRIGATOR
JACK STRAW
KLINOSTAT
LARVICIDE
LAWN-MOWER
LEAF-MOULD
LINE-FENCE
LIVESTOCK
MIDDLINGS
MILK-HOUSE
NEAT-HOUSE
NEAT-STALL
PALM-HOUSE
PASTURAGE
PEAT-STACK
PERENNIAL
PERPETUAL
PESTICIDE
PHOSPHATE
PINE-HOUSE

PITCHFORK
POTATO-PIT
QUERCETUM
RAT-POISON
REPOTTING
RICEFIELD
RICK-STAND
RICK-STICK
RING-FENCE
ROOT-HOUSE
SALICETUM
SCARECROW
SECATEURS
SEED-DRILL
SEED-FIELD
SEED-PLANT
SEPARATOR
SHEEP-COTE
SHEEPFOLD
SHEEP-HOOK
SHEEPWALK
SHEEP-WASH
SHRUBBERY
SPREADING
SPRINKLER
STACKYARD
STOCK-WHIP
STOCKYARD
STRAWYARD
SUBSOILER
SWINGTREE
TEA-GARDEN
THRASHING
THRESHING
THRUST-HOE
TRIHYBRID
TRUCK-FARM
TRUNCHEON
TURF-SPADE
UNDERSOIL
VINE-STOCK
VINTAGING
VITICETUM
WEEDICIDE
WHIP-GRAFT
WINDOW-BOX
WINNOWING
WORM-FENCE

10

AFTERGRASS
APICULTURE
BACK-GARDEN
BUSH-HARROW
CATTLE GRID
CHICKEN-RUN
CHURN-STAFF
CINDER-PATH
CROWN-GRAFT
CULTIVATOR
DEEP LITTER
DISC-HARROW
DISC-PLOUGH
DRAY-PLOUGH
DRY FARMING
EARTH-BOARD
EMBLEMENTS
EXTIRPATOR
FERTILISER
FISH-MANURE
FORCING-PIT
GARDEN PATH
GARDEN WALL
GREENHOUSE
GREENSWARD
HUSKING-BEE
INCUBATING
INCUBATION
IRRIGATION
LEY-FARMING
MEADOWLAND
MOULD-BOARD
MUCK-RAKING
MUTUAL WALL
NESTING-BOX
ORCHARDING
PADDY-FIELD
PARIS GREEN
PEASE-STRAW
PEA-TRAINER
PHEASANTRY
PLANTATION
PLOUGH-IRON
PLOUGHLAND
PLOUGH-TAIL
PLOUGH-TREE
PRODUCTION
PROPAGATOR
RADICATION
RICK-LIFTER

ROCK-GARDEN
ROOF-GARDEN
ROSE-GARDEN
SEWAGE-FARM
SHEEP-TRACK
SPRINKLING
STONE-BRASH
STRIPPINGS
STOVE-PLANT
SUBSOILING
SWINGLE-BAR
THORN-HEDGE
TOP-SOILING
WATER-GLASS
WEEDKILLER
WHEAT-FIELD
WINTER CROP

11

AFTERGROWTH
AGRARIANISM
AGRICULTURE
AGROBIOLOGY
BACILLICIDE
CHAFF-CUTTER
CHAIN-HARROW
COLUMBARIUM
COMPOST-HEAP
CRAZY PAVING
CROP-DUSTING
CROSS-TINING
CULTIVATION
DRILL-BARROW
DRILL-HARROW
DRILL-PLOUGH
EMBOWERMENT
FACTORY FARM
FLOWER-CLOCK
FRONT-GARDEN
GARDEN-GLASS
GARDEN GNOME
GARDEN PATCH
GRAFT HYBRID
GRASS-CUTTER
HAND-FEEDING
HARDY ANNUAL
HARVEST-HOME
HEAVY ROLLER
HILL-PASTURE
HORSE-LITTER

AGRICULTURE

HYDROPONICS
INGATHERING
INSECTICIDE
INSECTIFUGE
LEAF-CUTTING
LINSEED-CAKE
LINSEED-MEAL
MILKING-TIME
MOLE DRAINER
MONOCULTURE
MUSHROOMING
ORCHID-HOUSE
ORCHIDOLOGY
OSTRICH-FARM
PASTEURISER
PASTURELAND
PICKET-FENCE
PIGEON-HOUSE
PLOUGHSHARE
PLOUGH-STAFF
PLOUGH-STILT
POMICULTURE
POULTRY-FARM
POULTRY-YARD
PROPAGATION
PRUNING-BILL
PRUNING-HOOK
RABBIT-HUTCH
REAPING-HOOK
REED-DRAWING
RODENTICIDE
ROOT-PRUNING
RUBBING-POST
SERICULTURE
STEAM-PLOUGH
STOCKTAKING
STRAW-CUTTER
STUBBLE-RAKE
SWINGLETREE
SWING-PLOUGH
TANK-FARMING
TOP-DRESSING
TURFING-IRON
VERMICULITE
VINICULTURE
VITICULTURE
WATERING-CAN
WATERING-POT
WEEDING-FORK
WHEELBARROW
WHEEL-PLOUGH

WHIPPLETREE
WINE-GROWING
WIRE-NETTING
WOOL-GROWING
ZERO-GRAZING

12

AGRIBUSINESS
CONSERVATORY
CRADLE-SCYTHE
CROP-SPRAYING
FINGER-AND-TOE
FLORICULTURE
FLOWER-GARDEN
FORCING-HOUSE
GREEN FINGERS
HARVEST-FIELD
HOME-CROFTING
HORTICULTURE
HUMIFICATION
INSECT-POWDER
MARKET-GARDEN
MILKING-STOOL
MOLLUSCICIDE
ORCHARD-HOUSE
PARASITICIDE
PHYSIC GARDEN
PISCICULTURE
PRUNING-KNIFE
SHEEP-FARMING
SMALLHOLDING
STOCK-RAISING
STUBBLE-FIELD
SWINE-KEEPING
TRACE ELEMENT
TRANSHUMANCE
TRENCH-PLOUGH
TRUCK-FARMING
VERMIN-KILLER
WATER-CULTURE
WEEDING-TONGS
WHIP-GRAFTING
WINNOWING-FAN
WINTER-GARDEN

13

ARBORICULTURE

BOULTING-HUTCH
CAPRIFICATION
CARPET-BEDDING
CROSSBREEDING
CUCUMBER FRAME
DISSEMINATION
ELECTRIC FENCE
GREEN MANURING
ITALIAN GARDEN
KITCHEN-GARDEN
LAWN-SPRINKLER
MOWING-MACHINE
OSTREICULTURE
PALMIFICATION
PERSIAN POWDER
PRUNING-SHEARS
SHEEP-SHEARING
SOWING-MACHINE
STIRPICULTURE
STOCK-BREEDING
TEA-PLANTATION
THRESHING-MILL
TRANSPLANTING
WEEDING-CHISEL

14

COLLECTIVE FARM
CONTOUR FARMING
DRILL-HUSBANDRY
FACTORY FARMING
MILKING-PARLOUR
PASTEURISATION
REAPING-MACHINE
SPADE-HUSBANDRY
SUPERPHOSPHATE
THRESHING-FLOOR
VEGETABLE MOULD
WEEDING-FORCEPS

15

BORDEAUX MIXTURE
BURGUNDY MIXTURE
MARKET-GARDENING
TRANSPLANTATION
WINDOW-GARDENING

ANIMALS – BIRDS

3

AUK
COB
DAW
EMU
HEN
JAY
KEA
MAG
MAW
MEW
NUN
OWL
PEN
PIE
REE
TIT
TUI

4

BARB
BIRD
CIRL
COCK
COOT
CROW
DOVE
DUCK
ERNE
EYAS
FOWL
GUAN
GULL
HAWK
HERN
HUIA
IBIS
JACK
JYNX
KAKA
KITE
KIWI
KNOT
KORA
LARK
LOON
LORY
MINA
MONK
MULE

MYNA
PECK
PERN
PINK
POLL
RAIL
RHEA
ROOK
RUFF
RUNT
RYPE
SHAG
SKUA
SMEE
SMEW
SORA
SPOT
SWAN
TAHA
TEAL
TERN
TODY
WEKA
WREN

5

ARIEL
BOOBY
CAPON
CHICK
COLIN
CRANE
DIVER
DRAKE
DUMPY
EAGLE
EGRET
EIDER
FINCH
GALAH
GOOSE
GREBE
GRIPE
HENNY
HERON
HOBBY
HOMER
JÄGER
JUNCO
MACAW

MADGE
MANEH
MAVIS
MERLE
MURRE
MYNAH
NANDU
NELLY
NODDY
OUSEL
OUZEL
OWLET
OXEYE
PEGGY
PIPER
PIPIT
POAKA
POLLY
POULT
QUAIL
RAVEN
REEVE
ROBIN
ROTCH
SAKER
SARUS
SCAPE
SCRAY
SERIN
SHAMA
SNIPE
SOLAN
SQUAB
STARE
STINT
STORK
SWIFT
TEREK
TWITE
UMBRE
URUBU
VEERY
WADER
WAVEY

6

AMAZON
ANCONA
ARGALA
AUKLET

AVOCET
BANTAM
BARBET
BISHOP
BONXIE
BRAHMA
BUDGIE
BULBUL
CANARY
CHOUGH
CHUKOR
COCHIN
CONDOR
CORBIE
COUCAL
CUCKOO
CULVER
CURLEW
CYGNET
DARTER
DIPPER
DOPPER
DRONGO
DUCKER
DUIKER
DUNLIN
EAGLET
ELANET
FALCON
FULMAR
GAMBET
GANDER
GANNET
GARROT
GENTLE
GENTOO
GODWIT
GOONEY
GOSLET
GROUSE
HARELD
HERMIT
HOOPOE
HOUDAN
JABIRU
JACANA
KAKAPO
LANNER
LINNET
LORIOT
MAGPIE
MARTIN

MERLIN
MISSEL
MONAUL
MOPOKE
MOTMOT
MUSKET
ORIOLE
OSPREY
OX-BIRD
PARROT
PASTOR
PEA-HEN
PEEPER
PEEWIT
PETREL
PIGEON
PLOVER
POUTER
PUFFIN
PULLET
RED-CAP
REELER
ROCKER
ROLLER
RUMKIN
RUNNER
SAPPHO
SCAURY
SCOTER
SEA-COB
SEA-MEW
SEA-PIE
SHRIKE
SISKIN
SORAGE
SULTAN
TERCEL
THRUSH
TOMTIT
TOUCAN
TOWHEE
TROGON
TURBIT
TURKEY
WILLET
YAFFLE
YNAMBU
YUCKER

ANIMALS – BIRDS

7

ANT-BIRD
APTERYX
BABBLER
BARN OWL
BEE-KITE
BITTERN
BLUECAP
BLUE-EYE
BLUE JAY
BLUE-TIT
BOOBOOK
BULLBAT
BUNTING
BUSH-TIT
BUSTARD
BUZZARD
CATBIRD
CHEWINK
CHICKEN
COAL-TIT
COB-SWAN
COLIBRI
CORELLA
COTINGA
COURLIN
COURSER
COWBIRD
CRACKER
CREEPER
CROPPER
DORHAWK
DORKING
DOVEKIE
DOVELET
DUN-BIRD
DUNNOCK
EGG-BIRD
EMU-WREN
FANTAIL
FERN-OWL
FLAPPER
FLICKER
GADWALL
GOBBLER
GORCOCK
GORCROW
GOSHAWK
GOSLING
GRACKLE
GREYHEN

GREYLAG
GREY OWL
HACKLET
HALCYON
HAMBURG
HARRIER
HATCHER
HOATZIN
ICE-BIRD
JACAMAR
JACINTH
JACKDAW
JACOBIN
KAMICHI
KESTREL
KILLDEE
LAPWING
LAUGHER
LEGHORN
LICH-OWL
MALLARD
MANAKIN
MARABOU
MARTLET
MINIVET
MINORCA
MOORHEN
MUDLARK
NOCTULE
OIL-BIRD
ORTOLAN
OSTRICH
OVEN-TIT
PEACOCK
PEA-FOWL
PELICAN
PENGUIN
PINTAIL
PINNOCK
PINTADO
POCHARD
POE-BIRD
POULARD
POY-BIRD
PUTTOCK
QUETZAL
RAINBOW
REDPOLL
REDWING
ROOSTER
ROSELLA
RUDDOCK

SAKERET
SAW-BILL
SCOOPER
SEA-BIRD
SEA-CROW
SEA-DOVE
SEA-DUCK
SEA-FOWL
SEAGULL
SEA-HAWK
SEA-LARK
SERIEMA
SIRGANG
SKIMMER
SPARROW
SQUACCO
STANIEL
SUN-BIRD
SWALLOW
TANAGER
TATTLER
TINAMOU
TITLARK
TITLING
TOURACO
TUMBLER
VULTURE
VULTURN
WAGTAIL
WARBLER
WAX-BILL
WAX-WING
WHOOPER
WIDGEON
WOOD-OWL
WREN-TIT
WRYBILL
WRYNECK

8

AASVOGEL
AIGRETTE
ALCATRAS
AMADAVAD
ARAPUNGA
BALD-COOT
BALDPATE
BARNACLE
BATELEUR
BEE-EATER

BELL-BIRD
BERGHAAN
BLACKCAP
BLUEBIRD
BLUEWING
BOATBILL
BOAT-TAIL
BOBOLINK
BOB-WHITE
BRANCHER
BROWN OWL
CAGE-BIRD
CAGELING
CALL-BIRD
CAPUCHIN
CARACARA
CARGOOSE
CHURN-OWL
COCKATOO
COCK-BIRD
COCKEREL
CURASSOW
DABCHICK
DANDY-HEN
DIDAPPER
DIPCHICK
DOTTEREL
DUCKHAWK
DUCKLING
DUCKMOLE
DUNDIVER
EAGLE-OWL
FALCONET
FAUVETTE
FIRE-BACK
FIRE-BIRD
FISH-HAWK
FLAMINGO
FORKTAIL
GAME-BIRD
GAME-COCK
GAREFOWL
GARGANEY
GREENLET
GROSBEAK
GUACHARO
HACKBOLT
HANGBIRD
HANGNEST
HAWFINCH
HAZEL HEN
HEATH-HEN

HERNSHAW
HICKWALL
HORNBILL
HORSEMAN
KING-BIRD
KING-CROW
LANDRAIL
LANGSHAN
LANNERET
LORIKEET
LOVEBIRD
LYRE-BIRD
MACARONI
MAN-OF-WAR
MAORI HEN
MEGAPODE
MIRE-DRUM
MOORCOCK
MOORFOWL
MORE-PORK
MURRELET
MUSK-DUCK
MUTE SWAN
NESTLING
NIGHTJAR
NIGHT-OWL
NUTHATCH
OLD SQUAW
OVEN-BIRD
OX-PECKER
PARAKEET
PEA-CHICK
PERCOLIN
PETCHARY
PHEASANT
POORWILL
POPINJAY
PUFF-BIRD
RAIN-BIRD
RED-SHANK
REDSTART
REED-BIRD
REEDLING
REED-WREN
RICE-BIRD
RING-DOVE
RING-TAIL
ROCK-BIRD
ROCK-DOVE
ROCKETER
ROCK-LARK
SAGE-COCK

SAND-LARK
SCREAMER
SEA-EAGLE
SEA-SNIPE
SHAKE-BAG
SHELDUCK
SHOE-BILL
SILKTAIL
SKUA-GULL
SNOW-BIRD
SNOWY OWL
SONGBIRD
SORE-HAWK
STARLING
SURF-BIRD
SWIFTLET
TAPACULO
TAWNY-OWL
TELL-TALE
TERCELET
TERU-TERO
THRASHER
THRESHER
THROSTLE
TITMOUSE
TOUCANET
TRAGOPAN
TREMBLER
TROUPIAL
UMBRETTE
WATER-HEN
WHEATEAR
WHIMBREL
WHINCHAT
WHITECAP
WILD DUCK
WOOD-CHAT
WOODCOCK
WOOD-IBIS
WOODLARK
WOODWALE
WOOD-WREN
ZOPILOTE

9

ALBATROSS
ANT-THRUSH
BALD-EAGLE
BALDICOOT
BALTIMORE

BECCAFICO
BEEFEATER
BERGANDER
BLACKBIRD
BLACKCOCK
BLACKGAME
BLACKHEAD
BLACK SWAN
BLOOD-BIRD
BOWER-BIRD
BRAMBLING
BULLFINCH
CAMPANERO
CASSOWARY
CEDAR-BIRD
CHAFFINCH
CHICKADEE
CHICKLING
COAL-MOUSE
COCKATIEL
COCK-ROBIN
CORMORANT
CORNCRAKE
CROSSBILL
DANDY-COCK
DECOY-DUCK
DICKY-BIRD
EAGLE-HAWK
EIDER-DUCK
FIELDFARE
FIELD LARK
FIG-PECKER
FIRECREST
FLEDGLING
FLUTE-BIRD
FRIARBIRD
FROGMOUTH
GALLINAZO
GALLINULE
GERFALCON
GIER-EAGLE
GOLDCREST
GOLDEN-EYE
GOLDFINCH
GOOSANDER
GREY-GOOSE
GUILLEMOT
GUINEA-HEN
GYRFALCON
HEATHBIRD
HEATHCOCK
HEATH-FOWL

HEN-DRIVER
HERONSHAW
HIGH-FLIER
HONEY-BIRD
HORNED OWL
INCUBATOR
JACK-SNIPE
JENNY-WREN
KITTIWAKE
MALLEE-HEN
MALLEMUCK
MERGANSER
MEROPIDAN
MESSENGER
MIRE-SNIPE
MOUND-BIRD
NIGHT-BIRD
NIGHT-FOWL
NIGHT-HAWK
NUTJOBBER
NUTPECKER
ORPINGTON
OSSIFRAGA
OSSIFRAGE
OWL-PARROT
PADDY-BIRD
PARTRIDGE
PEREGRINE
PETAURIST
PHALAROPE
PINE-FINCH
PLUME-BIRD
PTARMIGAN
RAZOR-BILL
REDBREAST
RIFLE-BIRD
RING-OUSEL
ROCK-PIPIT
SABRE-WING
SALANGANE
SANDPIPER
SATIN-BIRD
SCALD-CROW
SCRUB-BIRD
SEA-PARROT
SEA-TURTLE
SEDGE-BIRD
SEDGE-WREN
SHELDRAKE
SHOVELLER
SKUNK-BIRD
SNAKEBIRD

SNOW-FINCH
SNOWFLAKE
SNOW-GOOSE
SOLITAIRE
SORE-EAGLE
SPOONBILL
STILT-BIRD
STINK-BIRD
STOCK-DOVE
STONECHAT
STONE-HAWK
STORM-BIRD
STORM-COCK
SWAN-GOOSE
SWART-BACK
SWORD-BILL
TALEGALLA
THICKHEAD
THICK-KNEE
TROCHILUS
TRUMPETER
TURKEY-HEN
TURNSTONE
UMBER-BIRD
WATER-BIRD
WATER-COCK
WATER-FOWL
WHALE-HEAD
WHITEHEAD
WHITEWING
WIDOW-BIRD
WILD GOOSE
WIND-HOVER
WOOD-SPITE
WYANDOTTE

10

ABERDEVINE
ANDALUSIAN
AUSTRALORP
BLUEBREAST
BLUETHROAT
BRENT-GOOSE
BRONZE-WING
BUDGERIGAR
BUFFLEHEAD
BURROW-DUCK
BUSH-SHRIKE
BUTTER-BIRD

7

ANIMALS – BIRDS

BUTTER-BUMP
CANARY-BIRD
CANVAS-BACK
CAPE PIGEON
CHIFF-CHAFF
CHITTAGONG
CROW-SHRIKE
DEMOISELLE
DICKCISSEL
DIDUNCULUS
DUNG-HUNTER
EMBER-GOOSE
FALLOW-CHAT
FLYCATCHER
FOUR-O-CLOCK
GOATSUCKER
GOONEY-BIRD
GREENFINCH
GREENSHANK
GREY PARROT
GROUND-DOVE
GUINEA-FOWL
HEATH-POULT
HEN-HARRIER
HERALD-DUCK
HONEY-EATER
HONEY-GUIDE
HOODED CROW
INDIGO BIRD
JUNGLE FOWL
KINGFISHER
KOOKABURRA
MALLEE-BIRD
MALLE-FOWL
MEADOW-LARK
MISSEL-BIRD
MOTH-HUNTER
MUTTON-BIRD
NIGHT-CHURR
NIGHT-HERON
NUTCRACKER
PARSON-BIRD
PETTICHAPS
PICK-CHEESE
PIPING CROW
POLL-PARROT
PRAIRIE-HEN
PRATINCOLE
QUAKER-BIRD
RACKET-TAIL
RAFTER-BIRD
RAIN-PLOVER

REED-THRUSH
REGENT-BIRD
RING-PLOVER
ROAD-RUNNER
ROCK-HOPPER
ROCK-PIGEON
RUBY-THROAT
RUNNER-DUCK
SADDLEBACK
SAGE-GROUSE
SAND-GROUSE
SAND-MARTIN
SCOTER DUCK
SCREECH-OWL
SEA-SWALLOW
SHEARWATER
SICKLE-BILL
SOLAN GOOSE
SONG-THRUSH
SORE-FALCON
SPIRIT-DUCK
STONE-SNIPE
SUN-BITTERN
TAILOR-BIRD
TROPIC-BIRD
TURKEY-COCK
TURTLE-DOVE
TYRANT-BIRD
VELVET-DUCK
WATER-OUSEL
WATTLE-BIRD
WEASEL-COOT
WEAVER-BIRD
WHISKY-JOHN
WHYDAH-BIRD
WILLOW-WREN
WONGA-WONGA
WOOD-GROUSE
WOODPECKER
WOOD-PIGEON
WOOD-THRUSH
YELLOW-BIRD
ZEBRA-FINCH

11

BLACKGROUSE
BRUSH-TURKEY
BUFFALO-BIRD
BUTCHER-BIRD
CARRION-CROW

CHANTICLEER
CIRL BUNTING
COCK-SPARROW
DRAGOON-BIRD
FALLOW-FINCH
FRIGATE BIRD
GAME-CHICKEN
GOLDEN EAGLE
GREEN LINNET
GROUND-ROBIN
HAZEL GROUSE
HERRING-GULL
HONEY-SUCKER
HUMMING-BIRD
JAVA SPARROW
KING-PENGUIN
KING-VULTURE
LAMMERGEIER
LAMMERGEYER
LEATHER-HEAD
MOCKING-BIRD
MOOR-BUZZARD
MUSCOVY-DUCK
NIGHTINGALE
PURPLE FINCH
REED-BUNTING
REED-SPARROW
REED-WARBLER
ROCK-SPARROW
ROYSTON CROW
SCISSOR-BILL
SCISSOR-TAIL
SCREECH-HAWK
SCRUB-TURKEY
SEA-DOTTEREL
SHELL-PARROT
SINGING-BIRD
SNOW-BUNTING
SONG-SPARROW
SPANISH FOWL
SPARROW-HAWK
STILT-PLOVER
STONE-CURLEW
STONE-FALCON
STONE-PLOVER
STORM-PETREL
SWALLOW-TAIL
TREE-CREEPER
WHITETHROAT
WOOD-SWALLOW
WOOD-WARBLER

8

12

BRAMBLE-FINCH
BRONZE-PIGEON
BURROWING-OWL
CAPERCAILLIE
CARDINAL-BIRD
COAL-TITMOUSE
COW BLACKBIRD
DRONGO-CUCKOO
DRONGO-SHRIKE
FALCON-GENTLE
FIGHTING COCK
GOLDEN PLOVER
GROUND-CUCKOO
GROUND-PIGEON
HEDGE-SPARROW
HEDGE-WARBLER
HOMING PIGEON
HONEY-BUZZARD
INDIAN RUNNER
MAN-OF-WAR-BIRD
MANDARIN DUCK
MARSH-HARRIER
MISSEL-THRUSH
MOUND-BUILDER
PAINTED SNIPE
PLYMOUTH ROCK
REED-PHEASANT
RIFLEMAN-BIRD
RING-DOTTEREL
SAGE-THRASHER
SAPPHIRE-WING
SEDGE-WARBLER

SERPENT-EATER
STANDARD-WING
STORMY-PETREL
TERCEL-JERKIN
THROSTLE-COCK
UMBRELLA-BIRD
VELVET-SCOTER
WATER-WAGTAIL
WHIP-POOR-WILL
WILLOW-GROUSE
YELLOW-HAMMER

13

ARGUS PHEASANT
BARNACLE-GOOSE
BOATSWAIN-BIRD
BUFF ORPINGTON
CARRIER-PIGEON
CHAPARRAL COCK
COACHWHIP-BIRD
COCK-OF-THE-ROCK
CROCODILE BIRD
CUTHBERT'S DUCK
HARLEQUIN DUCK
HEDGE-ACCENTOR
ICELAND FALCON
OYSTER-CATCHER
PLANTAIN-EATER
SCREECH-MARTIN
SCREECH-THRUSH
SECRETARY-BIRD
SHELL-PARAKEET

TURKEY-BUZZARD
WILLOW-WARBLER
WOOD-SANDPIPER
YELLOW-BUNTING
ZEBRA-PARAKEET

14

BABBLING THRUSH
BIRD-OF-PARADISE
BRAIN-FEVER BIRD
CHIMNEY-SWALLOW
EMPEROR PENGUIN
GOLDEN PHEASANT
GRIFFON VULTURE
PRAIRIE-CHICKEN
RHINOCEROS-BIRD
RHODE ISLAND RED
SATIN BOWER-BIRD
SILVER PHEASANT
SKUNK-BLACKBIRD

15

BALTIMORE ORIOLE
DARTFORD WARBLER
FIRE-CRESTED WREN
GOLD-CRESTED WREN
LAUGHING-JACKASS
PEACOCK-PHEASANT
PEREGRINE FALCON

ANIMALS – DEER

3	4		5		6	
		KUDU		MOOSE		IMPALA
		MUSK		ORIBI		INYALA
BOK	AXIS	ORYX	ADDAX	ROYAL	BOSBOK	KOODOO
DOE	BUCK	SIKA	BONGO	SABLE	CABRIE	NILGAI
ELK	DEER	STAG	ELAND	SAIGA	CHITAL	NILGAU
GNU	FAWN	THAR	GORAL	SASIN	DIK-DIK	PALLAH
KOB	HART		KAAMA	SEROW	DUIKER	REEBOK
ROE	HIND		MHORR		DZEREN	SAMBAR

9

ANIMALS – DEER

SAMBUR
WAPITI

7

BLAUBOK
BLESBOK
CARIBOU
CHAMOIS
CHIKARA
DEERLET
GAZELLE
GEMSBOK
GRYSBOK
HOG-DEER
KNOBBER
MADOQUA
MUNTJAC
MUNTJAK
RED-DEER
ROEBUCK
ROE-DEER
SPITTER
TRAGULE

8

ANTELOPE
BLUE-BUCK
BONTEBOK
BUSH-BUCK
CARIACOU
MULE-DEER
MUSK-DEER
PALEBUCK
REINDEER
STEENBOK
STEINBOK

9

BLACKBUCK
MOUSE-DEER
PRONGBUCK
PRONGHORN
SPRINGBOK
WATER-BUCK
WATER-DEER

10

CHEVROTAIN
FALLOW DEER
HARTEBEEST
OX-ANTELOPE
SPRINGBUCK
WILDEBEEST

11

BARKING DEER
JUMPING-DEER

12

GOAT-ANTELOPE
KLIPSPRINGER

13

SABLE ANTELOPE

ANIMALS – DOGS

3

CUR
DOG
POM
PUG
PUP

4

CHOW
DIEB
LYAM
MUTT
PEKE
SKYE

5

BITCH
BOXER
BRACH
CAIRN
CORGI
DHOLE
DINGO
HOUND
HUSKY
LAIKA
POOCH
PUPPY
RACHE
SPITZ
WHELP

6

BANDOG
BARKER
BASSET
BEAGLE
BORZOI
BOWWOW
BRIARD
CANINE
COCKER
COLLIE
GUN-DOG
JACKAL
JOWLER
LAPDOG
POODLE

PUG-DOG
PYE-DOG
RANGER
RATTER
SALUKI
SCOTTY
SETTER
TECKEL
TOY DOG
TUFTER
YAPPER
YELPER

7

BASENJI

BIRD-DOG
BOBTAIL
BRACHET
BULLDOG
BULL-PUP
CLUMBER
GRIFFON
HARRIER
LURCHER
MASTIFF
MONGREL
POINTER
SAMOYED
SAPLING
SHIH TZU
SPANIEL
STARTER

TERRIER
VOLPINO
WHIPPET
WILD DOG
WOLF-DOG

8

ALSATIAN
BLENHEIM
CHOW-CHOW
COACHDOG
ELKHOUND
FOXHOUND
GUIDE DOG
HOUSE-DOG
HYENA-DOG
KEESHOND
LABRADOR
LONG-TAIL
MALEMUTE
PAPILLON
PEKINESE
PINSCHER
PUPPY-DOG
SEALYHAM
SHEEPDOG
SPRINGER
WARRAGAL
WATCH-DOG
WATER-DOG
WIRE-HAIR

9

BADGER-DOG
BOARHOUND
BUCKHOUND
CHIHUAHUA
DACHSHUND
DALMATIAN
DEER-HOUND
DOBERMANN
DRAGHOUND
ESKIMO DOG
GAZE-HOUND

GREAT DANE
GREYHOUND
HARLEQUIN
KERRY BLUE
LHASA APSO
LYAM-HOUND
PARIAH DOG
PEKINGESE
POLICE-DOG
POODLE-DOG
RED SETTER
RETRIEVER
RIDGEBACK
SCHNAUZER
STAGHOUND
ST BERNARD
TOY POODLE
WOLFHOUND
YELLOW-DOG

10

BEDLINGTON
BLOODHOUND
FOX-TERRIER
ICELAND-DOG
MALTESE DOG
OTTER-HOUND
POMERANIAN
RACCOON-DOG
ROTTWEILER
SCHIPPERKE
SPOTTED DOG
TOY SPANIEL
TRACKER-DOG
TRUFFLE-DOG
WORKING DOG

11

AFGHAN HOUND
BASSET-HOUND
BLACK-AND-TAN
BULL-MASTIFF
BULL-TERRIER
CARRIAGE DOG

JACK RUSSELL
LAND-SPANIEL
SLEUTH-HOUND
TIBETAN APSO

12

BORDER COLLIE
CAIRN TERRIER
FIELD-SPANIEL
IRISH TERRIER
NEWFOUNDLAND
WATER-SPANIEL

13

AFFENPINSCHER
BEARDED COLLIE
BOSTON TERRIER
COCKER SPANIEL
DANDIE DINMONT
LION'S PROVIDER
SCOTCH TERRIER
ST BERNARD'S DOG
SUSSEX SPANIEL

14

CLUMBER SPANIEL
IRISH WOLFHOUND
TIBETAN TERRIER

15

ABERDEEN TERRIER
AIREDALE TERRIER
BLENHEIM SPANIEL
BRUSSELS GRIFFON
GOLDEN RETRIEVER
NORFOLK SPRINGER
SEALYHAM TERRIER
SPRINGER SPANIEL

ANIMALS – FISH, SEALS & CETACEANS

3

BAR
BIB
COD
DAB
EEL
GAR
HAG
IDE
LOB
ORC
RAY
TAI

4

BASS
BLAY
BRIT
BUTT
CARP
CHAD
CHAR
CHUB
CHUM
CLAM
COHO
CRAB
CUSK
DACE
DORY
DRUM
FISH
GOBY
GRIG
HAKE
HUSO
JACK
KELT
KETA
LANT
LING
LUCE
LUMP
MAID
MASU
MORT
OPAH
ORFE
PARR

PAUA
PEAL
PIKE
PINK
POPE
POUT
RUDD
RUFF
SALP
SCAD
SCAR
SCUP
SEAL
SHAD
SILD
SLUG
SOLE
TANG
TOPE
TUNA

5

ABLET
BLAIN
BLEAK
BREAM
BRILL
CISCO
COBIA
COLEY
CONCH
DORAD
DORIS
DORSE
ELOPS
ELVER
FLUKE
GAPER
GIBEL
GRUNT
GUPPY
HYDRA
LAKER
LOACH
LYTHE
MANTA
MONAD
MORAY
MORSE
NERKA

NURSE
OLIVE
ORMER
OTARY
PERAI
PERCH
PHOEA
PIPER
POGGE
POLYP
PORGY
POULP
POWAN
PRAWN
ROACH
ROKER
SAURY
SEPIA
SEWIN
SHARK
SKATE
SMELT
SMOLT
SNOEK
SNOOK
SPECK
SPRAT
SQUID
TENCH
TOGUE
TORSK
TROUT
TUNNY
WHALE
WHELK
WHIFF
WITCH

6

ALEVIN
ALLICE
BAGGIT
BALLAN
BARBEL
BEAGLE
BELUGA
BLENNY
BONITO
BOUNCE

BOWFIN
BRAISE
BRASSY
BURBOT
CARIBE
CHEVEN
COCKLE
COMBER
CONGER
CONNER
COWRIE
CUTTLE
CYPRID
DARTER
DIPNOI
DOCTOR
DORADO
DUGONG
DUN-COW
ELLOPS
FINNER
FOGASH
GANOID
GORAMY
GRILSE
GUNNEL
GURNET
HASSAR
LAUNCE
LIGGER
LIMPET
MAIGRE
MARLIN
MEDUSA
MEGRIM
MILTER
MINNOW
MORGAY
MUD-CAT
MULLET
MUSSEL
NATIVE
NEREID
NERITE
OYSTER
PALOLO
PLAICE
POLLAN
POLYPE
QUAHOG
REDEYE
REMORA

ROBALO
SALMON
SAMLET
SANDER
SARDEL
SAUGER
SAUREL
SCAMPI
SCAMPO
SEA-APE
SEA-BAT
SEA-BUN
SEA-CAT
SEA-COW
SEA-DOG
SEA-EAR
SEA-EEL
SEA-EGG
SEA-FOX
SEA-MAT
SEA-OWL
SEA-PIG
SEEDER
SEPHEN
SHANNY
SHINER
SHRIMP
SPONGE
SQUILL
STROMB
SUCKER
TARPON
TAUTOG
TURBOT
TWAITE
URCHIN
VOLUTE
WALRUS
WEEVER
WINKLE
WRASSE
YAPOCK
ZINGEL

7

ABALONE
ACALEPH
ACTINIA
ALEWIFE
ANCHOVY

ASTERID
AZURINE
BERGYLT
BLUBBER
BLUECAP
BUMMALO
CAPELIN
CATFISH
CAVALLY
CESTOID
CICHLID
CLUPEID
CODFISH
CODLING
COPEPOD
COTTOID
COWFISH
CRUCIAN
DOG-CRAB
DOGFISH
DOLPHIN
DUN-FISH
ECHINUS
EELPOUT
ESCOLAR
FANTAIL
FIDDLER
FINBACK
FINNOCK
FUR-SEAL
GARFISH
GARPIKE
GOLDEYE
GOURAMI
GRAMPUS
GRIBBLE
GROUPER
GROWLER
GRUNTER
GUDGEON
GURNARD
GWYNIAD
HADDOCK
HAGFISH
HALIBUT
HERLING
HERRING
HIRLING
HOG-FISH
HOMELYN
HYDROID
JEWFISH

12

LAMPERN
LAMPREY
LOBSTER
LUBFISH
MAHSEER
MANATEE
MEDUSAN
MOLLUSC
MONAXON
MONODON
MOONEYE
MORRHUA
MURAENA
NARWHAL
OAR-FISH
OCTOPUS
OSSETER
PANDORE
PEA-CRAB
PENTACT
PIDDOCK
PIG-FISH
PINFISH
PIRANHA
POLLACK
POMFRET
POMPANO
PORIFER
POUTING
QUINNAT
ROCK-COD
RORQUAL
ROTIFER
SADDLER
SAND-EEL
SARDINE
SAW-FISH
SCALLOP
SCULPIN
SEA-BASS
SEA-CALF
SEA-COCK
SEA-DACE
SEA-FISH
SEA-HARE
SEA-LION
SEA-MOSS
SEA-PIKE
SEA-SLUG
SEA-STAR
SEA-WIFE
SEA-WOLF

SEA-WORM
SHEDDER
SKEGGER
SKIPPER
SNAPPER
SOCKEYE
SPAWNER
SPONDYL
SPOUTER
STARLET
STERLET
SUN-FISH
TADPOLE
TIDDLER
TITLING
TOHEROA
TOP-KNOT
TORGOCH
TREPANG
TUBFISH
VENDACE
WALL-EYE
WHITING
WIDE-GAB

8

ALBACORE
ALBICORE
ARAPAIMA
ARK-SHELL
ASCIDIAN
ASTEROID
ATHERINE
BACHELOR
BAND-FISH
BARNACLE
BEAR'S-EAR
BLUEBACK
BLUEFISH
BOARFISH
BONY PIKE
BRISLING
BUCKLING
BULLHEAD
CACHALOT
CALAMARY
CORKWING
COW-PILOT
CRAWFISH
CRAYFISH
DEALFISH

DEER-HORN
DOG-WHELK
DRAGONET
DRUMFISH
EAGLE-RAY
EAR-SHELL
ECHINOID
ESCALLOP
EULACHON
FILE-FISH
FIN-WHALE
FLAT-FISH
FLOUNDER
FOULFISH
FOUR-EYES
FOX-SHARK
FROGFISH
GILLAROO
GILT-HEAD
GOATFISH
GOLDFISH
GRAYLING
GREYFISH
HAIR-SEAL
HAIR-TAIL
HALF-BEAK
HALICORE
HARDHEAD
HARP-SEAL
HORNBEAK
HORN-POUT
HUMPBACK
HYDRANTH
KABELJOU
KING-CRAB
KINGFISH
LAMANTIN
LANCELET
LAND-CRAB
LEMON-DAB
LIMNAEID
LUMPFISH
LUNG-FISH
MACKEREL
MEDUSOID
MENHADEN
MILLIONS
MONK-FISH
MONK-SEAL
MOON-FISH
MORAY-EEL
NAUTILUS

NINE-EYES
OPHIURID
OSTRACOD
PENNY-DOG
PHYSETER
PICKEREL
PILCHARD
PIPE-FISH
PIRARUCU
POLLIWOG
POLYAXON
PORPOISE
RED-BELLY
RHINODON
ROCK-COOK
ROCK-FISH
ROCKLING
RONCADOR
ROSE-FISH
SAIBLING
SAIL-FISH
SALMONET
SALMONID
SANDLING
SAND-STAR
SAW-SHARK
SCARFISH
SEA-ACORN
SEA-ADDER
SEA-BREAM
SEA-DEVIL
SEA-EAGLE
SEAHORSE
SEA-HOUND
SEA-JELLY
SEA-LEMON
SEA-LOACH
SEA-LUNGS
SEA-MOUSE
SEA-PERCH
SEA-ROBIN
SEA-SNAIL
SEA-SNAKE
SEA-SNIPE
SEA-SWINE
SEA-TROUT
SEECATCH
SEED-FISH
SERRANID
SHIP-WORM
SILUROID
SKIPJACK

SMEAR-DAB
SNAKE-EEL
STARFISH
STING-RAY
STURGEON
SURF-FISH
TARWHINE
THRESHER
TILEFISH
TOAD-FISH
TOP-SHELL
TREVALLY
TRIDACNA
TROUTLET
WHITLING
WOLF-FISH

9

AMBER-FISH
AMPHIOXUS
ANGEL-FISH
BARRACUDA
BATHYBIUS
BLACK BASS
BLACKFISH
BLINDFISH
BLUE WHALE
BRANDLING
BULL-TROUT
CHAVENDER
CIRRIPEDE
CONE SHELL
CONGER-EEL
CORAL-FISH
CORYPHENE
CRAB-EATER
CRAMP-FISH
CROSSFISH
DATE-SHELL
DEVIL-FISH
DOG-SALMON
EAR-COCKLE
FISH-LOUSE
GASPEREAU
GLASS-ROPE
GLOBE-FISH
GOLDFINNY
GOLDSINNY
GOLOMYNKA
GOOSE-FISH

ANIMALS – FISH, SEALS & CETACEANS

GREEN-BONE
HARP-SHELL
HORNWRACK
HORNYHEAD
HORSE-FOOT
HOTTENTOT
HOUND-FISH
HYALONEMA
JACULATOR
JELLYFISH
LAMP-SHELL
LANGOUSTE
LEMON-SOLE
MENOMINEE
MIDAS'S EAR
MILLEPORE
MUD-MINNOW
NOCTILUCA
OPHIUROID
PIKE-PERCH
PILOT-FISH
POND-SNAIL
PORBEAGLE
PORWIGGLE
RAZOR-BACK
RAZOR-CLAM
RAZOR-FISH
RED MULLET
ROCK-BORER
ROCK-PERCH
ROUND-FISH
SAIL-FLUKE
SALLEE-MAN
SAND-PRIDE
SAND-SCREW
SCALDFISH
SCALE-FISH
SEA-CANARY
SEA-DRAGON
SEA-LAWYER
SEA-NETTLE
SEA-ORANGE
SEA-SALMON
SEA-SLEEVE
SEA-SPIDER
SEA-SQUIRT
SEA-URCHIN
SHEAT-FISH
SHORE-CRAB
SMOOTH DAB
SNAIL-FISH
SNIPE-FISH

SOLENETTE
SPEARFISH
SPIKE-FISH
STINGAREE
STING-BULL
STING-FISH
SURMULLET
SWINE-FISH
SWORDFISH
SWORD-TAIL
THORNBACK
TROUTLING
TRUMPETER
TRUNK-FISH
TURBINATE
TUSK-SHELL
WHALE-CALF
WHITEBAIT
WHITEBASS
WHITEFISH
WHORE'S-EGG
WING-SHELL
WING-SNAIL

10

ACORN-SHELL
AMBLYOPSIS
ARCHER-FISH
AUGER-SHELL
BARRAMUNDA
BÊCHE-DE-MER
BITTERLING
BOMBAY DUCK
BOTTLE-FISH
BOTTLE-HEAD
BOTTLE-NOSE
BOTTOM-FISH
BROWN TROUT
BUTTER-FISH
CAMEO-SHELL
CANDLE-FISH
CESTRACION
COELACANTH
COFFER-FISH
COPPER-WORM
CRAIG-FLUKE
CTENOPHORE
CUTTLEFISH
CYCLOSTOME
DEMOISELLE

DOCTOR-FISH
DRAGON-FISH
ECHINODERM
FINGERLING
FLUTEMOUTH
FLYING FISH
GROUNDLING
HAMMER-FISH
HAMMERHEAD
HEART SHELL
HERMIT-CRAB
HYDROPOLYP
KING-SALMON
LAKE-LAWYER
LOGGERHEAD
LUMPSUCKER
MILLER'S DOG
MITRE-SHELL
MITTEN-CRAB
MOSSBUNKER
MUD-SKIPPER
NEEDLE-FISH
NETTLE-FISH
NIGGER-HEAD
NURSEHOUND
PARROT-FISH
PERIWINKLE
PILOT-WHALE
PLANOBLAST
PURPLE-FISH
PYCNOGONID
RABBIT-FISH
RAZOR-SHELL
RIBBON-SEAL
RIGHT-WHALE
ROBBER-CRAB
ROCK-SALMON
ROCK-TURBOT
ROUGH-HOUND
RUDDER-FISH
SACRED FISH
SADDLEBACK
SAND-DOLLAR
SAND-HOPPER
SAND-LAUNCE
SAND-SUCKER
SCRAG-WHALE
SEA-ANEMONE
SEA-BLUBBER
SEA-LEOPARD
SEA-POACHER
SEA-SERPENT

SEA-SURGEON
SEA-SWALLOW
SEA-UNICORN
SHEEP'S-HEAD
SHIP-HOLDER
SHOVEL-HEAD
SILVER-FISH
SIPUNCULID
SLEEVE-FISH
SPATANGOID
SPERM-WHALE
SPIDER-CRAB
SQUETEAGUE
STONE-BORER
SWAN-MUSSEL
TIGER-SHARK
TOOTH-SHELL
TOWER-SHELL
TUBULARIAN
TWAITE SHAD
VELVET-CRAB
VENUS-SHELL
WENTLETRAP
WHALE-SHARK
WHITE WHALE
XIPHOSURAN
XYLOPHAGAN

11

BELLOWS-FISH
BRINE-SHRIMP
BRITTLE-STAR
BUBBLE-SHELL
CAAING WHALE
CALLING-CRAB
DISCOPHORAN
DOLLY VARDEN
ELECTRIC EEL
ELECTRIC RAY
EURYPHARYNX
FIDDLER CRAB
FISHING-FROG
FLYING SQUID
HEART COCKLE
HEART URCHIN
HELMET-SHELL
HIPPOCAMPUS
HOLOTHURIAN
HORSE MUSSEL
KILLER WHALE

14

LAKE-HERRING
LEATHER-BACK
LEPIDOSIREN
MUSSEL-SHELL
NEMATOPHORE
OXYRHYNCHUS
PEACOCK-FISH
PEARL-MUSSEL
PEARL-OYSTER
PELICAN-FISH
PLUMULARIAN
PRICKLEBACK
REEF-BUILDER
RIVER-MUSSEL
ROCK-LOBSTER
SALMON-TROUT
SAND-SKIPPER
SEA-CRAWFISH
SEA-CRAYFISH
SEA-CUCUMBER
SEA-ELEPHANT
SEA-HEDGEHOG
SEA-SCORPION
SERPENT-STAR
SIPUNCULOID
SOCIAL WHALE
SOLDIER-CRAB
SPECTRE-CRAB
STICKLEBACK
SUCKING-FISH
SURGEON-FISH
TROUGH-SHELL
TRUMPET-FISH
WALKING-FISH
WHISTLE-FISH
WHITING-POUT

12

BALLANWRASSE
BASKING SHARK
COELENTERATE
DISCOMEDUSAN
ELEPHANT SEAL
FATHER-LASHER
FIGHTING FISH
GOLDEN SALMON
GROUND-FEEDER
MANTIS SHRIMP
MILLER'S-THUMB
MOUTH-BREEDER
PARADISE FISH
PARROT-WRASSE
PELICAN'S-FOOT
RAINBOW-TROUT
SAUCEPAN-FISH
SCABBARD-FISH
SCORPION-FISH
SEA-BUTTERFLY
SEA-PORCUPINE
SENTINEL CRAB
SERGEANT-FISH
SILVER SALMON
SPECTRE-SHRIMP
SPINDLE-SHELL
SPINY LOBSTER
TRUMPET-SHELL
UNICORN-SHELL
UNICORN-WHALE
VENUS'S GIRDLE

13

BURNETT SALMON
BUTTERFLY-FISH
DOG-PERIWINKLE
HEXACTINELLID
HORSE MACKEREL
KEYHOLE-LIMPET
LEATHER-JACKET
MACKEREL-GUIDE
MACKEREL-MIDGE
MACKEREL-SHARK
MERMAID'S-GLOVE
NORWAY HADDOCK
NORWAY LOBSTER
PILGRIM'S SHELL
SEA-GOOSEBERRY
SLIPPER LIMPET
THRESHER-SHARK
THRESHER-WHALE
VELVET-FIDDLER

14

SKELETON-SHRIMP

15

CROSSOPTERYGIAN
HAMMERHEAD SHARK
WHEEL ANIMALCULE

ANIMALS – GENERAL LAND ANIMALS

3	CUB	HOB	RAM	**4**	BOAR	EURO	JOEY	MOLE
	DAM	HOG	SOW		BUCK	EYRA	LAMB	NEAT
BAT	DOE	KID	YAK	ANOA	BULL	GAUR	LION	OONT
CAT	EWE	KIT	ZHO	ATOK	CALF	GOAT	LYNX	PACO
COW	FOX	PIG		BEAR	COON	IBEX	MINK	PEBA

15

ANIMALS –

PUMA
STOT
TAHR
TAIT
TANA
UNAU
URVA
WOLF
ZEBU
ZOBO

TAYRA
TIGER
TIGON
URIAL
VISON
ZERDA
ZHOMO
ZIBET
ZORIL
ZORRO

5

BALOO
BISON
CAMEL
CIVET
COATI
FITCH
FOSSA
GAYAL
GENET
HIPPO
HYENA
IZARD
KOALA
LIGER
LLAMA
MANIS
MANUL
OKAPI
OTTER
OUNCE
PANDA
PEKAN
PIGGY
RASSE
RATEL
RHINO
SABLE
SHEEP
SHOAT
SHREW
SKUNK
SLOTH
STIRK
STOAT
SWINE
TAKIN
TAPIR
TATOU

6

ALPACA
ANGORA
AOUDAD
ARGALI
BADGER
BHARAL
BOBCAT
COUGAR
COYOTE
CUS-CUS
DESMAN
ERMINE
FENNEC
FERRET
FOX-BAT
GRISON
HEIFER
JAGUAR
KALONG
KITTEN
MARGAY
MARTEN
MUSANG
MUSK-OX
OCELOT
OVIBOS
PIGLET
PORKER
POSSUM
RACOON
SERVAL
TELEDU
TENREC
VICUÑA
WEASEL
WOMBAT

7

ANT-BEAR
BANTENG
BEARCAT
BIGHORN
BLUE FOX
BRUSHER
BUFFALO
BULLOCK
BULL-PUP
BUSHCAT
CARACAL
CATTABU
CATTALO
CHEETAH
COW-CALF
ECHIDNA
FITCHET
FOUMART
GIRAFFE
GLUTTON
GRIZZLY
GUANACO
KEITLOA
KIDLING
LEOPARD
LINSANG
LIONESS
MARKHOR
MARMOSE
MEERKAT
MINIVER
NANDINE
OPOSSUM
PALM-CAT
PANTHER
PECCARY
PIG-DEER
PIGLING
POLECAT
RACCOON
SEA-BEAR
SOUNDER
SUN-BEAR
TIGRESS
WALLABY
WART-HOG
WILD CAT
ZAMOUSE

8

AARDVARK
AARDWOLF
ANT-EATER
BACTRIAN
BANGTAIL
BANXRING
BLACK-CAT
BLACK-FOX
BONASSUS
BULL-CALF
CACOMIXL
CARCAJOU
CAVICORN
DUCKBILL
EARTH-HOG
ELEPHANT
FRUIT-BAT
GOATLING
GREY WOLF
KANGAROO
KINKAJOU
LAMBLING
MONGOOSE
PANGOLIN
PLATYPUS
PORKLING
RINGTAIL
RIVER-HOG
SAPI-UTAN
SELADANG
SEROTINE
STAR-NOSE
STINKARD
SURICATE
TAMANDUA
TAMANOIR
TIGER-CAT
TODDY-CAT
WALLAROO
WILD BOAR
WOLFLING

9

ARMADILLO
BINTURONG
BLUE SHEEP
BROWN BEAR
CATAMOUNT

DELUNDUNG
DROMEDARY
EARTHWOLF
FLYING-FOX
GROUND-HOG
HAWKSBILL
HONEY-BEAR
ICHNEUMON
KOALA BEAR
MUSK-SHEEP
MUSK-SHREW
MUSTELINE
PADEMELON
PALM-CIVET
PHALANGER
POLAR BEAR
REARMOUSE
SAPI-OUTAN
SILVER-FOX
SLOTH-BEAR
STEERLING
THYLACINE
TIGER-WOLF
TREE-SHREW
WATER-MOLE
WEASEL-CAT
WHITE-BEAR
WOLVERENE
WOLVERINE
WOOD-SHOCK

10

BABIROUSSA
CACOMISTLE
CAMELOPARD
COATI-MUNDI
FREEMARTIN
GIANT PANDA
GOLDEN MOLE
HONEY-MOUSE
JAGUARUNDI
LEOPARD-CAT
LEOPARDESS
MEXICAN HOG
NOTORYCTES
OTTER-SHREW
PANTHERESS
PARADOXURE
PICHICIAGO
PINE-MARTEN

RHINOCEROS
RIVER-HORSE
SHREW-MOUSE
SPECTRE BAT
TIMBER-WOLF
VAMPIRE-BAT

11

BARBASTELLE
BEECH-MARTEN
GRIZZLY BEAR
HONEY-BADGER
MOUNTAIN-CAT
PIPISTRELLE
PRAIRIE-WOLF
SNOW-LEOPARD
STONE-MARTEN

12

CATAMOUNTAIN
CINNAMON-BEAR
FLITTER-MOUSE
HIPPOPOTAMUS
MOUNTAIN-GOAT
MOUNTAIN-LION
SERPENT-EATER
TREE-KANGAROO
WATER-BUFFALO

13

BRUSH-KANGAROO
MOUNTAIN-SHEEP
SQUIRREL-SHREW
STAR-NOSED MOLE

TASMANIAN WOLF

14

CLOUDED LEOPARD
HUNTING LEOPARD
STINKING BADGER
TASMANIAN DEVIL
VULPINE OPOSSUM

15

BLACK RHINOCEROS
FLYING-PHALANGER
WHITE RHINOCEROS
▬▬▬▬▬▬▬▬▬

ANIMALS – HORSES

3	PLUG	PUNCH	KICKER	COACHER	**8**
ASS	PONY	SCREW	LEADER	COURSER	BATHORSE
BAY	ROAN	STEED	LEAPER	GELDING	BRANCARD
COB	SIRE	WALER	MAIDEN	HEMIONE	COCKTAIL
DUN	ZEBU	ZEBRA	ONAGER	HOBBLER	GALLOPER
NAG			PAD-NAG	JACKASS	GALLOWAY
RIP	**5**	**6**	POSTER	KNACKER	HEMIONUS
	BIDET	BAYARD	RACKER	MUSTANG	HUNTRESS
	BURRO	BRONCO	RINGER	PALFREY	LED HORSE
4	CAPLE	BRUMBY	ROARER	PIEBALD	PACK-MULE
ARAB	FILLY	CANUCK	SORREL	PIT-PONY	PAD-HORSE
COLT	HINNY	CAYUSE	STAGER	PRANCER	PALOMINO
FOAL	HOBBY	CHASER	STAYER	RUNAWAY	ROADSTER
GREY	HORSE	DONKEY	SUMMER	SHAFTER	SCHIMMEL
HACK	JENNY	ENTIRE	TANGUN	SHELTIE	SKEWBALD
HOSS	KIANG	GARRON	TATTOO	SPANKER	STALLION
JACK	KULAN	GEE-GEE	TRACER	SUMPTER	WAR-HORSE
JADE	MOUNT	HOGGET	VANNER	SWINGER	WARRAGAL
MARE	PACER	HUNTER		THILLER	YEARLING
MOKE	PINTO	JENNET	**7**	TROTTER	ZEBRINNY
MULE	PIPER	JIBBER	CHARGER	WILD ASS	
				ZEBRASS	
				ZEBRULE	

17

ANIMALS – HORSES

9

CART-HORSE
COCK-HORSE
DRAY-HORSE
DZIGGETAI
FORE-HORSE
MALT-HORSE
MILL-HORSE
PACK-HORSE
PERCHERON
POSTHORSE
RACEHORSE
STUD-HORSE

RACKABONES
SHAFT-HORSE
SHIRE-HORSE
STAGE-HORSE
STONEHORSE
THILL-HORSE
TRACE-HORSE
TROOP-HORSE
WHEEL-HORSE

11

HIGH-STEPPER
SADDLE-HORSE

10

BLOOD-HORSE
CLYDESDALE
COACH-HORSE
LIPIZZANER

12

CLEVELAND BAY
DRAUGHT-HORSE

LIBERTY HORSE
SHETLAND PONY
SUFFOLK PUNCH
THOROUGHBRED

13

CARRIAGE HORSE
JERUSALEM PONY
STEEPLECHASER

14

STRAWBERRY ROAN

15

STABLE COMPANION

ANIMALS – INSECTS, ARACHNIDS & WORMS

3

ANT
BEE
BOT
BUG
DOR
FLY
KED
LOB
LUG
NIT
NUN

FRIT
GNAT
GRIG
HAWK
MITE
MOTH
PIUM
SLUG
TICK
WASP
WORM
ZIMB

4

BLUE
CLEG
FLEA

5

APHID
APHIS
ARGUS
AWETO

BRIZE
COMMA
DRAKE
DRONE
EGGAR
EGGER
EMMET
FLUKE
LEECH
LOUSE
MIDGE
NURSE
NYMPH
OUBIT
OWLET
OX-BOT
PIPER
SAUBA
SNAIL
Y-MOTH

ZEBUB

6

ACARID
ACARUS
ANT-COW
BEDBUG
BEETLE
BOTFLY
BREEZE
BUGONG
CADDIS
CAPSID
CHAFER
CHIGOE
CHIGRE
CHINCH
CICADA

COCCID
DAY-FLY
DOG-BEE
DOR-FLY
EARWIG
ELATER
GADFLY
GRU-GRU
HOP-DOG
HOP-FLY
HOPPER
HORNET
INSECT
INSTAR
JIGGER
LOCUST
LOOPER
MANTID
MANTIS
MAY-BUG

MAYFLY
MEASLE
MOTUCA
MUSCID
MYGALE
NASUTE
PALMER
PIERID
PSYCHE
RED ANT
SAW-FLY
SCARAB
SOW-BUG
SPIDER
TETTIX
TSETSE
WALKER
WEEVIL
WORKER
WOUBIT

18

7

ANNELID
ANT-LION
ARANEID
ARMY ANT
ASCARID
BEE-MOTH
BEET-FLY
BLOW-FLY
BOAT-FLY
BROMMER
BUZZARD
CESTODE
CESTOID
CLOCKER
CORNFLY
CRICKET
CULICID
CUTWORM
DEW-WORM
DOG-TICK
DUCK-ANT
EELWORM
EPEIRID
ERGATES
FIREFLY
GALL-FLY
GOLD-BUG
GOUTFLY
HAIR-EEL
HIVE-BEE
HOP-FLEA
HORNBUG
ICE-WORM
KALLIMA
KATYDID
LADYBUG
LADYCOW
LADYFLY
LOBWORM
LUGWORM
MAW-WORM
MEAT-FLY
NOCTUID
OESTRUS
OWL-MOTH
PHASMID
PILL-BUG
PISMIRE
PUG-MOTH
PYRALID

RAGWORM
RAT-FLEA
ROSE-BUG
SAND-FLY
SCIARID
SEA-WORM
SERPULA
SKEETER
SKIPPER
SNOW-FLY
SYRPHID
TABANID
TERMITE
WAX-MOTH
WOOD-ANT

8

ALDER-FLY
APHIDIAN
ARACHNID
ARMY WORM
ATTERCOP
BOLL-WORM
BOMBYCID
BOOKWORM
CASE-WORM
CERCARIA
CHELIFER
CORN-MOTH
CORNWORM
CRANE-FLY
CURCULIO
DART-MOTH
DIPTERAN
DOG-LOUSE
DYTISCID
ESCARGOT
FIREBRAT
FIREWORM
FLAG-WORM
FLAT-WORM
FLESH-FLY
FROTH-FLY
FRUIT-FLY
GALL-WASP
GAPEWORM
GEOMETER
GILT-TAIL
GLOW-WORM
GNATLING

GOAT-MOTH
GOLD-WASP
GREENFLY
HAIR-WORM
HAWK-MOTH
HELMINTH
HESPERID
HONEY-ANT
HONEY-BEE
HOOK-WORM
HORNTAIL
HORNWORM
HORSEFLY
HOUSE-FLY
HOVER-FLY
INCH-WORM
ITCH-MITE
LACE-WING
LADYBIRD
MEAL-WORM
MEALY-BUG
MILLIPED
MOSQUITO
MUCK-WORM
NEMATODE
NIGHT-FLY
OAK-EGGAR
OX-WARBLE
PASTE-EEL
PEDIPALP
PILE-WORM
PILL-WORM
PUSS-MOTH
QUEEN-BEE
RHODITES
RUBY-TAIL
SAND-DART
SAND-FLEA
SAND-WASP
SANDWORM
SAUBA-ANT
SCORPION
SEDGE-FLY
SHEEP-KED
SILKWORM
SKIPJACK
SLAVE-ANT
SNAKE-FLY
SNOW-FLEA
SPHINGID
STONE-FLY
TAPEWORM

TOXOCARA
TRICHINA
TUBE-WORM
VAPOURER
WALLFISH
WATER-BUG
WATER-FLY
WHEAT-EEL
WHEAT-FLY
WHIPWORM
WHITE ANT
WIRE-WORM
WOOD-MITE
WOOD-TICK
WOOD-WASP
WOODWORM

9

AMAZON-ANT
ARTHROPOD
BIRD-LOUSE
BLINDWORM
BLOOD-WORM
BOOKLOUSE
BRIMSTONE
BUMBLE-BEE
BUTTERFLY
CADDIS-FLY
CANTHARIS
CENTIPEDE
CHAETOPOD
CHURR-WORM
CLAVICORN
CLEARWING
COCCIDIUM
COCHINEAL
COCKROACH
COFFEE-BUG
CORN-BORER
CRAB-LOUSE
CUCKOO-FLY
DOODLEBUG
DOR-BEETLE
DRAGONFLY
EARTHWORM
EPHEMERID
EPHEMERON
ERGATANER
FLESHWORM
FLUKEWORM

FOREST-FLY
GALL-MIDGE
GEOMETRID
GHOST-MOTH
GOLDEN-EYE
GOURD-WORM
GRASS-MOTH
GYPSY-MOTH
HARVESTER
HESPERION
HODMANDOD
HUMBLE-BEE
JOINT-WORM
LITHISTID
LONGICORN
MILLIPEDE
NEMERTINE
NUT-WEEVIL
NYMPHALID
OIL-BEETLE
ORANGE-TIP
PEDICULUS
PHALANGID
PLANARIUM
PLUME-MOTH
POMACE-FLY
REARHORSE
RED SPIDER
ROBBER-FLY
ROUND-WORM
SAND-MASON
SHEEP-TICK
SHIELD-BUG
STRAW-WORM
STRONGYLE
SUGAR-MITE
TARANTULA
TIGER-MOTH
TIGER-TAIL
TORTRICID
TREMATODE
TSETSE-FLY
TUMBLE-BUG
TURNIP-FLY
VERMICULE
WARBLE-FLY
WATER-FLEA
WAX-INSECT
WHEAT-MOTH
WHEAT-WORM
WHIRLIGIG
WOOD-BORER

WOOD-LOUSE
WORKER-BEE

10

ANOPHELINE
ANTLER-MOTH
BARK-BEETLE
BIRD-SPIDER
BLACK WIDOW
BLISTER-FLY
BLUEBOTTLE
BOLL-WEEVIL
BURNET-MOTH
CABBAGE-FLY
CADDIS-WORM
CANKER-WORM
CARPET-MOTH
CECIDOMYIA
CHEESE-MITE
CHIRONOMID
COCKCHAFER
CODLIN-MOTH
CORN-THRIPS
CORN-WEEVIL
COTTONWORM
DEMOISELLE
DIGGER-WASP
DOLPHIN-FLY
DUNG-BEETLE
ERGATOGYNE
FEN-CRICKET
FRITILLARY
FROG-HOPPER
GALLEY-WORM
GOLD-BEETLE
GRAPE-LOUSE
GREEN-DRAKE
GRU-GRU WORM
GUINEA-WORM
HAIRSTREAK
HARVEST-BUG
HARVEST-FLY
HARVESTMAN
HEMIPTERAN
HESSIAN FLY
HORSELEECH
KITTEN-MOTH
LACKEY MOTH
LANTERN FLY
LAPPET MOTH

LEAF-CUTTER
LEAF-HOPPER
LEAF-INSECT
LIVER-FLUKE
MAGPIE MOTH
MINER'S WORM
MUSK-BEETLE
NOTODONTID
PALMER-WORM
PEACH-BLOOM
PINE-BEAUTY
PINE-BEETLE
PINE-CARPET
PINE-CHAFER
PLANT-LOUSE
RED ADMIRAL
RIBBON-WORM
ROSE-BEETLE
ROSE-CHAFER
ROVE-BEETLE
SALTIGRADE
SHEEP-LOUSE
SILVER-FISH
SMOTHER-FLY
SOLDIER ANT
SPANISH FLY
SPHINX-MOTH
SPRINGTAIL
STAG-BEETLE
THREAD-WORM
TURNIP-FLEA
VENEER-MOTH
VINEGAR-EEL
VINEGAR-FLY
VOETGANGER
WHEAT-MIDGE
WOLF-SPIDER
WOOLLY-BEAR

11

BITING-LOUSE
BLACK-BEETLE
BLADDER-WORM
BLOODSUCKER
BRISTLE-TAIL
BRISTLE-WORM
CABBAGE-MOTH
CABBAGE-WORM
CATERPILLAR
CLICK-BEETLE

CLOTHES-MOTH
COPROPHAGAN
CYSTICERCUS
DRACUNCULUS
EMPEROR MOTH
ERGATOMORPH
FROTH-HOPPER
GRASSHOPPER
GREENBOTTLE
HARVEST-MITE
HARVEST-TICK
LAMELLICORN
MEADOW-BROWN
MOLE-CRICKET
MONEY-SPIDER
OLIGOCHAETE
PAINTED LADY
SCALE-INSECT
SCHISTOSOME
SCORPION-FLY
SEA-LONG WORM
SHARD-BEETLE
STICK-INSECT
SWALLOW-TAIL
TIGER-BEETLE
TUSSOCK-MOTH
TYPOGRAPHER
TYROGLYPHID
UMBRELLA-ANT
UNICORN-MOTH
VINE-FRETTER
WALKING-LEAF
WALKING-TWIG
WATER-BEETLE

WATER-SPIDER
WOOD-FRETTER

12

BOOK-SCORPION
CABBAGE-WHITE
CHEESE-HOPPER
CINNABAR-MOTH
DERMATOPHYTE
DIADEM SPIDER
GROUND-BEETLE
HARVEST-LOUSE
ICHNEUMON FLY
MARBLED-WHITE
MONEY-SPINNER
SALLOW-KITTEN
SEXTON-BEETLE
SPRING-BEETLE
SQUIRREL-TAIL
WALKING-STICK
WALKING-STRAW
WATER-BOATMAN
WATER-STRIDER
WHIP-SCORPION
WHITE ADMIRAL
WOOD-ENGRAVER

13

BLISTER-BEETLE
BURYING-BEETLE

DADDY-LONG-LEGS
DIAMOND-BEETLE
GOLIATH-BEETLE
HARVEST SPIDER
HONEYCOMB-MOTH
HOTTENTOT'S GOD
LEATHER-JACKET
MEASURING-WORM
PRAYING INSECT
PRAYING MANTIS
PURPLE EMPEROR
SPECTRE-INSECT
TORTOISE-SHELL

14

AMBROSIA BEETLE
BEAR-ANIMALCULE
COLORADO BEETLE
DEATH'S-HEAD MOTH
GOOSEBERRY-MOTH
HERCULES BEETLE
SCORPION-SPIDER

15

ERGATANDROMORPH
LONGICORN BEETLE
WHIRLIGIG BEETLE

ANIMALS – MONKEYS & LEMURS

3	4	5		6	
APE	DOUC	CEBUS	LORIS	AYE-AYE	DOG-APE
SAI	MICO	CHIMP	MAGOT	BABOON	GIBBON
	MONA	DRILL	PONGO	BANDAR	GRISON
	SAKI	INDRI	POTTO	CHACMA	GRIVET
	TITI	JOCKO	SAJOU	COAITA	GUENON
	ZATI	LEMUR	TOQUE	COLUGO	HOWLER
					LANGUR
					MALMAG

ANIMALS – MONKEYS & LEMURS

MONKEY
PONGID
RHESUS
SAGUIN
SIMPAI
SPHINX
TEE-TEE
VERVET
WOW-WOW

TAMARIN
TARSIER
WISTITI

8

BUSH-BABY
DURUKULI
ENTELLUS
HYLOBATE
MANDRILL
MANGABEY
MARMOSET
MONGOOSE
TALAPOIN
WANDEROO

SACRED APE

10

ANGWANTIBO
ANTHROPOID
BARBARY APE
CHIMPANZEE

11

DIANA MONKEY
DOUROUCOULI
FLYING LEMUR
PLATYRRHINE
SATAN MONKEY

RHESUS MONKEY
SPECTRE-LEMUR
SPIDER-MONKEY

13

GALEOPITHECUS
SOOTY MANGABEY

14

CAPUCHIN MONKEY
SQUIRREL-MONKEY

7

GORILLA
GUEREZA
HALF-APE
HANUMAN
HOOLOCK
JACCHUS
MACAQUE
SAIMIRI
SAPAJOU
SIAMANG

9

BABACOOTE
ORANG-UTAN

12

BONNET-MONKEY
CYNOCEPHALUS

15

PROBOSCIS MONKEY

ANIMALS – REPTILES & AMPHIBIANS

3

ASK
ASP
BOA
EFT

5

ADDER
COBRA
DRACO
ELAPS
GECKO
KRAIT
MAMBA
SKINK
SNAKE
SWIFT
VARAN
VIPER

CAYMAN
DIPSAS
DRAGON
GAVIAL
GOANNA
IGUANA
LIZARD
MOLOCH
MUGGER
PYTHON
SLIDER
TURTLE
WORRAL

HOG-NOSE
MONITOR
RATTLER
REPTILE
SERPENT
TUATARA

MATAMATA
MENOPOME
MOCCASIN
MUD-PUPPY
PIT-VIPER
PLATANNA
RED-BELLY
SEA-SNAKE
SLOW-WORM
STELLION
SUCURUJÚ
SURUCUCU
TEGUEXIN
TERRAPIN
TORTOISE
TREE-FROG
WALL-NEWT
WATER-BOA

4

BOMA
EMYS
FROG
GILA
NAGA
NEWT
SEPS
TOAD

8

ANACONDA
BASILISK
BULLFROG
CERASTES
FROGLING
GALAPAGO
HICCATEE
JARARACA
LANGAHAR

6

AGAMID

7

AXOLOTL
FROGLET

9

ALLIGATOR
AMPHIBIAN
BERG-ADDER
BLINDWORM
BOOM-SLANG
CHAMELEON
CHELONIAN
COACHWHIP
CROCODILE
GALLIWASP
HAMADRYAD
HOOP-SNAKE
KING-COBRA
NOTOTREMA
PUFF-ADDER
RING-SNAKE
RIVER-JACK
ROCK-SNAKE
SAND-SNAKE
SEA-TURTLE
SPADE-FOOT

WHIP-SNAKE

10

BATRACHIAN
BLACK SNAKE
BUSHMASTER
COPPERHEAD
CORAL-SNAKE
FER-DE-LANCE
GLASS-SNAKE
GRASS-SNAKE
HELLBENDER
HORNED TOAD
NATTERJACK
SALAMANDER
SAND-LIZARD
THALASSIAN
THORN-DEVIL
TIGER-SNAKE
WALL-LIZARD
WATER-SNAKE

11

CARPET-SNAKE
CONSTRICTOR
COTTONMOUTH
FENCE-LIZARD
GARTER-SNAKE
GREEN TURTLE
HORNED VIPER
RATTLESNAKE
SURINAM TOAD

12

DRAGON-LIZARD
KOMODO DRAGON
KOMODO LIZARD
PLATANNA FROG
SPRING-KEEPER

13

FRILLED LIZARD
GIANT TORTOISE
MONITOR LIZARD
SERPENT-LIZARD
STELLIO LIZARD
WATER-MOCCASIN

14

BOA CONSTRICTOR
NATTERJACK TOAD
SNAPPING-TURTLE

15

CAPE NIGHTINGALE

ANIMALS – RODENTS

3

RAT

4

CAVY
CONY
HARE
JACK
MARA
PACA
PIKA
SKUG
VOLE

5

BOBAK
COYPU
DAMAN
HUTIA
HYRAX
MOUSE
URSON

6

AGOUTI
BEAVER
BOOMER
CASTOR

DASSIE
GERBIL
GOPHER
HACKEE
HOG-RAT
JERBOA
MARMOT
MURINE
NUTRIA
OAR-LAP
PIG-RAT
RABBIT
RODENT
SUSLIK
TAGUAN
TAPETI
URCHIN

7

ACOUCHY
HAMSTER
KLIPDAS
LAND-RAT
LEMMING
LEVERET
MEERKAT
MOLERAT
MUSK-RAT
ONDATRA
POTOROO
SONDELI

8

BLACK RAT
BLUE HARE
BROWN RAT
CAPYBARA
CHIPMUNK
DORMOUSE
HAMPSTER
HEDGEHOG
HEDGEPIG
MOUSEKIN
MUSK-CAVY
MUSQUASH
RIVER-HOG
SAND-MOLE
SEWELLEL

ANIMALS – RODENTS

SEWER-RAT
SQUIRREL
TUCUTUCO
VISCACHA
WATER-DOG
WATER-RAT
WHARF-RAT
WHISTLER

9

BANDICOOT
BEAVER RAT
CAMASS-RAT
CAPE-HYRAX
CHICKAREE
DEER-MOUSE
DESERT RAT
GRAPHIURE
GROUND-HOG

GUINEA-PIG
NORWAY RAT
PORCUPINE
REX RABBIT
WATER-VOLE
WOODCHUCK

10

CHINCHILLA
COTTONTAIL
DOLICHOTIS
FIELDMOUSE
JACK-RABBIT
MALABAR-RAT
ORINOCO HOG
PIPING HARE
POUCHED RAT
PRAIRIE-DOG
ROCK-BADGER

ROCK-RABBIT
SAGE-RABBIT
SPRING-HAAS
SPRING-HARE
WATER-MOUSE

11

BELGIAN HARE
JUMPING-HARE
KANGAROO-RAT
RED SQUIRREL
SPERMOPHILE
WISHTONWISH

12

GREY SQUIRREL
HARVEST MOUSE

JUMPING-MOUSE
MOUNTAIN-HARE
POCKET-GOPHER
POUCHED MOUSE

13

GOLDEN HAMSTER
WALTZING MOUSE

14

FLYING-SQUIRREL
GROUND-SQUIRREL
MOUNTAIN-BEAVER
RABBIT-SQUIRREL
SNOW-SHOE RABBIT

ARTS – BALLET & DANCING

3

ACT
BOB
BOP
HAY
HEY
HOP
JIG
PAS
SET

4

BALL
FADO
FRIS
HAKA
JETÉ
JIVE
JOTA
JUBA
KOLO
POLO
REEL
STEP
TRIP

5

BEBOP
BRAWL
CAROL
CONGA
DANCE
DISCO
FLING
GALOP
GLIDE
GOPAK
LIMBO
LOURE
MAMBO
PAVAN
POLKA
POULE
ROUND
RUMBA
SAMBA
STOMP

TANGO
TWIRL
TWIST
VALSE
VOLTA
WALTZ

6

ALMAIN
BALLET
BOLERO
BOSTON
BOURÉE
CANARY
CANCAN
CHA-CHA
CHASSÉ
COUPEE
DOSI-DO
ENCORE
FADING
FIGURE
FRISKA
KICK-UP
MASQUE
MAXIXE
MINUET
POINTE
REDOWA
SHIMMY
SPRING
VELETA

7

BEGUINE
CARIOCA
CLASSIC
COURANT
CSÁRDÁS
DANCING
DOS-Á-DOS
FARRUCA
FEATHER
FOOTING
FORLANA
FOUETTÉ
FOX-TROT
GAVOTTE
HALLING

HOEDOWN
LANCERS
LÄNDLER
MAILLOT
MAZURKA
MEASURE
MORESCO
MORISCO
ONE-STEP
PLANXTY
POLACCA
RAGTIME
ROMAIKA
ROUNDEL
ROUTINE
SHUFFLE
TRENISE
TWINKLE
TWO-STEP
ZIGANKA

8

ASSEMBLÉ
ATTITUDE
AUDITION
BALLROOM
BUNNY-HUG
CACHUCHA
CAKEWALK
CHACONNE
CORYPHEE
EGG-DANCE
ENSEMBLE
FAN DANCE
FANDANGO
FISHTAIL
FLAMENCO
FLIP-FLOP
GALLIARD
GLISSADE
HABANERA
HEY-DE-GUY
HORNPIPE
HULA-HULA
HUNT-BALL
ICE-DANCE
IRISH JIG
KANTIKOY
ORCHESIS
PANTALON

RACE-BALL
RIGADOON
SARABAND
SKIPPING
STOMPING
TAP-DANCE
TEA-DANCE
TELEMARK
WALTZING
WAR DANCE

9

ALLEMANDE
ARABESQUE
BACCHANAL
BERGAMASK
BOSSA NOVA
BREAKDOWN
BULL-DANCE
CLOG-DANCE
COTILLION
DANCE-HALL
ÉCOSSAISE
ELEVATION
ENTRECHAT
FARANDOLE
FOLK-DANCE
FORMATION
GALLOPADE
JITTERBUG
KATHAKALI
PAS DE DEUX
PASO DOBLE
PASSEPIED
PAUL JONES
PIROUETTE
POLONAISE
POUSSETTE
PROMENADE
QUADRILLE
QUICK-STEP
REHEARSAL
RING-DANCE
ROUNDELAY
SAND-DANCE
SICILIANA
SICILIANO
SPOT DANCE
STAG-DANCE
STEP-DANCE

TAMBOURIN
THREESOME
TRIPUDIUM
VARIATION
ZAPATEADO

10

BELLY-DANCE
CARMAGNOLE
CHARLESTON
CINQUE-PACE
CORROBOREE
EPAULEMENT
GAY GORDONS
GRAND MARCH
HOKEY-COKEY
ICE-DANCING
MASKED-BALL
MASQUERADE
ORCHESTICS
PETRONELLA
PIGEON-WING
REPERTOIRE
ROUNDABOUT
ROUND DANCE
SALTARELLO
SEGUIDILLA
SNAKE-DANCE
STRATHSPEY
SWORD-DANCE
TAP-DANCING
TARANTELLA
THÉ DANSANT
TORCH-DANCE
TURKEY-TROT
TYROLIENNE
WALK-AROUND

11

ANTISTROPHE
BLACK BOTTOM
CHOREOGRAPH
CRACOVIENNE
DINNER-DANCE
DISCOTHÈQUE
FIGURE-DANCE
LAMBETH WALK
MORRIS-DANCE

ARTS – BALLET & DANCING

PALAIS GLIDE
PAS REDOUBLÉ
PASTOURELLE
PERFORMANCE
SCHOTTISCHE
SHIMMY-SHAKE
SLOW FOX-TROT
SQUARE-DANCE
VARSOVIENNE

FOURSOME REEL
LABANOTATION
PASSY-MEASURE
SKIRT-DANCING
TRIPUDIATION
VIRGINIA REEL

12

ASSEMBLY ROOM
BALLETOMANIA
BREAK-DANCING
CHASSÉ-CROISÉ
CHOREOGRAPHY
COUNTRY DANCE
DIVERTIMENTO

13

BOSTON TWO-STEP
DOUBLE-SHUFFLE
EIGHTSOME REEL
HIGHLAND FLING
MORRIS-DANCING
ORCHESOGRAPHY
PALAIS DE DANCE
SQUARE-DANCING
VIENNESE WALTZ

14

COUNTRY DANCING
DRESS REHEARSAL
FANCY-DRESS BALL
JACK-IN-THE-GREEN

15

BALLROOM DANCING
CINDERELLA-DANCE
HESITATION WALTZ
INVITATION WALTZ
MILITARY TWO-STEP
ROGER DE COVERLEY
SOFT-SHOE SHUFFLE

ARTS – CINEMA

3

CAN
CUT
SET

4

BOOM
CAST
CLIP
EPIC
FILM
GATE
PART
REEL
RÔLE
RUSH
SHOT
TAKE
TONY

5

DRAMA
FOYER
FRAME
GENRE
MOVIE
OSCAR
PRINT
SCENE
SHOOT
SHORT
SPOOL
STUNT

6

CAMERA
CINEMA
COMEDY
DOUSER

FADE-IN
FLICKS
REMAKE
RETAKE
SCREEN
SCRIPT
SEQUEL
SERIAL
STRIPE
STUDIO
TALKIE
VIEWER
WEEPIE

7

BALCONY
BIT-PART
CARTOON
CIRCUIT
CLASSIC

CLOSE-UP
CREDITS
CUTTING
DUBBING
EFFECTS
EPISODE
EXCERPT
FADE-OUT
FILMDOM
FLEA-PIT
MATINÉE
MONTAGE
MUSICAL
PANNING
PICTURE
PREVIEW
QUICKIE
RELEASE
SHOWBIZ
STARDOM
TRAILER
WESTERN

8

BIOGRAPH
BIOSCOPE
CINERAMA
CRITIQUE
DIALOGUE
EPISCOPE
FILMLAND
LOCATION
LONG SHOT
NEWSREEL
PICTURES
SCENARIO
SEQUENCE
SHOOTING
SOB-STORY
SPROCKET
SUBTITLE
THRILLER
VIGNETTE
ZOETROPE

ZOOTROPE

SOUND-TRACK
TEAR-JERKER
WIDE SCREEN

SHOW BUSINESS
SILVER SCREEN
SOUND EFFECTS
STEREOPTICON

9

ANIMATION
BOX OFFICE
BURLESQUE
DIRECTION
FLASH-BACK
LOW COMEDY
MUTOSCOPE
PROGRAMME
PROJECTOR
SCREENING
SKINFLICK
SLAPSTICK
SOUND-FILM
VITASCOPE
VOICE-OVER
ZOECHROME

11

BLACK COMEDY
BLACK HUMOUR
CINEMASCOPE
CLIFFHANGER
DOCUMENTARY
DOLLY CAMERA
EPIDIASCOPE
FEATURE FILM
KINETOGRAPH
KINETOSCOPE
NEWS-THEATRE
PERFORMANCE
PICTURE-PLAY
TECHNICOLOR

13

CAMERA OBSCURA
CHARACTER PART
CINE-PROJECTOR
CINEMATOGRAPH
DRAMATISATION
GOLDEN THISTLE
MOTION PICTURE
MUSICAL COMEDY
NOUVELLE VAGUE
PICTURE-PALACE
SPROCKET-WHEEL

10

AVANT-GARDE
CINE-CAMERA
DOUBLE-TAKE
HORROR FILM
HORSE OPERA
KLIEG LIGHT
PRE-RELEASE
PRODUCTION
PROJECTION
SCREENPLAY
SCREEN TEST

12

CINÉMA VÉRITÉ
CLAPPERBOARD
CREDIT TITLES
DRIVE-IN MOVIE
FILM FESTIVAL
FILM PREMIÈRE
INTERMISSION
LANTERN SLIDE
MAGIC LANTERN
PICTURE-HOUSE
PRAXINOSCOPE

14

CINEMATOGRAPHY
DISSOLVING VIEW
MOVING PICTURES
SUPPPORTING RÔLE

15

ANIMATED CARTOON
PHENAKISTOSCOPE
SEMIDOCUMENTARY
SLAPSTICK COMEDY

ARTS – CRAFTS & HOBBIES

3

ART
KEY
PIN
SET

4

BUHL
CARD
CLAY
DARN

ETUI
FRET
FRIT
HAND
KANA
KERF

KNIT
LOOP
PURL
SLIP
TAIL

5

BATIK
BLOOM
CHINA
CRAFT

CUTCH
DELFT
DERBY
DOWEL
FLOSS
FLUTE

FRAME
GLAZE
GRAIN
HOBBY
INLAY
JAPAN

ARTS – CRAFTS & HOBBIES

JOINT
KYLIN
MAGOT
MINIM
MITRE
MODEL
MOULD
MOUNT
PASTE
PEARL
PICOT
PIQUÉ
PLAIN
PLATE
PRUNT
QUILT
SCARF
SMALT
SMEAR
SPODE
TENON

6

BISQUE
BONSAI
FINISH
JASPER
LUSTRE
MARBLE
MOSAIC
NEEDLE
NESHKI
NIELLO
OFFCUT
ORMOLU
OSIERY
PALLET
PEBBLE
PILLOW
PURFLE
RABBET
RAFFIA
RÉSEAU
SAGGAR
SÈVRES
SEWING
SHIPPO
SMALTO
STITCH
TARSIA

TRIFLE
VENEER
WICKER

7

BISCUIT
BLUNGER
BUNRAKU
CERAMET
CERAMIC
CHASING
COLLAGE
CROCHET
CRYSTAL
FABERGÉ
FAIENCE
FELTING
GOBELIN
HOUSING
IKEBANA
JOINERY
LACQUER
LAP-WORK
MACRAMÉ
MATTING
MEANDER
MEISSEN
MIXTION
MORTISE
NAILING
ORIGAMI
PASTIME
PATTERN
POTICHE
POTTERY
RUBBING
SAMPLER
SCHMELZ
TAMBOUR
TATTING
TURNING
VARNISH
VERMEIL
WEAVING

8

APPLIQUÉ
BASKETRY
BRAIDING

CERAMICS
CISELURE
COALPORT
COUCHING
DENTELLE
DOVETAIL
DOWEL-PIN
EGGSHELL
EMERY-BAG
FRET-WORK
GLYPTICS
GRAINING
HAIR-WORK
HALF-TEXT
HEEL-BALL
INTAGLIO
INTARSIA
IRONWARE
IRONWORK
KATAKANA
KNITTING
KNOTTING
KNOTWORK
KNURLING
KOFTGARI
KOFTWORK
LAID WORK
LAP-BOARD
LONGHAND
MAJOLICA
MANDARIN
MARBLING
OPEN-WORK
OVERFOLD
PENCRAFT
PETUNTZE
PLAITING
PLASTICS
PURFLING
REPOUSSÉ
RING-WORK
SCARFING
STUDWORK
TAPESTRY
TENT-WORK
TEXT-HAND
TOREUTIC
WEDGWOOD
WIREWORK
WOODWORK
WOOLWORK

9

BONE CHINA
CAMEO WARE
CARPENTRY
CHAMPLEVÉ
CHART-HAND
CHINAWARE
COURT-HAND
DELFTWARE
DRAWN-WORK
EX-LIBRISM
FAGGOTING
FANCYWORK
FOLK-CRAFT
GLASSWARE
GLASSWORK
GOFFERING
GROS POINT
GROUNDING
GUILLOCHE
HANDIWORK
HEM-STITCH
HOMECRAFT
KALAMKARI
KNEE-JOINT
LETTERING
MARQUETRY
METAL-WORK
MODELLING
NEEDLEFUL
OVERGLAZE
PARQUETRY
PATCHWORK
PHILATELY
PIQUÉ WORK
PLAINWORK
POKER-WORK
PORCELAIN
RICE-GRAIN
ROUNDHAND
SALT-GLAZE
SCALE-WORK
SCRIMSHAW
SCULPTURE
SGRAFFITO
SHELLWORK
SMALL-HAND
SPARTERIE
STEELWARE
STEELWORK
STITCHING

STONEWARE
STUMPWORK
TIE-DYEING
VENEERING
WORCESTER

10

APICULTURE
BACKSTITCH
BASKETWORK
BEEKEEPING
BRANCH-WORK
CANVAS-WORK
CARTOPHILY
CHARTREUSE
COLLECTION
CREWELLERY
CREWELWORK
CROCHETING
CROUCH-WARE
CROWN DERBY
DINANDERIE
DOWEL-JOINT
EMBOSSMENT
EMBROIDERY
FRENCH HEEL
FRENCH SEAM
GEM-CUTTING
GOLD-THREAD
HAIR-STROKE
HANDICRAFT
HOUSECRAFT
JAPANESERY
JAPANESQUE
JASPERWARE
LITHOGLYPH
LITHOPHANE
LOCK-STITCH
MATCHBOARD
MATCH-JOINT
MILLEFIORI
NEEDLE-BOOK
NEEDLE-CASE
NEEDLEWORK
OPEN-STITCH
PEACH-BLOOM
PEARL-WHITE
PEBBLEWARE
PENMANSHIP
PETIT POINT

PHILLUMENY
PIETRA DURA
PILLOW-LACE
PIN-CUSHION
PLASTICINE
PLASTILINA
QUEEN'S WARE
RENOVATION
REPOUSSAGE
ROPE-STITCH
RUSTIC-WARE
SAMIAN WARE
SAND-CASTLE
SCARF-JOINT
SMITHCRAFT
SPIDER-WORK
STAMP-ALBUM
STEM-STITCH
TARSIA-WORK
TENT-STITCH
TERRACOTTA
WATTLE-WORK
WHIP-STITCH
WICKERWORK

HOUSEWIFERY
MING POTTERY
NEEDLECRAFT
NEEDLE-POINT
NUMISMATICS
PICK-AND-PICK
PLASTIC CLAY
QUEEN-STITCH
RABBET-JOINT
RUNNING-HAND
SAMPLER-WORK
SATIN-STITCH
SATSUMA WARE
SCRATCH-WORK
SEMPSTERING
SERICULTURE
SPIDER-WHEEL
STEVENGRAPH
STITCHCRAFT
SUNG POTTERY
WHOLE-STITCH
WORSTED-WORK

SPIDER-STITCH
VASE-PAINTING

13

BLANKET STITCH
CABINET-MAKING
DARNING-NEEDLE
FEATHER-STITCH
FIGURE-CASTING
FIGURE-WEAVING
FLEMISH STITCH
FRIT PORCELAIN
GLASS-GRINDING
MATCHBOARDING
MODELLING CLAY
ORNAMENTATION
PASSEMENTERIE
PHELLOPLASTIC
PORCELAIN CLAY
RAILWAY-STITCH
SEMIPORCELAIN
SHELL-ORNAMENT
THROWING-TABLE
TORTOISE-SHELL
WILLOW PATTERN

11

BARBOLA WORK
BATTALIA PIE
BELL-RINGING
CABLE-STITCH
CALLIGRAPHY
CHAIN-STITCH
CHELSEA WARE
CHIP-CARVING
CLOISONNAGE
COPPERPLATE
CROCHET-HOOK
CROCHET-WORK
CROSS-STITCH
DELLA-ROBBIA
DRESDEN WARE
DOVETAILING
EARTHENWARE
FAMILLE ROSE
FANCY STITCH
GENTLE CRAFT

12

BASKET-MAKING
BLANC-DE-CHINE
BLIND TOOLING
BRASS RUBBING
BUTTERFLY-NET
CARTON-PIERRE
SEROPLASTICS
CHALCOGRAPHY
DO-IT-YOURSELF
DRESDEN CHINA
FAMILLE JAUNE
FAMILLE NOIRE
FAMILLE VERTE
FRENCH POLISH
GARTER-STITCH
GEM-ENGRAVING
GLYPTOGRAPHY
PAINTED CLOTH
PALAEOGRAPHY
PEARL-ESSENCE
POTICHOMANIA

14

COROMANDEL WORK
EBURNIFICATION
IVORY PORCELAIN
KNITTING-NEEDLE
SECRETARY HAND
TABERNACLE-WORK
WHEAT-EAR STITCH
XYLOPYROGRAPHY

15

LAPIS-LAZULI WARE
PORCELAIN CEMENT
STAMP-COLLECTING

ARTS – LITERATURE

3
ANA
PEN

4
BOOK
EPIC
HERO
MYTH
OPUS
PLOT
SAGA
TALE
TEXT
TOME
WORK

5
CENTO
CONTE
CYCLE
DIARY
DRAMA
ESSAY
FABLE
GENRE
NOVEL
PAPER
PIECE
PROSE
QUOTE
ROMAN
SCI-FI
SQUIB
STORY
STUDY
STYLE
SUMMA
THEME
TITLE

6
DONNÉE
LEGEND

MASQUE
MYTHUS
PARODY
PRÉCIS
SATIRE
SEQUEL
THESIS

7
AGONIST
AUTONYM
CHAPTER
CLASSIC
COMMENT
CONTEXT
EPISODE
EPITOME
EROTICA
EXCERPT
FICTION
FUSTIAN
HEROINE
HISTORY
LAMPOON
MÄRCHEN
MEMOIRS
MORCEAU
NOVELLA
ODYSSEY
PANDECT
PARABLE
PASSAGE
PEN-NAME
PREFACE
ROMANCE
SETTING
SUBPLOT
SUMMARY
TRILOGY
VERSION
VILLAIN
WESTERN
WRITING

8
ADESPOTA

ALLEGORY
ANALECTA
ANTI-HERO
APOLOGIA
APOLOGUE
CRITIQUE
EPILOGUE
EUPHUISM
FOLK-TALE
FOREWORD
HAMARTIA
JEREMIAD
LIBRETTO
LONGUEUR
NOUVELLE
NOVELISM
OPUSCULE
PASTICHE
PASTORAL
PROLOGUE
PROTASIS
RHETORIC
SYNOPSIS
THRILLER
TREATISE
WRITINGS

9
ALLOGRAPH
ANTI-NOVEL
BIOGRAPHY
CHARACTER
FAIRY TALE
HAGIOLOGY
LOVE STORY
MANNERISM
MONOGRAPH
MORAL TALE
NARRATIVE
NOVELETTE
OPUSCULUM
PARAGRAPH
POT-POURRI
PRODROMUS
PROLUSION
PSEUDONYM
QUOTATION
SAGA NOVEL
SITUATION

SQUIBBING
STORY LINE
SYMBOLISM
TETRALOGY
TROPOLOGY
UNDERPLOT
WHODUNNIT

10
BEAST FABLE
CLASSICISM
DÉNOUEMENT
GHOST STORY
INSTALMENT
LAMPOONERY
LITERATURE
LITEROSITY
MAGNUM OPUS
METAPHRASE
MISCELLANY
MONOGRAPHY
NATURE-MYTH
NOM DE PLUME
NON-FICTION
STYLISTICS
VILLAINESS

11
ANTI-HEROINE
CLIFFHANGER
COMPOSITION
DESCRIPTION
FINE WRITING
HISTORIETTE
LIFE HISTORY
MASTERPIECE
MYTHOGRAPHY
PASTORALISM
PURPLE PATCH
RENAISSANCE
ROMAN FLEUVE
THESIS NOVEL
TRANSLATION
WORD-PICTURE

ARTS – MUSIC – MUSICAL INSTRUMENTS

ARTS – MUSIC – MUSICAL INSTRUMENTS

TABORIN
TAMBOUR
TESTUDO
THEORBO
TIMBREL
TIMPANI
TIMPANO
TINKLER
TRUMPET
UKELELE
UKULELE
UPRIGHT
VIOLONE
WHISTLE

8

ARCHLUTE
AUTOHARP
BAGPIPES
BASS DRUM
BASS HORN
BASS TUBA
BASS VIOL
BOUZOUKI
CLAPPERS
CLARINET
CLAVECIN
CORNPIPE
CROMORNA
CROTALUM
DULCIMER
HANDBELL
HAND-HORN
HORNPIPE
JEW'S-HARP
KEY-BUGLE
KNACKERS
LANGSPEL
LYRA-VIOL
MANDOLIN
MARTENOT
MELODEON
MIRLITON
OLIPHANT
OTTAVINO
PAN-PIPES
PHORMINX
PIANETTE
POLYPHON
POST-HORN

PSALTERY
RECORDER
SIDE-DRUM
SQUIFFER
STICCADO
TAMBOURA
TENOROON
TRIANGLE
TRICHORD
TROMBONE
TYMPANUM
VIRGINAL
VOCALION
WALDHORN
ZAMBOMBA
ZAMPOGNA

9

ACCORDION
ALPENHORN
BABY GRAND
BALALAIKA
BANJULELE
BOMBARDON
BONGO-DRUM
BUGLE-HORN
CASTANETS
CHALUMEAU
CHIME BARS
CLARIONET
COACH-HORN
CORNEMUSE
CORNOPEAN
DECACHORD
DRONE-PIPE
DULCITONE
EUPHONIUM
FLAGEOLET
FLÛTE-À-BEC
HAND-ORGAN
HARMONICA
HARMONIUM
INTONATOR
JEW'S-TRUMP
KRUMMHORN
LANGSPIEL
MANDOLINE
MONOCHORD
NOSE-FLUTE
OCTACHORD

ORPHARION
PANTALEON
PIPE-ORGAN
PORTATIVE
PYROPHONE
REED-ORGAN
SAXOPHONE
SEMI-GRAND
SERAPHINE
SERINETTE
SNARE-DRUM
TENOR-HORN
TENOR-TUBA
TENOR-VIOL
VIBRAHARP
WASHBOARD
WELSH HARP
XYLOPHONE

10

BASS-FIDDLE
BASSET HORN
CHAIR-ORGAN
CHITARRONE
CHOIR-ORGAN
CLAVICHORD
CONCERTINA
CONTRABASS
COR ANGLAIS
DIDGERIDOO
DOUBLE-BASS
FLÜGELHORN
FORTEPIANO
FRENCH HORN
GRAND PIANO
HARMONICON
HEPTACHORD
HURDY-GURDY
KETTLE-DRUM
LIGHT-ORGAN
MINUTE-BELL
MOUTH-ORGAN
NUN'S-FIDDLE
OBOE D'AMORE
OPHICLEIDE
ORPHEOREON
PENTACHORD
PINAOFORTE
PIANO-ORGAN

SLEIGH-BELL
SOURDELINE
SOUSAPHONE
SQUEEZE-BOX
SYMPHONION
TAMBOURINE
VIBRAPHONE

11

AEOLIAN HARP
APOLLONICON
BARREL-ORGAN
CHORDOPHONE
CINEMA-ORGAN
CLAIRSCHACH
COLOUR ORGAN
FIPPLE-FLUTE
GERMAN FLUTE
HARPSICHORD
HUNTING-HORN
OCTAVE-FLUTE
ORCHESTRINA
ORCHESTRION
PLAYER PIANO
VIOLA D'AMORE
VIOLONCELLO
WOBBLE-BOARD

12

ALTO-CLARINET
ALTO-TROMBONE
CHAMBER ORGAN
CLAVICEMBALO
CONCERT-GRAND
COTTAGE PIANO
GLOCKENSPIEL
HAMMOND ORGAN
HARMONICHORD
HARMONIPHONE
METALLOPHONE
PANDEAN PIPES
PENNY-WHISTLE
SARRUSOPHONE
THEATRE ORGAN
TROMBA MARINA
UPRIGHT PIANO
VIOLA DA GAMBA

13

ALTO-SAXOPHONE
AMERICAN ORGAN
CONTRABASSOON
CONTRAFAGOTTO
DOUBLE-BASSOON
ELECTRIC ORGAN
HAMMERKLAVIER
MARINE TRUMPET
PANHARMONICON
PHYSHARMONICA

PIPELESS ORGAN
POSITIVE ORGAN
SLIDE TROMBONE
TINTINNABULUM
VALVE TROMBONE
VIOLA DA SPALLA

14

CLAVICYTHERIUM
ELECTRIC GUITAR

JINGLING JOHNNY
MUSICAL GLASSES
ORGAN-HARMONIUM
PIANO-ACCORDION
TENOR-SAXOPHONE

15

CHINESE PAVILION
CORNO DI BASSETTO

ARTS – MUSIC – MUSICAL TERMS

3	**4**				
AIR	ALTO	LIED	ROTA	ARSIS	DUMKA
ALT	ARIA	LILT	RUNE	BASSO	E-FLAT
BAR	BASS	LONG	SCAT	BATON	E-LA-MI
BIS	BEAT	MASS	SEXT	BEBOP	ELEGY
BOB	BELL	MEAN	SING	BELLY	ÉTUDE
BOP	BIND	MESE	SLUR	B-FLAT	F-CLEF
BOW	BOOK	MODE	SOLO	BLUES	F-FLAT
DOH	CLEF	MONO	SONG	BRASS	F-HOLE
DUO	CODA	MOOD	SOUL	BREVE	FIFTH
E-LA	DESK	MUTE	STOP	BUFFA	FLUTE
FAH	DUET	NECK	TAIL	BUFFO	FORTE
JIG	ECHO	NETE	TEXT	CANON	FUGUE
KEY	FADO	NOTE	TIME	CANTO	GAMBA
LAH	FA-LA	OPUS	TONE	CAROL	GAMUT
LAY	FLAT	PART	TRAD	CATCH	G-CLEF
MOD	FLUE	PEAL	TRIO	C-FLAT	G-FLAT
NUT	FORM	PIPE	TUBA	CHANT	GIGUE
OAT	FRET	PLAY	TUNE	CHECK	GRACE
PEG	FROG	PORT	TURN	CHIME	HURRY
PIN	GLEE	PUNK	VAMP	CHORD	INDEX
POP	HEAD	RAGA	VEIL	COMMA	INTRO
RAG	HEEL	RANK	WIRE	CONGA	IVORY
RAY	HYMN	REED	WOLF	CREDO	KLANG
RIB	JACK	REST	WORK	CROOK	KWELA
RUN	JAZZ	RIFF		D-FLAT	LARGE
SOH	JIVE	RING	**5**	DIRGE	LARGO
SOL	JUBA	RISE		DITAL	LASSU
TIE	KOLO	ROCK	A-FLAT	DITTY	LENTO
		ROLL	AGOGE	DOLCE	LIMMA
		ROOT		DRONE	LONGA

33

ARTS – MUSIC – MUSICAL TERMS

LOURE
LYRIC
MARCH
METER
MINIM
MOTET
MOTIF
MUSIC
MUZAK
NEUME
NINTH
NODDY
NONET
OCTET
OPERA
PAEAN
PAUSE
PAVAN
PEDAL
PIANO
PIECE
PITCH
POLKA
PRIME
PSALM
QUART
QUILL
QUINT
REPLY
RONDO
ROUND
SAMBA
SCALE
SCORE
SEGNO
SHARP
SHIFT
SIXTH
SLIDE
SOL-FA
SOUND
SPACE
SPINA
STAFF
STAVE
STICK
STOMP
STRUM
STYLE
SUITE
SWELL
SWING

TABLE
TANGO
TEMPO
TENTH
TENOR
THEME
THIRD
TITLE
TONIC
TONUS
TOUCH
TRIAD
TRILL
TRINE
TRITE
TROLL
TROPE
TUNER
TUTTI
TWANG
UP-BOW
VALUE
VALVE
VOCAL
VOICE
VOLTA
WAIST
WALTZ
YODEL

6

ACCORD
ADAGIO
ANSWER
ANTHEM
ARIOSO
A-SHARP
ATTACK
AUBADE
BALLAD
BEBUNG
BOLERO
BOOGIE
BOURÉE
BRIDGE
B-SHARP
BURDEN
CANTUS
CATGUT
CHAPEL
CHORUS

COLOUR
COURSE
C-SHARP
DAMPER
DIESIS
DITONE
D-SHARP
DUETTO
ECBOLE
EIGHTH
ENCORE
ENTRÉE
E-SHARP
FIASCO
FIGURE
FINALE
FIPPLE
FOURTH
F-SHARP
G-SHARP
HAMMER
HOPPER
HYPATE
JINGLE
KEY-PIN
LAMENT
LEGATO
LYRICS
LYRISM
MAXIXE
MEDLEY
MELODY
MINUET
MONODY
MONTRE
MORRIS
NASARD
NUMBER
OCTAVE
OTTAVA
PALATE
PAVANE
PEG-BOX
PERIOD
PHRASE
PIPING
PISTON
PLAINT
PNEUMA
PRAISE
PRESTO
PYCNON

QUAVER
RATTAN
REDOWA
REGGAE
REPEAT
RESULT
RHYTHM
SCRAPE
SECOND
SEPTET
SERIES
SESTET
SEXTET
SHANTY
SKETCH
SNATCH
SONATA
STAPLE
STEREO
STRAIN
STRING
TAMPON
TATTOO
THESIS
TIERCE
TIMBRE
TIRADE
TONGUE
TREBLE
TRILLO
TRIPLE
TRIPOD
TUNING
UNISON
UPBEAT
VELETA
VENTIL
VERSET
WARBLE
WINKER

7

ALLEGRO
ANDANTE
ARIETTA
ART FORM
ART-SONG
BACKING
BALANCE
BALLADE

BAROQUE
BASS-BAR
BATTUTA
BLUETTE
BOURDON
BOW-HAND
BRAVURA
CADENCE
CADENCY
CADENZA
CALYPSO
CANTATA
CANZONE
CARIOCA
CELESTE
CHAMADE
CHANSON
CHANTER
CHORALE
CLAPPER
CLASSIC
COMIQUE
COMPASS
CONCERT
CONCORD
CONSOLE
CORANTO
COUNTER
COUPLER
COURANT
COW-BELL
CSÁRDÁS
DESCANT
DISCORD
DOWNBOW
EPISODE
FANFARE
FERMATA
FISTULA
FOOTAGE
GAVOTTE
G-STRING
HALLALI
HARMONY
HUSHABY
JINGLET
KEY-DESK
KEYNOTE
LULLABY
MAZURKA
MEASURE
MEDIANT

34

MELISMA
MIDDLE C
MINIKIN
MIXTURE
MORDENT
MUSETTE
NATURAL
NEW WAVE
NONETTE
ORGANUM
PARTITA
PASSAGE
PIANISM
PIBROCH
PLAYING
PLECTRE
POLACCA
POP SONG
PRELUDE
QUALITY
QUARTET
QUINTET
RAGTIME
RASTRUM
RECITAL
REFRAIN
REPRISE
REQUIEM
REVERIE
RIPIENO
ROMANCE
RONDEAU
RONDINO
ROSALIA
ROULADE
SALICET
SANCTUS
SCHERZO
SCHISMA
SEPTUOR
SETTING
SEVENTH
SHADING
SINGING
SKIFFLE
SONG-HIT
SOPRANO
SORDINO
STICKER
STRETTO
STRINGS
SUBJECT

TANGENT
TANTARA
TIPPING
TIRASSE
TOCCATA
TRACKER
TREMOLO
TRENTAL
TRILOGY
TRIPLET
TRITONE
TRUMPET
TWELFTH
VAMPING
VIBRATO
VOICING
WAR-SONG
WIND-BAG
ZIGANKA

8

AGNUS DEI
ANTIPHON
ARPEGGIO
BACKFALL
BARITONE
BASS CLEF
BEL CANTO
BELL-ROPE
BERCEUSE
BLUE-NOTE
BOAT-SONG
BOB MAJOR
BOB MINOR
BOB ROYAL
BRINDISI
BURLETTA
CANTICLE
CANTICUM
CARILLON
CASTRATO
CATHISMA
CAVATINA
CHACONNE
CHEVALET
CHEVILLE
CONCERTO
COURANTE
CORONACH
CROMORNA

CROTCHET
DIAPASON
DIAPENTE
DIAPHONE
DOMINANT
DOWNBEAT
DOXOLOGY
DRUMHEAD
DUETTINO
DULCIANA
ENSEMBLE
ENTR'ACTE
EVENSONG
EXERCISE
FABURDEN
FALDERAL
FALSETTO
FANTASIA
FESTIVAL
FLAMENCO
FLOURISH
FLUE-PIPE
FLUEWORK
FOLK-ROCK
FOLK-SONG
FOLK-TUNE
FREE REED
FUGHETTA
HALF-NOTE
HALF-TONE
HARMONIC
HEADNOTE
HEMIOLIA
HOMOTONY
IDÉE FIXE
INTERVAL
KEYBOARD
KNEE-STOP
LICHANOS
LIGATURE
LOVE-SONG
MADRIGAL
MAJOR KEY
MAPSTICK
MEAN-TONE
MELODICS
MICROTON
MINOR KEY
MOVEMENT
MUSICALE
MUTATION
NOCTURNE

NONUPLET
NOTATION
OCTUPLET
OPEN NOTE
OPERETTA
OPUSCULE
ORATORIO
OSTINATO
OVERTONE
OVERTURE
PARAMESE
PARANETE
PART-SONG
PARTITUR
PASTICHE
PASTORAL
PAVILION
PEDALIER
PHRASING
PIPEWORK
PLECTRUM
POP MUSIC
POSITION
POSTLUDE
PRACTICE
PRELUDIO
REED-PIPE
REED-STOP
REGISTER
REPETEND
RHAPSODY
RHYTHMUS
RICERCAR
RIGADOON
SARABAND
SAW-TONES
SCHMALTZ
SEMITONE
SEQUENCE
SERENADE
SERENATA
SESTETTO
SEXTOLET
SINFONIA
SING-SONG
SIRVENTE
SOL-FAISM
SONATINA
SONG FORM
SOUNDING
SOUND-BAR
SOUND-BOX

SOURDINE
SPICCATO
STACCATO
STANDARD
STOPPING
SUBTONIC
SYMPHONY
TAIL-GATE
TERZETTO
THRENODY
TONALITY
TONE POEM
TONICITY
TRICHORD
UNA CORDA
VOCALISM
WALDHORN
WOLF-NOTE
WOODWIND
WREST-PIN
ZARZUELA

9

ALLEMANDE
ANDANTINO
ARABESQUE
BACCHANAL
BAGATELLE
BANDSTAND
BARCAROLE
BEAT MUSIC
BUGLE-CALL
BURLESQUE
CANTABANK
CANTILENA
CAPRICCIO
CASSATION
CHALUMEAU
CHARIVARI
CHEST-NOTE
CHEST-TONE
CONTRALTO
CRESCENDO
DANCE-TUNE
DEAD-MARCH
DIAZEUXIS
DITHYRAMB
DIXIELAND
DOUBLE-BAR
DRUMSTICK

DUMB-PIANO
DUODECIMO
EPINIKION
EXTEMPORE
FANFARADE
FARANDOLE
FIDDLE-BOW
FINGERING
FOLK-MUSIC
FULL ORGAN
FULL SCORE
GALLOPADE
GENERATOR
GLISSANDO
GONG-STICK
GRACE NOTE
GRADATION
GRANDSIRE
GREEK MODE
GRUPPETTO
HALF-CLOSE
HALF-SHIFT
HEXACHORD
HOMOPHONY
HONKY-TONK
IMBROGLIO
IMITATION
IMPROMPTU
INNER PART
INTERLUDE
INVENTION
KNEE-SWELL
KRUMMHORN
KUNSTLIED
LARGHETTO
LEGER-LINE
LEITMOTIV
MAJOR MODE
MAJOR TONE
MELOMANIA
METRONOME
MINIM REST
MINOR MODE
MINOR TONE
MODULATOR
MUSIC-RACK
MUSIC-ROLL
OBBLIGATO
OCTACHORD
OPEN SCORE
OPUSCULUM
ORGAN-PIPE

PARHYPATE
PARTITION
PASO DOBLE
PASTORALE
PERCUSSOR
PIANO-WIRE
PITCHFORK
PITCHPIPE
PIZZICATO
PLAINSONG
POLONAISE
POLYPHONY
PORT A BEUL
POT-POURRI
PRELUSION
PRINCIPAL
PROLATION
PSALM-TUNE
PYRAMIDON
QUADRILLE
QUODLIBET
REED-KNIFE
REHEARSAL
RENDERING
RENDITION
REPLICATE
RESONATOR
RIBATTUTA
ROCK'N'ROLL
ROUNDELAY
SELECTION
SEMANTRON
SEMIBREVE
SEPTIMOLE
SEPTUPLET
SEXTUPLET
SFORZANDO
SICILIANA
SICILIANO
SIGNATURE
SOFT PEDAL
SOLFEGGIO
SONGCRAFT
SONG-CYCLE
SOPRANINO
SOUND-BODY
SOUND-HOLE
SOUND-POST
SPIRITUAL
STRUMMING
SUBOCTAVE
TABLATURE

TAILPIECE
TAMBOURIN
TANTARARA
TARANTARA
TENOR CLEF
TESSITURA
THEME SONG
TOCCATINA
TONOMETER
TORCH-SONG
TREMOLANT
TROPARION
TUNING-KEY
TUNING-PEG
TUNING-PIN
TWELVE-ROW
UNDERNOTE
UNDERSONG
UNDERTONE
VARIATION
VOLUNTARY
VOX HUMANA
WALDFLUTE
WIND-CHEST
WOODWINDS

10

ACCIDENTAL
AFFETTUOSO
ATTUNEMENT
BINARY FORM
BITONALITY
BOB MAXIMUS
CANCIONERO
CANTATRICE
CANTO FERMO
CARMAGNOLE
CHEST-VOICE
CLARABELLA
CLASSICISM
COLORATURA
COMIC OPERA
COMMON TIME
COMPLEMENT
CONCERTINO
CONSONANCE
CONSONANCY
CORROBOREE
DANCE-MUSIC
DEMI-DITONE

DIGITORIUM
DIMINUENDO
DISSONANCE
DORIAN MODE
DOTTED NOTE
DOUBLE-FLAT
EISTEDDFOD
EMBOUCHURE
EPISTROPHE
ESCAPEMENT
EXPOSITION
EXPRESSION
FIGURATION
FINGERHOLE
FOREBITTER
GRAND OPERA
GROUND-BASS
HALLELUJAH
HEPTACHORD
HUMORESQUE
IASTIC MODE
INNER VOICE
INTERMEZZO
INTONATION
JAM SESSION
KLANG-FARBE
LEDGER-LINE
LIGHT MUSIC
LIGHT OPERA
LYDIAN MODE
MAINSTREAM
MAJOR SCALE
MAJOR THIRD
MASTER-WORK
MEDITATION
METROSTYLE
MINOR SCALE
MINOR THIRD
MINSTRELSY
MODULATION
MOUTH MUSIC
MOUTHPIECE
MUSICALITY
MUSICOLOGY
MUSIC-DRAMA
MUSIC-STAND
MUSIC-STOOL
NACHSCHLAG
OPERA SERIA
ORGAN-POINT
PARADIDDLE
PARAPHONIA

PATTER-SONG
PEDAL-BOARD
PEDAL-ORGAN
PEDAL-POINT
PENTACHORD
PERCUSSION
PIANO-STOOL
PIPED MUSIC
PLAIN-CHANT
PORTAMENTO
PROPORTION
QUADRUPLET
QUINTUPLET
RECITATIVE
RECITATIVO
REHEARSING
REPERTOIRE
REPETITION
RESOLUTION
RITARDANDO
RITORNELLO
ROCKABILLY
RONDOLETTO
SALICIONAL
SALTERELLO
SCHERZANDO
SCORDATURA
SCOTCH SNAP
SEGUIDILLA
SEMICHORUS
SEMIQUAVER
SONATA FORM
SOUND-BOARD
STRATHSPEY
SUBMEDIANT
SUPERTONIC
SUSPENSION
SWING-MUSIC
TABLE-MUSIC
TARANTELLA
TETRACHORD
THEME MUSIC
TOCCATELLA
TONIC SOL-FA
TONAL FUGUE
TRANSCRIPT
TRANSITION
TRANSPOSAL
TREBLE CLEF
TREMOLANDO
TRIPLE TIME
TRIPLICITY

TUNING-FORK
TWELVE-NOTE
TWELVE-TONE
TYROLIENNE
UNDECIMOLE
UNISONANCE
VIOLIN-CASE
VIRTUOSITY
VOCAL MUSIC
WALKAROUND
WATER-MUSIC

11

AEOLIAN MODE
ARRANGEMENT
AZIONE SACRA
BOTHY BALLAD
CAPRICCIOSO
CHANSONETTE
CHANTERELLE
CHECK-ACTION
COLOUR MUSIC
COMMON CHORD
COMPOSITION
CONCERTANTE
CONSECUTION
CRACOVIENNE
DECRESCENDO
DEVELOPMENT
DIATESSARON
DISCOGRAPHY
DODECAPHONY
DOUBLE-SHARP
FIDDLESTICK
FIGURED BASS
FINGERBOARD
FRENCH PITCH
FUNDAMENTAL
GERMAN SIXTH
GREAT OCTAVE
HUNTING-SONG
HYPERLYDIAN
KINDERSPIEL
LEADING NOTE
LOCRIAN MODE
MASTERPIECE
MUSIC-HOLDER
OPEN HARMONY
OPERA BOUFFE
PARTIAL NOTE

PART-WRITING
PASSACAGLIA
PASSING-NOTE
PEDAL-ACTION
PERFORMANCE
PIANO-PLAYER
PRESTISSIMO
PROGRESSION
PROPOSITION
QUARTER-NOTE
QUARTER-TONE
RALLENTANDO
RECESSIONAL
RIFACIMENTO
ROGUE'S MARCH
SCHOTTISCHE
SCOTCH CATCH
SMALL OCTAVE
SOLMISATION
SONGFULNESS
STEREOPHONY
SUBDOMINANT
SUPEROCTAVE
SYNCOPATION
TARATANTARA
TEMPERAMENT
TRANSPOSING
TRIDIAPASON
TRUMPET-CALL
TRUMPET-TONE
VARSOVIENNE
VOIX CÉLESTE
VOX ANGELICA

12

ACCIACCATURA
ALTALTISSIMO
ANTICIPATION
APPOGGIATURA
ARCO SALTANDO
AUGMENTATION
BOOGIE-WOOGIE
CANTUS FIRMUS
CHAMBER MUSIC
CHROMATICISM
CLOSE HARMONY
COMPOUND TIME
CONCERT PITCH
CONCERT WALTZ
COUNTERPOINT

ARTS – MUSIC – MUSICAL TERMS

COUNTER-TENOR
DIRECT MOTION
DIVERTIMENTO
DUTCH CONCERT
EPITHALAMION
EXTRAVAGANZA
FIDDLE-STRING
HEAD REGISTER
INTERMISSION
INTRODUCTION
ITALIAN SIXTH
KEY SIGNATURE
MEDIEVAL MODE
MELODIC MINOR
MEZZO-SOPRANO
MOTO PERPETUO
MUSICAL DRAMA
MUTATION STOP
NATURAL SCALE
OPEN DIAPASON
OPÉRA COMIQUE
PASSION MUSIC
PEDAL-CLAVIER
PERFECT FIFTH
PERFECT PITCH
PHRYGIAN MODE
POLYTONALITY
PRALLTRILLER
RECITING-NOTE
REGISTRATION
RESONANCE-BOX
RHYTHMOMETER
RHYTHMOPOEIA
SENSIBLE NOTE
SESQUIALTERA
SESQUITERTIA
SIGHT-PLAYING
SIGHT-READING

SIGHT-SINGING
THOROUGH BASS
TUNING-HAMMER
VIOLIN-STRING
VOX CAELESTIS
WEDDING-MARCH

13

ABSOLUTE PITCH
ACCOMPANIMENT
BALLAD CONCERT
BASSO PROFONDO
CHEST-REGISTER
COMMON MEASURE
FALSE RELATION
GREGORIAN MODE
HARMONIC MINOR
HARMONIC TRIAD
IMPROVISATION
INFINITE CANON
JANIZARY MUSIC
NEOCLASSICISM
OBLIQUE MOTION
ORCHESTRATION
PERFECT FOURTH
PLAGAL CADENCE
RANZ-DES-VACHES
SERIALISATION
SIGNATURE TUNE
STAFF-NOTATION
SUPERDOMINANT
SYMPHONIC POEM
TIME-SIGNATURE
TRANSCRIPTION
TRANSPOSITION

14

CHROMATIC SCALE
CONTRARY MOTION
COUNTER-SUBJECT
DEMI-SEMI-QUAVER
DOUBLE-STOPPING
FOUNDATION-STOP
GREGORIAN CHANT
INTERPRETATION
INTERNATIONALE
JUST INTONATION
MIXOLYDIAN MODE
NATIONAL ANTHEM
PERFECT CADENCE
PLANTATION SONG
PROGRAMME MUSIC
RECAPITULATION
REED-INSTRUMENT
WIND INSTRUMENT

15

CORNO DI BASSETTO
ELECTRONIC MUSIC
INCIDENTAL MUSIC
INSTRUMENTATION
INVERTED MORDENT
MUSIQUE CONCRÈTE
NEAPOLITAN SIXTH
PERFECT INTERVAL
SERIAL TECHNIQUE
TRADITIONAL JAZZ

ARTS – PAINTING, SCULPTURE & DRAWING

3	4					
		DAUB	IDOL	PLAN	VIEW	5
		DRAW	IKON	POSE	WASH	
ART	BUST	FORM	NUDE	TERM		BRUSH
HUE	CHIP	HERM	OILS	TINT		CAMEO
PEN	DADA	ICON	OLEO	TONE		CHALK

CONTÉ
DECAL
DRAFT
DRIER
EASEL
FITCH
FRAME
GENRE
GESSO
GROUP
HERMA
IDYLL
IMAGE
LIGHT
MODEL
MOUNT
MURAL
OP-ART
ORANT
PAINT
PANEL
PAPER
PIN-UP
PRINT
PUTTO
ROUGH
ROUND
SABLE
SCAPE
SCENE
SECCO
SEPIA
SHADE
SPECK
STUDY
STUMP
TITLE
TONDO
VALUE
VIRTU
VOLET

6

CANVAS
CHROMA
COLOUR
CRAYON
CUBISM
DESIGN
DOODLE

FIGURE
FRESCO
FUSAIN
GROUND
KITCAT
KITSCH
MARINE
MEDIUM
MEGILP
MOBILE
MOSAIC
NEEDLE
NIELLO
PALLET
PARIAN
PASTEL
PENCIL
PIN-MAN
POP-ART
POSING
POSTER
PUTOIS
RELIEF
SHADOW
SKETCH
STATUE
STROKE
STUDIO
VERISM

7

ART DECO
ATELIER
AUREOLE
BAROQUE
BAUHAUS
BOTTEGA
BOZZETO
CAMAIEU
CARTOON
CARVING
CLASSIC
COLLAGE
COMBINE
DADAISM
DIPTYCH
DRAUGHT
DRAWING
ÉCORCHÉ
ETCHING

EXHIBIT
FAUVISM
FOLK-ART
GLAZING
GOUACHE
GRAVING
IMPASTO
LINOCUT
MIMESIS
MONTAGE
MONTANT
MONTURE
MORDANT
MORISCO
ORPHISM
OUTLINE
PALETTE
PATTERN
PAYSAGE
PICTURE
PLASTIC
PREVIEW
PROFILE
RELIEVO
RILIEVO
SCENERY
SCOOPER
SCRAPER
SCUMBLE
SEA-VIEW
SHADING
SINOPIA
SIPOREX
SITTING
SPECKLE
STABILE
STENCIL
STIPPLE
SUBJECT
TABLEAU
TACHISM
TEMPERA
TINTING
TRACING
VARNISH
VEHICLE
WOODCUT

8

ACROLITH

ANAGLYPH
AQUATINT
ART AUTRE
CHARCOAL
COLOSSUS
DOODLING
DRY-POINT
DYNAMISM
ECCE HOMO
ESQUISSE
EXEMPLAR
EXTERIOR
FIGURINE
FROTTAGE
GRAFFITI
GRAFFITO
GRAPHICS
GROUPING
HALF-TINT
HATCHING
INTIMISM
KAKEMONO
LIKENESS
MAKIMONO
MANDORLA
MAQUETTE
MONOTINT
MORESQUE
MOVEMENT
MUSCLING
NOCTURNE
ORIGINAL
PAINT-BOX
PAINTING
PASTORAL
PENUMBRA
PLASTICS
PORTRAIT
PREDELLA
REMARQUE
SANGUINE
SEA-PIECE
SEASCAPE
SKYSCAPE
STAFFAGE
STATUARY
SYMMETRY
TONALITY
TRECENTO
TRIPTYCH
VELATURA
WATERING

WATER-POT
ZOOMORPH

9

ALLA PRIMA
ANASTASIS
ANTHEMION
AQUARELLE
ARABESQUE
BAS-RELIEF
BEAUX ARTS
BRUSH-WORK
CEROGRAPH
DEPICTION
DEPICTURE
DESIGNING
DISTEMPER
ENCAUSTIC
ENGRAVING
FRESCOING
GRISAILLE
GROTESQUE
LANDSCAPE
LAY-FIGURE
LETTERING
MAHLSTICK
MANNERISM
MAULSTICK
MEDALLION
MEZZOTINT
MINIATION
MINIATURE
MYRIORAMA
OBJET D'ART
OIL-COLOUR
OLD MASTER
OLEOGRAPH
PEN-AND-INK
PORTRAYAL
POT-BOILER
PRIMITIVE
SCULPTURE
SCUMBLING
SERIGRAPH
SKETCHING
SNOWSCAPE
STATUETTE
STILL-LIFE
STIPPLING
STRETCHER

39

ARTS – PAINTING, SCULPTURE & DRAWING

SYMBOLISM
TABLATURE
UNDERTINT
UNDERTONE
VORTICISM
WOODBLOCK
WORK OF ART
XYLOGRAPH
ZOOMORPHY
ZOOPHORUS

10

ALTARPIECE
ART NOUVEAU
ASSEMBLAGE
AUTOMATISM
AVANT-GARDE
BACKGROUND
BLOTTESQUE
CARICATURE
CIRE PERDUE
COMMISSION
DEFINITION
DISCOBOLUS
DOWNSTROKE
DRAWING-PEN
DRAWING-PIN
FIGURATION
FOREGROUND
FOUNDATION
GROUND-PLAN
HAIR-PENCIL
HALF-LENGTH
HEROIC SIZE
HIGH RELIEF
KINETIC ART
LITERALISM
LUMINARISM
MAINSTREAM
MASTER-WORK
MINIMAL ART
MONOCHROME
MONOCHROMY
MORBIDEZZA
NIGHTPIECE
OLEOGRAPHY
ORDONNANCE
ORTHOGRAPH
PAINT-BRUSH
PENCILLING

PHYLACTERY
PLASTIC ART
PLASTICINE
PLASTICITY
PLASTILINA
POLYCHROME
POLYCHROMY
RESOLUTION
RIVERSCAPE
ROMANESQUE
SERIGRAPHY
SILHOUETTE
SILK-SCREEN
STEEL-PLATE
SUPREMATISM
SURREALISM
TERRACOTTA
XYLOGRAPHY

11

ALTO-RILIEVO
CAVO-RILIEVO
CHIAROSCURO
CINQUECENTO
COLOURATION
COMPOSITION
DELINEATION
DIVISIONISM
FÊTE GALANTE
FOUND OBJECT
GLYPTOTHECA
GRAPHIC ARTS
ICHNOGRAPHY
ICONOGRAPHY
IMPASTATION
LITHOCHROMY
LOCAL COLOUR
MASTERPIECE
OIL-PAINTING
OLIGOCHROME
PAPIER-COLLÉ
PAPIER-MÂCHÉ
PERSPECTIVE
PLASTER CAST
POINTILLISM
PORTE-CRAYON
PORTRAITURE
POSTER-PAINT
PROTRACTION
PRIMITIVISM

RENAISSANCE
RETROUSSAGE
SAUCE-CRAYON
SCENOGRAPHY
SCRIVE-BOARD
SCULPTURING
SILVER-POINT
SOLID COLOUR
SPATTER-WORK
STENCILLING
STEREOGRAPH
SYNCHRONISM
TAUROBOLIUM
THERIOMORPH
TROMPE L'OEIL
WATER-COLOUR
WAX-PAINTING
WHOLE-LENGTH
WOOD-CARVING
ZOOMORPHISM

12

ARTIST'S PROOF
CHROMATICITY
CLAIR-OBSCURE
COLOUR SCHEME
CONSTRUCTURE
COUNTERLIGHT
DRAWING-BOARD
DRAWING-PAPER
DRAWING-TABLE
ICONOPHILISM
ILLUMINATION
ILLUSTRATION
LINE OF BEAUTY
MEZZO-RILIEVO
MIDDLE GROUND
NEOHELLENISM
ORNITHOMORPH
ORPHIC CUBISM
PALETTE-KNIFE
PARIAN MARBLE
PASSE-PARTOUT
PENCIL-SKETCH
PICTURE-FRAME
PORTRAIT-BUST
POSTER-COLOUR
REPRODUCTION
RISORGIMENTO
SCRAPER-BOARD

SELF-PORTRAIT
STENCIL-PLATE
STEREOCHROME
STEREOCHROMY
STEREOGRAPHY
SUPERREALISM
TORCHON PAPER
TRACING-PAPER
WALL-PAINTING

GLASS-PAINTING
GRATICULATION
ICHTHYOGRAPHY
ICONOMATICISM
IMPRESSIONISM
LINE-ENGRAVING
MURAL PAINTING
NAÏVE PAINTING
NEO-PLASTICISM
PRE-RAPHAELISM
RHODIAN SCHOOL
RHYPAROGRAPHY
VRAISEMBLANCE
WOOD-ENGRAVING

CHROMATOGRAPHY
CONSTRUCTIVISM
MIDDLE DISTANCE
PLASTER OF PARIS
PRIMARY COLOURS
QUATTROCENTISM
REPRESENTATION
STEEL-ENGRAVING
VANISHING POINT
WORKING-DRAWING

15

CANVAS-STRETCHER
LITHOCHROMATICS
PRE-RAPHAELITISM
ROMANTIC REVIVAL
SELF-PORTRAITURE
THUMBNAIL SKETCH

13

BELLE PEINTURE
CROSS-HATCHING
DRAWING-PENCIL
ETCHING GROUND
EXPRESSIONISM
FLEMISH SCHOOL

14

ACTION PAINTING

ARTS – POETRY

3	5	STAVE STICH	JINGLE LAISSE	7	PANTOUM PENNILL
BOB	ARSIS	TANKA	MIURUS	ALCAICS	PROSODY
LAY	CANTO	TITLE	MONODY	ART FORM	REFRAIN
ODE	CENTO	TRIAD	NOSTOS	BALLADE	RONDEAU
	DIVAN	VERSE	OCTAVE	BUCOLIC	SEMEION
	ELEGY	WHEEL	PASSUS	CAESURA	SEMIPED
4	ENVOY		PERIOD	CHOREUS	SESTINA
	EPODE		POETRY	COUPLET	SESTINE
DUAN	HAIKU	6	RHYTHM	DIMETER	SIXAINE
ECHO	ICTUS		RONDEL	DISTICH	SOTADIC
EPIC	IDYLL	AMORET	SCAZON	ECLOGUE	SPONDEE
EPOS	IONIC	BALLAD	SESTET	EPICEDE	STICHOS
FOOT	LIMMA	CHOREE	SONNET	EPIGRAM	STROPHE
IAMB	LYRIC	CRETIC	STANZA	EPISODE	TRIOLET
LINE	METRE	DACTYL	SYSTEM	FABLIAU	TRIPLET
LONG	OCTET	DIPODY	TENSON	GEORGIC	TRIPODY
MODE	PAEON	DIZAIN	TERCET	HOMERID	TRISEME
MORA	QUOTE	EPOPEE	THESIS	HUITAIN	TROCHEE
POEM	RHYME	GHAZAL		MEASURE	VERSING
SONG	RUN-ON	HAIKAI		METRICS	VIRELAY
TIME	STAFF	IAMBUS		OUTRIDE	

ARTS – POETRY

8

ANAPAEST
BACCHIUS
BALLADRY
BOBWHEEL
CANTICLE
CHEVILLE
CHOLIAMB
CHORIAMB
CLERIHEW
DOCHMIUS
DOGGEREL
EPILOGUE
EPITRITE
EPYLLION
GLYCONIC
HEXAPODY
KALEVALA
KYRIELLE
LIMERICK
LIPOGRAM
LYRICISM
MADRIGAL
MARINISM
MOLOSSUS
OCTAPODY
PALINODE
PASTORAL
PINDARIC
POETSHIP
PROLOGUE
QUATRAIN
SAPPHICS
SCANNING
SCANSION
SENARIUS
SONNETRY
STASIMON
SYNAPHEA
TERZETTA
TRIBRACH
TRIMETER
TRISTICH
TROCHAIC
VERSELET

9

AMPHIGORY
ANACRUSIS

ANTHOLOGY
ANTISPAST
ASCLEPIAD
CATALEXIS
CINQUAINE
COMPLAINT
DECASTICH
DISPONDEE
DITHYRAMB
DITROCHEE
EPINIKION
FIFTEENER
FREE VERSE
HEMISTICH
HEPTAPODY
HEXAMETER
HEXASTICH
LONG METRE
LYRIC POEM
MALE RHYME
MONOMETER
MONORHYME
MONOSTICH
OCTAMETRE
OCTASTICH
PARNASSUS
PAROEMIAC
PENTAPODY
POETICISM
POETICULE
PROSODIAN
QUOTATION
RHOPALISM
RICH RHYME
SIXTEENER
SONNETING
STORNELLO
SYLLABICS
SYNAPHEIA
TELESTICH
TERZA-RIMA
TETRAPODY
VERS LIBRE

10

AMPHIBRACH
AMPHIMACER
ASYNARTETE
BLANK VERSE
BOUTS RIMÉS

DOLICHURUS
ENJAMBMENT
FOURTEENER
HEPTAMETER
HEROIC POEM
METAPHRASE
OCTONARIAN
OTTAVA RIMA
PENTAMETER
PENTASTICH
POETASTERY
QUATORZAIN
RHYME-ROYAL
SHORT METER
STAVE-RHYME
STICHOLOGY
TETRAMETER
TETRASTICH
THEOTECHNY
VILLANELLE

11

ALEXANDRINE
ANTISTROPHE
BALLAD METRE
COMMON METRE
FLORILEGIUM
GALLIAMBICS
HEROIC VERSE
LINKED VERSE
LONG MEASURE
MOCK-HEROICS
OCTASTICHON
PARACROSTIC
PASTOURELLE
PENTHEMIMER
PETRARCHISM
PINDARIC ODE
RHYME-LETTER
RIDING-RHYME
SEPTENARIUS
STICHOMETRY

12

ANTIBACCHIUS
ARCHILOCHIAN
BALLADE ROYAL
EPITHALAMION

GENETHLIACON
HEPHTHEMIMER
HUDIBRASTICS
OCTOSYLLABIC
PROTHALAMION
PYTHIAN VERSE
SERVICE METRE
SONNETEERING
SPRUNG RHYTHM
STICHOMYTHIA
TRANSVERSION

13

ALCAIC STROPHE
FEMININE RHYME
HEROIC COUPLET
HETEROSTROPHY
METRIFICATION
MONOSTROPHICS
NONSENSE VERSE
PARNASSIANISM
POETIC LICENCE
REPORTED VERSE
SYLLABLE VERSE

14

ALLOIOSTROPHOS
CONCRETE POETRY
FEMININE ENDING
IDENTICAL RHYME
LIPOGRAMMATISM
LONGS-AND-SHORTS
MASCULINE RHYME
MILTONIC SONNET
PETRARCHIANISM
POLITICAL VERSE
PROCELEUSMATIC
RHYMING COUPLET
SESQUIPEDALITY
SONNET-SEQUENCE

15

FEMININE CAESURA
HENDECASYLLABLE
POULTERS' MEASURE
SERPENTINE VERSE

ARTS – TELEVISION, RADIO & RECORDS

3

HIT
JAM
POP
SET
WOW

4

BAND
BOOM
CAST
CLIP
DECK
DISC
EMMA
EMMY
FILM
GAIN
HI-FI
LINE
MIKE
MONO
MUSH
SHOW
SKIP
SLOT
SNOW
TAPE
TONE
WAVE

5

AMPEX
BLEEP
DRAMA
FIELD
FRAME
GHOST
NOISE
PANEL
PULSE
RADIO
RELAY
SOUND
STORY
TELLY
TRACK

VIDEO

6

AD-MASS
ADVERT
AERIAL
BEACON
CAMERA
COMEDY
DIPOLE
FADE-IN
FORMAT
GROOVE
LEAD-IN
MATRIX
NEEDLE
PICK-UP
RASTER
RECORD
REFLEX
REPEAT
REPLAY
SCREEN
SCRIPT
SERIAL
SERIES
SIGNAL
SINGLE
SKETCH
SLEEVE
STATIC
STEREO
STUDIO
STYLUS
TRANNY
VISION
WOOFER

7

ANTENNA
AUTOCUE
BLEEPER
CARRIER
CATHODE
CHANNEL
CLOSE-UP
CONSOLE
DISPLAY

DUBBING
EPISODE
EXCERPT
FADE-OUT
JUKE-BOX
MONITOR
NETWORK
PANNING
PHONE-IN
PICTURE
POP-SONG
READ-OUT
RELEASE
SCANNER
SKY-WAVE
SONG-HIT
SPEAKER
STARDOM
STATION
SYNTONY
TONE-ARM
TWEETER
VIEWING

8

AUDITION
BULLETIN
CASSETTE
CHAT-SHOW
DIALOGUE
EARPHONE
EPILOGUE
FLIP-SIDE
LONG-WAVE
MAGIC EYE
NEWSCAST
ORTHICON
PLAYBACK
POP-MUSIC
PREMIÈRE
PRESSING
RADIATOR
RECEIVER
RECORDER
SCANNING
SCANSION
SIDE-BAND
SMASH HIT
TELECAST
TELECINE

TELEFILM
TELETHON
TELETRON
WAVE-BAND
WIRELESS

9

AMPLIFIER
BLIND SPOT
BROADCAST
CIRCUITRY
EARPHONES
FORTY-FIVE
FREQUENCY
GOGGLE-BOX
HEADPHONE
HIT-PARADE
IDIOT CARD
INTERVIEW
LASER DISC
MICROWAVE
MODULATOR
PANEL GAME
PHONOGRAM
POP-RECORD
PROGRAMME
RADIOGRAM
RADIO WAVE
RECEPTION
RECORDING
SCREENING
SHORT-WAVE
SOAP OPERA
STORY LINE
TELEVISOR
TURNTABLE
VIDEOTAPE
VIDEO TUBE

10

BEAM SYSTEM
COMMENTARY
COMMERCIAL
CRYSTAL SET
DISTORTION
ELIMINATOR
EUROVISION
GOLDEN ROSE

GRAMOPHONE
HEADPHONES
IDIOT BOARD
INSTALMENT
LONG-PLAYER
MASS-MEDIUM
MEDIUM-WAVE
MICROPHONE
MODULATION
MULTIMEDIA
OSCILLATOR
PHONOGRAPH
PICK-UP HEAD
RESOLUTION
SOLAR NOISE
SOUND MIXER
STEAM RADIO
STEREOGRAM
SUPPRESSOR
TELECAMERA
TELESCREEN
TELEVÉRITÉ
TELEVISION
TIME SIGNAL
TRANSCRIPT
TRINISCOPE
VECTOGRAPH
WAVELENGTH
WHITE NOISE

11

ASPECT RADIO
CATCH-PHRASE
CAT'S-WHISKER
CHROMINANCE
DISCOGRAPHY
DOCUMENTARY
ELECTRON GUN
GAIN-CONTROL
LOUDSPEAKER
MICROGROOVE
MUSIC CENTRE
NEWSCASTING
NICKELODEON
OPEN CIRCUIT
OSCILLATION
PRESELECTOR
SMALL SCREEN
SPECTACULAR
TONE CONTROL

ARTS – TELEVISION, RADIO & RECORDS

TRANSMITTAL
TRANSMITTER
TRANSPONDER
VECTORSCOPE
VIDEO SIGNAL

REPRODUCTION
SCANNING-DISC
SEVENTY-EIGHT
SOUND EFFECTS
TAPE-RECORDER
TELEPROMPTER
TRANSMISSION

14

AUDIO-FREQUENCY
AUDIO-VISUAL AID
CATHODE-RAY TUBE
ELECTRON CAMERA
RADIO FREQUENCY
VIDEO FREQUENCY
VIDEO RECORDING

12

ACTION REPLAY
ANNOUNCEMENT
ATMOSPHERICS
BROADCASTING
CROSSCUTTING
EXTENDED PLAY
EXTRAVAGANZA
HIGH-FIDELITY
INTERFERENCE
MAGNETIC TAPE
PICTURE RATIO
PRESELECTION
RECEIVING-SET
RECORD PLAYER

13

BREAKFAST SHOW
CLOSED CIRCUIT
DRAMATISATION
HIGH-FREQUENCY
PIRATE-STATION
QUADRAPHONICS
SIGNATURE-TUNE
TAPE-RECORDING
TELERECORDING
TRANSCRIPTION
VIDEO RECORDER
WIRED WIRELESS

15

CABLE TELEVISION
DIRECTION-FINDER
RADIO-GRAMOPHONE
SEMI-DOCUMENTARY
SITUATION COMEDY
TRANSISTOR RADIO

ARTS – THEATRE

3

ACT
BOX
CUE
HIT
PIT
REP
RUN
SET

4

AUTO
BOOK
CAST
DAME

DOCK
DROP
EXIT
GRID
JUDY
LEAD
LOGE
MASK
MIME
OLIO
PART
PLAY
PLOT
PROP
RÔLE
SEAT
SHOW
SKIT
SPOT

TABS
TOUR
TURN
WING

5

ASIDE
CLOTH
CYCLE
DÉCOR
DRAMA
ENTRY
EXODE
FARCE
FIT-UP
FLIES

FLOAT
FLOOD
FOOTS
FOYER
HOUSE
LINES
LODGE
PANTO
PAPER
PIECE
PROPS
PUNCH
REVUE
SCENA
SCENE
SLIPS
SMASH
STAGE
STALL

STAND
STORY
STUDY
TITLE
TRICK
WINGS

6

ACTING
BOARDS
BRIDGE
BUMPER
BY-PLAY
BY-PLOT
CHORUS
CLAQUE

COMEDY
DRY RUN
ENCORE
FINALE
GRADIN
KABUKI
LINE-UP
MASQUE
MIMING
NUMBER
PARODY
PERIOD
PUPPET
REVIEW
SCRIPT
SCRUTO
SKETCH
STALLS
TROUPE

7

BALCONY
BENEFIT
BESPEAK
BIT-PART
CABARET
CIRCUIT
CLASSIC
COMPANY
CURTAIN
EFFECTS
EPISODE
GALLERY
GUIGNOL
HISTORY
HISTRIO
MACHINE
MATINÉE
MIMICRY
MIRACLE
MUMMERY
MUMMING
MUSICAL
MYSTERY
OVATION
PLAYLET
PREVIEW
READING
REVIVAL
REVOLVE
SCENARY
SCENERY
SEATING
SELL-OUT
SETTING
SHOWBIZ
SIDE-BOX
SNOW-BOX
STAGERY
STARDOM
STROPHE
SUBPLOT
TAKE-OFF
THEATRE
THE GODS
TRAGEDY
TRILOGY
VAMPIRE
VARIETY

8

APPLAUSE
AUDIENCE
AUDITION
BACKDROP
BOX-LOBBY
COULISSE
CRITIQUE
DIALOGUE
DROLLERY
DUMB-SHOW
ENSEMBLE
ENTERING
ENTR'ACTE
ENTRANCE
EPILOGUE
EPITASIS
FAUTEUIL
FESTIVAL
FREE-LIST
GRACIOSO
HISTRION
INTERACT
INTERVAL
LIGHTING
MONOLOGY
MORALITY
NAME-PART
PARTERRE
PASTORAL
PLAYBILL
PREMIÈRE
PROLOGUE
PROPERTY
PUPPETRY
SCENARIO
SET PIECE
SHOW-BILL
SMASH-HIT
STAGE-BOX
STAR-TRAP
THE HALLS
THRILLER
TRAVESTY
VIGNETTE
WARDROBE

9

BACK-CLOTH

BAIGNOIRE
BOX-OFFICE
BURLESQUE
CATCHWORD
CATHARSIS
CHARACTER
CLOAKROOM
COLUMBINE
COULISSES
CRUSH-ROOM
DRAMATICS
DROP-SCENE
EARLY DOOR
EPIC DRAMA
EPIRRHEMA
FLOOR-SHOW
FOOTLIGHT
FULL HOUSE
GREEN-ROOM
HAPPENING
HARLEQUIN
HYPNOTISM
INTERLUDE
LEITMOTIF
LEITMOTIV
LOW COMEDY
MELODRAMA
MESMERISM
MEZZANINE
MONODRAMA
MONOLOGUE
MUSIC-HALL
NIGHT-CLUB
ORCHESTRA
PANTALOON
PANTOMIME
PARABASIS
PERIAKTOS
PERSONAGE
PLAYHOUSE
PORTRAYAL
PROGRAMME
PROLUSION
PROMPT-BOX
PROMPTING
REHEARSAL
REPERTORY
SCENE-DOCK
SINGSPIEL
SITUATION
SLAPSTICK
SOLILOQUY

SOTTISIER
SPHENDONE
SPIRIT-GUM
SPOTLIGHT
STAGE-DOOR
STAGE-NAME
STAGE-PLAY
STAGINESS
STORY LINE
STRIP-CLUB
TETRALOGY
THEATRICS
THROW-AWAY
TITLE-RÔLE
TRIALOGUE
UNDERPLOT

10

AFTERPIECE
ANTI-MASQUE
APRON-STAGE
ARENA STAGE
AUDITORIUM
BOOK-HOLDER
CATASTASIS
CHORUS LINE
CLOSET-PLAY
DÉNOUEMENT
DRAMATURGY
FANTOCCINI
FIRST HOUSE
FIRST NIGHT
FOURTH WALL
HIPPODROME
IMPRESSION
MARIONETTE
MIMOGRAPHY
MUSIC-DRAMA
OMNIBUS BOX
PASQUINADE
PERIPETEIA
PRODUCTION
PROMPT-BOOK
PROMPT-COPY
PROMPT-SIDE
PROSCENIUM
PUPPET-PLAY
PUPPET-SHOW
REHEARSING
REPERTOIRE

45

ARTS – THEATRE

SCARAMOUCH
SHADOW-PLAY
SOUND-BOARD
STAGECRAFT
STAGE-FEVER
STRIP-TEASE
TAP-DANCING
VAUDEVILLE
WALK-AROUND
WALK-ON PART

SECOND HOUSE
SKIMMINGTON
STAGE-EFFECT
STAGE-FRIGHT
THEATRICALS
THEATRICISM
TRAGI-COMEDY
VARIETY SHOW
VENTRILOQUY
WALKING-PART

CURTAIN SPEECH
DEUS EX MACHINA
DRAMATISATION
HISTRIONICISM
IMPERSONATION
LITTLE THEATRE
LIVING THEATRE
MUSICAL COMEDY
SAFETY CURTAIN
SOUNDING-BOARD
TABLEAU VIVANT
THEATRICALISM
THEATRICALITY
VENTRILOQUISM

11

BLACK COMEDY
BLACK HUMOUR
CLIFFHANGER
CLOSET-DRAMA
COUNTER-TURN
CURTAIN CALL
DRAMATICISM
DROP-CURTAIN
EPIC THEATRE
GALANTY SHOW
GREASE-PAINT
HISTRIONICS
HISTRIONISM
HOUSE LIGHTS
IRON CURTAIN
LIVE THEATRE
MIRACLE PLAY
MISE-EN-SCÈNE
MYSTERY PLAY
PAINT-BRIDGE
PARASCENIUM
PASSION-PLAY
PERFORMANCE
POSTSCENIUM
PROBLEM PLAY
PUNCHINELLO
RIGGING LOFT
SCAFFOLDAGE

12

AMPHITHEATRE
BREECHES PART
CONSTRUCTURE
EXTRAVAGANZA
GRAND GUIGNOL
HARLEQUINADE
INTERMISSION
METHOD ACTING
MORALITY PLAY
NATIVITY PLAY
PEPPER'S GHOST
PROPERTY-ROOM
SHOW BUSINESS
SNEAK PREVIEW
STAGE WHISPER
STOCK COMPANY
STRAIGHT PART
STRAIGHT PLAY
SUMMER SEASON
THEATROMANIA
THEATROPHONE
TOTAL THEATRE

13

CHARACTER PART
COUP DE THÉÂTRE

14

CONSTRUCTIVISM
DRESS-REHEARSAL
INTERPRETATION
PROSCENIUM ARCH
REPRESENTATION
SCREAMING FARCE
STAGE DIRECTION
SUPPORTING RÔLE

15

CHARACTER ACTING
COMEDY OF MANNERS
FRONT OF THE HOUSE
LEADING BUSINESS
LEGITIMATE DRAMA
ORCHESTRA STALLS
PERFORMING RIGHT
SHADOW-PANTOMIME
SLAPSTICK COMEDY
STANDING OVATION

AVIATION TERMS

3

BAY
FIN
FIX
FLY
GUN
HOP
LEM
PAD
RIB
VOR
VTO
YAW

4

BANK
BODY
COWL
DECK
DIVE
DOPE
DRAG
FLAP
FLIP
HULL
JATO
KEEL
LIFT
LOOP
MACH
NOSE
PACK
PROP
PROW
RAID
RANK
ROOF
SKID
SPAN
SPAT
TAIL
TAXI
TRIM
VTOL
WING

5

AUDIO

BLITZ
BRAKE
CABIN
CHOCK
CHORD
DECCA
FLARE
FLY-BY
HEAVE
NAAFI
ORDER
PLANE
PRANG
PROBE
RADAR
ROTOR
SPACE
STACK
STAGE
STALL
STICK
STRUT
SURGE
WHEEL
WINGS

6

AIR-ARM
AIRWAY
BASKET
DECTRA
DROGUE
ELEVON
FAN-JET
FLIGHT
FLYING
GAS-BAG
GEORGE
GLITCH
HANGAR
MID-AIR
MODULE
OUTAGE
PARADE
POCKET
PUSHER
RADOME
REHEAT
ROCKET
RUDDER

RUNWAY
SLEEVE
SORTIR
STRIKE
TARGET
TARMAC
THRUST
VECTOR
VOLERY
VOYAGE
WASH-IN
YAWING

7

AILERON
AIR-BASE
AIRHOLE
AIR-LANE
AIR-LIFT
AIRLINE
AIR-LOCK
AIR-MISS
AIRPORT
AIR-RAID
AIRSTOP
BALLAST
BANKING
BLISTER
BOOSTER
CAPSULE
CEILING
CHASSIS
CHEVRON
COCKPIT
COMMAND
CONSOLE
CONTROL
COWLING
FAIRING
FLYOVER
FLY-PAST
FOOT-BAR
GONDOLA
GREMLIN
JUMP-OFF
LANDING
LIFT-OFF
MILK-RUN
MISSION
NACELLE

NAVARHO
PANCAKE
PAYLOAD
PONTOON
RE-ENTRY
RIGGING
RIP-CORD
SOARING
SPONSON
SURGING
TAKE-OFF
TAXIING
WASH-OUT
WING-TIP

8

AEROFOIL
AIR-BRAKE
AIR-COVER
AIRDROME
AIRFIELD
AIR FORCE
AIR POWER
AIRSCREW
AIR-SPACE
AIR-SPEED
AIRSTRIP
ALTITUDE
ATTITUDE
AVIATION
AVIONICS
BALLONET
BLACK BOX
BRIEFING
BURBLING
CAROUSEL
CONTRAIL
DOG-FIGHT
EJECTION
ELEVATOR
ENVELOPE
FREE-FALL
FUSILAGE
HELIPORT
HYDROSKI
JATO UNIT
JET-DRIVE
JOY-STICK
LONGERON
MOONSHOT

NOSE-CONE
NOSE-DIVE
PILOTAGE
PILOTING
SEADROME
SEAT-BELT
SIDE-SLIP
STACKING
STALLING
STRIP MAP
TAIL-BOOM
TAIL-SPIN
TRIMMING
VOLPLANE
WIND-CONE
WIND-SOCK
WING-FLAP
WING-SPAN
ZERO HOUR

9

AERODROME
AEROMOTOR
AEROSPACE
AIR-BRIDGE
AIR-POCKET
AIR-STRIKE
ASTRODOME
AUTOFLARE
BUFFETING
COUNT-DOWN
CRASH-DIVE
DASHBOARD
EMPENNAGE
EQUIPMENT
FLARE-PATH
FOOTPRINT
FORMATION
GLIDE-PATH
HELIDROME
HELISCOOP
HYDROFOIL
INSERTION
ION ENGINE
JET ENGINE
JET-STREAM
LOCALISER
MONOCOQUE
OUTRIGGER
OVERSHOOT

AVIATION TERMS

PARACHUTE
PERIMETER
POWER-DIVE
PROPELLER
SNEAK-RAID
SONIC BANG
SONIC BOOM
SUSTAINER
TOUCH-DOWN
VERTIPORT
WHIPSTALL

10

AEROBATICS
AERO-ENGINE
AIR-CUSHION
CONTRAPROP
GLIDE SLOPE
GREENHOUSE
GROUNDPLOT
MACH NUMBER
MOONSTRIKE
NAVIGATION
PATHFINDER
ROTOR-BLADE
SHOCK STALL
SHROUD-LINE
SPACE-PROBE
SPLASHDOWN
STABILISER
STATIC LINE
TARGET AREA
TEST-FLIGHT
TURBULENCE
UNDERSHOOT
WIND-SLEEVE
WIND-TUNNEL

11

AERONAUTICS
AEROSTATICS
AEROSTATION

AIR-CORRIDOR
AIR TERMINAL
AIR-UMBRELLA
COMPRESSION
DELAYED DROP
DIVE-BOMBING
EJECTOR SEAT
GROUND-SPEED
HEAT BARRIER
LANDING-BEAM
LANDING-GEAR
LEADING EDGE
NIGHT-FLYING
RECONNOITRE
RETROACTION
RETRO-ROCKET
ROCKET-MOTOR
SMOKE-TUNNEL
STAGING-POST
TALK-YOU-DOWN
TRIMMING TAB
VAPOUR TRAIL
WATER-TUNNEL
WING-LOADING

12

AERODYNAMICS
AIR-SEA RESCUE
ARRESTER HOOK
ASTRONAUTICS
BELLY-LANDING
CONTROL LEVER
CONTROL STICK
CONTROL TOWER
CRASH-LANDING
EARTHING TYRE
EQUILIBRATOR
HEDGE-HOPPING
LANDING-FIELD
LANDING-PLACE
LANDING-SPEED
LANDING-STRIP
LAUNCHING-PAD
PILOT-BALLOON

RETROPULSION
ROTOR-STATION
SERVO-CONTROL
SONIC BARRIER
SOUND BARRIER
SPACE-STATION

13

BOUNDARY LAYER
BURBLING POINT
CARPET-BOMBING
CONTACT FLIGHT
CONTROL COLUMN
FORCED LANDING
GROUND-CONTROL
JET-PROPULSION
LANDING-GROUND
PRESSURE-CABIN
SHOCK-ABSORBER
SPACE-PLATFORM
UMBILICAL CORD
UNDERCARRIAGE

14

AUTOMATIC PILOT
CONTROL SURFACE
DECCA FLIGHT LOG
FLIGHT-RECORDER
PROPELLER-BLADE
PROPELLER-SHAFT
RECONNAISSANCE
TALK-DOWN SYSTEM
WEIGHTLESSNESS

15

LANDING-CARRIAGE
THRESHOLD LIGHTS
VERTICAL TAKE-OFF

BELIEFS

3

FAD
ZEN

4

CULT
YOGA

5

CREED
DEISM
DOGMA
FAITH
ISLAM
JEWRY
KARMA
ODISM
TENET
ZOISM

6

BABISM
BELIEF
DUDISM
EGOISM
HERESY
HOLISM
HUMISM
HYLISM
LAXISM
MAOISM
MONISM
NUDISM
OBEISM
OPHISM
PAPISM
PURISM
RACISM
SEXISM
SHINTO
TAOISM
THEISM
THEORY
VEDISM
YOGISM

7

ATHEISM
ATOMISM
BAALISM
BAASKAP
BAHAISM
BIGOTRY
CARLISM
COMTISM
COSMISM
CULTISM
DUALISM
ÉLITISM
ESOTERY
EVANGEL
FADDISM
FASCISM
HEURISM
IDOLISM
JAINISM
JUDAISM
KANTISM
KENOSIS
KRYPSIS
LAMAISM
LEFTISM
LUDDISM
MARXISM
MOSAISM
MYTHISM
NAZIISM
ODYLISM
ORPHISM
OWENISM
PARSISM
PIETISM
REALISM
SAIVISM
SAKTISM
SCOTISM
SELFISM
SIKHISM
SIVAISM
SUFIISM
SUN-CULT
THEURGY
THOMISM
TITOISM
TORYISM
TSARISM
TYCHISM

UTOPISM
WORSHIP
ZIONISM

8

ACOSMISM
APOSTASY
ARIANISM
ATTICISM
AUTONOMY
BABELISM
BROWNISM
BUDDHISM
CACODOXY
CHARTISM
DEMONISM
DITHEISM
DOCETISM
DOCTRINE
DONATISM
DRUIDISM
DYNAMISM
ESCAPISM
ESSENISM
ETHICISM
EUGENISM
FAKIRISM
FAMILISM
FATALISM
FEMINISM
FINALISM
FUTURISM
GALENISM
GAULLISM
GEOLATRY
HEDONISM
HELOTISM
HINDUISM
HUMANISM
HYLACISM
IDEALISM
IDEOLOGY
IDOLATRY
ISLAMISM
JINGOISM
LEGALISM
LENINISM
LUNARISM
MAHDIISM
MAZDAISM

MINIMISM
MODALISM
MOLINISM
MONADISM
NATIVISM
NATURISM
NEGROISM
NIHILISM
OCCAMISM
OPHITISM
OPTIMISM
PACIFISM
PAGANISM
PANISLAM
PAPALISM
PHALLISM
POPULISM
PSYCHISM
PUSEYISM
QUIETISM
REGALISM
RELIGION
RIGORISM
ROMANISM
ROYALISM
RURALISM
SATANISM
SEMITISM
SOLARISM
SOLIDISM
SOMATISM
STOICISM
STUNDISM
TANTRISM
TIMONISM
TOTEMISM
TRIALISM
ULTRAISM
UNBELIEF
UNIONISM
VITALISM
WAHABISM

9

ANICONISM
ANIMATISM
APARTHEID
APRIORISM
AUTOLATRY
BABBITISM

BARBARISM
BIBLICISM
CAESARISM
CALVINISM
CAREERISM
CASUALISM
CATHARISM
CELTICISM
CHURCHISM
COBDENISM
COMMUNISM
COSMOGONY
DARWINISM
DEFEATISM
DISBELIEF
DITHELISM
DOGMATISM
DRACONISM
ECUMENISM
EGOTHEISM
ENCRATISM
EPEOLATRY
EPICURISM
EREMITISM
EROTICISM
ESOTERISM
ETHNICISM
EXTREMISM
FABIANISM
FALANGISM
FENIANISM
FETICHISM
FETISHISM
FEUDALISM
FORMALISM
FUSIONISM
GENTILISM
HEATHENRY
HEBREWISM
HELLENISM
HESYCHASM
HETAIRISM
HITLERISM
HYLOZOISM
IMMANENCY
IRVINGISM
ISMAILISM
JANSENISM
JESUITISM
LABOURISM
LOLLARDRY
LUTHERISM

BELIEFS

MAMMONISM
MECHANISM
MELIORISM
MENDELISM
MENTALISM
METHODISM
MISBELIEF
MITHRAISM
MODERNISM
MONERGISM
MONTANISM
MORMONISM
MOSLEMISM
MYSTICISM
MYTHICISM
NEPHALISM
OCCULTISM
ORANGEISM
ORIGENISM
ORLEANISM
ORTHODOXY
PANEGOISM
PANTHEISM
PARSEEISM
PAULINISM
PESSIMISM
PETRINISM
PHYSICISM
PLATONISM
PLURALISM
POUJADISM
POWELLISM
PRELATISM
QUAKERISM
QUIXOTISM
RABBINISM
RACIALISM
RANTERISM
REFORMISM
RITUALISM
ROUTINISM
SABBATISM
SABIANISM
SADDUCISM
SCIENTISM
SEXUALISM
SHAKERISM
SHAMANISM
SHINTOISM
SNAKE-CULT
SOCIALISM
SOLIPSISM

SOVIETISM
SPINOZISM
SPIRITISM
SUTTEEISM
SYMBOLISM
SYNERGISM
TELEOLOGY
TERMINISM
TEUTONISM
THANATISM
TRITHEISM
TUTIORISM
UTRAQUISM
VOLCANISM
VOODOOISM
VORTICISM
VULCANISM
ZEALOTISM
ZOOTHEISM

10

ANABAPTISM
ANTICIVISM
ANTITHEISM
ASCETICISM
ASIATICISM
ASTROLATRY
AUTOMATISM
AUTOTHEISM
AVERRHOISM
BANTINGISM
BARDOLATRY
BENTHAMISM
BOLSHEVISM
BOURBONISM
BRAHMANISM
BUCHMANISM
CAPITALISM
CHAUVINISM
CONCRETISM
EBIONITISM
EUHEMERISM
EVANGELISM
FANATICISM
FEDERALISM
FORTUITISM
FOURIERISM
FROEBELISM
GENEVANISM
GNOSTICISM

GRADUALISM
GRIFFINISM
GYMNOSOPHY
HAGIOLATRY
HEATHENISM
HELIOLATRY
HENOTHEISM
HETERODOXY
HIEROLATRY
HOBBIANISM
HUMORALISM
HYLOTHEISM
ICONOCLASM
ICONOLATRY
ICONOMACHY
ILLUMINISM
IMMORALISM
JACOBINISM
JACOBITISM
KANTIANISM
LAMARCKISM
LIBERALISM
LOLLARDISM
MESSIANISM
MODERATISM
MONARCHISM
MONETARISM
MONOGENISM
MONOTHEISM
NARCISSISM
NATURALISM
NAZARITISM
NEGATIVISM
NEUTRALISM
NOETIANISM
NOMINALISM
ORGANICISM
PACIFICISM
PANSLAVISM
PANSOPHISM
PARTIALISM
PATRIOTISM
PERSUASION
PHALLICISM
PHARISAISM
PHILOSOPHY
PLUTOLATRY
POLYGENISM
POLYTHEISM
POSITIVISM
PRAGMATISM
PURITANISM

PYRRHONISM
RADICALISM
RELATIVISM
RELATIVITY
REUNIONISM
REVIVALISM
RUSSIANISM
SARACENISM
SCEPTICISM
SECULARISM
SENSUALISM
SEPARATISM
SINECURISM
SOLIDARISM
SUN-WORSHIP
SWADESHISM
SYBARITISM
SYNCRETISM
TROTSKYISM
UTOPIANISM
VATICANISM
VIRTUALISM
WOLFIANISM

11

ADIAPHORISM
ADOPTIANISM
AGNOSTICISM
ANGELOLATRY
ANGLICANISM
APOLITICISM
APOLOGETICS
BACONIANISM
BONAPARTISM
BYZANTINISM
CATHOLICISM
CEREBRALISM
COENOBITISM
COLONIALISM
COMMUNALISM
COSMOTHEISM
CREATIONISM
DETERIORISM
DETERMINISM
DIPHYSITISM
DITHELETISM
ECUMENICISM
ERASTIANISM
ESCHATOLOGY
ESOTERICISM

EUDAEMONISM
EXTERNALISM
FIRE-WORSHIP
GALLICANISM
HEGELIANISM
HERO-WORSHIP
HIERARCHISM
HISTORICISM
HYLOPATHISM
ILLUSIONISM
IMMANENTISM
IMMEDIATISM
IMPERIALISM
INTUITIVISM
IRRIDENTISM
LUTHERANISM
MATERIALISM
MEDIEVALISM
MOHAMMEDISM
NAPOLEONISM
NATIONALISM
NEOPAGANISM
NEOVITALISM
NOVATIANISM
OBJECTIVISM
ORIENTALISM
PANISLAMISM
PANPSYCHISM
PARALLELISM
PELAGIANISM
PERSONALISM
PHENOMENISM
PHYSIOLATRY
PHYSITHEISM
PLYMOUTHISM
POSSIBILISM
PRETERITION
PRIMITIVISM
PROBABILISM
PROGRESSISM
PYTHAGORISM
RATIONALISM
RECHABITISM
REGIONALISM
RELATIONISM
RELIGIONISM
REVISIONISM
ROMANTICISM
SADDUCEEISM
SCIENTOLOGY
SCRIPTURISM
SINGULARISM

SOCINIANISM
SOTERIOLOGY
STAHLIANISM
SYSTEMATISM
TEETOTALISM
TELEOLOGISM
TETRATHEISM
THATCHERISM
THEANTHROPY
THEOSOPHISM
THERIOLATRY
TREE-WORSHIP
WESLEYANISM
ZEN BUDDHISM

12

AESTHETICISM
ANTI-SEMITISM
CHRISTIANISM
CHRISTIANITY
COLLECTIVISM
COLLEGIALISM
CONFUCIANISM
CONSERVATISM
CORPOREALISM
DEVIATIONISM
DISSENTERISM
ELEMENTALISM
EPICUREANISM
EPISTEMOLOGY
EVANGELICISM
EVOLUTIONISM
EXCLUSIONISM
EXPANSIONISM
FACTIONALISM
FEBRONIANISM
FREE-THINKING
HIPPOCRATISM
ICHTHYOLATRY
IMAGE-WORSHIP
IMMERSIONISM
INFLATIONISM
ISOLATIONISM
LAODICEANISM
LOW-CHURCHISM
MARCIONITISM
MUNICIPALISM
NEO-DARWINISM
NEONOMIANISM
NESTORIANISM
OBSCURANTISM

PANHELLENISM
PANSEXUALISM
PAROCHIALISM
PERPETUALISM
PHILISTINISM
PHILOSOPHISM
PRACTICALISM
PRECISIANISM
PROPAGANDISM
PSILANTHROPY
PSYCHOLOGISM
REDUCTIONISM
ROSMINIANISM
RUSSOPHILISM
SABELLIANISM
SALVATIONISM
SAMARITANISM
SECESSIONISM
SECTARIANISM
SEMI-ARIANISM
SPIRITUALISM
STERCORANISM
SUBJECTIVISM
TRADUCIANISM
TRANSFORMISM
UNITARIANISM
UNIVERSALISM
VOLUNTARYISM

13

ACCEPTILATION
ANTHROPOLATRY
ANTHROPOSOPHY
ANTIOCHIANISM
ANTISOCIALISM
APOCATASTASIS
ARISTOCRATISM
AUTO-EROTICISM
BERKELEIANISM
CATASTROPHISM
CATECHUMENISM
CEREMONIALISM
COMPATRIOTISM
CONCEPTUALISM
COSMOPOLITISM
DOCTRINAIRISM
ECUMENICALISM
ETHNOCENTRISM
FEUILLETONISM
FILIBUSTERISM

BELIEFS

FLAGELLANTISM
FRACTIONALISM
FUNCTIONALISM
GENERATIONISM
GEOCENTRICISM
HIGH-CHURCHISM
HILDEBRANDISM
IMMATERIALISM
IMPOSSIBILISM
INDETERMINISM
INDIVIDUALISM
INFALLIBILISM
IRRATIONALISM
LIBERATIONISM
MACHIAVELLISM
MALTHUSIANISM
MANICHAEANISM
MILLENNIALISM
MOHAMMEDANISM
MONARCHIANISM
MONOPHYSITISM
MONOTHELETISM
MORISONIANISM
NEO-LAMARCKISM
OCCASIONALISM
OCCIDENTALISM
PANSPERMATISM
PARTICULARISM
PERFECTIONISM
PHALANSTERISM
PHENOMENALISM
PROTECTIONISM
PROTESTANTISM
PRUDENTIALISM
REACTIONARISM
REPUBLICANISM
REVOLUTIONISM
SACERDOTALISM
SAINT-SIMONISM
SANITARIANISM
SCHOLASTICISM
SCRIPTURALISM
SEMI-BARBARISM
SOLIFIDIANISM
SPENCERIANISM
STRUCTURALISM

SUGGESTIONISM
THAUMATURGISM
THEANTHROPISM
TRACTARIANISM
TRADE UNIONISM
UNICAMERALISM
VEGETARIANISM
VOLTAIRIANISM
ZARATHUSTRISM

14

ALBIGENSIANISM
ANTI-JACOBINISM
AUGUSTINIANISM
EGALITARIANISM
ENCYCLOPAEDISM
EVANGELICALISM
EXISTENTIALISM
FUNDAMENTALISM
INDIFFERENTISM
INSPIRATIONISM
INTERACTIONISM
INTUITIONALISM
LEIBNITZIANISM
LIBERTARIANISM
MILLENARIANISM
MULTIRACIALISM
MYTHICAL THEORY
NECESSARIANISM
NIETZSCHEANISM
PAN-AMERICANISM
PERFECTIBILISM
PERIPATETICISM
PREDETERMINISM
PROBABILIORISM
PROGRESSIONISM
PROHIBITIONISM
PSILANTHROPISM
PYTHAGOREANISM
RASTAFARIANISM
RESTITUTIONISM
RESTORATIONISM
ROSICRUCIANISM

SABBATARIANISM
SACRAMENTALISM
SUBSTANTIALISM
TERRITORIALISM
THEOPASCHITISM
THERIOMORPHISM
TRADITIONALISM
TRINITARIANISM
TRIPERSONALISM
ULTRAMONTANISM
UTILITARIANISM
VALENTINIANISM
ZOROASTRIANISM

15

ANNIHILATIONISM
ANTICLERICALISM
ANTI-GALLICANISM
BACCHANALIANISM
CONFESSIONALISM
CONSERVATIONISM
EPISCOPALIANISM
EQUALITARIANISM
EXPERIENTIALISM
FIFTH-MONARCHISM
HUMANITARIANISM
INSTRUMENTALISM
INTELLECTUALISM
INTERVENTIONISM
INTRANSIGENTISM
NEO-CHRISTIANITY
NOTHINGARIANISM
PATRIPASSIANISM
PREFERENTIALISM
PREFORMATIONISM
PRESBYTERIANISM
PRESENTATIONISM
RESURRECTIONISM
SEMI-PELAGIANISM
SUPERNATURALISM
THERIANTHROPISM
TOTALITARIANISM

BUILDINGS – ARCHITECTURE & BUILDING TERMS

3

BAY
COB
EYE
FUR
HIP
KEY
LAG
LUM
MAT
NOG
PUG
RIB
SET
TIE

4

ADIT
ANTA
APSE
ARCH
BASE
BEAD
BEAM
BOND
CASE
COPE
COVE
CROP
CUSP
CYMA
DADO
DOME
DOOR
DRIP
DRUM
FLAG
FOIL
FRET
FROG
GROG
KAME
LADY
LATH
LEAD
LIST
NECK
NOOK
NOSE

OGEE
PANE
PIER
PILE
PISÉ
PLAN
PLOT
RAFT
RAGG
ROLL
ROOF
SITE
SKEW
SLAB
SLAT
SPAR
STOA
STUD
TIGE
TILE
TORE
VASE
VOID
WALL
WING
XYST

5

ADOBE
ANCON
ANNEX
ATTIC
BAULK
BÉTON
BLOCK
BOARD
BRICK
COMPO
CROWN
CRUCK
CRYPT
CURVE
DALLE
DORIC
EAVES
FLOOR
FLUTE
GABLE
GLASS

GLYPH
GROIN
GROUT
GUTTA
HANCE
HELIX
IONIC
JOIST
JUTTY
KNOSP
LABEL
LEDGE
LEVEL
LOTUS
MINAR
MOULD
M-ROOF
NERVE
NEWEL
NICHE
OGIVE
ORDER
ORIEL
OVOLO
OXEYE
PEGGY
PLATE
PORCH
PRINT
PUTTY
PYLON
QUEEN
QUIRK
QUOIN
RIDGE
ROUND
RYBAT
SCAPE
SHAFT
SLATE
SLYPE
SMALL
SOCLE
SPIRE
SPLAY
STONE
STRIA
STYLE
TABLE
TALON
TORUS
TRUNK

TUDOR
VAULT
VERGE
ZOCCO

6

ABACUS
ALCOVE
ANNEXE
ARCADE
ASHLAR
BATTEN
BILLET
BONDER
CANTON
CASING
CAULIS
CEMENT
CIPPUS
CLOSER
COFFER
COLUMN
CONCHA
COPING
CORBEL
CORNER
CORONA
COURSE
COVING
CRENEL
CULLIS
CUPOLA
DENTEL
DENTIL
DIAPER
DORTER
DOUBLE
DRY-ROT
EXEDRA
FAÇADE
FACING
FASCIA
FILLER
FILLET
FINIAL
FLY ASH
FRIEZE
GABLET
GAZEBO
GIRDER

GOTHIC
GRIFFE
GUNITE
GUTTER
HAUNCH
HEADER
HURTER
IMBREX
IMPOST
INVERT
LANCET
LAYING
LEDGER
LIERNE
LINTEL
LISTEL
MALTHA
MATRIX
METOPE
MODULE
MONIAL
MORTAR
MUTULE
NEBULE
NEEDLE
NOSING
OFFSET
PALLET
PARPEN
PATERA
PATTEN
PERRON
PILLAR
PLINTH
PODIUM
POMMEL
PORTAL
PURLIN
QUARRY
RAFTER
RECESS
REGLET
REGULA
RETURN
REVEAL
ROCOCO
ROSACE
RUBBLE
RUSTIC
SCHEME
SCOTIA
SCREED

SCROLL
SEVERY
SOFFIT
SOLIVE
SPRING
STAIRS
STOREY
STRIGA
STRING
STUCCO
SUMMER
TAENIA
TASSEL
TEGULA
THATCH
THOLOS
THOLUS
THROAT
THRUST
TIE-ROD
TILING
TIMBER
TORSEL
VALLEY
VOLUTE
WATTLE
WINDOW
XYSTUS

7

AILERON
AIR-TRAP
ANNULET
ANTEFIX
ARCHLET
ARCHWAY
AZULEJO
BALCONY
BALLOON
BAROQUE
BONDING
CABLING
CAPITAL
CAVETTO
CEILING
CHIMNEY
CLINKER
COB-WALL
COLUMEL
CONCAVE

BUILDINGS – ARCHITECTURE & BUILDING TERMS

CONSOLE
CORBEIL
CORNICE
COVELET
CROCKET
CUSHION
DIAGRAM
DIGLYPH
DISTYLE
DOORWAY
DORMANT
DOUCINE
DUCHESS
ECHINUS
ENTASIS
EUSTYLE
EXHEDRA
FEATHER
FESTOON
FLETTON
FLEURON
FLEXURE
FRONTAL
FRONTON
FURRING
FUSAROL
GLAZING
GRECQUE
GUICHET
HIP-KNOB
HIP-ROOF
HOUSING
HUTTING
KING-ROD
KLINKER
LACUNAR
LAGGING
LARMIER
LATHING
LATTICE
LUCARNE
LUM-HEAD
LUNETTE
MANSARD
MASONRY
MINARET
MOELLON
MULLION
NECKING
NERVURE
NULLING
NO-FINES

NOGGING
OUTWALL
PANNIER
PANTILE
PARAPET
PENDANT
PERSIAN
PLAFOND
PLASTER
PLYWOOD
PORTICO
PUGGING
PURLINE
QUARREL
RAGWORK
REEDING
RESPOND
RIBBING
RIB-WORK
RIDGING
ROOFING
ROOFTOP
ROSETTE
ROTUNDA
SAGITTA
SEXFOIL
SHINGLE
SIPOREX
SKEW-PUT
SLATING
SOLDIER
SOLIDUM
SQUINCH
STEEPLE
SUPPORT
SURBASE
SYSTYLE
TAILING
TALL-BOY
TAMBOUR
TELAMON
TERRACE
TESSERA
TESTUDO
TIE-BEAM
TRACERY
TRANSOM
TREFOIL
TRIMMER
TRUMEAU
VERANDA
VITRAIL

WALLING

8

ABUTMENT
ADJUTAGE
AIR-BRICK
AIR-DRAIN
AIRSHAFT
APOPHYGE
ASTRAGAL
BAGUETTE
BALUSTER
BANDELET
BANDAROL
BARTISAN
BELLCOTE
BUTTRESS
CANEPHOR
CARACOLE
CARYATID
CASEMENT
CHAPITER
CHAPTREL
CINCTURE
CLOISTER
CONCRETE
COUNTESS
CROSS-RIB
CYMATIUM
DANCETTE
DIASTYLE
DIPTEROS
DOGTOOTH
ENCARPUS
ENTRESOL
EPISTYLE
ERECTION
EXTRADOS
FEMERALL
FENESTRA
FIRE-CLAY
FLOORING
FOOTINGS
FRONTAGE
FRONTOON
GABLE-END
GARGOYLE
GROINING
GROUTING
HOUSETOP

IMPERIAL
INTERTIE
INTRADOS
ISODOMON
KEYSTONE
KING-BOLT
KINGPOST
KNURLING
MASCARON
MOULDING
OVERSAIL
PALMETTE
PARABEMA
PAVILION
PEDESTAL
PEDIMENT
PENTROOF
PILASTER
PILEWORK
PINNACLE
PLATBAND
PLATFORM
PRINCESS
PROPYLON
PROSTYLE
PUNCHEON
RAGSTONE
REAR-ARCH
RED BRICK
RERE-ARCH
ROCAILLE
ROCK WOOL
ROCK-WORK
ROOF-TREE
SEMI-DOME
SEPT-FOIL
SHOT-HOLE
SIDEPOST
SKEW-BACK
SKYLIGHT
SPANDREL
SPANDRIL
SPAN-ROOF
SPRINGER
STRINGER
STUDDING
STUDWORK
SUBBASAL
TERRAZZO
TESSELLA
TOP-STONE
TRIGLYPH

TYMPANUM
VAULTAGE
VAULTING
VERANDAH
VOMITORY
VOUSSOIR
WATTLING

9

AGGREGATE
AIR-JACKET
ALABASTER
ANGLE IRON
APSIDIOLE
ARCHIVOLT
BAND-STONE
BANQUETTE
BATH STONE
BAY WINDOW
BELVEDERE
BONDSTONE
BOW WINDOW
BRICKWORK
BRIQUETTE
CAPE DUTCH
CARTOUCHE
CENTERING
CHIPBOARD
CLAPBOARD
COLONNADE
CRIPPLING
CROSSBEAM
CROSSETTE
CROWN-POST
CROW-STEPS
CUL-DE-FOUR
CYMA RECTA
DECASTYLE
DRIP-STONE
DUCK-BOARD
DUTCH TILE
ELEVATION
EMBRASURE
EXTENSION
FASTIGIUM
FENESTRAL
FIREBRICK
FOLIATION
FOLIATURE
FREESTONE

FROSTWORK
GATE-HOUSE
GATE-TOWER
GOTHICISM
GUTTERING
HARDBOARD
HEADSTONE
HEXASTYLE
HEART-BOND
HYPOCAUST
INFILLING
JUT-WINDOW
LINEN-FOLD
LOOP-LIGHT
MALE-ORDER
MEZZANINE
MINKSTONE
MODILLION
MULTIFOIL
NEO-GOTHIC
OCTASTYLE
ONION-DOME
PANTILING
PARGETING
PENISTONE
PEPPER-BOX
PEPPER-POT
PERIDROME
PERISTYLE
PINEAPPLE
POZZOLANA
PRINCIPAL
QUEEN-POST
RIDGE-POLE
RIDGE-TILE
ROOFBOARD
ROOF-PLATE
ROUGHCAST
SADDLE-BAR
SCAGLIOLA
SCROLLERY
SHINGLING
SKEW-TABLE
SMALL LADY
SPRINGING
STAIRCASE
STANCHION
STONEWORK
STRAPWORK
STRETCHER
STRIATION
STRIATURE

STRUCTURE
STYLOBATE
TECTONICS
THATCHING
TILE-STONE
THOLOBATE
TIERCERON
TRIFORIUM
TROCHILUS
UNDERWORK
WAGON-ROOF
WALL-BOARD
WALL-PLATE
WATER-LEAF

10

ACROTERION
AIR-GRATING
ARAEOSTYLE
ARCHITRAVE
ASHLAR-WORK
ATTIC ORDER
BALCONETTE
BALL-FLOWER
BALUSTRADE
BARGE-BOARD
BOND-TIMBER
BRATTICING
BREAST WALL
BRICK-EARTH
BROWNSTONE
CAULICULUS
CAVITY WALL
CHIMNEY-CAN
CHIMNEY-POT
CHIMNEY-TOP
CINQUE-FOIL
CLERESTORY
COLLAR-BEAM
CORBELLING
CORINTHIAN
CROWN-GLASS
DAMP-COURSE
DITRIGLYPH
DORIC ORDER
EARTH-TABLE
EGG-AND-DART
FAN TRACERY
FEATHERING
FENESTELLA

FIBREBOARD
FIELDSTONE
FIRST FLOOR
FLOOR-BOARD
FOUNDATION
FRENCH ROOF
FRENCH SASH
GROUNDSELL
GROUNDSILL
HAMMER-BEAM
INSULATION
IONIC ORDER
JACK RAFTER
JERKINHEAD
LANCET-ARCH
MONKEY-TAIL
MOUCHARABY
NORMAN ARCH
ORDONNANCE
PARPEN-WALL
PEBBLE-DASH
PENCILLING
PENDENTIVE
PENTASTYLE
PLATE-GLASS
PROJECTION
PROPYLAEUM
PYRAMIDION
QUARTERING
QUATREFOIL
RIDGE-PIECE
ROMANESQUE
ROSE WINDOW
RUBBLEWORK
RUSTIC-WORK
SADDLEBACK
SADDLE-ROOF
SAFETY-ARCH
SASH WINDOW
SCROLLWORK
SETTLEMENT
SHEET-GLASS
SHUTTERING
SKEW-CORBEL
STEREOBATE
SUBSIDENCE
SUMMER-TREE
TETRASTYLE
THIRD FLOOR
TRABEATION
TRANSITION
VERGE-BOARD

WAGON-VAULT
WATER-JOINT
WATER-SPOUT
WATER-TABLE
WINDOW-PANE
WINDOW-SILL
WIRED-GLASS

11

BARGE-COUPLE
BARGE-STONES
BARREL-VAULT
BEAUMONTAGE
BEAVER BOARD
BLIND-STOREY
BROACH-SPIRE
CINQUECENTO
CONTRACTION
COPING-STONE
CORBEL-TABLE
CORNER-STONE
COUNTER-FORT
CURTAIN WALL
CYMA REVERSA
DODECASTYLE
ENGLISH BOND
ENTABLATURE
FAN VAULTING
FIRST STOREY
FLEMISH BOND
FOAM PLASTIC
FOUNDATIONS
GABLE-WINDOW
GAMBREL ROOF
GROUND FLOOR
GYPSUM BLOCK
HAMMER-BRACE
HAUTE ÉPOQUE
IMBRICATION
LINEN-SCROLL
MANSARD-ROOF
MARCHIONESS
OEIL-DE-BOEUF
ORIEL-WINDOW
PARPEN-STONE
PATERNOSTER
PENDANT-POST
PLASTER-WORK
PLASTIC CLAY
QUARREL-PANE

55

BUILDINGS — ARCHITECTURE & BUILDING TERMS

RIB-VAULTING
ROMAN CEMENT
ROOFING-TILE
RUBBLE-STONE
SECOND FLOOR
STILTED ARCH
STORM WINDOW
SURBASEMENT
THATCH-BOARD
THIRD STOREY
THREE-DECKER
TUDOR FLOWER
VISCOUNTESS
WATER-CEMENT
WHEEL-WINDOW
WINDOW-FRAME
WINDOW-GLASS

PALLADIANISM
PAVILION-ROOF
PLASTERBOARD
PSEUDO-GOTHIC
QUARTER-ROUND
RECESSED ARCH
SECOND STOREY
STAINED GLASS
STRING-COURSE
SUBARCUATION
SUBSTRUCTION
SUBSTRUCTURE
TESSELLATION
THROUGH-STONE
WEATHER-BOARD
WOOD-WOOL SLAB

QUATREFEUILLE
RELIEVING ARCH
SEGMENTAL ARCH
SOUND-BOARDING
STRAINING-BEAM
STRETCHER-BOND
SUBORDINATION
TOOTH-ORNAMENT
TRIUMPHAL ARCH
UNIVERSAL BEAM
WATTLE AND DAUB

14

ASBESTOS CEMENT
CASEMENT-WINDOW
CATHERINE-WHEEL
CORRUGATED IRON
CURTAIN-WALLING
DECORATED STYLE
FLYING BUTTRESS
GALVANISED IRON
LONGS-AND-SHORTS
OPUS LATERICIUM
PORTLAND CEMENT
QUEEN ANNE STYLE
SHOULDERED ARCH
SUPERELEVATION
SUPERSTRUCTION
SUPERSTRUCTURE
SYSTEM BUILDING

12

ARCHITECTURE
BOARD-MEASURE
BREASTSUMMER
CHIMNEY-PIECE
CHIMNEY-SHAFT
CHIMNEY-STACK
CLINKER-BLOCK
COLUMNIATION
CONSTRUCTION
CONSTRUCTURE
CRENELLATION
DORMER WINDOW
EARLY ENGLISH
EGG-AND-ANCHOR
ESPAGNOLETTE
FENESTRATION
FRENCH WINDOW
FRONTISPIECE
FROSTED-GLASS
FROST TRACERY
GEODESIC DOME
HOOD-MOULDING
INVERTED ARCH
LANCET-WINDOW
LOUVRE WINDOW
NECK-MOULDING

13

BATEMENT LIGHT
BUILDING-BLOCK
BUILDING-BOARD
CABLE-MOULDING
CHAIN-MOULDING
CHIMNEY-BREAST
COMPASS WINDOW
CONCRETE STEEL
COURSING-JOINT
CROSS-SPRINGER
CROSS-VAULTING
CTESIPHON ARCH
DILAPIDATIONS
DIMENSION WORK
DOUBLE-GLAZING
ELECTRO-CEMENT
ENCAUSTIC TILE
EXPANDED METAL
FERRO-CONCRETE
GOTHIC REVIVAL
GROIN-CENTRING
INTERPILASTER
LATTICE-GIRDER
LOW SIDE-WINDOW
MACHICOLATION
PERPENDICULAR
PORTLAND STONE

15

AERATED CONCRETE
CORINTHIAN ORDER
DISCHARGING ARCH
FOUNDATION STONE
HANGING BUTTRESS
INSULATING BOARD
QUADRIPARTITION
WEATHER-BOARDING

BUILDINGS – DWELLINGS & SHELTERS

3

BOX
COT
HUT
INN
KIP
PAD

4

BARN
BULK
BUTT
BYRE
CAMP
CASA
CAVE
CRIB
DIGS
DRUM
DUMP
FARM
FLAT
HALL
HIDE
HOLE
HOME
NEST
PENT
ROOF
SEAT
SEMI
SHED
TENT
YURT

5

ABODE
ADOBE
ANTRE
BOOTH
BOTHY
CABIN
COURT
CROFT
DACHA
HOTEL
HOUSE

HOVEL
HUMPY
HYDRO
IGLOO
KIOSK
KRAAL
LODGE
MANSE
MOTEL
PHARE
PLACE
RANCH
ROOMS
SHACK
STALL
STAND
TEPEE
TUPIK
VILLA
YAMEN
YOURT

6

AWNING
BED-SIT
BILLET
BUNKER
BURROW
CABANA
CASTLE
CHALET
DUGOUT
GARAGE
GRANGE
GUNYAH
HEARTH
HOSTEL
LEAN-TO
LOG-HUT
MAISON
MUD-HUT
PALACE
PHAROS
POSADA
PREFAB
PRIORY
QUINTA
RANCHO
REFUGE
REMISE

SAETER
SCONCE
SHANTY
STABLE
TEEPEE
WIGWAM

7

BASTIDE
CABOOSE
CARAVAN
CHÂTEAU
CONVENT
COTTAGE
COW-SHED
DEMESNE
EDIFICE
FLATLET
GRANARY
HIDEOUT
HOSPICE
KIBITKA
KIP-SHOP
KOLKHOZ
MANSION
MARQUEE
MIRADOR
NUNNERY
PENSION
PUP-TENT
RECTORY
RETREAT
SCHLOSS
SHELTER
SHIPPEN
UMBRAGE

8

AIR-HOUSE
BARRACKS
BELL-TENT
BUILDING
BUNGALOW
COAL-HOLE
DIGGINGS
DOMICILE
DWELLING

FUNK-HOLE
HACIENDA
HIDEAWAY
HIDYHOLE
HOME-FARM
HOSTELRY
HOTHOUSE
KIP-HOUSE
LODGINGS
LOG-CABIN
LOG-HOUSE
LOVE-NEST
MARQUISE
OUTHOUSE
PAVILION
QUARTERS
RIFLE-PIT
RONDAVEL
SHAMIANA
TENEMENT
TOOL-SHED
VICARAGE
WATCH-BOX
WOOD-HOLE
WOODSHED

9

ALMS-HOUSE
APARTMENT
BED-SITTER
BÉGUINAGE
BELVEDERE
BOATHOUSE
BOMBPROOF
BUNK-HOUSE
CART-HOUSE
COAL-HOUSE
DHARMSALA
DOSS-HOUSE
DUTCH BARN
FARMHOUSE
FARMSTEAD
FIREHOUSE
FLOPHOUSE
GATE-HOUSE
GATE-TOWER
HERMITAGE
HOME-CROFT
HOMESTEAD
HOSPITIUM
HOUSE-BOAT

LOCKHOUSE
LODGEMENT
LONG-HOUSE
MANOR-SEAT
MANSIONRY
MAST-HOUSE
MATTAMORE
MONASTERY
NEAT-HOUSE
NEAT-STALL
NISSEN HUT
ORPHANAGE
PALMHOUSE
PARSONAGE
PEEL-HOUSE
PENTHOUSE
PINE-HOUSE
RANCHERIA
RESIDENCE
RESIDENCY
REST-HOUSE
ROOT-HOUSE
SANCTUARY
SENTRY-BOX
TITHE-BARN
TOLL-BOOTH
TOLL-HOUSE
TOOLHOUSE
TOWN-HOUSE
TREE-HOUSE
WIND-BREAK
WOOD-HOUSE

10

BATHING-BOX
BATHING-HUT
BUS SHELTER
CANTONMENT
COACH-HOUSE
COUNTRY-BOX
DOWER-HOUSE
EARTH-HOUSE
FERRY-HOUSE
FRAME-HOUSE
GARDEN-SHED
GLASS-HOUSE
GLEBE-HOUSE
GREENHOUSE
GUEST-HOUSE
HABITATION

57

BUILDINGS – DWELLINGS & SHELTERS

HIBERNACLE
HUNTING-BOX
LIGHTHOUSE
LUMBER-CAMP
MAISONETTE
MANOR-HOUSE
PICTS' HOUSE
PIED-À-TERRE
PRAETORIUM
PRESBYTERY
PRINCIPIUM
QUONSET HUT
REST-CENTRE
STOREHOUSE
SUBTERRENE
TABERNACLE
WATCH-HOUSE

11

BRIDGE-HOUSE
COLD HARBOUR
COTTAGE ORNÉ
COUNTRY-SEAT
DAK BUNGALOW
GARDEN-HOUSE
HEAD-STATION
HIDING-PLACE
HUNTING-SEAT
INHABITANCY
ORCHID-HOUSE

OUTBUILDING
PHALANSTERY
PIT-DWELLING
PRISON-HOUSE
SCHOOLHOUSE
SERVICE-FLAT
SHOOTING-BOX
STATELY HOME
SUMMER-HOUSE
TIED COTTAGE
XENODOCHIUM

12

BACHELOR FLAT
COUNCIL-HOUSE
COUNTRY-HOUSE
HEADQUARTERS
HIBERNACULUM
HIGH-RISE FLAT
HUNTING-LODGE
INHABITATION
LAKE-DWELLING
LODGING-HOUSE
MANSION-HOUSE
ORCHARD-HOUSE
PILE-DWELLING
PORTER'S LODGE
PRIVATE HOTEL
ROOMING-HOUSE
TELEPHONE-BOX

13

ACCOMMODATION
ANCESTRAL HOME
BOARDING-HOUSE
DWELLING-HOUSE
DWELLING-PLACE
HIGH-RISE BLOCK
MAISON DE VILLE
OPEN-PLAN HOUSE
SHOOTING-LODGE

14

AIR-RAID SHELTER
BATHING-MACHINE
FALL-OUT SHELTER
TELEPHONE-KIOSK

15

ANDERSON SHELTER
DUPLEX APARTMENT
JERRY-BUILT HOUSE
SPLIT-LEVEL HOUSE
SUCCESSION HOUSE
TEMPERANCE HOTEL
▬▬▬▬▬▬▬▬▬

BUILDINGS – FACTORIES & SHOPS

3

INN
PIT
PUB

4

CAFÉ

CO-OP
FARM
HONG
KHAN
MART
MILL
MINE
MINT
SHOP

5

BOOTH
DAIRY
DEPOT
FORGE
HOUSE
KIOSK
LOCAL
PLANT

SALON
SERAI
STALL
STORE
WORKS

6

AGENCY

ARCADE
ASHERY
BAKERY
BAZAAR
BISTRO
BODEGA
BOOZER
BOTHAN
BRANCH
BUREAU

EATERY
FINERY
GARAGE
GODOWN
KNEIPE
LOGGIA
MARKET
OFFICE
OILERY
POSADA

PUBLIC
QUARRY
ROPERY
SMITHY
TAVERN
TAWERY
TILERY
VINTRY

SUTLERY
TANNERY
TAVERNA
TEA-SHOP
TIN-MINE
TOY-SHOP
TRIPERY
TURNERY

SALT-MINE
SEED-SHOP
SHOE-SHOP
SLAP-BANG
SLOP-SHOP
SMELTERY
SMITHERY
SNACK-BAR
SPINNERY
STANNARY
STONE-PIT
TAP-HOUSE
TEA-HOUSE
TEA-ROOMS
TICK-SHOP
TIDEMILL
TRY-HOUSE
TUCK-SHOP
WALK-MILL
WINE-SHOP
WOOL-MILL

PRINT-SHOP
REPERTORY
ROADHOUSE
ROPE-HOUSE
ROPEWORKS
SALT-WORKS
SALVATORY
SHALE-MINE
SHOT-TOWER
SNUFF-MILL
SOAP-WORKS
SPEAK-EASY
STRIP-MINE
SWEAT-SHOP
SWEET-SHOP
TALLY-SHOP
TIED HOUSE
TOLLBOOTH
TRATTORIA
TRIPE-SHOP
WAREHOUSE
WATER-MILL

7

ALBERGO
ALCÁZAR
ARSENAL
AUBERGE
BINDERY
BOILERY
BOTTEGA
BREWERY
BUVETTE
CANNERY
CANTEEN
CATTERY
CHOLTRY
COAL-PIT
DRIVE-IN
DUDDERY
EATERIE
FACTORY
FOUNDRY
GINNERY
GIN-SHOP
KENNELS
LAUNDRY
MALTING
MILK-BAR
NAILERY
NURSERY
PET-SHOP
PIE-SHOP
POP-SHOP
POT-SHOP
POTTERY
RETTERY
RUM-SHOP
SALTERN
SAW-MILL
SEX-SHOP
SHAMBLE
SHEBEEN
STATION

8

ABATTOIR
ALE-HOUSE
BALNEARY
BONE-MILL
BOOKSHOP
BOUTIQUE
BUTCHERY
CALENDRY
CLAY-MILL
COAL-MINE
COOKSHOP
CORN-MILL
CREAMERY
DRAM-SHOP
DYE-HOUSE
DYE-WORKS
EMPORIUM
ENTREPOT
FILATURE
FLAX-MILL
FRUITERY
GANG MILL
GAS-WORKS
GIN-HOUSE
GOLD-MINE
GRINDERY
GROG-SHOP
HACIENDA
IRON-MINE
JUNK-SHOP
KNACKERY
MALT-MILL
PAWNSHOP
PHARMACY
PIZZERIA
PLUMBERY
POT-HOUSE
PREMISES
PULP-MILL
REFINERY

9

BAKEHOUSE
BEER-HOUSE
BLEACHERY
BOOKSTALL
BOOKSTAND
BRASSERIE
BREW-HOUSE
CAFETERIA
CHOP-HOUSE
CLOTH-HALL
COOKHOUSE
COOPERAGE
CYCLE-SHOP
DOLLY-SHOP
DRUG-STORE
ESTAMINET
FLOUR MILL
FREE HOUSE
GIN-PALACE
GRIST-MILL
IRONWORKS
JOB CENTRE
LIBRAIRIE
MUSIC SHOP
NEWS-STAND
PAPER-MILL
PAPER-SHOP

10

ALCAICERÍA
BAKER'S SHOP
BRICKWORKS
BUCKET SHOP
CHAIN-STORE
COFFEE-SHOP
CONDENSERY
COPPER-MINE
CORNER SHOP
COTTON-MILL
DISTILLERY
DRYSALTERY
FISH-MARKET
GLASS-HOUSE
GLASSWORKS
GROCETERIA
LAUNDROMAT
LOAN-OFFICE
LUMBER-MILL
MARKET-HALL
MEAT-MARKET
MOBILE SHOP
OFF-LICENCE
OPEN MARKET
PÂTISSERIE
POST OFFICE

BUILDINGS – FACTORIES & SHOPS

POWDER MILL
POWER-HOUSE
POWER-PLANT
PRINT-WORKS
REPAIR-SHOP
REPOSITORY
RESTAURANT
RÔTISSERIE
SMOKE-HOUSE
SPORTS SHOP
STEELWORKS
STOREHOUSE
SUBSTATION
SUGAR-HOUSE
TRUST-HOUSE

11

ANTIQUE SHOP
BEAUTY SALON
BETTING-SHOP
BLEACH-FIELD
BONDED STORE
CHARCUTERIE
COFFEE-HOUSE
COFFEE-STALL
COPPER-WORKS
CRAZING MILL
DRAPER'S SHOP
EATING-HOUSE
FITTING-SHOP
FLESH-MARKET
FREIGHT-SHED
FULLING-MILL
GROCER'S SHOP
HYPERMARKET
IRON-FOUNDRY
LAUNDERETTE
LEAVING-SHOP
MANUFACTORY
MARKET-HOUSE

OFFICE BLOCK
PORTER-HOUSE
PUBLIC HOUSE
ROLLING-MILL
SUPERMARKET
TAILOR'S SHOP
TIMBER-WORKS
TUCKING-MILL
TYPE-FOUNDRY
WOOLLEN-MILL

12

BUTCHER'S SHOP
CARAVANSERAI
CHEMIST'S SHOP
CORN-EXCHANGE
CORNING-HOUSE
DELICATESSEN
DUTY-FREE SHOP
FASHION HOUSE
FLORIST'S SHOP
GARDEN CENTRE
GENERAL STORE
HABERDASHERY
MULTIPLE SHOP
POWER-STATION
SPINNING-MILL
TICKET AGENCY
TRADING HOUSE
TRAVEL AGENCY

13

BEAUTY PARLOUR
CHANDLER'S SHOP
COVERED MARKET
DRUGGIST'S SHOP
ESTABLISHMENT
JEWELLER'S SHOP

MULTIPLE STORE
PRINTING-HOUSE
SMELTING-HOUSE
SMELTING-WORKS
SUGAR-REFINERY
TIPPLING-HOUSE
TRANSPORT CAFÉ

14

BUREAU DE CHANGE
FILLING STATION
FRUITERER'S SHOP
FUNERAL PARLOUR
FURNITURE STORE
MASSAGE PARLOUR
NEWSAGENT'S SHOP
OUTFITTER'S SHOP
PRINTING-OFFICE
RECEIVING-HOUSE
REDUCTION WORKS
SERVICE STATION
SHOPPING CENTRE
SLAUGHTERHOUSE
STATIONER'S SHOP

15

BONDED WAREHOUSE
DEPARTMENT STORE
DRY-CLEANER'S SHOP
FISH-AND-CHIP SHOP
FISHMONGER'S SHOP
IRONMONGER'S SHOP
PAWNBROKER'S SHOP
RECEIVING-OFFICE
VEGETABLE-MARKET

BUILDINGS – FORTIFICATIONS

3

DUN
SAP
TOP

4

BAWN
BERM
BURG
DIKE
DYKE
FAST
FORT
HA-HA
KEEP
MOAT
MOON
RATH
RING
WALL
WING

5

AGGER
BOYAU
BROCH
FENCE
FOSSE
GAZON
GORGE
LIMES
MOTTE
MOUND
PIEND
REDAN
TALUS
TOWER
TRACE
WALLS
WORKS

6

ABATIS
BAILEY
BONNET

CASBAH
CASTLE
CORDON
DONJON
EPAULE
ESCARP
FLÈCHE
FRAISE
GABION
GLACIS
KASBAH
LAAGER
MERLON
REDUIT
SANGAR
SCONCE
TENAIL
TRENCH
TURRET
VALLUM
ZAREBA

7

ALCAZAR
BARMKIN
BARRAGE
BARRIER
BASTION
BATTERY
BRISURE
BULWARK
CASERNE
CHÂTEAU
CITADEL
CORBEIL
COUPURE
CUNETTE
CURTAIN
CUVETTE
DUNGEON
FLANKER
FORTLET
FOXHOLE
KREMLIN
LUNETTE
MIRADOR
MOINEAU
NURHAGE
OUTWORK
PANNIER

PARADOS
PARAPET
PILL-BOX
POLYGON
RAMPART
RAVELIN
REDOUBT
REMBLAI
SALIENT
SANDBAG
SURTOUT
TAMBOUR

8

BARBETTE
BARBICON
BARTISAN
BASTILLE
BRATTICE
CASEMATE
CAVALIER
DEFILADE
DEMI-LUNE
EARTH-BAG
ENCEINTE
ESTACADE
FIRE-STEP
FORTRESS
GARRISON
HEDGEHOG
HERISSON
HILL-FORT
HORNWORK
MARTELLO
MUNIMENT
ORILLION
PARALLEL
PENTAGON
PLATFORM
STOCKADE
TENAILLE

9

ACROPOLIS
BARRICADE
BASECOURT
BEACH-HEAD
CAPONIERE

CASTELLUM
CROWNWORK
DEMI-GORGE
EARTHWORK
FORTALICE
GABIONADE
GABIONAGE
GATE-TOWER
MUNITIONS
PEEL-TOWER
PONTLEVIS
REVETMENT
TENAILLON

10

BATTLEMENT
BLOCKHOUSE
BREASTRAIL
BREASTWORK
BRIDGEHEAD
COVERED WAY
DRAWBRIDGE
EPAULEMENT
FIRING-STEP
MILE-CASTLE
MUNIFIENCE
PORTCULLIS
ROUNDABOUT
SHIELD-WALL
SLIT-TRENCH
STRONGHOLD
TERREPLEIN
TÊTE-DE-PONT
TROU-DE-LOUP
WATCH-HOUSE
WATCH-TOWER

11

COUNTERMINE
CRÉMAILLÈRE
DEMI-BASTION
EMPLACEMENT
SIEGE-BASKET
STRONGPOINT

BUILDINGS – FORTIFICATIONS

12

COUNTER-GUARD
COUNTERSCARP
DEMI-DISTANCE
EMBATTLEMENT
ENTRENCHMENT
MAIDEN CASTLE
RETRENCHMENT

13

CHEVAL-DE-FRISE
FORTIFICATION
MACHICOLATION
MARTELLO TOWER
RETAINING WALL
VITRIFIED FORT
VITRIFIED WALL

14

COUNTER-BATTERY
MAIDEN FORTRESS
PRAETORIAN GATE

15

CIRCUMVALLATION
CONTRAVALLATION
COUNTER-APPROACH
FLOATING BATTERY

BUILDINGS – INSTITUTIONS & CHURCH BUILDINGS

3

GYM

4

BANK
CLUB
FANE
HALL
HOME
KIRK
NAOS
SHUL
TANA
TOPE

5

ABBEY
BATHS
COURT
CURIA
DIVAN
DUOMO
HOUSE

KAAVA
LYCÉE
MANSE
STUPA

6

ASHRAM
ASYLUM
BAGNIO
BEDLAM
BETHEL
BEULAH
CHAPEL
CHURCH
CLINIC
CRÈCHE
DAGOBA
DOUANE
FRIARY
HEROON
HOSTEL
LYCEUM
MANÈGE
MASJID
MORGUE
MOSQUE

MUSEUM
PAGODA
PALACE
PRIORY
SCHOOL
TEMPLE
VIHARA
VIMANA

7

ACADEMY
ALMONRY
COLLEGE
CONVENT
EMBASSY
HOSPICE
LAZARET
LIBRARY
MADRASA
MANDIRA
MINSTER
MISSION
NUNNERY
NURSERY
ORATORY
RETREAT

8

BASILICA
BETHESDA
CLOISTER
DELUBRUM
EXCHANGE
EXTERNAT
GURDWARA
HALL-MOOT
HOSPITAL
HOSTELRY
KACHAHRI
LAMASERY
LAW-COURT
MADHOUSE
MOOT-HALL
MORTUARY
PANTHEON
PECULIAR
REGISTRY
REST-HOME
SACELLUM
SEMINARY
SERAPEUM
TEOCALLI
TOWN-HALL
VICARAGE

ZIGGURAT

9

ALMA MATER
AREOPAGUS
ATHENAEUM
BARRACOON
BASECOURT
BEAD-HOUSE
BÉGUINAGE
CATHEDRAL
CLUBHOUSE
CONSULATE
DAY CENTRE
DAY SCHOOL
DEAD-HOUSE
DRILL-HALL
GUILDHALL
GYMNASUIM
HERMITAGE
HIGH COURT
INFIRMARY
INSTITUTE
JOSS-HOUSE
LAZARETTO
MAUSOLEUM

MONASTERY
MOOT-HOUSE
ORPHANAGE
PALAESTRA
PARSONAGE
PEST-HOUSE
POOR-HOUSE
PRYTANEUM
SICK-HOUSE
SKI-SCHOOL
SUCCURSAL
SYNAGOGUE
WORKHOUSE

10

CHARTREUSE
CHURCH-HALL
COURTHOUSE
CROWN-COURT
DAME-SCHOOL
FREE-SCHOOL
LIFE-SCHOOL
MARKET-HALL
MENTAL HOME
MONOPTEROS
OBSERVANCY
POLYCLINIC
POST OFFICE
PREP SCHOOL
PROTECTORY
REAL SCHOOL
ROCK-TEMPLE
SANATORIUM
STATE-HOUSE
TABERNACLE
UNIVERSITY
WATCH-HOUSE
WATER-WORKS
WEIGH-HOUSE

11

APPEAL COURT
BIBLIOTHECA
CHAPEL ROYAL
CREMATORIUM
CUSTOM-HOUSE
FIRE-STATION
FREE-AND-EASY
INSTITUTION

MARKET-HOUSE
MISSION-HALL
NIGHT-SCHOOL
NURSING HOME
OBSERVATORY
PIANO-SCHOOL
POLICE-COURT
POLYTECHNIC
PUBLIC BATHS
SAVINGS BANK
SENATE-HOUSE
SQUARSONAGE
STAVE-CHURCH
VILLAGE HALL
YOUTH HOSTEL

12

CHAPEL OF EASE
CHAPTER-HOUSE
CHARTERHOUSE
CHURCH-SCHOOL
COMMON SCHOOL
CONSERVATORY
COUNTY SCHOOL
DIVORCE COURT
HÔTEL DE VILLE
INFANT SCHOOL
INHALATORIUM
JUNIOR SCHOOL
KINDERGARTEN
LOCK-HOSPITAL
MEETING-HOUSE
MERCHANT BANK
MIDDLE SCHOOL
NORMAL SCHOOL
ORPHAN-ASYLUM
PARISH CHURCH
POLICE-OFFICE
PROCATHEDRAL
PUBLIC SCHOOL
RECORD OFFICE
RIDING SCHOOL
SENIOR SCHOOL
STAFF COLLEGE
STATION-HOUSE
SUNDAY SCHOOL

13

CHARITY-SCHOOL
COMMUNITY HOME

CONSERVATOIRE
CORONER'S COURT
COUNCIL SCHOOL
COURT OF HONOUR
ESTABLISHMENT
GRAMMAR SCHOOL
HOUSE OF REFUGE
LUNATIC ASYLUM
MOBILE LIBRARY
NURSERY SCHOOL
OPEN-AIR SCHOOL
POLICE-STATION
PRIMARY SCHOOL
PRIVATE SCHOOL
REAL GYMNASIUM
RIDING ACADEMY
ROYAL PECULIAR
SABBATH SCHOOL
SACRED COLLEGE
SESSIONS-HOUSE
SPONGING-HOUSE
STOCK EXCHANGE
SWIMMING BATHS

14

BOARDING-SCHOOL
LABOUR EXCHANGE
LENDING LIBRARY
MENTAL HOSPITAL
NATIONAL SCHOOL
PREACHING-HOUSE
PROVIDED SCHOOL
REGISTER OFFICE
REGISTRY OFFICE
WEATHER-STATION

15

BANKRUPTCY COURT
BUILDING SOCIETY
COLLEGIAL CHURCH
COMMUNITY CENTRE
COMMUNITY SCHOOL
COTTAGE HOSPITAL
LYING-IN HOSPITAL
PARLIAMENT-HOUSE
SECONDARY SCHOOL
TRAINING-COLLEGE
VOLUNTARY SCHOOL

BUILDINGS – ROOMS & INDOOR AREAS

3

BAR
DEN
LAB
LOO

4

AULA
CELL
HALL
HOLE
JOHN
LOFT
ROOM
SNUG
WARD
WELL

5

ATTIC
BERTH
BIBBY
BOWER
CABIN
CUDDY
DIVAN
ENTRY
FLOOR
FOYER
GRILL
HAREM
LAURA
LOBBY
ORIEL
PRIVY
SALON
SOLAR
STAGE
STUDY
SUITE
VAULT

6

ATRIUM
BED-SIT

BUREAU
CAMERA
CARREL
CELLAR
CHAPEL
CLOSET
DONJON
EXEDRA
FRATER
FRATRY
GARRET
LARDER
LAVABO
LOUNGE
OFFICE
PANARY
PANTRY
PAY-BOX
RUELLE
SALOON
SERAIL
STOREY
STUDIO
TOILET
URINAL
VESTRY
VINTRY
ZENANA

7

ATELIER
BAR-ROOM
BEDROOM
BOUDOIR
BOX-ROOM
BUTLERY
BUTTERY
CABINET
CABOOSE
CARVERY
CELLULE
CENACLE
CHAMBER
CUBICLE
DINETTE
DUNGEON
GALLERY
GENIZAH
GUNROOM
HALLWAY

KITCHEN
KURSAAL
LANDING
LIBRARY
MEGARON
NURSERY
OFFICES
ORATORY
PARLOUR
PASSAGE
PRONAOS
SANCTUM
SERVERY
SICK-BAY
SURGERY
TAP-ROOM
TEA-ROOM
THEATRE

8

ANTEROOM
AUDITORY
BALL-ROOM
BASEMENT
BASILICA
BATHROOM
BOX-LOBBY
CLOISTER
CLUBROOM
COCKLOFT
CONCLAVE
COOKROOM
CORRIDOR
DARK-ROOM
ENFILADE
HALFPACE
INTERIOR
LAVATORY
LOCUTORY
MAGAZINE
MESS-ROOM
NEWSROOM
PLAYROOM
PRESS-BOX
PULPITUM
PUMP-ROOM
REST-ROOM
SACRISTY
SALE-ROOM
SCULLERY

SERAGLIO
SHOWROOM
SICKROOM
SNUGGERY
SUDATORY
SURROUND
THALAMUS
TOILETTE
TOP FLOOR
TRAVERSE
UPSTAIRS
VESTIARY
WARDROBE
WARD-ROOM
WELL-ROOM
WORKROOM
WORKSHOP

9

ANCHORAGE
APARTMENT
BED-CLOSET
BREADROOM
CAMARILLA
CHART-ROOM
CHECKROOM
CLASSROOM
CLOAKROOM
CONCOURSE
COURTROOM
CRUSH-ROOM
CUBBY-HOLE
DORMITORY
FORECABIN
GARDEROBE
GLORY-HOLE
GREEN-ROOM
GRILL-ROOM
GUARD-ROOM
GUEST-ROOM
GYNAECEUM
HONEYCOMB
INGLE-NOOK
MEZZANINE
MUSIC-ROOM
OUBLIETTE
PAINT SHOP
PAY-OFFICE
PLATE-ROOM
PRESS-ROOM

PUBLIC BAR
RECLUSERY
REFECTORY
SACRARIUM
SALOON BAR
SICK-BERTH
SPARE ROOM
STACK-ROOM
STAFFROOM
STATEROOM
STILL-ROOM
STOCK-ROOM
STOREROOM
TRIFORIUM
VESTIBULE
WASH-HOUSE
WELL-HOUSE
WINE-VAULT

10

AUDITORIUM
BACKSTAIRS
BAR-PARLOUR
BEDCHAMBER
CASUAL WARD
COAL-CELLAR
COFFEE-ROOM
COMMON ROOM
DEEP FREEZE
DEPARTMENT
DINING-HALL
DINING-ROOM
DISPENSARY
DOWNSTAIRS
FIRST FLOOR
LABORATORY
LIVING-ROOM
LUMBER-ROOM
MISERICORD
PADDED CELL
PANOPTICON
PASSAGEWAY
PENETRALIA
POWDER-ROOM
REREDORTER
ROBING-ROOM
SADDLE-ROOM
SALUTATORY
SKY-PARLOUR
STABLE-ROOM

STATE-CABIN
STRONGROOM
SUDATORIUM
SUN-PARLOUR
TEPIDARIUM
THIRD FLOOR
THRONE-ROOM
TRICLINIUM
VESTIBULUM
VESTRY-ROOM
WINE-CELLAR

11

ANTECHAMBER
APODYTERIUM
AUCTION ROOM
BARRACK-ROOM
BARREL-HOUSE
BRIDAL SUITE
BOOKING-HALL
CHAPEL ROYAL
CHIMNEY-NOOK
COACH-OFFICE
COCKTAIL BAR
COMPARTMENT
CONTROL ROOM
CONVENIENCE
DRAWING-ROOM
FIRST STOREY
FITTING-ROOM
FRIGIDARIUM
GROUND FLOOR
HALF-LANDING
HARNESS-ROOM
KITCHENETTE
MACHINE-SHOP
MORNING-ROOM

OEIL-DE-BOEUF
ORDERLY ROOM
PAPER-OFFICE
PATTERN SHOP
PRIEST'S HOLE
READING-ROOM
SCRIPTORIUM
SECOND FLOOR
SERVICE-ROOM
SITTING-ROOM
SMOKING-ROOM
SOUP-KITCHEN
THIRD STOREY
UTILITY ROOM
WAITING-ROOM
WATER-CLOSET

12

ASSEMBLY HALL
ASSEMBLY ROOM
BILLIARD-ROOM
BRIDE-CHAMBER
CASUALTY WARD
CHANGING-ROOM
CONSERVATORY
COUNTING-ROOM
DELIVERY ROOM
DRESSING-ROOM
INCIDENT ROOM
OPISTHODOMUS
ORGAN-GALLERY
POWDER-CLOSET
PRESERVATORY
PRESS-GALLERY
PRIVY CHAMBER
PROPERTY ROOM
SECOND STOREY
SERVANTS' HALL

WASHING-HOUSE

13

BOOKING-OFFICE
CONDEMNED CELL
LADIES' GALLERY
MATERNITY WARD
RECEIVING-ROOM
RECEPTION-ROOM
REFRIGERATORY
TREATMENT ROOM
VIVISECTORIUM

14

BANQUETING HALL
BED SITTING-ROOM
COMMERCIAL ROOM
CONSULTING-ROOM
COUNCIL CHAMBER
FUNERAL PARLOUR
POWDER-MAGAZINE
SINGING-GALLERY
UNSADDLING ROOM
WITHERING-FLOOR

15

BARGAIN BASEMENT
DEPARTURE LOUNGE
PRESENCE-CHAMBER
REFRESHMENT-ROOM
SHOOTING-GALLERY
WITHDRAWING-ROOM

BUILDINGS – STRUCTURES

3

DAM
PEN
RIG

4

ARCH
DECK
DOCK
DYKE
GATE
KANG
LEAF
LOCK
MOLE
PIER
POLE
QUAY
SPUR
WALL
WEIR
WELL

5

CRANE
CROSS
DARGA
FENCE
FOLLY
FRAME
HOVEL
JETTY
KIOSK
LEVEE
PYLON
SHELL
STAGE
STALK
STAND
STILE
STILT
TORII
TOWER
WHARF

6

ANICUT
BEACON
BELFRY
BRIDGE
GANTRY
GOPURA
GROYNE
HURDLE
LASHER
LIGGER
MACHAN
OIL-RIG
PILLAR
REFUGE
SLUICE
STANCH
TORANA
TURRET

7

ATALAYA
BOLLARD
CALL-BOX
CHIMNEY
CLAPPER
CONDUIT
CULVERT
DECKING
DERRICK
GATEWAY
HYDRANT
LANTERN
LOCKAGE
MAYPOLE
MILL-DAM
OBELISK
PERGOLA
PONCEAU
PONTOON
POTENCE
PYRAMID
ROSTRUM
SEA-GATE
SEA-WALL
SOAP-BOX
STAGING
TERRACE
TREILLE

TRELLIS
VIADUCT

8

AQUEDUCT
CABLEWAY
CENOTAPH
ERECTION
FOUNTAIN
HOG-FRAME
ICE-APRON
LAMP-POST
LOCK-GATE
MONOLITH
MONUMENT
PIER-HEAD
POST-MILL
SCAFFOLD
STANDARD
TAIL-GATE
TETRAPOD
TIDE-GATE
TIDE-LOCK
TOLL-GATE
WELL-CURB
WELL-HEAD
WINDMILL

9

BANDSTAND
BELL-TOWER
CAMPANILE
CHAIN-PIER
COFFER-DAM
FLOODGATE
GASOMETER
LETTER-BOX
LINE-FENCE
LODGE-GATE
PILLAR-BOX
SALLYPORT
SENTRY-BOX
SIGNAL-BOX
STAND-PIPE
STRUCTURE
SWISS ROLL
TOTEM POLE
TREILLAGE

TURNSTILE
WASTE-GATE
WATER-GATE

10

BELL-TURRET
BREAKWATER
DECK-BRIDGE
FOOTBRIDGE
GRANDSTAND
LEAF-BRIDGE
LIGHTHOUSE
LIGHT-TOWER
RAFT-BRIDGE
ROAD-BRIDGE
ROUND TOWER
SKEW-BRIDGE
SLUICE-GATE
TEXAS TOWER
TOLL-BRIDGE
WATCH-TOWER
WATER CRANE
WATER-TOWER
WIRE-BRIDGE

11

CHAIN-BRIDGE
GANTRY CRANE
MARKET-CROSS
OIL-PLATFORM
PIVOT-BRIDGE
SCAFFOLDAGE
SCAFFOLDING
SWING-BRIDGE
TRUSS-BRIDGE
UNDERBRIDGE
WISHING-WELL

12

BAILEY BRIDGE
CONSTRUCTION
CONSTRUCTURE
FLYING BRIDGE
GIRDER BRIDGE
LANDING-STAGE
OUTER GATEWAY

13

BASCULE BRIDGE
FLOATING CRANE
LATTICE-BRIDGE
LIFTING-BRIDGE

MACHICOLATION
PONTOON-BRIDGE
RETAINING WALL
TELEGRAPH-POLE
TRESTLE-BRIDGE
TRUIMPHAL ARCH

14

FLOATING BRIDGE
SUPERSTRUCTURE

BUSINESS

3

BID
BUY
DUD
DUE
FEE
IOU
JOB
LOT
PAR
PAY
POP
RUN
TAB

4

AGIO
BANK
BILL
BOND
BOOM
CANT
CASH
CHOP
COST
DEAL
DEBT
DRUG
FARM
FILE
FIRM
FUND
GAIN
GIRO
HIRE
HYPE
KIND
KITE
LINE
LOAN
LOSS
MAKE
MEMO
NETT
PAWN
PERK
PLUG
PUFF
RING

RISE
RUIN
SALE
SIGN
SNIP
SPEC
SWAP
SWOP
TARE
TICK
TILL
TOLL
TRET
WAGE
WARE

5

AUDIT
BONUS
BOOKS
BRAND
CHECK
CLOFF
CRASH
DEBIT
DRAFT
DRIVE
ENTRY
FLIER
FLOAT
FLOOR
GILTS
GOODS
GROSS
HOUSE
ISSUE
LAY-BY
OFFER
ORDER
PITCH
PRICE
QUOTA
QUOTE
RAILS
RAISE
REJIG
ROUND
SCRIP
SHARE
SLUMP

SMASH
STOCK
STORE
TALLY
TERMS
TRADE
TRUCK
TRUST
VALUE
YIELD

6

ACCESS
ADVERT
AGENCY
AGENDA
AMOUNT
BARTER
BOODLE
BOURSE
BRANCH
BUREAU
BUYING
CHARGE
CHEQUE
CONTRA
CORNER
COUPON
CREDIT
CUSTOM
DEMAND
DOCKET
EXPORT
FILING
GROWTH
HIRING
IMPORT
IMPOST
INCOME
INDENT
JOB-LOT
LABOUR
LAUNCH
LEDGER
MARGIN
MARKET
MERGER
METAGE
MOTION
MUTUUM

NOTICE
OFFICE
OILERY
OMNIUM
ONCOST
OPTION
OUTAGE
OUTFIT
OUTLAY
OUTPUT
POLICY
POSTER
PROFIT
RECESS
REFUND
RENTAL
RESALE
RETAIL
RETURN
RIP-OFF
SALARY
SAMPLE
SLOGAN
SPIRAL
STAPLE
STOCKS
SUPPLY
SURVEY
TARIFF
TENDER
USANCE
VENDUE

7

ACCOUNT
ADVANCE
AFFAIRS
ALE-POLE
ALLONGE
ANNUITY
ARREARS
AUCTION
BACKLOG
BAD DEBT
BALANCE
BANKING
BARGAIN
BOUNCER
BROKAGE
BULLION

CANVASS
CAPITAL
CARTAGE
CHARTER
CLOSURE
COMBINE
COMPACT
COMPANY
CONCERN
CONSOLS
DAY-BOOK
DEALING
DEFICIT
DEPOSIT
ECONOMY
EMBARGO
EMPTION
EXPENSE
FEATURE
FINANCE
FUTURES
GILDING
GIMMICK
INN-SIGN
INVOICE
JOURNAL
LAYAWAY
LIAISON
LIMITED
MAKINGS
MERCERY
MILK-RUN
MILLING
MINUTES
NAME-DAY
NOTCHEL
OPENING
OVERBID
PASSAGE
PAY-BILL
PAY-ROLL
PEDLARY
PLACARD
PREMIUM
PRODUCT
PROJECT
PUB-SIGN
PUFFERY
RECEIPT
RÉCLAME
REDRAFT
RESERVE

SECONDS
SELLING
SERVICE
SKY-SIGN
SMALL AD
SPIN-OFF
SQUEEZE
STORAGE
SURPLUS
TAKINGS
TRADE-IN
TRADING
TRAFFIC
TRANCHE
VENTURE
VOUCHER
WAR LOAN
WARRANT

8

AGIOTAGE
AUDITING
BANK-BILL
BANK-BOOK
BANK-NOTE
BANK-RATE
BANKROLL
BASE RATE
BILL-BOOK
BILLHEAD
BLUE-CHIP
BOOK-DEBT
BRIDGING
BUSINESS
CABOTAGE
CALL-LOAN
CAMPAIGN
CASH-BOOK
CASH-FLOW
CHAFFERY
CO-AGENCY
COMMERCE
CONTANGO
CONTRACT
DELIVERY
DISCOUNT
DIVIDEND
DRY-GOODS
EQUITIES
ESTIMATE

EXCHANGE
EXPENSES
FILE COPY
FLAT RATE
FURRIERY
GIVEAWAY
GUARANTY
HARD SELL
HOARDING
INCREASE
INDUSTRY
INTEREST
KITE-MARK
KNOCKOUT
MILLINERY
MONOPOLY
ORDERING
PAR VALUE
PASS-BOOK
PAY-SHEET
PICKINGS
POUNDAGE
PRACTICE
PROPOSAL
PROSPECT
PURCHASE
RECEIPTS
RECOURSE
RENT-ROLL
SCHEDULE
SECURITY
SETTLING
SHARE-OUT
SHIPMENT
SHOP SIGN
SHOW-CARD
SHUT-DOWN
SIDE-LINE
SOFT SELL
SOLVENCY
SPENDING
STALLAGE
STRADDLE
SURVEYAL
SWAPPING
TAKE-OVER
TRANSFER
TRUCKAGE
TRUCKING
TURNOVER
UNIT COST
VENDIBLE

VIREMENT
WAGE-FUND

9

AGREEMENT
ARBITRAGE
ASSURANCE
BANK-PAPER
BANK-STOCK
BILLBOARD
BOX NUMBER
BRAND-NAME
BROKERAGE
BY-PRODUCT
CARD-INDEX
CATCHWORD
CHECK-LIST
COEMPTION
COMMODITY
COST PRICE
DEBENTURE
DEFERMENT
DEFLATION
DEMURRAGE
DICTATION
EXCHEQUER
EXPANSION
EXPORTING
FAIR TRADE
FLOTATION
FRANCHISE
FREE TRADE
GUARANTEE
HALF-SHARE
IMBALANCE
IMPORTING
INCREMENT
INDENTURE
INFLATION
INSURANCE
INTERVIEW
INVENTORY
KEEN PRICE
LIFE-TABLE
MAIL ORDER
MARKETING
MILK-ROUND
NAME BRAND
OLIGOPOLY
ORDER-BOOK

OUTGOINGS
OVERDRAFT
OVERHEADS
PATRONAGE
PENNY-BANK
PETTY CASH
PORTFOLIO
POST-ENTRY
PRICE-LIST
PRINCIPAL
PROMOTION
PUBLICITY
QUOTATION
RECESSION
RECKONING
REDUCTION
REFERENCE
REFLATION
REPAYMENT
RISK-MONEY
SALE-PRICE
SHOP-BOARD
SHROFFAGE
SIDE-ISSUE
SIGNBOARD
SOFT GOODS
SPECIALTY
STATEMENT
STOCK-LIST
STOCKPILE
TENDERING
TICKET-DAY
TRADE-MARK
TRADE-NAME
TRADE SALE
TRUST FUND
TURN-PENNY
UNIT TRUST
UTILITIES
VALUATION
VENDITION
WHITE SALE
WHOLESALE

10

AUTOMATION
BANK-CHEQUE
BANKRUPTCY
BEAR MARKET
BLOOD-MONEY

BUSINESS

BONDED DEBT
BONUS ISSUE
BUCKET SHOP
BULK-BUYING
BULL MARKET
CANVASSING
CASH-CREDIT
CATCH-PENNY
CHANGEOVER
CHEQUE-BOOK
COLLATERAL
COMMERCIAL
COMMISSION
CONFERENCE
CONSORTIUM
CONSPECTUS
CREDIT CARD
DATE-CODING
DEPOSITORY
DEPRESSION
DEPUTATION
DICTAPHONE
DICTOGRAPH
EMPLOYMENT
ENCASHMENT
ENGAGEMENT
ENTERPRISE
EVALUATION
FIRE-POLICY
FISCAL YEAR
FORCED SALE
FORWARDING
FREE SAMPLE
GRAVY TRAIN
HOME MARKET
INSOLVENCY
INSTALMENT
INVESTMENT
JOINT-STOCK
JUMBLE SALE
KITE-FLYING
LOSS-LEADER
MAIN CHANCE
MANAGEMENT
MEMORANDUM
MERCHANTRY
MONEY-MAKER
MORATORIUM
NEVER-NEVER
NON-PAYMENT
NOTE OF HAND
OLIGOPSONY

ORDER-PAPER
ORGANOGRAM
PAWN-TICKET
PERCENTAGE
PERPETUITY
PERQUISITE
PIGEON-HOLE
PREFERENCE
PRICE-LEVEL
PROMPT-NOTE
PROSPECTUS
REFUNDMENT
REPURCHASE
RESHIPMENT
SALE OF WORK
SALES DRIVE
SCRIP ISSUE
SECURITIES
SETTLEMENT
SKY-WRITING
SQUARE DEAL
SUBSIDIARY
SURVEYANCE
TALLY-TRADE
TRADE CYCLE
TRADE PRICE
TRUST STOCK
WAGE FREEZE
WAGE-PACKET
WITHDRAWAL

11

ACCOUNT-BOOK
ADVERTISING
APPOINTMENT
ASKING PRICE
BANK-BALANCE
BANKER'S CARD
BANK OF ISSUE
BARBER'S POLE
BARCLAYCARD
BIG BUSINESS
BILL OF SIGHT
BILL OF STORE
BLACK MARKET
BLANK CHEQUE
BOND-WASHING
BOOK-ACCOUNT
BOOKKEEPING
CASH-ACCOUNT

CASH-PAYMENT
CASH-RAILWAY
CITY COMPANY
CO-INSURANCE
COLD STORAGE
CONSIGNMENT
COUNTERBOND
COUNTERFOIL
COUNTERMARK
DEVALUATION
DOUBLE-ENTRY
DOWN-PAYMENT
ENDORSEMENT
ENGROSSMENT
EXPENDITURE
EXPORTATION
FAIR TRADING
FLUCTUATION
FOREPAYMENT
HOUSE OF CALL
IMPORTATION
INTERCHANGE
INTERCOURSE
KEY INDUSTRY
LAW-MERCHANT
LIFE ANNUITY
LIQUIDATION
LOAN SOCIETY
MARKET-PRICE
MARKET-VALUE
MERCHANDISE
MONEY-MAKING
MONEY-MARKET
MUTUAL FUNDS
NON-DELIVERY
NOTICE-BOARD
OVERBIDDING
OVERPAYMENT
OVER-TRADING
PACKAGE-DEAL
PAPER-CREDIT
PART-PAYMENT
PARTNERSHIP
PAWNBROKING
PIGNORATION
PILOT SCHEME
PROPOSITION
RE-EXPANSION
REPEAT ORDER
REQUISITION
RUMMAGE SALE
SALES LEDGER

SETTLING DAY
SINGLE-ENTRY
SINKING FUND
SPECULATION
SPONSORSHIP
STAFF SYSTEM
STOCK MARKET
STOCKPILING
STOCKTAKING
SUBCONTRACT
TAKE-OVER BID
TALLY-SYSTEM
TESTIMONIAL
TIME-BARGAIN
TRANSACTION
UNDERCHARGE
WAREHOUSING

12

AMALGAMATION
AMORTISATION
APPRECIATION
BALANCE-SHEET
BILL OF LADING
BOARD MEETING
BOUGHT LEDGER
BRAND LOYALTY
BRIDGING LOAN
BUYERS' MARKET
CAPITAL GAINS
CAPITAL GOODS
CHARTERPARTY
CIRCULAR NOTE
CLEARING BANK
CLOSE COMPANY
COMMON MARKET
CONGLOMERATE
CORRIDOR WORK
COST ANALYSIS
DEPRECIATION
DISBURSEMENT
DISCOUNT RATE
DUTCH AUCTION
DUTCH BARGAIN
EARLY CLOSING
EXPORT MARKET
FILING SYSTEM
FIXED CAPITAL
FLOATING DEBT
GOING CONCERN

HIRE PURCHASE
HORSE-TRADING
MERCANTILISM
MONEY-LENDING
MONEY-SPINNER
ORGANISATION
PASSING TRADE
PRICE-CURRENT
PRICE-CUTTING
PRICE-RIGGING
PRODUCTIVITY
PROFIT MARGIN
REINVESTMENT
RESERVE PRICE
SALESMANSHIP
SELLING-PRICE
SHARE-CAPITAL
STOCKBROKING
STOCK-JOBBERY
STOCK-JOBBING
STOCK-IN-TRADE
SUBHASTATION
TRADING-STAMP
TRANSIT TRADE
UNDERWRITING

FRANCHISEMENT
FRINGE BENEFIT
HEAVY INDUSTRY
INDUSTRIALISM
LIFE ASSURANCE
LIFE INSURANCE
LIGHT INDUSTRY
MARKETABILITY
MERCHANDISING
MISMANAGEMENT
OFF-RECKONINGS
ORDINARY SHARE
OVERVALUATION
PARENT COMPANY
PRODUCER GOODS
PUBLIC COMPANY
QUALIFICATION
READY-RECKONER
SANDWICH-BOARD
SELF-INSURANCE
SELLERS' MARKET
SHARP PRACTICE
STANDING ORDER
STOCK EXCHANGE
SWITCH SELLING
THREE-PER-CENTS
VISIBLE EXPORT
VISIBLE IMPORT

GROUP INSURANCE
HOLDING COMPANY
INERTIA SELLING
INSURANCE CLAIM
INVISIBLE TRADE
LETTER OF CREDIT
LETTRE DE CHANGE
LIMITED COMPANY
MARKET RESEARCH
OVERPRODUCTION
PRIVATE COMPANY
PUBLICITY STUNT
PYRAMID SELLING
REORGANISATION
TRAFFIC-RETURNS
UNDERVALUATION
VESTED INTEREST
WINDOW-DRESSING

15

BUILDING SOCIETY
BUSINESS MEETING
DEFERRED ANNUITY
DEFERRED PAYMENT
DIVIDEND-WARRANT
ENDOWMENT POLICY
ESCALATOR CLAUSE
FLOATING CAPITAL
GOLDEN HANDSHAKE
INVESTMENT TRUST
INVISIBLE EXPORT
INVISIBLE IMPORT
KNOCKOUT AUCTION
MARINE INSURANCE
MUTUAL INSURANCE
PREFERENCE SHARE
PREFERENCE STOCK
SPOT ADVERTISING
SUPPLY AND DEMAND
SUSPENSE ACCOUNT
UNDER-PRODUCTION
WAGES-FUND THEORY

13

ADVERTISEMENT
APPROPRIATION
BACKWARDATION
BUSINESS CYCLE
CARRIAGE TRADE
CHARGE ACCOUNT
CLEARING-HOUSE
COMMERCIALISM
CONSUMER GOODS
COUNTING-HOUSE
DOUBLE-DEALING
ECONOMISATION
ESTABLISHMENT
EXPRESS AGENCY
FINANCIAL YEAR
FIRE-INSURANCE

14

BALANCE OF TRADE
BILL OF EXCHANGE
BUREAU DE CHANGE
COST-ACCOUNTING
CURRENT ACCOUNT
DEFERRED SHARES
DEPOSIT ACCOUNT
DEPOSIT-RECEIPT
DIRECT DEBITING
EXPENSE ACCOUNT
EXPRESS COMPANY
FOUNDERS' SHARES
FREE ENTERPRISE

CLOTHING – CLOTHING TERMS

3

ARM
BOW
COP
CUP
CUT
EYE
FIT
FLY
FOB
HEM
JAG
LAP
LEG
NAP
PAD
PIN
RAG
RIB
RIG
RUN
SET
TAB
TAG
TOE
TON
ZIP

4

BALL
BAND
BELT
BONE
BURL
BUST
CUFF
DART
DRAG
ETUI
FALL
FLAP
FOLD
GARB
GEAR
GORE
HANG
HANK

HEEL
HIPS
HOOK
HOOP
KNEE
KNOT
LACE
LIFT
LINE
LIST
MODE
NECK
PEAK
PILE
POKE
POUF
PUFF
RAGS
REEL
SCYE
SEAM
SEAT
SIZE
SLIT
SNIP
SOLE
STUD
TACK
TAIL
TAPE
TEAR
TOGS
TRIM
TUCK
TUFT
VAMP
VENT
WALE
WEAR
WELT
YARN
YOKE

5

BANDS
BRACK
CHECK
CHEST

CLASP
CLOCK
CLUMP
DRESS
FILET
FLARE
FLASH
FRILL
GET-UP
GIGOT
GILET
GODET
INLET
INSET
JABOT
LABEL
LACET
LAPEL
MATCH
MITRE
MODEL
MORSE
MUFTI
PANEL
PATCH
PATTE
PEARL
PICOT
REFIT
RIDGE
RUCHE
SHANK
SHARP
SHIRR
SKEIN
SLASH
SPOOL
STRAP
STRIP
STYLE
TAILS
TRAIN
TRY-ON
TWEED
TWIST
UPPER
VITTA
V-NECK
VOGUE
WAIST
WEEDS

6

ALNAGE
ARMLET
ATTIRE
BARREL
BOBBIN
BOBBLE
BRACES
BUCKLE
BUSTLE
BUTTON
COPPIN
CREASE
FALLAL
FRINGE
GARTER
GATHER
GORING
GUSSET
HANDLE
HAT-PIN
INSOLE
LACING
LADDER
LAPPET
LINING
LIVERY
NEEDLE
NUMBER
OLIVET
OSPREY
OUTFIT
PIPING
POCKET
POMPOM
POUFFE
REVERS
RIBBON
RIG-OUT
ROBING
RUCKLE
RUFFLE
RUMPLE
RUNKLE
SEQUIN
SLEEVE
SMALLS
STAPLE
STITCH
STRAND
STRING

TAG-RAG
TASSEL
TEASEL
THREAD
TIE-PIN
TOE-CAP
TOGGLE
TOILET
TONGUE
TUCKER
TURN-UP
UNDIES
UPLIFT
WEEPER
WHITES
WOGGLE
ZIPPER
ZOSTER

7

APPAREL
ARMBAND
ARMHOLE
BANDEAU
CASUALS
CIVVIES
CLOBBER
CLOTHES
CORSAGE
COSTUME
COUTURE
ELASTIC
FALBALA
FALSIES
FASHION
FITTING
FLOUNCE
GALLOON
GALLOWS
GARMENT
HARNESS
HAT-BAND
HEEL-TAP
HEM-LINE
HIP-BELT
HOSIERY
LAYETTE
MEASURE

MIDRIFF
MODESTY
NÉGLIGÉ
NETSUKE
NEW LOOK
ODDMENT
ORPHREY
OUTSOLE
PADDING
PANNIER
PASSING
PATTERN
PICKING
PIN-TUCK
PLACKET
RAIMENT
REMNANT
RIBBING
RUCHING
SEATING
SELVAGE
SHOE-TIE
SNIPPET
SPANGLE
SPORRAN
SUITING
TACKING
TEXTURE
THIMBLE
TOGGERY
UNDRESS
VEILING
VESTURE
WEARING
WEBBING
WEFTAGE

8

BOOT-HOOK
BOOT-JACK
BOOT-LACE
BOX-PLEAT
BRASSARD
CINCTURE
CLOTHING
CREATION
ENSEMBLE
FASTENER

FILIGREE
FOOTGEAR
FOOTWEAR
FRILLIES
FROU-FROU
FURBELOW
GLAD RAGS
HAT-GUARD
HEAD-BAND
IMPROVER
INCH-TAPE
KNITWEAR
LINGERIE
LIRIPOOP
LONG-TOGS
MEN'S-WEAR
MOURNING
NECK-BAND
NECKLINE
NECKWEAR
PEARLIES
POLKA-DOT
POLO-NECK
POULAINE
PRANKING
PULL-BACK
QUILLING
RIBBONRY
ROSE-KNOT
RUFFLING
SCARF-PIN
SELVEDGE
SHIRRING
SHIRT-PIN
SHOE-LACE
SHOE-ROSE
SHOULDER
SLASHING
SMOCKING
SNIPPING
SOUTACHE
STAY-LACE
STAY-TAPE
SWISSING
TAPELINE
TOURNURE
TRIMMING
TURNBACK
TURNOVER
WARDROBE
WAXED END
WOOLLENS

9

CHAUSSURE
CHIN-STRAP
CUBAN HEEL
CYCLE-CLIP
DOG'S-TOOTH
FANDANGLE
FASTENING
FLY-BUTTON
FUR-COLLAR
GARNITURE
GATHERING
FUR-LINING
HEEL-PIECE
HIP-POCKET
INSERTION
INSIDE LEG
MILLINERY
NECK-PIECE
NIGHT-GEAR
OUTERWEAR
OVERCHECK
PAILLETTE
PASSEMENT
PEARL-EDGE
PETERSHAM
PIN-STRIPE
PRESS-STUD
RATIONALS
REFITMENT
SAFETY-PIN
SCARF-RING
SEPARATES
SHIRT-BAND
SHIRT-STUD
SHIRT-TAIL
SPIKE HEEL
STIFFENER
STITCHING
STRETCHER
SURCINGLE
SUSPENDER
SWEAT-BAND
TAILORING
TRAPPINGS
TROUSSEAU
UNDERWEAR
WAISTBAND
WAIST-BELT
WAISTLINE
WRISTBAND

10

BABY-RIBBON
BAND-STRING
BOONDOGGLE
BREAST-KNOT
BUTTON-HOLE
BUTTON-HOOK
CANONICALS
CHEVESAILE
COLLAR-BONE
COLLAR-STUD
CONFECTION
COTTON-REEL
DERNIER CRI
DÉSHABILLÉ
DRAW-STRING
ENCINCTURE
ENLACEMENT
FANCY DRESS
FOURCHETTE
FRENCH HEEL
GARMENTURE
HABILIMENT
HALTER-NECK
JARDINIÈRE
KNICK-KNACK
LADIES'-WEAR
LAVALLIÈRE
OUTFITTING
PIECE-GOODS
POCKET-HOLE
SHIRT-FRILL
SHIRT-FRONT
SHOE-BUCKLE
SHOESTRING
SLIT-POCKET
SMALL-WARES
SPORTSWEAR
STIFFENING
SUNDAY-BEST
SUSPENDERS
TASSELLING
TROUSER-LEG
TURTLE-NECK
UNDERLINEN
VEST-POCKET

11

APRON-STRING

BIAS BINDING
CO-ORDINATES
DRESS-LENGTH
DRESS-SHIELD
EMPIECEMENT
HAND-ME-DOWNS
HERRING-BONE
HOUND'S-TOOTH
LAWN SLEEVES
LOW NECKLINE
MEASUREMENT
NIGHT-ATTIRE
PATCH-POCKET
PEARL-BUTTON
PLACKET-HOLE
SEAMING-LACE
SHIRT-BUTTON
SHIRT-SLEEVE
SHOE-LATCHET
SHOULDER-PAD
SUCCINCTORY
TAPE-MEASURE
THIMBLE-CASE
TIGHT-LACING
TROUSER-CLIP
UNDERSLEEVE
WATCH-POCKET
WIDOW'S WEEDS
ZIP-FASTENER

12

ACCOUTREMENT
BUTTERFLY-BOW
HABERDASHERY
HALF-MOURNING
HAUTE COUTURE
KIMONO SLEEVE
NIGHT-CLOTHES
ODD-COME-SHORT
PAGODA SLEEVE
RAGLAN SLEEVE
REACH-ME-DOWNS
SHAWL-PATTERN
SHORT-CLOTHES
SLEEVE-BUTTON
SLOP-CLOTHING
SMALL-CLOTHES
STILETTO HEEL

CLOTHING – CLOTHING TERMS

STOCKING-FOOT
UNDERCLOTHES

13

DARNING-NEEDLE
HIGHLAND DRESS
KNICK-KNACKERY
MEASURING-TAPE

PRESS-FASTENER
PUDDING SLEEVE
RIDING-CLOTHES
SHOULDER-STRAP
SOCK-SUSPENDER
SUCCINCTORIUM
TROUSER-BOTTOM
TROUSER-BUTTON
TROUSER-POCKET
UNDERCLOTHING
UNISEX CLOTHES

14

KISSING-STRINGS
PAISLEY PATTERN
UNMENTIONABLES

15

HIGHLAND COSTUME

CLOTHING – FOOTWEAR & HOSIERY

3

GUM
SKI
SOX

4

BOOT
CLOG
HOSE
MULE
PUMP
SHOE
SOCK
SPAT
SPUR

5

DERBY
SABOT
SKATE
STILT
STOCK
WADER
WEDGE

6

ARCTIC
BOOTEE
BROGUE
BUSKIN
GAITER
GALOSH
GAMASH
JEMIMA
LOAFER
MUKLUK
NYLONS
OXFORD
PUTTEE
RACKET
SANDAL
SPIKES
TIGHTS

7

BLUCHER
BOOTLEG
BOTTINE
CASUALS
CHOPINE
COTHURN
CRACOWE
GUMBOOT

GUMSHOE
GYM SHOE
HIGH-LOW
LACE-UPS
LEGGING
MAILLOT
MINI-SKI
OXONIAN
PEEP-TOE
RUBBERS
SLIPPER
SNEAKER
SPATTEE
TOP-BOOT

8

BABOUCHE
BALMORAL
BOOTIKIN
CHAUSSES
FINNESCO
FLIP-FLOP
FOOTMUFF
GOLF SHOE
HALF-BOOT
JACK-BOOT
JODHPURS
LACE-BOOT
LEGGINGS

MOCASSIN
MOCCASIN
MOON-BOOT
MUCKLUCK
OVERSHOE
PABOUCHE
PANTOFLE
PLIMSOLL
SAND-SHOE
SLIP-SLOP
SNOW-BOOT
SNOW-SHOE
SOLLERET
SPLASHER
STOCKING
TRAINERS
VELSKOEN

9

ALPARGATA
ANKLE-BOOT
ANKLE-JACK
ANKLE-SOCK
BOBBY-SOCK
CLOUT-SHOE
COTHURNUS
COURT SHOE
FIELD-BOOT
FLESHINGS

GOLOE-SHOE
LEG-WARMER
SCARPETTO
STOCKINGS

10

BALLET-SHOE
BOVVER BOOT
ESPADRILLE
OXFORD SHOE
RIDING-BOOT
SKIN-TIGHTS
SQUARE-TOES
TENNIS-SHOE
WELLINGTON

11

COSSACK BOOT
HESSIAN BOOT
HOBNAIL BOOT
JODHPUR-BOOT
NETHERSTOCK
RUNNING-SHOE
SPATTERDASH
WELLINGTONS

12

ANTIGROPELOS
GALLIGASKINS
SURGICAL BOOT
SURGICAL SHOE
WINKLE-PICKER

13

BEETLE-CRUSHER
CARPET-SLIPPER
KLETTERSCHUHE
SLING-BACK SHOE

14

HIGH-HEELED SHOE
WELLINGTON-BOOT

15

HALF-WELLINGTONS

CLOTHING – GENERAL CLOTHING

3

ALB
BIB
BRA
MAC
MOB
OBI
RAG

4

BAGS
BELT
CAPA
CAPE
COAT
COPE
GOWN
HAIK
JACK
JUMP
KILT
MAIL
MAXI
MINI
MINK
MINO
MUFF
OILS
PEGS

PINK
RAMI
ROBE
SACK
SARI
SASH
SLIP
SLOP
SUIT
TOGA
TUTU
VEIL
VEST
WRAP

5

ACTON
AMICE
APRON
ARMET
CAMIS
CHAPS
CHOLI
CLOAK
CORDS
COTTA
CULET
CYMAR
DHOTI
DRESS

DUCKS
EPHOD
ETONS
FANON
FICHU
FROCK
FRONT
GILET
GLOVE
GREGO
G-SUIT
HABIT
JAMBE
JEANS
JUPON
KANZU
LAMMY
LEVIS
LONGS
LUNGI
MANTA
NAPPY
PALLA
PANTS
PARKA
PAVIS
PILCH
PINNY
RAMIE
SAGUM
SAYON
SHAWL

SHIFT
SHIRT
SKIRT
SLOPS
SMOCK
STAYS
STOLA
STOLE
TAILS
TALAR
TALMA
TANGA
THROW
TREWS
TRUSS
TUNIC
WAMUS

6

ABOLLA
ACHKAN
ANORAK
ARMOUR
BANIAN
BARROW
BASQUE
BEAVER
BIKINI
BLAZER
BLOUSE

BODICE
BOLERO
BRIEFS
BURKHA
BYRNIE
CAFTAN
CAMISE
CAPOTE
CESTUS
CHIMER
CHINOS
CHITON
CILICE
CORSET
CUISSE
DENIMS
DIAPER
DICKEY
DIRNDL
DOLMAN
DOMINO
EXOMIS
FANNEL
FLARES
GIRDLE
GORGET
GREAVE
GUSSET
HALTER
JACKET
JERKIN
JERSEY

JOSEPH
JUBBAH
JUMPER
KABAYA
KAROSS
KIMONO
KIRTLE
KNICKS
LORICA
MANTLE
MANTUA
MASCLE
MITTEN
MUU-MUU
OILERS
OUTFIT
PEPLOS
PEPLUM
PINNER
PONCHO
RAGLAN
REEFER
ROLL-ON
SABLES
SAKKOS
SARONG
SERAPE
SHORTS
SLACKS
SONTAG
STEP-IN
TABARD

CLOTHING – GENERAL CLOTHING

TIPPET
TONNAG
TRUNKS
T-SHIRT
TUXEDO
ULSTER
VAKASS
VISITE
WOOLLY
ZEPHYR
ZOUAVE

7

AILETTE
BALDRIC
BLANKET
BLOOMER
BLOUSON
BOX-COAT
BURDASH
BURNOUS
CAGOULE
CASSOCK
CASUALS
CAT-SUIT
CHEMISE
CHLAMYS
CHUDDER
CORSLET
COSTUME
CRAWLER
CUIRASS
CUTAWAY
DOUBLET
DRAWERS
FILIBEG
FUR COAT
G-STRING
GYM-SLIP
HAUBERK
HUMERAL
JAMBEAU
LAMBOYS
LEOTARD
MAE WEST
MAILLOT
MANIPLE
MANTEAU
MANTLET
MOZETTA

NIGHTIE
OVERALL
PAENULA
PALETOT
PALETTE
PALLIUM
PANOPLY
PANTIES
PEA-COAT
PEG-TOPS
PELISSE
PIERROT
PLACKET
POSTEEN
PYJAMAS
ROMPERS
RUBBERS
RUG-GOWN
SABATON
SARAFAN
SINGLET
SLICKER
SMICKET
SOUTANE
SPENCER
SURCOAT
SURTOUT
SWEATER
TALLITH
TANK-TOP
TEA-GOWN
TOP-COAT
TUCKERS
TUNICLE
TWIN-SET
UNIFORM
VAREUSE
WET-SUIT
WRAPPER
ZAMARRA

8

ARMATURE
AVENTAIL
BALL-GOWN
BASQUINE
BATH-ROBE
BENJAMIN
BLOOMERS
BRASSARD

BREECHES
BUFF COAT
CAMISOLE
CAPUCHIN
CARDIGAN
CARDINAL
CHASUBLE
CHAUSSES
CINGULUM
COD-PIECE
CORSELET
COVERALL
CULOTTES
DALMATIC
DJELLABA
DUST-COAT
ENSEMBLE
ETON SUIT
FLANNELS
GAMBESON
GAUNTLET
GYM-TUNIC
HIMATION
HIPSTERS
JODHPURS
JUMP-SUIT
KID-GLOVE
KNICKERS
LAVA-LAVA
LEATHERS
LIFEBELT
MACKINAW
MANTELET
MINI-KINI
MINK COAT
NANKEENS
NEGLIGEE
OIL-SKINS
OVERALLS
OVERCOAT
OVERSLIP
PADDLERS
PALATINE
PANNICLE
PAULDRON
PEARLIES
PECTORAL
PEIGNOIR
PELERINE
PINAFORE
PLASTRON
PRINCESS

PULLOVER
RAINCOAT
SACK-COAT
SCAPULAR
SEALSKIN
SLIP-OVER
SMOCK-TOP
SUBUCULA
SURPLICE
SWIM-SUIT
TAGLIONI
TAIL-COAT
TEE-SHIRT
TOURNURE
TROUSERS
UNDERSET
VAMBRACE
VAMPLATE
VESTMENT
ZOOT SUIT

9

AIR-JACKET
BACK-PIECE
BACK-PLATE
BALL-DRESS
BED-JACKET
BRASSIÈRE
BUSH-SHIRT
CHAIN-MAIL
CHEONG-SAM
COAT-DRESS
COAT-FROCK
CORDUROYS
CRINOLINE
DRAPE SUIT
DRESS-COAT
DRESS-SUIT
DUNGAREES
FROCK-COAT
GABERDINE
GALA-DRESS
GARIBALDI
GREATCOAT
HABERGEON
HACQUETON
HAIR-SHIRT
HOUSE-COAT
JOCKSTRAP
KNEE-CORDS
LOIN-CLOTH

LONG JOHNS
MACINTOSH
MAXI-SKIRT
MINI-SKIRT
MOLESKINS
NEWMARKET
NIGHT-GOWN
NIGHT-ROBE
OVERDRESS
OVERSKIRT
PANTALETS
PEA-JACKET
PETERSHAM
PETTICOAT
PHELONION
PLUS-FOURS
POLONAISE
POURPOINT
PRINCESSE
PRINCESSE
PROTECTOR
RAINPROOF
RA-RA SKIRT
REDINGOTE
REREBRACE
SACK-DRESS
SANBENITO
SIREN SUIT
SLAMMAKIN
SLOPPY JOE
SPACE-SUIT
STOMACHER
STUFF-GOWN
TEDDY SUIT
TRACK-SUIT
TUBE-SKIRT
TWEED SUIT
UNDERCOAT
UNDERGOWN
UNDERVEST
UNION SUIT
WAISTCOAT

10

BODY-WARMER
BOILER-SUIT
BRIGANDINE
BUFF JERKIN
BUSH-JACKET
BUSTER-SUIT
CARMAGNOLE
CATAPHRACT

76

CHAPARAJOS
CHEMISETTE
COAT-ARMOUR
COAT OF MAIL
CORK-JACKET
COTE-HARDIE
COURT-DRESS
COVERT COAT
CRINOLETTE
CUMMERBUND
DINNER-GOWN
DRAIN-PIPES
DRESS-SHIRT
DUFFEL-COAT
EMPIRE GOWN
ETON JACKET
FUSTANELLA
GENEVA GOWN
GRASS SKIRT
HALF-KIRTLE
HAND-ME-DOWN
HAREM SKIRT
HUG-ME-TIGHT
INDIA SHAWL
LEDERHOSEN
LIFE-JACKET
LOUNGE-SUIT
MACKINTOSH
MONKEY-SUIT
NIGHT-DRESS
NIGHT-SHIRT
OMOPHORION
OPERA-CLOAK
OXFORD BAGS
PALATINATE
PALUDAMENT
PANTALOONS
PLASTIC MAC
REVERSIBLE
RIDING-COAT
RIDING-ROBE
RIDING-SUIT
ROMPER-SUIT
ROQUELAURE
SAFARI-SUIT
SALOPETTES
SHIRT-DRESS
SMOCK-FROCK
SPONGE BAGS
SPORTS COAT
STICHARION
SWEAT-SHIRT

TRENCH-COAT
ULSTERETTE
UNDERDRESS
UNDERSHIRT
UNDERSKIRT
UNDERTUNIC
WAISTCLOTH
WATERPROOF
WINDJAMMER
WRAP-RASCAL

11

BABY'S NAPKIN
BATHING-SUIT
BATTLEDRESS
BELL-BOTTOMS
BOILED SHIRT
BOXER SHORTS
BREASTPLATE
BRITISH WARM
BUFFALO-ROBE
DIVING-DRESS
DOLLY VARDEN
FARTHINGALE
GAY DECEIVER
GENOUILLÈRE
GLOVE-SHIELD
HACKING-COAT
HOBBLE SKIRT
MATINÉE COAT
MENTONNIÈRE
MORNING-GOWN
MORNING-SUIT
PAIR OF STAYS
PANTALETTES
PILOT-JACKET
PLATE-ARMOUR
PONTIFICALS
RIDING-CLOAK
RIDING-GLOVE
RIDING-SKIRT
RUBBER GLOVE
SCALE-ARMOUR
SHELL-JACKET
SWAGGER-COAT
SWALLOW-TAIL
TROUSER-SUIT
TWEED JACKET
V-NECK JUMPER
WINDCHEATER

12

BATHING-DRESS
BEARING CLOTH
BODY STOCKING
CAMI-KNICKERS
CHASTITY BELT
CHESTERFIELD
CHRISOM-CLOTH
COMBAT JACKET
COMBINATIONS
CROPPED JEANS
DINNER-JACKET
DIVIDED SKIRT
DONKEY JACKET
DRESSING-GOWN
DRESSING-SACK
DRESS-UNIFORM
EVENING-DRESS
FATIGUE DRESS
KNEE-BREECHES
LONG TROUSERS
LUMBER-JACKET
MONKEY-JACKET
MORNING-DRESS
MOUSQUETAIRE
PAISLEY SHAWL
PALUDAMENTUM
PEDAL-PUSHERS
PRESSURE-SUIT
PYJAMA-JACKET
SAFARI-JACKET
SHIRTWAISTER
SHOULDER BELT
SKELETON SUIT
SPLINT-ARMOUR
SPORTS JACKET
SUIT OF ARMOUR
SUPERHUMERAL
TOPLESS DRESS
UNDERGARMENT
WEATHERPROOF
WEDDING-DRESS

13

BERMUDA SHORTS
BUTTON-THROUGH
CAMEL-HAIR COAT
COCKTAIL DRESS
EPITRACHELION
HACKING-JACKET

CLOTHING – GENERAL CLOTHING

INVERNESS CAPE
LEATHER JACKET
LIBERTY BODICE
MATINÉE JACKET
MOURNING-CLOAK
NORFOLK JACKET
PINAFORE-DRESS
PINAFORE-SKIRT
POWDERING-GOWN
PUFF-BALL SKIRT
REEFING-JACKET
ROBE-DE-CHAMBRE
SHEEPSKIN COAT
SHORT TROUSERS
SMOKING JACKET

STRAPLESS GOWN
SUSPENDER-BELT
TOGA PRAETEXTA
TRUNK-BREECHES
WATTEAU BODICE

14

BATHING-COSTUME
CHEST-PROTECTOR
CLAW-HAMMER-COAT
DRESSING-JACKET
GOING-AWAY DRESS
KNICKERBOCKERS

PYJAMA-TROUSERS
RIDING-BREECHES
SHAWL-WAISTCOAT
SHOOTING-JACKET
SWIMMING TRUNKS

15

BULLET-PROOF VEST
PEASECOD-CUIRASS
PNEUMONIA BLOUSE
POLO-NECK SWEATER
SWIMMING COSTUME

CLOTHING – HEADGEAR & NECKWEAR

3

BOA
CAP
FEZ
HAT
LID
LUM
MOB
TAJ
TAM
TIE
WIG

4

BAND
CAUL
COIF
COPE
COWL
HELM
HOOD
KEPI
MASK
POKE
RUFF

TILE
TOPI
VEIL

5

ARMET
BANDS
BERET
BUSBY
CAXON
CROWN
CURCH
DERBY
FICHU
FOGLE
GIBUS
MITRE
MUTCH
NUBIA
PAGRI
PLAID
PLUME
ROMAL
SCARF
SHAKO

SNOOD
STOCK
STOLE
TAMMY
TERAI
TIARA
TOPEE
TOQUE
TOWER
TUQUE
VISOR
VITTA
VIZOR
VOLET

6

ANADEM
BAG-WIG
BARRET
BEAVER
BERTHA
BOATER
BONNET
BOWLER
BOW-TIE

BRETON
BRUTUS
CALASH
CASQUE
CASTOR
CHOKER
CLAQUE
CLOCHE
COLLAR
COLLET
CORNET
CRAVAT
DIADEM
FEDORA
FILLET
GORGET
HEAUME
HELMET
INFULA
JAMPOT
KALPAK
KISS-ME
LAUREL
LUM-HAT
MADRAS
MESAIL
MOB-CAP

MODIUS
MORION
PANAMA
PERUKE
PILEUS
PINNER
POT-HAT
RED-HAT
SALLET
SUN-HAT
TIN-HAT
TITFER
TOP-HAT
TOPPER
TRILBY
TURBAN
VIZARD
WEEPER
WIMPLE

7

BASHLYK
BASINET
BELCHER
BIRETTA

BUZZ-WIG
BYCOKET
CALOTTE
CAPUCHE
CHAPEAU
CHAPLET
CHÉCHIA
CHIP-HAT
CHUDDAR
CIDARIS
CIRCLET
COMMODE
CORONAL
CORONET
EARMUFF
FLAT-CAP
FLAT-HAT
FRONTAL
GAS-MASK
HOMBURG
LEGHORN
MARABOU
MONTERO
MUFFLER
NECKLET
NECKTIE
ORARION

PERIWIG
PETASUS
PILL-BOX
PITH-HAT
PLATEAU
PLUG-HAT
SILK-HAT
SKID-LID
SOLA HAT
SOUBISE
SPENCER
STETSON
STICKUP
TALL HAT
TILE-HAT
TRICORN
VANDYKE
VEILING
WHIMPLE
YASHMAK

8

BABUSHKA
BALMORAL
BANDANNA
BEARSKIN
BLACK CAP
BONGRACE
BURGANET
CALYPTRA
CAPELINE
CARCANET
CHAPERON
CLOTH-CAP
CROWNLET
CRUSH-HAT
DALMAHOY
DRESS-TIE
EARMUFFS
FALDETTA
FONTANGE
FOOL'S CAP
FRONTLET
HAVELOCK
HEADBAND
HEADGEAR
KAFFIYEH
KALYPTRA
KERCHIEF
MANTILLA

MUSHROOM
NECK-BAND
NECKGEAR
NIGHTCAP
OPERA-HAT
PALATINE
PAPER-HAT
PUGGAREE
SILLY-HOW
SKULLCAP
SNAP-BRIM
SOMBRERO
STEPHANE
STRAW-HAT
TARBOOSH
THRUM-CAP

9

BALACLAVA
BARRET-CAP
BILLYCOCK
BLINDFOLD
BOWLER-HAT
BROAD-BRIM
COCKED HAT
COCK'S-COMB
COCKLE-HAT
COMFORTER
DOG-COLLAR
DUNSTABLE
FALSE FACE
FORAGE-CAP
GAS-HELMET
GLENGARRY
HEADCLOTH
HEAD-DRESS
HEADPIECE
IRON CROWN
MUFFIN-CAP
NECK-CLOTH
NITHSDALE
PANAMA-HAT
PEAKED CAP
PICCADILL
SAILOR-HAT
SCHOOL TIE
SHOVEL-HAT
SHOWER-CAP
SLOUCH-HAT
SOLITAIRE

SOU'-WESTER
SPHENDONE
STEENKIRK
STRING-TIE
SUN-BONNET
TARPAULIN
VICTORINE
VISOR-MASK
WIDE-AWAKE
ZUCCHETTO

10

BLUE-BONNET
CHIMNEY-POT
COLLARETTE
COLLEGE CAP
ETON COLLAR
FASCINATOR
FOUR-IN-HAND
GORGONEION
HEAD-HUGGER
HEADSQUARE
HUNTING-CAP
KILMARNOCK
LAMBREQUIN
LIBERTY CAP
MONTERO-CAP
MURAL CROWN
OXYGEN MASK
PICCADILLY
PICTURE-HAT
PITH-HELMET
POKE-BONNET
PORK-PIE HAT
RESPIRATOR
RIDING-HOOD
ROLL-COLLAR
SCARLET-HAT
SCRATCH-WIG
SMOKING CAP
SOLA HELMET
STEEPLE-HAT
THROAT-BAND
VIZARD-MASK
WING-COLLAR

11

BONNET-ROUGE

CHAPEAU-BRAS
CRASH-HELMET
DEERSTALKER
DOLLY VARDEN
FALLING BAND
KISS-ME-QUICK
MORTAR-BOARD
NECKERCHIEF
NIGHTINGALE
PHRYGIAN CAP
PICKELHAUBE
SMOKE-HELMET
TAM O'SHANTER
THROAT-LATCH
THROAT-STRAP
TRENCHER-CAP
TRIPLE CROWN
TYROLEAN HAT

12

CHEESE-CUTTER
FORE-AND-AFTER
MAZARINE HOOD
MOUSQUETAIRE
OLD SCHOOL TIE
SCOTCH BONNET
SQUIRREL-TAIL
STEEPLE-CROWN
STOVEPIPE HAT
TEN-GALLON HAT

13

FEATHER-BONNET

14

FIREMAN'S HELMET
KILMARNOCK COWL
MANDARIN COLLAR
PRESSURE-HELMET

15

BALACLAVA HELMET

CLOTHING – MATERIALS & FABRICS

3
ABA
ABB
FUR
HOG
KID
NAP
NET
PVC
REP
SAY
TAT
WEB

4
BAFT
BATT
BUFF
BURR
CALF
CIRÉ
COIR
CONY
CORK
CUIR
DOWN
DRAB
DUCK
ECRU
FELT
FLIX
FLUE
GIMP
HARN
JEAN
KELT
KEMP
LACE
LAMÉ
LAWN
LENO
LINT
MULL
NOIL
PACO
PIÑA
RACK
SILK
VAIR
WOOL

YUFT

5
ABAYA
ARRAS
ATLAS
BAIZE
BASAN
BEIGE
BRAID
BUDGE
CHINO
CLOTH
CRAPE
CRASH
CRÊPE
DENIM
DRILL
FANON
FITCH
FLOCK
FLOSS
FOULÉ
GAUZE
GUNNY
HARDS
JASPÉ
KHAKI
LINEN
LINER
LISLE
MOIRE
MUNGO
NINON
NYLON
ORRIS
OTTER
PANNE
PASHM
PERSE
PIQUÉ
PLAID
PLUSH
POINT
PRINT
RAYON
SABLE
SATIN
SCRIM
SERGE

SHEER
SKUNK
STUFF
SUEDE
SURAH
SURAT
TABBY
TAMIN
TERRY
TOILE
TULLE
TWEED
TWILL
UNION
VOILE
WEAVE
WIGAN

6
ALPACA
ANGORA
BAREGE
BEAVER
BOUCLÉ
BROCHÉ
BURLAP
BURNET
BURREL
BYSSUS
CADDIS
CALICO
CAMLET
CANVAS
CATGUT
CHINTZ
CLOQUÉ
COBERG
COTTON
COUTIL
CREPON
CREWEL
CUBICA
CYPRUS
DACRON
DAMASK
DIMITY
DOMETT
DOWLAS
DRALON
DUFFEL

DURANT
DURRIE
ERMINE
FABLON
FABRIC
FAILLE
FERRET
FRIEZE
GURRAH
HARDEN
HODDEN
HUMHUM
JAEGER
JERSEY
KERSEY
KINCOB
LAMPAS
LANUGO
LINING
LINSEY
LUSTRE
MADRAS
MEDLEY
MELTON
MERINO
MOHAIR
MOREEN
MOTLEY
MULMUL
MUSLIN
NUTRIA
OCELOT
PONGEE
POPLIN
RABBIT
RATINE
RIBBON
RUSSEL
RUSSET
SAMITE
SARONG
SATARA
SATEEN
SAXONY
SENDAL
SHODDY
SINDON
SKIVER
SONERI
TAMISE
TARTAN
T-CLOTH

THIBET
TICKEN
TISSUE
TRICOT
TUSSER
VELOUR
VELVET
VICUÑA
WADMAL
WINCEY
ZEPHYR
ZORINO

7
ALEPINE
BAGGING
BATISTE
BELTING
BOMBAST
BOX-CALF
BROCADE
BUCKRAM
BUNTING
CAMBRIC
CATSKIN
CHALLIS
CHAMOIS
CHARPIE
CHEVIOT
CHIFFON
CODILLA
COWHIDE
CYPRESS
DELAINE
DOE-SKIN
DOGSKIN
DORNICK
DRABBET
DROGUET
DRUGGET
EXTRACT
FAÇONNÉ
FELTING
FITCHET
FLANNEL
FOOTING
FOULARD
FRAYING
FUSTIAN
GALATEA

GALLOON
GENAPPE
GINGHAM
GOBELIN
GROGRAM
GUIPURE
HATTING
HEEL-TAP
HESSIAN
HOG-SKIN
HOLLAND
JAMDANI
JAP-SILK
KARAKUL
KHADDAR
KID-SKIN
KIP-SKIN
LEATHER
LEGHORN
LOCKRAM
MALINES
MARABOU
MATTING
MECHLIN
MEXICAN
MINIVER
MOROCCO
NACARAT
NANKEEN
NETTING
OILSILK
OILSKIN
OPOSSUM
ORGANZA
ORLEANS
OTTOMAN
PADDING
PAISLEY
PERCALE
PIGSKIN
PLASTIC
PRINTER
RABANNA
RACCOON
RAG-WOOL
RATTEEN
SACKING
SAFFIAN
SAGATHY
SATINET
SCHAPPE
SOW-SKIN

TABARET
TAFFETA
TEXTILE
TICKING
TIFFANY
TROLLEY
TUSSORE
VEILING
VESTING
WADDING
WOOLLEN
WOOLSEY
WORSTED
ZANELLA

8

ARMOZEEN
ARRASENE
BARATHEA
BARRACAN
BEARSKIN
BOBBINET
BONE-LACE
BOX-CLOTH
BUCKSKIN
CALFSKIN
CAMELINE
CASHMERE
CHENILLE
CHEVEREL
CONY-WOOL
CORDOVAN
CORDUROY
CORDWAIN
CORPORAL
COTELINE
COUTILLE
CRETONNE
DAMASSIN
DEERSKIN
DIAMANTÉ
DRABETTE
DRILLING
DUNGAREE
ÉOLIENNE
FROCKING
GAMBROON
GOATSKIN
GOLD-LACE
GOSSAMER

HAIRLINE
HOMESPUN
JACQUARD
JEANETTE
KNOTTING
KOLINSKY
LAMBSKIN
LUSTRING
MANTLING
MARCELLA
MAROCAIN
MAROQUIN
MATERIAL
MAZARINE
MOLESKIN
MOQUETTE
MUSLINET
MUSQUASH
NAINSOOK
NEAR-SILK
OILCLOTH
ORGANDIE
OSNABURG
PADUASOY
PLAIDING
PONY-SKIN
PRUNELLA
PRUNELLE
QUILTING
RICK-RACK
SARSENET
SÉALSKIN
SHAGREEN
SHALLOON
SHANTUNG
SHAWLING
SHEETING
SHIRTING
SHOT SILK
SICILIAN
SKIN-WOOL
SKIRTING
SQUIRREL
STUFFING
TABBINET
TAPESTRY
TARLATAN
TERYLENE
THICKSET
VELVERET
WAX-CLOTH
WHEELING

WHIPCORD
WHIPPING
WILD SILK
WOLF-SKIN

9

ASTRAKHAN
BALDACHIN
BALZARINE
BENGALINE
BLOND-LACE
BOMBAZINE
CALAMANCO
CAMEL-HAIR
CARMELITE
CARPETING
CASSIMERE
CHARMEUSE
CHEVRETTE
COTTONADE
COURTELLE
CREPOLINE
CRIMPLENE
CRINOLINE
EIDERDOWN
FIBROLINE
FILOSELLE
FINGERING
FLOSS SILK
FLOUNCING
FOLK-WEAVE
GABERDINE
GEORGETTE
GOLD-CLOTH
GRENADINE
GROSGRAIN
HAIRCLOTH
HORSEHAIR
HUCKABACK
KALAMKARI
LAMB'S-WOOL
LONG-CLOTH
MATELASSÉ
NITRO-SILK
ORGANZINE
OVERCHECK
PACK-CLOTH
PACKSHEET
PARAMATTA
PERCALINE

PERSIENNE
PETERSHAM
PIÑA-CLOTH
POINT-LACE
POLYAMIDE
POLYESTER
POLYTHENE
POLYVINYL
SACKCLOTH
SAIL-CLOTH
SATINETTE
SATIN JEAN
SHARKSKIN
SHEEPSKIN
SILVER-FOX
SLINKSKIN
STROUDING
SWANSDOWN
TARPAULIN
TENT-CLOTH
TOWELLING
VELOUTINE
VELVETEEN
VELVETING
WIRE-GAUZE
WOLVERINE
ZIBELLINE

10

BALBRIGGAN
BERLIN WOOL
BOBBIN-LACE
BOOK-MUSLIN
BROADCLOTH
BROCATELLE
CANDLEWICK
CIRCASSIAN
COLBERTINE
COTTON-WOOL
DEVIL'S DUST
FEARNOUGHT
FLORENTINE
GRASSCLOTH
HABIT-CLOTH
HODDEN-GREY
HOPSACKING
KENTE CLOTH
KERSEYMERE
MACKINTOSH
MIGNONETTE

CLOTHING – MATERIALS & FABRICS

MOUSSELINE
MUMMY-CLOTH
NEEDLECORD
PAPER-CLOTH
PASTE-GRAIN
PILOT-CLOTH
POPLINETTE
REVERSIBLE
RUSSEL-CORD
SEERSUCKER
SICILIENNE
STRAW-PLAIT
THREAD-LACE
THROWN-SILK
TIBET-CLOTH
TOILINETTE
TROUSERING
TUFTAFFETY
TUSSER-SILK
VELVET-PILE
WATER-TWIST
WINCEYETTE

11

BUFF-LEATHER
BUTTER-CLOTH
CHEESECLOTH
CLOTH OF GOLD
CUIR-BOUILLI
DRAP-DE-BERRY
DREADNOUGHT
EVERLASTING
FAIR-LEATHER
FLANNELETTE
HAMMERCLOTH
HONITON LACE

KENDAL-GREEN
LEATHERETTE
LEOPARD-SKIN
LEVANT LINEN
MARQUISETTE
MECHLIN LACE
NEEDLE-POINT
NETTLE-CLOTH
NUN'S-VEILING
OVERCOATING
PAPER-MUSLIN
SHOE-LEATHER
SPONGE-CLOTH
STOCKINETTE
TORCHON LACE
WASH-LEATHER
WATERED-SILK
WHITLEATHER

12

BRUSSELS LACE
BUTTER-MUSLIN
CAVALRY TWILL
CIRCASSIENNE
CRÊPE-DE-CHINE
DUCHESSE LACE
ELECTRIC SEAL
FIREPROOFING
LEATHER-CLOTH
MUTATION MINK
NEAT'S LEATHER
PACKING-SHEET
SLIPPER SATIN
SPLIT LEATHER
VALENCIENNES
VISCOSE RAYON

WAISTCOATING
WAXED LEATHER
WHITE LEATHER

13

AMERICAN CLOTH
BOULTING CLOTH
BRATTICE-CLOTH
CASEMENT-CLOTH
CHANTILLY LACE
CHROME-LEATHER
COVERT COATING
FOUNDATION-NET
FRENCH MOROCCO
LINSEY-WOOLSEY
MOURNING-STUFF
OUTING-FLANNEL
PATENT LEATHER
RUSSIA LEATHER
SHAMMY-LEATHER
WATERPROOFING

14

ARTIFICIAL SILK
HEATHER MIXTURE
MOROCCO LEATHER
PERSIAN MOROCCO

15

JAPANNED LEATHER
WEATHERPROOFING

COLOURS & DYES

3
BAY
DUN
DYE
HUE
JET
RED
TAN

4
ANIL
BLUE
BUFF
CYAN
DRAB
DUSK
FAWN
GOLD
GRAY
GREY
HAEM
LAKE
OPAL
PINK
PUCE
ROAN
ROSE
RUST
SAXE
TINT
TONE
WELD
WOAD

5
AMBER
AZURE
BEIGE
BLACK
BLUSH
BROWN
CHICA
CORAL
EOSIN
GRAIN
GREEN
HAZEL

HENNA
KHAKI
LEMON
LIVER
LOVAT
MAUVE
MUMMY
OCHRE
OLIVE
PANSY
PEACH
PERSE
PUTTY
ROUGE
SABLE
SEPIA
SHADE
SLATE
SMALT
STAIN
SUEDE
TAWNY
TINGE
UMBER
WHITE

6
ANATTO
ARCHIL
ARGENT
AUBURN
AURORA
AZO-DYE
BISTRE
BRONZE
CANARY
CERISE
CHROME
CLARET
COBALT
COLOUR
COPPER
CYANIN
DAMASK
FALLOW
FLAVIN
INDIGO
ISABEL
ISATIN
KAMALA

KERMES
LAC-DYE
MADDER
MALLOW
MAROON
MINIUM
MODENA
MURREY
ORANGE
ORCEIN
PASTEL
PTERIN
PURPLE
RÉSÉDA
ROUCOU
RUDDLE
RUSSET
SALMON
SHRIMP
SIENNA
SORREL
TITIAN
VIOLET
YELLOW

7
ALIZARI
ALKANET
ANILINE
ARGYRIA
AZURINE
CARMINE
CELADON
CITRINE
CORBEAU
CRIMSON
CUDBEAR
CYANINE
DARK RED
ETIOLIN
FILEMOT
GRIZZLE
JACINTH
LAC-LAKE
MAGENTA
MAUVINE
MELANIN
NACARAT
OLD GOLD

OLD ROSE
PARA-RED
PIGMENT
PONCEAU
SAFFRON
SCARLET
SKY-BLUE
TILE-RED
TURACIN
VERMEIL
XANTHIN

8
AMETHYST
BLOOD-RED
BRICK-RED
CAROTENE
CERULEIN
CINNAMON
COLORANT
CRAMOISY
DARK BLUE
DYESTUFF
FUCHSINE
GRIDELIN
GUNMETAL
HYACINTH
INDULINE
IRON-GREY
ISABELLA
JET-BLACK
LAVENDER
LUTEOLIN
MAHOGANY
MAZARINE
NAVY-BLUE
ORPIMENT
ORSEILLE
PEA-GREEN
PRIMROSE
PURPURIN
ROSE-PINK
SANGUINE
SANTALIN
SAP-GREEN
SAPPHIRE
TINCTURE
TURNSOLE
VERDITER
VIRIDIAN

9
AUBERGINE
BILIRUBIN
BLUE-BLACK
CARNATION
CHAMPAGNE
COCHINEAL
COLCOTHAR
COLOURING
CURCUMINE
DARK BROWN
DARK GREEN
DUTCH PINK
DYER'S WOAD
EUMELANIN
FIELD GREY
FLESH-PINK
FLESH-TINT
INDIAN RED
LAMP-BLACK
LIGHT BLUE
LITHOPONE
NIGROSINE
OLIVE DRAB
PEARL-GREY
PHTHALEIN
POMPADOUR
PRIMULINE
RHODAMINE
ROYAL BLUE
SAFFRANIN
SAGE-GREEN
SAXON BLUE
SLATE-GREY
SOLFERINO
STEEL-BLUE
STEEL-GREY
TANGERINE
TURKEY RED
TURQUOISE
UROCHROME
VERMILION
WHITE LEAD
ZINC OXIDE
ZINC-WHITE

10
ANILINE-DYE
ANTHOCLORE

COLOURS & DYES

AQUAMARINE
BERLIN BLUE
BILIVERDIN
CAROTENOID
CARTHAMINE
CHARTREUSE
COBALT-BLUE
COQUELICOT
DOVE-COLOUR
FLAKE-WHITE
HELIOTROPE
INDIGO BLUE
LIGHT BROWN
LIGHT GREEN
LIPOCHROME
MADDER-LAKE
OLIVE GREEN
OXFORD BLUE
PARIS GREEN
PEACH-BLOOM
PEARL-WHITE
PLUM-COLOUR
RED-SANDERS
RIFLE-GREEN
ROSANILINE
ROSE-COLOUR
SALMON-PINK
SMOKE-BLACK
SNUFF-BROWN
SPIRIT-BLUE

11

ANTHOCYANIN
BOTTLE-GREEN
BURNT-SIENNA
FLESH-COLOUR

FLUORESCEIN
FRENCH BERRY
KING'S-YELLOW
LEMON-YELLOW
LIVER-COLOUR
MOUSE-COLOUR
NATTIER BLUE
NIGRESCENCE
PEACOCK-BLUE
PHYCOCYANIN
PHYCOPHAEIN
POMPEIAN-RED
SANG-DE-BOEUF
SNUFF-COLOUR
STONE-COLOUR
STRAW-COLOUR
ULTRAMARINE
VENETIAN RED
WATER-COLOUR
YELLOW-EARTH
YELLOW-OCHRE
YOUNG FUSTIC

12

AIR-FORCE BLUE
ANTHOXANTHIN
CAPPAGH-BROWN
CHINESE WHITE
CHROME-YELLOW
DRAGON'S-BLOOD
ELECTRIC BLUE
EMERALD GREEN
LINCOLN GREEN
NAPLES YELLOW
PHYCOXANTHIN
PIGEON'S-BLOOD

PRUSSIAN BLUE
QUAKER-COLOUR
TURACOVERDIN
VANDYKE BROWN
VISUAL PURPLE
XANTHOPTERIN

13

CAMBRIDGE BLUE
CHLOROCRUORIN
GENTIAN VIOLET
LEMNIAN RUDDLE
MONASTRAL BLUE
PHTHALOCYANIN
PHYCOERYTHRIN
SCHEELE'S GREEN
SULPHUR-YELLOW
TITANIUM WHITE
TURQUOISE-BLUE

14

INVISIBLE GREEN
MONASTRAL GREEN
PARAROSANILINE
TURQUOISE-GREEN

15

DIMETHYLANILINE
LAPIS-LAZULI BLUE
PURPLE OF CASSIUS
WALLFLOWER BROWN

COMMUNICATIONS

3

BUG
DAK
DOT
FAX
GEE
GEN
KEY
PIP
SOS
STD

4

BLIP
CALL
CARD
CODE
DASH
DIAL
DOPE
LINE
LINK
MAIL
MEMO
NEWS
NOTE
PECK
PIPS
POST
SCAN
SIGN
SKIP
TAPE
WIRE

5

BLEEP
BREVE
CABLE
CODEX
CREED
DECCA
FLASH
LOCAL
MASER
MEDIA
MORSE
ORGAN

PHONE
RADAR
RADIO
RELAY
STAMP
TELEX
TRACT
TRUNK
VIDEO

6

AERIAL
BEACON
BLOWER
CIPHER
CLAVIS
DECTRA
ERRAND
HOMING
HOOK-UP
LETTER
LINK-UP
MAYDAY
MEDIUM
NOTICE
OUTPUT
PINGER
POSTER
REPORT
SENDER
SIGNAL
TANNOY
TICKER
TIC-TAC
WIGWAG

7

ADDRESS
AIR MAIL
ANTENNA
BLEEPER
CARRIER
CHANNEL
CLUTTER
EPISTLE
EXPRESS
FAN MAIL
HAND-SET

HOT LINE
LOW-DOWN
MAIL-BAG
MAIL-BOX
MAIL-CAR
MAIL-GIG
MAIL-VAN
MEGAFOG
MESSAGE
MISSIVE
MONITOR
NETWORK
NOTELET
PECKING
POSTAGE
POST-BAG
SCANNER
SIMPLEX
SPUTNIK
TIDINGS
WAR-DRUM

8

AEROGRAM
AGITPROP
AIRGRAPH
AREA CODE
BOOK-POST
BULLETIN
CIRCULAR
DESPATCH
DIALLING
DISPATCH
ENVELOPE
EXCHANGE
INTELSAT
INTERCOM
LAND-LINE
LAST POST
LIFE-LINE
MAIL-BOAT
MAIL-CART
NEWSCAST
NEWSROOM
PAMPHLET
PASTORAL
PAY-BOOTH
PAY-PHONE
PIPELINE
POSTCARD

POSTCODE
POSTMARK
RADIATOR
RECEIVER
REPEATER
SCANNING
TALK-BACK
TELEGRAM
TELESEME
TELETEXT
TELETYPE
TICK-TACK
TOLL-CALL
TRACKING
WIRELESS

9

AIR LETTER
BROADCAST
CABLEGRAM
CIPHER-KEY
DICTATION
EXTENSION
FIRST POST
GRAPEVINE
LETTER-BOX
LOCAL-CALL
MAIL-COACH
MAIL ORDER
MASS MEDIA
MAIL-PLANE
MAIL-TRAIN
MEGAPHONE
MICROGRAM
MINI-TRACK
MISREPORT
MORSE CODE
NEWS-FLASH
NEWSPAPER
NEWS-SHEET
OBEDIENCE
PARTY-LINE
PENNY-POST
PILLAR-BOX
RADIOGRAM
RESPONDER
SATELLITE
SCRAMBLER
SEMAPHORE
TELEGRAPH

TELEPHEME
TELEPHONE
TELEPHONY
TRUNK-CALL
TRUNK-MAIL
VIEWPHONE

10

BILLET-DOUX
COLLECTION
COMMUNIQUÉ
CRYPTOGRAM
DICTAPHONE
DICTOGRAPH
DROP-LETTER
ENCLYCLICAL
HELIOGRAPH
HYDROPHONE
INTERPHONE
LETTER-CARD
LOUD-HAILER
LOVE-LETTER
MASS MEDIUM
MEMORANDUM
MICROGRAPH
NEWSLETTER
OPEN LETTER
PARCEL POST
PAY-STATION
PHONOPHORE
PHOTOPHONE
PHOTOPHONY
PIGEON POST
POSTAL CODE
POSTAL TUBE
POST-LETTER
POST-OFFICE
POST-SCRIPT
PROPAGANDA
QUADRUPLEX
RADIOPHONE
ROUND ROBIN
SECOND POST
SHIP-LETTER
SIGNALLING
TELEGRAPHY
TELEVISION
TELEWRITER
TICKER-TAPE
TIME-SIGNAL

COMMUNICATIONS

VIDEOPHONE
WIGWAGGING

11

CHAIN-LETTER
CRYPTOGRAPH
FLAG-WAGGING
GENERAL POST
HELIOGRAPHY
INFORMATION
LOUDSPEAKER
MAIL-CATCHER
MAILING-CARD
MARCONIGRAM
NEWSCASTING
NOTICE-BOARD
RADIO BEACON
SMOKE SIGNAL
STEGANOGRAM
STORM SIGNAL
SURFACE MAIL
SWITCHBOARD
TAPE-MACHINE
TELEARCHICS
TELECONTROL
TELEMESSAGE
TELEPRINTER
TRANSLATION
TRANSMITTER
TRANSPONDER
TWO-WAY RADIO
WRONG NUMBER

12

BROADCASTING
DETECTOPHONE
DIALLING CODE

DIALLING TONE
MAIL CARRIAGE
NOTIFICATION
PICTURE-PHONE
POSTAGE-STAMP
RADAR-SCANNER
RADIOPHONICS
RADIO STATION
RECEIVING-SET
SIGN LANGUAGE
SPEAKING-TUBE
STENTORPHONE
STORM WARNING
TELAUTOGRAPH
TELERECORDER
THEATROPHONE
TRANSMISSION
WALKIE-TALKIE

13

BEGGING-LETTER
BUSH TELEGRAPH
CARRIER-PIGEON
COMMUNICATION
COUNTER-SIGNAL
EXPRESS LETTER
EXPRESS PACKET
EXPRESS PARCEL
HERTZIAN WAVES
LETTER MISSIVE
MESSENGER-WIRE
MONOTELEPHONE
POSTE RESTANTE
POST-OFFICE BOX
RADIOLOCATION
RADIOTELEGRAM
REBECCA-EUREKA
SPEAKING-CLOCK
TELAUTOGRAPHY

TELEGRAPH-POLE
TELEGRAPH-WIRE
TELERECORDING
TRUNK-DIALLING
VIDEO RECORDER

14

CIRCULAR LETTER
CORRESPONDENCE
COVERING LETTER
EPISTOLOGRAPHY
FINGER ALPHABET
FIRST-CLASS MAIL
PASTORAL LETTER
PHOTOTELEGRAPH
RADIOTELEGRAPH
RADIOTELEPHONE
RADIOTELEPHONY
SECONDARY RADAR
SOUNDING ROCKET
TELEGRAPH-CABLE
TELETYPESETTER
TELETYPEWRITER
VIDEO RECORDING

15

CABLE TELEVISION
EXPRESS DELIVERY
PERSONAL SERVICE
POISON PEN LETTER
RADIOTELEGRAPHY
SECOND-CLASS MAIL
SPEAKING-TRUMPET
TELEPHONE NUMBER
TRANSISTOR RADIO
WIRELESS STATION

COMPUTERS

3

BIT
BOX
BUG
HUB
JAM
JOB
KEY
LEG
MOS
ROW
RUN
SET
TAB
TAG
VDU

4

AREA
BAND
BASE
BAUD
BEAD
BEAT
BIAS
BYTE
CARD
CELL
CHAD
CODE
CORE
DATA
DECK
DISC
DISK
DRUM
FACE
FILE
FILM
GATE
GULP
HALT
JACK
LINK
LOOP
MARK
MASK
MODE
PACK
PAGE

PLUG
PORT
REEL
SCAN
SKIP
STEP
TANK
TAPE
TRAP
WORD
ZERO
ZONE

5

ADDER
ALGOL
ARRAY
BASIC
BATCH
BLANK
BLOCK
CARRY
CHAIN
CHART
CHECK
CLOCK
COBOL
CORAL
CYCLE
DETAB
DIGIT
DIODE
DRIFT
DRIVE
DUMMY
ENTRY
ERROR
FAULT
GROUP
INDEX
INPUT
LABEL
LOGIC
MODEM
MOUSE
ORDER
PATCH
PIXEL
RADIX
RANGE
ROUTE

SCALE
SPOOL
STACK
STORE
TABLE
TALLY
TIMER
TRACK
TRUNK
VIDEO

6

ACCESS
ADDEND
ANALOG
AUGEND
BRANCH
BUCKET
BUFFER
CATENA
CODING
FACTOR
FILTER
HEADER
LEADER
MATRIX
MEMORY
MODULE
NIBBLE
OUTPUT
PAGING
PASCAL
RECALL
RECORD
REPORT
RESULT
SCHEMA
SCREEN
SIZING
SOCKET
SORTER
STREAM
STRING
SUBSET
SYMBOL
SYSTEM
TOGGLE
VOLUME
X-PUNCH
Y-PUNCH

7

ADDRESS
ARCHIVE
BAR CODE
BURSTER
CAPSTAN
CHANNEL
CHAPTER
CHOPPER
CIRCUIT
CONSOLE
CONTROL
DECIMAL
DECODER
DISPLAY
DIVISOR
DUMPING
ELEMENT
EMITTER
ENCODER
END-MARK
FAILURE
FORTRAN
GARBAGE
HACKING
JOURNAL
KEYWORD
LIBRARY
LIMITER
MASKING
MINUEND
MONITOR
NUMERAL
OPERAND
OVERLAY
PACKAGE
PROCESS
PROGRAM
READ-OUT
RELEASE
ROUTINE
ROUTING
RUN TIME
SECTION
SEGMENT
SIMPLEX
SORTING
SPLICER
STACKER
STORAGE
SUMMARY

TEST-BED
TEST-RUN
TRIGGER
TYPE-BAR
UTILITY
ZONE BIT

8

ANALYSER
ANALYSIS
ARGUMENT
ASSEMBLY
AUTOCODE
BASE FILE
BLOCKING
BRIDGING
CAPACITY
CARD CODE
CARD FACE
CARD FEED
CODE HOLE
COLLATOR
COMPILER
COMPUTER
CONSTANT
CORE DUMP
CREATION
DATA BANK
DATA BASE
DATA UNIT
DECISION
DIRECTOR
DIVIDEND
DRUM MARK
EMULATOR
FEEDBACK
FLIP-FLOP
FLOWLINE
FUNCTION
HARDWARE
HOOT-STOP
INDEXING
INPUT LOG
KEYBOARD
KEY-PUNCH
LANGUAGE
LIGHT PEN
MAGAZINE
MODIFIER
NEGATION

COMPUTERS

OPEN LOOP
OPERATOR
PASSWORD
PINBOARD
PRINT-BAR
PRINT-OUT
PUNCHING
QUOTIENT
REAL TIME
RECOVERY
REGISTER
RESOLVER
ROW PITCH
RUN CHART
RUN PHASE
SAMPLING
SCANNING
SCAN RATE
SECURITY
SELECTOR
SEQUENCE
SOFTWARE
TAPE CORE
TAPE FEED
TAPE MARK
TAPE UNIT
TERMINAL
TEST DATA
TRANSFER
TRAPPING
TYPE-DRUM
UPDATING
VERIFIER
WORK AREA
WORK TAPE

9

AMPLIFIER
ARCHIVING
ASSEMBLER
BEAM STORE
BENCHMARK
BLANK TAPE
BOOTSTRAP
BREAKDOWN
BUDGETING
BYTE TRACK
CARD PUNCH
CATALOGUE
CHAIN CODE
CHARACTER

CONNECTOR
CONVERTER
DEBUGGING
DELAY-LINE
DIAGNOSIS
DIGITISER
DISC DRIVE
DISK DRIVE
DUPLEXING
ERASE HEAD
ERROR CODE
ERROR RATE
FAULT TIME
FLOWCHART
GENERATOR
HALF-ADDER
INDICATOR
INPUT AREA
INTERFACE
ITERATION
JACK PANEL
MULTIPLEX
OPERATION
ORDER CODE
OVERPUNCH
PAPER TAPE
PARITY BIT
PERIPHERY
PLUGBOARD
PROCESSOR
PULSE CODE
QUANTIZER
QUICKTRAN
RESET MODE
RETRIEVAL
RING-SHIFT
ROW BINARY
SELECTING
SEPARATOR
SIGN DIGIT
SPOT-PUNCH
STATEMENT
TABULATOR
TAPE-PUNCH
TIME STUDY
TOTAL TIME
TWIN-CHECK
WRITE HEAD
WRITE TIME
X-POSITION
Y-POSITION
ZONE DIGIT

10

ACCESS TIME
ADDRESSING
AREA SEARCH
AUDIT TRAIL
AUTOMATION
BINARY CELL
BINARY CODE
BIT PATTERN
BREAKPOINT
CALCULATOR
CARD-HOPPER
CARD-READER
CARD SYSTEM
CHECK DIGIT
CLOSED LOOP
COMMON AREA
COMPARATOR
DIRECT CODE
FACE-UP FEED
FALSE ERROR
FLOPPY DISC
FLOPPY DISK
LOGIC CHART
MACHINE RUN
MASTER CARD
MASTER FILE
ON-LINE FILE
PATCHBOARD
PERFORATOR
PROCESSING
PSEUDOCODE
REDUNDANCY
RELOAD TIME
REPERTOIRE
REPRODUCER
RESET CYCLE
SCHEDULING
SEARCH TIME
SIMULATION
SUBROUTINE
TABULATION
THROUGHPUT
TIMER CLOCK
TRANSDUCER
TRANSISTOR
TRANSITION
TRANSLATOR
TRUTH TABLE
TYPEWRITER
UNDERPUNCH

UNIT RECORD

11

BASE ADDRESS
BINARY DIGIT
BUFFER STORE
COMPUTERESE
CONTROL-CARD
CONTROL TAPE
CYBERNETICS
CYCLIC STORE
DATA CONTROL
DATA STORAGE
DESIGNATION
ELAPSED TIME
ENDWISE FEED
INFORMATION
INPUT DEVICE
INSTRUCTION
LATTICE FILE
MACHINE CODE
MULTIPLEXOR
PRINT FORMAT
PROGRAMMING
PUNCHED-CARD
PUNCHED TAPE
RECORD COUNT
REPLICATION
ROUNDING-OFF
TAPE LIBRARY
TARGET PHASE
TEST ROUTINE
TIME-SHARING
TOTAL SYSTEM
TRANSACTION
TRANSCRIBER

12

ABSOLUTE CODE
BACKING STORE
BINARY SEARCH
CARD-PUNCHING
CARD VERIFIER
CONTROL PANEL
DIGITAL CLOCK
DIGIT EMITTER
DISASSEMBLER
DYNAMIC STORE

FACE-DOWN FEED
FILE RECOVERY
FILM RECORDER
INHIBIT PULSE
INPUT PROGRAM
LEAPFROG TEST
LOGIC DIAGRAM
MAGNETIC-CARD
MAGNETIC CELL
MAGNETIC CORE
MAGNETIC DISC
MAGNETIC DISK
MAGNETIC DRUM
MAGNETIC TAPE
MULTIPLEXING
OUTPUT DEVICE
PUNCHING RATE
RANDOM ACCESS
RELATIVE CODE
RESPONSE TIME
SERIAL ACCESS
SPROCKET-HOLE
SYNCHRONIZER
TAPE VERIFIER
TRANSFER-CARD
TRANSFER TIME
VERIFICATION
VERTICAL FEED
WILLIAMS TUBE

BASIC LANGUAGE
DATA PROCESSOR
DECISION TABLE
DIGIT SELECTOR
DOCUMENTATION
DUPLEX CONSOLE
EFFECTIVE TIME
HOLLERITH-CARD
HOLLERITH CODE
JUSTIFICATION
LINEAR PROGRAM
OCTAL NOTATION
OUTPUT PROGRAM
REDUNDANT CODE
REMOTE CONSOLE
REPORT PROGRAM
RESIDUAL ERROR
SEQUENCE CHECK
SHIFT REGISTER
SPECIFICATION
STORAGE DEVICE
STORED PROGRAM
SYSTEMS DESIGN
TAPE TRANSPORT
TARGET PROGRAM
TRANSFER CHECK
VALIDITY CHECK
VARIABLE FIELD
WORD PROCESSOR

DOUBLE-PUNCHING
HYBRID COMPUTER
LOADING PROGRAM
MICROPROCESSOR
PERIPHERAL UNIT
PROCESS CONTROL
PROGRAM LIBRARY
PROGRAM STORAGE
PROGRAM TESTING
SERVICE ROUTINE
SIGNAL DISTANCE
SOURCE LANGUAGE
VIRTUAL ADDRESS

15

ABSOLUTE ADDRESS
ASSEMBLY PROGRAM
BI-STABLE CIRCUIT
COMPUTERISATION
COMPUTER PROGRAM
DATA PREPARATION
DIGITAL COMPUTER
EDGE-NOTCHED CARD
EDGE-PUNCHED CARD
INSTRUCTION CODE
MACHINE LANGUAGE
MULTIPLE ADDRESS
NUMERIC PUNCHING
OPERATING SYSTEM
OUTPUT BUS-DRIVER
RELATIVE ADDRESS
SPECIFIC ADDRESS
SYSTEMS ANALYSIS

13

ACOUSTIC STORE
ANALOG NETWORK
AVAILABLE TIME
BARREL-PRINTER

14

ANALOG COMPUTER
BINARY NOTATION
BOOLEAN ALGEBRA
DATA PROCESSING

CONTAINERS

3

ARK
BAG
BIN
BOX
CAN
CUP
DOP
FAT
HOD
JAG
JAR
JUG
KEG
KID
KIT
MUG
NET
NUT
PAN
PIN
POT
PYX
TIG
TIN
TUB
TUN
URN
VAT
WOK

4

BACK
BALE
BASS
BATH
BOWL
BUTT
CADE
CAGE
CASE
CASK
CELL
CHEF
COOP
CORF
COWL
CRIB
DISH
DIXY
ETNA
ETUI
EWER
FONT
GRIP
HORN
HUSK
INRO
JACK
KANG
KIER
KILN
KIST
LEAD
LEAP
LOTA
MILL
OLLA
OLPE
OVEN
PACK
PAIL
PECK
POKE
POME
SACK
SAFE
SKEP
SKIN
SKIP
TANK
TASS
TIDY
TILL
TOMB
TRAY
TRUG
TUBE
VASE
VIAL

5

AMBRY
AMPUL
BASIN
BILLY
BULSE
CABAS
CADDY
CHEST
CHURN
COUPE
CRATE
CREEL
CROCK
CRUET
CRUSE
CUPEL
CUVÉE
CYLIX
DIOTA
DIXIE
EMPTY
FLASK
FRAIL
GLASS
GLOBE
GOURD
HANAP
HUTCH
JERRY
JORAM
JORUM
KEEVE
LAVER
MOULD
OILER
PHIAL
POKAL
POUCH
PURSE
PYXIS
ROUND
SCRIP
SCULL
SERON
SHELL
STAND
STEAN
STEIN
STOCK
STOUP
TAZZA
TRUNK

6

ALUDEL
BARREL
BASKET
BEAKER
BEDPAN
BICKER
BOILER
BOTTLE
BUCKET
BUDDLE
BUSHEL
CACHET
CARAFE
CARBOY
CARTON
CASING
CASKET
CASTOR
CENSER
CHATTY
COFFER
COFFIN
COOKER
COOLER
COPPER
COTYLE
DIPPER
DOLIUM
DRAWER
EGG-BOX
ELUTOR
FIASCO
FILLER
FINGAN
FLACON
FLAGON
FOLDER
FRIDGE
FUNNEL
GAS-BAG
GAS-JAR
GOBLET
GOGLET
HAMPER
HATBOX
HAYBOX
HOLDER
ICEBOX
INKPOT
IN-TRAY
JAM-JAR
JAMPOT
KALPIS
KETTLE
KIBBLE
KIRBEH
KIT-BAG
LAGENA
LOCKER
MAGNUM
MANGER
MOCOCK
MONKEY
MORTAR
MUFFLE
NOGGIN
OCTAVE
OIL-CAN
PACKET
PARCEL
PATINA
PETARA
PIGGIN
PIPKIN
PITHOS
POCKET
POSNET
POTTLE
PUNNET
QUIVER
RAG-BAG
RED-BOX
RETORT
RHYTON
RUMMER
SACHET
SAGGAR
SCONCE
SHAKER
SHEATH
SHRINE
SIPHON
TAN-PIT
TAN-VAT
TAR-BOX
TEA-BAG
TEA-CUP
TEA-POT
TEA-URN
TIN-CAN
TIN-POT
TOY-BOX
TROUGH
TUREEN
VALISE
VESSEL
WALLET

7

AEROSOL
ALEMBIC
ALFORJA
AMPHORA
AMPOULE
AMPULLA
ASPERGE
BAGGAGE
BAND-BOX
BARRICO
BATH-TUB
BEAN-BAG
BEER-CAN
BEER-MUG
BRAN-TUB
BRAZIER
BREAKER
BRIMMER
BURETTE
CAISSON
CAKE-TIN
CANOPUS
CANTEEN
CAPSULE
CARRIER
CASSONE
CHALICE
CISTERN
COAL-BOX
COFFRET
COMPACT
CRESSET
CUE-CASE
CYATHUS
DUSTBIN
EYE-BATH
FIRE-PAN
FIRE-POT
FLACKET
FLASKET
FLY-BOOK
FONTLET
FREEZER
FURNACE
GAME-BAG
GAS-TANK
GLUE-POT
GOLF-BAG
GRAB-BAG
HANAPER

HANDBAG
HELL-BOX
HIP-BATH
HOLD-ALL
HOLSTER
HOP-SACK
INKHORN
INKWELL
LANTERN
LAUNDER
LEAGUER
LIVE-BOX
LOAF-TIN
LUGGAGE
MAIL-BAG
MAIL-BOX
MASH-TUB
MASH-VAT
MATRASS
MEASURE
MEAT-TUB
MESS-TIN
MUSK-BAG
NOSEBAG
OIL-BATH
OUT-TRAY
PACKAGE
PANNIER
PEN-CASE
PICKLER
PILL-BOX
PINT-POT
PIPETTE
PITCHER
PLAY-BOX
POOR-BOX
POST-BAG
POST-BOX
POTICHE
PUFF-BOX
RAMEKIN
REACTOR
RUNDLET
SALT-BOX
SALT-FAT
SAMOVAR
SANDBAG
SAND-BOX
SATCHEL
SCUTTLE
SEED-BOX
SEEDLIP

SHOE-BOX
SHOW-BOX
SHUTTLE
SKILLET
SKIPPET
SNOW-BOX
STAMNOS
STEEPER
TANKARD
TERRINE
THERMOS
TOBY-JUG
TOOL-BOX
TUCK-BOX
TUMBLER
UTENSIL
VITRINE
WANIGAN
WASH-POT
WASH-TUB
WATERER
WHEY-TUB
WINE-BAG
WINE-VAT
WORK-BAG
WORK-BOX

8

AQUARIUM
ATOMISER
BEARLEAP
BÉNITIER
BILLY-CAN
BINNACLE
BIRD-BATH
BIRDCAGE
BLACK BOX
BREAD-BIN
BRIEF-BAG
BRINE-PAN
CACHE-POT
CANISTER
CANNIKIN
CASSETTE
CAULDRON
CELLARET
CHAUFFER
CIBORIUM
CIGAR-BOX
COAL-HOLE
CYLINDER

DEMI-JOHN
DIGESTER
DILLY-BAG
DITTY-BAG
DITTY-BOX
DOLLY-TUB
ENVELOPE
FIGULINE
FLESH-POT
FOOT-BATH
GALLIPOT
GOATSKIN
GRACE CUP
GRASS-BOX
GREEN-BAG
HIP-FLASK
HONEYPOT
JEROBOAM
JERRY-CAN
JIFFY-BAG
KALAMDAN
KNAPSACK
KNIFE-BOX
LAY-STALL
LEKYTHOS
LUCKY-BAG
LUCKY-DIP
MATCHBOX
MEAL-POKE
METAL BOX
MING VASE
MONEY-BAG
MONEY-BOX
MONTEITH
MUSK-BALL
NAVICULA
NOTE-CASE
PAINT-BOX
PANCHEON
PANNIKIN
PAPER-BAG
PATCH-BOX
PEDAL-BIN
PIPE-CASE
PLANT-POT
POCHETTE
POMANDER
PRESSFAT
QUART-POT
REHOBOAM
RETICULE
ROSE-BOWL

RUCKSACK
SAND-BATH
SARATOGA
SCENT-BAG
SCHOONER
SCREWTOP
SEA-CHEST
SEED-TRAY
SLOP-PAIL
SNUFF-BOX
SOAP-DISH
SOLANDER
SOUSE-TUB
SPICE-BOX
STOCK-POT
SUITCASE
SWILL-TUB
SWING-BIN
TEA-CADDY
TEA-CHEST
TEST-TUBE
TOLL-DISH
TOUCH-BOX
TRASH-CAN
VASCULUM
VIVARIUM
WASH-BOWL
WASTE-BIN
WATER-BAG
WATER-JAR
WATER-POT
WINE-CASK
WINE-SKIN
WOOL-PACK

9

ALCARRAZA
ARYBALLOS
AUTOCLAVE
BAIN-MARIE
BAKING-TIN
BALAAM-BOX
BALLOT-BOX
BLACKJACK
BRIEF-CASE
BUTTER-BOX
CALANDRIA
CANTHARUS
CANVAS-BAG
CARPET-BAG

CONTAINERS

CASSEROLE
CHEESE-VAT
CLARET-JUG
COFFEE-POT
CONTAINER
CONVERTER
DIMITY-BAG
DISPENSER
DREDGE-BOX
DUFFEL-BAG
EEL-BASKET
FINING-POT
FLOWERPOT
GAS-BOTTLE
GASOMETER
GAS-RETORT
GRAVY-BOAT
GREYBEARD
HAVERSACK
HOOPED-POT
HOP-POCKET
HOUSEWIFE
ICE-BUCKET
INK-BOTTLE
JEWEL-CASE
KILDERKIN
LACHRYMAL
LETTER-BOX
LEYDEN JAR
LITTER-BIN
LOVING-CUP
MINIATURE
MONKEY-BAG
MONKEY-JAR
MUFFINEER
MUMMY-CASE
MUSIC-CASE
MUSIC-ROLL
MUZZLE-BAG
PAPER-CASE
PAPETERIE
PAY-PACKET
PEAT-CREEL
PENCIL-BOX
PEPPER-BOX
PEPPER-POT
PETRI DISH
PETROL-CAN
PEWTER-MUG
PIGGY-BANK
PILLAR-BOX
PINT-STOUP

PORRINGER
PORTFOLIO
POSSET-CUP
POUNCE-BOX
POWDER-BOX
POWDER-KEG
RELIQUARY
RESERVOIR
SADDLE-BAG
SAUCE-BOAT
SCHOOLBAG
SHEATHING
SNEEZE-BOX
SNUFF-DISH
SPONGE-BAG
STRING-BAG
STRONG-BOX
SUGAR-BOWL
TEA-KETTLE
TINDER-BOX
TRUNK MAIL
VANITY-BAG
VANITY-BOX
WATCHCASE
WATER-BATH
WATER-BUTT
WINDOW-BOX
WINE-GLASS
YARD OF ALE

10

AEROSOL CAN
AQUAMANILE
BAKING-TRAY
BEER-BARREL
BEER-BOTTLE
BELLARMINE
BISCUIT-TIN
BUCK-BASKET
BUTTER-DISH
CARRIER-BAG
CASSOLETTE
CHAMBER-POT
CHIP-BASKET
COAL-BUNKER
CRICKET-BAG
DEEP FREEZE
DINNER-PAIL
DOROTHY-BAG

FINGERBOWL
FIRE-BUCKET
FISH KETTLE
FLAG-BASKET
GARBAGE-CAN
HALF-BOTTLE
HAND-BASKET
HONEY-CROCK
JARDINIÈRE
JUNK-BOTTLE
LOBSTER-POT
MELTING-POT
METHUSELAH
MONSTRANCE
MUSIC-FOLIO
MUSTARD-POT
NÉCESSAIRE
NEEDLE-BOOK
NEEDLE-CASE
OLD SOLDIER
PACKING-BOX
PARTING-CUP
PEG-TANKARD
PENCIL-CASE
PEPPER-MILL
PERCOLATOR
PETROL TANK
PHYLACTERY
PLASTIC BAG
POUNCET-BOX
POWDER-HORN
RECEPTACLE
RELIQUAIRE
SABRETACHE
SALT-CELLAR
SAPLING-CUP
SEPTIC TANK
SODA-SIPHON
STIRRUP-CUP
SUCKING-CUP
SUGAR-BASIN
TABERNACLE
TEAR-BOTTLE
TOBACCO TIN
UNGUENTARY
VANITY-CASE
VAPOUR-BATH
VIOLIN-CASE
WAGE-PACKET
WARMING-PAN
WASH-BOTTLE
WASSAIL-CUP

WATER-GLASS
WINE-COOLER
WORK-BASKET

11

ASPERGILLUM
ASPERSORIUM
ATTACHÉ-CASE
BONBONNIÈRE
BRANDY-GLASS
BREAD-BASKET
CHRISMATORY
COAL-SCUTTLE
DISPATCH-BOX
DRIPPING-PAN
GAS CYLINDER
HARNESS-CASK
INCENSE-BOAT
LUNCH-BASKET
MUSIC-HOLDER
PACKING-CASE
PLATE-BASKET
PORTMANTEAU
POWDER-FLASK
ROASTING-TIN
SANDWICH-BOX
SARCOPHAGUS
SAUCE-BOTTLE
SCENT-BOTTLE
SCISSOR-CASE
SCUTTLE-BUTT
SEMBLING-BOX
SHOPPING-BAG
STANDING-CUP
TEA-CANISTER
THIMBLE-CASE
TROUT-BASKET
TWEEZER-CASE
VACUUM-FLASK
VINAIGRETTE
WASSAIL-BOWL
WASTE-BASKET
WATER-BARREL
WATER-BOTTLE
WATER-BOUGET
WATERING-CAN
WATERING-POT
WATER-MONKEY
WRITING-CASE

12

BOLOGNA PHIAL
CARDBOARD BOX
CHARTER-CHEST
CHEST-FREEZER
CHOCOLATE-BOX
CHRISTMAS-BOX
DRESSING-CASE
GLADSTONE BAG
GOLDFISH BOWL
JEWELLERY-BOX
LACHRYMAL URN
MICROCAPSULE
MOUSTACHE-CUP
OVERNIGHT BAG
PANTECHNICON
PEPPER-CASTER
PICNIC-BASKET
POLYTHENE-BAG
PORTE-MONNAIE
POWDERING-TUB
REFRIGERATOR
SAMPLE-BOTTLE
SEASONING-TUB
STANDING-BOWL
THERMOS FLASK

TOBACCO-POUCH
UNGUENTARIUM
WOULFE-BOTTLE

13

BISCUIT-BARREL
CIGARETTE-CASE
CLOTHES-BASKET
COLLECTING-BOX
COLLECTION-BOX
FEEDING-BOTTLE
FLORENCE FLASK
FRIDGE-FREEZER
INCENSE-BURNER
LAUNDRY-BASKET
MEDICINE CHEST
NORWEGIAN OVEN
OVERNIGHT CASE
PILGRIM-BOTTLE
POST-OFFICE BOX
POWDER-COMPACT
RESISTANCE-BOX
SUCKING-BOTTLE
SUGGESTION-BOX
TREASURE-CHEST

WARDROBE-TRUNK
WASHING-BOTTLE
WASTE-PAPER BIN

14

COCKTAIL-SHAKER
HOT-WATER BOTTLE
KNEADING-TROUGH
MAGNETIC BOTTLE
MEDICINE-BOTTLE
PRESSURE-COOKER
SACRAMENT-HOUSE
SAFE-DEPOSIT BOX
SHOPPING-BASKET
SMELLING-BOTTLE
WATERING-TROUGH
WINDOW-ENVELOPE

15

CIGARETTE-PACKET
MEDICINE-DROPPER

CRIME & PUNISHMENT

3

CAN
CAT
DAB
JOB
JUG
PEN
RAP
ROD
SOP

4

BEAT
BOOT
CANE
CELL
CLUE
CUFF
FINE
GAOL
HARD
JAIL
LASH
LIFE
NICK
PLOT
QUOD
RACK
RAID
RAMP
RAPE
SACK
SLAP
STIR
TIME
WELT
WHIP
WHOP

5

ALIBI
ARSON
BIRCH
BOUGH
BRIBE
CHAIR
CHOKY

CLINK
CRIME
CROSS
EXILE
FRAUD
GRAFT
HEIST
HORSE
JOUGS
KNOUT
LIBEL
LIMBO
MANOR
NOOSE
OFLAG
PATCH
SMACK
SNAPS
SPANK
STAKE
STICK
STRAP
SWISH
TAWSE
THEFT
THONG
USURY
WHACK
WHANG
WHEEL

6

ARREST
BIGAMY
CANGUE
CANING
CHAINS
CIPPUS
COOLER
DUPERY
DURESS
FELONY
FETTER
GIBBET
HIDING
HIJACK
HOBBLE
HOLD-UP
INCEST
INFAMY

LOCK-UP
MAIDEN
MOB-LAW
MURDER
NOYADE
PIRACY
PIZZLE
PRISON
RACKET
RAPINE
RAVAGE
RIP-OFF
SEARCH
SIMONY
SLANGS
SNATCH
STALAG
STOCKS
STRIPE
THRASH
THWACK
TICKET

7

ANARCHY
ASSAULT
BATTERY
BORSTAL
BRIBERY
CATASTA
CHABOUK
COMPLOT
CRUELTY
DACOITY
DARBIES
DEFAULT
DEICIDE
DOUCEUR
DUNGEON
FORFEIT
FORGERY
FRAME-UP
GALLOWS
HANGING
HOT SEAT
INQUIRY
KILLING
KNAVERY
KURBASH
LARCENY

LASHING
LECHERY
LEG-IRON
LOW TOBY
MANACLE
MANTRAP
MISDEED
MITTENS
MUGGING
OFFENCE
OUTRAGE
PENALTY
PENANCE
PERFIDY
PERJURY
PILLAGE
PILLORY
PIMPING
PLAGIUM
PLUNDER
PONCING
RIGGING
ROBBERY
ROGUERY
SACKING
SCOURGE
SHACKLE
SJAMBOK
SLAMMER
SLANDER
SLAYING
SLIPPER
STICK-UP
STIFLER
STRETCH
SUICIDE
SWINDLE
SWIPING
THUGGEE
TORTURE
TREASON
TRIGAMY
WARRANT
WELTING

8

ADULTERY
ATROCITY
AUTO-DA-FÉ
BIG HOUSE
BIRCH ROD

BOOTIKIN
BULLWHIP
BURGLARY
CHANTAGE
CRUCIFIX
DISGUISE
DULE-TREE
ENORMITY
FILCHING
FLOGGING
FOUL-PLAY
FURACITY
GARROTTE
GATE-FINE
GAUNTLET
GENOCIDE
HIGH TOBY
HOMICIDE
HOOSEGOW
INIQUITY
JUDGMENT
KOURBASH
LYNCHING
LYNCH-LAW
MEDICINE
MOUCHARD
OVERT ACT
PHOTOFIT
PLOTTING
POACHING
PRECINCT
PRESIDIO
PUNITION
QUILTING
REGICIDE
ROPE'S-END
RUSTLING
SABOTAGE
SCAFFOLD
SCOLDING
SEDITION
SENTENCE
SISERARY
SLAPPING
SPANKING
SPEEDING
STEALING
STRAP-OIL
STRIPING
SWISHING
THIEVERY
THIEVING

THUGGERY
THUGGISM
TRESPASS
VATICIDE
VILLAINY
WAR CRIME
WHACKING
WHIPLASH
WHIPPING
WHOPPING
WILD MARE

9

ABDUCTION
BLACKMAIL
BOWSTRING
BRIDEWELL
BRIGANDRY
BULLWHACK
CALABOOSE
CHICANERY
CLY-FAKING
COLLUSION
CRIME RATE
CRIME WAVE
DACOITAGE
DETECTION
DETENTION
DUPLICITY
EXECUTION
EXPULSION
EXTORTION
FLAGELLUM
FOOTPRINT
HANDCUFFS
HORSEWHIP
IDENTIKIT
IMPOSTURE
INDECENCY
KLEPHTISM
LOITERING
MACTATION
MATRICIDE
PARRICIDE
PATRICIDE
PILFERING
POISONING
PROLICIDE
PYROMANIA
RASP-HOUSE

RECEIVING
RECLUSION
REFRESHER
SACRILEGE
SCARPINES
SCRUMPING
SEA-ROVING
SLAUGHTER
SLAVE-FORK
SMUGGLING
STATEMENT
STRAPPADO
STRAPPING
SUSPICION
SWEETENER
SWINDLING
TANTALISM
TERRORISM
THRASHING
THWACKING
TOWELLING
TREACHERY
TREADMILL
TROUNCING
UXORICIDE
VANDALISM
WHIRLIGIG

10

BACK-HANDER
BANISHMENT
COMMITMENT
CONSPIRACY
CONSTRAINT
CONVICTION
CORRECTION
CORRUPTION
DECIMATION
DEFACEMENT
DISHONESTY
ENTHRALDOM
FRATRICIDE
GAS CHAMBER
GUILLOTINE
GUNRUNNING
HARD LABOUR
ILLEGALITY
IMMORALITY
IMMUREMENT
IMPALEMENT

IMPOSITION
INDUCEMENT
INFLICTION
INFRACTION
INTERNMENT
JUDICATION
KIDNAPPING
KINCHIN-LAY
LAPIDATION
LITTLE-EASE
LYDFORD LAW
MISCONDUCT
NEGLIGENCE
OPEN PRISON
PAEDERASTY
PALM-GREASE
PANOPTICON
PECULATION
PERVERSION
PILLIWINKS
PLAGIARISM
PLUNDERAGE
PLUNDERING
PRISON-YARD
PUNISHMENT
PURLOINING
RACHMANISM
RAVISHMENT
RECIDIVISM
REMAND HOME
RUM-RUNNING
SHEBEENING
SMOTHERING
SORORICIDE
STRANGLING
THROTTLING
THUMB-SCREW
TICKING-OFF
TRAITORISM
TYBURN-TREE
UNDERWORLD
URTICATION
VAPULATION
WRONG-DOING

11

BOOTLEGGING
CASTIGATION
CONFEDERACY
CONFINEMENT

CONJURATION
COUNTERPLOT
CRIMINOLOGY
CRUCIFIXION
DACTYLOGRAM
DECOLLATION
DEFALCATION
DEFRAUDMENT
DELINQUENCY
DEPORTATION
DESPOILMENT
ELIMINATION
ENCHAINMENT
ENDORSEMENT
ENSLAVEMENT
ENTHRALMENT
FINGERPRINT
FIRE-RAISING
FORCIPATION
FRAUDULENCE
FREEBOOTERY
FREEBOOTING
FUSTIGATION
GALLOWS-TREE
GANGSTERISM
HEINOUSNESS
HIGH TREASON
HOUSE-ARREST
INFANTICIDE
KNEE-CAPPING
LAW-BREAKING
LESE-MAJESTY
LIE DETECTOR
LIQUIDATION
MACHINATION
MALEFACTION
MALFEASANCE
MALPRACTICE
PERDUELLION
PIGEON-HOLES
PRISON-HOUSE
RE-ENACTMENT
SAFE-BLOWING
SHOP-LIFTING
SKULDUGGERY
SPREAD-EAGLE
STATE-PRISON
SUBORNATION
SUFFOCATION
THIRD DEGREE
TRAFFICKING
TRESPASSING

CRIME & PUNISHMENT

TYRANNICIDE
WOODEN HORSE

12

ARMED ROBBERY
BERTILLONAGE
BRAINWASHING
CHASTISEMENT
CONDEMNATION
CONFISCATION
CUCKING-STOOL
DEATH PENALTY
DECAPITATION
DESPOLIATION
DOPE-PEDDLING
DUCKING-STOOL
EMBEZZLEMENT
EXCRUCIATION
EXERCISE-YARD
FIRST OFFENCE
GRAND LARCENY
IMPRISONMENT
INCENDIARISM
INFRINGEMENT
KERB-CRAWLING
MALVERSATION
MANSLAUGHTER
MARCH-TREASON
MISDEMEANOUR
MOSS-TROOPING
PENALISATION
PENITENTIARY
PERPETRATION
PETTY LARCENY

PETTY TREASON
PROSTITUTION
RACKETEERING
REFORM SCHOOL
RESURRECTION
RITUAL MURDER
SAFE-BREAKING
SAFE-CRACKING
SHOPBREAKING
SNAFFLING-LAY
STRAIGHTENER
STRAIT-JACKET
WHIPPING-POST

13

ASSASSINATION
BODY-SNATCHING
CAPITAL MURDER
CAT-O'-NINE-TAILS
CONTRABANDISM
DRUG-SMUGGLING
ELECTRIC CHAIR
ELECTROCUTION
FALSIFICATION
FORCIBLE ENTRY
HANGING MATTER
HOUSE-BREAKING
INCARCERATION
INTERROGATION
INVESTIGATION
MOONLIGHT FLIT
PICK-POCKETING
POCKET-PICKING
ROGUES' GALLERY

SEARCH-WARRANT
SHEEP-STEALING
SIMPLE LARCENY
STREET-WALKING
TRANSGRESSION
TREASON FELONY

14

APPROVED SCHOOL
CAPITAL OFFENCE
COUNTERFEITING
CRIME PASSIONEL
DEVIL-ON-THE-NECK
FACINOROUSNESS
FINGERPRINTING
GROSS INDECENCY
JEDDART JUSTICE
PENAL SERVITUDE
PURSE-SNATCHING
RECONSTITUTION
RECONSTRUCTION
RIDING THE STANG
TRANSPORTATION
WRONGFUL ARREST

15

COMPOUND LARCENY
COUNTERFEISANCE
DAYLIGHT-ROBBERY
DETENTION CENTRE
STRAIT-WAISTCOAT

DEATH & DISASTER

3
END
PIT
URN

4
BANE
BIER
CIST
DOOM
EXIT
FALL
FATE
FIRE
GHAT
HELL
KEEN
LOSS
MOLE
MORT
OBIT
PALL
PILE
PYRE
RUIN
TOMB
WAKE

5
ASHES
CHAOS
CRYPT
DEATH
DIRGE
DYING
FLOOD
GRAVE
HAVOC
KNELL
LIMBO
MUMMY
PURGE
SHEET
SPEOS
STIFF
STONE
VAULT

6
CASKET
COFFIN
CORPSE
DEMISE
ENDING
EXEQUY
FAMINE
HEARSE
HEROON
LAMENT
MARKER
MAYHEM
MISHAP
MORGUE
PLAGUE
POGROM
SERDAB
SHROUD
SUTTEE
TREMOR
WREATH

7
CADAVER
CARCASE
CARCASS
CARNAGE
CHARNEL
CHUDDAR
CORTÈGE
DEBÂCLE
DECEASE
DECLINE
EPICEDE
EPITAPH
FUNERAL
LICHWAY
MAJESTY
MASTABA
OSSUARY
PASSING
QUIETUS
REMAINS
SCOURGE

8
ACCIDENT
CALAMITY
CATACOMB
CEMETERY
CENOTAPH
COT DEATH
CREMATOR
DEATH-BED
DISASTER
DISORDER
DISTRESS
DOOMSDAY
DROWNING
FATALITY
GENOCIDE
GOD'S ACRE
GOLGOTHA
HYPOGEUM
KIRKYARD
KISTVAEN
LICH-GATE
LYCH-GATE
LONG HOME
MASSACRE
MEMORIAL
MORTBELL
MORT-SAFE
MORTUARY
MOURNING
OBITUARY
OSSARIUM
OVERKILL
PANTHEON
SACELLUM

9
AVALANCHE
CATACLASM
CERE-CLOTH
CINERATOR
CREMATION
DEAD-HOUSE
DEAD-MARCH
DEATH-BELL
DEATH-BLOW
DEATH-DAMP
DEATH-FIRE
DEATH-MASK
DEATH-RATE
DEATH-ROLL
DEATH-SONG
DEATH-TRAP
DEPARTURE
EARTHFALL
EMBALMING
EMERGENCY
FACE-CLOTH
GRAVEYARD
HEADSTONE
HOLOCAUST
INTERMENT
LANDSLIDE
LAST RITES
LETHALITY
MAUSOLEUM
MEGADEATH
MORTALITY
MORTCLOTH
MORTSTONE
NECROLOGY
OBSEQUIES
PLAGUE-PIT
RUINATION
SEPULCHRE
SEPULTURE
SLAUGHTER
STICKY END
TOMBSTONE

10
BRAIN DEATH
CAMPO SANTO
CATAFALQUE
CHURCHYARD
CINERATION
DEATH-AGONY
DEATH-KNELL
DEATH'S DOOR
DEATH-THROE
DEATH-WATCH
DEATH-WOUND
EARTHQUAKE
EMBALMMENT
ENTOMBMENT
EXTINCTION
GRAVESTONE
IMMOLATION
INHUMATION

DEATH & DISASTER

MISFORTUNE
MUMMY-CLOTH
NECROPOLIS
PESTILENCE
PREDECEASE
STILL-BIRTH
ZOOTHAPSIS

LAST OFFICES
MORUBUNDITY
PASSING-BELL
RIGOR MORTIS
SARCOPHAGUS
TERMINATION
UNDERTAKING

11

BEREAVEMENT
BURIAL-PLACE
CATASTROPHE
CREMATORIUM
DEATH-RATTLE
DEATH-STROKE
DESTRUCTION
EARTH-TREMOR
EXANIMATION
EXTIRPATION
FUSILLATION
HEARSE-CLOTH
INCINERATOR
LAMENTATION
LAST HONOURS

12

BURIAL-GROUND
CHAPEL OF REST
CHARNEL-HOUSE
CONCREMATION
DEBT OF NATURE
DEPOPULATION
GRAVE-CLOTHES
HALF-MOURNING
INCINERATION
LIFELESSNESS
MOURNING-RING
NATURAL DEATH
OBLITERATION
PAUPER'S GRAVE
WINDING-SHEET

13

CEREBRAL DEATH
COMMEMORATION
EXTERMINATION
FUNERAL RITES
MOURNING-CLOAK
MOURNING-COACH
MOURNING-PIECE
MOURNING-STUFF
MUMMIFICATION
VIVISEPULTURE

14

SELF-IMMOLATION

15

CHAPELLE ARDENTE

DEITIES & MONSTERS

3

DIV
ELF
FAY
GOD
HEX
IMP
JAH
LAR
MAB
NIS
NIX
ROC

4

AITU
BOGY
BOYG
DEUS
FAUN
FUNG
HUMA
JANN
JINN
KAMI
OGRE
PERI
PIXY
PUCK
YAMA
YETI

5

AFRIT
ANGEL
BOGLE
DEITY
DEMON
DEUCE
DEVIL
DJINN
DRAKE
DRYAD
DUPPY
DWARF
ELFIN
FAERY

FAIRY
FETCH
FIEND
GEIST
GENIE
GHOST
GHOUL
GIANT
GNOME
HARPY
HOURI
JINNI
JOTUN
JUMBY
LAMIA
MARID
MONAD
NAIAD
NYMPH
OREAD
PIXIE
POWER
PYGMY
SAINT
SATYR
SILVA
SIREN
SNARK
SPOOK
SYLPH
TROLL
ZOMBI

6

AVATAR
BOOJUM
BUNYIP
CHERUB
DAEMON
DOUBLE
DRAGON
DYBBUK
EMPUSA
GARUDA
GENIUS
GOBLIN
JUMART
KELPIE
KOBOLD
KRAKEN

MANITO
MERMAN
NEREID
OGRESS
PANISK
PYTHON
SEA-GOD
SERAPH
SIMURG
SPHINX
SPIRIT
SUN-GOD
TANGIE
TARAND
THRONE
UNDINE
VIRTUE
VISION
WAR-GOD
WIVERN
WRAITH
WYVERN
ZOMBIE

7

BANSHEE
BROWNIE
BUGABOO
CENTAUR
CHIMERA
DEMIGOD
DEVILET
DEVLING
FEN-FIRE
GODDESS
GRIFFIN
GRIFFON
GRYPHON
HAUNTER
INCUBUS
KNOCKER
LAKSHMI
LUCIFER
MANITOU
MERMAID
MONSTER
MOON-GOD
OCEANID
PHANTOM

RAKSHAS
RUSALKA
RYE-WOLF
SANDMAN
SAVIOUR
SEA-KING
SEA-MAID
SILENUS
SPECTRE
SUCCUBA
SYLPHID
UNICORN
VAMPIRE
WARLOCK
WATCHER

8

BARGHEST
BASILISK
BEHEMOTH
DEMIURGE
DEMONESS
DIVINITY
DRAGONET
ERDGEIST
FAMILIAR
GIANTESS
IMMORTAL
ISENGRIM
LINDWORM
MONOPODE
PHANTASM
REVENANT
RIVER-GOD
SATYRESS
SATYRISK
SEA-DEVIL
SEA-HORSE
SEA-NYMPH
SEA-WOMAN
SUCCUBUS
SYLPHIDE
TENEBRIO
TUTELARY
VISITANT
WATER-COW
WATER-GOD
WEREWOLF

9

ARCHANGEL
BLUE DEVIL
BOTTLE-IMP
CACODEMON
DEMI-DEVIL
DOMINIONS
DRAGONESS
ELEMENTAL
FEE-FAW-FUM
HAMADRYAD
HELLHOUND
HIERARCHY
HOBGOBLIN
LEVIATHAN
MANTICORE
MERMAIDEN
NATURE-GOD
PHANTASMA
SAGITTARY
TRAGELAPH
WATER-BULL
WHITE-LADY
WOOD-NYMPH

10

BESOM-RIDER
CACODAEMON
COCKATRICE
CORN-SPIRIT
CRIO-SPHINX
GOLDEN CALF
HIPPOGRIFF
HIPPOGRYPH
LEPRECHAUN
MUMBO-JUMBO
ONOCENTAUR
RIVER-HORSE
SALAMANDER
SANTA CLAUS
SEA-GODDESS
SEA-MONSTER
SEA-SERPENT
SERPENT-GOD
SWAN-MAIDEN
THUNDER-GOD
WAR-GODDESS
WATER-HORSE
WATER-NIXIE

DEITIES & MONSTERS

WATER-NYMPH

11

AMPHISBAENA
DEMIGODDESS
HIPPOCAMPUS
HIRCOCERVUS
LUBBER FIEND
MOON-GODDESS
PATRON SAINT
POLTERGEIST
PSYCHAGOGUE
WATER-SPRITE

12

BANDERSNATCH
DOPPEL-GÄNGER
HEAVENLY HOST
HIPPOCENTAUR
LITTLE PEOPLE
PRINCIPALITY

13

GUARDIAN ANGEL
HOUSEHOLD GODS

14

FAIRY GODMOTHER
SERPENT-GODDESS

15

FLIBBERTIGIBBET
LOB-LIE-BY-THE-FIRE

DRINK — BEVERAGES

3

ALE
AVA
CHA
LAP
MUM
NOG
POP
TEA

4

AQUA
BEER
BOCK
BULL
CAFÉ
CHAR
COKE
COLA
FIZZ
FLIP
KAVA
MATÉ
MEAD
MILD
NIPA
PURL
SAKE
SODA

5

ASSAI
BOHEA
BOOZE
CIDER
COCOA
CRUSH
CUPPA
DRINK
HOGAN
HYSON
JUICE
JULEP
KEFIR
KVASS
LAGER
MOCHA

MORAT
NAPPY
NEGUS
PEKOE
PERRY
PUNCH
SHRUB
STOUT
TONIC
WATER

6

ALEGAR
BISHOP
BITTER
BURTON
CASSIS
CAT-LAP
CAUDLE
CHASER
CLOVES
COFFEE
CONGOU
COOPER
EGGNOG
ENTIRE
KUMISS
LIQUOR
LOVAGE
NECTAR
OOLONG
PORTER
POSSET
PTISAN
PULQUE
SALOOP
SHANDY
SQUASH
STINGO
TIPPER
WALLOP
ZYTHUM

7

BEEF-TEA
BREWAGE
CORDIAL
EGG-FLIP

EWE-MILK
FOUR-ALE
FUSTIAN
GUARANÁ
HERB-TEA
LIMEADE
MACE-ALE
MILD ALE
OCTOBER
PALE ALE
PERSICO
PILSNER
RATAFIA
ROSOLIO
SAGE-TEA
SCRUMPY
SELTZER
SHERBET
TWANKAY
UVA-URSI

8

ADAM'S ALE
ALE-BERRY
AMBROSIA
APERITIF
AUDIT ALE
BEVERAGE
BLACK TEA
BROWN ALE
CAFÉ NOIR
CAPER-TEA
CHINA TEA
CIDER-CUP
CIDERKIN
CLUB SODA
GREEN-TEA
HEAVY WET
HERB-BEER
HYDROMEL
ICE-WATER
LEMONADE
LIGHT ALE
NEAR-BEER
PERSICOT
PILSENER
RICE-BEER
ROOT-BEER
SENNA TEA
SKIMMING

SMALL-ALE
SOUCHONG
SWITCHEL
TAP-WATER

9

BADMINTON
CHERRYADE
CHOCOLATE
CHURN-MILK
CREAM SODA
DIET-DRINK
DILL-WATER
GINGERADE
GINGER ALE
GINGER POP
INDIAN TEA
LAGER BEER
LAMB'S-WOOL
LIME-JUICE
MARCH BEER
METHEGLIN
MILK-PUNCH
MILK-SHAKE
MILK-STOUT
MINT JULEP
MIRABILIS
ORANGEADE
PUMP-WATER
RICE-WATER
ROSA-SOLIS
RYE-COFFEE
SMALL-BEER
SODA WATER
TABLE-BEER

10

BEST BITTER
BROWN STOUT
BUTTERMILK
CAFÉ AU LAIT
CAFÉ FILTRE
CAMBRIC TEA
CAPILLAIRE
CAPPUCCINO
DARJEELING
GINGER BEER
HEATHER ALE

DRINK – BEVERAGES

HOP-BITTERS
HUMMING ALE
LEMON JUICE
MALT LIQUOR
PEPPERMINT
POPPY WATER
POUSSE-CAFÉ
RUMFUSTIAN
RUSSIAN TEA
SACK-POSSET
SHANDYGAFF
SPRUCE-BEER
TABLE-WATER
TONIC WATER
VICHY WATER

BARLEY-BROTH
BARLEY WATER
BITTER LEMON
BLACK VELVET
COCONUT-MILK
COOL-TANKARD
DOUBLE-STOUT
DRAUGHT BEER
IRISH COFFEE
LABRADOR TEA
LEMON SQUASH
ORANGE JUICE
PARAGUAY TEA
SKIMMED MILK
SPRING-WATER

ICE-CREAM SODA
MINERAL WATER
ORANGE SQUASH
SARSAPARILLA

13

AQUA CAELESTIS
AQUA-MIRABILIS
CERTIFIED MILK
GINGER CORDIAL
PRAIRIE OYSTER

11

APOLLINARIS

12

GAELIC COFFEE

14

ESPRESSO COFFEE

DRINK – BREWING & DRINKING TERMS

3

BAR
BAT
JAG
NIP
PEG
PIN
SIP
SUP
TAP
TOT

4

BARM
BASE
BODY
BREE
BREW
BUNG

DRAM
DRUM
FOAM
GULP
HEAD
HOPS
LEES
MALT
MARC
MASH
MUST
ORGY
PONY
PULL
RACE
RAPE
SHOT
SLUG
SNUG
STUM
SUCK
SWIG

TIFF
WASH
WORT

5

BINGE
BLOAT
BOOZE
DRAFF
DREGS
DRINK
DRUNK
FROTH
GRIST
GROUT
OPTIC
PINTA
PROOF
QUAFF
ROUND

SHIVE
SHORT
SNORT
SPLIT
SPREE
STAVE
STIFF
STILL
STRAW
SWILL
TOAST
TOP-UP
TWIST
USUAL
YEAST

6

BENDER
BOTHAN
BRACER

BUMPER
CELLAR
CHASER
DUNDER
GRAINS
GUZZLE
JIGGER
KNEIPE
MOTHER
MULTUM
PALATE
POMACE
POT-ALE
RAZZLE
RECIPE
REFILL
SALOON
SHAKER
SIPHON
SPIRIT
SPONGE
SWEETS

SWIPES
TEA-BAG
TIDDLY
TIPPLE
ULLAGE
ULLING

7

ALEMBIC
ALE-COST
BAGASSE
BOUQUET
BREWING
CAROUSE
CHANOYU
COBBLER
CORKAGE
DEBAUCH
DRAUGHT
EBRIETY

FERMENT
FUDDLER
GAUGING
GROUNDS
HEEL-TAP
LAMB-ALE
JIMJAMS
MALTASE
MALTOSE
MALT TEA
MASHING
MASH-TUB
MEASURE
SHICKER
SKINFUL
SNIFTER
SOTTING
SPARKLE
SPIRITS
SWALLOW
STENGAH
STINGER
SWIZZLE
TAPPING
TAPLASH
TAP-ROOM
TEA-LEAF
TICKLER
VENT-PEG
VINALIA
VINASSE
VINTAGE
WASSAIL
ZYMURGY

8

APERITIF
BEESWING
BRINDISI
BUN-FIGHT
CAROUSAL
DIONYSIA
DRINKING
FULLNESS
GRACE CUP
HANGOVER
HEAVY WET

HIP-FLASK
INFUSION
LIBATION
LOW WINES
MALT-DUST
NIGHTCAP
PELLICLE
PICK-ME-UP
POTATION
POT-STILL
PUB-CRAWL
QUENCHER
RACINESS
SEDIMENT
SNOOTFUL
SNUGGERY
SOBRIETY
STILLAGE
STILLING
STILLION
SWILLING
TEA-FIGHT
TEA-PARTY
TEETOTAL
VENT-PLUG
VINOSITY
WATERING

9

APPETISER
BEER-MONEY
CANE-TRASH
CELLARAGE
DECOCTION
EBRIOSITY
ELEVENSES
EPULATION
EYE-OPENER
INEBRIETY
MALT-FLOOR
MOONLIGHT
MOONSHINE
NEPHALISM
OENOMANIA
OENOPHILY
ON-LICENCE

PUBLIC BAR
RECTIFIER
REFRESHER
SALOON BAR
STILL-HEAD
STILL-ROOM
STIMULANT
SUNDOWNER
SWEET-WORT
TEMULENCE
TIPSINESS
WASSAILRY
WHITEWASH
WINE-PARTY
YARD OF ALE

10

ABSTINENCE
BACK-HANDER
BAR-PARLOUR
CELLAR-BOOK
CONCOCTION
DIPSOMANIA
DISTILLAND
DUTCH TREAT
IMBIBITION
INSOBRIETY
INTOXICANT
METHOMANIA
OLD SOLDIER
SHEBEENING
STILLATORY
STIRRUP-CUP
STRONG HEAD
TEMPERANCE
TODDY-STICK
WASSAILING

11

BACCHANALIA
BARREL-HOUSE
BOTTLE-PARTY
CLOSING TIME
COLD-WITHOUT

COMPOTATION
DRUNKENNESS
HALF-AND-HALF
INEBRIATION
LOCAL OPTION
OPENING TIME
PATENT STILL
PROHIBITION
REFRESHMENT
STRONG DRINK
TEETOTALISM
VINTAGE YEAR
WASSAIL-BOUT
WINE-BIBBING

12

DISTILLATION
DRINKING-BOUT
DRINKING-HORN
FERMENTATION
INTEMPERANCE
INTOXICATION
KATZENJAMMER
OPENING HOURS
SHORT MEASURE
SUPERNACULUM
SWIZZLE-STICK

13

COCKTAIL-STICK
DRINKING-STRAW
FORTIFICATION

14

REDISTILLATION
THIRST-QUENCHER

15

DELIRIUM TREMENS

DRINK – SPIRITS & COCKTAILS

3
DOP
GIN
RUM
RYE

4
FINE
GROG
OUZO
RAKI

5
BINGO
BRONX
BUMBO
BYRRH
HOOCH
MOBBY
NOYAU
PUNCH
RUMBO
SLING
SMOKE
TAFIA
TODDY
VODKA

6
ARRACK
BRANDY
CHASSE
CHICHA
COGNAC
CRUSTA
GENEVA
GIMLET
GRAPPA
HOOTCH
KIRSCH
KÜMMEL
MALIBU

MESCAL
METAXA
OLD TOM
PERNOD
PEYOTE
POTEEN
ROT-GUT
SCOTCH
WHISKY
ZOMBIE

7
ALCOHOL
AQUAVIT
BACARDI
BOURBON
CAMPARI
CURAÇAO
GIN-FIZZ
LIQUEUR
MARTINI
NEGRONI
PINK GIN
POTHEEN
QUETSCH
SAMSHOO
SIDECAR
SLOE-GIN
TEQUILA
WHISKEY

8
ABSINTHE
ADVOCAAT
ANISETTE
ARMAGNAC
CALVADOS
COCKTAIL
DAIQUIRI
DOG'S-NOSE
DRAMBUIE
EAU DE VIE
GALLIANO
GEROPIGA
GIN AND IT
GIN-SLING

HIGHBALL
HOLLANDS
HOT TODDY
KAOLIANG
PLAYMATE
RED BIDDY
RUM-PUNCH
RUM-SHRUB
SANGAREE
SCHIEDAM
SCHNAPPS
SNOWBALL
VERMOUTH

9
APPLE-JACK
AQUA-VITAE
BUCKS FIZZ
CAPE SMOKE
CLARET-CUP
COINTREAU
FIRE-WATER
MANHATTAN
RUSTY NAIL
RYE-WHISKY
SLIVOVITZ
WHITE LADY
WHIZZ BANG

10
BLOODY MARY
BRANDY GUMP
CHARTREUSE
CLOVER CLUB
CORN-BRANDY
CORN-WHISKY
FIRST NIGHT
JAMAICA RUM
MARASCHINO
MARC BRANDY
SQUARE-FACE
TOM COLLINS
USQUEBAUGH
VELVET KISS
WHISKY-SOUR

11
AGUARDIENTE
BENEDICTINE
BLACK VELVET
JOHN COLLINS
MILLIONAIRE
MOTHER'S RUIN
MOUNTAIN-DEW
NEAT ALCOHOL
PEACH-BRANDY
PROOF-SPIRIT
SCREWDRIVER
TOM-AND-JERRY
WATER OF LIFE
WHISKY-SLING
WHISKY TODDY

12
BRANDY-PAWNEE
CHERRY-BOUNCE
CHERRY BRANDY
CRÈME DE CACAO
CRÈME DE NOYAU
HUMPTY-DUMPTY
IRISH WHISKEY
KIRSCHWASSER
OLD-FASHIONED
POTATO-SPIRIT
SCOTCH WHISKY
SPIRIT OF WINE

13
APRICOT BRANDY
COBBLER'S PUNCH
CRÈME DE MENTHE
EAU DES CREOLES
FINE CHAMPAGNE
SHERRY COBBLER

14
AMERICAN BEAUTY
NAPOLEON BRANDY
TEQUILA SUNRISE

DRINK — WINE

3

VIN

4

ASTI
BOCA
FINO
FIZZ
GIRO
HOCK
PIAT
PORT
ROSÉ
SACK
TENT
WINE
ZUPA

5

AIGLE
CRÉPY
DORIN
ENFER
HEMUS
MÂCON
MÉDOC
MOSEL
NASCO
PERLA
PLONK
RUEDA
SOAVE
SORNI
XERES

6

ALOQUE
BARSAC
BEAUNE
BUBBLY
CANARY
CHINON
CLARET
DINGAC
DOCTOR

FRACIA
GRAVES
HUELVA
LISBON
MALAGA
MARFIL
MONICA
MUSCAT
OLIENA
OSTUNI
SHERRY
SIMKIN
VOLNAY
WEHLEN
YVORNE

7

ALICANT
BIKAVÉR
CATAUBA
CHABLIS
CHACOLI
CHIANTI
CLOBERG
COTESTI
DONNICI
FALERNO
HEURIGE
LESSONA
LUTOMER
MADEIRA
MALMSEY
MARSALA
MERCIER
MOSELLE
OENOMEL
OLOROSO
ORVIETO
PASSITO
PICOLIT
RECIOTO
RED WINE
RETSINA
RHENISH
SABLANT
SANGRIA
SCHLUCK
SETUBAL
SILLERY

SIMPKIN
TAURASI
TORBATO
VIÑA SOL
VIN ROSÉ
VOUVRAY

8

BAROLINO
BERGERAC
BORDEAUX
BROUILLY
BUCELLAS
BURGUNDY
CHARNECO
CORONATA
ERBALUCE
FRIULANO
LÁGRIMAS
LATISANA
LOG-JUICE
MORENITO
MOUNTAIN
MUSCADEL
MUSCADET
MUSCATEL
NICHOLAS
PALM-WINE
POL ROGER
PORT-WINE
RESINATA
RIESLING
SAUTERNE
ST JULIEN
SYLVANER
VIN BLANC
VIN ROUGE
WÜRZBURG
ZAGOROLO

9

ACHKARREN
AGLIANICO
ALBANELLO
BACHARACH
BOLLINGER

BOTTICINO
BURNT SACK
CABRIÈRES
CHAMPAGNE
DON CORTEZ
HERMITAGE
HIPPOCRAS
MAMERTINO
MANTONICO
MONT-REDON
POLCEVERA
RHINE-WINE
SAUVIGNON
TABLE-WINE
TARRAGONA
VALDADIGE
VINO SANTO
WHITE WINE

10

BEAUJOLAIS
BUTTAFUOCO
CHAMBERTIN
CONSTANTIA
GENEVRETTE
GINGER WINE
LOLL-SHRAUB
MANZANILLA
MATEUS ROSÉ
MONTEROSSO
PETER-SEE-ME
PIESPORTER
ROSÉ D'ANJOU
TAITTINGER
VERDICCHIO

11

AFFENTHALER
AMONTILLADO
BRISTOL-MILK
CURRANT-WINE
DOM PÉRIGNON
EDELZWICKER
LAVILLEDIEU
MOUTON CADET
NIERSTEINER
RÜDESHEIMER
SCUPPERNONG
STEINBERGER

DRINK – WINE

12

MARCOBRUNNER
SCHILLERWEIN
VALPOLICELLA
VIN ORDINAIRE

13

LIEBFRAUMILCH

MARTINA FRANCA
MOËT ET CHANDON
UNDHOF AUSLESE
VEUVE CLICQUOT

14

CASTEL DEL MONTE
ELDERBERRY WINE
GOOSEBERRY WINE

JOHANNISBERGER
MERLOT DI BERICI
MOSEL-SAAR-RUWER

15

GLADSTONE SHERRY
LACHRYMA CHRISTI

EDUCATION

3

ART
CSE
FEE
GCE
GYM
LAB
MUG

4

CANE
COED
CRAM
CRIB
DEMY
DESK
DUTY
EXAM
FAIL
FORM
GCSE
GULF
HALL
HOLS
MARK
MOCK
MODS
ORAL
PASS
POLL
PREP
ROLL
ROTE
SWOT
TERM
TEST

5

BREAK
CHAIR
CHALK
CLASS
CRAFT
DRAMA
DRILL
EASEL
ESSAY
EXEAT
EXTRA
FIRST
GAMES
GAUDY
GLOBE
GRADE
GRANT
GREEK
GRIND
HOUSE
IMPOT
LATIN
LINES
LODGE
LYCÉE
MATHS
MUSIC
ORACY
PAPER
PRIZE
RESIT
SHELL
SLATE
STICK
STUDY

6

A-LEVEL
BOTANY
CAMPUS
CANING
COURSE
CRAYON
CREDIT
CURSUS
DEGREE
DESIGN
EXAMEN
FRENCH
GATING
GERMAN
HOOKEY
HOSTEL
INTAKE
LESSON
LYCEUM
MONTEM
NATION
O-LEVEL
OPTIME
PENSUM
PERIOD
POETRY
PRELIM
PRIMER
READER
REMOVE
REPORT
SCHOOL
SCONCE
SMALLS
SPORTS
STREAM
THESIS
TRIPOS
TYPING
VULGUS

7

ALGEBRA
BANDING
BATTLES
BIOLOGY
BURSARY
COLLEGE
COMMONS
CONDUCT
COOKERY
CRAMMER
DANCING
DIPLOMA
ENGLISH
FACULTY
FAGGING
FLOORER
GEOLOGY
GRAMMAR
GREAT GO
HIGHERS
HISTORY
HONOURS
HYGIENE
ITALIAN
LAURELS
LECTURE
LETTERS
LOCKOUT
LOG-BOOK
MARKING

MAXIMUS
MINIMUS
PHYSICS
PLAY-WAY
POINTER
POTTERY
PREMIUM
PROJECT
READING
RUSSIAN
SATCHEL
SCIENCE
SEMINAR
SESSION
SETTING
SICK-BAY
SPANISH
SUBJECT
TESTING
TORPIDS
TRUANCY
TUITION
VARSITY
WEAVING
WRITING

8

ACTIVITY
AEGROTAT
COMMERCE
DEMYSHIP
ENCAENIA
EXERCISE
EXTENDER
EXTERNAT
FORM ROOM
GATE-FINE
GEOMETRY
HALF-TERM
HANDWORK
HOMEWORK
LAUREATE
LEARNING
LIRIPOOP
LITERACY
LITTLE GO
NUMERACY
NUMERALS
PASS MARK
PEDAGOGY

PLAYTIME
PROGRESS
QUESTION
REGISTER
REVISION
ROLL-CALL
SEMESTER
SEMINARY
SICK-ROOM
SPELLING
SWIMMING
SYLLABUS
TEACHING
TERM-TIME
TESTAMUR
TEXT-BOOK
TRAINING
TRUANTRY
TUTELAGE
TUTORAGE
TUTORIAL
TUTORING
VIVA VOCE
WOODWORK

9

ALMA MATER
ATHLETICS
BEHAVIOUR
BLACK BOOK
CHEMISTRY
CLASS-BOOK
CLASSROOM
CROCODILE
DALTONISM
DAY-SCHOOL
DETENTION
DICTATION
DORMITORY
ECONOMICS
EDUCATION
ENROLMENT
EXPULSION
FIRE-DRILL
GAUDEAMUS
GEOGRAPHY
GROUNDING
GYMNASIUM
HEURISTIC
HIGH TABLE
INSTITUTE

EDUCATION

LANGUAGES
LECTORATE
MASTERATE
MATRICULA
MECHANICS
MERIT MARK
METALWORK
PRACTICAL
PRIZE-LIST
PROGRAMME
PUPILLAGE
RECTORIAL
REFECTORY
REFRESHER
SCHOOLBAG
SCHOOL-DAY
SCHOOLING
SCRIPTURE
SHORTHAND
SOCIOLOGY
SPEECH DAY
SPORTS DAY
STAFFROOM
STREAMING
SUPPLICAT
TABLE-BOOK
TEST-PAPER
TIMETABLE
TRIMESTER
TUTORSHIP
VISUAL AID

10

ARITHMETIC
ATTENDANCE
AUTODIDACT
BARRING-OUT
BLACKBOARD
CHALKBOARD
COLLECTION
COLLOQUIUM
COMMON ROOM
COURSE-WORK
CURRICULUM
DISCIPLINE
DUAL SCHOOL
ELEVEN-PLUS
EXHIBITION
FRATERNITY
FRESHERDOM

GRADUATION
GYMNASTICS
HIGH SCHOOL
HOUSECRAFT
HOUSE-POINT
HUMANITIES
IMPOSITION
INTERNMENT
LABORATORY
LAUREATION
LECTORSHIP
LITERATURE
NEEDLEWORK
PEDAGOGICS
PEDAGOGISM
PLAYGROUND
POLL-DEGREE
PREFECTURE
PRELECTION
PROCTORAGE
PROSPECTUS
QUADRANGLE
REAL SCHOOL
RECREATION
REGISTRARY
SCHOOL-BELL
SCHOOL-BOOK
SCHOOL FEES
SCHOOL-ROOM
SCHOOL-TERM
SCHOOL-TIDE
SCHOOL-TIME
SCHOOLWORK
SPRING TERM
STATISTICS
SUMMER TERM
TECHNOLOGY
UNIVERSITY

11

BLACK MONDAY
BOOKKEEPING
CERTIFICATE
COEDUCATION
COMPOSITION
DIDACTICISM
DOUBLE-FIRST
EDIFICATION
EDUCABILITY
ELECTRONICS

ENGINEERING
EXAMINATION
HANDWRITING
HEDGE-SCHOOL
INSTRUCTION
LECTURESHIP
LIBERAL ARTS
MAGISTERIUM
MATHEMATICS
MODERATIONS
NATURE STUDY
NIGHT-SCHOOL
PARENTCRAFT
PEDAGOGUERY
POLYTECHNIC
PREFECTSHIP
PREPARATION
PROCTORSHIP
RESPONSIONS
RUSTICATION
SCHOLARSHIP
SCHOOLCRAFT
SCHOOL-GOING
SCHOOLHOUSE
STUDENTSHIP
TOWN AND GOWN
VALEDICTORY

12

COMMENCEMENT
COMMON SCHOOL
CONGREGATION
CROSS-COUNTRY
DIRECT METHOD
EXERCISE-BOOK
FLANNELGRAPH
FRESHMANSHIP
HUMAN BIOLOGY
INVIGILATION
KINDERGARTEN
MISBEHAVIOUR
MISEDUCATION
MULTIVERSITY
PHONIC METHOD
PROFESSORATE
PROGYMNASIUM
SENIOR OPTIME
STICK AND BOOK
TRIGONOMETRY

13

BACCALAUREATE
CHRISTMAS TERM
COMPREHENSIVE
DEMONSTRATION
GRAMMAR SCHOOL
HOME ECONOMICS
INFANTS' SCHOOL
MATRICULATION
NON-ATTENDANCE
NURSERY SCHOOL
OPEN-AIR SCHOOL
PRELIMINARIES
PROFESSORSHIP

QUALIFICATION
REAL GYMNASIUM
SCHOOL-LEAVING
VOCATIONALISM

14

HOME MANAGEMENT
MICHAELMAS TERM
NATIONAL SCHOOL
PROGRESS REPORT
PROVIDED SCHOOL
RECEPTION CLASS
SCHOOL-TEACHING

SPEECH TRAINING

15

BUSINESS STUDIES
COMBINATION ROOM
COMPUTER SCIENCE
DOMESTIC SCIENCE
REFRESHER COURSE
SCHOOLMASTERING
TEACHING MACHINE
VOLUNTARY SCHOOL

ENGINEERING & MINING

3

BAR
BIT
CAM
COG
CUT
DIE
DYE
EYE
GIB
GOB
HOD
HUB
JAW
JIB
JUD
KEY
KIP
LAG
LAP
NIP
NOG
OIL
ORE
PAN
PEG
PIG
PIN
PIT
RAM
REV
RIB
RIG
RIM
ROD
SET
SOW
TAP
TAW
TIP
TUB
TUP
TYE
VAN
WAX
WEB

4

ADIT
ARCH
AXLE
BAND
BANK
BELT
BOOM
BORE
BOSS
BROW
BUSH
BUTT
CAGE
CALX
CAST
CHIP
CLAM
CLOD
COCK
CONE
COOM
CRAB
CRIB
CULM
CURD
DAMP
DRAG
DRUM
DUCT
DUFF
DUST
DUTY
FACE
FLEX
FLOW
FLUX
FORK
FORM
FUSE
GALL
GEAR
GEAT
GOAF
GRAB
HEAD
HOOP
HOSE
HUSH
JACK
JOIN
KILN
KNEE
LEAR

LIFT
LINK
LODE
MELT
MESH
MINE
NAVE
OVEN
PACK
PAWL
PEEN
PILE
PLAY
PLUG
POLL
POST
PROP
PULP
PUMP
RACK
REED
REEF
RIND
RISE
ROAD
ROLL
SEAL
SEAM
SILL
SKIP
SLAB
SLAG
SLOT
SLUB
SLUG
SLUM
SPAN
SPIN
SPIT
STAY
STOP
SUMP
SWAG
SWIG
T-BAR
TEST
TILL
TRAP
TRIG
TUBE
TURN
TYMP

VANE
VEIN
WALL
WARP
WEAR
WEFT
WELD
WELL
WHIM
WHIP
WIRE
WOOF
WORM

5

BLANK
BLOCK
BRAKE
CABLE
CANAL
CHAIN
CHILL
CHUTE
CRAMP
CRANE
CRANK
CUPEL
DITCH
DOBBY
DOLLY
DOWEL
DRIFT
DROSS
FELLY
FIELD
FINES
FLASH
FLIER
FORGE
GEODE
GRASS
HEALD
HEAVE
HITCH
HUTCH
INGOT
JOINT
LADLE
LEASE
LEVEL

LEVER
LEWIS
MATTE
METAL
MODEL
MOULD
NOILS
PEDAL
PERCH
PITCH
PIVOT
PLANE
PLANT
PLATE
PROBE
PUNCH
QUILL
RATCH
ROTOR
SCALE
SCREW
SHAFT
SHEET
SHOOT
SKILL
SLAVE
SLIDE
SLING
SLIPE
SOLAR
SOUGH
SPARE
SPILE
SPILL
SPOIL
SPOKE
SPRAG
SPRUE
STACK
STALL
STEEN
STOOP
STOPE
STOUP
STRIP
STRUT
STUFF
STULL
STULM
SWASH
SWIFT
TERNE

TERTS
TOOTH
TRACE
T-RAIL
TRUNK
TRUSS
UNION
VALVE
WEDGE
WHEEL
WHELP
WHORL
WINCH
WINZE
WORKS

6

BOBBIN
BOILER
BONNET
BUCKET
BUDDLE
CAMBER
CLEVIS
CLUTCH
CRADLE
CRUSET
CULLET
CUT-OFF
CUTTER
DAMASK
DOCTOR
DOFFER
DREDGE
DUFFER
DYEING
ENAMEL
FILING
FILLET
FILTER
FLANGE
FORCER
GASKET
GAS-TAR
GETTER
GIBBET
GIRDER
GREASE
GROOVE
GROUND

GUSHER
HANDLE
HEARTH
HEDDLE
HOPPER
HURTER
INGATE
INTAKE
JIGGER
KEEPER
KEY-PIN
KEY-WAY
KILLAS
LAMINA
LEADER
LET-OFF
LIMING
LINGOT
MATRIX
MINING
MOBILE
MOCK-UP
MONKEY
MOTION
NIPPLE
NOZZLE
NUGGET
OIL-RIG
OUTPUT
PALLET
PICKLE
PIG-BED
PILLAR
PINION
PINTLE
PIPING
PISTON
PLACER
PLATEN
POPPET
POTASH
PULLEY
PUSHER
QUARRY
REBORE
REJECT
REMAKE
RESIST
RIFFLE
RIGGER
ROCKER
ROLLER

ROVING
RUBBER
RUNNER
SADDLE
SCORIA
SCOTCH
SHEAVE
SHIELD
SHODER
SLEEVE
SLIDER
SLIMES
SLUICE
SMOKER
SPEISS
SPIGOT
SPLINE
SPOILS
SPRING
STATOR
STOCKS
STRAIN
STRAKE
STRESS
STRIKE
STROKE
SUCKER
SWIVEL
TACKLE
TALLOW
TAN-PIT
TAN-VAT
TAPPET
TAWING
TEMPER
TENTER
THREAD
TORQUE
T-PLATE
TRÉMIE
TROMPE
TRY-OUT
TUBING
TUBULE
TURRET
TWITCH
UPCAST
WASH-UP
WINDER
WINDLE
WIRING
WORTLE

7

ADAPTOR
AIR-DUCT
AIR-LOCK
AIR-PIPE
AIR-TUBE
BAR-IRON
BASCULE
BEARING
BLUEING
BOLSTER
BONANZA
BOOSTER
BORINGS
BRACKET
BUTT-END
CAISSON
CASTING
CHAMFER
CHANNEL
CHAPLET
CHIMNEY
CLAY-PIT
CLINKER
COAL-BED
COAL-PIT
COOLANT
CRAMPET
CRANAGE
CREEPER
CULVERT
CUSHION
DABBING
DASH-POT
DAY-COAL
DERRICK
DIP-PIPE
DIP-TRAP
FACTURE
FAIRING
FERRULE
FOOTWAY
FORGING
FOUNDRY
FURNACE
GALLERY
GALLOWS
GAS-COAL
GAS-COKE
GAS-LIME
GAS OVEN

GEARING
GROMMET
GRUMMET
GUDGEON
HARD-PAN
HEADING
HOT WELL
INCLINE
JOURNAL
JOURNEY
KEY-SEAT
KING-PIN
LAGGING
LOW GEAR
MAGNETO
MANDREL
MEASURE
MELTING
MESHING
MILL-EYE
MILLING
MINERAL
MULLOCK
NAIL-ROD
OFF-SCUM
OFFTAKE
OIL-BATH
OIL-WELL
PACKING
PANNING
PATTERN
PAY-DIRT
PIG-IRON
PIG-LEAD
PIN-DUST
PINKING
PINNING
PIT-BROW
PITHEAD
PIT-PROP
PLASTIC
PLATING
PROJECT
RACE-WAY
RATCHET
REDUCER
REGULUS
ROSETTE
ROTATOR
SALT-PIT
SAND-BED
SANDING

SCALING
SCHLICH
SCISSEL
SECTION
SHAPING
SHUTTLE
SONDAGE
SOURING
SPILING
SPINDLE
SPOUTER
SPUTTER
STARTER
STEMPEL
STOPING
STUDDLE
TAGGERS
TAMPING
TAN-BARK
TANNAGE
TANNING
TAN-OOZE
TEMPLET
TENSION
TEST-BED
TIN MINE
TORSION
TREADLE
TRIBLET
TRIBUTE
TROMMEL
TRUCKLE
TRUNDLE
TUBBING
TURNERY
TURNING
VANNING
VITRICS
WARRANT
WEARING
WEAVING
WEDGING
WELDING
WINDAGE

8

ACIERAGE
AIR-VALVE
ASH-LEACH
BALLCOCK

111

ENGINEERING & MINING

BALL-RACE
BED-PLATE
BLOOMERY
BLOW-HOLE
BLOWPIPE
BOLT-HOLE
BOREHOLE
BRATTICE
CAM-SHAFT
CAM-WHEEL
CARRIAGE
CATENARY
CHAINLET
CHALK-PIT
CLACK-BOX
CLAP-SILL
COAL-FACE
COAL-MINE
COLLIERY
CRUCIBLE
CYLINDER
DAY-LEVEL
DIGGINGS
DIRECTOR
DOLLY-TUB
DOWNCAST
EDGE COAL
EFFLUENT
ENGINERY
FAN WHEEL
FEED-HEAD
FEED-PIPE
FILATURE
FIREDAMP
FIRE-TUBE
FLASHING
FLOODWAY
FLYWHEEL
FOLLOWER
FOUNDING
FRICTION
GAS-WATER
GOLD-DUST
GOLD-MINE
GOLD-RUSH
GOVERNOR
GRAINING
HEADGEAR
HEAT SINK
HIGH GEAR
HOISTWAY
IMPELLER

INDUSTRY
INJECTOR
INTAGLIO
IRON-MINE
ISOLATOR
JUNK-RING
LAY-SHAFT
LEACHING
LEASE-ROD
LEVERAGE
LICKER-IN
LINCHPIN
LINKWORK
LIVE-AXLE
LIXIVIUM
LONGWALL
MATTRESS
MILL-WORK
MOULDING
MULTIPLE
NOTCHING
OFFSORTS
OIL-FIELD
PAVEMENT
PEAK-LOAD
PEDESTAL
PIN-MAKING
PIPELINE
PIVOTING
PROOFING
PROSPECT
PUDDLING
PUMP-HEAD
PUMP-HOOD
PUMP-WELL
PURCHASE
RACKWORK
RAGWHEEL
REFINING
REFUSION
REVOLVER
RIM-BRAKE
ROTATION
SALT-MINE
SALT-WORK
SAND-BATH
SANDIVER
SAND-TRAP
SCAVENGE
SCUTCHER
SHAFTING
SHEETING

SLIME-PIT
SMELTING
SMOKE-BOX
SPITTING
SPOILAGE
SPROCKET
SPUR-GEAR
STACKING
STANNARY
STEATITE
STEENING
STEERING
STOP-COCK
STOPPING
STRADDLE
STREAMER
STRINGER
TAIL-PIPE
TEMPLATE
TIDE-MILL
TRUNNION
TUBE-WELL
TURNCOCK
UNDERSET
VEE-JOINT
VENT-PIPE
VIBRATOR
WALLSEND
WASH-DIRT
WATER-BOX
WATER-RAM
WEAR-IRON
WELDMENT
WELL-HOLE
WET ASSAY
WINDLASS
WIRE-ROPE
WOOL-CARD
WOOL-COMB
WORKINGS
WORM-GEAR
WRIST-PIN

9

AIR-BUBBLE
ANNEALING
ARCHETYPE
AUGER-HOLE
BAND-BRAKE
BAND-WHEEL

BASEPLATE
BELL CRANK
BEVEL-GEAR
BLACK DAMP
BLAST-HOLE
BLAST-PIPE
BLOW-VALVE
BLUEPRINT
BOWSTRING
BOX-GIRDER
CAPILLARY
CARBONADO
CHAIN-GEAR
CHAIN-PUMP
CLEARANCE
CLOCKWORK
COMPONENT
COPPERING
CRAMP-IRON
CRANKCASE
CROSS-HEAD
DAMASCENE
DEFLECTOR
DETORSION
DIAPHRAGM
DOODLE-BUG
DRAW-PLATE
DUCTILITY
ECCENTRIC
EXTRUSION
FEED-WATER
FILTER-BED
FLOTATION
FLOW CHART
FLOW SHEET
FOLIATION
FORK-CHUCK
FREE-WHEEL
GEAR-RATIO
GEAR-WHEEL
GETTERING
GLASS-GALL
GRUBSTAKE
HEADFRAME
HEADSTOCK
HEAPSTEAD
HEDDLE-EYE
HEMICYCLE
HOLDERBAT
IDLE-WHEEL
INHIBITOR
INJECTION

INTERLOCK
IRON-MOULD
LEASE-BAND
LIFT-SHAFT
LIQUATION
LUBRICANT
MACHINERY
MECHANICS
MECHANISM
METAL-WORK
MICROWIRE
MIDDLINGS
MILLSTONE
MILL-WHEEL
NOSE-PIECE
PAY-GRAVEL
PINCHCOCK
PIVOT-WORK
PUNCH-PROP
QUARRY-SAP
REGULATOR
RESISTANT
ROCK-SHAFT
SAND-BLAST
SAND-TABLE
SCOURINGS
SCREW-PILE
SCUTCHING
SEASONING
SHEET-IRON
SLIDE-REST
SMALL-COAL
SOAPSTONE
SPARE PART
SPLIT RING
SPRINGING
SPUR-WHEEL
STAR-WHEEL
STEAM-DOME
STEAM-PIPE
STEAM-PORT
STEAM-TRAP
STOCKWORK
STREAM-TIN
STRIP-MINE
SURFACING
TAN-LIQUOR
TAN-PICKLE
TAPPET-ROD
TENSILITY
TOLERANCE
TOUGHENER

TRUSS-BEAM
TURNTABLE
UNDERCAST
UNDERCLAY
VEINSTUFF
VIBRATION
WASTE-PIPE
WATER-CORE
WATER-PIPE
WATER-PUMP
WATER-SEAL
WHEEL-RACE
WHEELWORK
WHITE DAMP
WIRE GUAGE
WORKPIECE
WORM-WHEEL

10

ARC-WELDING
AUTOMATION
BLOCK-CHAIN
BRUSHWHEEL
CANTILEVER
CHAIN-CABLE
CHAIN-DRIVE
CLACK-VALVE
COMBUSTION
COSTEAN-PIT
CRANKSHAFT
DIE-SINKING
DONKEY-PUMP
EFFICIENCY
ENAMELLING
END-PRODUCT
FILLET WELD
FILTRATION
FLASH-BOARD
FLOAT GLASS
FLUID DRIVE
GOLD-WASHER
HUNTING-COG
HYDRAULICS
INSPECTION
IRON-MINING
JOURNAL-BOX
LAMINATION
LINK-MOTION
LUFFING-JIB
MACERATION

MALLEATION
MELTING-POT
METALLURGY
MICROMETRY
MINERAL OIL
MITRE-WHEEL
OVERLAYING
PILOT-PLANT
PIPE-LAYING
PITCH-WHEEL
PLANE-TABLE
PRODUCTION
PROPULSION
PUMP-HANDLE
REFRACTORY
REVOLUTION
REVOLVENCY
SAFETY-CAGE
SAFETY-LAMP
SAFETY-PLUG
SAFETY-STOP
SCREW-PLATE
SHEET-METAL
SLIDE-VALVE
SPRINGHEAD
SPUTTERING
STEAM-CHEST
STEAM-POWER
STEAM-PLATE
STREAM-GOLD
SWASH PLATE
SWING-STOCK
TACHOMETRY
TAPPET-RING
TECHNOLOGY
TENSION-ROD
TENTER-HOOK
TERNEPLATE
TOUGHENING
UNDERDRIVE
WATER-FRAME
WATER-LEVEL
WATER-MOTOR
WATER-POWER
WELL-BORING
YIELD POINT

11

BALL-BEARING
BELL-HOUSING

BEVEL-WHEELS
BREAST WHEEL
BUCKET-WHEEL
BUTTED JOINT
BUTT WELDING
CEMENTATION
CEMENT-STONE
CHOKING-COIL
COARSE METAL
COLD-CASTING
COLD-FORGING
COLD-WELDING
COMPENSATOR
COMPRESSION
COPPERPLATE
CROSS-GARNET
CUPELLATION
DAMASCENING
DAMASK-STEEL
DRIFT-MINING
DRIVING-BAND
DRIVING-GEAR
DROP-FORGING
ELECTRIC ARC
ENDLESS BELT
ENDLESS WORM
ENGINEERING
ESCAPE VALVE
FOLLOW-BOARD
GOLD-BEATING
GOLD-DIGGING
GRANULATION
LIXIVIATION
LUBRICATION
MACHINE-WORK
MANUFACTURE
MASTER-WHEEL
METALLIDING
MINERAL WOOL
MONKEY-WHEEL
MOULD-FACING
PELTON-WHEEL
PLASTICISER
PLATFORMING
POPPET-VALVE
PROSPECTING
QUARRY-WATER
RAW MATERIAL
RECUPERATOR
RIVET-HEARTH
RUNNING-GEAR
SAFETY-VALVE

ENGINEERING & MINING

SCREW-THREAD
SEAM-WELDING
SPINNERETTE
SPUR-GEARING
STEAM-JACKET
STUFFING-BOX
SWIVEL-JOINT
TOGGLE-JOINT
UPCAST-SHAFT
WALKING-BEAM
WATER-JACKET
WELL-SINKING
WIRE-DRAWING
WOOL-CARDING
WOOL-COMBING
WORKING-EDGE
WORKING-FACE
WORM-BEARING

12

ANTI-FRICTION
ASSEMBLY LINE
BASIC PROCESS
BLAST-FURNACE
BLOW-MOULDING
CANALISATION
CANTING-WHEEL
CHIMNEY-STALK
CIRCUMFUSION
COLD-MOULDING
COUNTER-DRAIN
COUNTERPOISE
COUNTERSHAFT
DECALESCENCE
DELIVERY-PIPE
DELIVERY-TUBE
DRAWING-TABLE
DRIVING-SHAFT
DRIVING-WHEEL
EDULCORATION
ENDLESS CHAIN
ENDLESS SCREW
EXPLOITATION
FRACTIONATOR
GAS-CONDENSER
GLASS-BLOWING

GLASS-CUTTING
GREASE-NIPPLE
GRIT-BLASTING
HYDRAULIC RAM
KNUCKLE-JOINT
LIQUEFACTION
LOAD-SHEDDING
METAL-WORKING
MODIFICATION
OFF-SCOURINGS
PANEL-BEATING
PANEL-WORKING
PERSIAN-WHEEL
PLUMMER-BLOCK
RATCHET-WHEEL
ROPE-DRILLING
SPARKING-PLUG
SPINDLE-WHORL
SQUIRREL-CAGE
STEAM-WHISTLE
STEERING-GEAR
STRENGTHENER
SULPHURATION
TAPPET-MOTION
TIN-STREAMING
UNDERPINNING
VARIABLE GEAR
VITRIFACTION
VITRIFACTURE
WASTE PRODUCT
WATER-BELLOWS
WHIP-AND-DERRY

13

BALL AND SOCKET
CHROME-PLATING
CHROME-TANNING
CONNECTING-ROD
COUNTER-WEIGHT
DECOMPRESSION
DOWNCAST-SHAFT
ENCAPSULATION
HYDRAULIC BELT
HYDRAULIC JACK
MECHANISATION
METALLISATION

NICKEL-PLATING
NON-PRODUCTION
PALLETISATION
PROVING GROUND
RACK AND PINION
REINFORCEMENT
SCORIFICATION
SMOKE-CONSUMER
SNIFTING-VALVE
SPECIFICATION
SPROCKET-WHEEL
STEAM-GOVERNOR
STRENGTHENING
VITRIFICATION
VULCANISATION
ZINCIFICATION

14

COUNTER-BALANCE
ELECTROGILDING
ELECTROPLATING
ELECTROWINNING
HYDRAULIC PRESS
MASS-PRODUCTION
OPEN-CAST MINING
PREFABRICATION
PRODUCTION LINE
SERVO-MECHANISM
SWINGLING-STOCK
TELEPROCESSING
UNIVERSAL JOINT
VIBROFLOTATION

15

ELECTRIC FURNACE
FOUR-STROKE CYCLE
FRICTION WELDING
HYDRAULIC MINING
LUBRICATED WATER
STOVE-ENAMELLING
TORQUE-CONVERTER

FINANCE – CURRENCY

3

BIT
BOB
DAM
ÉCU
FEN
FIN
KIP
LEK
LEU
LEV
MIL
ÖRE
PIE
PUL
SEN
SOL
SOU
WON
YEN
ZUZ

4

ANNA
BAHT
BUCK
CEDI
CENT
DIME
DOIT
DONG
DURO
JOEY
KOBO
KURU
KYAT
LION
LIRA
LWEI
MARK
MITE
OBOL
PARA
PAUL
PESO
PICE
PULA
QUID
RAND

REAL
REIS
RIAL
RIEL
RYAL
SYLI
TAKA
TALA
YUAN

5

ANGEL
ASPER
BEKAH
BELGA
BODEL
BROAD
BUTUT
CHIAO
COLON
CROWN
DARIC
DINAR
DUCAT
EAGLE
FIVER
FRANC
GERAH
GROAT
KRONA
KRONE
LEONE
LIARD
LIBRA
LIVRE
LOUIS
MOHUR
NAIRA
NOBLE
OBANG
PAISA
PAOLO
PENNY
PLACK
POUND
RIDER
RIYAL
ROYAL
RUBLE
RUPEE

SCEAT
SCUDO
SEMIS
SOLDO
SUCRE
TICAL
TIZZY
TOMAN
UNITE
ZAIRE
ZLOTY

6

AGOROT
AUREUS
BALBOA
BAWBEE
BENDER
BEZANT
COPECK
COPPER
COUTER
DALASI
DEANER
DÉCIME
DENIER
DIRHAM
DIRHEM
DODKIN
DOLLAR
DOUBLE
DRACHM
EKUELE
ESCUDO
FLORIN
FORINT
FRANIC
GOURDE
GROSZY
GUINEA
GULDEN
HALERU
HELLER
JITNEY
KOBANG
KOPECK
KORUNA
KWACHA
KWANZA
LEPTON

MANCUS
MARKKA
NICKEL
NICKER
OBOLUS
PAGODA
PESETA
PESEWA
ROUBLE
SEQUIN
SHEKEL
SHINER
STATER
STIVER
TANNER
TENNER
TESTER
TESTON
THALER
TICKEY
TUGRIK

7

AFGHANI
BOLIVAR
CARDECU
CAROLUS
CENTAVO
CENTIME
CÓRDOBA
CRUSADO
DRACHMA
GEORDIE
GUARANI
GUILDER
JACOBUS
LEMPIRA
MILLIME
MILREIS
MOIDORE
OUGUIYA
PATRICK
PFENNIG
PIASTRE
PISTOLE
QUARTER
QUETZAL
RINGGIT
RUDDOCK
SEXTANS

SMACKER
SOLIDUS
SPANKER
TAMBALA
TESTOON
TWO BITS
UNICORN
XERAFIN

8

CRUZEIRO
DENARIUS
DOUBLOON
DUCATOON
FARTHING
GROSCHEN
IMPERIAL
JOHANNES
KREUTZER
LOUIS-D'OR
MARAVEDI
MILLIÈME
NAPOLEON
NGULTRUM
PICAYUNE
PISTOLET
PORTAGUE
PORTIGUE
QINDARKA
QUADRANS
RENMINBI
SEMUNCIA
SESTERCE
SHILLING
SIXPENCE
SKILLING
STOTINKI
TENPENCE
TWOPENCE
ZECCHINO

9

BOLIVIANO
DANDIPRAT
DIDRACHMA
FIVEPENCE
FOURPENCE
HALF-CROWN

FINANCE – CURRENCY

HALFPENNY
LILANGENI
PISTAREEN
POUND COIN
POUND NOTE
RIX-DOLLAR
ROSE-NOBLE
SCHILLING
SOVEREIGN
SPUR ROYAL
ZWANZIGER

THREEPENCE

HALF-SOVEREIGN
MEXICAN DOLLAR
TENPENNY-PIECE
THREEPENNY BIT

11

BONNET-PIECE
DOUBLE-EAGLE
SPADE-GUINEA
SWORD-DOLLAR
TETRADRACHM

14

FIFTY-POUND NOTE
FIVEPENNY PIECE
FOURPENNY PIECE
HALF-A-SOVEREIGN
HONG KONG DOLLAR
THREEPENNY JOEY

12

ANTONINIANUS
DEUTSCHEMARK
PIECE OF EIGHT
TEN-POUND NOTE

10

BROADPIECE
HALF-A-CROWN
HALF-DOLLAR
KRUGERRAND
PENNY-PIECE
PORTCULLIS
REICHSMARK

13

FIVE-POUND NOTE

15

FIFTY-PENCE PIECE
TEN-SHILLING NOTE
TWENTY-POUND NOTE

FINANCE – MONETARY TERMS

3	4			GRAVY	STAKE
		LEVY	SUBS	GROSS	SUGAR
		MILL	TOLL	HEADS	SYCEE
BET	BILL	MINA	WAGE	INGOT	TAILS
COB	CASH	MINT	WHIP	LIKIN	TERMS
DUD	COIN	NETT		LOLLY	TITHE
DUE	COST	NOTE	5	LUCRE	TOKEN
FEE	DISC	PAYE		MODUS	TRONC
PAY	DOLE	PEAG	BANCO	MONEY	VALUE
POT	DUES	PELF	BATTA	ORDER	VERSO
PYX	DUMP	PILE	BRASS	PIECE	WAGER
RAP	DUTY	PONY	BREAD	PRICE	WAGES
SUB	FARE	RATE	CRORE	RAISE	WORTH
SUM	FINE	RENT	DOUGH	RATES	ZIMBI
TAX	FUND	REST	DUMMY	RENTE	
TIN	GALE	RISE	DUMPS	RHINO	6
TIP	GOLD	SCAT	FLOAT	SCREW	
VAT	HIRE	SCOT	GRAND	STACK	BOODLE
WAD	LAKH	STUB	GRANT		

CEDULA
CHANGE
COPPER
DOCTOR
DUFFER
EXCISE
FLIMSY
FUMAGE
HIDAGE
INCOME
MONKEY
OLIVET
PADUAN
PARITY
PAY-OFF
PAYOLA
POCKET
RANSOM
RATING
REBATE
REFUND
REMEDY
RENTAL
SALARY
SEA-PAY
SILVER
SPECIE
STUMER
SURTAX
TAXING
TOWAGE
VALUTA
VELLON
WAKIKI
WAMPUM

7

BENEFIT
BULLION
COINAGE
CUSTOMS
EXERGUE
FALDAGE
FULLAGE
GABELLE
GARNISH
HALF-PAY
HANDSEL
IMITANT
IMPREST
JACKPOT

LAND-TAX
LASTAGE
LENDING
LINEAGE
LOCKAGE
MILLING
MINTAGE
MOORAGE
OBVERSE
PAYMENT
PAY-ROLL
PENSION
PEW-RENT
PIERAGE
POLL-TAX
PONTAGE
PORTAGE
POSTAGE
PREMIUM
PRIMAGE
RAKE-OFF
RED-CENT
REEDING
REQUITE
REVENUE
REVERSE
ROULEAU
SAVINGS
SHEKELS
STIPEND
STORAGE
STOWAGE
SUBSIDY
SURPLUS
TANKAGE
TIPPING
TOLLAGE
TONNAGE
TRIBUTE
WARRANT
YARDAGE

8

BANK-BILL
BANK-NOTE
BANK-ROLL
BASE COIN
CORN-RENT
CURRENCY
DANEGELD
DONATION

EARNINGS
ENTRY FEE
EXCHANGE
FERRIAGE
FREE-COST
GATE-FINE
GRAINAGE
GRATUITY
HALF FARE
HARD CASH
HEAD RENT
HONORARY
HOT MONEY
HOUSE-TAX
INTEREST
KEY MONEY
KICKBACK
MINT-MARK
PENNY-FEE
PIN-MONEY
PITTANCE
PLANCHET
POOR-RATE
POUNDAGE
PROCEEDS
QUIT-RENT
RACK-RENT
RAG-MONEY
REQUITAL
RESERVES
RETAINER
SALES TAX
SHARE-OUT
SPOT CASH
SPY-MONEY
STERLING
STOPPAGE
SUPERTAX
TAXATION
TRANSIRE
TRUCKAGE
WAGONAGE
WARD-CORN
WATERAGE
WEIGHAGE
WHARFAGE
WINDFALL

9

AGISTMENT
BAKSHEESH

BANK-PAPER
CONSULAGE
DEATH DUTY
DEFLATION
DIRECT TAX
EASY MONEY
EMOLUMENT
EXCHEQUER
FACE VALUE
FACTORAGE
GATE-MONEY
GREENBACK
GROUNDAGE
HALF-PRICE
HARD MONEY
HEAD MONEY
HEARTH TAX
HOUSE-DUTY
INCOME TAX
INFLATION
LAGNIAPPE
LIGHT-DUES
LUCK-PENNY
NINEPENCE
OUTGIVING
OVERISSUE
PAY-PACKET
PENNY-RENT
PETTY CASH
POLL-MONEY
PORTERAGE
PRINCIPAL
READY CASH
REFLATION
REPAYMENT
RESOURCES
RING-MONEY
RISK-MONEY
STAMP DUTY
STRIKE-PAY
SURCHARGE
WATER-RATE
WHIP-ROUND
WINDOW TAX

10

CAPITATION
COLLECTION
DIRTY MONEY
DOLLAR AREA
EASTER DUES

117

FINANCE – MONETARY TERMS

EIGHTPENCE
EURO-DOLLAR
EXPRESS FEE
FOUND MONEY
FREIGHTAGE
GRANT-IN-AID
GREEN POUND
GROUND-RENT
HONORARIUM
KNIFE-MONEY
LEGACY DUTY
LIVING WAGE
LUCKY-PIECE
MONETARISM
MONEY-ORDER
PAPER MONEY
PETROMONEY
PETROPOUND
PREPAYMENT
PRESS-MONEY
PRESTATION
PRIVY-PURSE
PRIZE-MONEY
QUARTERAGE
READY MONEY
REAP-SILVER
REBATEMENT
RECOMPENSE
REMITTANCE
SECURITIES
SESTERTIUM
SETTLEMENT
SEVENPENCE
SHELL-MONEY
SHOESTRING
SIEGE-PIECE
SMART-MONEY
STAKE-MONEY
SUBVENTION
TABLE-MONEY
TOKEN-MONEY
TOUCH-PIECE

11

BIMETALLISM
CAPITAL LEVY
CIRCULATION
CONTINENTAL
CONTORNIATE
COUNTERFEIT

DANGER MONEY
DEVALUATION
ENTRANCE FEE
GRESHAM'S LAW
HARBOUR DUES
HEARTH-MONEY
HEARTH-PENNY
INDIRECT TAX
LEGAL TENDER
MAUNDY MONEY
NUMISMATICS
PETER'S PENCE
PETRODOLLAR
POCKET-MONEY
POCKET-PIECE
PORT-CHARGES
POSTAL ORDER
PROBATE DUTY
PROPERTY TAX
PURCHASE TAX
RATION-MONEY
REQUITEMENT
REVALUATION
SICK-BENEFIT
SMART-TICKET
SPONDULICKS
TAKE-HOME PAY
TRANSIT-DUTY
TURNOVER TAX

12

CURRENCY NOTE
DISBURSEMENT
EARNEST-MONEY
EARNEST-PENNY
EXCHANGE RATE
GOLD STANDARD
HARD CURRENCY
PASSAGE-MONEY
PAY-AS-YOU-EARN
RECOGNISANCE
REMUNERATION
RETAINING FEE
SEVERANCE PAY
SHARE-CAPITAL
SOFT CURRENCY
STATE PENSION
STERLING AREA
SUBSCRIPTION
TREASURY NOTE

TRIBUTE MONEY
UNDERPAYMENT

13

CONSIDERATION
DILAPIDATIONS
EIGHTEENPENCE
EXCHEQUER BILL
FIDDLER'S MONEY
INLAND REVENUE
MINT CONDITION
OLD AGE PENSION
PAR OF EXCHANGE
POST-WAR CREDIT
PURCHASE MONEY
REIMBURSEMENT
SPENDING MONEY
TRIAL OF THE PYX
VALUE-ADDED TAX
WIDOW'S PENSION

14

BUREAU DE CHANGE
DIRECT TAXATION
FIELD ALLOWANCE
PEPPERCORN RENT
PROMISSORY NOTE
REVALORISATION
SUCCESSION DUTY
SUPERANNUATION
SURRENDER VALUE
THREE-FARTHINGS
THREE-HALFPENCE
UNEARNED INCOME

15

CAPITAL GAINS TAX
CAPITATION GRANT
EASTER OFFERINGS
EXCHANGE CONTROL
GOLDEN HANDSHAKE
PROTECTION MONEY
PURCHASING POWER
REDUNDANCY MONEY
RESERVE CURRENCY
SPECIAL RETAINER
SUBSCRIPTION FEE

FOOD – CONFECTIONERY & DESSERTS

3

BUN
GUM
ICE
PIE

4

BABA
CAKE
CHOU
CONE
DROP
DUFF
FLAN
FOOL
PUFF
RICE
ROCK
RUSK
SAGO
SNAP
TART
WHIP

5

BOMBE
CANDY
COUPE
CRISP
FUDGE
ICING
JELLY
LOLLY
SCONE
SWEET
TANSY
WAFER

6

AFTERS
BONBON
BOUCHÉ
CACHOU
COMFIT
COOKIE
CORNET

CRISPS
DRAGÉE
DUNDEE
ÉCLAIR
FARINA
GÂTEAU
HALVAH
HUMBUG
JUJUBE
JUMBAL
JUNKET
MOUSSE
MUFFIN
NOUGAT
PARKIN
PASTRY
SORBET
SPONGE
SUNDAE
SWEETY
TOFFEE
TRIFLE
WAFFLE

7

ALCORZA
BANNOCK
BATH BUN
BISCUIT
BOURBON
BRIOCHE
CARAMEL
CHOC-ICE
CONFECT
CRACKER
CRUMPET
CUP-CAKE
DESSERT
FONDANT
ICED BUN
JAM PUFF
JAM TART
JANNOCK
MADEIRA
NAIL-ROD
OLYKOEK
PARFAIT
PIKELET
POPCORN
POPADUM

PRALINE
PRETZEL
PUDDING
RATAFIA
RUM BABA
RYE ROLL
SHERBET
SWEETIE
TAPIOCA
TARTLET
TEA-CAKE
TRUFFLE

8

ACID-DROP
APPLE-PIE
BULL'S-EYE
CONFETTI
CORN-BALL
CRACKNEL
DOUGHNUT
FROSTING
FRUIT-GUM
HARDBAKE
HARD TACK
ICE-CREAM
ICE-LOLLY
LICORICE
LOAF-CAKE
LOLLIPOP
MACAROON
MARZIPAN
MERINGUE
MINCE-PIE
NAPOLEON
NOISETTE
PANDOWDY
PASTILLE
PEAR-DROP
PLUM-CAKE
PLUM-DUFF
QUIDDANY
ROCK-CAKE
ROLY-POLY
ROSE-DROP
SEED-CAKE
SEMOLINA
SILLABUB
SLAB-CAKE
SNOWBALL

STICKJAW
SYLLABUB
TORTILLA
TURNOVER
WATER-ICE

9

ANGEL-CAKE
APPLE-TART
BARNBRACK
BRIDECAKE
BUBBLE-GUM
CHARLOTTE
CHERRY-PIE
CHOCOLATE
CREAM-CAKE
CREAM-HORN
DIGESTIVE
DROP-SCONE
EASTER EGG
FAIRY-CAKE
FANCY-CAKE
FRUIT-CAKE
FRUIT-TART
FRIEDCAKE
GARIBALDI
GENOA CAKE
GINGER-NUT
HONEYCOMB
JELLY-BABY
JEQUIRITY
LARDY CAKE
LAYER CAKE
LEMON-DROP
LIQUORICE
MADELEINE
NONPAREIL
PEARL-SAGO
PETIT FOUR
POUND-CAKE
SALLY LUNN
SHORTCAKE
SODA-SCONE
SPICE-CAKE
SPUN SUGAR
STICKY BUN
SUGAR-PLUM
SWEET-MEAT
SWISS ROLL
TIPSY CAKE

WAFER-CAKE
WARDEN PIE

10

BABA AU RHUM
BAKED APPLE
BATH OLIVER
BATTENBURG
BLANCMANGE
BRANDY-BALL
BRANDY-SNAP
CANDY FLOSS
CHEESECAKE
CHELSEA BUN
CHEWING-GUM
CONFECTION
CREAM-SLICE
CURRANT-BUN
CUSTARD-PIE
DUNDEE CAKE
DUNDERFUNK
ECCLES CAKE
FRANGIPANI
FRUIT SALAD
GINGER-CAKE
GINGER-SNAP
HOKEY-POKEY
JOHNNY-CAKE
PEACH MELBA
PEPPER-CAKE
PEPPERMINT
SEA-BISCUIT
SHERBET-DAB
SHORTBREAD
SIMNEL-CAKE
SPONGE-CAKE
SPOTTED DOG
SUGAR-CANDY
SWEET-STUFF
WALNUT-WHIP

11

ANISEED-BALL
BAKED ALASKA
BANANA SPLIT
BANBURY CAKE
BARLEY SUGAR
BOILED SWEET

119

FOOD – CONFECTIONERY & DESSERTS

BROWN GEORGE
CURRANT-CAKE
CUSTARD TART
FRUIT SUNDAE
GINGERBREAD
HOT CROSS BUN
JAM DOUGHNUT
MADEIRA CAKE
MARSHMALLOW
PLUM-PUDDING
PROFITEROLE
RICE-BISCUIT
RICE-PUDDING
SAFFRON-CAKE
SIMNEL-BREAD
SPOTTED DICK
SUET-PUDDING
TOFFEE-APPLE
TREACLE-TART
TUTTI-FRUTTI
WEDDING-CAKE
WINE-BISCUIT

12

APPLE-CRUMBLE
APPLE-FRITTER
APPLE STRUDEL
BAKED JAM-ROLL
BAKEWELL TART
BUTTERSCOTCH
CREAM CRACKER

CRÈME CARAMEL
CURRANT-JELLY
CUSTARD CREAM
DROPPED-SCONE
MAID OF HONOUR
PEARL-TAPIOCA
PORTLAND SAGO
SHERBET-LEMON
SHERRY TRIFLE
SHIP'S BISCUIT
SINGING HINNY
SPEARMINT GUM
SPONGE-FINGER
WATER-BISCUIT

13

APPLE-TURNOVER
BANANA-FRITTER
BUTTER-BISCUIT
CASTLE PUDDING
CHOCOLATE-DROP
CONFECTIONERY
DOLLY MIXTURES
FRUIT COCKTAIL
KISSING-COMFIT
LEMON MERINGUE
MARRONS GLACÉS
MILK CHOCOLATE
MILLEFEUILLES
NEAPOLITAN ICE
SPONGE-PUDDING

SUMMER PUDDING
TREACLE TOFFEE

14

BOURBON BISCUIT
CABINET-PUDDING
CHARLOTTE RUSSE
CHOCOLATE FLAKE
COLLEGE-PUDDING
GINGERBREAD-MAN
GOOSEBERRY-FOOL
GOOSEBERRY-TART
PARLIAMENT-CAKE
PEPPERMINT DROP
PETTICOAT-TAILS
PLAIN CHOCOLATE
PONTEFRACT-CAKE
RHUBARB-CRUMBLE
STEAMED PUDDING
TREACLE PUDDING
TURKISH DELIGHT

15

CHOCOLATE BUTTON
CHOCOLATE RIPPLE
MACARONI-PUDDING
QUEEN OF PUDDINGS
RASPBERRY RIPPLE

FOOD – CULINARY TERMS

3

FAT
KAI
ORT
PAT
TEA

4

BASE
BITE
DIET
DISH
FARE
FAST
FILL
FOOD
GRUB
HEEL
HERB
KEEP
LARD
MEAL
MENU
NOSH
PECK
SLAB
SNAP
SPIT
STIR
SUET
TACK
TANG
TUCK

5

BEANO
BOARD
CARTE
CHUCK
COVER
DEVIL
FEAST
GORGE
GRILL
GUSTO
ICING
LUNCH

ROAST
ROUND
SALAD
SCOFF
SCRAN
SLICE
SMACK
SNACK
SOUSE
SPICE
TABLE
TASTE
TWANG
YEAST

6

AFTERS
BAKING
BROACH
BRUNCH
BUFFET
COURSE
DAINTY
DICING
DINNER
DOUCET
EDIBLE
ENTRÉE
KAIKAI
LEAVEN
MORSEL
NACKET
OREXIS
PICKLE
PICNIC
PIPING
RATION
RECIPE
REGALE
RELISH
SETTER
SIMMER
SIPPET
SNATCH
SOLIDS
SPREAD
STAPLE
STODGE
SUPPER
TIFFIN

TITBIT
VIANDS

7

ALIMENT
BANQUET
BLOW-OUT
BOILING
CARVING
COCTION
COMMONS
COOKERY
COOKING
COOKOUT
CUISINE
DESSERT
EATABLE
ESSENCE
FILLING
FLAVOUR
FORMULA
GARNISH
GELATIN
HELPING
HIGH TEA
LIQUIDS
MEAT-TEA
PORTION
PROTEIN
RATAFIA
RATIONS
REGIMEN
SALTING
SAVOURY
SEA-FOOD
SERVICE
SERVING
SETTING
SIFTING
SLICING
SOUPÇON
SOUSING
SPICERY
SQUEEZE
STEWING
SUCCADE
TOPPING
VANILLA
VITAMIN
ZAKUSKA

8

ADDITIVE
À LA CARTE
APPETITE
BARBECUE
BRAISING
BROILING
BROWNING
BUN-FIGHT
CLAMBAKE
COCOA-FAT
CONSERVE
DÉJEUNER
DELICACY
DRESSING
ESCULENT
FAST FOOD
GELATINE
GLUTTONY
GRILLADE
GRILLING
GULOSITY
KICKSHAW
LEFT-OVER
LUNCHEON
MARINADE
MOUTHFUL
NUNCHEON
OPSONIUM
ORDINARY
PIQUANCY
PRESERVE
ROASTING
ROUGHAGE
SALADING
SCALDING
SEASONER
SIDE-DISH
SMÖRBRÖD
STIRRING
STOCK-POT
STUFFING
SUGARING
SUPPLIES
TOASTING
TURNSPIT
VICTUALS

9

ALMOND-OIL
APPETISER
BARMECIDE
BEANFEAST
BLANCHING
BREAKFAST
BUTTERFAT
COLOURING
CONDIMENT
EDIBILITY
ENTREMETS
EPULATION
FOODSTUFF
FULL-BOARD
GROCERIES
GUSTATION
HALF-BOARD
HOT-AND-HOT
ISINGLASS
LEAVENING
NUTRIMENT
NUTRITION
OPSOMANIA
PAPILLOTE
RÉCHAUFFÉ
REFECTION
SALAD HERB
SEASONING
SIDE-SALAD
STRAINING
SWEETNESS
THICKENER
WHOLEFOOD

10

AFTERTASTE
BAKING SODA
BILL OF FARE
CHOTA-HAZRI
COOKING-FAT
COOKING-OIL
DATE-CODING
DUTCH TREAT
FLAVOURING
FOOD VALUES
FORK SUPPER
FRICANDEAU
GASTROLOGY

121

FOOD – CULINARY TERMS

GASTRONOMY
GORMANDISM
INGREDIENT
IRON RATION
KITCHEN-FEE
MEAL TICKET
MIXED GRILL
MUTTON-SUET
NOURRITURE
PEACH-WATER
PLAT DU JOUR
PROVISIONS
PURVEYANCE
REGALEMENT
SALAD PLANT
SORBIC ACID
SPECIALITY
STAPLE DIET
SUSTENANCE
SWEETENING
SWEET TOOTH
TABLE D'HOTE
TENDERISER
THICKENING
TURNBROACH

11

BED AND BOARD

CHEF D'OEUVRE
COMESTIBLES
CONSISTENCY
COVER CHARGE
DEGUSTATION
GOURMANDISE
HORS D'OEUVRE
INEDIBILITY
NOURISHMENT
PARSON'S NOSE
PREPARATION
REFRESHMENT
REFRIGERANT
SELF-SERVICE
SMÖRGÅSBORD
SPREAD-EAGLE
SPUD-BASHING
VICTUALLAGE
WATER-SOUCHY
YEAST POWDER

12

AMERICAN PLAN
BAKING-POWDER
BOUQUET GARNI
DAIRY PRODUCE
DAIRY PRODUCT
DELICATESSEN

EUROPEAN PLAN
FORK LUNCHEON
HAUTE CUISINE
KITCHEN-STUFF
PANIFICATION
PRESERVATION
PRESERVATIVE
REFRESHMENTS
SHORT COMMONS

13

CUSTARD POWDER
MEALS-ON-WHEELS
REFRIGERATION

14

RUNNING-BANQUET

15

BED AND BREAKFAST
CONVENIENCE FOOD
LUNCHEON VOUCHER

FOOD – FRUIT, NUTS & BERRIES

3

COB
FIG
HAW
HIP
NUT

4

AKEE
BAEL

BITO
CRAB
DATE
GAGE
GEAN
KAKI
MAST
PEAR
PEPO
PILI
PINE
PLUM

SLOE
SNOW
TUNA
UGLI

5

ACORN
APPLE
ARECA
ASSAI
BERRY

BETEL
DRUPE
FRUIT
GOURD
GRAPE
GUAVA
JAFFA
LEMON
MANGO
MELON
MERRY
MOREL

NELIS
OLIVE
PAPAW
PEACH
PECAN
TOKAY

6

ACAJOU
ACHENE
ACINUS

ALMOND
ANANAS
BANANA
BEN-NUT
BEURRÉ
BIFFIN
CASHAW
CASHEW
CHERRY
CITRON
COB-NUT
DAMSON

DOG-HIP
EMBLIC
JUJUBE
KARAKA
KERNEL
LICHEE
LITCHI
LONGAN
LOQUAT
LYCHEE
MAMMEE
MEDLAR
MUSCAT
NARRAS
OIL-NUT
ORANGE
PAPAYA
PAWPAW
PEANUT
PIG-NUT
PIPPIN
POMELO
QUINCE
RENNET
RUSSET
SECKAL
TOMATO
WALNUT
WAMPEE
WARDEN

7

APRICOT
AVOCADO
BABASSU
BALDWIN
BILIMBI
BRINJAL
CATAWBA
COCONUT
CODLING
COSTARD
CRAB-NUT
CUMQUAT
EGG-PLUM
FILBERT
GENIPAP
GOAT-FIG
HAMBURG
HAUTBOY

HOG-PLUM
KUMQUAT
MALMSEY
MANJACK
MAY-DUKE
MORELLO
NAARTJE
NARTJIE
PARÁ NUT
PILI-NUT
PINGUIN
POMEROY
PUMPKIN
PUPUNHA
QUETSCH
RIBSTON
ROSE-HIP
RUDDOCK
SALIGOT
SATSUMA
SHEA-NUT
SOUR-SOP
TANGELO
VALONIA
WILDING
WINE-SAP

8

AGUACATE
ARECA-NUT
BAYBERRY
BERGAMOT
BETEL-NUT
BILBERRY
BLANQUET
BREADNUT
CALABASH
CAPRIFIG
CEDAR-NUT
CHESTNUT
COCOPLUM
COQUILLA
COWBERRY
CREAM-NUT
DATE-PLUM
DEW-BERRY
DOGBERRY
EARTHNUT
EGG-APPLE
EGG-FRUIT

FEN-BERRY
FOXBERRY
FOX-GRAPE
GOOSEGOG
GREENING
HANEPOOT
HAZEL-NUT
IVORY-NUT
JONATHAN
KALUMPIT
MAD-APPLE
MANDARIN
MULBERRY
MUSCADEL
MUSCATEL
MUSK-PEAR
MUSK-PLUM
PEARMAIN
PECAN-NUT
PLANTAIN
QUEENING
RAMBUTAN
SEBESTEN
SHADDOCK
SWEETING
SWEET-SOP
TIGER-NUT

9

ALGARROBA
AUBERGINE
BANEBERRY
BEACH-MAST
BLAEBERRY
BLUEBERRY
BRAZIL NUT
BUSH-FRUIT
BUTTERNUT
CANDLE-NUT
CANTALOUP
CARAMBOLA
CASHEW-NUT
CHERIMOYA
CHOKE-PEAR
COCO-DE-MER
COROZO NUT
CRAB-APPLE
CRANBERRY
CROW-BERRY
DEERBERRY

GREENGAGE
GROUND-NUT
HAANEPOOT
HINDBERRY
ILLIPE NUT
INDIAN FIG
JACK-FRUIT
JENNETING
JOHN-APPLE
JUNEBERRY
KING-APPLE
KIWI FRUIT
LOVE-APPLE
MANZANITA
MELOCOTON
MOCKER-NUT
MONKEY-NUT
MUSK-MELON
MYROBALAN
NASEBERRY
NECTARINE
NONPAREIL
ORTANIQUE
PERSIMMON
PHYSIC-NUT
PINEAPPLE
PISTACHIO
POPPERING
RASPBERRY
REDSTREAK
ROSE-APPLE
RUSSETING
SASKATOON
SNOW-BERRY
SOAPBERRY
SORB-APPLE
SOUARI-NUT
STAR-APPLE
TANGERINE
VICTORINE
WALL-FRUIT
WILD-GRAPE
WINEBERRY

10

BLACKBERRY
BLACKHEART
BLADDER-NUT
BREADFRUIT
BUFFALO-NUT

FOOD – FRUIT, NUTS & BERRIES

CHERRY-PLUM
CHOKEBERRY
CLEMENTINE
CLOUDBERRY
CONFERENCE
CORALBERRY
DAMASK PLUM
ELDERBERRY
FIRST-FRUIT
FRENCH PLUM
GOOSEBERRY
GRANADILLA
GRENADILLA
GRAPEFRUIT
IDAEAN VINE
JARGONELLE
LOGANBERRY
MANGOSTEEN
MARKING-NUT
MUSSEL-PLUM
PALMYRA-NUT
PEPPERCORN
PICK-CHEESE
POME-CITRON
QUARRENDER
REDCURRANT
RHINE-BERRY
ROWAN-BERRY
SALAL-BERRY
SCALD-BERRY
SOUR ORANGE
STONE-FRUIT
STRAWBERRY
SUGAR-APPLE
SWEET-WATER
TREE-TOMATO
WATER-LEMON
WATER-MELON
WHITEHEART
WILD CHERRY
YOUNGBERRY

CANDLE-BERRY
CHOKECHERRY
CITRUS FRUIT
CLEARING-NUT
COFFEE-BERRY
EATING-APPLE
GOLDENBERRY
GRANNY SMITH
HUCKLEBERRY
INDIAN BERRY
JAMAICA PLUM
MALAKATOONE
MAMMEE APPLE
MONKEY-BREAD
NAVEL-ORANGE
OSAGE-ORANGE
PIGEON-BERRY
POMEGRANATE
POMPELMOOSE
POTATO-APPLE
PRICKLY-PEAR
QUANDONG-NUT
QUINSY-BERRY
SALMON-BERRY
SAPUCAIA-NUT
SCUPPERNONG
SWEET ORANGE
YELLOW BERRY

12

BITTER ORANGE
BLACKCURRANT
BRAMBLE-BERRY
COOKING-APPLE
CUISSE-MADAME
CUSTARD-APPLE
GROUND-CHERRY
HOTTENTOT FIG
MAMMEE-SAPOTA
PASSION-FRUIT
PERSIAN BERRY
RACCOON-BERRY
SASSAFRAS-NUT
SEASIDE-GRAPE
SERVICE-BERRY
VICTORIA PLUM

WHORTLEBERRY
WINTER-CHERRY
WINTER-CLOVER

13

ALLIGATOR PEAR
BLADDER-CHERRY
BULLOCK'S-HEART
CATHERINE PEAR
DOUBLE-COCONUT
HONEYDEW-MELON
HORSE-CHESTNUT
KANGAROO-APPLE
MARMALADE PLUM
POPPERING PEAR
QUEENSLAND-NUT
RIBSTON PIPPIN
SAPODILLA PLUM
SEEK-NO-FURTHER
SEVILLE ORANGE
ST ANTHONY'S NUT
SWEET-CHESTNUT
WATER-CHESTNUT

14

ALLIGATOR APPLE
BARBADOS CHERRY
BLENHEIM ORANGE
CALABASH NUTMEG
CAPE GOOSEBERRY
JAPANESE MEDLAR
MANDARIN ORANGE
PARTRIDGE-BERRY
RIPSTONE PIPPIN
VEGETABLE IVORY
WORCESTER-BERRY

15

GOLDEN DELICIOUS
MOUNTAIN BRAMBLE
SPANISH CHESTNUT
VEGETABLE MARROW

11

ANCHOVY-PEAR
BLACK WALNUT
BLOOD ORANGE
BOYSENBERRY

FOOD – GENERAL FOOD

3

AVA
BAP
DIP
EGG
GUR
JAM
PAP
PIE
POY
PUD
SOP
SOY
WAD

4

BRAN
BRIE
CHIP
CURD
DILL
EDAM
FLAN
GHEE
HASH
LOAF
MACE
MASH
MEAL
MUSH
OATS
OKRA
OLEO
OLIO
PÂTÉ
PEEL
PONE
RICE
RIND
ROLL
ROUX
RUSK
SAGE
SALT
SAMP
SKYR
SLAW
SOUP
STEW

WHEY

5

ASPIC
AZYME
BAGEL
BASIL
BREAD
BROSE
BROTH
BUTTY
CABOC
CHIVE
CLOVE
CREAM
CRÊME
CRISP
CRUMB
CRUST
CURRY
DOUGH
FARCE
FLOUR
GOUDA
GRAIN
GRAVY
GRIST
GRITS
GROAT
GRUEL
GUMBO
HONEY
HOOSH
JELLY
KABOB
KEBAB
MARGE
MATZO
MEBOS
PASTA
PASTE
PASTY
PATTY
PILAU
PIZZA
PRUNE
PURÉE
ROOTY
SALMI
SAUCE

SHCHI
SOUSE
STOCK
SUGAR
SYRUP
THYME
TOAST
WIMPY

6

BANGER
BATTER
BISQUE
BORSCH
BURGOO
BUTTER
CANAPÉ
CASSIA
CATSUP
CECILS
CEREAL
CHEESE
CHILLI
COBURG
COMPOT
CROÛTE
DAMPER
DUNLOP
FAGGOT
FONDUE
FROISE
GINGER
HAGGIS
HOMINY
HOT DOG
HOTPOT
JUNKET
KANTEN
KONFYT
MEALIE
MUESLI
NECTAR
NOCAKE
NOODLE
NUTMEG
OMELET
ORGEAT
OXTAIL
PAELLA
PANADA

PASTRY
PEPPER
PICKLE
PINOLE
POLONY
POTAGE
QUICHE
RAGOUT
RAISIN
RED-DOG
RELISH
SALAMI
SEA-PIE
SKILLY
SPREAD
TAMALE
TSAMBA
YAOURT
YOGURT

7

BAY LEAF
BLEWITS
BLOOMER
BOTARGO
BOUILLI
BOURSIN
CARAMEL
CAYENNE
CHAPATI
CHEDDAR
CHICORY
CHOWDER
CHUTNEY
COB-LOAF
COMPOTE
COWHEEL
CROÛTON
CURRANT
CUSTARD
DARIOLE
FRITTER
FRITURE
GNOCCHI
GOULASH
GRUYÈRE
HARICOT
JAGGERY
KEBBOCK
KETCHUP

LASAGNE
MEAT-PIE
MELBURY
MILK-SOP
MUSTARD
OREGANO
PANCAKE
PANOCHA
PAP-MEAT
PAPRIKA
PARSLEY
PEA-SOUP
PIMENTO
PLUM JAM
POLENTA
POLLARD
POPCORN
PORK-PIE
POTTAGE
PUDDING
RAMEKIN
RAREBIT
RAVIOLI
RISOTTO
RISSOLE
SAPSAGO
SAUSAGE
SAVELOY
SCALLOP
SCOLLOP
SOUFFLÉ
STILTON
STRUDEL
SULTANA
SUPPAWN
TABASCO
TARTINE
TERRINE
TREACLE
TRUFFLE
VANILLA
VINEGAR
YOGHURT

8

ALLSPICE
AMBROSIA
BAKEMEAT
BÉCHAMEL
BEL PAESE

FOOD – GENERAL FOOD

BOUILLON
CARDAMOM
CHOP-SUEY
CHOW-MEIN
CINNAMON
COLESLAW
CONSOMMÉ
COUSCOUS
CRUDITÉS
DEMERARA
DOUGHBOY
DRIPPING
DUMPLING
EMMENTAL
FEDELINI
FISHBALL
FISHCAKE
FLAPJACK
FLUMMERY
FRIED EGG
FRUMENTY
HALF-LOAF
HOTCHPOT
JULIENNE
KAOLIANG
KEDGEREE
KROMESKY
LOBLOLLY
MACARONI
MARJORAM
MATELOTE
MEAT-BALL
MILK-LOAF
MOLASSES
MOUSSAKA
MUSHROOM
OLIVE OIL
OMELETTE
OREGANUM
PARMESAN
PEMMICAN
PIECRUST
PORRIDGE
PRUNELLO
PURSLANE
QUENELLE
RACAHOUT
RICE-SOUP
ROSEMARY
RYE-BREAD
RYE-FLOUR
SALAD OIL

SANDWICH
SHRED-PIE
SLAPJACK
SOFT ROLL
SOY SAUCE
SQUAB-PIE
STUFFING
SUKIYAKI
TARRAGON
TEA-BREAD
TURMERIC
WHITE-POT
ZWIEBACK

ANTIPASTO
BAKED BEAN
BÉARNAISE
BEEF-BROTH
BEET-SUGAR
BOILED EGG
BREAD-CORN
BROOM-CORN
BROWN RICE
CAMEMBERT
CANE-SUGAR
CASSAREEP
CASSEROLE
CASSOULET
CHIPOLATA
CLAPBREAD
COCK-BROTH
COLCANNON
CORN-BREAD
CORN-FLOUR
CROISSANT
CROQUETTE
CROUSTADE
DAMSON JAM
DATE-SUGAR
DIET-BREAD
DIKA-BREAD
EGG-POWDER
EWE-CHEESE
FISH-PASTE
FISH-SAUCE
FRICASSEE
GALANTINE

GALINGALE
GOA BUTTER
GRAVY-SOUP
GRENADINE
HAMBURGER
HIVE-HONEY
HUMBLE-PIE
IRISH STEW
JARLSBERG
LAVA-BREAD
LEICESTER
LEMON CURD
LEMON PEEL
LOAF-SUGAR
LOBSCOUSE
LUMBER-PIE
LUMP-SUGAR
LYMESWOLD
MACÉDOINE
MARGARINE
MARMALADE
MEAT-PASTE
MINCEMEAT
MINT-SAUCE
MUSCOVADO
NUT-BUTTER
ONION SOUP
PALM-SUGAR
PEASE-MEAL
PEASE-SOUP
POT-LIQUOR
POT POURRI
PUFF-PASTE
RAISED PIE
REVALENTA
RICE-FLOUR
ROCK-TRIPE
ROQUEFORT
RUM-BUTTER
SCOTCH EGG
SOURDOUGH
SOYA FLOUR
SPAGHETTI
SUCCOTASH
SUGAR-LOAF
SWEET-CORN
VOL-AU-VENT
WHEAT-CORN
WHEATGERM
WHOLEMEAL
WILD HONEY
WOOD-HONEY

APPLE SAUCE
APRICOT JAM
BARLEYCORN
BEEFBURGER
BLACK BREAD
BLANQUETTE
BLUE-CHEESE
BREAD-CRUMB
BREADSTUFF
BROWN BREAD
BROWN SAUCE
BROWN SUGAR
BUCK-RABBIT
CAERPHILLY
CANNELLONI
CAPER-SAUCE
CASSUMUNAR
CELERY SOUP
CHAUDFROID
CORNFLAKES
CORNSTARCH
CRACKLINGS
CRUSTY ROLL
DAIRY-CREAM
DERBYSHIRE
DIKA-BUTTER
EGG-ON-TOAST
FANCY BREAD
FISH-FINGER
FLESH-BROTH
FLORENTINE
FRENCH LOAF
FRIED-BREAD
GORGONZOLA
HAMBURGHER
HODGEPODGE
HOTCHPOTCH
ICING SUGAR
INDIAN MEAL
JARDINIÈRE
LANCASHIRE
MACONOCHIE
MALAGUETTA
MAPLE-SYRUP
MAYONNAISE
MINESTRONE
MOZZARELLA
ORANGE PEEL
OXTAIL SOUP
PALM-BUTTER

PEASE-BROSE
PICCALILLI
PICKLED EGG
POACHED EGG
POTATO-CHIP
PUDDING-PIE
PUFF-PASTRY
SAGE CHEESE
SALAD-CREAM
SALMAGUNDI
SAUERKRAUT
SHEA-BUTTER
SHISH KEBAB
SOUP-MAIGRE
STRACCHINO
TOMATO SOUP
TURTLE SOUP
VERMICELLI
WATER-GRUEL
WHEAT-BERRY
WHITE BREAD
ZABAGLIONE

11

BAKED POTATO
BURNT ALMOND
CARAWAY-SEED
CASTER SUGAR
CHEESE-STRAW
CHICKEN SOUP
CLAM-CHOWDER
COTTAGE LOAF
COULOMMIERS
CREAM-CHEESE
CURRANT-LOAF
CURRY-POWDER
DOUBLE CREAM
FOUR-POUNDER
FRANKFURTER
FRENCH BREAD
FRENCH-FRIED
FRENCH STICK
FRENCH TOAST
GARAM MASALA
GOLDEN SYRUP
HOG'S PUDDING
HORSE-RADISH
INDIAN BREAD
KOKUM BUTTER
LEMON CHEESE

MAHWA BUTTER
MORNAY SAUCE
OLLA-PODRIDA
OYSTER-PATTY
PÉRIGORD PIE
POTATO-CRISP
RATATOUILLE
ROAST POTATO
SAUSAGE-MEAT
SAUSAGE-ROLL
SCOTCH BROTH
STRONG FLOUR
STRONG WHEAT
SUET-PUDDING
TOMATO SAUCE
VICHYSSOISE
VINAIGRETTE
WELSH RABBIT
WENSLEYDALE

12

BEANS-ON-TOAST
BLACK-PUDDING
BLOOD-PUDDING
CHEESEBURGER
CLOTTED CREAM
CLUB SANDWICH
COCKIELEEKIE
CORNISH PASTY
CRESCENT ROLL
CURRANT BREAD
DAMSON CHEESE
GARLIC-BUTTER
HASTY PUDDING
JACKET POTATO
MANGO CHUTNEY
MILK-PORRIDGE
MULLIGATAWNY
MUSHROOM SOUP
OPEN SANDWICH
PEANUT BUTTER
PEASE-PUDDING
PICKLED ONION
PROCESSED PEA
PUMPERNICKEL
QUARTERN LOAF
RAISED PASTRY
RASPBERRY JAM
SCRAMBLED EGG

SHEPHERD'S PIE
SOUBISE SAUCE
TARAMASALATA
TARTARE SAUCE
TRIPLE-DECKER
VELOUTÉ SAUCE
WHIPPED CREAM
WHITE-PUDDING

13

BOUILLABAISSE
CAYENNE PEPPER
COCONUT-BUTTER
CONDENSED MILK
CORIANDER-SEED
COTTAGE CHEESE
FRENCH MUSTARD
GOOSEBERRY JAM
JAMAICA PEPPER
MUSTARD PICKLE
OLEO-MARGARINE
PALESTINE SOUP
PEASE-PORRIDGE
PRAIRIE-OYSTER
SALAD DRESSING
STANDARD BREAD
STRAWBERRY JAM
TOAD-IN-THE-HOLE
TOMATO KETCHUP

14

BOLOGNA SAUSAGE
BREAD-AND-BUTTER
CRANBERRY SAUCE
ENGLISH MUSTARD
MACARONI CHEESE
MOCK TURTLE SOUP
PÂTÉ DE FOIS GRAS
PICKLED CABBAGE
QUICHE LORRAINE
SCOTCH WOODCOCK
TRIPE AND ONIONS
WHOLEMEAL BREAD
WORCESTER SAUCE

15

BLACKCURRANT JAM

FOOD – GENERAL FOOD

BUBBLE AND SQUEAK
DEVONSHIRE CREAM
EGGS IN MOONSHINE

MUSTARD AND CRESS
REDCURRANT JELLY
RESURRECTION-PIE

SHORTENING-BREAD
WIENER SCHNITZEL

FOOD – MEAT & FISH

3

COD
CUT
DAB
EEL
FAT
HAM
LEG
RIB
ROE

4

BARD
BEEF
CHOP
CRAB
DUCK
FISH
FOWL
GAME
HAKE
HARE
HOCK
JERK
LAMB
LEAN
LOIN
MEAT
NECK
PORK
RUMP
SHIN
SIDE
SOLE

SPAM
TUNA
VEAL
WING

5

BACON
BELLY
BRAWN
BULLY
CAPON
FILET
FLANK
GIGOT
GOOSE
HEART
JERKY
JOINT
LIVER
MINCE
OFFAL
PRAWN
QUAIL
ROAST
SCRAG
SKATE
SKIRT
SLINK
SNAIL
SPRAT
SQUID
STEAK
TRIPE
TROUT
WHELK

6

BREAST
COCKLE
COLLAR
CUTLET
FILLET
FINNAN
FLITCH
FUMADO
GAMMON
GROUSE
HASLET
KIDNEY
KIPPER
MUSSEL
MUTTON
OLIVES
OYSTER
PIGEON
PLAICE
RABBIT
RASHER
SADDLE
SALMON
SCAMPI
SHRIMP
TARGET
TONGUE
TURBOT
TURKEY
TURTLE
WINKLE

7

ANCHOVY

BEEF-HAM
BILTONG
BLOATER
BRISKET
BROILER
BUMMALO
CAVIARE
CHARQUI
CHICKEN
HADDOCK
HALIBUT
HARSLET
HERRING
KNUCKLE
LARDOON
LOBSTER
LONG-PIG
OCTOPUS
OX-LIVER
PANDORE
POULTRY
QUARTER
RED MEAT
ROOSTER
SARDINE
SCALLOP
SIRLOIN
SURLOIN
TOPSIDE
TREPANG
TROTTER
VENISON
WHITING

8

BULL-BEEF

CHUMP END
CRAYFISH
ESCALOPE
ESCARGOT
FLOUNDER
FOIE GRAS
HUNG-BEEF
LAMB CHOP
LEMON-DAB
MACKEREL
NECKBEEF
NOISETTE
OX-TONGUE
PHEASANT
PILCHARD
PORK-CHOP
POT-ROAST
SALT-BEEF
SCRAG-END
SEA-STICK
SHOULDER
SPARE RIB
UNDERCUT

9

AITCHBONE
BEEFSTEAK
BLADEBONE
BULLY-BEEF
CHUMP CHOP
CÔTELETTE
CRACKLING
CRACKNELS
DOVER SOLE
ENTRECÔTE
FORCEMEAT

GRENADINE
HABERDINE
HAMBURGER
LEMON-SOLE
MINCEMEAT
MUTTON-HAM
PARTRIDGE
PETTITOES
POPE'S NOSE
PTARMIGAN
ROAST-BEEF
ROAST-LAMB
ROAST-PORK
RUMP-STEAK
SCHNITZEL
SHELLFISH
STOCKFISH
TOURNEDOS
WHITEBAIT
WHITEBASS
WHITE MEAT

10

BEEFBURGER
BOMBAY DUCK
BROWN TROUT
CHUCK-STEAK
CORNED BEEF
HORSEFLESH
JELLIED EEL
JERKED-MEAT
JUGGED HARE
LAMB-CUTLET
MUTTON-CHOP
PERIWINKLE
RED HERRING
ROCK-SALMON
ROCK-TURBOT
ROMAN SNAIL
SILVERSIDE
SPATCHCOCK
SPITCHCOCK

SQUETEAGUE
SWEETBREAD
T-BONE STEAK
TENDER-LOIN
VEAL-CUTLET
WONGA-WONGA

11

BARON OF BEEF
FILET MIGNON
FILLET STEAK
MINUTE STEAK
PARSON'S NOSE
PORTERHOUSE

12

HARVEST-GOOSE

LUNCHEON-MEAT
MUTTON-CUTLET
NORFOLK CAPON
RAINBOW-TROUT
STREAKY BACON
WHITE HERRING

13

AYLESBURY DUCK
CHÂTEAUBRIAND
SHIELD OF BRAWN
SMOKED HADDOCK

14

PICKLED HERRING

FOOD – VEGETABLES

3

COS
PEA
YAM

4

BEAN
CHOU
COLE
KALE
LEEK
NEEP
SOYA
SPUD
TARO

5

CHARD
CHIVE
CIBOL
COCCO
COLZA
CRESS
FLUKE
NAVEW
ONION
ORACH
PULSE
SAVOY
SWEDE

6

BATATA

CARROT
CELERY
COW-PEA
ENDIVE
FRIJOL
GARLIC
GREENS
KUMARA
LABLAB
LEGUME
LENTIL
LOVAGE
MARROW
MURPHY
POTATO
PRATIE
RADISH
RUNNER
SPROUT
TOMATO

TURNIP

7

CABBAGE
CARDOON
CHICORY
COLLARD
GHERKIN
GOA BEAN
HARICOT
LETTUCE
PARSNIP
PUMPKIN
RAMPION
SALSIFY
SHALLOT
SKIRRET
SPINACH

8

BEETROOT
BORECOLE
BROCCOLI
CELERIAC
CHICK-PEA
COLE-WORT
CUCUMBER
ESCHALOT
HASTINGS
KOHLRABI
LIMA-BEAN
MUSHROOM
RUTABAGA
SCALLION
SOYA-BEAN
SPLIT PEA
TUCKAHOE
ZUCCHINI

FOOD – VEGETABLES

9

ARTICHOKE
ASPARAGUS
AUBERGINE
BREADROOT
BROAD-BEAN
CHICKLING
COLOCYNTH
COURGETTE
CURLY-KALE
FLAGEOLET
GARDEN PEA
HORSE-BEAN
NEW POTATO
PIGEON-PEA
RED PEPPER
ROUNCEVAL
SUGAR-BEAN
SWEETCORN
TREE-ONION
VEGETABLE

KING EDWARD
LOCUST-BEAN
RED CABBAGE
RUNNER-BEAN
SCORZONERA
SCOTCH KALE
STRING-BEAN
SWISS CHARD
WATER-CRESS
WELSH ONION

11

CAULIFLOWER
CURLY-GREENS
EGYPTIAN PEA
FRENCH ONION
GREEN PEPPER
HARICOT BEAN
SCARLET-BEAN
SPRING ONION
SWEET-POTATO
WEBB'S WONDER

10

BUTTER-BEAN
COS LETTUCE
FRENCH BEAN
GREENSTUFF
KIDNEY-BEAN

12

COLOQUINTIDA
CORN ON THE COB
INDIAN TURNIP
KIDNEY-POTATO

MARROWFAT PEA
MARROW-SQUASH
SAVOY CABBAGE
SPANISH ONION
SPRING GREENS
WHITE CABBAGE
YELLOW PEPPER

13

ASPARAGUS TIPS
PRAIRIE-TURNIP
SCARLET-RUNNER
SPRING CABBAGE

14

BRUSSELS SPROUT
CABBAGE-LETTUCE
CHICKLING-VETCH
GLOBE ARTICHOKE
ICEBERG LETTUCE

15

VEGETABLE-MARROW

FUELS, LIGHTS & FIRE

3

ASH
COB
DIP
GAS
LOG
LOX
OIL
RAY

4

BEAM
BULB
BURN
COAL
COKE
CROW
DERV
FIRE
FUEL
FUNK
GLOW
HEAT
KILN
LAMP
LEAR
LINK
OAST
OVEN
PEAT
PUNK
SLUT
SOOT
SPOT
WICK
WOOD

5

ASHES
BLAZE
CERGE
DEVIL
EMBER
FLAME
FLARE
FLASH
FLINT

FLOAT
FOOTS
FORGE
FUMES
FUSEE
GLARE
GLEAM
GLINT
JUICE
LIGHT
MATCH
METHS
SHAFT
SHEEN
SHINE
SMOKE
SPARK
SPILL
STICK
STOVE
TAPER
TORCH
VESTA

6

BATTEN
BEACON
BENZOL
BOILER
BOUGIE
BURGEE
BURNER
BUTANE
CANDLE
CANNEL
COCKLE
COOKER
CUPOLA
DAZZLE
DIMMER
EMBERS
ETHYNE
FAGGOT
FINERY
FIRING
FULGOR
FUSAIN
GAS-JET
HEATER
HEXANE

HYDYNE
LAMPAD
LUSTRE
MANGEL
MANTLE
MARKER
MAROON
OCTANE
OIL-GAS
PENCIL
PETROL
PRIMUS
REFLET
SCONCE
SCORCH
SUN-RAY
TALLOW
TINDER
WARMTH
WINKER

7

ARC-LAMP
ASTATKI
BENZINE
BENZOLE
BITUMEN
BONFIRE
BRAZIER
BURNING
CARBIDE
CINDERS
CLINKER
COAL-GAS
COAL-OIL
COAL-TAR
COMBUST
CRESSET
ELEMENT
FIDIBUS
FLASHER
FLICKER
FOG-LAMP
FURNACE
GASAHOL
GAS-BUOY
GAS-FIRE
GAS-LAMP
GASOHOL
GAS-OVEN

GAS-RING
GEORDIE
GLIMMER
GLISTEN
GLITTER
HEATING
LAMPION
LANTERN
LIGHTER
LIGNITE
LUCENCY
LUCIFER
LUCIGEN
METHANE
OIL-LAMP
PADELLA
PENDANT
PIT-COAL
PROPANE
ROASTER
ROCK-OIL
SEA-FIRE
SHIMMER
SPARKLE
SUNBEAM
SUN-LAMP
TWINKLE

8

ARC-LIGHT
BALE-FIRE
BARBECUE
BLOWLAMP
BULL'S-EYE
CALOR GAS
CAMP-FIRE
CHARCOAL
CONGREVE
CREMATOR
CRUDE OIL
DAVY-LAMP
DICE-COAL
DIGESTER
DRY LIGHT
FIRE-WOOD
FLAMBEAU
FLAMELET
FULGENCY
GASALIER
GASLIGHT

GASOLENE
GASOLINE
GAS-POKER
GAS-STOVE
GLOWLAMP
HEADLAMP
HOME-FIRE
ICE-BLINK
IGNITION
INCENSOR
KEROSENE
KEROSINE
KINDLING
LAMBENCY
LIGHTING
LIME-KILN
LOCOFOCO
LUMINANT
LUMINARY
MARSH-GAS
MATCHBOX
METHANOL
MOONBEAM
NEED-FIRE
NEON LAMP
OPEN FIRE
PARAFFIN
PHOTOGEN
PILOT-JET
PORT-FIRE
PRODUCER
RADIANCE
RADIANCY
RADIATOR
REAR-LAMP
RED LIGHT
SCALDINO
SHALE OIL
SIDE-LAMP
SMOULDER
SPARKLER
SPARKLET
SPLINTER
SPOTLAMP
STREAMER
SUNBURST
SUNLIGHT
SUNSHINE
TAN-BALLS
TANDOORI
THERMITE
TORCHÈRE

FUELS, LIGHTS & FIRE

TRIPTANE
VESUVIAN
WAX-LIGHT
WILDFIRE
WOOD-COAL

9

ACETYLENE
BENZOLINE
BLIND-COAL
BLOCK-COAL
BOTTLE-GAS
BRICK-KILN
BROWN COAL
CANDLE-END
CONVECTOR
CORPOSANT
EPIPOLISM
FIREBRAND
FIRELIGHT
FIRE-STICK
FLASH-BULB
FLOOD-LAMP
FOOTLIGHT
GAS-BURNER
GAS-COOKER
GAS-MANTLE
GLORY-HOLE
HEADLIGHT
HIGHLIGHT
KITCHENER
LAMPADARY
LAMP-GLASS
LAMPLIGHT
LIGHT-BULB
LIGHTNING
LIMELIGHT
LONG-SIXES
LUMINAIRE
LUMINANCE
MATCHWOOD
MODERATOR
MOONLIGHT
MOONSHINE
NEON LIGHT
NIGHTFIRE
OIL-BURNER
PETROLEUM
PHOTOGENE
RADIATION

REAR-LIGHT
RUSHLIGHT
SCINTILLA
SIDELIGHT
SMALL COAL
SNOW-BLINK
SOLID FUEL
SPARKLING
SPOTLIGHT
STARLIGHT
STARSHINE
STEAM-COAL
STOP-LIGHT
TAIL-LIGHT
TALLOW-DIP
TWINKLING
VEILLEUSE
VERY LIGHT
WATCH-FIRE
XENON LAMP

10

AMBER LIGHT
ANTHRACITE
ATOMIC FUEL
BACK-BOILER
CAKING COAL
CANDLE COAL
CANDLEWICK
CANNEL-COAL
CHANDELIER
CHERRY-COAL
COMBUSTION
CONVECTION
CROSSLIGHT
DESTRUCTOR
EFFULGENCE
ERADIATION
FAIRY LIGHT
FIXED LIGHT
FLASHLIGHT
FLOODLIGHT
FOREST FIRE
FOSSIL FUEL
GAS-FURNACE
GLANCE-COAL
GREEN LIGHT
iLLUMINANT
KLIEG LIGHT
LAMP-BURNER

LIGHTENING
LUMINATION
LUMINOSITY
MATCHSTICK
MINER'S LAMP
NATURAL GAS
NIGHT-LIGHT
NIGHT-TAPER
PHOTOFLOOD
PILOT-LIGHT
PROMETHEAN
REFLECTION
REFULGENCE
REFULGENCY
ROCKET FUEL
RUSH-CANDLE
SAFETY LAMP
SHORT-SIXES
SODIUM LAMP
SPIRIT-LAMP
SPLINT-COAL
STREET-LAMP
SUN-RAY LAMP
TORCHLIGHT
WATCH-LIGHT
WOOD-SPIRIT

11

BEDSIDE-LAMP
BENGAL LIGHT
CANDESCENCE
CANDLE-LIGHT
CORUSCATION
DARK-LANTERN
ELECTRICITY
FATUOUS FIRE
FETCH-CANDLE
FIRELIGHTER
FULGURATION
HOUSE LIGHTS
IGNIS FATUUS
ILLUMINATOR
INCINERATOR
INCREMATION
INFLAMMABLE
LAMP-CHIMNEY
LAMPLIGHTER
LIGHTER FUEL
MINERAL COAL
MOULD-CANDLE

NUCLEAR FUEL
PILOT-BURNER
READING-LAMP
REFLEX LIGHT
RIDING-LIGHT
SAFETY LIGHT
SAFETY-MATCH
SEARCHLIGHT
SMOULDERING
SPERM-CANDLE
ST ELMO'S FIRE
WIND-FURNACE

12

BUNSEN-BURNER
ELECTRIC FIRE
FLAMMABILITY
FLUORESCENCE
HARBOUR-LIGHT
ILLUMINATION
INCINERATION
LUCIFER-MATCH
LUMINESCENCE
MARKER BEACON
NEON LIGHTING
NOCTILUCENCE
OLYMPIC FLAME
OLYMPIC TORCH
PARAFFIN LAMP
PLATINUM LAMP
STANDARD LAMP
STORM-LANTERN
TALLOW-CANDLE
TANTALUM-LAMP
TRAFFIC-LIGHT
WILL-O'-THE-WISP

13

CONFLAGRATION
DRUMMOND LIGHT
ELECTRIC LIGHT
ELECTRIC TORCH
FRIAR'S LANTERN
GATHERING-COAL
GATHERING-PEAT
HURRICANE-LAMP
INCANDESCENCE
INCENSE-BURNER

MICROWAVE OVEN
PARAFFIN STOVE
REDUCING FLAME
RUNNING LIGHTS
SCINTILLATION
SMOKELESS FUEL
STRIP-LIGHTING
TURNIP-LANTERN

14

AVIATION SPIRIT
BITUMINOUS COAL
CARBURETTED GAS
CHINESE LANTERN
ELECTRIC COOKER
INFLAMMABILITY
SENSITIVE FLAME
STREET-LIGHTING

15

ELECTRIC FURNACE
OXY-CALCIUM LIGHT
PHOSPHORESCENCE
SMELTING-FURNACE
THRESHOLD LIGHTS

GEOGRAPHY — GEOGRAPHICAL TERMS

3

AIT
ALP
BAR
BAY
BED
BEN
BOG
CAY
COL
CWM
DUN
FEN
GAT
GEO
GUT
HOE
KEY
KOP
MAN
MAP
NAB
PAN
RAS
RUN
SEA
SOG
SPA
TOR

4

AXIS
BANK
BECK
BENT
BERG
BORE
BRAE
BROW
BUND
BURN
CAPE
CARR
COMB
CONE
COVE
CRAG
DALE
DEAN

DELF
DELL
DENE
DOAB
DOWN
DRUM
DUMP
DUNE
EAST
EDDY
EYOT
FALL
FELL
FIRN
FLOE
FORD
FRET
GAPÓ
GHAT
GILL
GLEN
GRID
GULF
HARD
HEAD
HILL
HOLM
HOLT
HOOK
HOPE
INCH
ISLE
KHOR
KHUD
KNOT
KYLE
LAKE
LAVA
LEAD
LIDO
LINE
LINN
LOCH
LODE
MAIN
MERE
MESA
MOOR
MOSS
MULL
NAZE
NECK

NESS
PACK
PARK
PASS
PEAK
PIKE
POLE
POND
POOL
PORT
PURL
QUAG
RACE
REEF
RILL
RISE
SCAR
SCAW
SHAW
SIDE
SKAW
SLOB
SOAK
SPIT
SPUR
SUDD
TARN
TIDE
VALE
VENT
VLEI
WADI
WASH
WELL
WEST
WOOD

5

ABYSS
ARÊTE
ATLAS
BASIN
ATOLL
BAYOU
BEACH
BIGHT
BLUFF
BRAKE
BROAD
BROOK

BRUSH
BUTTE
CAIRN
CANAL
CHAIN
CHASM
CHINE
CLEVE
CLIFF
COMBE
COOMB
COPSE
CREEK
CREST
DELPH
DELTA
DONGA
EAGRE
FIORD
FJORD
FLASH
FLEET
FLUME
FORCE
FOUNT
GEOID
GHYLL
GLADE
GLIDE
GLOBE
GORGE
GROVE
GULCH
GULLY
GUYOT
HEATH
HITHE
HURST
INLET
ISLET
KLOOF
KNOLL
LAYER
LEVEE
LOUGH
MARCH
MARSH
MONTE
MOUND
MOUNT
MOUTH
NORTH

OASIS
OCEAN
OX-BOW
PINCH
PITCH
PLACE
PLAYA
POINT
POORT
POUND
RANGE
REACH
RIDGE
RIVER
SALSE
SCALP
SCARP
SCRUB
SELVA
SHELF
SHOAL
SHOLA
SHORE
SLADE
SLOPE
SLUMP
SOUND
SOUTH
STACK
STEEP
STRIP
SWALE
SWAMP
SWELL
SWIFT
SWIRE
TAIGA
URMAN
VERGE
WATER
WOODS
ZANJA

6

ARROYO
ASCENT
BANKER
BARROW
BORDER

BOTTOM
BOUNDS
CALLOW
CANYON
CIRQUE
CLOUGH
COMMON
CORRIE
COTEAU
COULÉE
COURSE
CRATER
CUESTA
DEFILE
DESERT
DIMBLE
DINGLE
DIVIDE
EJECTA
FOREST
FRAZIL
GEYSER
GULLET
GULLEY
HEIGHT
HOLLOW
ICE-CAP
ICE-PAN
INFALL
ISLAND
JUNGLE
KOPPIE
KRANTZ
LAGOON
LASHER
MASSIF
MIRAGE
MORASS
MUSKEG
NEEDLE
NULLAH
NYANZA
OFFSET
OSTIUM
PETARY
RAPIDS
RAVINE
RILLET
RISING
RUNLET
RUNNEL
SADDLE

SALINA
SCROBE
SEA-BED
SEA-ICE
SIERRA
SKERRY
SLEECH
SLOUGH
SOURCE
SPRING
SPRUIT
STRAIT
STRAND
STRATH
STREAM
SUMMIT
SURVEY
TONGUE
TROPIC
VALLEY
VORAGO
YARPHA

7

CASCADE
CHANNEL
CLIMATE
CONTOUR
COPPICE
CORCASS
CURRENT
DECLINE
DESCENT
DRY-WASH
EQUATOR
ESTUARY
EURIPUS
FRESHET
GLACIER
GROWLER
HACHURE
HARBOUR
HILLOCK
HILLTOP
HOGBACK
HORIZON
HOT WELL
HUMMOCK
ICE-BELT

ICEBERG
ICE-FLOE
ICE-FOOT
ICE-PACK
IGARAPÉ
INCLINE
ISOBATH
ISOGRAM
ISTHMUS
LAKELET
LOWLAND
MACHAIR
MAMELON
MUD-FLAT
MUD-LAVA
MUD-LUMP
NARROWS
NUNATAK
OUTFALL
PACK-ICE
PASSAGE
PEAT-BED
PEAT-BOG
PLATEAU
POLYNIA
QUARTER
RIVULET
SALTING
SALT-PAN
SAND-BAR
SEA-BANK
SEA-LINE
SEA-LOCH
SEAPORT
SKYLINE
SNOWCAP
SPA-WELL
SPINNEY
STRAITS
TERRAIN
THALWEG
THICKET
THWAITE
TIDE-WAY
TOMBOLO
TORRENT
TROPICS
UPGRADE
VERSANT
VOLCANO
WASH-OUT
YARDANG

8

ALLUVION
AVULSION
BARRANCO
BERGFALL
BOUNDARY
BROOKLET
CATARACT
CAUSEWAY
CLEARING
CONFINES
CREVASSE
DATE-LINE
DOLDRUMS
DRIFT-ICE
EFFLUENT
EMINENCE
EMISSARY
ERUPTION
FERNSHAW
FIELD-ICE
FOOTHILL
FORELAND
FORESTRY
FOUNTAIN
FRONTIER
HEADLAND
HIGHLAND
HILLSIDE
HOG'S-BACK
ICE-FIELD
ICE-LEDGE
ICE-WATER
INFLUENT
ISOGONIC
LANDMARK
LATITUDE
LITTORAL
MERIDIAN
MILLPOND
MILLRACE
MOUNTAIN
OVERFALL
PARALLEL
PEAT-BANK
PEAT-MOOR
PINNACLE
QUAGMIRE
RIVER-BED
RIVERWAY
SAND-BANK

SAND-DUNE
SAND-HILL
SASTRUGA
SCARPING
SEA-BASIN
SEA-BEACH
SEA-CLIFF
SEA-FRONT
SEA-LEVEL
SEA-MARGE
SEA-MOUNT
SEASHORE
SHELL-ICE
SNOWLINE
SODA-LAKE
SOFFIONI
TAILRACE
TIDEMARK
TOPOLOGY
TOPONYMY
TURLOUGH
WATER-GAP
WATERWAY
WELL-HEAD
ZASTRUGA

9

ACCLIVITY
ANABRANCH
ANTIPODES
BACKWATER
BILLABONG
BRUSHWOOD
CARTOGRAM
CATCHMENT
COASTLINE
COPSEWOOD
CORAL-REEF
DECLIVITY
DOWNGRADE
EARTHFALL
EFFLUENCE
ELEVATION
EVERGLADE
FORESHORE
GAZETTEER
GEOGRAPHY
GREENWOOD
HEADWATER
ISOCHRONE
ISOCLINAL

GEOGRAPHY – GEOGRAPHICAL TERMS

LONGITUDE
MAP-MAKING
NORTH-EAST
NORTH POLE
NORTH-WEST
OAKENSHAW
OROGRAPHY
OX-BOW LAKE
PANHANDLE
PENEPLAIN
PENINSULA
PLACENAME
PRECIPICE
QUICKSAND
RAZOR-BACK
RE-ENTRANT
RELIEF MAP
RESERVOIR
RIVER-BANK
RIVER-HEAD
RIVERSIDE
SALT-MARSH
SAND-BREAK
SEA-BREACH
SEA-STRAND
SHIP-CANAL
SHORELINE
SNOW-FIELD
SOUTH-EAST
SOUTH POLE
SOUTH-WEST
STREAM-ICE
STREAMLET
SUGAR-LOAF
TIDAL BORE
TRIBUTARY
VULCANISM
WATERFALL
WATER-HEAD
WATER-HOLE
WATER-LINE
WATERSHED
WATERSIDE

10

CHERSONESE
CINDER-CONE
COLATITUDE
CONFLUENCE
CONTOUR MAP
CORDILLERA
CRATER-LAKE
DEBOUCHURE
EMBANKMENT
EMBOUCHURE
ESCARPMENT
GLACIATION
GNAMMA HOLE
HARBOUR-BAR
HEADSTREAM
HEMISPHERE
LAND-SPRING
MAINSTREAM
MAP-READING
MILL-STREAM
MUD-VOLCANO
OCEAN-BASIN
PANCAKE-ICE
PERMAFROST
PILLOW-LAVA
POPULATION
PROJECTION
PROMINENCE
PROMONTORY
RAIN-FOREST
RIFT VALLEY
RIVER-MOUTH
SADDLEBACK
SALT-SPRING
SEMICIRQUE
STREAMLING
TIMBER-LINE
TOPOGRAPHY
UNDERCLIFF
UNDERGROVE
WATER-PLANE

WATERSMEET
WELL-SPRING

11

ARCHIPELAGO
BARRIER REEF
CARTOGRAPHY
CHOROGRAPHY
CONTOUR LINE
CORAL-ISLAND
DERELICTION
EXPLORATION
FORESTATION
HYDROSPHERE
ISOGEOTHERM
LIGNUM SCRUB
LIGNUM SWAMP
MALLEE-SCRUB
MINERAL WELL
MOUNTAIN-TOP
NUÉE ARDENTE
ORIENTATION
POLAR CIRCLE
RIVER-BOTTOM
SPILL-STREAM
VOLCANIC ASH
VOLCANIC MUD
VULCANICITY
VULCANOLOGY
WATERCOURSE

12

ARCTIC CIRCLE
ARTESIAN WELL
CALENDAR-LINE
CYPRESS-SWAMP
DISTRIBUTARY
EMBRANCHMENT
MOUNTAIN-SIDE

RIVER-TERRACE
VOLCANIC DUST
WATER-PARTING
WINTER-BOURNE

13

AFFORESTATION
CARDINAL POINT
DEFORESTATION
GEOMORPHOLOGY
GRID REFERENCE
HANGING VALLEY
MAGNETIC NORTH
MAGNETIC POLES
MANGROVE SWAMP
MINERAL SPRING
MOUNTAIN-CHAIN
MOUNTAIN-RANGE
POLAR DISTANCE
PRIME MERIDIAN
THERMAL SPRING
WEEPING-SPRING

14

FLOATING ISLAND
HORSE LATITUDES
TROPIC OF CANCER

15

ANTARCTIC CIRCLE
BURNING MOUNTAIN
FOLDED MOUNTAINS
MAGNETIC EQUATOR
SENSIBLE HORIZON

GEOGRAPHY — REGIONS & COMMUNITIES

3

GAU
MIR
PAH
SEE
SPA
WEN

4

AREA
BELT
BOSK
BURG
BUSH
CAMP
CITY
CLAN
DEME
DORP
FLAT
HOLM
LAND
NOME
PALE
PARK
PORT
POST
PUNA
RACE
RAND
RAPE
RIDE
SEAT
SLUM
SOKE
TOWN
VEGA
VELD
WARD
WOLD
ZONE

5

ALDEA
BASIN
BORGO
BOURG

BRUSH
BURGH
CHASE
CLIME
COAST
DUCHY
KAROO
KARST
KRAAL
LANDE
LATHE
LIMIT
LLANO
MANOR
MARCH
PAMPA
PATCH
PLAIN
REALM
REICH
SHIRE
SOKEN
STATE
SUBAH
TALUK
TRACT
TRIBE
VELDT
VERGE
WASTE
WEALD

6

ARCTIC
BARONY
BIZONE
BOSCAT
BUSTEE
CANTON
CENTRE
COLONY
COUNTY
DESERT
DOMAIN
EMPIRE
ESTATE
EYALET
FOREST
GHETTO
HAMLET

INLAND
JUNGLE
LEVANT
NATION
OBLAST
OFFING
ORIENT
PAMPAS
PARAMO
PARISH
PEOPLE
POLDER
PUEBLO
RANCHO
REGION
RESORT
RIDING
SANJAK
SIRCAR
STEPPE
SUBURB
TAHSIL
THORPE
TUNDRA
UPLAND
WARREN
ZILLAH

7

BARRENS
BOGLAND
BOROUGH
BOSCAGE
CAPITAL
CIRCUIT
COMMUNE
COUNTRY
DIOCESE
DUKEDOM
EARLDOM
EMIRATE
ENCLAVE
EPARCHY
EXCLAVE
EXPANSE
FAR EAST
FAR WEST
FENLAND
FLY-BELT
HUNDRED

INNINGS
KAMPONG
KHANATE
KIBBUTZ
KINGDOM
LOWLAND
MAREMMA
MIDLAND
MISSION
MOSHAVA
NEOGAEA
NEW TOWN
OIL-BELT
OUTBACK
OUTPOST
PARGANA
PHALANX
PRAIRIE
PURLIEU
QUARTER
REGENCY
RESERVE
RIVIERA
ROYALTY
SATRAPY
SAVANNA
SEAPORT
SEASIDE
SOCIETY
STEPPES
SUBURBS
SUBZONE
TROPICS
VILAYET
VILLAGE

8

BACKVELD
BAD LANDS
BUSHVELD
CAATINGA
CONURBIA
DEER PARK
DISTRICT
DIVISION
DOCKLAND
DOMINION
DOWNLAND
DUST-BOWL
EAST-LAND

ENVIRONS
FAR NORTH
FAR SOUTH
FAUBOURG
FORELAND
FREE-CITY
GAS-FIELD
HOLY CITY
HOLY LAND
HOMELAND
HOME-TOWN
IMPERIUM
INTERIOR
KIRKTOWN
MAINLAND
MOFUSSIL
MONARCHY
MOORLAND
NEAR EAST
NOMARCHY
OCCIDENT
OIL-FIELD
OPEN TOWN
PARKLAND
PHALANGE
POST-TOWN
PRESERVE
PROVINCE
QUEENDOM
REPUBLIC
SAVANNAH
SEABOARD
SEACOAST
SHEADING
SLOBLAND
SUBURBIA
TIME ZONE
TOPARCHY
TOWNSHIP
WOODLAND

9

ANTARCTIC
ARCHDUCHY
ARCTOGAEA
BACKWOODS
BAILIWICK
BANTUSTAN
BISHOPRIC
BORGHETTO

GEOGRAPHY — REGIONS & COMMUNITIES

CALIPHATE
CANAL ZONE
CHAPARRAL
CHINA-TOWN
CITY STATE
COALFIELD
COMITATUS
CONTINENT
CROWN LAND
DEEP SOUTH
DRIFT-LAND
EPARCHATE
FREE STATE
GHOST TOWN
GOLD-FIELD
GRASSLAND
GREEN BELT
HEARTLAND
HEATHLAND
INNER CITY
INTERZONE
KHEDIVATE
LAKE-BASIN
MARSHLAND
OUTPARISH
OUTSKIRTS
OVERSPILL
PRINCEDOM
PROVINCES
RANCHERIA
RESIDENCY
SACHENDOM
SCRUBLAND
SHOGUNATE
SHORE-SIDE
STORM BELT
SUBREGION
SULTANATE
TABLELAND
TERRITORY
UP-COUNTRY
VISCOUNTY
WAPENTAKE
WASTELAND

10

BORDERLAND
COSMOPOLIS
COUNTY TOWN
DEPARTMENT

EPISCOPATE
FATHERLAND
FRIGID ZONE
GARDEN CITY
GRAND DUCHY
HEMISPHERE
HINTERLAND
MARKET TOWN
METROPOLIS
MOTHERLAND
NO-MAN'S-LAND
OLD COUNTRY
PALAEOGAEA
PALATINATE
PENTAPOLIS
PINE-BARREN
PIT VILLAGE
POSSESSION
PRINCIPATE
PUBLIC LAND
RIVER-BASIN
SETTLEMENT
SHANTY TOWN
SUBKINGDOM
SUBTROPICS
SUPER-STATE
TETRAPOLIS
THIRD WORLD
TORRID ZONE
WILDERNESS

11

AMPHICTYONY
ARCHDIOCESE
ARCHDUKEDOM
BACK-COUNTRY
BUFFER STATE
BUILT-UP AREA
CAPITAL CITY
CONURBATION
COUNTRYSIDE
GAME RESERVE
HUSBANDLAND
LATIFUNDIUM
MEGALOPOLIS
POST-VILLAGE
RESERVATION
SOVEREIGNTY
SUBDISTRICT
TETRARCHATE

12

APOSTOLIC SEE
CONSTITUENCY
DIAMOND-FIELD
GAME PRESERVE
GARRISON TOWN
HEALTH RESORT
LANDGRAVIATE
LATIN QUARTER
MUNICIPALITY
NATIONAL PARK
POLAR REGIONS
PRINCIPALITY
PROTECTORATE
SUBCONTINENT

13

ARCHBISHOPRIC
CATCHMENT AREA
COUNTY BOROUGH
DEPRESSED AREA
MOTHER-COUNTRY
OUTSETTLEMENT
RURAL DISTRICT
SATELLITE TOWN
TEMPERATE ZONE
URBAN DISTRICT

14

ARRONDISSEMENT
BANANA REPUBLIC
COUNTY PALATINE
DISTRESSED AREA
RESTRICTED AREA
SATELLITE STATE
TRUST TERRITORY

15

ARCHIEPISCOPATE
DEVELOPMENT AREA
METROPOLITANATE

HERALDRY & LINEAGE

3

BAR
FUR
LAW
LIS
SOL
VOL

4

ARMS
BAND
BASE
BEND
DELF
FRET
GAMB
GARB
GOLP
LINE
LION
ORLE
PALE
PEAN
PILE
POMP
RACE
RITE
STEM
TILT
TREE
VAIR
VANE
VERT
WEEL

5

AZURE
BADGE
BATON
CHAMP
CHIEF
CREST
CROSS
DWALE
EAGLE
FESSE
FIELD

FUSIL
GARBE
GEMEL
GERBE
GIRON
GULES
GYRON
JOUST
LABEL
LISTS
METAL
MOTTO
NAVEL
ORDER
PHEON
POINT
QUEUE
REBUS
SABLE
SCARP
SCROG
STOCK
TENNÉ
TITLE
TORSE
TRICK

6

ARGENT
ARMORY
BANNER
BEZANT
BILLET
BLAZON
BORDER
CANTON
CHARGE
COTISE
DEVICE
DEXTER
DRAGON
EMBLEM
ETOILE
FLANCH
GARTER
LIONEL
MANCHE
MASCLE
MOLINE
MULLET

NORROY
PARADE
RIBBON
RITTER
RITUAL
RUSTRE
SEA-DOG
SHIELD
SPROUT
SQUARE
TABARD
TATTOO
WIVERN
WYVERN

7

ALERION
ANNULET
BEARING
BENDLET
BORDURE
BRISURE
CHEVRON
COTTISE
DESCENT
DISPLAY
DUBBING
DYNASTY
ENDORSE
ESCROLL
ESTOILE
GRIFFIN
LEOPARD
LINEAGE
LIONCEL
LOZENGE
MAJESTY
MARTLET
NOMBRIL
PAGEANT
PEERAGE
POTENCÉ
QUARTER
RED HAND
SALTIRE
SATYRAL
SEA-LION
TILTING
TITLING
TOURNEY

TRANGLE
TREFOIL
TRUNDLE
UNICORN

8

ACCOLADE
ANCESTRY
ARMORIAL
BANDEROL
BLAZONRY
CHIVALRY
CRESCENT
CROWNING
DANCETTE
DOUBLING
ESCALLOP
GAUNTLET
GRANDEUR
HERALDRY
HEREDITY
HERISSON
JOUSTING
MANTLING
OPINICUS
ORDINARY
PALMERIN
PEDIGREE
PRIMROSE
PUNDONOR
QUINTAIN
QUIXOTRY
SANGLIER
SEA-HORSE
SINISTER
STANDARD
TANISTRY
TILT-YARD
TINCTURE
TRESSURE

9

ABATEMENT
BLUE BLOOD
EIGHTFOIL
ELEVATION
GENEALOGY
GILT SPURS

HATCHMENT
JESSERANT
KNIGHTAGE
LIONCELLE
MATRILINY
PAGEANTRY
PARENTAGE
PAS D'ARMES
PHYLOGENY
POSTERITY
SPEAR-SIDE
SUPPORTER
TEKNONYMY
TRUNCHEON

10

BASTARD-BAR
BLOOD-ROYAL
BLOODY HAND
BLUE MANTLE
BLUE RIBBON
CINQUE-FOIL
COAT OF ARMS
COCKATRICE
COMPLEMENT
DIFFERENCE
EMBLAZONRY
ESCUTCHEON
FAMILY TREE
FESSE-POINT
FETTERLOCK
FLEUR-DE-LIS
HERALDSHIP
IMPALEMENT
KNIGHTHOOD
MATROCLINY
PORTCULLIS
PRECEDENCE
PRECEDENCY
PRECEPTORY
PROCESSION
QUARTERING
QUATRE-FOIL
QUINTE-FOIL
ROUGE CROIX
STALL-PLATE
SUCCESSION
SURMOUNTER
TOURNAMENT
VISITATION

HERALDRY & LINEAGE

11

ACHIEVEMENT
BAR-SINISTER
DIMIDIATION
DISTAFF SIDE
DOUBLE-EAGLE
ENGRAILMENT
ENNOBLEMENT
FIMBRIATION
HONOUR-POINT
INVESTITURE
PROGENITURE
RAGGED STAFF
ROUGE DRAGON
SPINDLE-SIDE
SPREAD-EAGLE

SUBORDINARY
SUPERCHARGE
SURMOUNTING

12

AUGMENTATION
BEND-SINISTER
EMBLAZONMENT
ENTHRONEMENT
GOLDEN FLEECE
INESCUTCHEON
ORDER OF MERIT
PATRILINEAGE
PHYLOGENESIS
SON ET LUMIÈRE

SPEAR-RUNNING

13

BATON-SINISTER
POINT OF HONOUR
PRIMOGENITURE

14

CATHERINE-WHEEL
DRAGON-STANDARD
KNIGHT-ERRANTRY
PROGENITORSHIP

HOLES

3

DIP
EYE
GAP
PIT
VUG

4

CAVE
DENT
DINT
FENT
FLAW
GAPE
GEAT
HOLE
KICK
LEAK
NICK
NOCK
NOOK
PORE
RENT
RIFT
RIMA
SLIT
SLOT
VENT
VOID
WELL

5

ABYSS
CHASM
CHINK
CLEFT
CRACK
DITCH
GRIKE
HATCH

JUDAS
MOUTH
NOTCH
SPACE
SPLIT
SPOUT
TREMA

6

CAVERN
CAVITY
CRANNY
CRATER
DIMPLE
EYELET
GROTTO
HIATUS
HOLLOW
INDENT
LACUNA
OSTIUM
OUTLET
PIERCE
RAVINE
RECESS
SAWPIT
SQUINT
STIGMA
SULCUS
TRENCH

7

AIRHOLE
ARMHOLE
CONCAVE
CREVICE
EYE-HOLE
FISSURE
FORAMEN
FOXHOLE
GAS-WELL

GUNPORT
HORNITO
HOUSING
INKWELL
KEYHOLE
MANHOLE
MORTISE
MUD-HOLE
OIL-WELL
OPENING
ORIFICE
OSTIOLE
PINHOLE
PITFALL
PITTING
POTHOLE
RAT-HOLE
ROW-PORT
SAND-PIT
SAW-GATE
SAW-KERF
SCUPPER
SCUTTLE
SPY-HOLE
SWALLET
SWALLOW
VACANCY

8

APERTURE
BLOW-HOLE
BOLT-HOLE
BORE-HOLE
BUNG-HOLE
BUNG-VENT
DENE-HOLE
DRAW-WELL
DUST-HOLE
FEMERALL
FUMEROLE
FUNKHOLE
HATCHWAY
HELL-HOLE

HIDY-HOLE
KILN-HOLE
KNOT-HOLE
LOOPHOLE
NAIL-HOLE
PEAT-HOLE
PEEP-HOLE
PLUG-HOLE
PORTHOLE
PUNCTULE
PUNCTURE
SAND-HOLE
SCISSURE
SHOT-HOLE
SINK-HOLE
SNAKE-PIT
SOFFIONI
SPARK-GAP
SPIRACLE
TROCHLEA
VENT-HOLE
WELL-HOLE
WORM-HOLE

9

AUGER-HOLE
BLACK HOLE
CONCAVITY
CREEP-HOLE
CUBBY-HOLE
DRAIN-HOLE
DREAMHOLE
EMPTINESS
GLORY-HOLE
HAWSEHOLE
JUDAS-HOLE
MOUSE-HOLE
OUBLIETTE
PERTUSION
PUNCH-HOLE
RIVET-HOLE
SHELL-HOLE
SIGHT-HOLE

SMOKE-HOLE
SOUND-HOLE
SPOUT-HOLE
STERN-PORT
STOKE-HOLE
THUMB-HOLE
TOUCH-HOLE
WHITE HOLE

10

DEPRESSION
DIMPLEMENT
EXCAVATION
EYELET-HOLE
FINGERHOLE
GULLEY-HOLE
HAGIOSCOPE
PIGEON-HOLE
POCKET-HOLE

11

GRUMMET-HOLE
INDENTATION
LUBBER'S HOLE
PERFORATION
PLACKET-HOLE
PRIEST'S HOLE
SHELL-CRATER
SWALLOW-HOLE

12

GIANT'S KETTLE
PUNCTULATION
PUNCTURATION

13

INSPECTION-PIT

HOROLOGY

3

FOB
KEY

4

BELL
DIAL
FACE
JACK
STEM
TICK
TIME

5

ALARM
BEZEL
CHIME
CLOCK
FUSEE
GLASS
INDEX
LARUM
LIGNE
SHADE
SNAIL
STAFF
STYLE
TIMER
VERGE
WATCH
WHEEL
WORKS

6

BUTTON
CHIMER
DETENT
GNOMON
HAMMER
HUNTER
PALLET
PILLAR

RIBBON
SPRING
STROKE
TICKER
TURNIP
WINDER

7

BALANCE
CHAPTER
CRYSTAL
LUNETTE
POTENCE
SPINDLE
SUNDIAL
TICKING

8

FOB-WATCH
HEART CAM
HOROLOBE
HOROLOGY
HOUR-HAND
MOVEMENT
PENDULUM
PIN-WHEEL
REPEATER
RING-DIAL
SOLARIUM
TICK-TOCK
TIME-BALL
TIPSY-KEY
WATCH-KEY

9

ALARM-BELL
CLEPSYDRA
CLOCK-FACE
DIAL-PLATE
GNOMONICS
GOLD WATCH

HOROMETRY
HOUR-GLASS
HOURPLATE
LARUM-BELL
REGULATOR
SAND-GLASS
STOP-WATCH
TIMEPIECE
WALL-CLOCK
WATCHCASE

10

ALARM-CLOCK
CHRONOLOGY
COUNT-WHEEL
DUTCH CLOCK
ESCAPEMENT
HAIR-SPRING
HALF-HUNTER
HOROGRAPHY
HOROLOGIUM
HYDROSCOPE
LEVER-WATCH
MAINSPRING
MINUTE-DROP
MINUTE-HAND
QUARTER-BOY
REGULATION
SCAPE-WHEEL
SECOND-HAND
SNAIL-WHEEL
SWING-WHEEL
TIMEKEEPER
WATCH-CLOCK
WATCH-GLASS
WATER-CLOCK
WATER-GLASS
WRIST-WATCH

11

ATOMIC CLOCK
CHRONOMETER
CHRONOMETRY

CHRONOSCOPE
COMPENSATOR
CUCKOO-CLOCK
ESCAPE-WHEEL
FLOWER-CLOCK
GNOMONOLOGY
MASTER-CLOCK
MINUTE-GLASS
MINUTE-WATCH
QUARTER-JACK
QUARTZ CLOCK
QUARTZ WATCH
TURRET-CLOCK
WATCH-SPRING

12

BALANCE-WHEEL
DIGITAL CLOCK
DIGITAL WATCH
PATTERN-WHEEL
WATCH-CRYSTAL

13

CARRIAGE CLOCK
LONG-CASE CLOCK
LUMINOUS WATCH
SPEAKING-CLOCK

14

COUNTER-BALANCE
WATCHMAN'S CLOCK

15

SECONDS-PENDULUM
SYNCHRONISATION

HOUSEHOLD – CLEANING & WASHING

3

DYE
MOP
PIG
RUB

4

BATH
SOAK
SOAP
SODA
SUDS
SWAB
WASH
WIPE

5

BLOOM
BROOM
BRUSH
CLOTH
GLOSS
LOOFA
LYSOL
METHS
MOP-UP
RINSE
SCOUR
SCRIM
SCRUB
SHINE
STEEP
TOWEL
TURPS
WATER
WIPER
WRING

6

BLANCO
BLEACH
BUFFER
DUBBIN
DUSTER
DYEING
FINISH
LATHER
LOOFAH

LUSTRE
POLISH
PUMICE
RUBBER
SHAMMY
SHOWER
SLUICE
SPIRIT
SPONGE
STARCH
WASH-UP
WIPING

7

BATHING
BEESWAX
BUFFING
CLEANER
DUSTING
DUST-PAN
FLANNEL
HYGIENE
LAUNDRY
LEATHER
RINSING
SCOURER
SOAKING
SWABBER
TERSION
TICKLER
TORCHON
WASHING
WHITING
ZIMOCCA

8

ABLUTION
BLACKING
CAMSTONE
CHLORIDE
CLEANING
CLEANSER
FUMIGANT
HAT-BRUSH
HEELBALL
LAVATION
PIPECLAY
POLISHER

SCOURING
SOAP-BALL
SOAPSUDS
SOFTENER
SOFT SOAP
SQUEEGEE
STAINING
STEEPING
SWILLING
WASH-BALL
WHITENER
WRINGING

9

BATH-BRICK
BATH-TOWEL
BLACKLEAD
BOOTBLACK
DETERGENT
DETERSION
DISH-CLOTH
DISH-WATER
DUST-BRUSH
FUMIGATOR
HAND-TOWEL
POLISHING
POPE'S HEAD
SHOE-BRUSH
SHOWERING
SOFTENING
TURK'S HEAD
WASHING-UP
WHITENING

10

ABSTERGENT
ABSTERSION
ABSTERSIVE
BOOT-POLISH
DECOLORANT
FLOORCLOTH
FUMIGATING
FUMIGATION
SHOE-POLISH
SOAP-BUBBLE
SOAP-POWDER
TOILET-SOAP
TURPENTINE
YELLOW-SOAP

11

CASTILE SOAP
COAL-TAR SOAP
DRY-CLEANING
FACE-FLANNEL
HEARTH-BRUSH
HEARTH-STONE
METAL POLISH
PUMICE-STONE
SCOURING-PAD
SPANISH SOAP
SPRING-CLEAN
WASHING-BLUE
WASHING-SODA
WASH-LEATHER
WINDSOR SOAP

12

BARRIER-CREAM
BRISTOL BRICK
CARBOLIC SOAP
CLOTHES-BRUSH
DISINFECTANT
PLATE-LEATHER
TURKISH TOWEL

13

CARPET-BEATING
CLEANING-BRUSH
FEATHER-DUSTER
SHAMMY-LEATHER
VACUUM-CLEANER
WASHING-POWDER

14

CHAMOIS-LEATHER
SCRUBBING-BRUSH
SPRING-CLEANING

15

BLEACHING POWDER
WASHING-UP LIQUID

143

HOUSEHOLD – FITTINGS & APPLIANCES

3

BAR
BIN
FAN
HOB
JET
KEY
LUM
MAT
NET
PAD
PEG
POT
RUG
TAP
TUB
URN

4

BATH
BOLT
BULB
BUMF
COWL
CURB
DADO
DOOR
EXIT
FLUE
FUSE
GATE
GONG
GRID
HOOD
IRON
JAMB
KALI
KNOB
LAMP
LEAF
LINE
LINO
LOCK
MAIN
OVEN
PACE
PIER
PIPE
PLUG

PUFF
RACK
RAIL
RASP
RISE
RISP
SAFE
SASH
SILL
SINK
SLAT
SLIP
SNAP
STEP
TANK
TICK
TIDY
TILE
TRAP
UNIT
VEIL
VENT
VICE
WARD
WELL

5

AIRER
ALARM
BASIN
BIDET
BLIND
CHEEK
CHICK
CLOCK
COVER
DÉCOR
DRAIN
DRAPE
DRIER
DRYER
DUVET
FLIER
GLASS
GLOBE
GRATE
GRILL
HATCH
HINGE
INGLE

JERRY
LATCH
LEDGE
LIGHT
MIXER
NEWEL
PANEL
PLATE
POINT
POKER
POTTY
PRESS
PUNKA
QUILT
RADIO
RANGE
RIGOL
RISER
SHADE
SHEET
SHELF
SHOJI
STACK
STAIR
STAND
STILE
STOEP
STOVE
TATTY
THROW
TREAD
U-TRAP
U-TUBE
VIDEO
VINYL

6

AERIAL
ASH-BIN
ASH-CAN
ASH-PAN
ASH-PIT
AWNING
BLOWER
BOILER
BONNET
BUTTON
BUZZER
CANOPY
CARPET

CASTOR
COOKER
COPPER
CORONA
COVING
DAMPER
DIMMER
DIPPER
DORMER
DOUCHE
DRAPES
DURRIE
FAUCET
FENDER
FLIGHT
FRIDGE
FRIEZE
GAS-TAP
GEYSER
GRILLE
GUTTER
HAT-PEG
HEARTH
HEATER
HOT TAP
ICE-BOX
KEEPER
LAVABO
LIGGER
LOUVRE
LUSTRE
MAIDEN
MANGLE
MANTEL
MIRROR
MUNTIN
NOSING
PARURE
PELMET
PILLOW
PIPAGE
PIPING
PLAQUE
PSYCHE
RAPPER
RUNNER
SCONCE
SCREEN
SHOWER
SOCKET
SPIGOT
SPREAD

STAIRS
STEREO
SWITCH
TABLET
TOILET
UPTAKE
WASHER
WICKET
WILTON
WINDOW

7

ADAPTOR
AERATOR
ANDIRON
ASH-HOLE
ASH-TRAY
BATH-TUB
BEDDING
BEDTICK
BELLOWS
BIBCOCK
BLANKET
BLENDER
BOLSTER
BOOK-END
BOX-IRON
BRACKET
CAT-FLAP
CHAMBER
CISTERN
CLICKET
COLD TAP
COMMODE
CONDUIT
CONSOLE
CORK-MAT
CORNICE
CURTAIN
CUSHION
DOORMAT
DOORWAY
DRAINER
DUST-BIN
DUST-PAN
ELEMENT
FIRE-BAR
FIREDOG
FIRE-PAN
FITMENT

FITTING
FIXTURE
FLY-TRAP
FREEZER
FUSE BOX
GAS-FIRE
GAS-LAMP
GAS-MAIN
GAS-OVEN
GAS-PIPE
GAS-RING
GAS-TRAP
GRATING
HAT-RACK
HEATING
HIP-BATH
HUMIDOR
JACUZZI
JIB-DOOR
KEYHOLE
KNEELER
KNOCKER
LAGGING
LATTICE
LEG-REST
MUNTING
NIGGARD
OVERLAY
PADLOCK
PARQUET
PLAY-PEN
PLUNGER
POSTERN
POT-HOOK
SAD-IRON
SHUTTER
SUN-LAMP
SWEEPER
TAMBOUR
TICKLER
TOASTER
TRAMMEL
TRESTLE
TRINGLE
TRIPPET
TUMBLER
VALANCE
VENTANA
VENTING
VITRAGE
WASH-POT
WASH-TUB

8

ASH-STAND
BACK DOOR
BACK GATE
BANISTER
BEDCOVER
BELL-PULL
BELL-PUSH
BIN-LINER
BOOK-RACK
CASEMENT
CATCH-PIT
CHECK-KEY
COAL-FLAP
COAT-RACK
CORK-TILE
COVERLET
CUPBOARD
CUSPIDOR
DOORBELL
DOORKNOB
DOORNAIL
DOORPOST
DOOR-SILL
DOORSTEP
FANLIGHT
FIRE-BACK
FIRESIDE
FLAT-IRON
FLUSH-BOX
FLYPAPER
FOOT-BATH
GASALIER
GAS-GLOBE
GAS-METER
GAS-POKER
GAS-STOVE
GATE-POST
GRIDIRON
HALF-DOOR
HALL-DOOR
HANDRAIL
HANGINGS
HEADREST
HOT PLATE
JALOUSIE
KEY-PLATE
KNIFE-BOX
LIGHTING
LINOLEUM
MAIN-DOOR

MATTRESS
MEAT-SAFE
OVERFLOW
PEAR-PUSH
PEDESTAL
PILOT-JET
PIPE-RACK
PORTIÈRE
RADIATOR
SASH-CORD
SASH-DOOR
SHELVING
SIDE-DOOR
SIDE-GATE
SIDEPOST
SIDE-STEP
SINK UNIT
SITZ-BATH
SKIRTING
SKYLIGHT
SOIL-PIPE
SPILLWAY
SPITTOON
STAIR-ROD
STAIRWAY
STOP-COCK
SUN-BLIND
SUN-SHADE
TANTALUS
TAPESTRY
TRAP-DOOR
TRAP-FALL
TRASH-CAN
TRAVERSE
TURNCOCK
UNDERLAY
WAINSCOT
WALL UNIT
WASTE-BIN
WATER-TAP
WIRELESS
YALE LOCK

9

ASH-BUCKET
AXMINSTER
BAY WINDOW
BEDSPREAD
BOOKSHELF
BOOKSTAND

BOW WINDOW
CARPET-ROD
CHUBB LOCK
COAL-PLATE
COMFORTER
CUSHIONET
DOOR-PLATE
DOWN QUILT
DRAIN-PIPE
DRAIN-TILE
DRAIN-TRAP
DRAPERIES
DUST-COVER
DUST-SHEET
EIDERDOWN
EXTRACTOR
FIRE-ALARM
FIRE-GRATE
FIREGUARD
FIRE-IRONS
FIRE-PLACE
FRONT DOOR
GAS-BURNER
GAS-COOKER
GAS-HEATER
GAS-MANTLE
GIRANDOLE
GOGGLE-BOX
GUTTERING
HAIR-DRIER
HAIR-DRYER
HAND-BASIN
HEARTH-RUG
JACK TOWEL
LAMPSHADE
LETTER-BOX
LIGHT-BULB
LIQUEFIER
LUMINAIRE
NAME-PLATE
NIGHT-BELL
PALAMPORE
PALLIASSE
PANELLING
PARTITION
PARTY-WALL
PIER-GLASS
PLAQUETTE
PLATE-RACK
PLATE-RAIL
POT-HANGER
PURDONIUM

HOUSEHOLD – FITTINGS & APPLIANCES

RADIOGRAM
ROOF-GUARD
SASH-FRAME
SCUNCHEON
SIDELIGHT
SMELL-TRAP
SMOKE-JACK
SNOW-GUARD
SPICE-RACK
SPIN-DRIER
STAIRCASE
STAIRFOOT
STAIRHEAD
STAIR-WELL
STEAM-IRON
STEP-STONE
STINK-TRAP
STOVEPIPE
SWING-DOOR
THRESHOLD
TOWEL-RACK
TOWEL-RAIL
TRAP-STAIR
VEE-GUTTER
WALL-CLOCK
WALLPAPER
WASH-BASIN
WASH-BOARD
WASTE-PIPE
WATER-BUTT
WATER-MAIN
WATER-PIPE
WINDOW-BAR
WINDOW-BOX
WIRE-GUARD

10

ALARM-CLOCK
BEDCLOTHES
BUTTERY-BAR
CANDELABRA
CATCH-BASIN
CELLAR-FLAP
CHAMBER-POT
CHANDELIER
CLOSE-STOOL
CLOTHES-PEG
COAT-HANGER
CORK-CARPET
CURTAINING

CURTAIN-ROD
DEEP-FREEZE
DINNER-GONG
DISHWASHER
DOOR-HANDLE
DUMB-WAITER
FIRE-BASKET
FIRE-ESCAPE
FIRESCREEN
FIRE-SHOVEL
GARBAGE CAN
GAS-BRACKET
GRAMOPHONE
HUMIFIFIER
INGLE-CHEEK
LACE-PILLOW
LAMBREQUIN
LAMPHOLDER
LIQUIDISER
LOOSE-COVER
MANTELTREE
NEEDLE-BATH
NET-CURTAIN
NIGHT-LATCH
NIGHT-LIGHT
NOTCH-BOARD
OVERMANTEL
PEAR-SWITCH
PERSIENNES
PHONOGRAPH
PICTURE-ROD
PILLOW-CASE
PILLOW-SLIP
PILOT-LIGHT
PLUNGE BATH
POWER-POINT
PUSH-BUTTON
ROSE-WINDOW
RÔTISSERIE
RUSH-HOLDER
SAFETY-FUSE
SALAMANDER
SASH-WINDOW
SEPTIC TANK
SHOWER-BATH
SHUTTERING
SMOKE-BOARD
SOLAR PANEL
SPRING-LOCK
STAIR-TOWER
STENCH-TRAP
STEREOGRAM

STRAP-HINGE
STREET-DOOR
STRIP-LIGHT
SWING-SHELF
TELEVISION
THUMB-LATCH
TIME-SWITCH
TOILET-ROLL
TOWEL-HORSE
TRAP-LADDER
UPHOLSTERY
VAPOUR-BATH
VENTILATOR
WANDER PLUG
WARMING-PAN
WATER-SPOUT
WINDOW-PANE
WINDOW-SASH
WINDOW-SILL

11

BEDSIDE-LAMP
BRIDGE-BOARD
CANDELABRUM
CANDLESTICK
CHEVAL-GLASS
CLOTHES-LINE
CLOTHES-POLE
CLOTHES-PROP
COMMON STAIR
CORNICE-HOOK
CORNICE-RAIL
COUNTERPANE
CURTAIL-STEP
CURTAIN-RING
DOLLY SWITCH
DOOR-KNOCKER
ELECTROLIER
FINGERPLATE
FOLDING-DOOR
FURNISHINGS
GAS-FITTINGS
HEARTH-STONE
ITALIAN IRON
JUNCTION-BOX
KITCHEN-SINK
KITCHEN UNIT
LATCH-STRING
LOUVRE-BOARD
MANTELPIECE

MANTEL-SHELF
MOISTURISER
MORTICE-LOCK
MOSQUITO NET
PICTURE-CORD
PICTURE-RAIL
PICTURE-WIRE
PILOT-BURNER
READING-LAMP
ROLLER-BLIND
ROLLER-TOWEL
SERVICE-PIPE
SERVICE-WIRE
SLEEPING-BAG
SLEEVE-BOARD
SPACE-HEATER
STAIR-CARPET
STAIR-TURRET
STORM-WINDOW
STRING-BOARD
STRING-PIECE
SWING-HANDLE
TOILET-CLOTH
TOILET-COVER
TOILET-GLASS
TUMBLE-DRIER
WAINSCOTING
WASTE-BASKET
WINDOW-BLIND
WINDOW-FRAME
WINDOW-GLASS
WIRELESS SET

12

ANTIMACASSAR
BREAKFAST BAR
BUTTERY-HATCH
CANDLE-HOLDER
CHEST-FREEZER
CHIMNEY-BOARD
CLOTHES-HORSE
CLOTHES-PRESS
COOKING-RANGE
CORK-LINOLEUM
CUSHION-COVER
DORMER-WINDOW

ELECTRIC FIRE
EXTINGUISHER
EXTRACTOR FAN
FESTOON-BLIND
HEATER-SHIELD
INDOOR AERIAL
INSTALLATION
IRONING-BOARD
KITCHEN-RANGE
LIGHT-FITTING
LIGHTNING-ROD
LOOKING-GLASS
LOUVRE-WINDOW
MAGAZINE RACK
MASTER-SWITCH
PANEL-HEATING
PARQUET-FLOOR
PERSIAN BLIND
PICTURE-FRAME
RECORD-PLAYER
REFRIGERATOR
ROASTING-JACK
ROCKER SWITCH
SERVICE HATCH
SOLAR-HEATING
SPACE-HEATING
STANDARD LAMP
STORM-SHUTTER
SWINGING-POST
TAPE RECORDER
TURKEY CARPET
WAINSCOTTING
WEATHER-STRIP
WINDOW-SCREEN

13

BATEMENT LIGHT
CANDLE-SNUFFER
CARPET-SWEEPER
CLOTHES-BASKET
COMPASS-WINDOW
DOUBLE-ADAPTOR
DOUBLE-GLAZING
DRAINING-BOARD
DRAUGHT-SCREEN
EMERGENCY EXIT

FRIDGE-FREEZER
INTERIOR GRATE
KIDDERMINSTER
MEDICINE-CHEST
MICROWAVE OVEN
PARTITION-WALL
PAVEMENT LIGHT
PERSIAN CARPET
PICTURE-WINDOW
REVOLVING DOOR
SEWING MACHINE
SHOWER-CURTAIN
SKIRTING-BOARD
SMOOTHING IRON
STRIP-LIGHTING
TELEVISION SET
TOILET-SERVICE
VACUUM-CLEANER
VENETIAN BLIND
VIDEO RECORDER
WASH-HAND BASIN
WINDOW-CURTAIN

14

ANGLE-POISE LAMP
BRUSSELS CARPET
CASEMENT WINDOW
CENTRAL HEATING
ELECTRIC HEATER
HOT-WATER BOTTLE
SPRING-MATTRESS
WARM-AIR HEATING
WASHING MACHINE
XMAS DECORATION

15

AIR-CONDITIONING
CASEMENT-CURTAIN
COMBINATION LOCK
ELECTRIC BLANKET
IMMERSION HEATER
PARLIAMENT-HINGE
PICTURE-MOULDING

147

HOUSEHOLD – FURNITURE

3

ARM
BED
BOX
COT
LEG
PEW

4

BUNK
CRIB
DESK
DOSS
FORM
LEAF
POUF
SEAT
SOFA
WING

5

BENCH
CHAIR
COUCH
DIVAN
EASEL
PALKI
STAND
STOOL
SUITE
TABLE

6

AIR-BED
BOX-BED
BUFFET
BUREAU
CANOPY
CARVER
CRADLE
DRAWER
LITTER
LOCKER
LOUNGE
LOWBOY

PALKEE
POUFFE
PUT-U-UP
ROCKER
SETTEE
SETTLE
TEAPOY
TESTER
THRONE
TOILET

7

ALMIRAH
ANTIQUE
ARMOIRE
BEDPOST
BOX-SEAT
BUNK-BED
CABINET
CAMP-BED
CHARPOY
COMMODE
CONSOLE
COUNTER
DOS-À-DOS
DOWN-BED
FLY RAIL
HAMMOCK
HASSOCK
LEG-REST
LOUNGER
NORIMON
OTTOMAN
REED-BED
SEATING
SICK-BED
SOFA-BED
TALLBOY
TENT-BED
TROLLEY
TRUCKLE
TRUNDLE
VIS-À-VIS
WHATNOT

8

ALEBENCH
ARMCHAIR

BASSINET
BEDSTEAD
BED-TABLE
BOOK-CASE
BRIDE-BED
BUNK-BEDS
CARRY-COT
CHAIR-BED
CHAIR-LEG
CUPBOARD
DIVAN-BED
FAUTEUIL
FIELD-BED
FLOCK-BED
HATSTAND
LOO-TABLE
LOVE-SEAT
LUG-CHAIR
MONOPODE
PEMBROKE
PLANK-BED
PRESS-BED
RECLINER
SHERATON
TABLE-LEG
TABLE-TOP
TABOURET
TEA-TABLE
TWIN-BEDS
VANITORY
VARGUEÑO
WARDROBE
WATER-BED

9

BANQUETTE
CABRIOLET
CAMP-CHAIR
CAMP-STOOL
CANE-CHAIR
CARD-TABLE
COATSTAND
DAVENPORT
DECK-CHAIR
DEVONPORT
DUTCH WIFE
EASY-CHAIR
FOOTSTOOL
FURNITURE
GARDEROBE

HALLSTAND
HEAD-BOARD
HEADCHAIR
HIGH-CHAIR
PALANQUIN
PIER-TABLE
SECRETARY
SETTLE-BED
SHAKE-DOWN
SIDEBOARD
SIDE-TABLE
SOFA-TABLE
SPRING-BED
SPRING-BOX
TABLE-LEAF
TÊTE-À-TÊTE
WASH-STAND
WORK-BENCH
WORK-TABLE

10

CANTERBURY
CHIFFONIER
DUMB-WAITER
ELBOW-CHAIR
ESCRITOIRE
FEATHER-BED
FOUR-POSTER
MUSIC-STOOL
NIGHT-CHAIR
NIGHT-STOOL
PIANO-STOOL
SECRETAIRE
TEA-TROLLEY
TRICLINIUM
TRUCKLE-BED
TRUNDLE-BED
WEDDING-BED
WINDOW-SEAT

11

BASKET-CHAIR
CARVER-CHAIR
CHIPPENDALE
COFFEE-TABLE
DINING-TABLE
DINNER-TABLE
DINNER-WAGON

HEPPLEWHITE
MARRIAGE-BED
MOSES BASKET
PERIOD PIECE
READING-DESK
ROLL-TOP DESK
STANDING-BED
STUDIO COUCH
SWIVEL-CHAIR
TOILET-TABLE
WRITING-DESK

CONSOLE-TABLE
DRAWING-TABLE
FOLDING CHAIR
NEST OF TABLES
ROCKING-CHAIR
TROLLEY-TABLE
WINDSOR-CHAIR
WRITING-TABLE

UMBRELLA-STAND

14

BREAKFAST-TABLE
CHEST OF DRAWERS
RECLINING-CHAIR

12

BEDROOM SUITE
BEDSIDE TABLE
CHAISE-LONGUE
CHESTERFIELD

13

BATHROOM SUITE
BONHEUR-DU-JOUR
DRAW-LEAF TABLE
DRESSING-TABLE
FILING-CABINET
PIECRUST TABLE
RECLINING-SEAT

15

DINING-ROOM SUITE
GATE-LEGGED TABLE
OCCASIONAL TABLE
THREE-PIECE SUITE

HOUSEHOLD – TABLEWARE & UTENSILS

3	**4**	**5**		
CUP	BOAT	ASHET	FRIER	SCOOP
JUG	BOWL	CHINA	GLASS	SHAPE
MAT	COSY	COUPE	HANAP	SIEVE
MUG	DISH	COVER	JORAM	SLICE
PAN	FORK	CRUET	JORUM	SPOON
POT	RING	DICER	KNIFE	TAMIS
URN	TRAY	DOILY	LADLE	TAMMY
WOK	ZARF	FLUTE	PLATE	TAZZA
			PYREX	TIMER
			QUERN	WHISK

HOUSEHOLD – TABLEWARE & UTENSILS

6

BEETLE
BOTTLE
CARAFE
CARVER
COPITA
CURATE
EGG-CUP
FINGAN
GOBLET
JAGGER
KETTLE
MUFFIN
NAPKIN
OPENER
PADDLE
PEELER
POPPER
POSNET
POT-LID
PUSHER
RHYTON
RUMMER
SALVER
SAUCER
SCONCE
SERVER
SHAKER
SILVER
SKEWER
SPIDER
TEA-CUP
TEA-POT
TEA-SET
TEA-URN
THIBLE
TRIVET
TUREEN

7

BALLOON
CHARGER
CHIP-PAN
COASTER
COCOTTE
CRACKLE
CUTLERY
ÉCUELLE

EGG-COSY
EPERGNE
FLASKET
FLIP-DOG
GRIDDLE
MESS-TIN
MILK JUG
PAP-BOAT
PIE-DISH
POACHER
PLATTER
RAMEKIN
SAMOVAR
SERVICE
SKILLET
SPATULA
STEWPAN
STEWPOT
TALLBOY
TEA-COSY
TEA-TRAY
TERRINE
TOBY-JUG
TUMBLER
UTENSIL

8

BREAD-BIN
COLANDER
CROCKERY
DECANTER
DUCHESSE
EGG-GLASS
EGG-SLICE
EGG-SPOON
EGG-TIMER
EGG-WHISK
HAND-MILL
JELLY BAG
MONTEITH
OILCLOTH
OVENWARE
PANCHEON
PAP-SPOON
PATTY-PAN
POT-STICK
SAUCEPAN
SLOP-BOWL
SOUP-DISH

SQUEEZER
STOCK-POT
STRAINER
TABLE-MAT
TEA-BOARD
TEA-CLOTH
TEA-SPOON
TEA-TOWEL
TRENCHER

9

BAKESTONE
BUTTER-BOX
CAKE-STAND
CANTHARIS
CHINAWARE
COFFEE-CUP
COFFEE-POT
DINNER-SET
DISH-COVER
DUTCH OVEN
EGG-BEATER
FISH-KNIFE
FISH-SLICE
FRYING-PAN
GLASSWARE
GOLD-PLATE
GRAVY-BOAT
HORNSPOON
ICE-BUCKET
KNIFE-REST
LOVING-CUP
MUFFINEER
PEPPER-POT
PORRINGER
POSSET-CUP
PUNCH-BOWL
SALT-SPOON
SAUCE-BOAT
SERVIETTE
SLOP-BASIN
SOUP-PLATE
SOUP-SPOON
STRAW-STEM
SUGAR-BOWL
TABLEWARE
TEA-KETTLE
TEA-THINGS
TIN-OPENER

TOAST-RACK
TORMENTOR
TRAY-CLOTH
WINE-GLASS

10

APPLE-CORER
AVENTURINE
BAKING-TRAY
BREAD-BOARD
BUTTER-BOAT
BUTTER-DISH
CHOP-STICKS
COFFEE-MILL
CORN-POPPER
CRUET-STAND
CRUMB-CLOTH
DILDO-GLASS
ENTRÉE DISH
FINGERBOWL
FISH-CARVER
FISH-KETTLE
FISH-TROWEL
FRUIT-KNIFE
HOLLOW-WARE
JELLY-MOULD
KNIFE-BOARD
MOUSSELINE
MUSTARD-POT
NAPKIN-RING
PERCOLATOR
PUNCH-LADLE
ROLLING PIN
SALAD-PLATE
SALT-CELLAR
SOUP-TUREEN
SUGAR-BASIN
SUGAR-TONGS
TABLE-CLOTH
TABLE-COVER
TABLE-KNIFE
TABLE-LINEN
TABLE-SPOON
TEA-SERVICE
TODDY-LADLE
TOUCH-PLATE
TUPPERWARE
WAFER-IRONS
WAFER-TONGS

WAFFLE-IRON
WASSAIL-CUP
WATER-GLASS
WATER-PLATE

TABLE-NAPKIN
TEA-EQUIPAGE
VINAIGRETTE
WASSAIL BOWL
WOODEN SPOON

TOASTING-IRON

11

BRANDY-GLASS
BUTTER-KNIFE
BUTTER-PLATE
CENTRE-PIECE
CHAFING-DISH
DUCHESSE SET
EARTHENWARE
JAGGING-IRON
KETTLE-CLOTH
NUTCRACKERS
PLATE-WARMER
SAUCE-BOTTLE
SILVER-PLATE
SUPPER-CLOTH

12

APOSTLE SPOON
BOTTLE-OPENER
BOTTLE-SLIDER
BREAKFAST-SET
BUTTER-COOLER
CARVING-KNIFE
CHEESE-GRATER
DESSERT-SPOON
FISH-STRAINER
LIQUEUR-GLASS
MAZARINE DISH
MOUSTACHE-CUP
TOASTING-FORK

13

BOTTLE-COASTER
CHOPPING-BOARD
CHOPPING-KNIFE
DINNER-SERVICE
LEMON-SQUEEZER
MAZARINE PLATE
PORRIDGE-STICK

14

COCKTAIL SHAKER
DESSERT-SERVICE
ORANGE-SQUEEZER
PRESSURE COOKER

INSTRUMENTS & GAUGES

3
LOG

4
RULE
VIAL

5
BEVEL
GAUGE
GLASS
GROMA
LEVEL
METER
NORMA
PLUMB
RULER
SCALE
SIREN
SIZER

6
ABACUS
ALIDAD
ETALON
FINDER
GUNTER
LOGGER
SCALER
SCALES
SECTOR
SEEKER
SQUARE
STADIA
STROBE

7
AMMETER
ANEROID
BALANCE
BINOCLE
COHERER
COMPASS

DIOPTER
ELLWAND
MEASURE
MONITOR
PELORUS
SCANTLE
SEXTANT
SOUNDER
TRANSIT
T-SQUARE
VERNIER

8
DIAGRAPH
DIP-STICK
DIVIDERS
DRAW-TUBE
ECHOGRAM
FOOT-RULE
GAS-METER
GYROSTAT
INCH-TAPE
IRISCOPE
LOG-GLASS
LUXMETER
METEWAND
METEYARD
MYOGRAPH
ODOGRAPH
ODOMETER
OHMMETER
OTOSCOPE
OXIMETER
QUADRANT
RHEOCORD
RHEOSTAT
SPYGLASS
TAPELINE
UDOMETER
VIAMETER
WAYWISER
WET METER

9
AEROGRAPH
AEROMETER
ALTIMETER
AMBULATOR

ASPIRATOR
ASTROLABE
ATMOMETER
AUXOMETER
BAROGRAPH
BAROMETER
BAROSCOPE
BOLOMETER
BONING-ROD
CALLIPERS
COELOSTAT
COMPASSES
CRYOMETER
CRYOSCOPE
CYMOGRAPH
DIP-CIRCLE
DIP-SECTOR
DOODLE-BUG
DOSIMETER
EIDOGRAPH
ENDOSCOPE
ENGYSCOPE
ERGOGRAPH
ERGOMETER
ERIOMETER
FLOWMETER
FOCIMETER
GRADUATOR
GYROSCOPE
HAEMOSTAT
HELIOSTAT
HODOMETER
HOUR-GLASS
HYDROSTAT
HYGRODEIK
HYGROSTAT
INDICATOR
KONIMETER
KONISCOPE
KYMOGRAPH
LIGHT-MILL
LYSIMETER
MACHMETER
MANOMETER
MARIGRAPH
MEGASCOPE
MEKOMETER
METESTICK
METRONOME
MICROGRAM
NAVIGATOR
NILOMETER

NOCTURNAL
OENOMETER
ONCOMETER
OPTOMETER
OSMOMETER
PEDOMETER
PERIMETER
PERISCOPE
PLUMB-LINE
PLUMB-RULE
POLYGRAPH
POROSCOPE
POTOMETER
PYROMETER
PYROSCOPE
RAIN-GAUGE
REFLECTOR
REFRACTOR
RHEOCHORD
RHEOMETER
RING-GAUGE
SAND-GLASS
SET SQUARE
SLIDE-RULE
SOMASCOPE
STADIA-ROD
TASIMETER
TAXIMETER
TELEMETER
TELESCOPE
TIDE-GAUGE
TONOMETER
VOLTMETER
VOLUMETER
WATTMETER
WAVE-METER
WIND-GAUGE
XYLOMETER
XYLOPHONE
ZYMOMETER

10
ACIDIMETER
ALMACANTAR
ALTAZIMUTH
ANEMOGRAPH
ANEMOMETER
ARAEOMETER
AUDIOMETER
BATHOMETER
BATHYMETER

BINOCULARS
CLINOMETER
COLLIMETER
COMPARATOR
CROSS-STAFF
CRYOPHORUS
CYANOMETER
CYCLOGRAPH
CYCLOMETER
CYSTOSCOPE
DECLINATOR
DENSIMETER
DIAGOMETER
DROSOMETER
DUMPY-LEVEL
EQUATORIAL
EUDIOMETER
FATHOMETER
GAUGE-GLASS
GAUGING-ROD
GONIOMETER
GRADIENTER
GRAVIMETER
HELIOGRAPH
HELIOMETER
HELIOSCOPE
HELIOTROPE
HYDROMETER
HYDROSCOPE
HYETOGRAPH
HYETOMETER
HYGROGRAPH
HYGROMETER
HYGROSCOPE
HYPSOMETER
ICONOMETER
INSTRUMENT
INTEGRATOR
MICROGRAPH
MICROMETER
MICROSCOPE
NEPHOGRAPH
NEPHOSCOPE
NITROMETER
OMBROMETER
OPISOMETER
OPSIOMETER
ORIENTATOR
PACHYMETER
PANTOGRAPH
PAPER-GAUGE
PAPER-RULER

PELVIMETER
PHOTOMETER
PIEZOMETER
PLANE-TABLE
PLANIMETER
PLANOMETER
PROTRACTOR
PULSIMETER
PULSOMETER
PYCNOMETER
RADIOGRAPH
RADIOMETER
SIDEROSTAT
SPIROGRAPH
SPIROMETER
STABILISER
STATOSCOPE
STEAM-GAUGE
STORM-GLASS
TACHOGRAPH
TACHOMETER
TACHYMETER
TASEOMETER
TEINOSCOPE
THEODOLITE
THERMOSTAT
TINTOMETER
TRIBOMETER
TROMOMETER
URINOMETER
VARIOMETER
VIBROGRAPH
VIBROMETER
VISCOMETER
VOLTAMETER
WATER-GAUGE
WATER-GLASS
WATER-LEVEL
WATER-METER
WEATHER-BOX

11

ACTINOMETER
ALKALIMETER
AUSCULTATOR
AUXANOMETER
CALORIMETER
CARDIOGRAPH
CHLORIMETER
CHLOROMETER

CHROMOSCOPE
CHRONOGRAPH
CHRONOSCOPE
COLORIMETER
COMET-FINDER
CORONOGRAPH
DENDROMETER
DICHROSCOPE
DYNAMOGRAPH
DYNAMOMETER
ECHO-SOUNDER
FEELER-GAUGE
FLUOROSCOPE
GRADIOMETER
GYROCOMPASS
HELICOGRAPH
INTOXIMETER
LIE-DETECTOR
MAP-MEASURER
METEOROGRAM
ODONTOGRAPH
OPEIDOSCOPE
PLUVIOMETER
POLARIMETER
POLARISCOPE
PSYCHOGRAPH
PSYCHOMETER
QUANTOMETER
RANGEFINDER
SALINOMETER
SCLEROMETER
SEISMOGRAPH
SEISMOMETER
SEISMOSCOPE
SPEEDOMETER
SPHEROMETER
SPIRIT-LEVEL
STEREOMETER
STETHOSCOPE
STRABOMETER
STROBOSCOPE
SWINGOMETER
TACHEOMETER
TAPE-MEASURE
THERMOGRAPH
THERMOMETER
THERMOSCOPE
TORQUE-METER
TORSIOGRAPH
TROCHOMETER
VAPORIMETER
VECTORSCOPE

INSTRUMENTS & GAUGES

VOLUMOMETER
ZYMOSIMETER

12

AETHRIOSCOPE
BOW-COMPASSES
BREATHALYSER
CATHETOMETER
COUNTER-GAUGE
DECLINOMETER
EBULLIOSCOPE
EFFUSIOMETER
ELECTROGRAPH
ELECTROMETER
ELECTROSCOPE
ELLIPSOGRAPH
ENDOSMOMETER
EVAPORIMETER
EXTENSOMETER
FIELD GLASSES
GALACTOMETER
GALVANOMETER
GALVANOSCOPE
GUNTER'S CHAIN
GUNTER'S SCALE
HARMONOGRAPH
HARMONOMETER
INCLINOMETER
KERAUNOGRAPH
LARYNGOSCOPE
MAGNETOGRAPH
MAGNETOMETER
MEASURING-ROD
METEOROGRAPH
MICROBALANCE
MYRINGOSCOPE
NEPHELOMETER
OSCILLOSCOPE
PERAMBULATOR
PSYCHROMETER
RADIO-COMPASS
RHYTHMOMETER

SCINTILLATOR
SENSITOMETER
SLIDING SCALE
SPECTROGRAPH
SPECTROMETER
SPECTROSCOPE
SPHYGMOGRAPH
SPHYGMOMETER
SPHYGMOPHONE
SPHYGMOSCOPE
STRAIGHT-EDGE
VERNIER SCALE
VISCOSIMETER
WEATHER-GLASS
WEATHER-HOUSE
ZENITH SECTOR

13

ACCELEROMETER
ALCOHOLOMETER
COUNTING FRAME
DIAGONAL SCALE
DIAPHANOMETER
DIFFUSION-TUBE
DIPPING-NEEDLE
DIPLEIDOSCOPE
ENCEPHALOGRAM
GEIGER-COUNTER
INCLINATORIUM
MICRODETECTOR
PERPENDICULAR
PHONAUTOGRAPH
PNEUMATOMETER
POTENTIOMETER
PROSPECT-GLASS
PYRHELIOMETER
REFRACTOMETER
SACCHARIMETER
SACCHAROMETER
SPRING-BALANCE
STALAGMOMETER
SYMPIESOMETER

TACHISTOSCOPE
THERMOBALANCE
TRANSIT-CIRCLE
VOLUMENOMETER
WEATHEROMETER

14

ABSORPTIOMETER
CIRCUMFERENTOR
DIFFRACTOMETER
DIVIDING-ENGINE
ENCEPHALOGRAPH
GEOTHERMOMETER
INTERFEROMETER
KINETHEODOLITE
MERIDIAN CIRCLE
OPHTHALMOMETER
OPHTHALMOSCOPE
PARALLEL RULERS
RADAR ALTIMETER
RADIO ALTIMETER
RADIO TELESCOPE
SCINTILLOMETER
SCINTILLOSCOPE
SPINTHARISCOPE
STRABISMOMETER
TORSION-BALANCE
WATER-BAROMETER

15

BONING-TELESCOPE
ELECTROMYOGRAPH
HYETOMETROGRAPH
KATATHERMOMETER
MAGNIFYING GLASS
MINIMISING-GLASS
PHASE-MICROSCOPE
RADIO-GONIOMETER
SOLAR MICROSCOPE
ULTRAMICROSCOPE

LANGUAGE – GRAMMAR & PHONETICS

3

DOT
MOT
PUN

4

BULL
CANT
CASE
DASH
DUAL
FORM
LONG
MODE
MOOD
MUTE
NOUN
OGAM
PAST
POSY
ROOT
RUNE
SIGN
STEM
STOP
SURD
TERM
VERB
WORD

5

BLANK
COLON
COMMA
ENTRY
GLIDE
GRADE
IMAGE
INFIX
IRONY
MEDIA
NASAL
OGHAM
POINT
POWER
QUERY
QUOTE

SCHWA
SHEVA
TENSE
THEME
TILDE
TREMA
TROPE
VELAR
VOICE
VOWEL

6

ABLAUT
ACCENT
ADVERB
AORIST
APORIA
APTOTE
ASPECT
BATHOS
CLAUSE
CLICHÉ
CLIMAX
CLINCH
COPULA
CRASIS
DATIVE
DIESIS
ECBOLE
ENDING
ESSIVE
ETYMON
FUTURE
GENDER
GERUND
HIATUS
HOWLER
HYBRID
HYPHEN
LABIAL
LENGTH
LETTER
MACRON
MEMBER
NEUTER
NUMBER
OBJECT
PENULT
PERIOD
PERSON

PHRASE
PLURAL
PREFIX
SEGHOL
SIMILE
STRESS
STROKE
SUFFIX
SUPINE
SYNTAX
TENUIS
TMESIS
TONEME
UMLAUT
VOCULE
ZEUGMA

7

ACRONYM
ADJUNCT
ANALOGY
ANTONYM
APAGOGE
APHESIS
APOCOPE
ASTEISM
AUXESIS
CADENCE
CEDILLA
CORONIS
DICTION
DIGRAPH
DIPHONE
ECHOISM
ECTASIS
ELISION
EPAGOGE
EPICENE
EPIGRAM
EPITHET
EROTEMA
EROTEME
ETACISM
FLEXION
FORMANT
FUTHORK
GRAMMAR
HOMONYM
IMAGERY
INITIAL

ITACISM
JUSSIVE
LITOTES
MEANING
MEIOSIS
METONYM
MIMESIS
NEOLOGY
NUMERAL
OXYTONE
PARADOX
PARONYM
PARSING
PASSIVE
PATRIAL
PERFECT
PHONEME
POSTFIX
PRESENT
PRONOUN
RECTION
SIGNARY
SPIRANT
SUBJECT
SYNESIS
SYNONYM
SYSTOLE
VARIANT
VIRGULE
VOCABLE
WORDING

8

ABLATIVE
ABSOLUTE
ALPHABET
ANALYSIS
ANAPHORA
ANTITHET
APHORISM
APODOSIS
ASPIRATE
BETACISM
BILABIAL
CHIASMUS
CLAUSULA
COMPOUND
DEPONENT
DIALLAGE
DIAPHONE

DIASTOLE
DIEGESIS
ELLIPSIS
EMPHASIS
ENALLAGE
ENCLISIS
ENCLITIC
EROTESIS
FEMININE
FULL STOP
FUNCTION
GENITIVE
GRAPHEME
GUTTURAL
IDIOLECT
ILLATIVE
IOTACISM
LACONISM
LANGUAGE
LOCATIVE
METAPHOR
METONYMY
MODIFIER
MORPHEME
MUTATION
NEGATIVE
OPTATIVE
OXYMORON
PARABOLE
PARADIGM
PARAGOGE
PARAGRAM
PARALLEL
PAROEMIA
PARONYMY
PARTICLE
PHRASING
PLATEASM
PLEONASM
POLYSEME
POLYSEMY
POSITIVE
PROTASIS
QUANTITY
QUESTION
RELATIVE
SENTENCE
SIBILANT
SINGULAR
SOLECISM
SPELLING
SYLLABLE

155

LANGUAGE – GRAMMAR & PHONETICS

SYMPLOCE
SYNONYMY
TRIGRAPH
TRIPHONE
TRIPTOTE
UNIVOCAL
VOCALISM
VOCATIVE
VOLITIVE

9

ACCIDENCE
ACROPHONY
ADJECTIVE
AFFRICATE
ALLOMORPH
ALLOPHONE
ANAPTYXIS
ASSONANCE
ASYNDETON
ATTRIBUTE
AUXILIARY
CAUSATIVE
CONDITION
CONJUGATE
CONSONANT
DIAERESIS
DIPHTHONG
DISSIMILE
DOG-LETTER
ENTHYMEME
EPITHESIS
EPIZEUXIS
EQUIVOQUE
ETYMOLOGY
EUPHEMISM
EXPLETIVE
EXPLOSIVE
EXTENSION
FORMATIVE
FORM CLASS
FRICATIVE
GERUNDIVE
GRADATION
GRIMM'S LAW
HAPLOLOGY
HEAD RHYME
HENDIADYS
HETERONYM
HOMOGRAPH

HOMOPHONE
HYPALLAGE
HYPERBOLE
HYPOTAXIS
IDIOTICON
IMPERFECT
IMPLOSION
INCEPTIVE
INCREMENT
INFLEXION
INTENSIVE
INVERSION
LEVELLING
MAJOR TERM
MARROWSKY
MASCULINE
METAPLASM
MONOPTOTE
MUMPSIMUS
NEOLOGISM
NEOTERISM
NONCE-WORD
NUNNATION
OBJECTIVE
OBSTRUENT
OCCLUSIVE
PALILLOGY
PARAGRAPH
PARATAXIS
PARTITIVE
PAST TENSE
PHILOLOGY
PHONETICS
PHONOGRAM
POLYPHONE
POTENTIAL
PREDICATE
PREFIXION
PRETERITE
PRIMITIVE
PRIVATIVE
PROCLITIC
PROLEPSIS
PROTHESIS
REFLEXIVE
RHOTACISM
RHYME-WORD
RUNE-STAVE
SEGHOLATE
SEMANTEME
SEMICOLON
SEMIVOWEL

SIBILANCE
SIGMATISM
SUMPSIMUS
SYLLABARY
SYLLABISM
SYLLEPSIS
SYNCHISIS
SYNIZESIS
TAUTOLOGY
VERBALISM
VERBALITY

10

ABSCISSION
ACCUSATIVE
ANASTROPHE
ANTECEDENT
ANTEPENULT
ANTICLIMAX
ANTITHESIS
APHAERESIS
APOPHTHEGM
APOSTROPHE
APPOSITION
ASPIRATION
CIRCUMFLEX
COMITATIVE
COMMON NOUN
COMPARISON
COMPLEMENT
COPULATIVE
CORREPTION
DECLENSION
DEFINITION
DERIVATION
DERIVATIVE
DIMINUTIVE
DISYLLABLE
ECPHONESIS
ECTHLIPSIS
ENANTIOSIS
EPENTHESIS
EPEXEGESIS
EPIPHONEMA
EPISTROPHE
EXPRESSION
FINITE VERB
GLOSSOLOGY
GLOTTOLOGY
GOVERNMENT

HOLOPHRASE
HYPERBATON
IMPERATIVE
INCHOATIVE
INDICATIVE
INFINITIVE
INFLECTION
INFLECTIVE
INTONATION
LACONICISM
LAMBDACISM
LEXICOLOGY
LINGUISTRY
METALEPSIS
METAPHRASE
METATHESIS
MULTIVOCAL
NOMINATIVE
NOUN CLAUSE
PARAPHRASE
PARATHESIS
PAROXYTONE
PARTICIPLE
PEJORATIVE
PERIEGESIS
PHONOGRAPH
PLUPERFECT
POLYSEMANT
POSSESSIVE
PREFIXTURE
PROPER NOUN
PROSTHESIS
QUIESCENCE
RESOLUTION
SOUND-SHIFT
SPOONERISM
SYNAERESIS
SYNALOEPHA
SYNECDOCHE
TETRAPTOTE
TRIPHTHONG
VERBAL NOUN
VERNER'S LAW
VOCABULARY
VOWEL POINT

11

ACTIVE VOICE
ACUTE ACCENT
AFFRICATION

AFFRICATIVE
AMPHIBOLOGY
ANACOLUTHIA
ANACOLUTHON
ANADIPLOSIS
ANTIPHRASIS
ANTONOMASIA
APOCOPATION
APOSIOPESIS
CATACHRESIS
COHORTATIVE
COMPARATIVE
CONJUGATION
CONJUNCTION
CONNOTATION
CONTRACTION
DECLINATION
DISJUNCTIVE
DISYLLABISM
ENLARGEMENT
EPANALEPSIS
EPICHEIREMA
FIRST PERSON
FUTURE TENSE
GLOTTAL STOP
GRAVE ACCENT
HETEROCLITE
HYPERBOLISM
HYPHENATION
HYPOSTROPHE
HYPOTYPOSIS
LABIODENTAL
LINGUISTICS
MALAPROPISM
MIDDLE VOICE
MISSPELLING
MONOPHTHONG
OBLIQUE CASE
PARALEIPSIS
PARALLELISM
PARENTHESIS
PARANOMASIA
PAST PERFECT
PENULTIMATE
PERIPHRASIS
PERISSOLOGY
PHONETICISM
PHRASEOLOGY
PREDICATION
PREPOSITION
PRETERITION
PUNCTUATION

REGULAR VERB
SUBJUNCTIVE
SUBSTANTIVE
SUCTION STOP
SUPERLATIVE
SVARABHAKTI
SYNCHORESIS
SYNOECIOSIS
TAUTOLOGISM
TERMINOLOGY
THIRD PERSON
TRISYLLABLE

12

ABBREVIATION
ABSTRACT NOUN
ALLITERATION
ANTIMETABOLE
ASSIBILATION
COMMON GENDER
CONCRETE NOUN
CONSTRUCTION
DEASPIRATION
DECASYLLABLE
DENTILINGUAL
DEPONENT VERB
DIRECT OBJECT
DIRECT SPEECH
DISTRIBUTIVE
GNOMIC AORIST
GRAMMATICISM
INESSIVE CASE
INTERJECTION
MONOSYLLABLE
OCTOSYLLABLE
ONOMATOPOEIA
ORTHOTONESIS
PART OF SPEECH
PASSIVE VOICE
PERFECT TENSE
PERISPOMENON
POLYSYLLABLE
POLYSYNDETON
POSTPOSITION
PRESENT TENSE
PROSOPOPOEIA
QUESTION-MARK
SECOND PERSON
SYNECDOCHISM
VOCALISATION

WORD-BUILDING

13

BACK-FORMATION
COGNATE OBJECT
EPANADIPLOSIS
ETHICAL DATIVE
FALSE QUANTITY
FOLK-ETYMOLOGY
FREQUENTATIVE
FUTURE-PERFECT
HOMEOTELEUTON
INTERPUNCTION
INTERROGATIVE
IRREGULAR VERB
MIXED METAPHOR
MORPHOPHONEME
OMNIBUS CLAUSE
ONOMATOPOESIS
OVERSTATEMENT
PARASYNTHESIS
PARASYNTHETON
POLYSYLLABISM
POLYSYNTHESIS
PRONUNCIATION
PROPAROXYTONE
QUADRILITERAL
REDUPLICATION
REFLEXIVE VERB
SUCTIONAL STOP
SYLLABICATION
SYNECPHONESIS
TETRASYLLABLE
TRILITERALISM
VERBALISATION
VISIBLE SPEECH
VOWEL MUTATION

14

ANTIMETATHESIS
CLOSED SYLLABLE
CONSTRUCT STATE
DODECASYLLABLE
DOUBLE ENTENDRE
FIGURE OF SPEECH
HAPAX LEGOMENON
HYPERCATALEXIS
IMPERATIVE MOOD

LANGUAGE – GRAMMAR & PHONETICS

IMPERFECT TENSE
INDICATIVE MOOD
INDIRECT OBJECT
INDIRECT SPEECH
INVERTED COMMAS
LEXICAL MEANING
MANUAL ALPHABET
PAST PARTICIPLE
POLYSYNTHETISM
POSSESSIVE CASE
QUADRISYLLABLE
QUOTATION-MARKS
REPORTED SPEECH
SIMPLE SENTENCE

TRANSITIVE VERB
UNDERSTATEMENT
VOWEL GRADATION

15

COMPLEX SENTENCE
CONJUNCTIVE MOOD
DEFINITE ARTICLE
DIACRITICAL MARK
ETHICAL GENITIVE

EXCLAMATION MARK
HISTORIC PRESENT
PARAGOGIC FUTURE
PAULO-POST-FUTURE
PERSONIFICATION
POLYSYLLABICISM
PORTMANTEAU-WORD
PROPERISPOMENON
PUNCTUATION MARK
RELATIVE PRONOUN
SPLIT INFINITIVE
SUBJUNCTIVE MOOD
SYLLABIFICATION

LANGUAGE – LANGUAGES & DIALECTS

3
BAT
GIZ
IBO
IDO
NEO
TWI

4
AINU
COPT
ERSE
GEËZ
MANX
NORN
PALI
SERB
SHAN
THAI
TUPI
URDU
ZULU

5
ARYAN
AZTEC
BANTU
CARIB
CZECH
DORIC
DUTCH
FANTI
GREEK
GUJAR
GUMBO
HINDI
HUSKY
IDIOM
IONIC
IRAQI
IRISH
KAREN
KHMER
KOINE
KUO-YÜ
LADIN
LATIN

LINGO
MALAY
MAORI
NORSE
ORIYA
OSCAN
PUNIC
ROMIC
SAKAI
SAXON
SCOTS
SHONA
SUOMI
SWISS
TAMIL
TATAR
TURKI
UZBEG
UZBEK
WELSH
WOLOF
XHOSA
YAKUT

6
ARABIC
BASQUE
BASUTO
BERBER
BRETON
CELTIC
CREOLE
CYMRIC
DANISH
ESKIMO
FRENCH
GAELIC
GALLIC
GERMAN
GOTHIC
GULLAH
HEBREW
HERERO
IONIAN
KABYLE
KAFFIR
LADINO
LYDIAN

MAGYAR
MANCHU
MEDIAN
MICMAC
MONGOL
NOVIAL
OSTYAK
PAKHTU
PATOIS
PERSIC
PIDGIN
POLISH
PUSHTU
ROMAIC
ROMANY
SCOTCH
SCOUSE
SHELTA
SLOVAK
SYRIAC
TELUGU
TONGUE
TSWANA
TUAREG
TUNGUS

TUSCAN
UGRIAN
YORUBA

7
AMHARIC
ARABIAN
ARAMAIC
ARMORIC
AVESTAN
AVESTIC
BENGALI
BRITISH
BURMESE
CATALAN
CHINESE
CHINOOK
CHOCTAW
CORNISH
DIALECT
ENGLISH
FINNISH
FLEMISH

158

FRISIAN
GAULISH
GUARANI
HITTITE
IRANIAN
ITALIAN
KALMUCK
KANNADA
KENNICK
KENTISH
LAPPISH
LETTISH
MALAYAN
MALTESE
MARATHI
MEXICAN
NAHUATL
PEHLEVI
PERSIAN
PRÂKRIT
PUNJABI
QUECHUA
ROMANCE
ROMANIC
RUSSIAN
RUTHENE
SAMNITE
SAMOYED
SEMITIC
SERBIAN
SIAMESE
SPANISH
SWAHILI
SWEDISH
TAGÁLOG
TIBETAN
TURKISH
UMBRIAN
VOLAPÜK
WALLOON
WENDISH
YIDDISH

8

AMERICAN
ARMENIAN
AUSTRIAN
BALINESE
BATAVIAN
BOG-LATIN

BOHEMIAN
BULGARIC
CHALDAIC
CHEROKEE
CUMBRIAN
DOG-LATIN
EGYPTIAN
ESTONIAN
ETHIOPIC
ETRUSCAN
GADHELIC
GUERNSEY
GUJARATI
HAWAIIAN
JAPANESE
KANARESE
KOLARIAN
LANGUAGE
LAW LATIN
LOW LATIN
MAEONIAN
MALAGASY
MANDAEAN
MANDARIN
MANDINGO
NEO-LATIN
NEPALESE
OLD NORSE
PHRYGIAN
POLABIAN
RABBINIC
ROMANSCH
ROMANIAN
RUMANIAN
SANSKRIT
SCOTTISH
SCYTHIAN
SLAVONIC
TEUTONIC
VOLSCIAN
YUGOSLAV

9

AFRIKAANS
BARAGOUIN
BULGARIAN
CASTILIAN
DRAVIDIAN
ESPERANTO
FRANGLAIS

HIGH DUTCH
HUNGARIAN
ICELANDIC
LANDSMAAL
LANGUE D'OC
LATE LATIN
LOW GERMAN
MALAYALAM
MALAYSIAN
MONGOLIAN
NORWEGIAN
PROVENÇAL
ROUMANIAN
RUTHENIAN
SAMARITAN
SARDINIAN
SINHALESE
UKRAINIAN
VARANGIAN
WEST SAXON

10

ANDALUSIAN
ANGLO-SAXON
AUSTRALIAN
CIRCASSIAN
DEVANAGARI
FOLK-SPEECH
HIGH GERMAN
HINDUSTANI
JOURNALESE
LANGUE D'OIL
LANGUE D'OUI
MELANESIAN
OCCIDENTAL
OLD ENGLISH
PHOENICIAN
PORTUGUESE
SERBO-CROAT
VERNACULAR
VIETNAMESE

11

BELORUSSIAN
COMPUTERESE
EPIC DIALECT
INTERGLOSSA
INTERLINGUA

LINGOA GERAL
MIDDLE LATIN
MODERN LATIN
MOESO-GOTHIC
OLD PRUSSIAN
ROCK ENGLISH
YUGOSLAVIAN

12

BASIC ENGLISH
DEAD LANGUAGE
IONIC DIALECT
KING'S ENGLISH
LINGUA FRANCA
METALANGUAGE
MOTHER-TONGUE
NORMAN-FRENCH
NORTHUMBRIAN
PLATT-DEUTSCH
TELEGRAPHESE
TONE LANGUAGE

13

NEO-MELANESIAN
OXFORD ENGLISH
PIDGIN-ENGLISH
QUEEN'S ENGLISH
RHAETO-ROMANIC
SATEM LANGUAGE
SERBO-CROATIAN

14

CLASSICAL LATIN
LIVING LANGUAGE

15

CZECHOSLOVAKIAN
RECEIVED ENGLISH
ROMANCE LANGUAGE
STANDARD ENGLISH

LANGUAGE – TALK & COLLOQUIALISM

3

FIB
GAB
GAG
GAS
LIE
LIP
ROT
SAW
SAY

4

BOSH
BUNK
CANT
CHAT
GIBE
JEER
JEST
JIBE
JOKE
QUIP
RANT
TALE
TALK
TOSH
WIND

5

ABUSE
ADAGE
AD LIB
ARGOT
ASIDE
BILGE
CHAFF
CRACK
GNOME
HOOEY
LYING
MAXIM
MOTTO
PI-JAW
PRATE
QUOTE
RECAP
REPLY

SALLY
SLANG
SPIEL
STORY
TRIPE

6

ANSWER
BANTER
BON MOT
BUNKUM
BYWORD
DENIAL
DRIVEL
EULOGY
FEELER
GABBLE
GAMMON
GOSSIP
HOMILY
HOT AIR
IONISM
JABBER
JARGON
JAWING
MUTTER
NATTER
PATTER
PHRASE
PIFFLE
PRAISE
REMARK
REPORT
RETORT
SAYING
SERMON
SPEECH
TATTLE
THREAT
TIRADE
TRUISM

7

ADDRESS
APOLOGY
BALONEY
BLARNEY
BLATHER

BLETHER
BOMBAST
CHATTER
CHINWAG
COMMENT
COMMUNE
FIBBING
GASSING
HEARSAY
LALLING
LECTURE
OBLOQUY
ORATION
PALAVER
PARABLE
PEP TALK
PRATING
PRATTLE
PROVERB
QUIBBLE
QUOTING
RANTING
READING
RECITAL
RIPOSTE
SARCASM
SLANDER
TALKING
TWADDLE
TWATTLE

8

ANECDOTE
ARCHAISM
AVERMENT
BABY-TALK
BACKCHAT
BADINAGE
BALLYHOO
BLABBING
BOASTING
BRAGGING
CHATTING
CHITCHAT
CLAPTRAP
COLLOQUY
CONVERSE
CUSS-WORD
CYNICISM
DIALOGUE

DIATRIBE
DICACITY
DORICISM
DUALOGUE
ELENCHUS
EPANODOS
EXCURSUS
EXORDIUM
GABBLING
GOSSIPRY
GRAECISM
GRASSING
HARANGUE
HEBRAISM
HECKLING
IDIOTISM
IRISHISM
LATINISM
LOCUTION
MUMBLING
NEGROISM
NONSENSE
OUTBURST
OUTFLING
PARLANCE
POLONISM
PROSAISM
QUESTION
RAILLERY
RELATION
REPARTEE
REVILING
RHETORIC
SAXONISM
SEMITISM
SINICISM
SLACK-JAW
SPEAKING
SWEARING
TATTLING
TOMMYROT
UTTERING
VERBIAGE

9

ANGLICISM
ASSERTION
BACK-SLANG
CATCH-WORD
CRITICISM

CROSS-TALK
DICTATION
DIRTY WORD
DISCOURSE
ELOQUENCE
EMPTY TALK
FACUNDITY
GALLICISM
GARRULITY
GASCONADE
GERMANISM
GIBBERISH
GOSSIPING
INSOLENCE
INFORMING
INVECTIVE
ITALICISM
ITERATION
JABBERING
LALLATION
LECTURING
MACROLOGY
MONOLOGUE
MUTTERING
NARRATING
NARRATION
NATTERING
OUTGIVING
PHILIPPIC
POPPYCOCK
PRATTLING
QUIBBLING
REJOINDER
SALES TALK
SET SPEECH
SMALL TALK
SOLILOQUY
STATEMENT
STRICTURE
SUMMING-UP
SWEAR-WORD
SYRIACISM
TABLE-TALK
TÊTE-À-TÊTE
TWATTLING
UTTERANCE
VOGUE WORD
WISECRACK
WITTICISM

10

ALLEGATION
ALLOCUTION
BALDERDASH
BRITISHISM
CHATTERING
DISCURSION
DISCUSSION
DOUBLE-TALK
DULCILOQUY
EXPOSITION
EXPRESSION
FUNNY STORY
GAINSAYING
HEBRAICISM
HIBERICISM
IMPUGNMENT
ITALIANISM
LOGORRHOEA
MAUNDERING
MISQUOTING
MISREADING
MULTILOQUY
OPPUGNANCY
OROTUNDITY
OUTPOURING
PARAENESIS
PERIPHRASE
PERORATION
PERSIFLAGE
PLEASANTRY
PROSAICISM
PROTREPTIC
RECITATION
REFUTATION
REPETITION
SCOTTICISM
SOMNILOQUY
WEASEL-WORD
YACKETY-YAK

11

ACCLAMATION

AFFIRMATION
AMERICANISM
BRAGGADOCIO
DECLAMATION
DECLARATION
DOUBLE-DUTCH
EJACULATION
ELABORATION
ENUNCIATION
EXHORTATION
EXPATIATION
EXPLANATION
EXPLICATION
FULMINATION
HISPANICISM
MALEDICTION
NORTHERNISM
OBSERVATION
OFFICIALESE
PERIPHRASIS
PRATTLEMENT
REITERATION
RODOMONTADE
ROGUES' LATIN
SOUTHERNISM
STULTILOQUY
VALEDICTION

12

ANNOUNCEMENT
ANNUNCIATION
CONVERSATION
DIALECTICISM
DIRECT SPEECH
DISSERTATION
FIDDLE-FADDLE
GIBBLE-GABBLE
GOBBLEDEGOOK
HIBERNIANISM
OLD WIVES' TALE
PROCLAMATION
RHYMING SLANG
SOMNILOQUISM

SPEECH-MAKING
STRAIGHT TALK
TITTLE-TATTLE
VITUPERATION
VOCIFERATION

13

CIRCUMAMBAGES
COLLOQUIALISM
CONFABULATION
CONVERSAZIONE
EXPOSTULATION
HOUSEHOLD WORD
INTERLOCUTION
MAGNILOQUENCE
MULTILOQUENCE
PLAIN SPEAKING
PRONOUNCEMENT
PROVERBIALISM
PROVINCIALISM
REMONSTRATION
SOMNILOQUENCE
VERNACULARISM

14

CIRCUMLOCUTION
LOADED QUESTION
PRITTLE-PRATTLE
RECAPITULATION
STULTILOQUENCE
TITTLE-TATTLING

15

EXTEMPORISATION
LEADING QUESTION
STRAIGHT TALKING

LEGAL TERMS

3

ACT
BAN
BAR
FEE
LAW
LET
LOT
SAC
SOC
USE

4

BAIL
BANC
BILL
BOND
BOOT
CASE
CHOP
CODE
DEED
DOCK
EYRE
FACT
FEME
FEUD
FIAT
FINE
FOUD
GELD
JURY
LEET
LIEN
MARK
MISE
MOOT
MORA
OATH
OYER
PAIS
PLEA
RIOT
RULE
SILK
SOKE
SUIT
TAIL
TERM

TOLT
TORT
USES
VETO
WILL
WRIT

5

ALIBI
ANNAT
ARRÊT
AVOUÉ
BENCH
BLAME
BRIEF
BULLA
BYLAW
CAUSE
CHOSE
CLAIM
COMPO
COSTS
COUNT
COURT
COVER
CRIME
CURIA
DOWER
DOWRY
DROIT
EDICT
ENTRY
FEOFF
FETWA
FOLIO
FORUM
FUERO
GAVEL
GEMOT
GOODS
GRANT
GUILT
ISSUE
LEASE
LIBEL
MANOR
MERCY
MULCT
ORDER
PARTY

PLAIN
PRIVY
PROOF
QUEST
REMIT
RIDER
RIGHT
SOKEN
SUING
SWEAR
TALES
TERCE
TITHE
TITLE
TRIAL
TRUST
VENUE
VISNE
VOUCH
WASTE
WRONG

6

ACCESS
ACTION
ANGARY
APPEAL
ARREST
ASSETS
ASSIZE
ASYLUM
AVOWAL
AVOWRY
BOUNTY
BREACH
BYE-LAW
BYRLAW
CAMERA
CARNET
CAVEAT
CHALAN
CHARGE
CLAUSE
CORVÉE
COTTAR
CURFEW
CY PRES
DECREE
DELICT
DEMAND

DEMISE
DIGEST
DOCKET
ENTAIL
EQUITY
ESCROW
ESSOIN
ESTATE
EXCUSE
EXPIRY
EXTENT
FEALTY
FIRMAN
GUILTY
HERIOT
HIDAGE
INDENT
INFAMY
JAGHIR
LACHES
LEGACY
LENITY
MATTER
MERITS
MOTION
MURAGE
NONAGE
OUSTER
OWELTY
PARAGE
PARDON
PATENT
PAVAGE
PERMIT
PLAINT
PLEDGE
PUTURE
REALTY
RECORD
REMAND
REMISE
REPEAL
RETURN
REVIEW
SCRIPT
SEA-LAW
SEIZIN
SOCAGE
STRESS
SUBFEU
SUDDER
SURETY

TENURE
TROVER
WAIVER

7

ALCALDE
ALIMONY
AMNESTY
ASSIZES
BASE FEE
BEQUEST
BROCARD
BURGAGE
CALUMNY
CAPTION
CAPTURE
CASE-LAW
CAUTION
CESSION
CHAMBER
CHARTER
CHATTEL
CIRCUIT
CODICIL
CONACRE
CORNAGE
CORN-LAW
CORRODY
CUSTODY
CUSTOMS
DAMAGES
DANELAW
DEDIMUS
DEFAULT
DEFENCE
DEODAND
DETINUE
DEVISAL
DIVORCE
DOSSIER
ESCHEAT
ESCUAGE
ESSOYNE
ESTOVER
ESTREAT
EXHIBIT
FALDAGE
FEE TAIL
FICTION
FORFEIT

FOUDRIE
HANAPER
HEARING
HONOURS
HUNDRED
INQUEST
ISONOMY
JURY-BOX
JUSTICE
LAND-LAW
LATITAT
LAW-BOOK
LAW-LIST
LAWSUIT
LETTING
LICENCE
MAJORAT
MANDATE
MERCHET
MORMAOR
NONSUIT
OFFENCE
OPENING
PANNAGE
PENALTY
PERJURY
POOR-LAW
PORTION
PRECEPT
PREMISE
PREMISS
PRISAGE
PROBATE
PROCESS
PROTEST
PROVISO
PURVIEW
QUARTER
REALITY
RECITAL
RELEASE
REPLEVY
RESIDUE
RESPITE
RETRIAL
REVIVOR
RIOT ACT
RUNDALE
SCAVAGE
SCUTAGE
SEIZURE
SERFDOM

SESSION
SEVERAL
SOCCAGE
SOREHON
STATUTE
SUBJECT
SUMMARY
SUMMONS
TALLAGE
TENANCY
TESTACY
TITHING
TONTINE
VACATUR
VERDICT
VESTING
VOUCHER
WARRANT

8

ADDENDUM
ADVOCACY
ANNEXURE
ANTINOMY
APPANAGE
ARTICLES
AUDIENCE
AVERMENT
BACKBOND
BAIL-BOND
BAIL-DOCK
BAILMENT
BARRATRY
BESTOWAL
BREVIATE
CAPACITY
CHAMBERS
CHAMPART
CHANCERY
CHATTELS
CITATION
CIVIL LAW
CLEMENCY
COGNOVIT
CONTEMPT
CONTRACT
COPYHOLD
COURT-DAY
COURTESY
COVENANT
COVERAGE

DEED POLL
DELATION
DOCUMENT
DONATION
DOTATION
EASEMENT
ENACTION
ESTOPPEL
EVICTION
EVIDENCE
FEME SOLE
FRANK-FEE
FREEHOLD
GAME LAWS
GRAVAMEN
GREAT FEE
GUARANTY
HEADNOTE
HELOTAGE
HORNGELD
HOTCHPOT
INNOCENT
INNUENDO
INSTANCE
JOINTURE
JUDGMENT
LEGAL AID
LEGALISM
LEGALITY
LENIENCE
LENIENCY
LIEGEDOM
LIMITARY
LOCATION
MAJORITY
MANDAMUS
MARITAGE
MESSUAGE
MINORITY
MISTRIAL
MITTIMUS
MODALITY
MONITION
MOOT CASE
MORTGAGE
MORTMAIN
MUNIMENT
NOMOLOGY
NON-CLAIM
NON-ENTRY
NOVERINT
ORDINARY

PALIMONY
PANDECTS
PAPER-DAY
PARTICLE
PECULIUM
PENDICLE
PERNANCY
PETITION
PETTY BAG
PLACITUM
PLEADING
POST-OBIT
PRACTICE
PROCLAIM
PROPERTY
REBUTTAL
RECOVERY
REFERRAL
RELATION
REMITTAL
REPLEVIN
REPRIEVE
RESIDUUM
REVISION
ROMAN LAW
SANCTION
SEDERUNT
SESSIONS
SPONSION
SUBLEASE
SUBPOENA
SUZERAIN
SWEARING
TAIL MALE
TENANTRY
TENEMENT
TENENDUM
TERMINER
TESTATUM
TEST-CASE
THIRLAGE
TRANSFER
TRIBUNAL
TRUE BILL
USUFRUCT
VALIDITY
VASSALRY
VAVASORY
VOIR DIRE
WARD-MOTE
WARDSHIP
WARRANTY

LEGAL TERMS

9

ABATEMENT
ACCESSION
ACQUITTAL
ADEMPTION
ADMINICAL
AFFIDAVIT
ANNULMENT
ASSUMPSIT
ATTAINDER
AUTHORITY
AVIZANDUM
AVOCATION
BAILIWICK
CAPITULAR
CASSATION
CAUTIONARY
CHALLENGE
CHAMPERTY
COLLUSION
COMMITTAL
COMMONAGE
COMMON LAW
COMPLAINT
CONDITION
COPYRIGHT
COROLLARY
COURT-CASE
COURT-LEET
COURT-ROLL
COURTROOM
COVERTURE
CROSS-BILL
DESERTION
DILIGENCE
DISCHARGE
DISMISSAL
DISTRAINT
EJECTMENT
EMBRACERY
ENDOWMENT
ESTOPPAGE
EXECUTION
FEE SIMPLE
FEOFFMENT
FEUDALISM
FEUDALITY
FIDUCIARY
FOLK-RIGHT
FORESTAGE
FOREST LAW

FREE-BENCH
FRITHBORH
FUNGIBLES
GAVELKIND
GUARANTEE
HEDGE-BOTE
HIGH COURT
HOUSE-BOTE
HOUSE-CARL
HUE AND CRY
INDEMNITY
INDENTURE
INJUSTICE
INNOCENCE
INSTITUTE
INTESTACY
INUREMENT
JUDGEMENT
JUDICIARY
LEASEHOLD
LEGAL YEAR
LIABILITY
LIBELLING
LICENSURE
LOCAL VETO
MAINPRISE
MISCHARGE
MOOTCOURT
MOVEABLES
NON-ACCESS
OBJECTION
OBREPTION
OCCUPANCY
OPEN COURT
ORDINANCE
OWNERSHIP
PATRIMONY
PENAL LAWS
PLEADINGS
PRECEDENT
PREJUDICE
PRESCRIPT
PRINCIPLE
PRIVILEGE
PROBATION
PROCEDURE
PROVISION
PUBLIC LAW
PURGATION
QUERIMONY
QUIT-CLAIM
QUITTANCE

RECAPTION
REDDENDUM
REFERENCE
REFRESHER
REHEARING
REJOINDER
REMAINDER
REMISSION
REMITMENT
REPRIEVAL
RES GESTAE
REVERSION
SEARCH-FEE
SERJEANTY
SEVERALTY
SHIRE-MOOT
SHOW TRIAL
SOKEMANRY
SPECIALTY
STATUS QUO
STYLE-BOOK
SUMMING-UP
SURRENDER
TESTAMENT
TESTATION
TESTIMONY
THEFTBOOT
TITLE-DEED
TRANSUMPT
TRUST-DEED
VASSALAGE

10

ABJURATION
ABROGATION
ACCUSATION
ADJUDGMENT
ALLEGATION
AMERCEMENT
APPEARANCE
ARRESTMENT
ARRIÈRE-BAN
ARROGATION
ASSESSMENT
ASSIGNMENT
ATTACHMENT
BANKRUPTCY
BILL OF SALE
BIRTHRIGHT
CERTIORARI

CESSIONARY
COGNISANCE
COMPETENCE
COMPLICITY
COMPROMISE
CONFESSION
CONSTRAINT
CONTRAHENT
CONVEYANCE
COTTIERISM
COURT-BARON
COURTHOUSE
CROWN COURT
CULVERTAGE
DECLARATOR
DECREE NISI
DEFAMATION
DEFEASANCE
DEPOSITION
DEPUTATION
DETAINMENT
DETRACTION
DEVASTAVIT
DISCLAIMER
DISTRINGAS
DUCHY COURT
ENFACEMENT
ENJOINMENT
ENTAILMENT
ESCHEATAGE
EXHUMATION
FACTUALITY
FEME COVERT
FOOT OF FINE
FORFEITURE
HILARY TERM
IMPOUNDAGE
IMPUTATION
INCITEMENT
INDICTMENT
INDUCEMENT
INJUNCTION
INNER HOUSE
INQUIRENDO
INVOCATION
JUDICATION
JUDICATURE
KING'S BENCH
KING'S PEACE
KNIGHT'S FEE
LAND VALUES
LATITATION

LEGITIMACY
LIFE-ESTATE
LITIGATION
MAGISTRACY
MEMORANDUM
MIDJOINDER
MISPRISION
MORATORIUM
NEGLIGENCE
NOMOGRAPHY
NON-JOINDER
OBJURATION
OBLIGATION
OBSERVANCE
OCCUPATION
OUTER HOUSE
PERSONALTY
POSTLIMINY
PRAEMUNIRE
PRIVATE LAW
PRIZE COURT
REAL ESTATE
RECOUPMENT
RECUSATION
REGULATION
RELAXATION
RESCISSION
RIGHT OF WAY
SECURITIES
SETTLEMENT
STATE TRIAL
STATUTE LAW
STILLICIDE
SUBLETTING
SUBMISSION
SUBSECTION
SUBTENANCY
SUCCESSION
SUGGESTION
SURETYSHIP
SURROGATUM
SURVIVANCE
SUSPENSION
SUZERAINTY
TENANTSHIP
TRANSCRIPT
UNDERLEASE
VALIDATION
VILLEINAGE
WARRANTING
WITNESS-BOX
WRITTEN LAW

11

ACTIVE TRUST
ADJOURNMENT
AFFIRMATION
APPEAL COURT
ARBITRAMENT
ARBITRATION
ARRAIGNMENT
ASSIGNATION
ATTESTATION
BILL OF COSTS
BRIBERY OATH
CERTIFICATE
CHARGE-SHEET
CIVIL RIGHTS
COMMON FORMS
COMPOSITION
CONDONATION
CONFUTATION
CONSERVANCY
CONSIGNMENT
CORPORATION
COUNTER-PLEA
COUNTER-ROLL
COUNTY COURT
CRIMEN FALSI
CROSS ACTION
CULPABILITY
DECLARATION
DECLINATURE
DEFORCEMENT
DELIVERANCE
DEVASTATION
DISPOSITION
EMPHYTEUSIS
ENCUMBRANCE
ENFEOFFMENT
ENFORCEMENT
ENGROSSMENT
ENTITLEMENT
ESTREPEMENT
EXCULPATION
EXONERATION
EXTENUATION
FORBIDDANCE
FORECLOSURE
FRANK-PLEDGE
HOME-CIRCUIT
IMMOVEABLES
IMPEACHMENT
IMPROBATION

INCULPATION
INFANGTHIEF
INFEUDATION
INFORMATION
INHERITANCE
INNER TEMPLE
INQUISITION
JURY-PROCESS
LANDLORDISM
LEADING CASE
LEGAL ACTION
LEGAL TENDER
LEGISLATION
LEGISLATIVE
LEGISLATURE
LOCAL OPTION
MAINTENANCE
MALFEASANCE
MANCIPATION
MISFEASANCE
MISPLEADING
OBSTRUCTION
OBTESTATION
OPEN VERDICT
OUTER TEMPLE
PATENT-RIGHT
PATENT-ROLLS
PATROONSHIP
PETITIONING
POLICE COURT
PRE-AUDIENCE
PRECONTRACT
PREJUDGMENT
PRESENTMENT
PRESUMPTION
PROCURATORY
PROHIBITION
PROSECUTION
PUBLIC WRONG
PUPILLARITY
PURPRESTURE
QUEEN'S BENCH
QUO WARRANTO
RECOMMITTAL
RELEASEMENT
REPLICATION
REQUEST NOTE
RES JUDICATA
RESTRICTION
RETROACTION
SCIRE FACIAS
SELF-DEFENCE

LEGAL TERMS

STATUTE-BOOK
STELLIONATE
STIPULATION
SUBCONTRACT
SUBROGATION
SUBTRACTION
SUPERSEDEAS
SUPERSEDERE
SURREBUTTAL
SURREBUTTER
SURROGATION
TENANT-RIGHT
TERM OF YEARS
TESTIMONIAL
TRINITY TERM
TRUSTEESHIP
TRUST ESTATE
USUFRUCTARY
WIDOW'S BENCH

12

ADJUDICATION
APPURTENANCE
AUGMENTATION
BENCH-WARRANT
BEQUEATHMENT
CALUMNIATION
CAUSE CÉLÈBRE
CHARTER-PARTY
CIVIL LIBERTY
CODIFICATION
COMPENSATION
COMPERGATION
CONSTITUTION
CONSULTATION
CONSUMMATION
CONVEYANCING
COUNTER-CLAIM
DIFFAREATION
DIJUDICATION
DISCLAMATION
DISTRAINMENT
DIVORCE COURT
ESTRANGEMENT
EXPECTATIONS
EXPROMISSION
FEIGNED ISSUE
FEUDAL SYSTEM
FRANKALMOIGN
GENERAL ISSUE

GRAND ASSIZES
HABEAS CORPUS
HARD SWEARING
HEREDITAMENT
IMPERTINENCE
INTERCESSION
INTROMISSION
JOINT-TENANCY
JUDGMENT-DEBT
JUDGMENT-HALL
JUDGMENT-SEAT
LAND TRANSFER
LEGALISATION
LEGITIMATION
MAIDEN ASSIZE
MISADVENTURE
NON-COMMITTAL
NON-RESIDENCE
ONUS PROBANDI
OUTFANGTHIEF
PARTY-VERDICT
PEACE-WARRANT
POINT OF ORDER
PRECOGNITION
PRECONDITION
PREJUDGEMENT
PRESCRIPTION
PRIVATE WRONG
PROBATE COURT
PROCLAMATION
PROMULGATION
PROSCRIPTION
PROTESTATION
QUARE IMPEDIT
RATIFICATION
RECOGNISANCE
RECONVEYANCE
RETAINING FEE
RIGHT OF ENTRY
ROUGH JUSTICE
SAVING CLAUSE
SPECIAL TRUST
SUBFEUDATION
SUPREME COURT
SURREJOINDER
TRANSUMPTION
TRUSTEE-STOCK
UNDERLETTING
UNDERTENANCY
VENIRE FACIAS

13

ANCIENT LIGHTS
ANIMADVERSION
AUDITA QUERELA
BORSTAL SYSTEM
BURDEN OF PROOF
BURGH OF BARONY
CO-INHERITANCE
CONSIDERATION
CORONER'S COURT
CORPUS DELICTI
COUNTERCHARGE
COURT OF APPEAL
DISPOSSESSION
DOCUMENTATION
EMINENT DOMAIN
EXPROPRIATION
FRANK-TENEMENT
GENERAL LEGACY
JURISPRUDENCE
JUSTIFICATION
KANGAROO COURT
KNIGHT SERVICE
LAND-OWNERSHIP
LETTERS-PATENT
MATERIAL ISSUE
MERCANTILE LAW
NON-APPEARANCE
NULLIFICATION
PETTY SESSIONS
PREJUDICATION
PREVARICATION
PRIMOGENITURE
QUALIFICATION
RECRIMINATION
REVENDICATION
RIGHT OF APPEAL
SEARCH WARRANT
SEQUESTRATION
SOLICITORSHIP
SUMMER SESSION
TESTIFICATION
TRANSCRIPTION
TREASURE TROVE
TRIAL BY ORDEAL
TRIAL BY RECORD
ULTIMUS HAERES
VALUATION ROLL
VEXATIOUS SUIT
WAGER OF BATTLE
WATCHING BRIEF

WINTER SESSION
WRIT OF INQUIRY

14

COMMON RECOVERY
COMPLETION DATE
CONDITIONAL FEE
DISINHERITANCE
DOUBLE JEOPARDY
EXTINGUISHMENT
FIFTH AMENDMENT
FORISFAMILIATE
GENERAL WARRANT
GRAND SERJEANTY
LETTER OF THE LAW
McNAGHTEN RULES
PERSONAL RIGHTS
PETTY SERJEANTY

QUARTER-SESSION
QUEEN'S EVIDENCE
RECEIVING-ORDER
SENATUS CONSULT
SPECIAL LICENCE
SPECIAL VERDICT
SPECIFIC LEGACY
SUBINFEUDATION
ULTIMOGENITURE

15

BANKRUPTCY COURT
BREACH OF PROMISE
CHAMBER PRACTICE
COMMERCIAL COURT
COUNTER-EVIDENCE
COUNTER-SECURITY

COURT OF REQUESTS
DECREE OF NULLITY
DISTRESS WARRANT
EXEMPLIFICATION
HEARSAY EVIDENCE
IDENTIFICATIONS
IMMATERIAL ISSUE
INDEMNIFICATION
JUSTICES' JUSTICE
LEADING QUESTION
LETTERS ROGATORY
MAJORITY VERDICT
POWER OF ATTORNEY
QUARTER-SESSIONS
RENT RESTRICTION
SECUNDOGENITURE
SEPARATION ORDER
SPECIAL PLEADING
WRIT OF PRIVILEGE

MACHINES

3
FAN
GIN

4
GRAB
JACK
LIFT
LOOM
MILL
MULE
PUMP
TILL

5
ADDER
BALER
BORER
CHURN
CRANE
CREED
DEVIL
DRIER
DRYER
ENIAC
ERNIE
FRAME
HOIST
JENNY
LATHE
MIXER
MOTOR
MOWER
NORIA
PLANT
PRESS
PUNCH
QUERN
ROBOT
RONEO
ROVER
SIREN
TELEX
VIDEO
WINCH
XEROX

6
BINDER
BLOWER
BOWSER
COPIER
CUTTER
DEVICE
DIGGER
DREDGE
DYNAMO
ENGINE
FANNER
HARROW
HEADER
JIGGER
LAPPER
LEGGER
LINTER
MANGLE
MILKER
MINCER
OLIVER
PACKER
PEELER
PICKER
PLOUGH
PULPER
RAM-JET
REAPER
SAKIEH
SCALES
SEEDER
SHEERS
STOKER
TWILLY
WASHER
WINDER

7
AUTOMAT
BALANCE
BLUNGER
BOULTER
BREAKER
BRICOLE
CAPSTAN
CRAMMER
CROPPER
CRUSHER

CYCLONE
DREDGER
EJECTOR
EXCITER
GIG-MILL
JUKE-BOX
KNOTTER
MACHINE
OIL-MILL
OIL-PUMP
POTCHER
PRINTER
PUG-MILL
QUILTER
RIVETER
SHADOOF
SIROCCO
SPINNER
STAPLER
STARTER
STEAMER
TUMBLER
TURBINE
WRINGER

8
BEER-PUMP
CALENDER
COMPUTER
CONVEYOR
DOLLY-TUB
DRAGLINE
EARPHONE
ELEVATOR
EPISCOPE
ESPRESSO
FEED-PUMP
FILATORY
FOOT-PUMP
GAS-MOTOR
HAND-LOOM
HAND-MILL
HEAT-PUMP
IRON LUNG
JIB-CRANE
JIG-BORER
LAZY-JACK
LIFT-PUMP
LINOTYPE
MONOTYPE

MOTOR-JET
OIL-PRESS
PULP-MILL
PULSATOR
PURIFIER
RECORDER
SAND-PUMP
SHREDDER
TELETYPE
THROSTLE
TURBO-JET
VIBRATOR
WALK-MILL
WINDMILL

9
AIR-ENGINE
APPARATUS
AUDIPHONE
AUTOMATON
CHECK-TILL
DASH-WHEEL
DISPENSER
DROP-PRESS
EARPHONES
ESCALATOR
EXCAVATOR
EXTRACTOR
FLOWER-BOLT
GANG PUNCH
GAS-ENGINE
GENERATOR
HAND-PRESS
HARVESTER
HEADPHONE
HOP-PICKER
HORSE-MILL
HYDROPULT
INCUBATOR
JET-ENGINE
LACE-FRAME
LAP-ROLLER
LAWN-MOWER
LOCOMOTOR
MACERATOR
MACHINERY
OIL-ENGINE
OPTOPHONE
PERFECTOR
PHOTOSTAT

POLYGRAPH
POWER-LOOM
PROJECTOR
RADIOGRAM
SCRIBBLER
SEPARATOR
SIGMATRON
SIMULATOR
SLOT-METER
SPIN-DRIER
STEELYARD
STONE-MILL
SUGAR-MILL
TELEPHONE
TOMOGRAPH
TOTALISER
TREADMILL
TURBO-PROP
VITASCOPE
WATER-MILL
WATER-PUMP
WELL-BORER
WINE-PRESS

10

BEAM-ENGINE
CALCULATOR
CENTRIFUGE
COAL-CUTTER
COFFEE-MILL
COMPRESSOR
CORN-HUSKER
CYCLOSTYLE
DICTAPHONE
DICTOGRAPH
DISHWASHER
DROP-HAMMER
DUMB-WAITER
DUPLICATOR
EXSICCATOR
FEED-HEATER
GALVANISER
GAS-TURBINE
GRAMOPHONE
GUILLOTINE
HEADPHONES
HEAT ENGINE
MASTICATOR
MIMEOGRAPH
MOTOR-MOWER

PASSIMETER
PETROL PUMP
PHONOGRAPH
PHONOPHORE
PILE-DRIVER
POWER-LATHE
POWER-PRESS
PULP-ENGINE
PULSOMETER
PULVERISER
QUARTZ-MILL
RADIOPHONE
REPRODUCER
ROSE-ENGINE
SCREW-PRESS
SELF-BINDER
SEPARATORY
SERVO-MOTOR
STEAM-CRANE
STEAM-NAVVY
STEREOGRAM
STERILISER
TILT-HAMMER
TRAVELATOR
TRAVOLATOR
TREAD-WHEEL
TRIP-HAMMER
TURBULATOR
TYPEWRITER
VACUUM-PUMP
VENTILATOR
WATER-MOTOR
WATER-WHEEL
WOOL-CARDER
WOOL-COMBER
WOOL-PICKER

11

ANNUNCIATOR
BACON-SLICER
BARKER'S MILL
BRAMAH-PRESS
CASH-RAILWAY
CHAFF-CUTTER
CHAFF-ENGINE
CHEESE-PRESS
CHEESE-WRING
COMPTOMETER
CONTRIVANCE
CONTRAPTION

COTTON-PRESS
DOUBLE-ENDER
EPIDIASCOPE
GRASS-CUTTER
LETTER-PRESS
MACHINE-TOOL
NICKELODEON
PAPER-CUTTER
PAPER-FEEDER
PASTEURISER
PATERNOSTER
PHOTO-COPIER
PSEUDOSCOPE
REGENERATOR
ROCK-BREAKER
ROLLING-MILL
ROPE-MACHINE
ROTARY PRESS
SLOT-MACHINE
STEAM-DIGGER
STEAM-ENGINE
STEAM-HAMMER
STEAM-PLOUGH
STEAM-SHOVEL
STEREOSCOPE
STIRRUP-PUMP
TELEPRINTER
TOTALISATOR
TREE-BICYCLE
TUMBLE-DRIER
TURBINE-PUMP
TURBO-RAM-JET
WATER-COOLER
WATER-ENGINE
WEIGHBRIDGE
WHEEL-CUTTER

12

ARITHMOMETER
CASH-REGISTER
CONVEYOR-BELT
COPYING-PRESS
DECOMPRESSOR
DIESEL ENGINE
DONKEY-ENGINE
DRAWING-FRAME
ELECTROMOTOR
EXTRACTOR FAN
FRUIT MACHINE
JACOB'S-LADDER

MACHINES

JACQUARD LOOM
LUFFING CRANE
MANDREL LATHE
MARBLE-CUTTER
MONKEY-ENGINE
MONKEY-HAMMER
PACKING-PRESS
PETROL ENGINE
PETTER ENGINE
POTTER'S LATHE
POTTER'S WHEEL
PRINTING-PRESS
RADIAL ENGINE
RAM-JET ENGINE
RECIPROCATOR
RECORD-PLAYER
ROTARY ENGINE
STAMPING-MILL
STAMP-MACHINE
STEAM-TURBINE
STONE-BREAKER
TAPE-RECORDER
TURNING LATHE
WATER-TURBINE
WHIP-AND-DERRY
WORKING-MODEL

13

ADDING-MACHINE
AIR-COMPRESSOR
CASH-DISPENSER
CONCRETE-MIXER
CYLINDER-PRESS
DISINTEGRATOR

DRAUGHT-ENGINE
DRILLING-LATHE
DRILLING-PRESS
ELECTRIC MOTOR
GRABBING CRANE
HEAT EXCHANGER
HYDRAULIC JACK
KIDNEY MACHINE
MOWING-MACHINE
QUILTING-FRAME
SEWING-MACHINE
SLIPFORM PAVER
SOWING-MACHINE
SPINNING JENNY
SPINNING-WHEEL
STOCKING-FRAME
THRESHING-MILL
VACUUM-CLEANER
VIDEO RECORDER
VOTING MACHINE
WHIRLING-TABLE
WINDING-ENGINE

14

ANALOG COMPUTER
BLOCK AND TACKLE
BURLING-MACHINE
CARDING-MACHINE
COMPOUND ENGINE
CONTAINER CRANE
FOLDING-MACHINE
HYDROEXTRACTOR
MANIFOLD-WRITER

MILKING-MACHINE
MILLING MACHINE
ONE-ARMED BANDIT
PLANING-MACHINE
PNEUMATIC DRILL
REAPING-MACHINE
STIRLING ENGINE
TALKING-MACHINE
TELETYPESETTER
TELETYPEWRITER
TRACTION-ENGINE
VENDING MACHINE
WASHING-MACHINE

15

CRIMPING-MACHINE
DIGITAL COMPUTER
DRILLING-MACHINE
ELECTRONIC BRAIN
FRANKING-MACHINE
INFERNAL MACHINE
KNITTING-MACHINE
MOVING STAIRCASE
PHENAKISTOSCOPE
PRINTING-MACHINE
SLOTTING-MACHINE
STAPLING-MACHINE
STRETCHING-FRAME
TEACHING MACHINE
ULTRA-CENTRIFUGE
WEIGHING-MACHINE
WHIRLING-MACHINE

MEDICINE – HOSPITAL TERMS

3

CUT
JAB
MOP

4

CARE
CASE
CURE
DIET
DOSE
DRIP
GERM
LINT
ORAL
PACK
PLUG
SCAN
SHOT
SWAB
TENT
TERM
WARD
X-RAY

5

BIRTH
BRACE
CROWN
ENEMA
ETHER
GAUZE
GRAFT
LANCE
LYSIS
PATCH
PLATE
PRICK
PROBE
PULSE
RALLY
SCORE
SETON
SLING
SMEAR
SPICA
STALL

STUPE
TAXIS
TRUSS
VIRUS

6

BOUGIE
BRIDGE
CAUTER
CLINIC
COURSE
CRADLE
CRISIS
CYESIS
DOSAGE
DOSSIL
EMBOLY
GARROT
GAVAGE
GURNEY
HEALTH
LABOUR
LANCET
LAVAGE
MORGUE
NEEDLE
PELOID
PLEXOR
REMEDY
SCREEN
SEEKER
SHEATH
SPLINT
STITCH
STYLET
SUTURE
SYSTEM
TAMPON
TRACER
TREPAN
TROCAR
XYSTER

7

AIR-BATH
ALGESIA
ASEPSIS
AUTOPSY

BANDAGE
BANDEAU
BANTING
BIOPSIS
BOOSTER
CANNULA
CAUTERY
CHARPIE
CHECK-UP
CONTACT
CULTURE
CURETTE
CUTTING
DILATOR
EYE BANK
FILLING
FISTULA
FORCEPS
FORMULA
FUNICLE
HEALING
IMPLANT
INFARCT
INHALER
LAZARET
LYING-IN
MASSAGE
MEDICAL
MICROBE
MIMESIS
MUD-BATH
MYOGRAM
NURSING
OTOLOGY
PELICAN
PESSARY
PLASTER
PLEDGET
PLUGGER
POROSIS
PROBANG
PTERION
REGIMEN
RELAPSE
REVIVAL
SCALPEL
SCANNER
SECTION
SICK-BAY
SICK-BED
SOUFFLE
SPATULA

SPATULE
STRIDOR
SURGERY
SWADDLE
SYMPTOM
SYRINGE
SYSTOLE
THEATRE
THERAPY
TORSION
UROLOGY
WADDING

8

ABORTION
ACCIDENT
AGAR-AGAR
BACILLUS
BACTERIA
BED-TABLE
BISTOURY
CAPELINE
CASEBOOK
CASE-WORK
CATHETER
CENTESIS
COLOTOMY
COMPRESS
CORN-CURE
COSMESIS
CROW-BILL
DELIVERY
DIALYSIS
DIASTOLE
EPIDEMIC
EFFUSION
ERETHISM
EXCISION
FARADISM
FIRST AID
GERIATRY
HOSPITAL
HYPALGIA
IMMUNITY
INCISION
INCISURE
IRON LUNG
JAW LEVER
LIGATION
LIGATURE

LOBOTOMY
LUXATION
MEDICINE
MERYCISM
METHYSIS
MIND-CURE
MISBIRTH
MORTUARY
MYOGRAPH
NECROPSY
NOSOLOGY
ONCOLOGY
ONCOTOMY
OTOSCOPE
OUTBREAK
OVERDOSE
OXIMETER
PATHOGEN
PEDICURE
PELOLOGY
PHARMACY
PLASTICS
PLUGGING
PODIATRY
POULTICE
PULMOTOR
RECOVERY
REFERRAL
REST-CURE
RHONCHUS
SCALPRUM
SCAPULAR
SEDATION
SEROCITY
SICK-LIST
SICKROOM
SINAPISM
SKIAGRAM
SKIATRON
SOLUTION
SOUNDING
SPECIMEN
SPECULUM
SPHYGMUS
STOPPING
SYNDROME
T-BANDAGE
TENOTOMY
TOCOLOGY
TOMOGRAM
TORCULAR
TRACTION

MEDICINE – HOSPITAL TERMS

TREPHINE
URETHANE
UROSCOPY
VIROLOGY
VULSELLA
ZOOGRAFT

9

AFTERCARE
AIR-SPLINT
ALLOPATHY
ANALGESIA
ANAMNESIS
ANAPLASTY
ANCILLARY
AUTOGRAFT
AUTOPHONY
BLOOD-AGAR
BLOOD BANK
BLOODHEAT
BLOOD TEST
CAESAREAN
CATAPLASM
CHIROPODY
COLLODION
COLOSTOMY
CONTAGION
CORDOTOMY
CURETTAGE
CYSTOTOMY
DENTISTRY
DEPLETION
DEPRESSOR
DIAGNOSIS
DIASTASIS
DIATHERMY
DIATHESIS
DICROTISM
DONOR CARD
DOSIOLOGY
DRAW-SHEET
EMERGENCY
ENDOSCOPY
EUTHANASY
FLUOTHANE
FOETICIDE
GALVANISM
GRAVIDITY
HALOTHANE
HELCOLOGY

HOMOGRAFT
IATROGENY
IATROLOGY
IDIOPATHY
IMPACTION
INCUBATOR
INFECTION
INHALATOR
INJECTION
INSECTION
INTENTION
IRRIGATOR
ISOLATION
JACTATION
LACTATION
LAZARETTO
LEPROSERY
LEUCOTOME
LEUCOTOMY
LISTERISM
LITHOLOGY
LITHOTOME
LITHOTOMY
LIVE-BIRTH
MICROTOME
MICROTOMY
MIDWIFERY
NEUROLOGY
OPERATION
OSTEOTOME
OSTEOTOMY
PACEMAKER
PAEDIATRY
PATHOLOGY
PREGNANCY
PRODROMUS
PROGNOSIS
PULSE-RATE
PULSE-WAVE
RADIOGRAM
RASPATORY
REPLETION
REPOSITOR
RESECTION
RESONANCE
RETENTION
RETRACTOR
RHINOLOGY
SEX-CHANGE
SIALOGRAM
SICK-HOUSE
SKIAGRAPH

SKIASCOPY
SMEAR TEST
SOMASCOPE
STITCHING
STRETCHER
SULCATION
SUSPENSOR
SYNOSOSIS
SYNTHESIS
TAMPONADE
TENACULUM
TOMOGRAPH
TONOMETER
TOPECTOMY
TREATMENT
TWIN-BIRTH
URINOLOGY
UROGRAPHY
UTEROTOMY
VASECTOMY
WASSERMAN
WATER-CURE
ZOOPLASTY

10

ADENECTOMY
AMPUTATION
ANTISEPSIS
ARTHROLOGY
ASEPTICISM
AUTOPLASTY
BALNEOLOGY
BARIUM MEAL
BLOOD COUNT
BLOOD GROUP
CARDIOGRAM
CHILDBIRTH
CHLOROFORM
COMMISSURE
CONCOCTION
COTTON-WOOL
CRANIOTOMY
CROSS-BIRTH
CYSTOSCOPE
CYSTOSCOPY
DANGER-LIST
DIAGNOSTIC
DIORTHOSIS
DISCISSION
DISCUSSION

DISPENSARY
DISPERSION
DISSECTION
EMBRYOTOMY
EMBRYULCIA
EMOLLITION
ENTEROLOGY
ENTEROTOMY
EPISIOTOMY
EUTHANASIA
EVACUATION
EXTRACTION
GASTROLOGY
GASTROTOMY
GERIATRICS
GUILLOTINE
HEPATOLOGY
HERNIOLOGY
HERNIOTOMY
HOMEOPATHY
HYDROPATHY
HYMENOLOGY
HYPALGESIA
HYPODERMIC
INCUBATION
INDUCEMENT
INFARCTION
INSPECTION
INSPIRATOR
INTERNMENT
INTUBATION
IRIDECTOMY
KISS OF LIFE
LAPAROTOMY
LEPROSERIE
LIGNOCAINE
LITHOCLAST
LITHOTRITY
MASTECTOMY
MIASMOLOGY
MYCOPLASMA
NATURE-CURE
NECROSCOPY
NEPHROLOGY
NEPHROTOMY
NEUROPATHY
NOSOGRAPHY
OBSTETRICS
OPOTHERAPY
ORTHOCAINE
ORTHOPTICS
OSTEOCLAST

OSTEOPATHY
OVARIOTOMY
OVERDOSAGE
OXYGENATOR
OXYGEN TENT
PASTEURISM
PATHOGNAMY
PELVIMETRY
PERCUSSION
PHLEBOTOMY
PLEXIMETER
PLEXIMETRY
POST MORTEM
PROSTHESIS
PROTECTIVE
PSYCHIATRY
PUERPERIUM
PULSIMETER
QUARANTINE
QUICKENING
RADIOGRAPH
RADIOSCOPY
RADIUM BOMB
RESOLUTION
RETRACTION
RHINOSCOPE
RHINOSCOPY
SANATORIUM
SIDE-EFFECT
SPIROGRAPH
SPIROMETER
SPIROMETRY
SPIROPHORE
STERILISER
STILL-BIRTH
STIMULATOR
STRABOTOMY
SUBCULTURE
SUCCUSSION
SUTURATION
THERMOGRAM
THUMB-STALL
TOMOGRAPHY
TOURNIQUET
TRANSPLANT
TREPANNING
URINOMETER
UTERECTOMY

11

ABLACTATION

ACUPRESSURE
ACUPUNCTURE
ANAESTHESIA
ANAESTHESIS
ANAESTHETIC
APPLICATION
ARTERIOTOMY
ATTENUATION
AUSCULTATOR
BIOFEEDBACK
BREECH BIRTH
CARDIOGRAPH
CASE HISTORY
CEPHALOTOMY
CHONDROLOGY
CIRCULATION
COAGULATION
CONFINEMENT
CONSULTANCY
CONTRACTION
CORN-PLASTER
COSMETOLOGY
CRANIOGNOMY
CRANIOMETRY
CREPITATION
CRYOSURGERY
CRYOTHERAPY
DECUMBITURE
DEEP THERAPY
DIAGNOSTICS
DIAPHORESIS
DISLOCATION
DUTCH LIQUID
ENTERECTOMY
ENTEROSTOMY
ENUCLEATION
EVENTRATION
FINGER-STALL
FLUOROSCOPY
FOMENTATION
FOOT-PLASTER
GASTRECTOMY
GASTROSTOMY
GEOMEDICINE
GYNAECOLOGY
HABITUATION
HAEMATOLOGY
HAEMOSTATIC
HEPATECTOMY
HOSPITAL BED
HYSTEROLOGY
HYSTEROTOMY

INCARNATION
INOCULATION
INSUFFLATOR
JACTITATION
KINESIPATHY
LACTESCENCE
LARYNGOLOGY
LARYNGOTOMY
LAUGHING-GAS
LEPROSARIUM
LITHOLAPAXY
LITHOTRITOR
MAMMOGRAPHY
MICROCOCCUS
MIND-HEALING
MISCARRIAGE
MOXIBUSTION
MUSTARD-BATH
NATUROPATHY
NEPHRACTOMY
NURSING HOME
ORCHIECTOMY
ORTHODONTIA
ORTHOGENICS
OSTEOCLASIS
OSTEOGRAPHY
OSTEOPLASTY
PAEDIATRICS
PARTURITION
PATHOGRAPHY
PELOTHERAPY
PERIODONTIA
PHYSICIANCY
PLASTER CAST
PREPARATION
PROPHYLAXIS
PROSTHETICS
RADIOGRAPHY
RETINOSCOPY
RHINOPLASTY
SABURRATION
SEROTHERAPY
SEX-REVERSAL
SIALOGRAPHY
SICK-NURSING
SPHYGMOGRAM
SPHYGMOLOGY
SPIRILLOSIS
SPLENECTOMY
STETHOSCOPE
STETHOSCOPY
STOMACH-PUMP

STRABOMETER
SYPHILOLOGY
SYRINGOTOMY
TEMPERATURE
THERMOGRAPH
THERMOMETER
THERMOMETRY
TRACHEOTOMY
TRANSFUSION
TREPANATION
URANOPLASTY
VACCINATION
VARIOLATION
VENESECTION
VENEREOLOGY
X-RAY THERAPY
ZOOGRAFTING

12

ACCOUCHEMENT
APPENDECTOMY
AUSCULTATION
BIRTH CONTROL
BLOODLETTING
CASUALTY WARD
CATHODOGRAPH
CHEMOTHERAPY
CHILDBEARING
CHIROPRACTIC
CIRCUMCISION
COMPLICATION
CONSULTATION
CURIETHERAPY
CYCLOPROPANE
DISINFECTION
DRAINAGE-TUBE
DUODENECTOMY
EMOLLESCENCE
ENANTIOPATHY
EPIDEMIOLOGY
EXACERBATION
EXPLANTATION
EXSANGUINITY
FEVER THERAPY
FREEZING-DOWN
GINGIVECTOMY
HEALTH CENTRE
HELIOTHERAPY
HETEROPLASTY
HYDROTHERAPY

MEDICINE – HOSPITAL TERMS

HYPERALGESIA
HYPNOTHERAPY
HYSTERECTOMY
IMMUNISATION
IMPLANTATION
INCRASSATION
KERATOPLASTY
LARYNGOPHONY
LARYNGOSCOPE
LARYNGOSCOPY
LATENT PERIOD
MERCY KILLING
MINISTRATION
MYRINGOSCOPE
NARCOTHERAPY
NEUROANATOMY
NEUROSURGERY
NIPPLE-SHIELD
NITROUS OXIDE
ODONTOGRAPHY
OOPHORECTOMY
ORCHIDECTOMY
ORTHODONTICS
ORTHOPAEDICS
PAEDODONTICS
PARACENTESIS
PECTORILOQUY
PERIODONTICS
PHAGOCYTOSIS
PHARYNGOTOMY
PHOTOTHERAPY
PLACENTATION
PRESCRIPTION
RADIOTHERAPY
RECUPERATION
RESUSCITATOR
RETINA CAMERA
RETROCESSION
RETROPULSION
RÖNTGENOGRAM
SCARIFICATOR
SERUM THERAPY
SHOCK THERAPY
SPERMATOLOGY
SPHYGMOSCOPE
SPLENISATION
SUCCUSSATION
SURGEON'S KNOT
THERAPEUTICS
THERMIC LANCE
THERMOGRAPHY
TONSILLOTOMY

TRACHEOSCOPY
TRACHEOSTOMY
VENEPUNCTURE

13

ACCOMMODATION
ACTINOTHERAPY
ADENOIDECTOMY
AMNIOCENTESIS
ANTISEPTICISM
BACTERIOLYSIS
BALNEOTHERAPY
BLOOD PRESSURE
CAUTERISATION
CONTRACEPTION
CONTRACEPTIVE
CONVALESCENCE
CYTODIAGNOSIS
DECOMPRESSION
DEFERVESCENCE
DEFIBRINATION
ENCEPHALOTOMY
ENDOCRINOLOGY
EPIPHENOMENON
EXTRAVASATION
FIELD HOSPITAL
IMMUNOTHERAPY
INCARCERATION
INTENSIVE CARE
ISOLATION WARD
KIDNEY MACHINE
KINESITHERAPY
MATERNITY HOME
MATERNITY WARD
MUSCLE-READING
OPHTHALMOLOGY
ORGANOTHERAPY
PHARMACEUTICS
PHARMACOPOEIA
PHARYNGOSCOPE
PHARYNGOSCOPY
PHYSIOTHERAPY
PNEUMONECTOMY
POROUS PLASTER
PROBE-SCISSORS
PROSTHODONTIA
PSYCHOSURGERY
PSYCHOTHERAPY
PYRETOTHERAPY

RESUSCITATION
REVACCINATION
RÖNTGENOSCOPY
SALPINGECTOMY
SCARIFICATION
SECTION-CUTTER
SELF-INFECTION
SPACE MEDICINE
SPEECH THERAPY
SPHYGMOGRAPHY
STERILISATION
SWADDLING BAND
SYMPATHECTOMY
SYMPHYSEOTOMY
SYMPHYSIOTOMY
TISSUE CULTURE
TOLERANCE DOSE
TONSILLECTOMY
TRACER ELEMENT
TRANSPLANTING
TRAUMATONASTY
TREATMENT ROOM
TWILIGHT SLEEP

14

APPENDICECTOMY
AUTORADIOGRAPH
BREECH DELIVERY
CALLIPER SPLINT
CHOLECYSTOTOMY
DISSECTING ROOM
ELECTROTHERAPY
ENDORADIOSONDE
ENTEROCENTESIS
HISTOPATHOLOGY
IATROCHEMISTRY
LUMBAR PUNCTURE
MENTAL HOSPITAL
METHYL CHLORIDE
MUSTARD PLASTER
NEUROPATHOLOGY
OPERATING TABLE
OPHTHALMOMETRY
OPHTHALMOSCOPE
OPHTHALMOSCOPY
PERIODONTOLOGY
PLASTER OF PARIS
PLASTIC SURGERY
PSYCHONOSOLOGY

REHABILITATION
RHESUS-NEGATIVE
RHESUS-POSITIVE
SHOCK TREATMENT
STAPHYLORRAPHY
STRABISMOMETER
SWADDLING-CLOTH
SYMPTOMATOLOGY
TELERADIUM UNIT
TRICHOBACTERIA
ULTRAMICROTOME
WASSERMAN'S TEST

15

AUTORADIOGRAPHY
CHOLECYSTECTOMY
CHOLECYSTOSTOMY
CLINICAL LECTURE
CLINICAL SURGERY
COTTAGE HOSPITAL
ENCEPHALOGRAPHY
HEART TRANSPLANT
HIPPOCRATIC OATH
INTROSUSCEPTION

MALPRESENTATION
MASS RADIOGRAPHY
MICRODISSECTION
ORGAN TRANSPLANT
PSYCHOCHEMISTRY
RADIUM TREATMENT
RÖNTGENOTHERAPY
STICKING PLASTER
TUBERCULISATION
XERORADIOGRAPHY

MEDICINE – HUMAN ANATOMY

3

ARM
EAR
EYE
GUM
GUT
HAM
HIP
JAW
LAP
LEG
LIP
ORB
RIB
RIM
ROD
SAC
TOE
VAS

4

ANUS
ARCH
AXIS
AXON
BACK
BODY

BONE
BROW
BULB
BUST
CALF
CAUL
CHIN
CHOP
CONE
COXA
CUSP
CYST
DERM
DISC
DRUM
DUCT
FACE
FALX
FIST
FOOT
GENA
GLIA
GULA
GUMS
GUTS
HAIR
HAND
HEAD
HEEL
HOCK

IRID
IRIS
JOWL
KNEE
LENS
LIEN
LIMB
LOBE
LOIN
LUNG
NAIL
NAPE
NECK
NOSE
PALM
PATE
PITH
PONS
PORE
PULP
RETE
RIMA
ROOT
RUMP
SEAT
SHIN
SIDE
SKIN
SOLE
TEAT

ULNA
UVEA
VEIN
VENA
VOLA
WOMB

5

ALULA
ANCON
ANKLE
ANVIL
AORTA
ATLAS
BELLY
BONES
BOSOM
BRAIN
CANAL
CHEEK
CHEST
CHOPS
COLON
CREST
CROWN
CUTIS
DIGIT
ELBOW

FEMUR
FLESH
FOSSA
FOVEA
FRAME
FRONT
GLAND
GORGE
GROIN
GYRUS
HEART
HELIX
HILUM
HYMEN
HYOID
ILEUM
ILIUM
INCUS
INDEX
INION
JOINT
JUGAL
LIVER
MALAR
MAMMA
MEDIA
MOLAR
MOTOR
MOUTH
NASAL

NATES
NAVEL
NERVE
NUCHA
ORBIT
ORGAN
OVARY
PELMA
PENIS
PINNA
PLANT
PSOAS
PUBES
PUBIS
PUPIL
QUICK
RAMUS
SCALA
SCALP
SINEW
SINUS
SKULL
SPINA
SPINE
TALUS
THIGH
THUMB
TIBIA
TOOTH
TORSO

MEDICINE – HUMAN ANATOMY

TRUNK
UVULA
VAGUS
VALVE
VELUM
VOMER
VULVA
WAIST
WRIST
ZYGON

6

AIR-SAC
AMNION
ANTRUM
AREOLA
ARMPIT
ARTERY
AXILLA
BEHIND
BICEPS
BIG TOE
BOTTOM
BOWELS
BREAST
BREGMA
BRIDGE
CAECUM
CANINE
CARPAL
CARPUS
CAVITY
CERVIX
CHIASM
COCCYX
COELOM
COLUMN
CONCHA
CORIUM
CORNEA
CORTEX
CRUTCH
CUSPID
DERMIS
DIPLOE
DORSUM
EARLAP
EYELID
EYE-PIT
FAUCES

FIBRIL
FIBULA
FINGER
FLEXOR
FORNIX
FRENUM
FUNDUS
GIRDLE
GULLET
HALLUX
HAMMER
HAUNCH
HUCKLE
INSTEP
INSULA
KIDNEY
LABIUM
LAMBDA
LARYNX
LEADER
LINGUA
LUNULA
MARROW
MATRIX
MEATUS
MEDIUS
MEMBER
MENINX
MENTUM
MID-GUT
MID-LEG
MUSCLE
MYELON
NASION
NEURON
NIPPLE
ORBITA
PALATE
PAPULA
PAUNCH
PELVIS
PERONE
PLANTA
PLEURA
PLEXUS
PODIUM
POLLEX
RADIUS
RECTUM
RECTUS
RETINA
ROTULA

SACRUM
SCLERA
SCRUFF
SEPTUM
SEROSA
SOCKET
SOLEUS
SPLEEN
STAPES
SULCUS
TARSAL
TARSUS
TEMPLE
TENDON
TENSOR
TESTIS
THENAR
THORAX
THROAT
THYMUS
TISSUE
TONGUE
TONSIL
TRAGUS
ULNARE
URETER
UTERUS
VAGINA
VENTER
VENULE
VERMIS
VERTEX
VESICA
VESSEL
VILLUS
VISCUS
VOMICA
ZYGOMA

7

ABDOMEN
ADENOID
ADRENAL
ALVEARY
AMPULLA
ANATOMY
ANNULAR
AURICLE
BLADDER
BRISKET

BUTTOCK
CANTHUS
CENTRUM
CHORION
CHOROID
CINEREA
COCHLEA
CONDYLE
CRANIUM
CRICOID
CUTICLE
DECIDUA
DENTARY
DILATOR
EAR-BONE
EARDRUM
EAR-HOLE
ENDERON
ENTERON
ERECTOR
EXCITOR
EYE-BALL
EYEBROW
EYELASH
FISSURE
FORCEPS
FOREARM
FOSSULA
FOVEOLA
GLENOID
GLOTTIS
GLUTEUS
GRISTLE
HIND-GUT
HIP-BONE
HUMERUS
HUNKERS
INCISOR
ISCHIUM
JAWBONE
JEJUNUM
JUGULAR
KNEE-CAP
KNEE-PAN
KNUCKLE
LACTEAL
LAXATOR
LEVATOR
LOCULUS
MALLEUS
MAMILLA
MASTOID

MAXILLA
MEDULLA
MIDRIFF
MYRINGA
NAIL-BED
NOSTRIL
OBELION
OCCIPUT
ORIFICE
OSSICLE
OTOCYST
OTOLITH
OVIDUCT
PAPILLA
PAROTID
PATELLA
PERIOST
PHALANX
PHALLUS
PHARYNX
PREPUCE
PROOTIC
PUDENDA
PUNCTUM
PUTAMEN
PYLORUS
RADIALE
RIB-BONE
SACCULE
SALPINX
SCAPULA
SCROTUM
SPONDYL
STERNUM
STIRRUP
STOMACH
STYLOID
SYNAPSE
TEAR-BAG
TENDRON
THYROID
TOE-NAIL
TONSILS
TRACHEA
TRICEPS
TRUE RIB
URACHUS
URETHRA
UTRICLE
VESICLE
VISCERA
WEASAND

8

ABDUCTOR
ADENOIDS
ADJUSTOR
ALVEOLUS
AMYGDALA
APPENDIX
APTERIUM
BACKBONE
BACKSIDE
BICUSPID
BILE-DUCT
BLIND-GUT
BRAINPAN
BRONCHIA
BRONCHUS
BUTTOCKS
CEREBRUM
CLAVICLE
CLITORIS
CONARIUM
CORACOID
DUODENUM
ELEVATOR
END ORGAN
EXTENSOR
EYE-TOOTH
FALSE RIB
FOREHEAD
FORESKIN
FOSSETTE
GALL-DUCT
GANGLION
GATE-VEIN
GENITALS
GLABELLA
GLANDULE
GLUTAEUS
HAIRLINE
HINDHEAD
HIP-JOINT
HYPODERM
INNER EAR
JAW-TOOTH
LIGAMENT
LOWER LIP
MAMMILLA
MANDIBLE
MASSETER
MEMBRANE
MENISCUS

MESODERM
MIDBRAIN
MODIOLUS
MOTORIUM
NECK-BONE
NERVE-END
OCCLUSOR
OMOHYOID
OMOPLATE
OMPHALOS
PALATINE
PANCREAS
PAVILION
PEDUNCLE
PERINEUM
PERIOTIC
PERONEUS
PETROSAL
PHALANGE
PIA MATER
PISIFORM
PLACENTA
PLATYSMA
PRE-MOLAR
PRENASAL
PRONATOR
PROSTATE
PUDENDUM
PULVINAR
QUADRATE
RADICULE
RUMP-BONE
SACCULUS
SERRATUS
SESAMOID
SHIN-BONE
SHORT-RIB
SHOULDER
SINCIPUT
SKELETON
SKULLCAP
SPERMARY
SPLENIUM
SPLENIUS
STAPHYLE
STRIATUM
TASTE-BUD
TEAR-DUCT
TEMPORAL
TESTICLE
THALAMUS
THROTTLE

TURBINAL
TYMPANIC
TYMPANUM
UNDER-JAW
UNDERLIP
UPPER LIP
VENA CAVA
VERTEBRA
VESICULA
VIBRISSA
VINCULUM
VOICE-BOX
WINDPIPE

9

ANTIHELIX
ARTERIOLE
ATTOLLENT
AUGMENTOR
BLADE-BONE
BLIND SPOT
BRAINCASE
CALCANEUM
CAPILLARY
CAPITULUM
CARTILAGE
CHEEK-BONE
CHOLECYST
CLAUSTRUM
COMPLEXUS
CORPUSCLE
DEPRESSOR
DIAPHRAGM
DIAPHYSIS
DURA MATER
EMUNCTORY
ENDOSTEUM
EPIDERMIS
EPIPHYSIS
EYE-STRING
FINGERTIP
FLOCCULUS
FORE-BRAIN
FORETOOTH
FUNDAMENT
FUNICULUS
FUNNY BONE
GENITALIA
GLADIOLUS
HAMSTRING

HIND-BRAIN
HYOID BONE
INTESTINE
INTROITUS
INVOLUCRE
KNEE-JOINT
LABYRINTH
MALLEOLUS
MANUBRIUM
MESENTERY
MIDDLE EAR
MILK-GLAND
MILK-MOLAR
MILK-TOOTH
MYLOHYOID
NERVE-CELL
NEUROGLIA
OBTURATOR
OLECRANON
OPTIC LOBE
ORGANELLE
OSTEODERM
PERFORANS
PERINAEUM
POSTERIOR
PREHALLUX
QUADRATUS
RETRACTOR
RIDGE-BONE
SARTORIUS
SCARFSKIN
SCLEROTIC
SHARE-BONE
SPADE-BONE
SPERMATIC
SPHINCTER
SQUAMOSAL
STAPEDIUS
STERNEBRA
SUPINATOR
SYNERGIST
TEAR-GLAND
TENTORIUM
THIGH-BONE
THUMBNAIL
TIGHTENER
TRABECULA
TRAPEZIUM
TRAPEZOID
TRIFACIAL
UMBILICUS
URANISCUS

177

MEDICINE – HUMAN ANATOMY

UTRICULUS
VENTRICLE
VESTIBULE
WHIRL-BONE

10

ACETABULUM
ADAM'S APPLE
AFTERBIRTH
AIR-BLADDER
ANTITRAGUS
AORTIC ARCH
ARYTAENOID
ASTRAGALUS
BODY CAVITY
BONE-MARROW
BREASTBONE
BUCCINATOR
CANNON BONE
CEREBELLUM
COLLAR-BONE
COMPRESSOR
CORRUGATOR
ENCEPHALON
EPIGLOTTIS
EPISTERNUM
EPITHELIUM
EPONYCHIUM
FINGERNAIL
FONTANELLE
FONTICULUS
FOREFINGER
FOURCHETTE
GLANS PENIS
GREY MATTER
HAUNCH BONE
HEMISPHERE
HINGE-JOINT
HUCKLE-BONE
HYPODERMIS
INTESTINES
LACHRYMALS
LIMB-GIRDLE
MAIDENHEAD
MARROW-BONE
MESENTERON
METACARPUS
METATARSUS
MYOCARDIUM
NERVE-FIBRE

NEURAL ARCH
NEUROLEMMA
OESOPHAGUS
PELVIC ARCH
PERFORATUS
PERIOSTEUM
PERITONEUM
PINEAL BODY
PORTAL VEIN
PREFRONTAL
PREMAXILLA
PRESTERNUM
PROMONTORY
PROTRACTOR
PULP-CAVITY
QUADRICEPS
SACROILIAC
SALT-CELLAR
SENSE-ORGAN
SOFT PALATE
SPERMADUCT
SPERMIDUCT
SPINAL CORD
STOMODAEUM
TRIGEMINAL
TRIQUETRUM
TROCHANTER
VENTRICULE
VOCAL CORDS
YELLOW-SPOT

11

APONEUROSIS
ARCHENTERON
BLOOD-VESSEL
CANALICULUS
CANINE TOOTH
CONJUNCTIVA
CONSTRICTOR
DIAPOPHYSIS
DUPLICATURE
ENARTHROSIS
ENDOCARDIUM
ENDOMETRIUM
EPIGASTRIUM
ETHMOID BONE
FLOATING RIB
GALL-BLADDER
HAEMATOCELE
HIPPOCAMPUS

INDEX-FINGER
JUGULAR VEIN
KNUCKLE-BONE
MACULA LUTEA
MASTOID BONE
MEDIASTINUM
MITRAL VALVE
MULTICUSPID
MUSCULATURE
NAVEL-STRING
NERVE-CENTRE
NERVE-ENDING
ORBICULARIS
PARAMASTOID
PARANEPHROS
PARATHYROID
PERICARDIUM
PERICRANIUM
PERIDESMIUM
PERINEURIUM
PINEAL GLAND
PONS VAROLII
PROCEREBRUM
PROCTODAEUM
RADIAL NERVE
SACROCOSTAL
SKELETOLOGY
SOLAR PLEXUS
SPINAL CANAL
SPINAL CHORD
STIRRUP-BONE
SUBSCAPULAR
TORTICOLLIS
VAS DEFERENS
VASODILATOR
VENTRICULUS
VOCAL CHORDS
WISDOM-TOOTH

12

ALVEOLAR ARCH
BREAST-GIRDLE
DIVERTICULUM
ENDOSKELETON
EPENCEPHALON
FORAMEN MAGNA
HYPOGASTRIUM
HYPOTHALAMUS
INTERMAXILLA
MAMMARY GLAND

MOUNT OF VENUS
PARAQUADRATE
PARASPHENOID
PARIETAL BONE
PELVIC GIRDLE
PERIOTIC BONE
PORTAL SYSTEM
RADIAL ARTERY
SCISSOR-TOOTH
SHOULDER-BONE
SPHENOID BONE
SPINAL COLUMN
SPINAL MARROW
SPLINTER-BONE
STOMATODAEUM
THORACIC DUCT
VERTEBRATION
XIPHISTERNUM
ZYGAPOPHYSIS

13

ADIPOSE TISSUE
ADRENAL CORTEX
ADRENAL GLANDS
CAROTID ARTERY
CHEMORECEPTOR
DELTOID MUSCLE
ELASTIC TISSUE
EXCRETORY DUCT
FALLOPIAN TUBE
FEMORAL ARTERY
GASTROCNEMIUS
GLANS CLITORIS
HYPOCHONDRIUM

LACHRYMAL DUCT
MESENCEPHALON
NAVICULAR BONE
NERVOUS SYSTEM
OCCIPITAL BONE
OPTIC THALAMUS
PARENCEPHALON
PERICHONDRIUM
PITUITARY BODY
PROPRIOCEPTOR
PROSTATE GLAND
PUNCTUM CAECUM
SHOULDER-BLADE
SPLANCHNOCELE
UMBILICAL CORD
ZYGOMATIC ARCH

14

ACHILLES' TENDON
BRACHIAL ARTERY
CORONARY ARTERY
DIGESTIVE TRACT
DUCTLESS GLANDS
EUSTACHIAN TUBE
FALLOPIAN TUBES
FENESTRA OVALIS
INNOMINATE BONE
INNOMINATE VEIN
LACHRYMAL GLAND
MASTOID PROCESS
MAXIMUS GLUTEUS
MUCOUS MEMBRANE
PECTORAL GIRDLE

PERMANENT TOOTH
PITUITARY GLAND
PLEURAPOPHYSIS
PROSENCEPHALON
PSEUDOMEMBRANE
PTERYGOID PLATE
RHINENCEPHALON
SAGITTAL SUTURE
SCAPHOCEPHALUS
SEROUS MEMBRANE
SHOULDER-GIRDLE
SPRING-LIGAMENT
SYLVIAN FISSURE
TROCHLEAR NERVE
WANDERING NERVE
XIPHIHUMERALIS
ZYGOMATIC FOSSA

15

ALIMENTARY CANAL
CRYSTALLINE LENS
DIGESTIVE SYSTEM
EUSTACHIAN VALVE
FENESTRA ROTUNDA
LUMBRICAL MUSCLE
MEDULLARY SHEATH
OCCIPITAL ARTERY
PULMONARY ARTERY
RHOMBENCEPHALON
VASOCONSTRICTOR
VERTEBRAL COLUMN
ZYGOMATIC MUSCLE
▬▬▬▬▬▬▬

MEDICINE — ILLNESSES & ABNORMALITIES

3	ILL	WEN	AIDS	CHAP	GASH	KIBE	POCK
	MAL		BLEB	CLAP	GOUT	LISP	PUNA
BUG	PIP	4	BOIL	CLOT	GRIP	LUES	RÂLE
CUT	PIT		BUBO	COLD	HACK	LUMP	RASH
FIT	POX	ACHE	BUMP	COMA	HEAD	ONYX	RICK
FLU	TAP	ACNE	BURN	CORN	HURT	PAIN	ROSE
GYP	TIC	AGUE	CAST	CYST	ITCH	PANG	SCAB

MEDICINE — ILLNESSES & ABNORMALITIES

SCAR
SORE
STYE
TURN
WART
WIND
YAWS

5

ATONY
BENDS
BLAIN
BREAK
CHILL
COLIC
COUGH
CRAMP
CRICK
CROUP
FAINT
FAVUS
FELON
FEVER
FLUSH
FUGUE
GRAZE
GUMMA
HEART
HIVES
ILEUS
LEPRA
LIVER
LUPUS
MANIA
MOUSE
MUMPS
MYOMA
PAINS
PALSY
PEARL
PILES
PLICA
POLIO
PRICK
PSORA
QUALM
RUPIA
SCALD
SCORE
SCURF

SHOCK
SMART
SOPOR
SPASM
SPRUE
STING
STONE
SWEAT
SWOON
TABES
TALPA
THROE
TINEA
ULCER
VARIX
VARUS
VIBEX
WORMS
WOUND

6

ACEDIA
ALALIA
ALBUGO
ALEXIA
ALOGIA
AMELIA
ANGINA
ANOXIA
ANURIA
APHTHA
APNOEA
ASTHMA
ATAXIA
ATTACK
AUTISM
BOW-LEG
BRUISE
BUNION
CALIGO
CALLUS
CANCER
CANKER
CARIES
CECITY
CHOREA
COMEDO
CORYZA
DARTRE
DENGUE

DROPSY
ECTOPY
ECZEMA
EPULIS
FAVISM
FESTER
FRENZY
FURFUR
GOITRE
GRAVEL
GRIPES
GRIPPE
GROWTH
HERNIA
HERPES
HIPPUS
INJURY
IODISM
IRITIS
JET-LAG
LESION
LICHEN
LIPOMA
LUNACY
MALADY
MEGRIM
MORULA
MYOPIA
MYOSIS
NANISM
NAUSEA
NEBULA
OEDEMA
OTALGY
OTITIS
OZAENA
PAPULA
PHOBIA
PIMPLE
PLAGUE
PLAQUE
POP-EYE
PTOSIS
QUINSY
RABIES
RANULA
RED-GUM
RHEXIS
SCORCH
SCRAPE
SCURVY
SEPSIS

SHINER
SPRAIN
SQUINT
STASIS
STITCH
STRAIN
STRESS
STROKE
STRUMA
TARTAR
TETANY
THEISM
THRUSH
TRANCE
TRAUMA
TUMOUR
TWINGE
TWITCH
TYPHUS
ULITIS
ULOSIS
UROSIS
VALGUS
VOMITO
WHITES
WRENCH
XEROMA
ZOSTER

7

ABOULIA
ABSCESS
ACCIDIE
ACIDITY
ADENOMA
AILMENT
ALGESIS
ALLERGY
AMENTIA
AMNESIA
ANAEMIA
ANGIOMA
ANOSMIA
ANTHRAX
APEPSIA
APHAGIA
APHASIA
APHONIA
APLASIA
APRAXIA

ASCITES
ATRESIA
ATROPHY
BEDSORE
BLISTER
BULIMIA
CACHEXY
CATARRH
CHANCRE
CHOLERA
COCK-EYE
COLITIS
CREWELS
DISEASE
DYSURIA
EARACHE
ECTHYMA
ECTOPIA
EMPYEMA
EQUINIA
FIBROID
FIBROMA
FISTULA
FLUXION
FOOTROT
FOX-EVIL
GUMBOIL
GUM RASH
HARE-LIP
HIP-GOUT
ICTERUS
ILEITIS
ILLNESS
JIMJAMS
LEPROSY
LEUCOMA
LIMOSIS
LOCKJAW
LUMBAGO
MADNESS
MAIDISM
MALACIA
MALAISE
MALARIA
MEASLES
MILK-LEG
MORPHEW
MYALGIA
MYCOSIS
MYIASIS
NEUROMA
OBESITY

ONYCHIA
OTALGIA
PARESIS
PIMPLES
PINK-EYE
PODAGRA
POLYPUS
PORRIGO
PRURIGO
PURPLES
PURPURA
PUSTULE
PYAEMIA
PYREXIA
PYROSIS
QUARTAN
RICKETS
ROSEOLA
RUBELLA
RUBEOLA
RUPTURE
SABURRA
SARCOMA
SCABIES
SCOTOMA
SCRATCH
SEIZURE
SERPIGO
SOROCHE
STAMMER
STUTTER
SUNBURN
SURDITY
SYCOSIS
SYNCOPE
TALIPES
TENTIGO
TERTIAN
TETANUS
TORMINA
TRAVAIL
TRISMUS
TYLOSIS
TIMPANY
TYPHOID
URAEMIA
UVEITIS
VAPOURS
VARIOLA
VARIOLE
VERRUCA
VERRUGA

VERTIGO
VIROSIS
WALL-EYE
WHITLOW
WRY-NECK
XERASIA
XEROSIS
ZYMOTIC

8

ACIDOSIS
ACROTISM
ADENITIS
ADYNAMIA
AGRAPHIA
AGUE-CAKE
AIR-BENDS
ALASTRIM
ALBINISM
ALGIDITY
ALOPECIA
ANASCARA
ANEURYSM
ANOREXIA
AORTITIS
APOPLEXY
APOSITIA
APYREXIA
ASPHYXIA
ASTHENIA
ATHEROMA
ATROPISM
BACKACHE
BERIBERI
BLACK EYE
BLACKOUT
BLOCKAGE
BONE-ACHE
BOTULISM
CACHEXIA
CALCULUS
CANITIES
CARDITIS
CARUNCLE
CATARACT
CHIRAGRA
CHLOASMA
CHYLURIA
CLOTTING
CLUB-FOOT

CORONARY
COXALGIA
CRAB-YAWS
CYANOSIS
CYNANCHE
CYSTITIS
DANDRUFF
DAY-SIGHT
DEAFNESS
DEBILITY
DELIRIUM
DIABETES
DIPLOPIA
DIURESIS
DUMBNESS
DWARFISM
DYSCHROA
DYSLEXIA
DYSMELIA
DYSPNOEA
EMBOLISM
EMPTYSIS
EMPYESIS
ENURESIS
EPILEPSY
ERGOTISM
ERUPTION
ERYTHEMA
ETHERISM
FACE-ACHE
FAINTING
FIBROSIS
FLAT-FOOT
FRACTURE
FURUNCLE
GANGRENE
GLANDERS
GLAUCOMA
GRAND MAL
HAY FEVER
HEADACHE
HEAT-SPOT
HEMIOPIA
HIDROSIS
HOOK-WORM
HYDROPSY
HYSTERIA
IMPETIGO
INGROWTH
INSANITY
INSOMNIA
ISCHEMIA

ISCHURIA
JAUNDICE
KALA-AZAR
KYLLOSIS
KYPHOSIS
LIENTERY
LORDOSIS
LUMPY-JAW
LYMPHOMA
MAL DE MER
MARASMUS
MASTITIS
MELANISM
MIGRAINE
MORBILLI
MUTENESS
MYCETOMA
MYELITIS
MYOSITIS
NARCOSIS
NECROSIS
NEOPLASM
NEURITIS
NEUROSIS
ODONTOMA
ORCHITIS
OSTEITIS
OVARITIS
PALUDISM
PANDEMIA
PARANOIA
PAROXYSM
PEARL EYE
PELLAGRA
PETECHIA
PETIT MAL
PHIMOSIS
PHLEGMON
PHTHISIC
PHTHISIS
PLANURIA
PLETHORA
PLEURISY
PLUMBISM
POCKMARK
PRIAPISM
PROGERIA
PROLAPSE
PRUNELLA
PRURITUS
PSELLISM
PSILOSIS

MEDICINE — ILLNESSES & ABNORMALITIES

PTYALISM
PYELITIS
RACHITIS
RAPHANIA
RECTITIS
RHINITIS
RINGWORM
ROSE-DROP
ROSE-RASH
SCALDING
SCARRING
SCIATICA
SCIRRHUS
SCLEREMA
SCLEROMA
SCROFULA
SCYBALUM
SEMICOMA
SHINGLES
SICKNESS
SINUITIS
SIRIASIS
SMALLPOX
SNIFFLES
SNIFTERS
SNUFFLES
SORENESS
SPLINTER
STAGGERS
STEATOMA
STENOSIS
STOPPAGE
STRABISM
SUDAMINA
SWELLING
SWOONING
SYNECHIA
SYPHILIS
TENESMUS
TERATOMA
THLIPSIS
THROMBUS
TINNITUS
TOXAEMIA
TRACHOMA
TREMBLES
TROPHESY
TUBERCLE
UTERITIS
UVULITIS
VITILIGO
VOLVULUS

VOMITING
VULVITIS
WATER-POX
WHITE-LEG
WINDBURN
XANTHOMA
ZOONOSIS

9

ACARIASIS
AGALACTIA
AMAUROSIS
AMBLYOPIA
ARTERITIS
ARTHRITIS
ASYNERGIA
ATHETOSIS
ATONICITY
BELLYACHE
BILHARZIA
BLACKHEAD
BLINDNESS
BLOOD-CLOT
CACHAEMIA
CALENTURE
CALVITIES
CAMP-FEVER
CARBUNCLE
CARCINOMA
CARNOSITY
CATALEPSY
CATAPLEXY
CHANCROID
CHILBLAIN
CHLOROSIS
CHOLAEMIA
CHOLELITH
CICATRICE
CIRRHOSIS
COCAINISM
COMPLAINT
CONCHITIS
CONDYLOMA
CONTAGION
CONTUSION
CRETINISM
CROTALISM
CYSTOCELE
DALTONISM
DEFLUXION

DEFORMITY
DIAPYESIS
DIARRHOEA
DYSCHROIA
DYSCRASIA
DYSENTERY
DYSPEPSIA
DYSPHAGIA
DYSPHONIA
DYSPHORIA
DYSTHESIA
DYSTHYMIA
DYSTROPHY
ECHOLALIA
ECLAMPSIA
ECTROPION
ECTROPIUM
EMPHLYSIS
EMPHYSEMA
ENCANTHIS
ENTERITIS
ENTROPION
EPISTAXIS
ERYTHRISM
EXANTHEMA
EXOSTOSIS
FEBRICULE
FLUOROSIS
FRENCH POX
FROSTBITE
GALL-STONE
GAOL-FEVER
GASTRITIS
GATHERING
GIDDINESS
GIGANTISM
GLOSSITIS
HAEMATOMA
HALITOSIS
HAMMER-TOE
HAY ASTHMA
HEADINESS
HEARTBURN
HEMIOPSIA
HEPATITIS
HORDEOLUM
HYDRAEMIA
HYDROCELE
HYPEREMIA
HYPINOSIS
HYSTERICS
IMBALANCE

INFECTION
INFIRMITY
INFLUENZA
ISCHAEMIA
JAIL-FEVER
KERATITIS
KING'S-EVIL
KLIEG EYES
LATHYRISM
LEAD COLIC
LEUKAEMIA
LITHIASIS
LITHOCYST
LOOSENESS
MADAROSIS
MAL DU PAYS
MELANOSIS
MELANURIA
MEPHITISM
MESCALISM
MICROPSIA
MISGROWTH
MONGOLISM
MORBIDITY
MYDRIASIS
MYXOEDEMA
NARCOTISM
NEPHRALGY
NEPHRITIS
NEPHROSIS
NERVINESS
NEURALGIA
NOSE-BLEED
NYSTAGMUS
OBSTRUENT
OCCLUSION
OLIGAEMIA
ONYCHITIS
OTORRHOEA
OUTGROWTH
OVERREACH
PAPILLOMO
PARACUSIS
PARALALIA
PARALEXIA
PARALOGIA
PARALYSIS
PAROTITIS
PEMPHIGUS
PERTUSSIS
PHLEBITIS
PHOSSY-JAW

PHOTOPSIA
PHRENITIS
PLEURITIS
PNEUMONIA
POMPHOLYX
PORPHYRIA
PRESBYOPY
PROCTITIS
PROLAPSUS
PROPTOSIS
PSORIASIS
PSYCHOSIS
PTERYGIUM
PYORRHOEA
QUOTIDIAN
RETINITIS
REVULSION
RHINOLITH
ROCK FEVER
SAPRAEMIA
SATURNISM
SCALD-HEAD
SCLERITIS
SCLEROSIS
SCOLIOSIS
SEPTICITY
SHIP-FEVER
SIALOLITH
SIDEROSIS
SILICOSIS
SINGULTUS
SINUSITIS
SPANAEMIA
SPHACELUS
SPLENITIS
SQUINT-EYE
SQUINTING
STEATOSIS
STEGNOSIS
STIFF-NECK
STIFFNESS
STRANGURY
STRUMITIS
SUNSTROKE
SWIVEL-EYE
SYMPTOSIS
SYNOVITIS
SYPHILOMA
TAENIASIS
TARANTISM
TARSALGIA
TOOTHACHE

TORULOSIS
TRICHOSIS
TUBERCULE
TYPHLITIS
URTICARIA
VAGINITIS
VARICELLA
VARIOLOID
VENTOSITY
WORM-FEVER
WRIST-DROP
XENOMENIA
XEROSTOMA
ZINC-COLIC

10

ABREACTION
ACROMEGALY
AFFLICTION
AFTERPAINS
ALCOHOLISM
ALLOCHIRIA
ANHELATION
ANTIADITIS
ARTHRALGIA
ASBESTOSIS
ASCARIASIS
ASYSTOLISM
ATELEIOSIS
BAGASSOSIS
BATTLE SCAR
BLACK DEATH
BLEPHARISM
BLOODY-FLUX
BOTTLE-NOSE
BRAIN DEATH
BRAIN FEVER
BRONCHITIS
BYSSINOSIS
CARCINOSIS
CARDIALGIA
CARPHOLOGY
CELLULITIS
CEPHALAGRA
CEPHALITIS
CEREBRITIS
CHICKEN-POX
CHLORALISM
CINCHONISM
COMMON COLD

CONCUSSION
CONGESTION
CONTRECOUP
CRAPULENCE
DEAF-MUTISM
DELIRATION
DEPRESSION
DERMATITIS
DIPHTHERIA
DIPSOMANIA
DISABILITY
DUODENITIS
DYSGRAPHIA
EBURNATION
ECCHYMOSIS
ECHOPRAXIA
ECHOPRAXIS
ECTOMORPHY
EMACIATION
EMMETROPIA
ENTEROCELE
ENTEROLITH
EPICANTHUS
ERYSIPELAS
FATTY HEART
FIBROSITIS
FILARIASIS
FLATULENCE
FLESH-WOUND
FRAMBOESIA
GALL-STONES
GASTRALGIA
GINGIVITIS
GLYCOSURIA
GONORRHOEA
GROGGINESS
HAEMATOSIS
HAEMATURIA
HEART-BLOCK
HEATSTROKE
HEMIANOPIA
HEMICRANIA
HEMIPLEGIA
HOARSENESS
HYPERAEMIA
HYPOSTASIS
HYSTERITIS
ICHTHYOSIS
IMBECILITY
IMPEDIMENT
INSOLATION
INTERTRIGO

IRRITATION
LACERATION
LACHRYMALS
LARYNGITIS
LASSA FEVER
LEONTIASIS
LUNG CANCER
MALIGNANCY
MALTA FEVER
MARSH FEVER
MELANAEMIA
MENINGIOMA
MENINGITIS
MOLYBDOSIS
MONILIASIS
MONOPLEGIA
MONORCHISM
MORPHINISM
MOUSE-SIGHT
MULLIGRUBS
MYRINGITIS
NARCOLEPSY
NEPHRALGIA
NETTLE-RASH
NEUROLYSIS
NICOTINISM
NYCTALOPIA
ODONTALGIA
OOPHORITIS
OPHTHALMIA
ORNITHOSIS
ORTHOPNOEA
OVERSTRAIN
OVERSTRESS
PANARITIUM
PAPILLITIS
PAPULATION
PARAMNESIA
PARAPHASIA
PARAPLEGIA
PARARTHRIA
PARONYCHIA
PESTILENCE
PHAGEDAENA
PHLEBOLITE
PHLEGMASIA
PHOCOMELIA
PITYRIASIS
PLAGUE-SORE
PLAGUE-SPOT
POLLENOSIS
POLYDIPSIA

MEDICINE – ILLNESSES & ABNORMALITIES

PRESBYOPIA
PROCIDENCE
PROCTALGIA
PROSTATISM
PSELLISMUS
QUEASINESS
RHEUMATICS
RHEUMATISM
RHINOLALIA
RHINOPHYMA
SCARLATINA
SCISSOR-LEG
SCLERIASIS
SCOTODINIA
SEBORRHOEA
SHELLSHOCK
SIDERATION
SKIN CANCER
SORE THROAT
SPASTICITY
STAPHYLOMA
STEATOCELE
STEREOPSIS
STIBIALISM
STOMATITIS
STRABISMUS
SYRINGITIS
TABESCENCE
TACHYPNOEA
TEICHOPSIA
THANATOSIS
THROMBOSIS
TOOTH DECAY
TRACHEITIS
TRAUMATISM
TRENCH-FOOT
TRICHIASIS
TUBERCULUM
TUMESCENCE
TYMPANITES
TYMPANITIS
ULCERATION
URETERITIS
URETHRITIS
VAGINISMUS
VALVULITIS
VARICOCELE
VARICOSITY
VESICATION
WATER-BRASH
WHEEZINESS
WIND-DROPSY

XANTHOPSIA
XERODERMIA
XEROSTOMIA
YELLOW JACK

11

ABNORMALITY
AIR-SICKNESS
ALBUMINURIA
AMENORRHOEA
ANAPHYLAXIS
ANTHRACOSIS
ASTIGMATISM
BARBADOS LEG
BILIOUSNESS
BLEPHARITIS
BLOODY-SWEAT
BRADYCARDIA
BROMIDROSIS
BRONZED SKIN
BULLET-WOUND
CEPHALALGIA
CHALKSTONES
CLEFT PALATE
CONSUMPTION
DEHYDRATION
DERANGEMENT
DISABLEMENT
DISTRACTION
DRUNKENNESS
DUMDUM FEVER
DYSFUNCTION
ENCHONDROMA
ENGORGEMENT
EPITHELIOMA
EVENTRATION
EXCRESCENCE
FARMER'S LUNG
GARGANTUISM
GLOSSODYNIA
GUTTA SERENA
HAEMOPHILIA
HAEMOPTYSIS
HAEMORRHAGE
HEART ATTACK
HEART TREMOR
HEBEPHRENIA
HECTIC FEVER
HEMERALOPIA
HEMIANOPSIA

HYDROPHOBIA
HYDROTHORAX
HYPEREMESIS
HYPERINOSIS
HYPERPHAGIA
HYPOSTROPHE
HYPOTENSION
HYPOTHERMIA
IDIOGLOSSIA
INDIGESTION
INFESTATION
JUNGLE FEVER
KIDNEY-STONE
KWASHIORKOR
LANCINATION
LARYNGISMUS
LEUCORRHOEA
LIPOMATOSIS
LYCANTHROPY
MAD STAGGERS
MASTOIDITIS
MENINGOCELE
MICTURITION
MONOBLEPSIS
MYOCARDITIS
NECROBIOSIS
NERVOUSNESS
NEUROTICISM
OBSTIPATION
OBSTRUCTION
PACHYDERMIA
PALPITATION
PARAGRAPHIA
PARAPHRAXIA
PARAPHRAXIS
PARACITOSIS
PARATYPHOID
PAROTIDITIS
PEDICULOSIS
PEPTIC ULCER
PERIOSTITIS
PERITONITIS
PHARYNGITIS
PHTHIRIASIS
PLEURODYNIA
PNEUMONITIS
PRICKLY-HEAT
PROSTATITIS
PSITTACOSIS
PUTRID FEVER
RHABDOMYOMA
RHINORRHOEA

SALPINGITIS
SCLEROTITIS
SCRUB-TYPHUS
SEASICKNESS
SEPTICAEMIA
SIALORRHOEA
SIDEROPENIA
SLIPPED DISC
SPINA BIFIDA
SPONDYLITIS
STAPHYLITIS
STOMACH-ACHE
STONE-BRUISE
TABEFACTION
TACHYCARDIA
TENNIS ELBOW
TETRAPLEGIA
THERMOLYSIS
THYROIDITIS
TONSILLITIS
TRAVAIL-PAIN
TRAVAIL-PANG
TRENCH-FEVER
TRICHINOSIS
TUBERCULOMA
TURGESCENCE
WAR NEUROSIS
WHISKY-LIVER
YELLOW FEVER

12

AEROEMBOLISM
AERONEUROSIS
ANACATHARSIS
ANENCEPHALIA
APPENDICITIS
ARCUS SENILIS
ATHLETE'S FOOT
AVITAMINOSIS
BLENNORRHOEA
BREAST CANCER
BUTTON-SCURVY
CEREBROTONIA
CHILDCROWING
COLOSTRATION
COLLYWOBBLES
CONSTIPATION
CRYSTALLITIS
DAY-BLINDNESS
DEBILITATION

DEXTROCARDIA
DICHROMATISM
DIPHTHERITIS
DRACONTIASIS
DYSAESTHESIA
ENCEPHALITIS
ENDOCARDITIS
ENDOMETRITIS
ENTERIC FEVER
ENTEROPTOSIS
EUNUCHOIDISM
EXOPHTHALMIA
FALLEN ARCHES
FEVERISHNESS
FIBRILLATION
GASTRIC FEVER
GROWING-PAINS
GYNAECOMASTY
HAEMATEMESIS
HAEMORRHOIDS
HALLUCINOSIS
HAMARTHRITIS
HEART DISEASE
HEART-FAILURE
HEAT-APOPLEXY
HEPATISATION
HIATUS HERNIA
HOMESICKNESS
HYDRARGYRISM
HYPERACIDITY
HYPERIDROSIS
HYPERPYREXIA
HYPERSARCOMA
HYPERSTHENIA
HYPERTENSION
HYPERTHERMIA
HYPOCHONDRIA
ILIAC PASSION
INCONTINENCE
INFLAMMATION
INSULIN SHOCK
INTOXICATION
INTUMESCENCE
KIDNEY-STONES
LEUCOCYTOSIS
LYMPHANGITIS
MALFORMATION
MALNUTRITION
MERCURIALISM
MESOTHELIOMA
MONGOLOID EYE
MONOCHROMASY

NEPHROPTOSIS
NEURASTHENIA
NOSE-BLEEDING
OPHTHALMITIS
OPISTHOTONOS
OSTEOMALACIA
OTOSCLEROSIS
PALPITATIONS
PANARTHRITIS
PANCREATITIS
PARAESTHESIA
PARAPHIMOSIS
PARKINSONISM
PERICARDITIS
PERINEURITIS
PHOSPHATURIA
PNEUMOTHORAX
PURBLINDNESS
QUADRIPLEGIA
RHINORRHAGIA
SAND-FLY FEVER
SCARLET FEVER
SCLERODERMIA
SHOOTING PAIN
SHOULDER-SLIP
SICK-HEADACHE
SMOKER'S COUGH
SPERMATOCELE
SPLENIC FEVER
SPLENOMEGALY
STRONGYLOSIS
STRYCHNINISM
SUBNORMALITY
SYNARTHROSIS
TRICHINIASIS
TUBERCULOSIS
TUNNEL VISION
TYPHOID FEVER
VARICOSE VEIN
VIRUS DISEASE
VOMITURITION
WEANING-BRASH
WRITER'S CRAMP

13

ACTINOMYCOSIS
BRACHYDACTYLY
BUBONIC PLAGUE
CARDIAC ARREST

CEREBRAL DEATH
CHOLECYSTITIS
COMBAT FATIGUE
CONNIPTION FIT
CONSUMPTIVITY
DIAPHRAGMITIS
DISFIGUREMENT
DOWN'S SYNDROME
DUODENAL ULCER
DYSMENORRHOEA
ELEPHANTIASIS
ENCEPHALOCELE
FOOD POISONING
GALACTORRHOEA
GALACTOSAEMIA
GERMAN MEASLES
GREEN SICKNESS
GYNAECOMASTIA
HALLUCINATION
HEEBIE-JEEBIES
HYDROCEPHALUS
HYPERHIDROSIS
HYPERMETROPIA
HYPERSARCOSIS
HYPOGLYCAEMIA
IMPACTED TOOTH
IMPERFORATION
INDISPOSITION
LABYRINTHITIS
LEAD-POISONING
LEISHMANIASIS
LEPTOSPIROSIS
LEUCOCYTHEMIA
MINER'S ANAEMIA
MONONUCLEOSIS
MORPHINOMANIA
MORTIFICATION
NERVOUS TWITCH
OSTEOMYELITIS
PAEDOMORPHISM
PAINTER'S COLIC
PANOPHTHALMIA
PARAPSYCHOSIS
PARROT DISEASE
PERIGASTRITIS
PERIHEPATITIS
PERITYPHLITIS
PLICA POLONICA
POLIOMYELITIS
POLYCYTHAEMIA
POTT'S FRACTURE
RHINOSCLEROMA

MEDICINE – ILLNESSES & ABNORMALITIES

SALMONELLOSIS
SELF-INFECTION
SIGHTLESSNESS
SNOW-BLINDNESS
SOLDIER'S HEART
STRANGULATION
ST VITUS'S DANCE
SYNCHONDROSIS
TABES DORSALIS
TIC-DOULOUREUX
TOXOPLASMOSIS
UNDULANT FEVER
VISCEROPTOSIS
WHOOPING-COUGH
WORD-BLINDNESS
XANTHOCHROMIA
XEROPHTHALMIA

14

ACARINE DISEASE
ACHONDROPLASIA
ALOPECIA AREATA
ANGINA PECTORIS
BRIGHT'S DISEASE
BRITISH CHOLERA
BRONCHIECTASIS
CAISSON DISEASE
CARCINOMATOSIS
CERVICAL CANCER
CHOLELITHIASIS
CONJUNCTIVITIS
CYSTIC FIBROSIS
DERBYSHIRE-NECK
ENDEMIC DISEASE
FALSE PREGNANCY
FLOATING KIDNEY
FROZEN SHOULDER
GLANDULAR FEVER

HEART CONDITION
HOUSEMAID'S KNEE
HYDRONEPHROSIS
HYPERAESTHESIA
HYPERCALCAEMIA
HYPERGLYCAEMIA
HYPERNATRAEMIA
LEUCOCYTOPENIA
LOBAL PNEUMONIA
LOCOMOTOR ATAXY
MINER'S PHTHISIS
MONOCHROMATISM
MUCOVISCIDOSIS
NIGHT-BLINDNESS
OLIGOCYTHAEMIA
ORGANIC DISEASE
OSTEO-ARTHRITIS
PINS AND NEEDLES
PNEUMOCONIOSIS
PSEUDAESTHESIA
PSYCHONEUROSIS
PUERPERAL FEVER
QUARTAN MALARIA
RELAPSING FEVER
REMITTENT FEVER
RHEUMATIC FEVER
RIVER BLINDNESS
SIMPLE FRACTURE
SLEEPY-SICKNESS
SPERMATORRHOEA
SPIROCHAETOSIS
ST ANTHONY'S FIRE
TELANGIECTASIS
THYROTOXICOSIS
TRICHINISATION
TRICHOMONIASIS
TRICHOPHYTOSIS
TROPHONEUROSIS
WATER ON THE KNEE
WHIPLASH INJURY

15

ADDISON'S DISEASE
ANKLYOSTOMIASIS
ANOREXIA NERVOSA
ATHEROSCLEROSIS
BLACKWATER FEVER
BORNHOLM DISEASE
COLOUR-BLINDNESS
CONSUMPTIVENESS
DELIRIUM TREMENS
DOUBLE PNEUMONIA
FALLING SICKNESS
FALSE CONCEPTION
FIRST DEGREE BURN
FROG IN THE THROAT
GASTROENTERITIS
HIP-JOINT DISEASE
HODGKIN'S DISEASE
HYPERADRENALISM
HYPERTHYROIDISM
HYPOCHONDRIASIS
LONG SIGHTEDNESS
MORNING-SICKNESS
NEAR SIGHTEDNESS
ONYCHOCRYPTOSIS
OPHTHALMOPLEGIA
PANOPHTHALMITIS
PERFORATED ULCER
PHENYLKETONURIA
SCHISTOSOMIASIS
SCRIVENER'S PALSY
TERMINAL ILLNESS
THIRD DEGREE BURN
TIME-ZONE DISEASE
TRYPANOSOMIASIS
UNCONSCIOUSNESS
VENEREAL DISEASE
WATER ON THE BRAIN

MEDICINE – MEDICATION & DRUGS

3

FIX
HOP
KEF
LSD
POT
TEA

4

BALL
BALM
BENJ
COKE
CURE
DOPE
DRUG
HEMP
IRON
JUNK
MOXA
PILL
SKAG
SNOW
SOMA

5

ALOES
BHANG
BOLUS
CRACK
CUBEB
DAGGA
DINIC
DROPS
FANGO
GANJA
GRASS
GUACO
HORSE
JALAP
LYMPH
OPIUM
PICRA
PUKER
PURGE
RUSMA
RUTIN
SALEP

SALTS
SALVE
SENNA
SERUM
SETON
SPEED
STEEL
STUFF
TONGA
TONIC
UPPER
VOMIT

6

ARNICA
BALSAM
BEZOAR
CERATE
DOWNER
ELIXIR
EMETIC
EMETIN
EVIPAN
FORMOL
GARGLE
GINGER
GURJUN
HEROIN
HYPNIC
IODINE
KAOLIN
LOTION
MATICO
MUMMIA
OPIATE
PELLET
PEPSIN
PHYSIC
PILULE
POTION
POWDER
PTISAN
REMEDY
SALINE
SIMPLE
STANCH
TABLET
THEINE
TISANE
TOXOID
TROCHE

VALIUM

7

ANODYNE
ANTACID
ARAROBA
ASEPTIC
ASPIRIN
ATABRIN
BITTERS
CALMANT
CALOMEL
CALUMBA
CARDIAC
CLYSTER
COCAINE
CODEINE
COPAIBA
CORDIAL
CURE-ALL
DAPSONE
DIASONE
DRASTIC
DRAUGHT
ECBOLIC
EPITHEM
EUCAINE
EUGENOL
EYE-WASH
GENTIAN
GINSENG
GUANINE
GUARANÁ
HASHISH
HEPARIN
HIRUDIN
HYPNONE
ICE-PACK
INHALER
INSULIN
LIBRIUM
LINCTUS
LOZENGE
MENTHOL
MERCURY
METOPON
MISHMEE
MORPHIA
NERVINE
NOSTRUM

OPORICE
PANACEA
PANADOL
PATULIN
PEP-PILL
PHILTRE
PLACEBO
QUININE
REVIVER
RHATANY
SCOURER
SECONAL
SQUILLS
STEROID
STYPTIC
SWEATER
THERIAC
TURPETH
UNCTION
UNGUENT
VACCINE
VERONAL

8

ANTIDOTE
APERIENT
ATARAXIC
BANTHINE
BLUE PILL
CAFFEINE
CAMOMILE
CANNABIS
COLD PACK
COMPOUND
COMPRESS
CORAMINE
CURARINE
DIAPENTE
DIURETIC
DRENCHER
EAR-DROPS
ECCRITIC
ELATERIN
EPULOTIC
EVACUANT
EXCITANT
EYE-DROPS
EYE-SALVE
EYE-WATER
FORMALIN

GOOFBALL
GUAIACUM
HIDROTIC
HYOSCINE
INHALANT
INOCULUM
LAUDANUM
LAXATIVE
LENITIVE
LICORICE
LINCTURE
LINIMENT
LIP-SALVE
LOOSENER
LOVE-DRUG
LUNGWORT
MAGNESIA
MECONIUM
MEDICINE
MERSALYL
METOPRYL
MEZEREON
MORPHINE
NARCOTIC
NAUSEANT
NEMBUTAL
NEOMYCIN
NICOTINE
OINTMENT
PASTILLE
PECTORAL
PICK-ME-UP
PINKROOT
POULTICE
PROCAINE
QUIETIVE
RELAXANT
ROBORANT
SANTONIN
SEDATIVE
SENNAPOD
SHARK-OIL
SICKENER
SPECIFIC
STOVAINE
TETRONAL
TINCTURE
VALERIAN
VARIDASE
VASELINE
VIRICIDE
ZERUMBET

187

MEDICINE – MEDICATION & DRUGS

9

ANALGESIC
ANTITOXIN
ANTRYCIDE
BARBITONE
BASILICON
BIRTH PILL
BLACK DROP
BLACK-WASH
CASSAREEP
CASTOREUM
CASTOR-OIL
CATHARTIC
CEPHALATE
COAGULANT
COLD-CREAM
COLLYRIUM
COLOCYNTH
CORTISONE
COUGH-DROP
DEMULCENT
DIGITALIS
ELECTUARY
EMOLLIENT
EMPLASTIC
EPHEDRINE
EXCIPIENT
FEBRIFUGE
FOLIC ACID
GALENICAL
GERMICIDE
GUANAZOLO
HECOGENIN
HISTAMINE
INUNCTION
JABORANDI
LARGACTIL
LIQUORICE
LIVERWORT
LOVE-CHARM
LOVE-JUICE
MARIHUANA
MARIJUANA
MEPACRINE
METHADONE
MODURETIC
MOUTH-WASH
MYDRIATIC
NARCOTINE
NEPHRITIC
NOSE-DROPS

OBSTRUENT
OBTUNDENT
OESTROGEN
OPODELDOC
PALUDRINE
PAREGORIC
PENTOTHAL
PETHIDINE
PRONTOSIL
PURGATIVE
RADIO PILL
RESERPINE
RESISTANT
SALVARSAN
SASSAFRAS
SNAKEROOT
SOPORIFIC
SPEED-BALL
STIMULANT
STOMACHIC
SUDORIFIC
TARAXACUM
TRUTH DRUG
VERMICIDE
VERMIFUGE
VULNERARY

10

ACRIFLAVIN
ANTAGONIST
ANTIBIOTIC
ANTISEPTIC
ASTRINGENT
AUREOMYCIN
BELLADONNA
BENZEDRINE
BENZOCAINE
CHLORODYNE
CHLOROQUIN
CHOLOGOGUE
COLCHISINE
COUGH-SWEET
COUGH-SYRUP
DEPRESSANT
DETOXICANT
DISCUTIENT
DISPERSANT
DUTCH DROPS
ECCOPROTIC
ECPHRACTIC

EMPHRACTIC
EMPLASTRON
ENKEPHALIN
EPSOM SALTS
EXHILARANT
GOLDEN-SEAL
GRAMICIDIN
HIERA-PICRA
HIPPOMANES
HYPODERMIC
INDIAN HEMP
INHALATION
INTERFERON
ISONIAZIDE
LIGNOCAINE
LOVE-POTION
MEDICAMENT
MEDICATION
METHEDRINE
MEXICAN TEA
MILK OF LIME
MITHRIDATE
NUMBER NINE
PAIN-KILLER
PALLIATIVE
PEARL-WHITE
PENICILLIN
PETROLATUM
PHENACITIN
POLYCHREST
PSILOCYBIN
SPANISH FLY
STRAMONIUM
TERRAMYCIN
THIOPENTAL
TROCHISCUS
TRUTH SERUM
TUBERCULIN
WITCH-HAZEL
WORM-POWDER
YELLOW-WASH

11

AMINOBUTENE
AMPHETAMINE
AMYL NITRATE
ANTIPYRETIC
APHRODISIAC
APOMORPHINE

ARQUEBUSADE
BACTERICIDE
BARBITURATE
BITTER EARTH
BORACIC ACID
CARMINATIVE
CHRYSAROBIN
COD-LIVER OIL
CULVER'S ROOT
CYCLOSERINE
DESERPIDINE
DIAPHORETIC
DIASCORDIUM
DIATESSORON
EMBROCATION
EMMENAGOGUE
EXPECTORANT
EYE-OINTMENT
FOMENTATION
HYOSCYAMINE
IPECACUANHA
LAUREL-WATER
LINSEED-MEAL
LITHOTRITIC
MALT-EXTRACT
MASTICATORY
MEPROBAMATE
NIKETHAMIDE
OIL OF CLOVES
PARACETAMOL
PARALDEHYDE
PROGESTOGEN
PTYALAGOGUE
PURPLE HEART
REJUVENATOR
RESTORATIVE
RESTRINGENT
RESUSCITANT
SALK VACCINE
SAL VOLATILE
SCOPOLAMINE
SCURVY-GRASS
SLIPPERY ELM
SUPPOSITORY
SUPPURATIVE
SYRUP OF FIGS
THALIDOMIDE
THIOPENTONE
TOLBUTAMIDE
TRYPANOCIDE
VASODILATOR
VASOPRESSIN

VASOPRESSOR
VITAMIN PILL

12

ALEXIPHARMIC
ANTIPERIODIC
ANTIPRURITIC
ANTIRACHITIC
ANTITHROMBIN
BALSAM OF TOLU
BLACK DRAUGHT
CANTHARIDINE
CARAWAY SEEDS
COLD COMPRESS
COLOQUINTIDA
COUGH-LOZENGE
COUGH-MIXTURE
DECONGESTANT
DOVER'S POWDER
ERYTHROMYCIN
FOLK-MEDICINE
FRIAR'S BALSAM
GALACTAGOGUE
GRISEOFULVIN
HALLUCINOGEN
HEROIC REMEDY
JESUITS' DROPS
LUNAR CAUSTIC
LYSERGIC ACID
MINERAL JELLY
NORADRENALIN
PANPHARMACON
PARASITICIDE
PAREIRA BRAVA
PHLEGMAGOGUE
PROPHYLACTIC
ROCHELLE-SALT
SABIN VACCINE
SARSAPARILLA

SLEEPING-PILL
SODIUM AMYTAL
STERNUTATIVE
STILBOESTROL
STREPTOMYCIN
STROPHANTHUS
SULPHONOMIDE
TARTAR EMETIC
TESTOSTERONE
TRYPAFLAVINE
ZINC OINTMENT

13

ANAPHRODISIAC
ANTHELMINTHIC
ANTICOAGULANT
ANTIHISTAMINE
ANTISCORBUTIC
ANTISPASMODIC
APOPHLEGMATIC
BACTERIOLYSIN
BRONCO-DILATOR
CASSIA FISTULA
CHLOROMYCETIN
CULVER'S PHYSIC
DANGEROUS DRUG
FERTILITY DRUG
GENTIAN VIOLET
GONADOTROPHIN
KNOCKOUT DROPS
MATERIA MEDICA
OIL OF LAVENDER
PURGING CASSIA
PYRIMETHAMINE
SALICYLIC ACID
SMELLING SALTS
STYPTIC PENCIL
SYNTHETIC DRUG
TRANQUILLISER

14

ALEXIPHARMAKON
ANDROMEDOTOXIN
ANTAPHRODISIAC
ANTICONVULSANT
ANTIDEPRESSANT
ANTIODONTALGIC
ANTIPHLOGISTIC
CALAMINE LOTION
CHAULMOOGRA OIL
CHLORAL HYDRATE
CHLORPROMAZINE
CORTICO-STEROID
CORTICO-TROPHIN
GREGORY'S POWDER
HICKERY-PICKERY
KAOLIN POULTICE
LIQUID PARAFFIN
MILK OF MAGNESIA
PATENT MEDICINE
PETROLEUM JELLY
PHARMACEUTICAL
PHENOBARBITONE
ROCHELLE-POWDER
SEIDLITZ POWDER
SLEEPING-TABLET
SULPHANILAMIDE
SULPHAPYRIDINE
SULPHATHIAZOLE
SURGICAL SPIRIT

15

ANABOLIC STEROID
COUNTER-IRRITANT
GREGORY'S MIXTURE
SLEEPING-DRAUGHT
SULPHAGUANIDINE
VASOCONSTRICTOR

MILITARY TERMS

3

BAR
BAY
FOE
KIT
PIP
SAP
WAR

4

ALLY
ARMY
AXIS
BASE
CAMP
DUMP
DUTY
FILE
FLAG
GONG
LEVY
LINE
LIST
MESS
MINE
NATO
PARK
PLAN
POST
PUSH
RAID
RANK
REAR
ROLL
ROUT
STAR
TAPS
TRAP
WING

5

BADGE
BATON
CACHE
CADRE
CARRY
CLASP

CREST
CROSS
DECOY
DEMOB
DEPOT
DRAFT
DRILL
EAGLE
ENEMY
ÉTAPE
FIELD
FLANK
FLARE
FLASH
FORAY
GUARD
ISSUE
LEAVE
LINES
LURCH
MARCH
MEDAL
MÊLÉE
NAAFI
ONSET
ORDER
PARTY
PEACE
PIVOT
RADAR
RANGE
RECCE
ROUTE
SALLY
SALVO
SIEGE
SLASH
STACK
STAND
STONK
SWOOP
TRUCE
WEDGE
WINGS

6

ACTION
AFFAIR
AMBUSH
ATTACK

BANNER
BATTLE
BEACON
BILLET
BOUNTY
BREVET
CALL-UP
CHARGE
COLUMN
COMBAT
DEFEAT
DOUBLE
DRY RUN
EMBLEM
ENSIGN
ERSATZ
FIZZER
GROUND
KIT-BAG
LIMBER
MANUAL
MORALE
MUSTER
MUTINY
ONRUSH
ORDERS
PARADE
PARLEY
PATROL
PICKET
POCKET
RAFALE
RAPPEL
RATION
RELIEF
RESCUE
REVIEW
RIBBON
ROSTER
SALUTE
SCREEN
SECTOR
SIGNAL
SORTIE
SQUARE
STORES
STRAFE
STRIPE
TARGET
TATTOO
TICKET
TRENCH

VOLLEY

7

AIR-DROP
ARMOURY
ARSENAL
BAGGAGE
BARRAGE
BATTERY
BISCUIT
BIVOUAC
BLIGHTY
BRACKET
CANTEEN
CHEVRON
COLD WAR
COLOURS
COMMAND
CRUSADE
DEFENCE
ECHELON
ENOMOTY
EPAULET
FALL-OUT
FOX-HOLE
HUTMENT
JANKERS
LANDING
LATRINE
LIAISON
MEDALET
MISSION
OUTFALL
OUTPOST
PANNIER
PHALANX
PINCERS
PIP EMMA
POTENCE
PRESENT
RAG-FAIR
RATIONS
REPULSE
RETREAT
REVERSE
SAND-BAG
SAPHEAD
SCALADE
SCALADO
SERVICE

SNIPING
SUPPORT
SURPLUS
TACTICS
THEATRE
TURN-OUT
VICTORY
WARFARE
YOMPING

8

ALL-CLEAR
ALLIANCE
ARMY LIST
ASSEMBLY
BARRACKS
BLINDAGE
BLOCKADE
BLOOD-TAX
BRIEFING
CAMISADO
CAMPAIGN
CASUALTY
CITATION
CIVIL WAR
COLLAPSE
CONQUEST
DEMOTION
DESPATCH
DISPATCH
ENFILADE
ESCALADE
FATIGUES
FIELD DAY
FIGHTING
FORE-RANK
FUNK-HOLE
FURLOUGH
GARRISON
GRATUITY
HARDWARE
INSIGNIA
INVASION
LANDWEHR
LAST POST
LOCKSTEP
LODGMENT
MAGAZINE
MARCHING
MATÉRIEL

MILITARY
MUSKETRY
NUMERALS
OPEN TOWN
ORDNANCE
PALISADE
PASSWORD
PRESIDIO
QUARTERS
RECOVERY
REGISTER
REVEILLE
RIFLE-PIT
ROLL-CALL
SALUTING
SENTRY-GO
SHELLING
SHOOTING
SKIRMISH
SLASHING
STANDARD
STOCKADE
STORMING
STRATEGY
STRENGTH
SUBBASAL
SUPPLIES
THE FRONT
TRAINING
UMBRELLA
WAR CLOUD
WHEELING
ZERO HOUR

9

ABOUT-FACE
ABOUT-TURN
AMBUSCADE
ARMISTICE
ARTILLERY
ATOMIC WAR
ATTENTION
BEACHHEAD
BILLETING
BLOOD-BATH
BLOODSHED
BUGLE-CALL
CANNONADE
CEASE-FIRE
CHALLENGE

CROSSFIRE
DECURSION
DESERTION
DETENTION
DISCHARGE
ENROLMENT
EPAULETTE
EQUIPMENT
EXCURSION
EXEMPTION
FIRE-POWER
FIRST POST
FORMATION
FOUR-BY-TWO
FUSILLADE
GOOSE-STEP
INCURSION
IRON CROSS
LANDSTURM
LEFT-WHEEL
LIGHTS OUT
LOGISTICS
MANOEUVRE
MARCH PAST
MEDALLION
MILITARIA
MINE-FIELD
MUNIMENTS
MUNITIONS
OBJECTIVE
OFFENSIVE
ONSLAUGHT
OPEN ORDER
OPERATION
PACK-DRILL
PREDICTOR
PROMOTION
ROUTE-STEP
SAND-TABLE
SERREFILE
SHELLFIRE
SLOW MARCH
SPEARHEAD
STAFF-DUTY
STRATAGEM
SURRENDER
SWORD-KNOT
WATCHWORD
WHITE FLAG

10

ACTIVE LIST
APPROACHES
BLITZKRIEG
BOMB-CRATER
BRIDGEHEAD
CAMOUFLAGE
CASHIERING
CASUS BELLI
COMMISSION
CONTRABAND
CRIME-SHEET
DEAD GROUND
DECAMPMENT
DECORATION
DEFILEMENT
DEPLOYMENT
DISCIPLINE
DISPATCHES
DUTY ROSTER
ENCAMPMENT
ENGAGEMENT
ENLISTMENT
EVACUATION
EXPEDITION
FIELD TRAIN
FIRING LINE
GLASS-HOUSE
GUARD-HOUSE
INDIAN FILE
INSPECTION
INVALIDING
INVESTMENT
LIMITED WAR
MANOEUVRES
MARTIALISM
MILITARISM
MUSTER-ROLL
NO MAN'S LAND
NUCLEAR WAR
OCCUPATION
PATROLLING
PICKET-DUTY
QUARTERING
QUICK MARCH
RIFLE-RANGE
RIGHT-ABOUT
ROUTE-MARCH
SECONDMENT
SENTRY-DUTY
SHELLSHOCK

SIEGECRAFT
SIEGE-TRAIN
SIGNALLING
SOLDIERING
TARGET AREA

11

AIGUILLETTE
ARMOUR-PLATE
BATTLEFIELD
BESIEGEMENT
BOMBARDMENT
COMPO RATION
COUNTERMAND
COUNTERSIGN
DEFERRED PAY
DEMARCATION
DISARMAMENT
DISBANDMENT
EMBARKATION
ENTRAINMENT
FATIGUE-DUTY
FLAG OF TRUCE
FORCED MARCH
GEORGE MEDAL
GERM WARFARE
IMPEDIMENTA
OUTQUARTERS
PENETRATION
PURPLE HEART
RECONNOITRE
RECRUITMENT
REQUISITION
RETIRED LIST
RUNNING FIRE
SEARCHLIGHT
SKIRMISHING
SMOKE-SCREEN
STAGING AREA
STAGING-BASE
SURROUNDING

12

CANNON FODDER
CAPITULATION
CHURCH-PARADE
CONSCRIPTION
COUNTERMARCH

MILITARY TERMS

COURT-MARTIAL
COVERING FIRE
FIELD BATTERY
FIELD COLOURS
FIELD KITCHEN
FLYING COLUMN
HEADQUARTERS
HOLLOW SQUARE
INDIRECT FIRE
LINE OF BATTLE
MAIDEN BATTLE
MALTESE CROSS
MOBILISATION
PARADE-GROUND
REDEPLOYMENT
RE-ENGAGEMENT
RE-ENLISTMENT
RETRENCHMENT
SEALED ORDERS
SHOCK TACTICS
SIEGE TACTICS
SIEGE WARFARE
STATE OF SIEGE
SURVEILLANCE
WATERING-CALL

ASSAULT COURSE
ATOMIC WARFARE
BARRACK-SQUARE
BATTLE FATIGUE
BELEAGUERMENT
COUNTER-ATTACK
COUNTER-PAROLE
CROIX DE GUERRE
DEMONSTRATION
DISENGAGEMENT
FIELD HOSPITAL
FLYING COLOURS
JUNIOR SERIVCE
KIT INSPECTION
LISTENING-POST
MILITARY CROSS
MILITARY MEDAL
ORDER OF BATTLE
PITCHED BATTLE
SABRE-RATTLING
SCORCHED EARTH
SOLDIERLINESS
SPIT AND POLISH
SQUARE-BASHING
SUBORDINATION
TRENCH WARFARE
VANTAGE-GROUND
VICTORIA CROSS

AMMUNITION DUMP
BALANCE OF POWER
BALLOON BARRAGE
DEMOBILISATION
DISEMBARKATION
FIELD ARTILLERY
INFRASTRUCTURE
LEGION D'HONNEUR
MARCHING ORDERS
PINCER MOVEMENT
PYRRHIC VICTORY
RECONNAISSANCE
REINFORCEMENTS
RIGHT-ABOUT FACE
STANDING ORDERS
WINTER QUARTERS

15

CASUALTY STATION
CHEMICAL WARFARE
DIRECTION FINDER
DISCHARGE PAPERS
DRESSING-STATION
INSUBORDINATION
MARRIED QUARTERS
NATIONAL SERVICE
OBSERVATION POST
SUBSTANTIVE RANK

13

ACTIVE SERVICE
ARTICLES OF WAR

14

ACTION STATIONS

NAUTICAL TERMS

3

BOW
BOX
EBB
FID
GUY
JIB
LEE
LOG
LUG
NIP
OAR
RAM
RIB
RIG
RIP
SEA
SOS
TOP
TOW
WAY
YAW

4

BACK
BANK
BASE
BEAM
BELL
BEND
BOOM
BOWS
BULK
BUNK
BUNT
BUOY
CANT
CLEW
COLT
CORD
DECK
DIVE
DOCK
EAST
EYES
FAKE
FISH
FLAG
FLAT

FLOW
FOAM
GAFF
GYBE
HARD
HEAD
HELM
HOLD
HULL
KEEL
KITE
KNOT
LAST
LEAD
LEAK
LINE
LIST
LOOM
LOOP
LUFF
MAIN
MARK
MAST
MESS
NAVY
NOCK
OARS
PACK
PEAK
PIPE
POOP
PORT
PROW
QUAY
RAID
RAIL
RAKE
RANK
RATE
REAR
REEF
ROLL
ROPE
RUNG
SAIL
SCUD
SIDE
SKID
SLEW
SNUB
SPAR
STAY

STEM
STEP
SURF
SWAB
TACK
TIDE
TILT
TIRE
TRIM
TUCK
VANG
WAKE
WALE
WASH
WAVE
WELL
WEST
WIND
WING
YARD

5

APRON
ASDIC
BERTH
BIBBY
BILGE
BITTS
BLADE
BLOCK
BOARD
BRAIL
BRINE
CABIN
CABLE
CARGO
CARRY
CHAIN
CHART
CHIME
CLEAT
CLOTH
COACH
CREST
CUDDY
DAVIT
DEPTH
DRIFT
FLAKE
FLEET

FLOAT
FLUKE
GENOA
GRIPE
HANCE
HATCH
HAVEN
HAWSE
HELIX
HITCH
HOIST
KEDGE
LAGAN
LEECH
LIGAN
LIGHT
LORAN
LURCH
MOUSE
NAAFI
NORTH
OAKUM
OCEAN
ORDER
ORLOP
PERCH
PITCH
PLUMB
PRIZE
RADAR
RAKER
RANGE
RAZEE
REACH
REFIT
RHUMB
ROACH
ROADS
ROPES
ROTOR
ROYAL
SALVO
SCOPE
SCREW
SCULL
SHEER
SHEET
SHOAL
SONAR
SOUTH
SPOON
SPRAY

SPRIT
STACK
STERN
STOCK
SURGE
SWEEP
SWELL
THOLE
TRICK
TRUSS
WAIST
WATCH
WHARF
WHEEL
WHELP
WRECK

6

ANCHOR
ARMADA
BATTEN
BATTLE
BEACON
BECKET
BILLOW
BITTER
BONNET
BOTTOM
BOW-OAR
BRACES
BRIDGE
BUFFER
BUMKIN
BUNKER
BURDEN
CANVAS
CAREEN
COMBER
CONVOY
COURSE
CRUISE
DODGER
DROGUE
EARING
ENSIGN
FATHOM
FENDER
FIDDLE
FO'C'SLE
FUNNEL

GALLEY
GAMMON
GASKET
GROUND
GUNNEL
HAMPER
HAWSER
JETSAM
JIGGER
KEDGER
LADING
LASKET
LAUNCH
LAY-DAY
LEEWAY
MARINA
MARINE
MARKER
MAYDAY
MID-SEA
MIZZEN
MUSLIN
MUTINY
NORMAN
PADDLE
PARADE
PARREL
POPPET
RATING
RATLIN
REVIEW
RIDING
ROLLER
ROPERY
ROPING
RUDDER
SALOON
SALUTE
SCREEN
SEA-BED
SEAWAY
SHEETS
SIGNAL
SORTIE
STEEVE
STORES
STRAKE
TACKLE
TARGET
THROAT
THWART
TILLER

NAUTICAL TERMS

TIMBER
TINGLE
TROUGH
ULLAGE
VOLLEY
VOYAGE

7

AIR-LOCK
BACKING
BALLAST
BEAM-END
BEAM SEA
BEARING
BLISTER
BOLLARD
BOWLINE
BREAKER
BULWARK
BUNTING
BUOYAGE
BURDENS
CABOOSE
CALKING
CAPSTAN
CATHEAD
CAT-HOLE
CAT'S-PAW
CHANNEL
CHEVRON
CITADEL
COCKPIT
COMMAND
COMPASS
CORDAGE
COUNTER
CRAMPON
CREEPER
CRESSET
CRINGLE
CURRENT
DAYMARK
DOCKAGE
DOCKING
DOGVANE
DRAUGHT
DRY-DOCK
DRY LAND
DUNNAGE
EASTING

EBB-TIBE
EMBARGO
FAIRWAY
FEATHER
FIDDLEY
FISHERY
FLOTSAM
FOG-BELL
FOGHORN
FORETOP
FOUNDER
FREIGHT
FUTTOCK
GANGWAY
GAS-BUOY
GRAPNEL
GUN DECK
GUNPORT
GUNWALE
GUY-ROPE
HALYARD
HARBOUR
HEAD SEA
HEADWAY
HORIZON
JIB-BOOM
JIB-STAY
KEELAGE
KEELSON
KILLICK
KNITTLE
LANDING
LANIARD
LANYARD
LASTAGE
LATTICE
LAZARET
LEE-GAGE
LEE SIDE
LEE TIDE
LEEWARD
LIMBERS
LISTING
LOADING
LOG-BOOK
LOG-CHIP
LOG-LINE
LOG-REEL
LOW TIDE
LUFFING
LUGSAIL
MAINTOP

MARLINE
MARLING
MOORAGE
MOORING
MUD-HOOK
MUZZLER
NUN-BUOY
OPEN SEA
OROPESA
OUTFLOW
OUTHAUL
OUTPORT
PAINTER
PASSAGE
PENNANT
PLEDGET
PLUMMET
POOPING
PORT BOW
PUSH-OFF
QUARTER
QUAYAGE
RATLINE
REEFING
REPULSE
RIGGING
RIPTIDE
ROLLING
ROWLOCK
ROW-PORT
RUMMAGE
SAGGING
SAILING
SALVAGE
SCUPPER
SCUTTLE
SEA-CARD
SEA-COCK
SEA-FOAM
SEA-LANE
SEA-LEGS
SEA-MARK
SEA-PASS
SEA-ROOM
SEAWARD
SEA-WING
SEXTANT
SHALLOW
SHIPLAP
SHIPWAY
SHROUDS
SICK-BAY

SINKING
SKYSAIL
SLIPWAY
SNOTTER
SNUBBER
SOUNDER
SPANKER
SPENCER
SPONSON
STATION
STEMSON
STOPPER
STOWAGE
STOWING
SURGING
SWALLOW
TABLING
TACKING
THE DEEP
TIDE-RIP
TILTING
TONNAGE
TOP DECK
TOPMAST
TOPSAIL
TOWLINE
TOWROPE
TRYSAIL
VEERING
VICTORY
WAFTAGE
WAVELET
WAVESON
WESTING
WET-DOCK
WHISKER
WHISTLE
WOOLDER
YARD-ARM

8

APLUSTRE
APPROACH
BACKWASH
BARBETTE
BARNACLE
BARRATRY
BEAM-ENDS
BEARINGS
BELL-BUOY

BINNACLE
BLOCKADE
BOARDING
BOAT-DECK
BOAT-HOOK
BOAT-LOAD
BOBSTAYS
BOLT-ROPE
BOOM-IRON
BOWSPRIT
BRIEFING
BULKHEAD
BULWARKS
BUNTLINE
CATAPULT
CAULKING
COAMINGS
COASTING
CROSSING
CRUISING
CUT-WATER
DEADWOOD
DECK-LAOD
DOCK-DUES
DOCKYARD
DOG-WATCH
DOLDRUMS
DOWN-HAUL
DRABBLER
DRIFTAGE
DRIFTING
DRUMHEAD
EVEN KEEL
FIFE-RAIL
FLOATAGE
FLOTILLA
FOOT-ROPE
FOREBITT
FORE-BODY
FOREDECK
FOREFOOT
FOREMAST
FOREPEAK
FORESAIL
FORESHIP
FORESTAY
FOREWIND
FREE PORT
GANTLINE
GARBOARD
GRIDIRON
HALF-TIDE

HALLIARD	PORT BEAM	TRIMMING	DOGSHORES
HANDRAIL	PORTHOLE	UNDERTOW	DRIFT-SAIL
HARPINGS	PORTOLAN	UPMAKING	DRIFTWOOD
HATCHWAY	QUAYSIDE	WALL-KNOT	EYE-SPLICE
HEAD-BOOM	RAFT-PORT	WARD-ROOM	FALSE KEEL
HEADFAST	RAFT-ROPE	WATERAGE	FLOOD-TIDE
HEADRAIL	RAT-GUARD	WATERWAY	FLOORHEAD
HEADWIND	REEF-BAND	WELL-DECK	FLYING JIB
HEAVY SEA	REEF-KNOT	WHARFAGE	FOG-SIGNAL
HIGH SEAS	RING-TAIL	WHITECAP	FORE-BRACE
HIGH TIDE	ROPEWORK	WINDLASS	FORECABIN
HORNPIPE	ROUND-TOP	WIND-SAIL	FORESHORE
HORSE-BOX	RUMBELOW	WINDWARD	FOUR BELLS
JETTISON	SAIL-ROOM	WOOLDING	FREE BOARD
JURYMAST	SAIL-YARD	WRECKAGE	GANGBOARD
KECKLING	SEA-BRIEF		GANGPLANK
LARBOARD	SEA-CRAFT		GIRTHLINE
LEAD-LINE	SEA-FIGHT	**9**	GOOSE-WING
LEE-BOARD	SEA-FLOOR		HALF-BOARD
LEE-SHORE	SEA-FROTH	AFTER-DECK	HALF-HITCH
LIFEBELT	SEA-POWER	ANCHORAGE	HAWSEPIPE
LIFE-BUOY	SEA-SPRAY	ANCHORING	HEADLINES
LIFE-LINE	SEA-STOCK	BACK-BOARD	HEADREACH
LIVE-WELL	SHALLOWS	BACKSTAYS	HIGH WATER
LOAD-LINE	SHIP-LOAD	BILGE-KEEL	HOLYSTONE
LOGBOARD	SHIPMENT	BILGE-PUMP	HOUSE-FLAG
LOG-GLASS	SHIPPING	BILLBOARD	HOUSE-LINE
LOG-SLATE	SHIPYARD	BLUE PETER	HYDROFOIL
LOW WATER	SHOALING	BLUE WATER	ICE-ANCHOR
LUCKY-BAG	SHORT SEA	BOAT-DRILL	JACK-BLOCK
MAGAZINE	SNUBBING	BREADROOM	JACK-STAFF
MAIN-BOOM	SONOBUOY	BREECHING	JACK-STAYS
MAIN-DECK	SOUNDING	BROADSIDE	KENTLEDGE
MAINMAST	SOUTHING	BUNKERING	LAUNCHING
MAINSAIL	SPAR-DECK	CAREENAGE	LAZARETTO
MAINSTAY	STAYSAIL	CHAIN-BOLT	LOG-ROLLER
MAINYARD	STEERAGE	CHART-ROOM	LOWER DECK
MANIFEST	STEERING	CHASE-PORT	MAINBRACE
MASTHEAD	STERNSON	CLEARANCE	MAINSHEET
MESS-DECK	STERNWAY	CLEW-LINES	MANOEUVRE
MOONSAIL	STOWDOWN	CLOVE-HOOK	MAROONING
MOORINGS	STRINGER	COMPANION	MESSENGER
NAVALISM	TACKLING	CORPOSANT	MIZZEN-TOP
NAVARCHY	TAFFRAIL	CRINOLINE	MONK'S SEAM
NAVICERT	TELL-TALE	CROSSJACK	MONOCOQUE
NAVY-LIST	TEMPLATE	CROSSTREE	MOONRAKER
NAVY-YARD	THE BRINY	CROW'S NEST	MOULD-LOFT
NEAP TIDE	THE DRINK	DAVY JONES	OUTHAULER
NORTHING	THOLE-PIN	DECK-CARGO	OUTRIGGER
OVERHAUL	TIDE-RACE	DECK-HOUSE	PADDLE-BOX
OVERSEAS	TOPSIDES	DEMURRAGE	PARBUCKLE
PERIPLUS	TRACKAGE	DEPARTURE	PERISCOPE

NAUTICAL TERMS

PIANO-WIRE
PORTOLANO
PREVENTER
PROMOTION
PROPELLER
PUDDENING
RECKONING
RED DUSTER
RED ENSIGN
REEF-POINT
REFITMENT
RHUMB-LINE
ROADSTEAD
ROYAL MAST
ROYAL NAVY
SAIL-CLOTH
SAILORING
SALLYPORT
SALT WATER
SCHNORKEL
SCRIMSHAW
SEA-ANCHOR
SEA-BATTLE
SEAFARING
SEA-LETTER
SEMAPHORE
SHEATHING
SHIPBOARD
SHIP'S HOLD
SHIPWRECK
SHOAL-MARK
SICK-BERTH
SMOKE-SAIL
SNORT-MAST
SONAR BUOY
SOUNDINGS
SPINDRIFT
SPINNAKER
SPRITSAIL
STAMP-NOTE
STANCHION
STARBOARD
STATEROOM
STERN-FAST
STERN-PORT
STERN-POST
STOKE-HOLD
STORM-CONE
STORM-DRUM
STORM-SAIL
STORM-STAY
TARPAULIN

TIDE-WATER
TIMENOGUY
TOP-HAMPER
TURK'S HEAD
UNDERDECK
UPPER DECK
WASH-BOARD
WATCH-BILL
WATER-FLOW
WATER-LINE
WATERMARK
WATER-SAIL
WHALEBACK
WHIPSTAFF
WRING-BOLT

10

AFTER-HATCH
AFTER-SAILS
ANCHOR BUOY
ANCHOR HOLD
BILGE-WATER
BLUE ENSIGN
BOTTOM BECK
BRIDGE DECK
CHAIN-PLATE
CLEW-GARNET
CLOVE-HITCH
COAL-BUNKER
COMMISSION
CROSSPIECE
EIGHT BELLS
ENGAGEMENT
ENGINE ROOM
ENLISTMENT
ESCUTCHEON
FATHOM-LINE
FIDDLEHEAD
FIGUREHEAD
FLIGHT-DECK
FLOAT-BOARD
FORECASTLE
FORECOURSE
FREIGHTAGE
HARBOURAGE
HUSBANDAGE
JIGGER-MAST
JOLLY ROGER
JURY-RUDDER
KNEE-TIMBER
LATEEN SAIL

LEAD-ARMING
LIFE-JACKET
LIFE-MORTAR
LIFE-ROCKET
LIGHTERAGE
LIGHTHOUSE
LOGGERHEAD
MAIN-COURSE
MARINE SOAP
MARKER BUOY
MARTINGALE
MIZZEN-MAST
MIZZEN-SAIL
MONKEY-GAFF
MONKEY-RAIL
MONKEY-ROPE
MUSTER ROLL
NAVIGATING
NAVIGATION
NIGHT-WATCH
PILOT-HOUSE
PORT OF CALL
POWDER-ROOM
QUARANTINE
QUARTERING
ROPE-LADDER
ROUND-HOUSE
SALOON-DECK
SAMSON POST
SEAMANSHIP
SEA-SERVICE
SHEEP-SHANK
SHOAL-WATER
SHORE-LEAVE
SIGNALLING
SKYSCRAPER
SMALL CRAFT
SMOKE-STACK
SPOONDRIFT
SPRING TIDE
SQUARE KNOT
SQUARE-SAIL
STABILISER
STATE-CABIN
STAY-TACKLE
STERN-CHASE
STERN-FRAME
SUBMERSION
SUPERCARGO
TABERNACLE
TARGET AREA
TILLER-ROPE

TORPEDO-NET
TREATY PORT
TURTLEBACK
UPPERWORKS
VISITATION
WATER-LEVEL
WATER-PLANE
WEATHER-BOW
WHEEL-HOUSE
WHITE-WATER
WRING-STAFF

11

ADVANCE NOTE
ANCHOR-STOCK
BELAYING PIN
BOOT-TOPPING
BOTTLE-CHART
BOWER-ANCHOR
BOWLINE KNOT
CARRICK BEND
CENTRE-BOARD
CHAFING-GEAR
CHAIN LOCKER
COMPASS CARD
COMPASS ROSE
DEBARKATION
DECK-PASSAGE
DOCK-WARRANT
DRIFT-ANCHOR
ECHO-SOUNDER
EMBARKATION
ESCAPE HATCH
FIDDLE BLOCK
FIRE-CONTROL
FLOOR TIMBER
FORETOPMAST
GAFF-TOPSAIL
GRAVING-DOCK
GROUND-SWELL
HARBOUR-DUES
HARNESS-CASK
IMPRESSMENT
LANDING DECK
LAZY PAINTER
LEADER-CABLE
LOXODROMICS
LUBBER'S HOLE
LUBBER'S LINE
MAINTOPMAST

MAINTOPSAIL
MARINE STORE
MARLIN-SPIKE
MIDDLE-WATCH
MONKEY-BLOCK
MOORING-MAST
NETT TONNAGE
PADDLE-BOARD
PADDLE-SHAFT
PADDLE-WHEEL
PARREL TRUCK
PORT OF ENTRY
QUARTER-DECK
QUARTER-WIND
RECONNOITRE
RECRUITMENT
RETIRED LIST
RHUMB-COURSE
RIDING-LIGHT
RING-STOPPER
RUNNING-KNOT
SAMSON'S POST
SEASICKNESS
SHEET-ANCHOR
SHIP'S PAPERS
SLIDING-KEEL
SLIDING-SEAT
SMOKE SCREEN
SNATCH-BLOCK
SOUNDING-ROD
SPREAD-EAGLE
STEERAGE-WAY
ST ELMO'S FIRE
STERN-SHEETS
STORM SIGNAL
TILLER-CHAIN
TORPEDO-BOOM
TORPEDO TUBE
TOWING-BITTS
TRIATIC STAY
WAIST-ANCHOR
WEATHER-GAGE
WEATHER-HELM
WEATHER-ROLL
WEATHER-SIDE
WHITE ENSIGN

12

ACTION RADIUS
AIR-SEA RESCUE

ARRESTER GEAR
BETWEEN-DECKS
BILL OF HEALTH
BILL OF LADING
BREECHES-BUOY
BROAD PENNANT
CAULKING-IRON
CLINCHER-WORK
COLLISION-MAT
COMPANIONWAY
CONNING-TOWER
COUNTER-BRACE
COURT-MARTIAL
DISPLACEMENT
ECHO-SOUNDING
FLOATING DOCK
FLYING BRIDGE
FUTTOCK-PLATE
GROSS TONNAGE
GROUND-TACKLE
HARBOUR LIGHT
JACOB'S LADDER
LANDING-STAGE
MAIDEN VOYAGE
MARINE BOILER
MARINE ENGINE
MARINE STORES
MARLINE-SPIKE
MINESWEEPING
MIZZEN-COURSE
MORNING-WATCH
NAUTICAL MILE
NAVAL COMMAND
NAVIGABILITY
NETT REGISTER
ORTHODROMICS
PLIMSOLL LINE
PLIMSOLL MARK
PRIVATEERING
RECOMMISSION
RE-ENGAGEMENT
RE-ENLISTMENT
RESPONDENTIA
RHUMB-SAILING
SHIPBUILDING
SHIPPING LANE
SHIPPING LINE
SNUBBING-POST
SOUNDING-LEAD
SOUNDING-LINE
SPANKING BOOM
SPEAKING-TUBE

SPILLING-LINE
STARBOARD BOW
STREAM-ANCHOR
STUDDING-SAIL
SUBMARINE PEN
SWINGING-BOOM
TOURIST CLASS
TRANSHIPMENT
TRANSHIPPING
UNDERCURRENT
WATER-BALLAST
WEATHER-BOARD
WEATHER-CLOTH
WEATHER-GLASS

13

AUDIO-LOCATION
BRIDGE-OF-BOATS
COMPASS SIGNAL
DEAD RECKONING
FIDDLER'S GREEN
FLOATING LIGHT
GRAPPLING-IRON
GROSS REGISTER
HARBOUR-LIGHTS
HIGH-WATER MARK
HURRICANE DECK
JACK-CROSSTREE
LAUNCHING-WAYS
LIFE-PRESERVER
MALLEMAROKING
ORDER OF BATTLE
PERPENDICULAR
PORTOLAN CHART
PROMENADE DECK
RE-EMBARKATION
RUNNING LIGHTS
SAILING ORDERS
SEAWORTHINESS
SHIP'S REGISTER
STARBOARD BEAM
STEERING-WHEEL
TWIDDLING-LINE
WEATHER-ANCHOR

14

BOATSWAIN'S PIPE
COALING STATION

NAUTICAL TERMS

COMPANION-HATCH
COMPASS-BEARING
COUNTER-CURRENT
COURSE-PLOTTING
DAVIS APPARATUS
DISEMBARKATION
FLAG OF DISTRESS
FORE-AND-AFT SAIL
FUTTOCK-SHROUDS
GARBOARD STRAKE
GYROSTABILISER
LETTER-OF-MARQUE
MUSHROOM-ANCHOR
PARLIAMENT-HEEL

POWDER MAGAZINE
PROPELLER-BLADE
PROPELLER-SHAFT
QUARANTINE FLAG
QUARTER-GALLERY
RECONNAISSANCE
RUNNING RIGGING
SCREW-PROPELLER
SHIFTING-BOARDS
SUBMERSIBILITY
SUPERSTRUCTURE
SWIVEL-ROWLOCKS
TOPGALLANT MAST
TRANSVERSE WAVE

15

COMPANION-LADDER
MARINE INSURANCE
MARINER'S COMPASS
MERCHANT SERVICE
MIDDLE-STITCHING
NATIONAL SERVICE
NAUTICAL ALMANAC
OPERATION ORDERS
RAINBOW DRESSING
STANDING-RIGGING
STEAM-NAVIGATION
VICTUALLING-BILL
VICTUALLING-YARD

OCCULTISM

3

ART
HEX
LEO
LOT
OBI
ORB

4

AURA
DOOM
FATE
JU-JU
MANA
MOLI
OATH
OMEN
RUNE
SIGN
STAR
TABU
TIKI
TWIG

5

ARIES
AUGUR
AZOTH
CHARM
CURSE
DUPPY
GHOST
GHOUL
GOETY
GUIDE
HOUSE
HYLEG
LARVA
LEMUR
LIBRA
MAGIC
MAMBO
OBEAH
OUIJA
POWER
SHADE

SIGIL
SPELL
SPOOK
TABOO
TAROT
TOTEM
UMBRA
VIRGO
V'SIT
WEIRD
ZOMBI

6

AMULET
APPORT
AUGURY
BAETYL
CABIRI
CANCER
DOUBLE
DYBBUK
FETISH
GEMINI
GNOSIS
HOODOO
KISMET
MASCOT
OBEISM
OCCULT
ORACLE
PISCES
PLANET
POTION
PYTHON
SCHEME
SÉANCE
SHADOW
SORTES
SPIRIT
SYMBOL
TAURUS
TELESM
TRANCE
TRIGON
VISION
VOODOO
WRAITH
XOANON
ZODIAC
ZOMBIE

7

ABRAXAS
ARCANUM
AUSPICE
BALDRIC
CABBALA
CONJURY
CONTROL
DESTINY
DEVILRY
EIDOLON
EVIL EYE
FETICHE
FORTUNE
GRAMARY
HAUNTER
HEY-PASS
MALISON
MANSION
MYALISM
PHANTOM
PHILTRE
PORTENT
PRESAGE
SCRYING
SEXTILE
SIGNARY
SORCERY
SPECTRE
TELERGY
THEURGY
VAMPIRE

8

ANATHEMA
AQUARIUS
BLACK ART
BODEMENT
CHURINGA
DEVILDOM
DEVILISM
EXORCISM
FORECAST
GEOMANCY
GRIMOIRE
GRISGRIS
HAUNTING
HOKY-POKY
LIGATURE

MEDICINE
MYOMANCY
NATIVITY
OBEAHISM
PARALLAX
PENTACLE
PHANTASM
PISHOGUE
PROPHECY
PSYCHICS
QUARTILE
REVENANT
SATANISM
SPOOKERY
SYNASTRY
TALISMAN
VISITANT
VISITING
WITCHERY
WITCHING
WIZARDRY
ZOMBIISM
ZOOMANCY

9

ASCENDANT
ASTROLOGY
BELOMANCY
BLACK MASS
CAPRICORN
CEROMANCY
CONJURING
DEVILMENT
DIABLERIE
DIABOLOGY
ECTOPLASM
ELEMENTAL
EMANATION
EVOCATION
FAITH-CURE
FOREGLEAM
FORETOKEN
GYROMANCY
HALLOWE'EN
HEY-PRESTO
HOROSCOPE
HOROSCOPY
INFLUENCE
JETTATURA
LOVE-CHARM

MARANATHA
OCCULTISM
OENOMANCY
PALMISTRY
PENTAGRAM
PENTALPHA
PHANTASMA
PRODROMUS
PYROMANCY
RAIN-STONE
RUNECRAFT
SHAMANISM
SORTILEGE
SORTILEGY
TAROT-CARD
TELEPATHY
THE OCCULT
THEOMANCY
TRIPUDIUM
VAMPIRISM
VOODOOISM
WARLOCKRY
WITCH HUNT
WITCH-KNOT

10

APPARITION
ASTRAL BODY
AXINOMANCY
BLACK MAGIC
CAPNOMANCY
CARTOMANCY
CLEROMANCY
DISPOSITOR
DIVINATION
DUKKERIPEN
EXALTATION
EXECRATION
FOREBODING
GRAPHOLOGY
HIEROMANCY
HIEROSCOPY
HOCUS-POCUS
HYDROMANCY
LINE OF LIFE
LITHOMANCY
LUCKY CHARM
LUCKY STONE
MUMBO-JUMBO
NECROMANCY

199

OCCULTISM

NIGHT-SPELL
NUMEROLOGY
OCCULTNESS
OPPOSITION
OUIJA BOARD
PHENOMENON
PLANCHETTE
PREDICTION
PROGNOSTIC
PSYCHOGRAM
PSYCHOPOMP
SIXTH SENSE
SPODOMANCY
STARGAZING
SUGGESTION
THE UNKNOWN
TRIPLICITY
VISITATION
WHITE MAGIC
WITCHCRAFT

ONEIROSCOPY
ONYCHOMANCY
PATERNOSTER
POLTERGEIST
PREMONITION
PRESAGEMENT
PROPHESYING
PSYCHOGRAPH
PSYCHOMETER
PSYCHOMETRY
RHABDOMANCY
SECOND-SIGHT
SEEING-STONE
SOOTHSAYING
SPECTRALITY
SPECTROLOGY
SPIRIT WORLD
TELEKINESIS
TEPHROMANCY
THOUGHT-WAVE
WEREWOLFISM
WITCH'S-BROOM
XENOGLOSSIA

SUPERNATURAL
SUPERSTITION
SYMBOLOLATRY
SYNECDOCHISM
TABLE-TURNING
TELAESTHESIA
VATICINATION
VITATIVENESS

13

CLAIRAUDIENCE
CRYSTAL-GAZING
DACTYLIOMANCY
DISEMBODIMENT
HARUSPICATION
MANIFESTATION
METAMORPHOSIS
OMOPLATOSCOPY
PREORDAINMENT
PSI-PHENOMENON
PSYCHOKINESIS
REINCARNATION
SEXTILE ASPECT
SPIRIT-RAPPING
SUGGESTIONISM

11

ABRACADABRA
ASTRAL PLANE
BEWITCHMENT
BIBLIOMANCY
BOTANOMANCY
CAPRICORNUS
CHEIROGNOMY
CHIEROMANCY
CONJURATION
CRITHOMANCY
CRYSTAL-BALL
DIVINING-ROD
ENCHANTMENT
FOREREADING
FOREWARNING
FORTUNE-BOOK
GASTROMANCY
HAND OF GLORY
HARIOLATION
HEPATOSCOPY
IMPRECATION
INCANTATION
LYCANTHROPY
MALEDICTION
METAPHYSICS
MIND-READING
ONEIROMANCY

12

ASTRAL SPIRIT
CLAIRVOYANCE
COSCINOMANCY
COUNTERCHARM
DOPPEL-GÄNGER
FAITH-HEALING
FIENDISHNESS
HAUNTED HOUSE
INVULTUATION
LAMPADOMANCY
METAPSYCHICS
NATURAL MAGIC
OMPHALOMANCY
ORNITHOMANCY
ORNITHOSCOPY
PORTE-BONHEUR
PRECOGNITION
PRESENTIMENT
PSYCHIC FORCE
PSYCHOGRAPHY
SCAPULIMANCY
SIGNIFICATOR
SLATE-WRITING
SPIRITUALISM
STAR-BLASTING

14

AUTO-SUGGESTION
CRYPTAESTHESIA
CRYSTALLOMANCY
FORTUNE-TELLING
METEMPSYCHOSIS
RETROCOGNITION
WALPURGIS NIGHT
WHEEL OF FORTUNE
WITCHES' SABBATH

15

ONEIROCRITICISM
PROGNOSTICATION
PSYCHIC RESEARCH
SUPERNATURALISM
THERIOMORPHOSIS

PARLIAMENT & POLITICS

3

ACT
AYE
GAG
LAW
NAY
RAJ
YEA

4

AXIS
BILL
BULL
COUP
DIET
FISC
GAIN
MOOT
PACT
PAIR
PINK
POLL
RULE
SEAT
VETO
VOTE
WHIP

5

BOULE
CABAL
COUNT
DRAFT
EDICT
EXILE
FLOOR
GEMOT
HOUSE
IRADE
JUNTA
LOBBY
ORDER
PAPER
PARTY
PLANK
PORTE
POWER

RÉGIE
SPLIT
STATE
UKASE
UNION
WITAN

6

BALLOT
BUDGET
CARTEL
CAUCUS
CENSUS
CLAUSE
COLONY
COUPON
DEBATE
DECREE
ENOSIS
LABOUR
LEAGUE
MOTION
OFFICE
PAPACY
PLACET
POLICY
QUORUM
RECALL
RECESS
RED-BOX
REFORM
RÉGIME
RENVOI
REPORT
RESULT
RETURN
RULING
SENATE
SIRCAR
SOVIET
SPEECH
SUPPLY
SWARAJ
TICKET
TREATY
VOTING

7

ADDRESS

APPARAT
BOROUGH
CABINET
CHAMBER
CHAPTER
CHARTER
CLOSURE
CLOTURE
COMITIA
COUNCIL
DÉTENTE
DIARCHY
DICTATE
DIETINE
EMBARGO
ENCLAVE
ENTENTE
FACTION
FASCISM
FORMULA
GALLERY
GANGWAY
HANSARD
LIBERAL
MACHINE
MANDATE
MARXISM
MEASURE
MISRULE
MISSION
NAZIISM
NEUTRAL
NOVELLA
ORATION
PAIRING
PASSAGE
PITTISM
PLUMPER
POLLING
PRIMARY
READING
RE-COUNT
REDRAFT
RED TAPE
REGIMEN
REMANET
REVENUE
SESSION
SITTING
SOAP-BOX
STATISM
STATUTE

SUBSIDY
TACKING
THE LEFT
TORYISM
TSARISM
ZIONISM

8

ALLIANCE
ALTERNAT
ASSEMBLY
ASSIENTO
AUTARCHY
AUTONOMY
BLUE BOOK
CARD-VOTE
CHARTISM
CLAWBACK
CONGRESS
DEED POLL
DÉMARCHE
DIRIGISM
DIVISION
DOMINION
ELECTION
FOLKMOOT
FREE VOTE
HECKLING
HEGEMONY
HOME RULE
HUSTINGS
MAJORITY
MANIFEST
MINISTRY
MINORITY
MONARCHY
OLD GUARD
PARTYISM
PETITION
PHALANGE
PLATFORM
POLITICS
PREAMBLE
PROCLAIM
PROTOCOL
QUESTION
QUIRINAL
REGIMENT
REPUBLIC
REVANCHE

SAFE SEAT
SANCTION
SCHEDULE
SCRUTINY
SIGNORIA
SINN FEIN
SUFFRAGE
SUMMITRY
SYNARCHY
THEARCHY
THE RIGHT
THE STATE
TREASURY
TRIARCHY
UNIONISM
WHIGGERY
WHIGGISM
WOOLSACK

9

ADMIRALTY
AMENDMENT
AUTOCRACY
BACKBENCH
BALLOT-BOX
CAMARILLA
CITY STATE
CIVIL LIST
COALITION
COBDENISM
COMINFORM
COMINTERN
COMMITTEE
CORRIDORS
COUP D'ÉTAT
DEMOCRACY
DESPOTISM
DIPLOMACY
DOLLAR GAP
DULOCRACY
ENACTMENT
ETHNARCHY
EXCHEQUER
EXECUTIVE
EXEQUATUR
EXILEMENT
EXPANSION
FRANCHISE
GYNOCRACY
HEPTARCHY

PARLIAMENT & POLITICS

HIERARCHY
INDICTION
INTERDICT
ISOPOLITY
KINGCRAFT
MANIFESTO
MOBOCRACY
MONEY-BILL
MONOCRACY
NOMOCRACY
OLIGARCHY
ORDER-BOOK
PARTITION
PARTY-LINE
PENTARCHY
PLURALITY
PLUTOLOGY
PLUTONOMY
POLYARCHY
PORTFOLIO
PRESIDIUM
PRIVILEGE
PROCEDURE
RULE OF LAW
SET SPEECH
SLUSH FUND
SOCIALISM
SPLIT VOTE
STALINISM
STRAW POLL
SYNEDRION
SYNEDRIUM
TERRITORY
THE CENTRE
THEOCRACY
TIMOCRACY
TORY PARTY
VOX POPULI
WAR OFFICE
WELFARISM
WITCH-HUNT

10

BANISHMENT
BLOCK GRANT
BY-ELECTION
CAPITALISM
COMMISSION
CONFERENCE
CONSISTORY

CONVENTION
COUNTY SEAT
CROSSBENCH
DELEGATION
DEPARTMENT
DEPENDENCY
DEPUTATION
DESPATCHES
DEVOLUTION
DISPATCHES
DUUMVIRATE
FEDERATION
FILIBUSTER
FRONT BENCH
GALLUP POLL
GOVERNANCE
GOVERNMENT
GREEN PAPER
GUILLOTINE
HAGIOCRACY
HETERONOMY
HIEROCRACY
HOME OFFICE
INDEXATION
LIBERALISM
LOG-ROLLING
LOWER HOUSE
MARTIAL LAW
MATRIARCHY
MEMORANDUM
MODERATISM
MONARCHISM
MONETARISM
NEUTRALISM
NEUTRALITY
NOMINATION
OCHLOCRACY
OPPOSITION
ORDER PAPER
PARLIAMENT
PARNELLISM
PATRIARCHY
PEACE-PARTY
PLAID CYMRU
PLEBISCITE
PLURAL VOTE
PLUTOCRACY
PORNOCRACY
POSTAL VOTE
PRESIDENCY
PRIVATE ACT
PRIVY PURSE

PROTECTION
PSEPHOLOGY
RADICALISM
RE-ELECTION
REFERENDUM
REFORM BILL
REGULATION
RESOLUTION
REVANCHISM
SATYAGRAHA
SECULAR ARM
SEPARATION
SEPARATISM
SETTLEMENT
STATECRAFT
STATE-HOUSE
STATE-PAPER
STATUTE LAW
TROTSKYISM
UPPER HOUSE
WHIGGARCHY
WHITE PAPER
WORLD POWER

11

ADJOURNMENT
ARISTOCRACY
BACKBENCHES
BALLOT-PAPER
BUFFER STATE
BUREAUCRACY
CASTING-VOTE
CONDOMINIUM
CROWN COLONY
DEPORTATION
DEVOLVEMENT
DIRECTORATE
DISPATCH-BOX
DISSOLUTION
ENABLING ACT
ERGATOCRACY
EXTRADITION
GENERAL LINE
GEOPOLITICS
GERRYMANDER
HATTI-SHERIF
IDENTIC NOTE
IMPEACHMENT
KING'S SPEECH
LABOUR PARTY

LEGISLATION
LEGISLATIVE
LEGISLATURE
MAJORITAIRE
McCARTHYISM
MEMBER'S BILL
MEMBER STATE
MERITOCRACY
NATIONALISM
NEGOTIATION
OBSTRUCTION
PHYSIOCRACY
POLICE STATE
POLITICKING
PREMIERSHIP
PRIVATE BILL
PROROGATION
PTOCHOCRACY
PUBLIC FUNDS
PUBLIC PURSE
REPORT STAGE
RETALIATION
ROYAL ASSENT
SECRETARIAT
SENATE-HOUSE
SINN FEINISM
SOVEREIGNTY
SQUIREARCHY
STATUTE-BOOK
STRATOCRACY
TECHNOCRACY
TRIUMVIRATE
WITENAGEMOT

12

BILL OF RIGHTS
CIVIL SERVICE
COLLECTIVISM
COLONISATION
COMMAND PAPER
COMMONWEALTH
CONSERVATISM
CONSERVATIVE
CONSTITUENCY
CONSTITUTION
DESPOTOCRACY
DICTATORSHIP
ENABLING BILL
EXPATRIATION
FIRST READING

FLOATING DEBT
FLOATING VOTE
GERONTOCRACY
GYNAECOCRACY
HOUSE OF LORDS
INDEPENDENCY
INTELLIGENCE
INTERDICTION
KAKISTOCRACY
LAISSEZ-FAIRE
LAW OF NATIONS
LAW OF THE LAND
LIBERAL PARTY
LOWER CHAMBER
MACHTPOLITIK
MAIDEN SPEECH
MARGINAL SEAT
NATIONAL DEBT
NON-ALIGNMENT
PAROCHIALISM
PEDANTOCRACY
PLENIPOTENCE
POINT OF ORDER
POLLING-BOOTH
POPULAR FRONT
PRESS-GALLERY
PRIVY COUNCIL
PROCLAMATION
PROTECTORATE
QUEEN'S SPEECH
RADICAL PARTY
RATIFICATION
REPATRIATION
SECOND BALLOT
SOCIAL CREDIT
SPEECH-MAKING
SPOILS SYSTEM
SUBCOMMITTEE
THIRD READING
TRANSFER-VOTE
TREASURY BILL
TRIPARTITION
UPPER CHAMBER
WAYS AND MEANS
WELFARE STATE
WOMEN'S RIGHTS

13

CONFEDERATION
COUNTY COUNCIL

FOREIGN OFFICE
FRANCHISEMENT
IDENTIC ACTION
INLAND REVENUE
LADIES' GALLERY
MACHIAVELLISM
MISGOVERNMENT
NATIONAL FRONT
ORDER OF THE DAY
PARLIAMENTING
PARTY-POLITICS
PLENARY POWERS
POCKET BOROUGH
POWER POLITICS
PRIVATISATION
QUADRUMVIRATE
RAPPROCHEMENT
REPUBLICANISM
ROTTEN BOROUGH
SANSCULOTTISM
SECOND CHAMBER
SECOND READING
SHADOW CABINET
SPLINTER PARTY
STANDING RULES
STATESMANSHIP
STRAIGHT FIGHT
SUMMIT MEETING
TEN MINUTE RULE
THALASSOCRACY
THREE-LINE WHIP
TREASURY BENCH
UNICAMERALISM
VANSITTARTISM
VOTE OF CENSURE
VOTE-SPLITTING
VOTING MACHINE

14

ADMINISTRATION
BLOCKING MOTION
CABINET COUNCIL
CABINET MEETING
CENTRALISATION
COLONIAL OFFICE
COLONIAL SYSTEM
COMMITTEE STAGE
COUNTERMEASURE
CUMULATIVE VOTE
DEMONETISATION

ELECTIONEERING
EXCLUSION ORDER
GERRYMANDERING
HAUTE POLITIQUE
HOUSE OF COMMONS
INTERPELLATION
LETTER OF MARQUE
LOCAL AUTHORITY
NATURALISATION
NEOCOLONIALISM
ORDER IN COUNCIL
PLUTO-DEMOCRACY
POLLING-STATION
PSEPHOANALYSIS
RECONSTITUTION
SANSCULOTTERIE
SELF-GOVERNMENT
SOCIAL CONTRACT
SOCIAL SECURITY
STANDING ORDERS
STRAIGHT TICKET
TWO-PARTY SYSTEM
VICE-PRESIDENCY

15

ACT OF PARLIAMENT
ALTERNATIVE VOTE
COMITY OF NATIONS
DOLLAR DIPLOMACY
ENFRANCHISEMENT
FAMILY ALLOWANCE
FULL-DRESS DEBATE
GENERAL ELECTION
LOCAL GOVERNMENT
NATIONALISATION
NON-INTERVENTION
PARLIAMENTARISM
PETITION OF RIGHT
PRIMARY ASSEMBLY
PRIMARY ELECTION
PUBLIC OWNERSHIP
ROYAL COMMISSION
SELECT COMMITTEE
SOCIAL DEMOCRACY
SOCIAL INSURANCE
STATE DEPARTMENT
TOTALITARIANISM
WHISTLE-STOP TOUR
WORKING MAJORITY

PEOPLE – BELIEVERS

3

FAN
JEW
RED
WET

4

BABI
JAIN
NAZI
SIKH
SUFI
TORY
WHIG
YOGI

5

ARIAN
BAHAI
BIGOT
DEIST
DRUID
FAKIR
HADJI
HINDU
LATIN
OVIST
PAGAN
ROMAN
SAIVA
SAKTA
SHIAH
STOIC
SUNNI
UNIAT
VEGAN
YOGIN
ZOIST

6

BABIST
COMMIE
DANITE
DOCETE
DUNKER

ESSENE
FABIAN
FENIAN
GUEBRE
HEBREW
HOLIST
HUMEAN
HUMIST
HUNKER
HYLIST
JESUIT
JEWESS
LAXIST
MAOIST
MARIAN
MONIST
MOONIE
MORMON
MOSLEM
MUSLIM
NUDIST
OPHITE
PAPIST
PARSEE
PURIST
QUAKER
RACIST
RANTER
SABIAN
SEXIST
SHAKER
SHIITE
TAOIST
THEIST
UNIATE
VEDIST
WAHABI
YEZIDI
ZEALOT
ZENDIK

7

APOSTLE
ASCETIC
ATHEIST
ATOMIST
AZYMITE
BAALITE
BAHAIST
BAPTIST

BENNITE
BRAHMAN
CARLIST
CASUIST
CHAUVIN
COMTIST
CONVERT
COSMIST
CULTIST
DADAIST
DERVISH
DEVOTEE
DUALIST
ÉLITIST
EPICURE
FADDIST
FASCIST
FEDERAL
GENEVAN
GNOSTIC
HEATHEN
HERETIC
HOBBIST
HUSSITE
INFIDEL
JACOBIN
JUDAIST
KANTIST
KARAITE
LAMAIST
LEAGUER
LEFTIST
LIBERAL
LOCKIAN
LOCKIST
LOLLARD
LUDDITE
MARXIST
MYTHIST
NEUTRAL
NOETIAN
OWENIST
OWENITE
PATARIN
PATRIOT
PAULIAN
PEELITE
PIETIST
PITTITE
PLENIST
PURITAN
RADICAL

RAPPIST
RAPPITE
REALIST
SARACEN
SCEPTIC
SCOTIST
SECTARY
SELFIST
SIVAITE
SUNNITE
THOMIST
TITOIST
TSARIST
UTOPIAN
UTOPIST
WOLFIAN
ZETETIK
ZIONIST

8

ADHERENT
AESTHETE
AGNOSTIC
ANGLICAN
APOSTATE
ARMINIAN
BACONIAN
BELIEVER
BROWNIST
BUDDHIST
CALENDER
CATHOLIC
CAVALIER
CHARTIST
CHILIAST
DARBYITE
DEMOCRAT
DEMONIST
DISCIPLE
DITHEIST
DOCETIST
DONATIST
DRUIDESS
DUKHOBOR
DYNAMIST
EBIONITE
ERASTIAN
ESCAPIST
ETHICIST
EUGENIST

FAMILIST
FATALIST
FEMINIST
FINALIST
FOLLOWER
FREUDIAN
FUTURIST
GALANIST
GALLICAN
GAULLIST
GLASSITE
GROUPIST
HEDONIST
HEGELIAN
HEURETIC
HUGUENOT
HUMANIST
HYLICIST
IDEALIST
ISLAMITE
JACOBITE
JINGOIST
JUDAISER
LEGALIST
LENINIST
LENINITE
LEVELLER
LOCOFOCO
LOYALIST
LUNARIST
LUTHERAN
MAHDIIST
MANICHEE
MARONITE
MAZDAIST
MINIMIST
MODALIST
MODERATE
MOLINIST
MORAVIAN
NATIVIST
NATURIST
NAZARENE
NAZARITE
NEOPAGAN
NIHILIST
NUTARIAN
OCCAMIST
OPTIMIST
PACIFIST
PAPALIST
PARTISAN

PELAGIAN
PHARISEE
POPULIST
PSYCHIST
PUSEYITE
QUEENITE
QUIETIST
RACOVIAN
RECUSANT
RED-SHIRT
REFORMER
REGALIST
RIGHTIST
RIGORIST
ROMANIST
ROYALIST
RURALIST
SADDUCEE
SATANIST
SEMITIST
SHAFIITE
SOCINIAN
SOLARIST
SOLIDIST
SOMATIST
STUNDIST
SWADDLER
SWADESHI
SYBARITE
TABORITE
TANTRIST
TIMONIST
TOTEMIST
TRIALIST
TRUE BLUE
ULTRAIST
UNIONIST
UTOPIAST
VITALIST
WAHABITE
WESLEYAN

9

ADVENTIST
ANICONIST
APPELLANT
APRIORIST
AUGUSTINE
BACCHANAL
BALAAMITE

BIBLICIST
BOLSHEVIK
CABBALIST
CAESARIST
CALIXTINE
CALVINIST
CAREERIST
CARTESIAN
CATHARIST
CHRISTIAN
COBDENITE
COCAINIST
COENOBITE
COMMUNARD
COMMUNIST
CONFESSOR
CONFORMER
DARWINIAN
DEFEATIST
DIETARIAN
DIPHYSITE
DISSENTER
DITHELETE
DOGMATIST
EMANATIST
ENCRATITE
EPICUREAN
EROTICIST
EUTYCHIAN
EXARCHIST
EXTREMIST
FALANGIST
FETICHIST
FETISHIST
FEUDALIST
FORMALIST
FUSIONIST
GHIBELINE
GIRONDIST
GREGORIAN
GYMNOSOPH
HARMONIST
HARMONITE
HEBREWESS
HELLENIST
HESYCHAST
HETAIRIST
HITLERITE
HOME RULER
HOMOUSIAN
HYLOZOIST
IDEOLOGUE

IRVINGITE
JANSENIST
LABOURIST
LUTHERIST
MAMMONIST
MECHANIST
MELIORIST
MENDELIAN
MENNONITE
MENSHEVIK
MENTALIST
METHODIST
MILLENARY
MITHRAIST
MODERNIST
MONTANIST
MUSSULMAN
MYTHICIST
NEONOMIAN
NEPHALIST
NEPTUNIST
NESTORIAN
NOTIONIST
OCCULTIST
OCTOBRIST
OLIVERIAN
ORANGEMAN
ORIGENIST
ORLEANIST
PANEGOIST
PANTHEIST
PAULICIAN
PAULINIST
PESSIMIST
PEW-HOLDER
PHYSICIST
PLATONIST
PLURALIST
POLITIQUE
POUJADIST
POWELLIST
PRECISIAN
PRELATIST
PRETERIST
PRIMITIVE
PROFESSOR
PROSELYTE
QUAKERESS
RABBINIST
RABBINITE
RACIALIST
RASKOLNIK

RECHABITE
REFORMIST
RITUALIST
ROSMINIAN
ROUNDHEAD
ROUTINIST
SABELLIAN
SAMARITAN
SCIENTIST
SE-BAPTIST
SECTARIAN
SEMI-ARIAN
SEXUALIST
SHAMANIST
SHINTOIST
SIBYLLIST
SOCIALIST
SOLIPSIST
SPINOZIST
SPIRITIST
SWARAJIST
SYMBOLIST
TERMINIST
TETRADITE
TEUTONIST
THANATIST
THEURGIST
TRADUCIAN
TRITHEIST
TUTIORIST
UNITARIAN
UTRAQUIST
VAISHNAVA
VISIONIST
VOLCANIST
VOODOOIST
VORTICIST
VULCANIST
ZWINGLIAN

10

ABIOGENIST
ANABAPTIST
ANTINOMIAN
ANTITHEIST
ASHKENAZIM
AUTOMATIST
AUTONOMIST
AUTOTHEIST
AVERRHOIST

PEOPLE – BELIEVERS

BENTHAMITE
BLACKSHIRT
BOLLANDIST
BOLSHEVIST
BOURBONIST
BUCHMANITE
BULLIONIST
CAMERONIAN
CAPERNAITE
CAPITALIST
CATECHUMEN
CHAUVINIST
CHURCH-GOER
CLEMENTINE
COMSTOCKER
CONFORMIST
CONVERTITE
ETERNALIST
EUHEMERIST
EVANGELIST
FACTIONARY
FACTIONIST
FEDERALIST
FLUVIALIST
FORTUITIST
FREE-FOODER
FREE-TRADER
FROEBELIAN
FRUITARIAN
GRADUALIST
HANOVERIAN
HENOTHEIST
HERRNHUTER
HUMORALIST
HYLOTHEIST
ICONOCLAST
IDEOLOGIST
IDOLOCLAST
IMMORALIST
KARMATHIAN
KENOTICIST
LAMARCKIAN
LEFT-WINGER
LEGITIMIST
LIBERALIST
LIMITARIAN
MALTHUSIAN
MANICHAEAN
MARCIONIST
MARCIONITE
MAXIMALIST
MESSIANIST

MINIMALIST
MOHAMMEDAN
MONARCHIAN
MONARCHIST
MONETARIST
MONOGENIST
MONOTHEIST
MORISONIAN
NATURALIST
NEUTRALIST
NOMINALIST
ORGANICIST
PACIFICIST
PANSLAVIST
PANSOPHIST
PARNELLITE
PARTIALIST
PASSIONIST
PAULIANIST
PHALANGIST
PHALLICIST
PHYSIOCRAT
POLYGENIST
POLYTHEIST
POSITIVIST
PRAGMATIST
PRE-ADAMITE
PROTESTANT
PTOLEMAIST
PYRRHONIST
RELATIVIST
REPUBLICAN
REUNIONIST
REVANCHIST
REVIVALIST
RUSSELLITE
SANHEDRIST
SANITARIAN
SCHISMATIC
SCHOLASTIC
SECULARIST
SENSUALIST
SEPARATIST
SINECURIST
SINN FEINER
SOLIDARIST
SOLIFIDIAN
SPARTACIST
SPERMATIST
SUFFRAGIST
SYNCRETIST
TECHNOCRAT

THEODICEAN
TRACTARIAN
TRIDENTINE
TRIPHYSITE
TROTSKYIST
TROTSKYITE
UNBELIEVER
VATICANIST
VEGETARIAN
VIRTUALIST
VOLTAIRIAN
WALDENSIAN
WORSHIPPER
WYCLIFFITE

11

ABECEDARIAN
ALBIGENSIAN
ANTIBURGHER
BONAPARTIST
CAMPBELLITE
CEREBRALIST
COLONIALIST
COMMUNALIST
COMMUNICANT
COSMOGENIST
CREATIONIST
CROSSBEARER
DEMOCRATIST
DETERMINIST
DILUVIALIST
DISBELIEVER
DISSENTIENT
DISUNIONIST
DOCTRINAIRE
EGALITARIAN
EUDAEMONIST
EVANGELICAL
FREETHINKER
GLADSTONIAN
HETEROUSIAN
HISTORICIST
HOMOIOUSIAN
HYLOPATHIST
ILLUSIONIST
IMMANENTIST
INDEPENDENT
IRRIDENTIST
LIBERTARIAN
MATERIALIST
MEDIEVALIST

MILLENARIAN
MISBELIEVER
MONOPHYSITE
MONOTHELETE
MUSSULWOMAN
MUTATIONIST
NAPOLEONIST
NATIONALIST
NEGATIONIST
NEO-CATHOLIC
NEOVITALIST
NIETZSCHEAN
NOTIONALIST
NOVATIONIST
NULLIFIDIAN
OBJECTIVIST
OLD CATHOLIC
ORTHODOX JEW
PANISLAMIST
PANPSYCHIST
PARALLELIST
PARISHIONER
PARLOUR PINK
PERIPATETIC
PERSONALIST
PHANTASIAST
PHENOMENIST
PHYSIOLATER
PHYSITHEIST
PLYMOUTHIST
PLYMOUTHITE
POSSIBILIST
PROBABILIST
PROGRESSIST
PROGRESSIVE
PYTHAGOREAN
RASTAFARIAN
RATIONALIST
REACTIONARY
REACTIONIST
REGIONALIST
RELATIONIST
RELIGIONIST
REMONSTRANT
REVISIONIST
RIGHT-WINGER
ROMANTICIST
ROSICRUCIAN
SABBATARIAN
SANDEMANIAN
SANSCULOTTE
SCRIPTURIST

SINGULARIST
SOUL-SLEEPER
SYSTEMATIST
TEETOTALLER
TELEOLOGIST
TETRATHEIST
THEOSOPHIST
UTILITARIAN
VALENTINIAN
ZEN BUDDHIST
ZOROASTRIAN

12

BEHAVIOURIST
CHORIZONTIST
COLLECTIVIST
CONFESSORESS
CONFUCIANIST
CONSERVATIVE
CONTAGIONIST
CORPOREALIST
CREMATIONIST
DEFLATIONIST
DEVIATIONIST
DIVERSIONIST
DOCTRINARIAN
EQUALITARIAN
EVOLUTIONIST
EXCLUSIONIST
EXPANSIONIST
EXTENSIONIST
FACTIONALIST
FUTILITARIAN
GYMNOSOPHIST
HUMANITARIAN
IMAGE-BREAKER
IMMERSIONIST
INFLATIONIST
INTRUSIONIST
INTUITIONIST
ISOLATIONIST
JEFFERSONIAN
MACMILLANITE
METAMORPHIST
MUGGLETONIAN
NEO-CHRISTIAN
NEO-DARWINIAN
NOTHINGARIAN
OBSCURANTIST
PAEDOBAPTIST

PANHELLENIST
PANSEXUALIST
PARTITIONIST
PATRIPASSIAN
PERPETUALIST
PHILOSOPHIST
PRACTICALIST
PRECISIONIST
PRESBYTERIAN
PROPAGANDIST
REDUCTIONIST
RELATIVITIST
SACRAMENTARY
SALVATIONIST
SECESSIONIST
SEMI-PELAGIAN
SPIRITUALIST
STERCORANIST
SUBJECTIVIST
SUBLAPSARIAN
THEOPASCHITE
TOTALITARIAN
TRADUCIANIST
TRANSFORMIST
UBIQUITARIAN
UNIVERSALIST
VOLUNTARYIST

13

ANGLO-CATHOLIC
ANTIQUITARIAN
ANTISOCIALIST
ANYTHINGARIAN
ASSUMPTIONIST
AUTHORITARIAN
CATASTROPHIST
COMPULSIONIST
CONCEPTUALIST
CONVULSIONARY
CONVULSIONIST
DESTRUCTIVIST
DEVOLUTIONIST
EMIGRATIONIST
ESCHATOLOGIST
FEUILLETONIST
FRACTIONALIST
FUNCTIONALIST
GREEK ORTHODOX
GRUMBLETONIAN
HEMEROBAPTIST

HUNTINGDONIAN
HUTCHINSONIAN
IMMATERIALIST
IMPOSSIBILIST
INDETERMINIST
INDIVIDUALIST
INFALLIBILIST
INNOVATIONIST
IRRATIONALIST
LIBERATIONIST
MACHIAVELLIAN
MILLENNIALIST
NEO-LAMARCKIAN
NONCONFORMIST
OCCASIONALIST
OPPOSITIONIST
PANSPERMATIST
PARTICULARIST
PERFECTIONIST
PHALANSTERIAN
PHALANSTERIST
PHENOMENALIST
PHILADELPHIAN
PROTECTIONIST
PRUDENTIALIST
REACTIONARIST
REVELATIONIST
REVOLUTIONIST
ROMAN CATHOLIC
SACERDOTALIST
SAINT-SIMONIAN
SAINT-SIMONIST
SCHWENKFELDER
SCRIPTURALIST
SEPARATIONIST
SUCCESSIONIST
SUGGESTIONIST
SUN-WORSHIPPER
SWEDENBORGIAN
THAUMATURGIST
THEANTHROPIST
TRADE UNIONIST
UNDULATIONIST
UNICAMERALIST
ZARATHUSTRIAN

14

ANTIMONARCHIST
CONVOCATIONIST
CORPUSCULARIAN

PEOPLE – BELIEVERS

DESTRUCTIONIST
EPISTEMOLOGIST
EXISTENTIALIST
FIRE-WORSHIPPER
FUNDAMENTALIST
INDIFFERENTIST
INFRALAPSARIAN
INSPIRATIONIST
INTEGRATIONIST
INTERACTIONIST
INTUITIONALIST
LATITUDINARIAN
LATTER-DAY SAINT
MINISTERIALIST
PERFECTIBILIAN
PERFECTIBILIST
PREDESTINARIAN
PREMILLENARIAN
PROBABILIORIST
PROGRESSIONIST
PROHIBITIONIST
PSILANTHROPIST
REFORMATIONIST
REPUDIATIONIST
RESTITUTIONIST

RESTORATIONIST
RESTRICTIONIST
RETALIATIONIST
SACRAMENTALIST
SACRAMENTARIAN
SCHWENKFELDIAN
SEGREGATIONIST
SOCIAL DEMOCRAT
SUBSTANTIALIST
SUPRALAPSARIAN
TARIFF-REFORMER
TERRITORIALIST
TRADITIONALIST
TREE-WORSHIPPER
TRINITARIANIST
TRIPERSONALIST
ULTRAMONTANIST
UNIFORMITARIAN

15

ANTHROPOSOPHIST
ANTITRINITARIAN
CHRISTADELPHIAN

CONFESSIONALIST
CONSERVATIONIST
CONVENTIONALIST
CRYPTO-CHRISTIAN
CRYPTO-COMMUNIST
DEGENERATIONIST
DEVIL-WORSHIPPER
FIFTH-MONARCHIST
INTELLECTUALIST
INTERVENTIONIST
INTRANSIGENTIST
JEHOVAH'S WITNESS
LIBERAL UNIONIST
LITTLE ENGLANDER
PARLIAMENTARIAN
PLYMOUTH BROTHER
POST-MILLENARIAN
PREFERENTIALIST
PREFORMATIONIST
PRESENTATIONIST
PROCESSIONALIST
RESURRECTIONIST
SECOND-ADVENTIST
SUPERNATURALIST

PEOPLE – CLERGY & MONASTICS

3

DOM
FRA
NUN

4

ABBA
ABBÉ
BAPU
COPT
COWL
CURÉ
DEAN
GURU

IMÂM
LAMA
MAGE
MONK
PAPA
POPE
SUFI
YOGI

5

ABBOT
BARBE
BENET
BONZE
CANON

CHELA
CLARE
CLERK
DRUID
ELDER
FAKIR
FRATE
FRIAR
MAGUS
MINIM
MUFTI
PADRE
PRIOR
RABBI
SADHU
SOFTA
SWAMI

VICAR
YOGIN

6

ABBESS
BISHOP
CANTOR
CLERGY
CLERIC
CULDEE
CURATE
DEACON
DIPPER
DIVINE
DOCTOR

DOPPER
ESSENE
EXARCH
FATHER
FLAMEN
FRATER
HERMIT
JESUIT
JUMPER
LECTOR
LEVITE
LUCUMO
MARIST
MARTYR
MOTHER
MULLAH
MYSTIC

NOVICE
PALMER
PARSON
PASTOR
PRIEST
PRIMUS
RANTER
READER
RECTOR
RED-HAT
SANTON
SCRIBE
SERVER
SEXTON
SISTER
VERGER
VESTAL

VOTARY
ZYMITE

TEMPLAR
TITULAR
UNALIST

PREACHER
PRIORESS
PROVISOR
REVEREND
SALESIAN
SEMINARY
SIDESMAN
SIN-EATER
SKY-PILOT
SQUARSON
SUBPRIOR
SUPERIOR
SYRIARCH
TALAPOIN
TERTIARY
THEATINE
THE CLOTH
THURIFER
TRAPPIST
URSULINE
VARTABED
VICARESS
VICE-DEAN
VOTARESS

CONFESSOR
CORDELIER
DALAI LAMA
DEACONESS
DIGNITARY
DOMINICAN
GOSPELLER
GREY FRIAR
GYROVAGUE
HIEROCRAT
INCUMBENT
LAMPADARY
LAY READER
LAY RECTOR
LAY SISTER
LIGUORIAN
LITURGIST
MENDICANT
MISSIONER
MONSIGNOR
NOVITIATE
OBSERVANT
OFFICIANT
ORATORIAN
PATRIARCH
PEW-OPENER
PILLARIST
POSTULANT
PRECENTOR
PREDICANT
PREDIKANT
PRELATESS
PRESBYTER
PRIESTESS
PROZYMITE
PULPITEER
RECOLLECT
RECTORESS
RELIGIEUX
RELIGIOUS
RURAL DEAN
SACRISTAN
SEXTONESS
SHAVELING
SIMEONITE
SUBCANTOR
SUBDEACON
SUCCENTOR
SUFFRAGAN
THEOLOGER
THEOLOGUE
VESTRYMAN

7

ACOLYTE
ALFAQUI
ASCETIC
AZYMITE
BEGHARD
BÉGUINE
BRAHMAN
BROTHER
CALOYER
CHANTER
CHORIST
CLUNIAC
DERVISH
DIGNITY
DOMINIE
GENERAL
GOLIARD
HOLY JOE
HYMNIST
INTONER
JACOBIN
LIMITER
MAR-TEXT
MAURIST
MUEZZIN
ORDINEE
OSTIARY
PAULINE
PIARIST
PILGRIM
PONTIFF
PRELACY
PRELATE
PRIMATE
PROPHET
PROVOST
RECLUSE
REGULAR
SACRIST
SECEDER
SECULAR
SERVITE
SHRIVER
STYLITE
SUBDEAN
SWINGER

8

ACOEMETI
ANTIPOPE
BACCHANT
BASILIAN
BEADSMAN
BEAU-PÈRE
BRETHREN
CANONESS
CANONIST
CAPUCHIN
CARDINAL
CHAPLAIN
CHOIRBOY
CHOIRMAN
CHORAGUS
CORYBANT
CRUCIFER
DIOCESAN
DRUIDESS
ECCLESIA
EMINENCE
EXORCIST
HOLINESS
IGNATIAN
INCENSER
INITIATE
LAY VICAR
LECTRESS
MAN OF GOD
MARABOUT
MATHURIN
MINISTER
MINORESS
MINORITE
MONASTIC
NEOPHYTE
OFFICIAL
OLIVETAN
ORDAINER
ORDINAND
ORDINANT
ORDINARY
PENITENT
PONTIFEX
POPELING

9

AMBROSIAN
ANCHORESS
ANCHORITE
ARCH-DRUID
ARYA SAMAJ
AYATOLLAH
BACCHANTE
BARNABITE
BISHOPESS
BLACK MONK
BLACK POPE
BOY BISHOP
CARMELITE
CATECHIST
CELEBRANT
CELESTINE
CELLARIST
CHANTRESS
CHARTREUX
CHORISTER
CHURCHMAN
CLERGYMAN
COENOBITE
COENOBIUM

PEOPLE – CLERGY & MONASTICS

10

ARCHBISHOP
ARCHDEACON
ARCH-FLAMEN
ARCH-PRIEST
BEADSWOMAN
BERNARDINE
BLACK FRIAR
CARTHUSIAN
CATHOLICOS
CISTERCIAN
CLOISTERER
CLOISTRESS
CONCLAVIST
CONVENTUAL
ECCLESIAST
EVANGELIST
FRANCISCAN
GILBERTINE
HIEROPHANT
HIGH PRIEST
ILLUMINATE
JACK PRIEST
LAY BROTHER
LICENTIATE
MASS PRIEST
MINOR CANON
MISSIONARY
MYSTAGOGUE
NORBERTINE
PREBENDARY
PROLOCUTOR
PSALMODIST
RELIGIONER
REVIVALIST
SANCTIFIER
SCHOLASTIC
SEMINARIAN
SEMINARIST
SERMONISER
SOLEMNISER
SUBCHANTER
THEOLOGIAN
THEOLOGIST
WHITE FRIAR

11

ABBEY-LUBBER

ARCH-PRELATE
AUGUSTINIAN
AUSTIN FRIAR
BENEDICTINE
CAMALDOLITE
CHURCHWOMAN
CLASS-LEADER
CLERGYWOMAN
COMMENDATOR
CONSECRATOR
DEVIL-DODGER
DEVOTIONIST
ECCLESIARCH
HEDGE-PARSON
HEDGE-PRIEST
HIERONYMITE
IGNORANTINE
INFIRMARIAN
INTERCESSOR
INTERVENTOR
MEKHITARIST
MONSEIGNEUR
OBEDIENTARY
PANCHEN LAMA
PARISH CLERK
POPE'S KNIGHT
PRECENTRESS
PROBATIONER
RELIGIONARY
SCEUOPHYLAX
SUBPRIORESS
SUPERIORESS
TIRONENSIAN
TRAPPISTINE
VICAR-CHORAL
VICAR-FORANE

12

CAMP-PREACHER
CANON REGULAR
CANON SECULAR
CHURCHWARDEN
CIRCUIT-RIDER
DEAN OF ARCHES
ECCLESIASTIC
HOT GOSPELLER
LOW-CHURCHMAN
METROPOLITAN
OBSERVANTINE

PARISH PRIEST
PENITENTIARY
PREMONSTRANT
QUALIFICATOR
REDEMPTORIST
RESIDENTIARY
TENT-PREACHER
VICAR-GENERAL

13

ARCHIMANDRITE
CHURCH-OFFICER
CONCEPTIONIST
CRUTCHED FRIAR
DEVOTIONALIST
FIELD-PREACHER
HIGH-CHURCHMAN
HIGH PRIESTESS
KNIGHT TEMPLAR
LOCAL PREACHER
POSSESSIONATE
REDEMPTIONIST
SISTER OF MERCY
SPIRITUAL PEER
TITULAR BISHOP

14

APOSTOLIC VICAR
CHURCH ORGANIST
DEVIL'S ADVOCATE
MOTHER SUPERIOR
PARISH MINISTER
PREACHING FRIAR
REVEREND MOTHER
SUPERINTENDENT
VICAR-APOSTOLIC

15

PERPETUAL CURATE
SCRIPTURE-READER
SUFFRAGAN BISHOP
WHIRLING DERVISH

PEOPLE – CRIMINALS

3

DIP
GUN
LAG
PAD

4

FAKE
HOOD
THUG

5

BRAVO
CROOK
DIVER
FAKER
FELON
FENCE
FRAUD
LIFER
RAPER
ROVER
STALL
THIEF

6

APACHE
BADDIE
BADMAN
BANDIT
BRIBER
COINER
CON-MAN
DACOIT
DIPPER
FORÇAT
FORGER
GUNMAN
HAIDUK
HIT-MAN
KILLER
KLEPHT
LATRON
LOOTER
MUGGER

OLD LAG
OUTLAW
PICKER
PIRATE
PUSHER
RAIDER
RAMPER
RAPIST
RAPTOR
RIFLER
ROBBER
RUNNER
SEA-RAT
SLAYER
SWIPER
TRUSTY
USURER
VANDAL

7

ABACTOR
ABETTOR
BRIGAND
BURGLAR
CATERAN
CONVICT
CORSAIR
CULPRIT
ESCAPEE
FILCHER
FIREBUG
FOOTPAD
GORILLA
GRAFTER
HEISTER
HOODLUM
LADRONE
LAND-RAT
MAGSMAN
MOBSTER
NUT-HOOK
PINDARI
PLOTTER
POACHER
RAVAGER
RUSTLER
SCALPER
SEA-WOLF
SPEEDER
SPOILER

STEALER
STIFLER
SUICIDE
TRAITOR
VILLAIN

8

ABDUCTOR
APPROVER
ARSONIST
ASSASSIN
BIGAMIST
CLY-FAKER
COLLUDER
CRIMINAL
CUTPURSE
ESCAPADO
FUGITIVE
GANGSTER
GAOL-BIRD
HIJACKER
JAIL-BIRD
LARCENER
LIBELLER
MARAUDER
MURDERER
OFFENDER
PERJURER
PETERMAN
PILFERER
PILLAGER
PLAGIARY
PLUG-UGLY
POISONER
PRISONER
RAMPSMAN
RANSOMER
RAPPAREE
RAVISHER
RECEIVER
REGICIDE
RIVER-RAT
SABOTEUR
SCELERAT
SEA-ROVER
SIMONIAC
SIMONIST
SMUGGLER
SUBORNER
SWAGSMAN

SWINDLER
TRUQUEUR
VATICIDE

9

ABSCONDER
ACCESSORY
ADULTERER
ANARCHIST
ARCH-FELON
AREA-SNEAK
AUTOLYCUS
BACKSTALL
BANDOLERO
BUCCANEER
CRACKSMAN
CUT-THROAT
DEFAULTER
DESPOILER
EMBEZZLER
FALSIFIER
FRAUDSTER
GUN-RUNNER
KIDNAPPER
LARCENIST
MAN-SLAYER
MATRICIDE
MURDERESS
PAEDERAST
PARRICIDE
PATRICIDE
PECULATOR
PERVERTER
PÉTROLEUR
PICK-PURSE
PLUNDERER
PRINCIPAL
PRIVATEER
PURLOINER
RACKETEER
RANK-RIDER
RANSACKER
RUM-RUNNER
SALLEE-MAN
SEA-ROBBER
SHEBEENER
SLANDERER
SMOTHERER
SPADASSIN
SPOLIATOR

PEOPLE – CRIMINALS

STRANGLER
THROTTLER
TRAITRESS
TRIGAMIST
UXORICIDE
WRONG-DOER

PYROMANIAC
RECIDIVIST
RICK-BURNER
SHOPLIFTER
SNEAK-THIEF
TRAFFICKER
TRESPASSER
TRIGGERMAN
VILLAINESS

BODY-SNATCHER
BUNKO-STEERER
DRUG-SMUGGLER
EXTERMINATOR
FILIBUSTERER
HOUSE-BREAKER
MISDEMEANANT
PEACE-BREAKER
SCAPEGALLOWS
SHEEP-STEALER
SWELL-MOBSMAN
TRANSGRESSOR

10

ACCOMPLICE
ADULTERESS
ARCH-PIRATE
BOOTLEGGER
BUSHRANGER
CAT-BURGLAR
CONJURATOR
CONTACT MAN
DECALCATOR
DELINQUENT
DOPE-PEDLAR
ELIMINATOR
EXTIRPATOR
FILIBUSTER
FIRE-RAISER
FREEBOOTER
FREE-TRADER
HATCHET MAN
HIGHBINDER
HIGHWAYMAN
HORSE-THIEF
INCENDIARY
LAND-PIRATE
LAW-BREAKER
LIQUIDATOR
MAN-STEALER
MOONSHINER
PÉTROLEUSE
PICK-POCKET
PLAGIARIST

11

ARCH-TRAITOR
ARCH-VILLAIN
BLACK-FISHER
BLACKMAILER
CATTLE-THIEF
CONSPIRATOR
EXTORTIONER
GALLOWS-BIRD
KERB-CRAWLER
MOONLIGHTER
MOSS-TROOPER
MOTOR-BANDIT
PERPETRATOR
PROBATIONER
SACRILEGIST
SAFE-BREAKER
SAFE-CRACKER
SEDITIONARY
SHOPBREAKER
SLAUGHTERER
SNATCH-PURSE
SNATCH-THIEF
SNOW-DROPPER

12

BABY-SNATCHER

13

CONSPIRATRESS
CONTRABANDIST
CORRUPTIONIST
COUNTERFEITER
FIRST-OFFENDER
PRISON-BREAKER
PRIVATEERSMAN
PURSE-SNATCHER
STATE-PRISONER

14

BLACK MARKETEER

15

HOMICIDAL MANIAC
MALPRACTITIONER
RESURRECTIONIST
RESURRECTION-MAN

PEOPLE – ELDERLY PEOPLE

3

ELD
HAG
OOM

4

FOGY
MUFF

5

BLIMP
CROCK
CRONE
DOBBY
DOYEN
ELDER
FOGEY
SIBYL

6

BELDAM
BUFFER
CODGER

DOTARD
DUFFER
DUGOUT
FOSSIL
GAFFER
GAMMER
GEEZER
MATRON
NESTOR
OLD BOY
OLD MAN
RIBIBE

7

DOYENNE
OLD HAND
OLD MAID
OLDSTER
OLD WIFE
RETIREE
VETERAN

8

DODDERER
HARRIDAN
HOARHEAD

OLD FOGEY
OLD-TIMER
OLD WOMAN

9

FOGRAMITE
GERIATRIC
GREYBEARD
MATRIARCH
MUMPSIMUS
OLD STAGER
PATRIARCH
PENSIONER

10

FUDDY-DUDDY
METHUSELAH
PENSIONARY
SUGAR-DADDY
WHITE-BEARD

11

CENTENARIAN
CROTCHETEER

OLD BACHELOR

12

ANTEDILUVIAN
DARBY AND JOAN
NONAGENARIAN
OCTOGENARIAN
OUT-PENSIONER
SEXAGENARIAN
SUPERANNUATE

13

SENIOR CITIZEN

14

ELDER STATESMAN
SEPTUAGENARIAN

15

OLD AGE PENSIONER

PEOPLE – ENTERTAINERS

3

DUO
HAM
PRO

4

ALMA

ALTO
BAND
BARD
BASS
CAST
DIVA
LEAD
STAR
TRIO
TURN

5

ACTOR
BASSO
BUFFA
CLOWN
COMBO
COMIC
DROLL
EXTRA

FIFER
GROUP
HEAVY
MIMER
MIMIC
OCTET
PIPER
TENOR
WAITS

6

ARTIST
BUGLER
BUSKER
CHORUS
DANCER
DISEUR
FLUTER
GEISHA

GUISER
GUSLAR
HARPER
HORNER
JESTER
LEADER
LUTIST
LYRIST
MUMMER
NAUTCH

PEOPLE – ENTERTAINERS

OBOIST
PLAYER
SEPTET
SEXTET
SINGER
STOOGE
TOOTER
TROUPE
VAMPER
VIBIST
VIOLER

7

ACROBAT
ACTRESS
ARTISTE
AUGUSTE
BUFFOON
CELLIST
COMIQUE
COMMÈRE
COMPANY
COMPÈRE
CORNIST
CROONER
DISEUSE
DRUMMER
FARCEUR
FEED-MAN
FIDDLER
FLUTIST
FUGUIST
GAMBIST
GAMELAN
GLEEMAN
HARPIST
HETAIRA
JUGGLER
MAESTRO
PIANIST
PIERROT
POP STAR
QUARTET
QUINTET
SCRAPER
SECONDO
SHOWMAN
SOLOIST
SOPRANO
STARLET

TABORER
TROLLER
TROUPER
TUMBLER
VIOLIST
WALTZER
WARBLER

8

BAGPIPER
BALANCER
BANDSMAN
BANJOIST
BARITONE
BOTHYMAN
CAROLLER
CASTRATO
COMEDIAN
CONJUROR
DANSEUSE
DUETTIST
ENSEMBLE
FARCEUSE
FIGURANT
FILM STAR
FLAUTIST
FRONT MAN
JONGLEUR
LUTANIST
MAGICIAN
MELODIST
MERRYMAN
MIMESTER
MIMICKER
MINSTREL
MUSICIAN
ORGANIST
PIANISTE
POP GROUP
POSTURER
RAGTIMER
REED BAND
SHOWGIRL
SONGSTER
STAR TURN
STRIPPER
STUNTMAN
TANGOIST
TENORIST
THESPIAN

TOP-LINER
VIRTUOSA
VIRTUOSO
VOCALIST
WALKER-ON
WHISTLER
YODELLER

9

ANCHORMAN
BALLADEER
BALLADIST
BALLERINA
BRASS BAND
CAMPANIST
CANTABANK
CELEBRITY
CEMBALIST
CHANTEUSE
CITHARIST
CONDUCTOR
CONTRALTO
COURT-FOOL
CYMBALIST
DANCE BAND
ECDYSIAST
FAGOTTIST
FAN DANCER
FIGURANTE
FIRE-EATER
GUITARIST
HAMFATTER
HARMONIST
HYPNOTIST
JOCULATOR
LION-TAMER
MESMERIST
ORCHESTRA
PANTALOON
PERFORMER
PIERRETTE
PIFFERARO
PLAY-ACTOR
POP SINGER
PORTRAYER
POSTURIST
PRESENTER
PRINCIPAL
PSALTRESS
PUPPETEER

RHYTHMIST
RIPIENIST
ROCK GROUP
SERENADER
SHANTYMAN
SOPRANINO
SOPRANIST
SOUBRETTE
STEEL BAND
TAP-DANCER
THEORBIST
TIMPANIST
TRAGEDIAN
TRUMPETER
TYMPANIST
VIOLINIST
VOLTIGEUR

10

BALLET-GIRL
BANDLEADER
BANDMASTER
BASSOONIST
BEAR-LEADER
BELL-RINGER
CANTATRICE
CHORUS-GIRL
CHORUS-LINE
CLOG-DANCER
COMÉDIENNE
CORNETTIST
DRAG-ARTIST
FIRE-WALKER
FOLK-DANCER
FOLK-SINGER
GLEEMAIDEN
GO-GO DANCER
GUT-SCRAPER
HARMONISER
HORSE-TAMER
KNOCKABOUT
LEADING MAN
NAUTCH-GIRL
ONE-MAN BAND
PERSONATOR
PIROUETTER
PRIMA DONNA
QUADRILLER
RING-MASTER
ROPE-WALKER

SCAT-SINGER
SONGSTRESS
STEP-DANCER
SYMPHONIST
SYNCOPATOR
TAXI-DANCER
THRENODIST
TROMBONIST
TROUBADOUR
UNDERACTOR
UNDERSTUDY
UNICYCLIST
VIGNETTIST
WIRE-DANCER
WIRE-WALKER

11

ACCOMPANIST
BARNSTORMER
BELLY-DANCER
BROADCASTER
CARILLONIST
CAROL-SINGER
CHANSONNIER
CLAVECINIST
COURT-JESTER
DANCING-GIRL
ENTERTAINER
EQUILIBRIST
FUNAMBULIST
ILLUSIONIST
LEADING LADY
LIMBO-DANCER
MATINÉE IDOL
MINNESINGER
MONOLOGUIST
OPERA-DANCER
OPERA-SINGER
PANTOMIMIST

PIANO-PLAYER
PLAY-ACTRESS
POLYPHONIST
SAXOPHONIST
SIGHT-PLAYER
SIGHT-SINGER
STAGE-PLAYER
STILT-WALKER
STRAIGHT MAN
STRIP-TEASER
TORCH-SINGER
TRAGEDIENNE
XYLOPHONIST

12

ACCORDIONIST
ACTOR-MANAGER
BALLET-DANCER
CLARINETTIST
COUNTER-TENOR
ESCAPOLOGIST
FUNAMBULATOR
HARMONIUMIST
IMPERSONATOR
JUVENILE LEAD
KNIFE-THROWER
MEZZO-SOPRANO
MILITARY BAND
MORRIS-DANCER
ORGAN-GRINDER
POSTURE-MAKER
PRESTIGIATOR
PRINCIPAL BOY
SNAKE-CHARMER
STAND-UP COMIC
TRICK CYCLIST
VARIATIONIST
VAUDEVILLIAN
VIBRAPHONIST

13

BASSO-PROFONDO
CALYPSO SINGER
CONTORTIONIST
CONTRAPUNTIST
CORPS DE BALLET
IMPRESSIONIST
KETTLEDRUMMER
MEISTERSINGER
ORCHESTRALIST
PANTOMIME DAME
POSTURE-MASTER
STRAIGHT-ACTOR
SUPERNUMERARY
TRAPEZE ARTIST
VENTRILOQUIST
VIOLONCELLIST

14

CHARACTER ACTOR
FLAMENCO DANCER
PRIMA BALLERINA
SWORD-SWALLOWER

15

CHRISTY-MINSTREL
HARMONICA-PLAYER
INSTRUMENTALIST
PRESTIDIGITATOR
RECORDING ARTIST
SONG-AND-DANCE MAN
STRAIGHT-ACTRESS
STROLLING PLAYER
SUPPORTING ACTOR
TIGHT-ROPE WALKER

PEOPLE – FOOLS

3

ASS
BUG
LOB
LOG
MUG
NIT
NUT
OAF
OWL
SAP

4

BERK
BOOB
CASE
CLOD
CLOT
DOLT
DOPE
DUPE
FOOL
GAWK
GOAT
GOOF
GOON
GOOP
GULL
GUMP
HICK
JERK
KOOK
LOON
MUFF
MUTT
PUNK
RUBE
SWAB
TWIT

5

BLOCK
BOOBY
CHUMP
CLOWN
CLUNK
DUMMY

DUNCE
GAWKY
GOLEM
GOOSE
IDIOT
LOOBY
LOONY
MOONY
MORON
NINNY
PRUNE
SCHMO
SILLY
SOFTY
SPOON
STOCK
TWERP
WALLY
YOKEL

6

BODGER
BOODLE
BUFFER
CRETIN
CUCKOO
DIMWIT
DONKEY
DUFFER
GALOOT
GANDER
GAUPUS
GOOSEY
JESTER
JOSKIN
KOOKIE
LURDAN
MADCAP
MADMAN
MOPOKE
NIG-NOG
NITWIT
NOODLE
NUTTER
OXHEAD
PUDDEN
RUSTIC
SAWNEY
SPOONY
SUCKER

THICKO
TURNIP
ZOMBIE

7

BALADIN
BOTCHER
BUFFOON
BUMPKIN
BUNGLER
BUZZARD
CHARLIE
COXCOMB
DIZZARD
DULLARD
FALL-GUY
FAT-HEAD
FOOZLER
FUMBLER
GUDGEON
HALF-WIT
HAWBUCK
HUMDRUM
JACKASS
JOHNNIE
JUGGINS
LOG-HEAD
MADLING
MANGLER
MUGGINS
NATURAL
NEBBISH
NUT-CASE
PIFFLER
PILLOCK
PINHEAD
POT-HEAD
PUDDING
SCHMUCK
SCHNOOK
TOMFOOL
WANT-WIT
WASH-OUT

8

ABDERITE
BONEHEAD
BORN FOOL

BULL-CALF
CLODPATE
CLODPOLL
CRACKPOT
DOTTEREL
DUMB-BELL
FLATHEAD
FRENETIC
GOOSE-CAP
HEADCASE
IGNORANT
IMBECILE
JACK-FOOL
JOLTHEAD
LIRIPIPE
LIRIPOOP
MOONCALF
NUMSKULL
OMADHAUN
SOFTHEAD
SOFTLING
SOFT MARK
TOM-NODDY
WISEACRE
WISELING

9

APRIL-FOOL
BESOMHEAD
BLOCKHEAD
BLUNDERER
CAPOCCHIA
CHAW-BACON
GOTHAMITE
IGNORAMUS
JOBERNOWL
JOCULATOR
MOONRAKER
PANTALOON
SCHLEMIEL
SCREWBALL
SIMPLETON
THICKHEAD
THICKSKIN

10

BEETLEHEAD
BUFFLEHEAD

CHANGELING
CLODHOPPER
CRACKBRAIN
DUMB BLONDE
DUNDERHEAD
DUNDERPATE
ILLITERATE
JOLTERHEAD
LOGGERHEAD
MUDDLEHEAD
MUTTONHEAD
NINCOMPOOP
PUDDEN-HEAD
RATTLEHEAD
SHEEP'S-HEAD
SILLY-BILLY
THICK-SKULL
WOODEN-HEAD

11

COMPLETE ASS
FEATHER-HEAD
FEATHER-PATE
KNOW-NOTHING
LEATHER-HEAD
RATTLE-BRAIN

12

FEATHER-BRAIN
SCATTER-BRAIN
SEMI-IMBECILE
VILLAGE IDIOT

13

LAUGHING-STOCK
PROPER CHARLIE

14

COUNTRY BUMPKIN

PEOPLE – GENERAL PEOPLE

3

APE
BIT
BOD
CAT
COB
COD
DAB
DOG
FAG
FAW
FOE
FOP
GAY
GUN
GUY
HEN
HER
HIM
HOB
JOB
LAG
MAN
MEN
NOB
ONE
OWL
PET
RUM
SHE
SIR
SRI
WAG

4

BINT
BIRD
BOOR
BUCK
CARD
CHAI
CHAL
CHAP
CLAM
COCK
COVE
DAME
DISH
DOER
DOLL
DOVE
DOWD
DUDE
DUMP
FARE
FOLK
FRAU
FROW
GENT
GINK
GOER
GRIG
HAWK
HEIR
HELP
HERR
HIND
HOBO
HOMO
HOST
LIER
LUMP
MA'AM
MAID
MALE
MISS
MOPE
NAME
ONER
PAWN
PEER
PLEB
POOF
PREY
PUNK
QUIZ
RAKE
RAMP
RYOT
SCAB
SEER
SIRE
SOUL
STAG
TIER
TIRO
TOFF
TOOL
TUAN
USER
WAIF
WARD

5

ADEPT
ADULT
AGENT
AIDER
ALIEN
ASKER
AUGUR
BEING
BELLE
BLADE
BLOKE
BLOND
BLOOD
BRICK
BROAD
BUYER
BWANA
CAGOT
CEORL
CHICK
CISSY
CIVVY
COMIC
COVER
CRANK
CRUSH
CUTIE
CROWD
DANDY
DEVIL
DINER
DOLLY
DONEE
DOYEN
DOZER
DUCKS
DUCKY
DUMPY
EATER
ELECT
ÉLITE
ENEMY
EPOTE
EQUAL
EXILE
FAIRY
FATTY
FIXER
FLEER
FREAK
FREER
FRUIT
FRUMP
GAPER
GAZER
GIANT
GLUER
GONER
GUEST
HATER
HAVER
HAZER
HE-MAN
HIKER
HIRER
HIVER
HODGE
HOMME
HUMAN
ISSEI
JOKER
JUROR
KILTY
KISAN
LAITY
LAKER
LEPER
LIKER
LIVER
LOCAL
LONER
LOPER
LOSER
MADAM
MAJOR
MAKER
MASON
METIC
MIMIC
MIXER
MOLLY
MOPUS
MOVER
MOWER
MUFTI
MUSER
NABOB
NAMER
NANCY
NOMAD
NO-ONE
NOTER
OWNER
PANSY
PARER
PARTY
PAYEE
PAYER
PEACH
PIECE
PIKER
PILER
PIVOT
PLEBS
PLIER
PODGE
POKER
POMMY
POPSY
PORER
POSER
PROXY
QUEEN
QUEER
QUEUE
RAKER
RATER
RAVER
RIDER
RISER
RIVAL
ROVER
SAHIB
SAVER
SCRAG
SEÑOR
SHEEP
SHIER
SHYER
SIDER
SISSY
SKIRT
SPADO
SPARK
SPORT
SQUAB
STRAY
SWELL
SYBIL
SYLPH
TAKER
TAMER
TAPER
THEIC
TIMER
TOWER
TOWNY
TOYER
TRAMP
TRIER
TRULL
TRUMP
URGER
VOTER
WADER
WAKER
WOMAN
WOMEN
WRECK

6

ALUMNA
ALUMNI
AMBLER
ANYONE
AUDILE
BALKER
BAR-FLY
BEARER
BEAUTY
BEGGAR
BIBBER
BIDDER
BLONDE
BLOWZE
CALLER
CAMPER
CAPTOR
CASUAL
CLIENT
COAXER
CODDLE
CODGER
COEVAL
CONCHY
COOKIE
COUPLE
CUFFIN
CUPMAN
DAMSEL
DARNER

217

PEOPLE – GENERAL PEOPLE

DAUBER	HUNKER	MILADY	PRETTY	SHRIMP
DEBTEE	HURLER	MILORD	PROSER	SIFTER
DEBTOR	INVERT	MINCER	PRUNER	SIGNER
DEFIER	ISSUER	MISTER	PULLER	SIGNOR
DIETER	JERKER	MODIST	PUNTER	SIPPER
DOWSER	JIGGER	MODERN	PURGER	SIRRAH
DRAWEE	JOSHER	MONKEY	PUSHER	SIRRAH
DRAWER	JUNGLI	MOONER	PUTTER	SITTER
DRIVER	JURANT	MOPPET	QUEUER	SLICER
DUENNA	KEY MAN	MORTAL	QUOTER	SLIDER
EARNER	KHANUM	MUSHER	RAISER	SMILER
ÉMIGRÉ	KIDDER	MUZHIK	RAMMER	SMITER
ENVIER	KILTIE	NABBER	RANGER	SMOKER
ESCORT	KISSER	NATIVE	RAPPER	SOCMAN
EUNUCH	KNOWER	NEEDER	RASPER	SOLVER
EXEMPT	KUMARI	NICKER	READER	SPARER
FAGGOT	LAGGER	NOBODY	REELER	SPHINX
FASTER	LANDER	NODDER	REJECT	SQUARE
FAUTOR	LAPPER	NOVICE	RENTER	SQUIRE
FEEDER	LARKER	NURSER	RESTER	STEWER
FELLAH	LASTER	ODDITY	RÊVEUR	STOOGE
FELLER	LAUDER	OLD BOY	RINGER	STOWER
FELLOW	LAYMAN	OLD MAN	RINSER	SUITOR
FEMALE	LEASER	OPENER	RIPPER	SUPPER
FENMAN	LENDER	OPTANT	RISKER	SWAYER
FIGURE	LESSEE	ORPHAN	ROAMER	TANNER
FINDER	LESSOR	OUSTER	ROCKER	TASKER
FLAYER	LETTER	PAKEHA	ROMPER	TEARER
FOLDER	LICKER	PARIAH	ROOMER	TENANT
FRIAND	LODGER	PARROT	ROOTER	TENDER
GABBER	LOLLER	PARSER	ROUSER	TENTER
GADFLY	LOOKER	PARTER	ROUTER	TERMOR
GAGGER	LOVELY	PASSER	RUBBER	TESTEE
GAINER	LUBBER	PATRON	RUSHER	TESTER
GALLIO	LUSTER	PAUPER	SALVOR	TIMIST
GENTRY	MADAME	PAUSER	SCREAM	TIPPER
GETTER	MAENAD	PAWNEE	SEEKER	TOILER
GNAWER	MAGNET	PAWNER	SEIZER	TOP DOG
GUIDER	MAGPIE	PEELER	SELLER	TOPPER
GUSHER	MAIDEN	PEG-LEG	SENDER	TOWNEE
HAULER	MARKER	PELTER	SENHOR	TRACER
HEARER	MAROON	PEOPLE	SEÑORA	TRUSTY
HEAVER	MASHER	PERSON	SETTER	TUBBER
HELPER	MASKER	PETTER	SEXPOT	TUGGER
HEP-CAT	MASQUE	PICKER	SHADOW	TURNER
HERMIT	MASSES	PITIER	SHAKER	UNDOER
HIGH-UP	MATRON	PLACER	SHAPER	UNIPEG
HOAXER	MEALER	POLLER	SHARER	UNITER
HOCKER	MEDIUM	POPPER	SHEILA	VARIER
HOLDER	MEMBER	POSTER	SHIKSA	VENDEE
HOMBRE	MENDER	POURER	SHORER	VENDOR
HOPPER	MENIAL	POUTER	SHOWER	VIATOR
				VICTIM

VIEWER	CITIZEN	FEASTER	JURYMAN	NOTHING
VIRGIN	CLAIMER	FIXTURE	KINDLER	OBLIGEE
VISILE	CLUBMAN	FLÂNEUR	KING-PIN	OBLIGOR
VULGUS	COMPANY	FLOATER	KNEELER	ODDBALL
WAHINE	COMPEER	FORAGER	KNITTER	OFFERER
WALKER	CONTACT	FREEMAN	KNOCKER	OLD BEAN
WANTER	COUNSEL	FRIANDE	KNOTTER	OLD CHAP
WARNER	COXCOMB	FRISKER	LAGGARD	OLD GIRL
WASHER	CRACKER	FURIOSO	LANDMAN	OLD HAND
WEARER	CREATOR	GOGGLER	LEARNER	OMITTER
WEIRDO	CRUMPET	GRAFTER	LEGATEE	ONANIST
WILLER	CUCKOLD	GRANGER	LEGATOR	OPPIDAN
WINCER	CYCLIST	GRANTEE	LESBIAN	ORARIAN
WINDER	DABBLER	GRANTER	LIE-ABED	ORGIAST
WINKER	DALLIER	GRANTOR	LIGHTER	OUTCAST
WINNER	DAMOSEL	GREMIAL	LIMITER	OUTLIER
WISHER	DANGLER	GRIEVER	LOATHER	PADDLER
WITTOL	DAZZLER	GRIPPER	LORETTE	PARADOX
WRETCH	DELATOR	GROUPER	LOUNGER	PATRIAL
	DENIZEN	GROUPIE	LOW-BROW	PATRIOT
	DEVISEE	GROWN-UP	LUBBARD	PEASANT
7	DEVISER	GUESSER	LUNCHER	PERUSER
	DEVISOR	GUZZLER	LURCHER	PIERCER
ABUTTER	DIALLER	HABITUÉ	MACHINE	PILGRIM
ACCUSER	DIE-HARD	HAGGLER	MADE MAN	PIONEER
ADAPTER	DIVIDER	HAS-BEEN	MAGNATE	PITCHER
ADVISER	DIVINER	HAVE-NOT	MANGLER	PIVOTER
ADVISOR	DREAMER	HAYSEED	MAN-JACK	PLAITER
ALIENEE	DRINKER	HEIRESS	MANKIND	PLANTER
ALIENOR	DROWNER	HEPSTER	MARCHER	PLAYBOY
ALUMNUS	DWELLER	HERITOR	MARRIER	PLEADER
AMENDER	ECHOIST	HIGGLER	MASQUER	PLEASER
ANCIENT	EDIFIER	HIPSTER	MENFOLK	PLEDGEE
ANONYMA	EIDETIC	HITCHER	MIGRANT	PLEDGER
ANYBODY	EJECTOR	HOARDER	MILK-SOP	PLEDGOR
APPOSER	ELECTOR	HOBBLER	MINGLER	PLODDER
ARCH-FOE	EMPTIER	HOMAGER	MISDOER	PLOTTER
AROUSER	ENACTOR	HOSTAGE	MOBSMAN	PLUGGER
ASSURER	ENDURER	HOSTESS	MONITOR	PLUNGER
BEATNIK	ENJOYER	HOTSPUR	MOOCHER	POINTER
BIG SHOT	ENTERER	IGNITER	MOORMAN	POPULUS
BOARDER	EPICURE	IGNORER	MOUNTER	PORTMAN
BUCOLIC	ERECTOR	IMBIBER	MOURNER	POUNDER
BUMPKIN	EREMITE	IMPUTER	MUFFLER	PRAISER
BURGESS	EVACUEE	INCOMER	MUNCHER	PRANCER
BYWONER	EXCITER	INDUCER	MYNHEER	PRESSER
CAJOLER	EXHALER	INHALER	NATURAL	PRONEUR
CAPTIVE	EXHUMER	INSIDER	NEUTRAL	PROPHET
CAT'S-PAW	EXODIST	INTRANT	NIBBLER	PROTÉGÉ
CAVEMAN	EXPOSER	INVITEE	NOMINEE	PSYCHIC
CHAPPIE	FAILURE	INVITER	NON-USER	PUNCHER
CHARMER	FANTAST	IRONIST	NOTABLE	PUNSTER

PEOPLE – GENERAL PEOPLE

PURSUER
PUZZLER
QUAFFER
QUERIST
QUESTER
QUIZZER
RAMBLER
REBUKER
RECLUSE
REDHEAD
REDUCER
REFUGEE
REFUSER
REFUTER
REGULAR
RELATOR
RENEWER
RENTIER
REPINER
REPLIER
RESCUER
RESIDER
REVERER
RÊVEUSE
REVIVER
RIDDLER
RUNAWAY
SALUTER
SAMPLER
SCALDER
SCALPER
SCEPTIC
SCHEMER
SCOOPER
SCOURER
SCRAPER
SCREWER
SECEDER
SECULAR
SEETHER
SENHORA
SERVILE
SETTLER
SHAMMER
SHEDDER
SHOPPER
SIGNORA
SKIPPER
SLAPPER
SLASHER
SLEEPER
SLICKER

SLIMMER
SLINGER
SLINKER
SLIPPER
SLITTER
SLUBBER
SLUMMER
SMASHER
SMELLER
SMOTHER
SMUDGER
SNARLER
SNIPPER
SNOOZER
SNUBBER
SOCAGER
SOCIATE
SOCIETY
SOKEMAN
SOMEONE
SOOTHER
SPANKER
SPARTAN
SPELLER
SPENDER
SPILLER
SPONGER
SPONSOR
SPOOFER
SPORTER
SPURRER
STAMPER
STAND-BY
STANDER
STAND-IN
STEEPER
STEERER
STEPPER
STICKER
STILLER
STOOPER
STOPPER
STRAYER
STREWER
STRIKER
STRIVER
STROKER
STUDENT
STUDIER
STUFFER
STUNNER
SUBJECT

SUCCESS
SULTANA
SUSPECT
SWAGMAN
SWAPPER
SWEARER
SWEATER
SWEEPER
SWILLER
SWINGER
SWISHER
SWOPPER
TAPERER
TARRIER
THANKER
THINKER
THROWER
TICKLER
TIPPLER
TOUCHER
TOURIST
TOW-HEAD
TRACKER
TRAILER
TRAINEE
TREADER
TREATER
TREKKER
TRIBADE
TRIMMER
TRIPPER
TROPIST
TRUDGER
TRUSTEE
TRUSTER
TRYSTER
TUMBLER
TWIRLER
UNIFIER
UNKNOWN
VAGRANT
VILLEIN
VISITEE
VISITOR
VOUCHEE
VOUCHER
VOYAGER
WAKENER
WAR HAWK
WATCHER
WAVERER
WEIRDIE

WETBACK
WHEELER
WHETTER
WHIFFER
WHIPPER
WHIRLER
WIELDER
WIGGLER
WITNESS
WOBBLER
WORRIER
WRINGER
YIELDER

8

ABHORRER
ABSENTEE
ACCEPTOR
ACCORDER
ADJUSTER
AMBIVERT
ANSWERER
APPEARER
APPROVER
ARRESTEE
ARRESTER
ASCENDER
ASPIRANT
ASSENTER
ASSENTOR
ASSIGNEE
ASSIGNOR
ATTENDER
ATTESTOR
BACCHANT
BACHELOR
BAILSMAN
BANKRUPT
BARNACLE
BEANPOLE
BEGINNER
BIG NOISE
BIG WHEEL
BOHEMIAN
BONDSMAN
BORDERER
BORROWER
BREATHER
BRINKMAN
BRUNETTE

CAROUSER
CASTAWAY
CAVALIER
CELIBATE
CHAIRMAN
CHAMPION
CHAPERON
CIVILIAN
CLAIMANT
CLUBBIST
COCKEREL
COLONIST
COMMONER
COMMUTER
COMPLIER
CONFIDER
CONSOLER
CONSUMER
CONVEYOR
CO-TENANT
COTTAGER
COURTIER
CREATRIX
CREDITOR
CUSTOMER
DECEASED
DECEDENT
DEMONIAC
DEMURRER
DEPONENT
DETAINEE
DETAINER
DEVIATOR
DIGESTER
DISPONEE
DISPONER
DISPOSER
DIVORCEE
DOG'S-BODY
DUMPLING
EMBRACER
EMIGRANT
EMULATOR
ENCLOSER
ENDORSEE
ENDORSER
ENJOINER
ENQUIRER
ENTAILER
EPISTLER
ERRORIST
EUPHUIST

EVERYMAN	INQUIRER	ONLOOKER	REASONER	SCRUPLER
EXAMINEE	INSPIRER	OPPOSITE	REBUTTER	SCUTTLER
EXCEPTOR	INSURANT	OPSIMATH	RECANTER	SEARCHER
EXECUTER	INVERTER	OPTIMIST	RECEIVER	SECONDER
EXECUTOR	INVESTOR	ORIGINAL	RECKONER	SEÑORITA
EXPIRANT	LAME DUCK	OUTSIDER	RECLINER	SETTER-UP
EXPLORER	LANDLADY	OUTVOTER	RECOILER	SHADOWER
EXTENDER	LANDLORD	OVERDOER	REDEEMER	SHIELDER
FAVOURER	LANDSMAN	OVERLIER	REFUNDER	SHOREMAN
FLAUNTER	LEGATARY	PACIFIER	REGAINER	SHRINKER
FLINCHER	LEVELLER	PAMPERER	REGARDER	SKELETON
FOLLOWER	LICENSEE	PARCENER	REJECTOR	SKINHEAD
FOREGOER	LIEGEMAN	PARDONER	REJOICER	SLAVERER
FORESTER	LINGERER	PARROTER	RELEASEE	SMALL FRY
FOUR-EYES	LISTENER	PARTAKER	RELEASER	SOLECIST
FRANKLIN	LITERATE	PASSER-BY	RELEASOR	SOLITARY
FRÄULEIN	LITIGANT	PATENTEE	REMITTEE	SOMEBODY
FREEDMAN	LIVE-WIRE	PEDALLER	REMITTER	SORROWER
FRONT MAN	LOBBYIST	PENITENT	RENDERER	SPECIMEN
FROWSTER	LONE WOLF	PICKETER	RENEGUER	SPINSTER
FUGITIVE	LOOKER-IN	PIVOT-MAN	REPAIRER	SPLASHER
GABELLER	LOOKER-ON	PLAINANT	REPEALER	SPLITTER
GADABOUT	LUMBERER	PLAY-GIRL	REPEATER	SPREADER
GAVELMAN	LUXURIST	PLEBEIAN	REPELLER	SQUATTER
GEORGIAN	MACARONI	POLEMIST	REPENTER	SQUINTER
GIANTESS	MANDATOR	POLLSTER	REPLACER	SQUIRTER
GO-GETTER	MARCHMAN	PLIGHTER	REPROVER	STALWART
GRISETTE	MARSH-MAN	PONDERER	REQUIRER	STANCHER
HABITANT	MAVERICK	POPINJAY	REQUITER	STARTLER
HASTENER	MEMSAHIB	POTTERER	RESENTER	STRAINER
HAUSFRAU	MIGRATOR	PREPARER	RESIDENT	STRANGER
HIGHER-UP	MILITANT	PRESAGER	RESIGNER	STREAKER
HILLFOLK	MIMICKER	PRESUMER	RESOLVER	STRINGER
HONOURER	MODIFIER	PRISONER	RESORTER	STROLLER
HUMANITY	MONOGLOT	PRIZE-MAN	RESTORER	STUMBLER
HUMORIST	MONSIEUR	PROCURER	RETAINER	SUBURBAN
IMAGINER	MORALIST	PROFITER	REVEALER	SUFFERER
IMITATOR	MOTORIST	PROMISEE	REVELLER	SUITRESS
IMPARTER	NAMESAKE	PROMISER	REVERIST	SUNDERER
IMPELLER	NANCY-BOY	PROMISOR	REVERSER	SUPERIOR
IMPLORER	NEWCOMER	PROMPTER	REWARDER	SURMISER
IMPONENT	NIGHT-OWL	PROPOSER	RIVERAIN	SURVIVOR
IMPROVER	NUMBERER	PROSAIST	ROADSTER	SWAGSMAN
INCEPTOR	NURTURER	PROSPECT	ROTARIAN	TALESMAN
INDICTEE	OBJECTOR	PROTÉGÉE	ROTURIER	TAX EXILE
INDULGER	OBLIGANT	PROVIDER	RUMMAGER	TAX-PAYER
INFECTOR	OBSCURER	PUNISHER	RUNABOUT	TELEPATH
INFERIOR	OBSERVER	PURIFIER	SABOTIER	TENDERER
INFLAMER	OBTAINER	QUAVERER	SAUCE-BOX	TESTATOR
INFLATOR	OCCUPANT	QUEEN-BEE	SCORCHER	THREADER
INITIATE	OCCUPIER	RATIFIER	SCRAWLER	THWACKER
INLANDER	OLD THING	REALISER	SCREENER	THWARTER

PEOPLE – GENERAL PEOPLE

TONTINER
TOTTERER
TOWNSMAN
TRAMPLER
TREMBLER
TROUNCER
TWIDDLER
TWINKLER
TWITCHER
TYPIFIER
UNDERDOG
UNDERMAN
UNFOLDER
UNLOADER
UNMASKER
UNPACKER
UNVEILER
UPHOLDER
UPLANDER
UPLIFTER
UTILISER
VAGABOND
VANISHER
VAVASOUR
VENDEUSE
VENTURER
VERIFIER
VILLAGER
VISITANT
VIVIFIER
WALLOPER
WANDERER
WARRENER
WATCH-DOG
WAYFARER
WAY-MAKER
WEAKLING
WELCOMER
WET-NURSE
WHEEEDLER
WHIZZ-KID
WONDERER
WRIGGLER

9

ABANDONEE
ABROGATOR
ABSTAINER
ACCEPTANT
ADVERSARY

ANNUITANT
APOLOGIST
APPELLANT
APPLICANT
ARCH-ENEMY
ARCHIMAGE
ARRAIGNER
ASSISTANT
ASSOCIATE
AUGMENTER
AUTARKIST
BACCHANAL
BACCHANTE
BICYCLIST
BLIND DATE
BON VIVANT
BOURGEOIS
BYSTANDER
CABALLERO
CANDIDATE
CAUTIONER
CHAFFERER
CHARACTER
CHEVALIER
CITIZENRY
CLIENTELE
CLUBWOMAN
COADJUTOR
COHERITOR
COLLEAGUE
COMFORTER
COMMUNITY
CONCUBINE
CONFIDANT
CONFIDENT
CONQUEROR
CONSERVER
CONSIGNEE
CONSIGNER
CONSORTER
CONSTRUER
CONSULTEE
CONSULTER
CONSULTOR
CONTRIVER
CONVERTER
COURTESAN
COVER GIRL
DARE-DEVIL
DARK HORSE
DECLARANT
DEFENDANT

DELIVERER
DEMANDANT
DENOUNCER
DESCENDER
DISSECTOR
DISSIDENT
DIVINATOR
DOCTORAND
DOLLY-BIRD
EARLY BIRD
EARTHLING
ECCENTRIC
EDWARDIAN
EMMETROPE
ENCHANTER
ENERGUMEN
ENGROSSER
ENLIVENER
EXCHANGER
EXECUTANT
EXECUTRIX
EXHIBITOR
EXPECTANT
EXPLAINER
EXQUISITE
EXTRACTOR
EXTROVERT
FASHIONER
FAVOURITE
FELLOW-MAN
FEUDALIST
FIREBRAND
FIRST-BORN
FLATTERER
FLESHLING
FOREIGNER
FORGETTER
FORTIFIER
FREE AGENT
FREEMASON
FREE-RIDER
FREEWOMAN
FULL-BLOOD
FURNISHER
FURTHERER
GAINSAYER
GARNISHEE
GARNISHER
GENTLEMAN
GENTLEMEN
GEOMANCER
GO-BETWEEN

GRATIFIER
GREENHORN
GUARANTOR
HARBINGER
HARBOURER
HEADLINER
HEARKENER
HEIR-AT-LAW
HELLHOUND
HERMITESS
HIGH-FLIER
HILL-BILLY
HOI POLLOI
HOMECOMER
HOSTELLER
HUMBUGGER
IDEALISER
IMMIGRANT
IMMOLATOR
IN-BETWEEN
INCOGNITA
INCOGNITO
INCREASER
INDWELLER
INHERITOR
INITIATOR
INNOVATOR
INTESTATE
INTROVERT
ITINERANT
JACULATOR
JOINT-HEIR
JOINTRESS
JOURNEYER
JURYWOMAN
JUSTIFIER
LADIES' MAN
LANDOWNER
LAZZARONE
LEG-PULLER
LIBELLANT
LIP-READER
LITTLE MAN
MAFFICKER
MAMMONITE
MANNERIST
MENDICANT
MISFEASOR
MITIGATOR
MODULATOR
MOLLIFIER
MONEY-BAGS

MORALISER
MORTGAGEE
MORTGAGOR
MORITIFIER
MOTIVATOR
MULTIPARA
MULTITUDE
MUSCLE-MAN
MYSTIFIER
NAIL-BITER
NEIGHBOUR
NIGHT-BIRD
NOCTURNAL
NOMINATOR
NONENTITY
NON-MEMBER
NONPAREIL
NON-PERSON
NON-SMOKER
NOURISHER
NULLIFIER
NULLIPARA
NUMBER ONE
OBSCURANT
OBSERVANT
ODD-MAN-OUT
OLD FELLOW
OUTLANDER
OUTRUNNER
OVERRULER
PACHYDERM
PARACLETE
PARCENARY
PART-OWNER
PARTY-GOER
PASSENGER
PEASANTRY
PENCILLER
PENDICLER
PERCEIVER
PEREGRINE
PERFORMER
PERMITTER
PERSONAGE
PERSONNEL
PERSUADER
PERTURBER
PESSIMIST
PEW-HOLDER
PICNICKER
PLAINTIFF
PLAYTHING

PLURIPARA
PLUTOCRAT
POKER-FACE
PORTRAYER
POSSESSOR
POSTPONER
PRACTISER
PRANKSTER
PRECURSOR
PREFERRER
PREDICTOR
PREHENSOR
PRESENTEE
PRESENTER
PRESERVER
PRETENDER
PREVENTER
PRIMIPARA
PROCEEDER
PROFFERER
PROLONGER
PROPELLER
PROPONENT
PROSCRIPT
PROTESTER
PROTESTOR
PURCHASER
QUALIFIER
QUIETENER
RAG-PICKER
RAIN-MAKER
RATEPAYER
REASSURER
RECIPIENT
RECOVEREE
RECOVERER
RECOVEROR
REDRESSER
REFRESHER
REHEARSER
RENOVATOR
REQUESTER
RESEMBLER
RESPECTER
RESPONDER
RESTARTER
RETRIEVER
REVELATOR
RUMINATOR
SALOONIST
SATURNIAN
SAUNTERER

SCAPEGOAT
SCARECROW
SCRAMBLER
SCRATCHER
SCREWBALL
SCRIBBLER
SENHORITA
SENSATION
SEPARATOR
SETTER-OFF
SETTER-OUT
SHANTYMAN
SHELTERER
SHORTENER
SHOVELLER
SIGHTSEER
SIGNALLER
SIGNATORY
SIGNORINA
SIMULATOR
SINGED CAT
SIX-FOOTER
SLOW-COACH
SLUMBERER
SMATTERER
SOCIALITE
SOJOURNER
SOLITAIRE
SPECTATOR
SPRINKLER
SQUABBLER
STARGAZER
STRAGGLER
STRETCHER
STUPEFIER
SUBLESSEE
SUBLESSOR
SUBLETTER
SUBMITTER
SUBTENANT
SUCCEEDER
SUCCESSOR
SUCCOURER
SUGGESTER
SUNBATHER
SUPPLIANT
SUPPORTER
SURFEITER
SURPRISER
SURROGATE
SUSPENDER
SUSTAINER

SWALLOWER
SYMBOLIST
TARNISHER
TELLURIAN
TESTATRIX
TESTIFIER
TIGHTENER
TOLERATOR
TRAVELLER
TRAVERSER
TRIBUTARY
TRICYCLER
TRIUMPHER
TUNNELLER
UITLANDER
UNDERLING
UPBRAIDER
VENERATOR
VICTORIAN
VISIONARY
VISITRESS
VISUALIST
VOLUNTARY
VOLUNTEER
WARRANTEE
WARRANTER
WARRANTOR
WASSAILER
WEEK-ENDER
WITNESSER
WOMANKIND
WOMENFOLK
WORLDLING

10

ANTAGONIST
APOLOGISER
ART STUDENT
BANQUETEER
BOBBYSOXER
BOND-HOLDER
CHAIRWOMAN
CHALLENGER
COADJUTRIX
COLLATERAL
COMANCHERO
COMPATRIOT
COMPOTATOR
CONFIDANTE
CO-OPERATOR

PEOPLE – GENERAL PEOPLE

CO-PARCENER
COUNTRYMAN
COVENANTEE
COVENANTOR
DAPPERLING
DAYDREAMER
DEFORCIANT
DEMOISELLE
DILETTANTE
DISCOVERER
DIVINERESS
DOWN-AND-OUT
DUTCH UNCLE
EAR-WITNESS
ECONOMISER
EFFEMINATE
ELIMINATOR
ELUCIDATOR
EMPIRICIST
ENCOURAGER
ENUMERATOR
EPISTOLIST
ERADICATOR
EXPATRIATE
EYE-WITNESS
FAINT-HEART
FASCINATOR
FASHIONIST
FORETELLER
FRANCHISER
FREEDWOMAN
FREEHOLDER
FREQUENTER
FUND-HOLDER
GAME TENANT
GASTRONOME
GASTROSOPH
GENERALIST
GENERATION
GENTLEFOLK
GEOPHAGIST
GLAMOUR BOY
GOLDILOCKS
GOOD-LOOKER
GRAND JUROR
HEART-THROB
HITCH-HIKER
HOMOSEXUAL
HUMAN BEING
IMPENITENT
IMPROVISER
INCULCATOR

INDIVIDUAL
INHABITANT
INHERITRIX
INSTITUTOR
INTEGRATOR
INTERCEDER
INTERPOSER
INTRODUCER
JACK-A-DANDY
LADY-KILLER
LAND-LUBBER
LANGUISHER
LIFE-TENANT
LITERALIST
LISTENER-IN
LOVE-MONGER
LOWER CLASS
LUCUBRATOR
MAINTAINER
MALCONTENT
MAN OF STRAW
MEDIOCRITY
MELIORATOR
MERRYMAKER
MONEY-MAKER
MONOGAMIST
MONOPOLIST
NAMBY-PAMBY
NON-CONTENT
NON-STARTER
NOTABILITY
OPINIONIST
ORIGINATOR
OUTDWELLER
OVERBIDDER
OVERLANDER
OVERTURNER
PAINSTAKER
PALL-BEARER
PAPER TIGER
PARADOXIST
PARAPHRAST
PARTIALIST
PAST-MASTER
PATHFINDER
PEDESTRIAN
PENETRATOR
PERCIPIENT
PERFORATOR
PETITIONER
PILGARLICK
PILLIONIST

PIPE-SMOKER
POLEMICIST
POPSY-WOPSY
POPULATION
PRAGMATIST
PREMONITOR
PREPARATOR
PRETENDANT
PROCLAIMER
PROFICIENT
PROHIBITOR
PROMENADER
PROPHESIER
PROPHETESS
PROPOUNDER
PROPRIETOR
PROSCRIBER
PROTRACTOR
PULVERISER
PUNCTUATOR
QUAESTUARY
QUANTIFIER
QUESTIONER
QUICK-FIRER
RAIN-DOCTOR
RECOGNISER
RECONCILER
REGISTRANT
REPATRIATE
REPOSITORY
REPROACHER
REPUDIATOR
REQUISITOR
RESPONDENT
RESTITUTOR
RESTRAINER
RUBBER-NECK
SACRIFICER
SCHLIMAZEL
SENSUALIST
SIMPLIFIER
SLAVE-OWNER
SLEEPY-HEAD
SNUFF-TAKER
SOLICITANT
SOLITARIAN
SOLIVAGANT
SOOTHSAYER
SORTILEGER
SPECULATOR
STARVELING
STAY-AT-HOME

STIMULATOR
STIPULATOR
SUBSCRIBER
SUBSIDIARY
SUBSTITUTE
SUPERSEDER
SUPPLANTER
SUPPLICANT
SURMOUNTER
SYMBOLISER
SYMMETRIAN
SYNTHETIST
TEA-DRINKER
TELEPHONER
TELEVIEWER
TEMPORISER
TENDERFOOT
TENDERLING
TERMINATOR
THE ACCUSED
TIMBER-TOES
TITILLATOR
TOWNSWOMAN
TRANSACTOR
TRANSFEREE
TRANSFEROR
TRANSFUSER
TRICHROMAT
TRICHROMIC
TRICYCLIST
UNRAVELLER
UNDERLAYER
UPPER CLASS
UPPER CRUST
VANQUISHER
VICEGERENT
VINDICATOR
VISUALISER
VOETGANGER
VOLAPUKIST
VOLUPTUARY
WALLFLOWER
WELL-WISHER
WINE-BIBBER
WITHDRAWER
WITHHOLDER
WORKAHOLIC

11

ABBREVIATOR

ABECEDARIAN
BEAUTY QUEEN
BENEFICIARY
BILLIONAIRE
BLUE-EYED BOY
BOURGEOISIE
CHAIN-SMOKER
CHANCE-COMER
CHEIRONOMER
CITY-SLICKER
CO-INHERITOR
COMPLAINANT
COMPURGATOR
CONCOMITANT
CONFEDERATE
CONSERVATOR
CONSOLATRIX
CONSUMMATOR
CONTRIBUTOR
COUNTRY-FOLK
CRACKERJACK
DELUSIONIST
DENUNCIATOR
DEPOPULATOR
DRAM DRINKER
EAGER BEAVER
ELIZABETHAN
EMBELLISHER
ENCHANTRESS
EQUIVOCATOR
ESTABLISHER
EXAGGERATOR
FAITH-HEALER
FAULT-FINDER
FEMME FATALE
FIRST-FOOTER
FOOTSLOGGER
FORESTALLER
FORETHINKER
FRONT-RANKER
FROTH-BLOWER
GARGANTUIST
GASTROLOGER
GENTLEWOMAN
GLAMOUR GIRL
GLAMOUR PUSS
HABILITATOR
HARUM-SCARUM
HEAVYWEIGHT
HIGH-STEPPER
HOUSEHOLDER
IDEOPRAXIST

INAUGURATOR
INHABITRESS
INHERITRESS
INTERCEPTER
INTERCESSOR
INTERMEDIUM
INTERROGANT
INTERRUPTER
INTERVIEWEE
INVIGORATOR
LAKE-DWELLER
LEASEHOLDER
LIGHTWEIGHT
LOGOMACHIST
MASQUERADER
MIDDLE CLASS
MILLIONAIRE
MISINFORMER
MOLLYCODDLE
MONOPOLISER
MYCOPHAGIST
NIGHT-WALKER
NOBODY'S FOOL
NONDESCRIPT
NON-RESIDENT
NON-UNIONIST
OPPORTUNIST
OSTREOPHAGE
OWNER-DRIVER
PACIFICATOR
PARAPHRASER
PARTICIPANT
PARTITIONER
PAYING GUEST
PERIPATETIC
PERPETUATOR
PERQUISITOR
PERSONALITY
PERSONIFIER
PERTURBATOR
PETITIONIST
PIPE-DREAMER
PLAIN-DEALER
POPULARISER
PRAGMATISER
PREDECESSOR
PREOCCUPANT
PRIZE-WINNER
PROGRESSIVE
PROLETARIAN
PROLETARIAT
PROPITIATOR

PROTAGONIST
PURIFICATOR
QUESTIONARY
QUESTIONIST
RECOMMENDER
REGENERATOR
REMUNERATOR
REPLACEMENT
REPLENISHER
REPREHENDER
REPRESENTER
RESURRECTOR
RESUSCITANT
REVERSIONER
RUNNING MATE
SECOND-RATER
SELF-MADE MAN
SETTER-FORTH
SHAREHOLDER
SIGHT-READER
SLAVE-HOLDER
SNAPSHOOTER
SOCIETARIAN
SOLUTIONIST
SOMNIVOLENT
SPECIALISER
SPECULATRIX
SQUIREARCHY
STALL-READER
STOCKHOLDER
STRAP-HANGER
SUBORDINATE
SUBURBANITE
SUFFRAGETTE
SURRENDEREE
SURRENDERER
SURRENDEROR
SURVEILLANT
SWEATER-GIRL
SYMPATHISER
SYNDICALIST
TAUTOLOGIST
TELEPATHIST
TELESCOPIST
TERRESTRIAL
THANKSGIVER
TOOTH-PICKER
TORCH-BEARER
TOWN-DWELLER
TOWNSPEOPLE
TRAIN-BEARER
TRANSFERRER

TRANS-SEXUAL
TRENCHERMAN
TRENDSETTER
TRUTH-TELLER
UNDERBIDDER
UNDERLETTER
UNDERSELLER
UNDERTENANT
UNDERVALUER
UNFORTUNATE
VACATIONIST
VATICINATOR
VOORTREKKER
WHIPPING-BOY
WITHSTANDER

12

ANIMADVERTER
BACHELOR-GIRL
BOBBY-DAZZLER
COLLABORATOR
COMMEMORATOR
COMMISERATOR
COMPLIMENTER
CONQUISTADOR
CONSERVATRIX
CONSIGNATORY
CONSOLIDATOR
CONTEMPLATOR
CONTEMPORARY
CONVIVIALIST
CO-RESPONDENT
COSMOPOLITAN
COUNTRYWOMAN
CROWN-WITNESS
EPISTOLARIAN
EXCURSIONIST
EX-SERVICEMAN
FATHER-FIGURE
FELLOW-MEMBER
FEMME DU MONDE
FEMME SAVANTE
FIRST-NIGHTER
GASTRONOMIST
GASTROSOPHER
GESTICULATOR
GLOBE-TROTTER
HELIOGRAPHER
HETEROSEXUAL
HOLIDAYMAKER

PEOPLE – GENERAL PEOPLE

IMPROPRIATOR
IMPROVISATOR
INCORPORATOR
INTERCHANGER
INTERCIPIENT
INTERMEDIARY
INTERPOLATOR
INTERROGATOR
JUSTIFICATOR
LEADING LIGHT
LETTER-WRITER
MADEMOISELLE
MAN-ABOUT-TOWN
MIGRATIONIST
MIRROR-WRITER
MISCEGENATOR
MISINFORMANT
MOTHER-FIGURE
MOTOR-CYCLIST
NOCTAMBULIST
NON-COMBATANT
NOUVEAU RICHE
OFFICE-HUNTER
OFFICE-SEEKER
PANTOPHAGIST
PARTICIPATOR
PERAMBULATOR
PEREGRINATOR
PERSEVERATOR
PILLION-RIDER
POLICY-HOLDER
PRECIPITATOR
PRECISIONIST
PRIMIGRAVIDA
PRIMOGENITOR
PROPRIETRESS
RECIPROCATOR
RECRIMINATOR
REDEMPTIONER
RESUSCITATOR
REVERSIONARY
ROUGH DIAMOND
SECLUSIONIST
SEQUESTRATOR
SOPHISTICATE
SPIRIT-RAPPER
SUBTERRANEAN
SUPPLEMENTER
SYNCHRONISER
TENANT-AT-WILL
TRADITIONIST

TRANSMIGRANT
UNDERSTANDER
VELOCIPEDIST
VINDICATRESS
WATER-DIVINER
WATER-DRINKER
WAY-PASSENGER
WEAKER VESSEL
WILL-O'-THE-WISP
WOOL-GATHERER
WORKING CLASS

13

BARGAIN-HUNTER
CONGRATULATOR
CONVENTIONIST
DECK-PASSENGER
DERIVATIONIST
DEUTEROGAMIST
DEUTERONOMIST
DISCRIMINATOR
FEATHERWEIGHT
FELLOW-CITIZEN
FINGER-POINTER
FLOATING VOTER
FOUNDER-MEMBER
GAME-PRESERVER
HUNGER-MARCHER
HUNGER-STRIKER
IMPROVISATRIX
INOPPORTUNIST
INTERMEDIATOR
MAN OF THE WORLD
MILLIONAIRESS
NIGHT-WANDERER
NONCONFORMIST
NON-SPECIALIST
ONYCHOPHAGIST
OWNER-OCCUPIER
PHILOSOPHISER
PREDESTINATOR
PRIMOGENITRIX
PROVERBIALIST
RAINBOW-CHASER
RECONSTRUCTOR
REMITTANCE-MAN
RHABDOMANTIST
SIMPLIFICATOR
SOPHISTICATOR

SPRING-CLEANER
STRIKE-BREAKER
SUPERNUMERARY
THOUGHT-READER
TRANSMIGRATOR
UNDERSTRAPPER
WINDOW-SHOPPER

14

CABIN PASSENGER
DISCIPLINARIAN
DOUBTING THOMAS
FELLOW-CREATURE
FELLOW-TOWNSMAN
MAN IN THE STREET
MAN OF THE MOMENT
MISINTERPRETER
NON-COMMUNICANT
OPPOSITE NUMBER
PLATINUM BLONDE
PLEASURE-SEEKER
PRACTICAL JOKER
PROCRASTINATOR
PROGNOSTICATOR
QUADRAGENARIAN
REQUISITIONIST
SENTIMENTALIST
TOTAL ABSTAINER

15

CIRCUMNAVIGATOR
DISPLACED PERSON
EXPERIMENTALIST
FELLOW-TRAVELLER
FEMME INCOMPRISE
FLIBBERTIGIBBET
LAY IMPROPRIATOR
MATERIAL WITNESS
PLATITUDINARIAN
QUINQUAGENARIAN
SALOON-PASSENGER
SLEEPING PARTNER
UNKNOWN QUANTITY
WOMAN OF THE WORLD

PEOPLE – JUVENILES

3

BOY
BUB
BUD
CUB
DEB
DUX
FAG
GAL
IMP
KID
LAD
MOD
TED
TOT

4

ARAB
BABE
BABY
BRAT
CHIT
COED
COLT
GIRL
LASS
MISS
MITE
PAGE
PUNK
PUSS
ROMP
WAIF
WARD

5

BAIRN
BAJAN
BUCKO
CADET
CHILD
FILLY
GAMIN
GUIDE
ISSUE
KIDDY
KNAVE

MARDY
MINOR
MISSY
NYMPH
PETTY
PUPIL
ROVER
SCOUT
SONNY
YOUTH

6

BEJANT
BURSCH
CHERUB
DAMSEL
DAY-BOY
ENFANT
EPHEBE
FIZGIG
GAMINE
GIGLET
HOYDEN
INFANT
JUNIOR
LADDIE
LASSIE
MAIDEN
MASTER
NIPPER
PATHIC
PICKLE
POT-BOY
RANGER
ROCKER
SENIOR
SHAVER
TOMBOY
URCHIN

7

BAMBINO
BOARDER
BROWNIE
CALLANT
CALL-BOY
COLLEEN
DAY-GIRL

DRAW-BOY
ETONIAN
FLAPPER
GOSSOON
GOWNBOY
GRUMMET
HEAD BOY
HELLION
HERDBOY
INGÉNUE
KINCHIN
LINKBOY
MONITOR
NEWSBOY
NYMPHET
PAGE-BOY
PAPOOSE
POSTBOY
PREFECT
SAND-BOY
SCHOLAR
SHIP-BOY
SHOP-BOY
STUDENT
TODDLER
WAR BABY
WHIFFET
WOLF-CUB
YOUNKER

8

AIR-SCOUT
BANTLING
BENJAMIN
BLUECOAT
BOY SCOUT
CABIN-BOY
CATAMITE
CHILDREN
CHRISTOM
COCKEREL
COLLEGER
COMMONER
CUB SCOUT
DÉBUTANT
GREYCOAT
HEAD GIRL
HORSE-BOY
JUVENILE
KILLCROP

KNIFE-BOY
LITTLING
MAN-CHILD
PAPER-BOY
SALOPIAN
SEA-SCOUT
SHOP-GIRL
SPRINGAL
SUCKLING
TEDDY BOY
TEENAGER
TRILLING
UNDERBOY
WEANLING

9

BACKFISCH
CHILD-WIFE
CLASSMATE
COLLEGIAN
DÉBUTANTE
FLEDGLING
FOUNDLING
GIRL GUIDE
GOLDEN BOY
GOOSE-GIRL
HARROVIAN
JACK-A-LENT
LOVE-CHILD
MAJORETTE
MONITRESS
MONTHLING
NAME-CHILD
NURSELING
OFFICE-BOY
OFFSPRING
PAPER-GIRL
PLOUGHBOY
PRINCEKIN
SCHOOLBOY
SEA-RANGER
SEX-KITTEN
SPRINGALD
STABLE-BOY
STEPCHILD
STREET-BOY
STRIPLING
TEDDY GIRL
YOUNGSTER

10

ABITURIENT
ADOLESCENT
BABE-IN-ARMS
BAR MITZVAH
CARTHUSIAN
CHANGELING
CHILD-BRIDE
CLAPPERBOY
DAY-BOARDER
DAY-SCHOLAR
JACKANAPES
LUCKY-PIECE
NURSE-CHILD
OFFICE-GIRL
PICCANINNY
PREPOSITOR
READING-BOY
SCHOOLGIRL
SCHOOL-MAID
SCHOOL-MATE
STREET-ARAB
SUBPREFECT
WYKEHAMIST

11

BLUE-EYED BOY
CLASSFELLOW
COLLEGIANER
GILDED YOUTH
GUTTERSNIPE
HALBSTARKER
HOBBLEDEHOY
SCHOOL-CHILD
TEENYBOPPER
WHIPPING-BOY

12

CHILD PRODIGY
FOUNDATIONER
MESSENGER-BOY
POWDER-MONKEY
PROBLEM CHILD
SCHOOLFELLOW
SCHOOL-FRIEND
SCHOOL-LEAVER
TEST-TUBE BABY
VENTURE SCOUT

PEOPLE – JUVENILES

13

DRUM MAJORETTE
JEUNESSE DORÉE
LATCHKEY CHILD
MESSENGER-GIRL

14

ENFANT TERRIBLE
GENTLEMAN CADET
PARLOUR-BOARDER

SCHOOL-CHILDREN
WARD IN CHANCERY
WHIPPERSNAPPER
YOUTH HOSTELLER

PEOPLE – LEADERS

3

AGA
BAN
BEY
DEY
DUX
VIP

4

AMIR
CHAM
COCK
CZAR
DUCE
EMIR
HEAD
IMÂM
KAID
KHAN
KING
LORD
NAIK
RAJA
RANI
SHAH
TSAR
VALI

5

AKELA
CHIEF

GHAZI
KALIF
MAHDI
MAYOR
MOGUL
MPRET
PASHA
QUEEN
RAJAH
RANEE
RULER
SHEIK
ZUPAN

6

BIG POT
BIGWIG
CAESAR
CALIPH
CONSUL
DESPOT
DYNAST
EPARCH
EXARCH
FÜHRER
GERENT
GUIDER
HETMAN
HUZOOR
INDUNA
LEADER
MASTER
MIKADO
PANDIT

PESHWA
PRINCE
REGENT
SACHEM
SATRAP
SHEIKH
SHERIF
SHOGUN
SULTAN
TUCHUN
TYCOON
TYRANT

7

AGA KHAN
BIG SHOT
CACIQUE
CAPITAN
CAPTAIN
CATAPAN
ELECTOR
EMPEROR
EMPRESS
GAEKWAR
GENERAL
HEADMAN
KHALIFA
MAGNATE
MAHATMA
MONARCH
MUGWUMP
NOMARCH
PREMIER
SCOUTER

SEA-KING
SHEREEF
SUPREMO
TOPARCH
VICEROY
VOIVODE
WARLORD

8

AUTOCRAT
BROWN OWL
CAPITANO
CAUDILLO
CHAIRMAN
CHIEFESS
CONSULAR
CZARITSA
DICTATOR
ETHNARCH
GOVERNOR
HEPTARCH
HIERARCH
KAIMAKAM
MARGRAVE
MONOCRAT
MUQADDAM
OLIGARCH
OVERLORD
PADISHAH
PENTARCH
PHYLARCH
SAGAMORE
SUBAHDAR
SUZERAIN

TAXIARCH
TETRARCH
THEOCRAT
TSARITSA

9

BIG CHEESE
CASTELLAN
CHÂTELAIN
CHIEFTAIN
CHILIARCH
CONDUCTOR
CUB-MASTER
DEMAGOGUE
ELECTRESS
HEADWOMAN
IMPERATOR
LADY MAYOR
LANDGRAVE
LOGOTHETE
MAHARAJAH
MAHARANEE
MATRIARCH
NUMBER ONE
OCHLOCRAT
PARAMOUNT
PATRIARCH
PENDRAGON
PLUTOCRAT
POTENTATE
PRESIDENT
PRINCIPLE
PROTECTOR
SERASKIER

SOVEREIGN
SULTANESS
TAOISEACH
TRIERARCH
TYRANNESS

10

AUTARCHIST
CARAVANEER
CHAIRWOMAN
CHANCELLOR
CHÂTELAINE
FIGUREHEAD
HERESIARCH
PANJANDRUM
RAJPRAMUKH
RINGLEADER
STRATOCRAT

TEAM-LEADER

11

CHAIRPERSON
CHEER-LEADER
GRAND VIZIER
HEAD OF STATE
HEPTARCHIST
PEDANTOCRAT
PROTECTRESS
SCOUT-MASTER
TURCOPOLIER

12

CHIEFTAINESS
PRESIDENTESS

PRINCE REGENT

13

ADMINISTRATOR
COCK-OF-THE-WALK
GENERALISSIMO
PRIME MINISTER

14

MERCHANT PRINCE

15

GOVERNOR-GENERAL
YOUTH-CLUB LEADER

PEOPLE – NATIONALS & TRIBESPEOPLE

3	CELT	MOOR	ADENI	HINDU	OSCAN
	CREE	PICT	ALEUT	HUSKY	PADDY
GIN	DAGO	POLE	ANGLE	IRAQI	POMAK
GOY	DANE	RIFF	ARYAN	KAFIR	PYGMY
HUN	DYAK	SARD	ASIAN	KAREN	RAYAH
JAP	EBON	SCOT	AZTEC	KHMER	ROMAN
JAT	ESTH	SERB	BANTU	LATIN	SABRA
JEW	FINN	SHAN	BOONG	LIMEY	SAKAI
KRU	GAEL	SLAV	CARIB	LUBRA	SAUDI
NIP	GAUL	SORB	CREEK	MAORI	SAXON
PAT	GOTH	THAI	CROSS	MASAI	SHONA
ROM	HOVA	TUPI	CUBAN	METIF	SICAN
YID	IMPI	TURK	CYMRY	METIS	SIKEL
	INCA	WEND	CZECH	MOGUL	SIOUX
4	JOCK	YANK	DRUSE	MUNDA	SUDRA
	KROO	ZULU	FANTI	MYALL	SWEDE
AINU	KURD	ZUÑI	FRANK	NEGRO	SWISS
ARAB	LAPP		GIPSY	NILOT	TAFFY
BALT	LETT		GREEK	NISEI	TAMIL
BANT	MAYA	**5**	GRIFF	OMANI	TATAR
BOER	MEDE		GYPSY	ORIYA	TURKI
BRIT	MICK	ABUNA	HAIKH	OSAGE	UZBEG

PEOPLE – NATIONALS & TRIBESPEOPLE

UZBEK
VEDDA
VLACH
WOLOF
XHOSA
YAKUT
ZAMBO

6

AFGHAN
ALMAIN
ALPINE
AMAZON
ANDEAN
APACHE
ASCIAN
AUSSIE
BASQUE
BASUTO
BERBER
BRETON
BRITON
BULGAR
CANUCK
COMARB
CREOLE
CRETAN
DIGGER
DORIAN
ESKIMO
FIJIAN
GADHEL
GASCON
GENTOO
GERMAN
GITANA
GITANO
GOIDEL
GRINGO
GRIQUA
GULLAH
GURKHA
HAMITE
HEBREW
HERERO
INDIAN
JEWESS
KABYLE
KAFFIR
KENYAN

KIKUYU
KOREAN
LADINO
LEVITE
LIBYAN
LYDIAN
MAGYAR
MANCHU
MEDIAN
MESTEE
MICMAC
MINOAN
MOHAWK
MONGOL
NATIVE
NAVAHO
NESIOT
NILOTE
NORDIC
NORMAN
NUBIAN
OSTYAK
PADUAN
PAPUAN
PARIAH
PARIAN
PATHAN
PAWNEE
PUEBLO
RED-MAN
ROMANY
SABINE
SALIAN
SAMIAN
SAMIOT
SAMOAN
SANNUP
SCOUSE
SEMITE
SENECA
SHERPA
SIWASH
SLOVAK
SOMALI
SOVIET
SYRIAN
TELUGU
TEUTON
THEBAN
TONGAN
TROJAN
TSWANA

TUAREG
TUNGUS
TUSCAN
TYRIAN
UGRIAN
VAISYA
VANDAL
VIKING
YANKEE
YEMENI
YORUBA

7

ACADIAN
ACHAEAN
AEOLIAN
AFRICAN
AMERIND
ANGEVIN
ANGOLAN
ARABIAN
ASIATIC
BELGIAN
BENGALI
BRYTHON
BURMESE
BUSHMAN
CAIRENE
CATALAN
CHALDEE
CHILEAN
CHINESE
CHOCTAW
CITIZEN
COCKNEY
COSSACK
CYPRIOT
FLEMING
FRENCHY
FRISIAN
GAMBIAN
GENEVAN
GENOESE
GEORDIE
GRECIAN
GUARANI
HAITIAN
HARIJAN
HELLENE
HESSIAN

HITTITE
IBERIAN
IRANIAN
IRISHER
ISHMAEL
ISMAILI
ISRAELI
ITALIAN
ITALIOT
JUDAEAN
KALMUCK
KUWAITI
LAOTIAN
LATVIAN
LLANERO
LOCRIAN
LOMBARD
MALAYAN
MALTESE
MANTUAN
MANXMAN
MESTIZA
MESTIZO
MÉTISSE
MEXICAN
MOABITE
MOHICAN
MOORESS
MORESCO
MORISCO
MULATTA
MULATTO
NEGRESS
NEGRITO
NEGROID
NICAEAN
OSMANLI
OTTOMAN
PAPHIAN
PERSIAN
PUNJABI
PYTHIAN
QUASHEE
QUECHUA
REDSKIN
RIFFIAN
ROOINEK
RUSSIAN
RUTHENE
SAMIOTE
SAMNITE
SAMOYED

SARACEN
SENUSSI
SERBIAN
SHAWNEE
SIAMESE
SIENESE
SLOVENE
SORBIAN
SPARTAN
SWAHILI
SWITZER
SZEKLER
TAGÁLOG
TIBETAN
TSIGANE
TZIGANI
UMBRIAN
VAUDOIS
VEDDOID
WALLOON
ZAMBIAN
ZANTIOT
ZINCALA
ZINCALO
ZINGARA
ZINGARO

8

ALBANIAN
ALGERIAN
ALGERINE
ALSATIAN
AMERICAN
ANDORRAN
ANTIGUAN
ARMENIAN
ARMENOID
ASSYRIAN
ATHENIAN
AUSTRIAN
BALINESE
BATAVIAN
BAVARIAN
BERMUDAN
BISCAYAN
BOEOTIAN
BOHEMIAN
BOLIVIAN
CABOCEER
CAMBRIAN

CANADIAN
CATHAYAN
CHALDEAN
CHEROKEE
CLANSMAN
CONGOESE
CORSICAN
DALESMAN
DEVONIAN
DUTCHMAN
EGYPTIAN
EPHESIAN
ESTONIAN
ETRUSCAN
EURASIAN
EUROPEAN
FANARIOT
FERINGHI
FILIPINO
GALILEAN
GEORGIAN
GHANAIAN
HABITANT
HAWAIIAN
HONDURAN
INDIGENE
IRISHMAN
IROQUOIS
ISLANDER
ISLESMAN
JAMAICAN
JAPANESE
JAVANESE
JEBUSITE
JUGOSLAV
KANARESE
KASHMIRI
LEBANESE
LEVANTER
LIBERIAN
LONDONER
MAEONIAN
MAHRATTA
MALAGASH
MALAGASY
MALAWIAN
MAMELUCO
MANDAEAN
MANDINGO
MILESIAN
MORAVIAN
MOROCCAN

NATIONAL
NAZARENE
NEGRILLO
NEPALESE
NIGERIAN
NORSEMAN
OCTOROON
ORCADIAN
ORIENTAL
OUTCASTE
PALEFACE
PAREOEAN
PARISIAN
PARTHIAN
PEKINESE
PERUVIAN
PHRYGIAN
POLABIAN
POLONIAN
PRUSSIAN
PYRENEAN
QUADROON
ROMANIAN
RUMANIAN
SALOPIAN
SAVOYARD
SCANDIAN
SCOTSMAN
SCYTHIAN
SEMINOLE
SHAGROON
SICILIAN
SICULIAN
SIKELIOT
SILESIAN
SPANIARD
SUDANESE
SYBARITE
TAHITIAN
TEUCRIAN
TOWNSMAN
TUNISIAN
TURKOMAN
TYROLEAN
TYROLESE
TYRRHENE
ULTONIAN
VENETIAN
VIENNESE
VISIGOTH
VOLSCIAN
WARRAGAL

WELSHMAN
YUGOSLAV
ZIGEUNER

9

ABORIGINE
AFRIKANER
AFRO-ASIAN
ALGONQUIN
ARGENTINE
ARMORICAN
BALTOSLAV
BARBADIAN
BERGAMASK
BLACKFOOT
BOSTONIAN
BRAZILIAN
BRITISHER
BULGARIAN
BYZANTINE
CAMBODIAN
CARIBBEAN
CASTILIAN
CAUCASIAN
CEYLONESE
COLOMBIAN
CONGOLESE
DAMASCENE
DRAVIDIAN
EAST-ENDER
EASTERNER
ENGLANDER
ETHIOPIAN
FINLANDER
FRENCHMAN
GALWEGIAN
GRENADIAN
HALF-BREED
HALF-CASTE
HEBRIDEAN
HESPERIAN
HIBERNIAN
HIMYARITE
HOLLANDER
HOTTENTOT
HUNGARIAN
ICELANDER
IROQUOIAN
ISRAELITE

JORDANIAN
LAPLANDER
LONGOBARD
LOWLANDER
MALAYSIAN
MANCUNIAN
MAN OF KENT
MANXWOMAN
MAURITIAN
MISCEGENE
MISCEGINE
MONGOLOID
MUSCOVITE
NABATAEAN
NEW YORKER
NIGRITIAN
NORWEGIAN
OSTROGOTH
PAKISTANI
PEKINGESE
PERISCIAN
PHANARIOT
PLAINSMAN
PROVENÇAL
QUINTROON
RED INDIAN
RHODESIAN
RIPUARIAN
ROUMANIAN
RUTHENIAN
SABELLIAN
SAMARITAN
SARDINIAN
SASSENACH
SCOTCHMAN
SINHALESE
SLAVONIAN
SLOVENIAN
SPRINGBOK
SRI LANKAN
STAGIRITE
TANGERINE
TANZANIAN
TASMANIAN
TRIBESMAN
UKRAINIAN
ULSTERMAN
URUGUAYAN
VARANGIAN
WESTERNER
YIDDISHER
ZANZIBARI

PEOPLE – NATIONALS & TRIBESPEOPLE

10

ABERDONIAN
ABORIGINAL
ABYSSINIAN
ANGLO-SAXON
AUSTRALIAN
AUTOCHTHON
BABYLONIAN
BLACKAMOOR
BOG-TROTTER
CALEDONIAN
CLANSWOMAN
COPPERSKIN
CORNISHMAN
COSTA RICAN
COUNTRYMAN
DUTCHWOMAN
EAST INDIAN
ENGLISHMAN
EURAFRICAN
FLORENTINE
GLASWEGIAN
GUATEMALAN
HANOVERIAN
HIGHLANDER
INDONESIAN
IRISHWOMAN
ISHMAELITE
ISLESWOMAN
KENTISH MAN
LITHUANIAN
MAINLANDER
MELANESIAN
MONÉGASQUE
NEAPOLITAN
NICARAGUAN
NORTHERNER
OCCIDENTAL
PANAMANIAN
PATAGONIAN
PARAGUAYAN
PARISIENNE
PHILISTINE
PHILLIPIAN
PHOENICIAN
POLYNESIAN
POMERANIAN
PORTUGUESE

ROCK-LIZARD
SCILLONIAN
SCOTSWOMAN
SENEGALESE
SERBO-CROAT
SHETLANDER
SOUTHERNER
SQUAREHEAD
THAILANDER
TOWNSWOMAN
TRAMONTANE
TRIDENTINE
TYRRHENIAN
VENEZUELAN
VIETNAMESE
WELSHWOMAN
WEST INDIAN
WOODLANDER
ZAPOROGIAN
ZIMBABWEAN

11

ANGLO-INDIAN
ANGLO-NORMAN
BANGLADESHI
BELORUSSIAN
BLACKFELLOW
CONTINENTAL
FRENCHWOMAN
GALLOVIDIAN
GREENLANDER
HETEROSCIAN
LANCASTRIAN
MARSHLANDER
MAURETANIAN
MELANOCHROI
MICRONESIAN
PALESTINIAN
SCOTCHWOMAN
TRIBESWOMAN
TRINIDADIAN
ULSTERWOMAN
UNTOUCHABLE
WESTPHALIAN
XANTHOCHROI
YUGOSLAVIAN

12

AFRO-AMERICAN
AUSTRALASIAN
CAPE COLOURED
CORNISHWOMAN
COUNTRYWOMAN
CZECHOSLOVAK
ENGLISHWOMAN
EURO-AMERICAN
FRONTIERSMAN
GIBRALTARIAN
LIVERPUDLIAN
NETHERLANDER
NEW ENGLANDER
NEW ZEALANDER
NORTHUMBRIAN
PRE-DRAVIDIAN
QUARTER-BLOOD
ROCK-SCORPION
SAUDI-ARABIAN
SCANDINAVIAN
SCATTERMOUCH
YORKSHIREMAN

13

ANGLO-AMERICAN
BLANKET INDIAN
BLANKET KAFFIR
KNICKERBOCKER
PELOPONNESIAN
PHILADELPHIAN
SERBO-CROATIAN

14

AMERICAN INDIAN
ANGLO-ISRAELITE
FRENCH CANADIAN
SYROPHOENICIAN

15

NORTH-COUNTRYMAN

PEOPLE – NOBILITY

3

DOM
DON
RAS
REX
SIR

4

CZAR
DAME
DOÑA
DUKE
EARL
GRAF
HEIR
INCA
KHAN
KING
LADY
LORD
PEER
RAJA
RANA
RANI
SHAH
TSAR

5

ARD-RI
BARON
BEGUM
BOYAR
COUNT
LAIRD
LIEGE
MIRZA
NAWAB
NEGUS
NIZAM
NOBLE
OMRAH
QUEEN
RAJAH
RANEE
ROYAL
THANE

6

DAIMIO
ERRANT
GRÄFIN
JUNKER
KAISER
KNIGHT
LUCUMO
MIKADO
PESHWA
PRINCE
RAJPUT
REGENT
REGINA
SHERIF
SHOGUN
SQUIRE
SULTAN
VIDAME
YEOMAN

7

ARD-RIGH
ARMIGER
BARONET
CONSORT
CZARINA
DAUPHIN
DOWAGER
DUCHESS
ELECTOR
EMPEROR
EMPRESS
ESQUIRE
GRANDEE
HIDALGA
HIDALGO
INFANTA
INFANTE
KARLING
KINGLET
LAW-LORD
MARQUIS
MONARCH
PALADIN
PEERESS
PHARAOH
ROYALET
ROYALTY

TITULAR
TSARINA

8

ARCHDUKE
ATHELING
BANNERET
BARONESS
CO-REGENT
COUNTESS
DUKELING
EUPATRID
FAINÉANT
HOSPODAR
INTERREX
KINGLING
LIFE-PEER
MAHARAJA
MAHARANI
MARCHESA
MARCHESE
MARGRAVE
MARQUESS
MARQUISE
MONSIEUR
NOBILITY
NOBLEMAN
OVERKING
PADISHAH
PALATINE
PRINCESS
QUEENLET
SEIGNEUR
TSARITSA
VISCOUNT

9

BRETWALDA
CESAREVNA
ELECTRESS
FREELANCE
GRAND DUKE
LANDGRAVE
LIEGE-LORD
MAGNIFICO
MAHARAJAH
MAHARANEE
PALSGRAVE

PATRICIAN
PRINCEKIN
PRINCELET
SOVEREIGN
SULTANESS
WALDGRAVE

10

ADELANTADO
ARISTOCRAT
BARONETESS
DAUPHINESS
NOBLEWOMAN
PRIEST-KING
PRINCELING
RHINEGRAVE
TSAREVITCH

11

ARCHDUCHESS
ARISTOCRACY
CESAREVITCH
CROWNED HEAD
CROWN PRINCE
EARL MARSHAL
LANDGRAVINE
LIFE-PEERESS
MARCHIONESS
MONSEIGNEUR
PALSGRAVINE
QUEEN-MOTHER
QUEEN-REGENT
VISCOUNTESS
WALDGRAVINE

12

EARL PALATINE
GRAND DUCHESS
HEIR-APPARENT
KNIGHT-ERRANT
PRINCE-BISHOP
PRINCE-REGENT
QUEEN-CONSORT
QUEEN-DOWAGER
QUEEN-REGNANT
RHINEGRAVINE
TEMPORAL PEER

PEOPLE – NOBILITY

13
COUNT PALATINE
PRINCE-CONSORT
PRINCESS-ROYAL
SPIRITUAL PEER

14
DOWAGER DUCHESS
KNIGHT-BACHELOR
KNIGHT-BANNERET
PRINCE-IMPERIAL

15
HEIR-PRESUMPTIVE

PEOPLE – PATIENTS

4
CASE
MUTE

NYMPHO
VECTOR
VICTIM

5
AMENT
DOPER
DUMMY
DWARF
HEADS
IDIOT
LAZAR
LEPER
MYOPE
MYOPS

6
ADDICT
ALBINO
CRETIN
DURGAN
EXTERN
HECTIC
INMATE
JUNKIE
MADMAN
MANIAC
MELANO
MIDGET
MONGOL
MYOPIC

7
AMPUTEE
BLEEDER
CARRIER
CONTACT
CRIPPLE
CYCLOID
DEVIATE
HOP-HEAD
INVALID
LAMETER
LUNATIC
MANIKIN
MATTOID
MINIKIN
PATIENT
PHOBIST
RALLIER
SCIATIC
SPASTIC
SUBJECT
TALIPED

8
ACID-HEAD
ALLOPATH
AMNESIAC
ANOREXIC

APHASIAC
ATHETOID
BLINKARD
BLUE BABY
CASUALTY
DEAF-MUTE
DÉTRAQUÉ
DIABETIC
DYSLEXIC
IMBECILE
MANNIKIN
NEURITIC
NEUROTIC
PRESBYTE
RELAPSER
SCHIZOID
SEMI-MUTE

9
ALCOHOLIC
ARTHRITIC
ASTHMATIC
BEDLAMITE
DÉTRAQUÉE
DICHROMAT
DOPE-FIEND
DRUG-FIEND
DYSPEPTIC
EPILEPTIC
EUNUCHOID
GERIATRIC
GUINEA-PIG
INCURABLE
IN-PATIENT

INSOMNIAC
MAINLINER
MONGOLOID
NARCOTIST
NEUROPATH
NYCTALOPS
PARALYTIC
PARANOIAC
PELLAGRIN
PHRENETIC
PRESBYOPE
PSYCHOTIC
RHEUMATIC
SILICOTIC
SOCIOPATH

10
DRUG-ADDICT
DYSTHYMIAC
HEMIPLEGIC
HOMONCULUS
ISCHURETIC
NYMPHOLEPT
OPIUM-EATER
OPSOMANIAC
OUT-PATIENT
PARAPLEGIC
PHOTOPHOBE
PSYCHOPATH
SOMNAMBULE
SYPHILITIC
THEOMANIAC
ZOOPHILIST

11

ANTHOMANIAC
CONSUMPTIVE
EROTOMANIAC
GLUE-SNIFFER
GYNAECOMAST
HEBEPHRENIC
LYCANTHROPE
MELANCHOLIC
MICROCEPHAL
MONOCHROMAT
MYTHOMANIAC
OPIUM-SMOKER
SLEEP-WALKER
THEOPHOBIST
TOXIPHOBIAC
WALKING-CASE

12

CONVALESCENT
DYSAESTHETIC
ETHEROMANIAC
HAEMOPHILIAC
HEBEPHRENIAC
KLEPTOMANIAC
MEGALOMANIAC
MELANCHOLIAC
NYMPHOMANIAC
SCHIZOPHRENE
SOMNAMBULANT
SOMNAMBULIST

13

DEXTROCARDIAC
HYPOCHONDRIAC

MENTAL PATIENT
MOUTH-BREATHER
NEURASTHENIAC
SCHIZOPHRENIC
SOMNAMBULATOR
STRETCHER-CASE

14

HYPOCHONDRIAST
MORPHINOMANIAC
VALETUDINARIAN

15

MANIC-DEPRESSIVE

PEOPLE – RELATIVES & FRIENDS

3

AMI
BUD
COZ
DAD
JOY
KIN
MAN
MUM
NAN
OOM
PAL
POP
SIB
SIS
SON

4

ALLY
AMIE

AUNT
BABY
BEAU
BRER
CHUM
DEAR
FOLK
FRAU
GRAN
HEIR
LASS
LOVE
MAMA
MATE
MOLL
NANA
PAPA
PARD
QUAD
QUIN
SIRE
TRIN
TWIN

WARD
WIFE

5

BELLE
BRIDE
BUDDY
CHILD
CHUCK
CRONY
CULLY
DADDY
DEARY
DOTER
DUTCH
FEMME
FLAME
FOLKS
GOODY
GROOM
HAREM

HONEY
HUBBY
IN-LAW
ISSUE
LOVER
MAMMA
MAMMY
MATER
MUMMY
NANNA
NANNY
NIECE
PATER
POPPA
ROMEO
SCION
SONNY
SPARK
SPRIG
SQUAW
SUGAR
SWAIN
SWEET

TRINE
UNCLE
VROUW
WIDOW
WOMAN
WOOER

6

AGNATE
AUNTIE
BEL AMI
BON AMI
CHUMMY
COBBER
COHEIR
COUPLE
COUSIN
CUPMAN
DEARIE
ELOPER
EPIGON

FAMILY
FATHER
FELLOW
FIANCÉ
FRIEND
GODSON
GRANNY
MARROW
MISSUS
MOTHER
NEPHEW
OLD MAN
PARENT
POPPET
RELICT
SISTER
SPOUSE
STEADY
SUITOR

PEOPLE – RELATIVES & FRIENDS

7

ACUSHLA
ADMIRER
AMORINO
AMORIST
AMOROSA
AMOROSO
BASTARD
BELOVED
BEST MAN
BROTHER
COGNATE
COMPANY
COMPEER
COMRADE
CONSORT
DARLING
DEAREST
DON JUAN
DOWAGER
FIANCÉE
GALLANT
GENITOR
GOODMAN
GRANDAD
GRANDMA
GRANDPA
HEIRESS
HUSBAND
KINDRED
KINFOLK
KINSMAN
NAME-SON
OLD LADY
PARDNER
PARTNER
PROGENY
SIBLING
SPONSOR
STEPSON
TRIPLET
WIDOWER

8

AMORETTO
ANCESTOR
BEGETTER
BENEDICK

CASANOVA
CHILDREN
CICISBEO
CONFRÈRE
DAUGHTER
DECAPLET
DIGAMIST
ESPOUSER
FAMILIAR
FANCY MAN
FOREBEAR
FOSTERER
GENERANT
GENETRIX
GODCHILD
GOODWIFE
GRANDSON
GUARDIAN
HELPMATE
HELPMEET
HENCHMAN
INTENDED
INTIMATE
KINSFOLK
LADY-LOVE
LOTHARIO
MESSMATE
MISTRESS
NEWLY-WED
NONUPLET
OCTUPLET
OLD FLAME
OLD WOMAN
PARAMOUR
PIRRAURU
PLAYMATE
PRECIOUS
RELATION
RELATIVE
ROMANCER
ROOM-MATE
SHIPMATE
SIDE-KICK
SON-IN-LAW
SUITRESS
TALLYMAN
TEAM-MATE
TOVARISH
TRIPLING
TRUE-LOVE
WAR-WIDOW
WORK-MATE

9

BEDFELLOW
BELLE AMIE
BELLE-MÈRE
BETROTHED
BOYFRIEND
BRIDE'S-MAN
BULLY-ROOK
CLASSMATE
COHABITEE
COHEIRESS
COMMENSAL
COMPANION
CONFIDANT
DEPENDANT
DREAMBOAT
ENAMORADO
FAMILY MAN
FOSTER-SON
GENERATOR
GODFATHER
GODMOTHER
GODPARENT
GOLF-WIDOW
GRAND-AUNT
GRANDMAMA
GRANDPAPA
GREAT-AUNT
GROOMSMAN
HALF-BLOOD
HOUSE-MATE
INAMORATA
INAMORATO
KID-SISTER
KINSWOMAN
LOVE-MAKER
MATRIARCH
OFFSPRING
PATRIARCH
PEN-FRIEND
PEW-FELLOW
PROCREANT
SEPTUPLET
SEXTUPLET
STEPCHILD
VALENTINE

10

BEST FRIEND

BETTER HALF
BRIDEGROOM
BRIDE'S-MAID
COHABITANT
CONFIDANTE
CONNECTION
DESCENDANT
FANCY WOMAN
FELLOW-HEIR
FOREFATHER
FOSTERLING
FULL-COUSIN
FULL-SISTER
GENERATRIX
GIRLFRIEND
GOOD-FELLOW
GRANDCHILD
GRAND-NIECE
GRAND-UNCLE
GRASS-WIDOW
GREAT-NIECE
GREAT-UNCLE
HALF-SISTER
KID-BROTHER
KITH AND KIN
MAVOURNEEN
NEXT FRIEND
PIGEON-PAIR
PLAYFELLOW
PROCREATOR
PROGENITOR
QUADRUPLET
QUINTUPLET
ROOM-FELLOW
SCHOOL-MATE
SECOND SELF
STEPFATHER
STEPMOTHER
STEP-PARENT
STEPSISTER
SWEETHEART
TALLYWOMAN
TWIN-SISTER
WORK-FELLOW

11

BOSOM FRIEND
CLOSE FRIEND
CONFEDERATE
CROSS-COUSIN

FATHER-IN-LAW
FIRST COUSIN
FOSTER-CHILD
FULL-BROTHER
GODDAUGHTER
GRANDFATHER
GRANDMOTHER
GRAND-NEPHEW
GRANDPARENT
GREAT-NEPHEW
HALF-BROTHER
HEMPEN WIDOW
HONEYMOONER
HOUSE-FATHER
HOUSE-MOTHER
MOTHER-IN-LAW
PROCHAIN AMI
PROGENITRIX
SIAMESE TWIN
SISTER-IN-LAW
STEPBROTHER
TWIN-BROTHER

12

ACQUAINTANCE
BLOOD-BROTHER

BROTHER-IN-LAW
COUSIN GERMAN
FAMILY CIRCLE
FOSTER-FATHER
FOSTER-MOTHER
FOSTER-PARENT
FOSTER-SISTER
GANDER-MOONER
ILLEGITIMATE
MUTUAL FRIEND
POT-COMPANION
PROGENITRESS
SCHOOL-FRIEND
SECOND COUSIN
SIAMESE TWINS
STEPDAUGHTER

13

BLOOD-RELATION
BLOOD-RELATIVE
BOON COMPANION
BROTHER-GERMAN
COUNTRY COUSIN
DAUGHTER-IN-LAW
FLESH AND BLOOD
FOSTER-BROTHER

GANGSTER'S MOLL
GRANDCHILDREN
GRANDDAUGHTER
GREAT-GRANDSON
GUARDIAN ANGEL
IDENTICAL TWIN
KISSING COUSIN
MATERFAMILIAS
PATERFAMILIAS

14

FOSTER-DAUGHTER
IDENTICAL TWINS
PARABIOTIC TWIN
WIDOW-BEWITCHED

15

DRINKING PARTNER
GREAT-GRANDCHILD
ONE-PARENT FAMILY
PARABIOTIC TWINS
STABLE COMPANION
UNMARRIED MOTHER

PEOPLE – SERVICES PEOPLE

3	**4**		**5**			
		POST		GHAZI	PADRE	SQUAD
		SALT		GUARD	PARTY	STAFF
ACE	ARMY	SIKH	ANZAC	HORSE	PILOT	TAXIS
ATS	CREW	SWAD	BOSUN	JAWAN	PIPER	TOMMY
COX	EXON	UNIT	BUFFS	JOLLY	POILU	TROOP
ERK	FOOT	WAAC	CADET	JONTY	POINT	TURCO
GOB	JACK	WAAF	CADRE	LIMEY	PONGO	UHLAN
MAN	MATE	WARD	CHIPS	MAJOR	PROVO	
MEN	NAIK	WING	CORPS	MATLO	RANKS	
NCO	NAVY	WRAC	DRAFT	MIDDY	SEPOY	**6**
RAF	PARA	WRAF	FIFER	MINER	SOWAR	
TAR	PEON	WREN	FLIER	NIZAM	SPAHI	AIRMAN

PEOPLE – SERVICES PEOPLE

ALPINO
AMAZON
ARCHER
ARNAUT
ASKARI
ATAMAN
BATMAN
BOMBER
BOWMAN
BUFFER
BUGLER
BUKSHI
COHORT
CORNET
DETAIL
ENSIGN
ESCORT
FORCES
GALOOT
GUARDS
GUIDON
GUNNER
GURKHA
HUSSAR
JAUNTY
LANCER
LASCAR
LEGION
LOOPER
MARINE
MARKER
MARQUE
MASTER
NON-COM
OLD MAN
PATROL
PATRON
PICKET
PULTUN
PURSER
RANGER
RANKER
RATING
RED-CAP
RED-HAT
REEFER
REGENT
REITER
RIGGER
ROOKIE
SAILOR
SAPPER

SEABEE
SEA-DOG
SEAMAN
SENTRY
SERANG
SIRDAR
SKYMAN
SNIPER
SNOTTY
SPARKS
SQUARE
STOKER
SWADDY
TINDAL
TOPMAN
TROOPS
WAR-DOG
YEOMAN
ZOUAVE

7

ADMIRAL
AIR-CREW
AVIATOR
BERSERK
BILLMAN
BRIGADE
CAPTAIN
CAVALRY
CHINDIT
COLONEL
COMPANY
CO-PILOT
COSSACK
DRAFTEE
DRAGOON
DRUMMER
ECHELON
FEDAYEE
FOOTMAN
GENERAL
HOPLITE
HUSSARS
JACKMAN
JACK-TAR
JEMADAR
KAVASSE
LASHKAR
MANIPLE
MARINER

MARSHAL
MATELOT
MILITIA
NAVARCH
OFFICER
OLD SALT
ORDERLY
PANDOUR
PATROON
PELTAST
PHALANX
PIKEMAN
PIONEER
PLATOON
PRICKER
PRIVATE
RECRUIT
REDCOAT
REGULAR
SADDLER
SEA-LORD
SEBUNDY
SECTION
SHIPMAN
SKIPPER
SOLDADO
SOLDIER
SOWARRY
SUBADAR
SURGEON
SWITZER
TERRIER
TROOPER
VEDETTE
VETERAN
WAISTER
WARRIOR

8

ADJUTANT
AIR FORCE
AIRWOMAN
ARMOURER
AVIATRIX
BANDSMAN
BATWOMAN
BIMBASHI
BOSTANGI
BRASS HAT
CAMISARD

CAVALIER
CHAPLAIN
CHASSEUR
COMMANDO
CORPORAL
COXSWAIN
CRUSADER
DECURION
DIVISION
DOG'S-BODY
DOUGHBOY
ENGINEER
FOREWARD
FUGLEMAN
FUSILIER
GARRISON
GREYCOAT
GUNLAYER
HAVILDAR
HELMSMAN
HORSEMAN
INFANTRY
IRONSIDE
JANIZARY
KILLADAR
LEADSMAN
LINESMAN
LOYALIST
MAMELUKE
MARKSMAN
MESSMATE
OBSERVER
OUTGUARD
OUTRIDER
PARTISAN
PIOU-PIOU
REAR RANK
RED-SHIRT
REGIMENT
RESERVES
RIFLEMAN
RISALDAR
SEACUNNY
SEAFARER
SEA FORCE
SENTINEL
SERGEANT
SHIPMATE
SILLADAR
SNOWDROP
SOLDIERY
SPEARMAN

SQUADDIE
SQUADRON
STICK-MAN
STRELITZ
TETRARCH
TIMARIOT
TIMONEER
TOP BRASS
VANGUARD
WARD-ROOM
WAR-HORSE
WHEELMAN
YEOMANRY

9

AIR-GUNNER
ARMY CORPS
ARTIFICER
ARTILLERY
ASTRONAUT
AUXILIARY
BATTALION
BOATSWAIN
BRIGADIER
CANNONEER
CENTURION
COMBATANT
COMMANDER
COMMODORE
CONSCRIPT
COSMONAUT
DESERT RAT
DRUM-MAJOR
ESTAFETTE
FIFE-MAJOR
FIRST MATE
FOOT-GUARD
FREELANCE
GALIONGEE
GAULEITER
GOLDSTICK
GRENADIER
GUARDSMAN
GUERRILLA
HOME GUARD
IRREGULAR
KSHATRIYA
LANCE-JACK
LAND FORCE
LEGIONARY

LIFEGUARD
LOWER DECK
LUFTWAFFE
MAN-AT-ARMS
MAQUISARD
MERCENARY
MUSKETEER
NAVIGATOR
NUMBER ONE
OUT-SENTRY
PAYMASTER
PIPE-MAJOR
PISTOLEER
PRIVATEER
PRIZE-CREW
REAR-GUARD
RECRUITER
RED DEVILS
RESERVIST
SAILOR-MAN
SERREFILE
SHELLBACK
SIGNALLER
SIGNALMAN
SKY-TROOPS
STEERSMAN
SUBALTERN
TARGETEER
TASK FORCE
TASK GROUP
THIRD MATE
TORPEDOER
TRIERARCH
TURCOPOLE
VEXILLARY
VOLTIGEUR
VOLUNTEER
WEHRMACHT

10

ABLE SEAMAN
AFTER-GUARD
AIDE-DE-CAMP
AIR-MARSHAL
AIR-OFFICER
ARMED FORCE
BLUEJACKET
BOMBARDIER
BROWNSHIRT
BUNDESWEHR

CADET CORPS
CAMEL CORPS
CAMERONIAN
CAMPAIGNER
CARABINIER
CAVALRYMAN
COMMANDANT
CUIRASSIER
DETACHMENT
FOEDERATUS
GALLOGLASS
GROUND CREW
GUN-CAPTAIN
HACKBUTEER
HALBERDIER
HIGH-RANKER
HORSE-GUARD
JAVELIN-MAN
LANSQUENET
LIBERTY-MAN
LIEUTENANT
LIGHT-HORSE
MARTIALIST
MIDSHIPMAN
MILITIAMAN
OLD SOLDIER
OTHER RANKS
PARATROOPS
PRAETORIAN
REAR-GUNNER
RIFLE CORPS
RITTMASTER
SEA-CAPTAIN
SEA-SOLDIER
SECOND MATE
SERVICEMAN
SHIP-MASTER
STAFF CORPS
SUBMARINER
TAIL-GUNNER
THE HEAVIES
TIRAILLEUR
TORPEDOIST
VOETGANGER
WARDMASTER

11

AIR-MECHANIC
ARMY OFFICER
ARQUEBUSIER

ARTILLERIST
BASHI-BAZOUK
BEACH-MASTER
BERSAGLIERI
BLACK-AND-TAN
CASTLE-GUARD
COLOUR-PARTY
CONDOTTIERE
CONTINENTAL
CORPS D'ÉLITE
CROSSBOWMAN
CULVERINEER
FIELD-CORNET
FIRING PARTY
FIRING SQUAD
FLAG-CAPTAIN
FLAG-OFFICER
FLYING CORPS
FLYING PARTY
FOOT-SOLDIER
FOREMASTMAN
GALLOWGLASS
HIGH ADMIRAL
HORSE GUARDS
INFANTRYMAN
LANDSKNECHT
LEATHERNECK
LEGIONNAIRE
MITRAILLEUR
PARATROOPER
PICKET-GUARD
PORT-ADMIRAL
POST-CAPTAIN
QUARTER-JACK
RANK AND FILE
REAR-ADMIRAL
ROYAL MARINE
SHOCK-TROOPS
STORM-TROOPS
TERRITORIAL
TOMMY ATKINS
TOP-SERGEANT
VEXILLATION
VICE-ADMIRAL
VICE-MARSHAL

12

ADVANCE GUARD
AIR-COMMODORE
AIRCRAFTSMAN

239

PEOPLE –

ARTILLERY-MAN
AWKWARD SQUAD
BRASS-BOUNDER
BRIGADE-MAJOR
FATIGUE-PARTY
FIELD-MARSHAL
FIELD OFFICER
FIRST OFFICER
GENERAL STAFF
GROUP-CAPTAIN
HORSE SOLDIER
MAJOR-GENERAL
MAN-OF-WAR'S-MAN
MASTER-AT-ARMS
MILITARY BAND
MOUSQUETAIRE
MUSTER-MASTER
NAVAL BRIGADE
NAVAL OFFICER
NON-COMBATANT
NON-EFFICIENT
PETTY OFFICER
PILOT-OFFICER
POWDER-MONKEY
QUARTER-GUARD
RECONNOITRER
SALVAGE CORPS
SHARPSHOOTER
SHIELD-BEARER
SHIP'S CAPTAIN
SQUARE-BASHER
STAFF-OFFICER
STORM-TROOPER
THIRD OFFICER
TRUMPET-MAJOR
WATCH-OFFICER

13

ARMY COMMANDER
BEETLE-CRUSHER
BRANCH-OFFICER
BREVET COLONEL

DESPATCH-RIDER
DISPATCH-RIDER
DRILL-SERGEANT
FLYING OFFICER
FOREIGN LEGION
KAMIKAZE PILOT
LANCE-CORPORAL
LANCE-SERGEANT
LEADING SEAMAN
LIGHT-HORSEMAN
LIGHT INFANTRY
MACHINE-GUNNER
MASTER MARINER
NATIONAL GUARD
PRISONER OF WAR
QUARTER-GUNNER
QUARTERMASTER
SAILING-MASTER
SCHUTZSTAFFEL
SECOND OFFICER
SENIOR OFFICER
SENIOR SERVICE
SERGEANT-MAJOR
STAFF-SERGEANT
STORMING PARTY
SUBLIEUTENTANT
WING-COMMANDER

14

AIRCRAFTSWOMAN
AIR VICE-MARSHAL
BOATSWAIN'S MATE
CAPTAIN-GENERAL
COLONEL-IN-CHIEF
COLOUR-SERGEANT
COMPANY OFFICER
FLAG-LIEUTENANT
FLIGHT-ENGINEER
FLIGHT-SERGEANT
GENERAL OFFICER
HORSE ARTILLERY
LIAISON OFFICER

MASTER-SERGEANT
MEDICAL OFFICER
MILITARY POLICE
ORDERLY OFFICER
ORDINARY SEAMAN
PANZER DIVISION
PROVOST-MARSHAL
ROYAL ARTILLERY
ROYAL TANK CORPS
SHIP'S CARPENTER
SQUADRON-LEADER
STANDARD-BEARER
STURMABTEILUNG
URBAN GUERRILLA
WARRANT-OFFICER

15

ADJUTANT-GENERAL
AIR CHIEF-MARSHAL
AIR FORCE OFFICER
BOARDING-OFFICER
FIRST LIEUTENANT
GAZETTED OFFICER
GENTLEMAN-AT-ARMS
HOUSEHOLD TROOPS
LANCE-BOMBARDIER
LORD HIGH ADMIRAL
ORDERLY CORPORAL
ORDERLY SERGEANT
PARACHUTE TROOPS
PLATOON SERGEANT
PRAETORIAN GUARD
PROTOSPATHARIUS
PROVOST-SERGEANT
QUARTERMISTRESS
SADDLER-CORPORAL
SADDLER-SERGEANT
SECOND-IN-COMMAND
SERGEANT-DRUMMER
STRETCHER-BEARER

PEOPLE – SOUNDMAKERS

5

CRIER
PULER
RAVER
SAYER
SNEAK

6

ARGUER
BARKER
BAWLER
CALLER
CHIDER
CURSER
GABBER
GAS-BAG
GASCON
GASPER
GOSSIP
HOWLER
HUMMER
IDOIST
KEENER
LISPER
MOANER
MOOTER
ORATOR
OVATOR
PRATER
PUFFER
QUOTER
RANTER
RAPPER
RINGER
ROARER
SIGHER
SINGER
SNORER
SOBBER
STATER
TALKER
TAPPER
TOLLER
VOICER
WAILER
WEEPER
WHINER
YAPPER

7

BABBLER
BERATER
BOASTER
CACKLER
CHEERER
CLACKER
CLAPPER
CLICKER
COUGHER
CROAKER
DRAWLER
GABBLER
GIGGLER
GROANER
GROWLER
GRUNTER
HECKLER
JANGLER
LAUGHER
MOUTHER
MUMBLER
OPPOSER
ORATRIX
PHRASER
PRAISER
RECITER
RELATER
REPLIER
SAGAMAN
SCOLDER
SHOUTER
SNAPPER
SNARLER
SNEEZER
SNORTER
SPEAKER
SPIELER
SPOUTER
STENTOR
SWEARER
TATTLER
THUMPER
UTTERER
WARBLER
WHEEZER
WHOOPER
WIND-BAG

8

AFFIRMER
ANSWERER
ASSERTER
ASSERTOR
BANTERER
BELLOWER
BIG-MOUTH
BRAGGART
CAVILLER
CONFEREE
EULOGIST
EXHORTER
GAMMONER
HOMILIST
IMPUGNER
INFORMER
JABBERER
MURMURER
MUTTERER
NARRATOR
NATTERER
OBSERVER
OBJECTOR
OPPUGNER
PALTERER
PLEONAST
POLEMIST
PRATTLER
PREACHER
QUAVERER
QUIBBLER
REMARKER
RETORTER
RHAPSODE
SCREAMER
SHRIEKER
SNUFFLER
SQUALLER
SQUAWKER
SQUEAKER
SQUEALER
TELL-TALE
THRUMMER
TITTERER
TWADDLER
TWATTLER
VOCALIST
WHISTLER
YODELLER

9

ADDRESSER
ADDRESSOR
ANNOUNCER
APOLOGIST
APPLAUDER
BARRACKER
CHATTERER
CLAMOURER
CLATTERER
DECLAIMER
DRIVELLER
EXPOSITOR
EXPOUNDER
GAINSAYER
HARANGUER
JARGONIST
LOUD-MOUTH
MAUNDERER
MISQUOTER
PALAVERER
RACONTEUR
RENOUNCER
SCREECHER
SLANDERER
SNIGGERER
SNIVELLER
SPUTTERER
SQUELCHER
STAMMERER
STUTTERER
THUNDERER
TWITTERER
WHIMPERER
WHISPERER

10

CHATTERBOX
COLLOCUTOR
COLLOQUIST
DECLAIMANT
DIATRIBIST
DISCURSIST
ELABORATOR
ENUNCIATOR
EXPATIATOR
FILIBUSTER
GASCONADER
LUCUBRATOR

PEOPLE – SOUNDMAKERS

MONOLOGIST
ORTHOEPIST
PANEGYRIST
PARABOLIST
PERSIFLEUR
POLEMICIST
PRATTLE-BOX
PROCLAIMER
PROLOCUTOR
PRONOUNCER
RACONTEUSE
RHAPSODIST
SPLUTTERER
SYMPOSIAST
TALE-BEARER
TALE-TELLER

DISSERTATOR
ESPERANTIST
PROLOCUTRIX
PROMULGATOR
RHETORICIAN
SPEECH-MAKER
SPELL-BINDER
STERNUTATOR
STORY-TELLER
THEOLOGISER
VITUPERATOR
VOCIFERATOR

REMONSTRATOR
SLANG-WHANGER
SOMNILOQUIST

13

COLLOQUIALIST
FIDDLE-FADDLER
RECITATIONIST
TITTLE-TATTLER
VALEDICTORIAN
VERNACULARIST

11

ARTICULATOR
BRAGGADOCIO

12

BLABBERMOUTH
COMMUNICATOR
CONFABULATOR
EXPOSTULATOR
FILIBUSTERER
INTERLOCUTOR

14

INTERLOCUTRESS

15

CONVERSATIONIST

PEOPLE – SPORTSPEOPLE

3

ACE
COX
GUN
OAR
PRO
SUB

4

BACK
BLUE
COLT
CREW
HALF
PACK
PINK
PONE

PROP
ROPE
SEED
SHOT
SIDE
SKIP
SLIP
TAIL
TEAM

5

BOXER
CHAMP
CHEAT
COACH
COVER
DIVER
DUMMY

EIGHT
HIKER
JÄGER
JUDGE
LOSER
MAKER
MID-ON
MILER
OMBRE
PACER
POINT
RACER
RIDER
RIVAL
ROVER
ROWER
SCOUT
SKIER
SLIPS
SQUAD

6

ANCHOR
ANGLER
ARCHER
ATTACK
BACKER
BATTER
BEATER
BETTER
BIDDER
BILKER
BOATER
BOWLER
BOWMAN
CADDIE
CAMPER
CENTRE
CHASER
CUEIST

CURLER
DEALER
DRIVER
DRY BOB
ELEVEN
ÉQUIPE
ESPADA
FENCER
FISHER
FOWLER
GILLIE
GOALIE
GOLFER
HAND-IN
HAWKER
HEELER
HITTER
HOOKER
HUDDLE
HUNTER

HURLER
JOCKEY
JOGGER
JUMPER
JUNIOR
KEEPER
KICKER
LEAPER
LINE-UP
LOBBER
LONG-ON
LOOPER
LUNGER
MARKER
MID-OFF
NOVICE
OPENER
PLAYER
PUNTER
PUTTER

RABBIT
RUNNER
SCORER
SEAMER
SECOND
SERVER
SKATER
STAYER
STROKE
SURFER
TORERO
UMPIRE
VICTOR
WALKER
WET BOB
WINGER
WINNER

7

ALSO-RAN
AMATEUR
ATHLETE
BACK ROW
BASEMAN
BATSMAN
BATTERY
BAULKER
BEAGLER
BLUFFER
BOATMAN
BRIDLER
BRUISER
CAPTAIN
CATCHER
CLIMBER
COURSER
CYCLIST
DEFENCE
ENTRANT
FIELDER
FIGHTER
FINE LEG
FLY-HALF
FORWARD
GAMBLER
GHILLIE
GYMNAST
HAND-OUT
HARRIER
HURDLER

JOUSTER
LONG-LEG
LONG-OFF
MARSHAL
MATADOR
MONTERO
OARSMAN
PARTNER
PICADOR
PITCHER
POLOIST
QUOITER
RALLIER
RAMBLER
REFEREE
RESERVE
RODSTER
SAMNITE
SHOOTER
SKIPPER
SKIRTER
SLEDGER
SLOGGER
SPARRER
SPINNER
SPOORER
STALKER
STARTER
STEWARD
STOPPER
STRIKER
STUMPER
SURFMAN
SWEEPER
SWIMMER
TACKLER
TAIL-END
THROWER
TRAINER
VAULTER
WAGERER
YACHTER

8

ABSEILER
AQUANAUT
ATTACKER
CANOEIST
CHAMPION
CHASSEUR

CORRIVAL
COXSWAIN
CRAGSMAN
DECLARER
DEFENDER
DRIBBLER
FALCONER
FINALIST
FINESSER
FOURSOME
FRONT ROW
FULL-BACK
HALF-BACK
HALF-BLUE
HORSEMAN
HUNTRESS
HUNTSMAN
LEFT-BACK
LEFT-HALF
LINESMAN
LONG-SLIP
LONG-STOP
MARKSMAN
OFFICIAL
OLYMPIAN
OPPONENT
OUTFIELD
OUTSIDER
PISCATOR
POSSIBLE
POTHOLER
PROBABLE
PUGILIST
PUNTSMAN
RABBITER
REINSMAN
RUNNER-UP
SELECTOR
SHIKAREE
SHORT LEG
SHUFFLER
SKY-DIVER
SNIGGLER
SOUTHPAW
SPRINTER
STAND-OFF
TEAM-MATE
THIRD MAN
TOREADOR
UNDERDOG
VICTRESS
VOLLEYER

WATERMAN
WING-HALF
WRESTLER

9

ANCHORMAN
ARCHERESS
BLACK BELT
BROWN BELT
COMBATANT
CONTENDER
CRICKETER
CUP-WINNER
DRAG RACER
EIGHTSMAN
FAVOURITE
FIELDSMAN
FIRST SLIP
FISHERMAN
FLY-FISHER
FLYWEIGHT
FOX-HUNTER
FREE-DIVER
GLADIATOR
HOT RODDER
ICE-SKATER
INFIELDER
JUDICATOR
LAMPADIST
LINE-JUDGE
LONG-FIELD
NAVIGATOR
NET-PLAYER
OARSWOMAN
PACEMAKER
PISCATRIX
POT-HUNTER
PRE-EMPTOR
QUALIFIER
RELAY TEAM
RETIARIUS
RETRIEVER
SCRUM-HALF
SEA-ANGLER
SHAMATEUR
SHORT-SLIP
SHORT-STOP
SKIN-DIVER
SKY-JUMPER
SPORTSMAN

243

PEOPLE – SPORTSPEOPLE

SQUARE LEG
STROKE-OAR
SWORDSMAN
TACTICIAN
TAIL-ENDER
THIRD SLIP
THROWSTER
TOURNEYER
TRAVERSER
WHIPPER-IN
WHITE BELT
YACHTSMAN

10

ALL-ROUNDER
AQUAPLANER
BACK-MARKER
BALLOONIST
BASEBALLER
CARD-PLAYER
CENTRE-BACK
CENTRE-HALF
CHALLENGER
COMPETITOR
CONTESTANT
CORINTHIAN
COVER POINT
DART-PLAYER
DECATHLETE
DICE-PLAYER
EQUESTRIAN
EXTRA COVER
FAST BOWLER
FOOTBALLER
FORE-CADDIE
FREE-FISHER
GOALKEEPER
GOAL-KICKER
GROUNDSMAN
GYMNASIAST
HANG-GLIDER
HIGH JUMPER
HORSEWOMAN
INSIDE LEFT
LEFT-HANDER
LEFT-WINGER
LION-HUNTER
LONG JUMPER
MARATHONER
MARKSWOMAN

OPPOSITION
OUTFIELDER
OVERBIDDER
PACE-SETTER
PIG-STICKER
POOL-PLAYER
SCRIMMAGER
SCRUMMAGER
SCUBA-DIVER
SEAM BOWLER
SECOND SLIP
SHOWJUMPER
SHOT-PUTTER
SILLY MID-ON
SILLY POINT
SLOW BOWLER
SPIN BOWLER
STEWARDESS
STRIKER-OUT
SUBSTITUTE
TENT-PEGGER
TOBOGGANER
TOUCH-JUDGE
TRANSFEREE
TWELFTH MAN
WATER-SKIER
WIND-SURFER

11

ADJUDICATOR
BULLFIGHTER
CHEER-LEADER
CHESS-PLAYER
CUP-FINALIST
DEERSTALKER
FRONT-RUNNER
GRAND MASTER
GROUND STAFF
HEAVYWEIGHT
HURDLE-RACER
INSIDE RIGHT
LIGHTWEIGHT
MOUNTAINEER
OUTSIDE LEFT
PANCRATIAST
PARACHUTIST
PARTICIPANT
PENTATHLETE
PIGEON-FLIER

PINCH-HITTER
POLE-VAULTER
PRIZE-WINNER
PROP-FORWARD
RALLY-DRIVER
RIGHT-HANDER
RIGHT-WINGER
ROCK-CLIMBER
RUGBY-PLAYER
SILLY MID-OFF
SLIP-FIELDER
SPORTSWOMAN
STONEWALLER
SWORDPLAYER
TOBOGGANIST
TOXOPHILITE
UNDERBIDDER
VICE-CAPTAIN
WHIST-PLAYER

12

BANDERILLERO
BANTAM-WEIGHT
BOTTLE-HOLDER
BRIDGE-PLAYER
CLOSE CATCHER
CLOSE FIELDER
EQUESTRIENNE
FIGURE-SKATER
HORSE-TRAINER
MIDDLEWEIGHT
NET-CORD JUDGE
OUTSIDE RIGHT
PENALTY-TAKER
PRIZE-FIGHTER
PROFESSIONAL
RACING-DRIVER
ROLLER-SKATER
SALMON-FISHER
SEMI-FINALIST
SHARPSHOOTER
SKATEBOARDER
TENNIS-PLAYER
THREE-QUARTER
TRAMPOLINIST
TRIPLE JUMPER
WEIGHT-LIFTER
WELTERWEIGHT
WICKET-KEEPER

13

BACKSWORDSMAN
BIG-GAME HUNTER
BUTTER-FINGERS
CENTRE-FORWARD
CORNER MARSHAL
CRUISERWEIGHT
DISCUS-THROWER
DRAUGHT-PLAYER
DRUM MAJORETTE
FEATHER-WEIGHT
INSIDE FORWARD

INTERNATIONAL
NIGHT-WATCHMAN
RECORD-BREAKER
SHOOTING PARTY
SNOOKER-PLAYER
SPEEDWAY RIDER
STEEPLECHASER

14

BASE-LINE PLAYER
BILLIARD-MARKER

BILLIARD-PLAYER
MARATHON RUNNER
MASTER OF HOUNDS
MOSQUITO-WEIGHT
OUTSIDE FORWARD

15

SPARRING PARTNER
SQUARE LEG UMPIRE

PEOPLE – UNDESIRABLES

3

BAG
BUM
CAD
CAT
COW
CUR
DOG
DUD
EEL
FOX
FUG
HAG
HOG
HUN
MOB
NUT
OAF
PIG
PRO
PUP
RAG
RAT
RED
RIP
SOD
SOT
SOW
YOB

4

BAWD
BEAR
BOOR
BORE
BRAT
CUSS
DRAB
DUCK
FINK
FUNK
GOTH
HEEL
JADE
JILT
JINX
LIAR
LOON
LOUT
LUSH
MAGE
MINX
MOLE
MOLL
MULE
NARK
NOSE
OGRE
PAIN

PEST
PILL
PIMP
PRIG
RAFF
RAKE
RAMP
ROUÉ
SCUM
SLOB
SLUG
SLUT
SMUG
SNAP
SNOB
SOAK
SPIV
SWAD
TART
TICK
TOAD
TOUT
TURK
TYKE
USER
VAMP
WASP
WEED
WINO
WOLF

WORM

5

BEAST
BESOM
BITCH
BROAD
BROCK
BRUTE
BUCKO
BULLY
BUTCH
CHEAT
CHUFF
CHURL
CREEP
CRONE
CYNIC
DEVIL
DOPER
DRÔLE
DRONE
DRUNK
DUPER
FIEND
FLIRT
GHOUL
GIBER

GRASS
HARPY
HOUND
HOURI
HUNKS
HUSSY
IDLER
JIBER
JONAH
JUDAS
KNAVE
KULAK
LEECH
LOUSE
MADAM
MAGUS
MARDY
MEANY
MISER
MIXER
MOPSY
NOSER
OGLER
PEACH
PIKER
PLANT
PONCE
PRIER
PRUDE
PRYER

PUPPY
QUACK
QUEAN
RANDY
REBEL
ROGUE
ROUGH
ROWDY
SCALD
SCAMP
SCOLD
SCREW
SHARK
SHREW
SIGHT
SKELM
SKITE
SKULK
SKUNK
SNAIL
SNAKE
SNEAK
SNIDE
SNOOP
SOUSE
SQUIT
STICK
STIFF
SWASH
SWINE

TABBY
TEASE
TIGER
TOADY
TOPER
TOUGH
TRAMP
TROUT
TWERP
VEXER
VIPER
VIXEN
WHORE
WITCH
YAHOO
YOBBO

6

ABUSER
ANIMAL
BASHAW
BEGGAR
BELDAM
BONNET
BOOZER
BUGGER
BUMMER
BUNTER

PEOPLE – UNDESIRABLES

CADGER
CANTER
CARPER
CHOUSE
COGGER
CON-MAN
COPIER
COWARD
CRAVEN
CRAVER
CURSER
DESPOT
DODGER
DOSSER
DRAGON
EGOIST
ENVIER
FIBBER
FIDGET
FORCER
FRIGHT
FUSSER
GAS-BAG
GIGOLO
GORGON
GOSSIP
GRIPER
GROPER
GROUCH
HAMMER
HARLOT
HECTOR
HEELER
HELLER
HOOKER
HOOTER
JACKAL
JEERER
KIDDER
LAP-DOG
LECHER
LOAFER
LURKER
MEANIE
MENACE
MILKER
MINION
MISERY
MOCKER
MOHOCK
MOUSER
MUCKER

MUFFIN
NAGGER
NICKER
NIPPER
NOCENT
OBI-MAN
PANDER
PEDANT
PEEPER
PHONEY
PICKLE
PICK-UP
PIRATE
PLAGUE
POSEUR
PSEUDO
PUSHER
RABBLE
RAG-BAG
RAIDER
RAMROD
RASCAL
RIBALD
RINGER
RIOTER
RIPPER
ROTTER
RUINER
SADIST
SATRAP
SAVAGE
SCRUFF
SETTER
SHAVER
SHOVER
SINNER
SKIVER
SLAVER
SLOUCH
SLOVEN
SMARTY
SNITCH
SNUDGE
SQUIRT
STARER
SUCKER
TAPPER
TARTAR
TEASER
TERROR
TOUTER
TRUANT

TSOTSI
TYRANT
UNDOER
VANDAL
VARLET
VIRAGO
VOYEUR
WANTON
WASTER
WEASEL
WHINER
WIZARD
WOWSER
WRETCH
YES-MAN
ZENDIK

7

A BAD HAT
A BAD LOT
ANANIAS
AVENGER
BADMASH
BAGGAGE
BASTARD
BAULKER
BIGHEAD
BLABBER
BLEEDER
BOASTER
BOBADIL
BOUNDER
BRAWLER
BUMBLER
BUTCHER
CAITIFF
CALIBAN
CHEATER
CHICKEN
COCOTTE
COPY-CAT
CRACKER
CRAWLER
CRINGER
CRY-BABY
CULLION
CULPRIT
DASTARD
DAWDLER
DEFILER

DELILAH
DELUDER
DEMIREP
DIDDLER
DRIFTER
DROP-OUT
DRUMMER
DRY-FIST
EGOTIST
ENTICER
EXACTOR
FIDDLER
FLASHER
FLEECER
FLEERER
FLOOSIE
FOISTER
FOPLING
FUSS-POT
GARBLER
GLUTTON
GRABBER
GRASPER
GROBIAN
GROUPIE
HALLION
HANGDOG
HIGH-HAT
HOODLUM
HOTHEAD
HUSTLER
IMPOSER
INCITER
INGRATE
INJURER
JARKMAN
JEZEBEL
KILLCOW
KILLJOY
KNOW-ALL
LEWDSBY
LUDDITE
LUMPKIN
MARPLOT
MEDDLER
MONSTER
MOOCHER
MOUTHER
MUGWUMP
NIGGARD
NIGGLER
NOBBLER

PAPHIAN
PARVENU
PEACOCK
PEASANT
PIDDLER
PINCHER
PLOTTER
POSEUSE
PROWLER
PUCELLE
PUTTOCK
QUELLER
QUITTER
RAG-DOLL
REPTILE
REVILER
ROAD-HOG
ROISTER
RUFFIAN
RUFFLER
SAVE-ALL
SCAMPER
SCHEMER
SCOFFER
SCORNER
SCROOGE
SCULPIN
SEDUCER
SERPENT
SHARPER
SHIFTER
SHIRKER
SHOCKER
SHOW-OFF
SHYLOCK
SKULKER
SLACKER
SNAPPER
SNEAKER
SNEAK-UP
SNEERER
SNIFFER
SNOOPER
SNUBBER
SO-AND-SO
SPIELER
SPITTER
SPOILER
SPONGER
SPOUTER
SPURNER
SQUARER

STINGER	BRAGGART	MAKEBATE	SLUGGARD
STINKER	BUSYBODY	MALIGNER	SLYBOOTS
STINTER	CABALLER	MAN-EATER	SMOOTHIE
STIRRER	CACAFOGO	MARAUDER	SNATCHER
STODGER	CALL-GIRL	MAR-SPORT	SNEAKSBY
SWANKER	CANNIBAL	MARTINET	SNIFFLER
SWEARER	CHICANER	MILITANT	SNITCHER
SWEATER	CLAWBACK	MISCHIEF	SORCERER
TAUNTER	COCKTAIL	MOLESTER	SOURPUSS
TEMPTER	CONNIVER	MUCK-WORM	SPALPEEN
TOSSPOT	COQUETTE	MYRMIDON	SPITFIRE
TRAITOR	CREATURE	NEPOTIST	SPRAWLER
TRICKER	DEFECTOR	NIGHT-MAN	SQUEAKER
TRIFLER	DESERTER	NUISANCE	SQUEALER
TRIMMER	DESIGNER	OBI-WOMAN	STICKLER
TROLLOP	DOGBERRY	OBTRUDER	STINKARD
TWISTER	DO-GOODER	OFFENDER	STOWAWAY
UPSTART	DOLLY-MOP	PARASITE	STRUMPET
USURPER	DRUNKARD	PERISHER	STRUTTER
VAMPIRE	ENSLAVER	PESTERER	SUCCUBUS
VAUNTER	EVIL-DOER	PICAROON	TABBY-CAT
VAURIEN	FANFARON	POLLUTER	TAMPERER
VILLAIN	FINE LADY	POLTROON	TARTUFFE
VULTURE	FLIP-FLOP	PROCURER	TEARAWAY
WANGLER	FOMENTER	PRODIGAL	TELL-TALE
WARLOCK	FRIBBLER	PRODITOR	TENEBRIO
WASTREL	GRIZZLER	PROFANER	TIGHTWAD
WELSHER	GRUMBLER	PROFUSER	TORTURER
WILDCAT	HANGER-ON	PROVOKER	TOUGH-GUY
WIND-BAG	HARASSER	QUIDNUNC	TOUGH-NUT
WISE GUY	HARD CASE	QUISLING	TRADUCER
WRECKER	HARDFACE	RAKEHELL	TROUBLER
WRESTER	HARRIDAN	RECREANT	TRUCKLER
WRONGER	HECTORER	RECUSANT	TURNBACK
WRONG 'UN	HEDGEHOG	RENEGADE	TURNCOAT
ZOILIST	HEN-HUSSY	RENEGADO	TWO-TIMER
	HINDERER	REVENGER	UPSETTER
	HIRELING	REVOLTER	VENEREAN
8	HOOLIGAN	RIFF-RAFF	VILIFIER
	HUCKSTER	RINGSTER	VIOLATOR
AGITATOR	IMPOSTOR	RUMOURER	VITIATOR
ALARMIST	INCENSOR	RUNAGATE	WATER-RAT
ATTACKER	INFORMER	SCIOLIST	WAYLAYER
BANGSTER	INSULTER	SCORPION	WHIFFLER
BARNACLE	INTRUDER	SCOURGER	WHIPJACK
BARRATOR	KIBITZER	SCRUBBER	
BESOGNIO	KOMITAJI	SIMPERER	
BETRAYER	LARRIKIN	SKIPJACK	
BIG-MOUTH	LAYABOUT	SLATTERN	**9**
BLAZONER	LEVANTER	SLOUCHER	
BLIGHTER	LEWDSTER	SLOWBACK	AGGRESSOR
BORACHIO	LOITERER	SLOWPOKE	ANARCHIST
			ARCH-FIEND

PEOPLE – UNDESIRABLES

ARRIVISTE
ASSAILANT
ASSAULTER
BACKBITER
BARATHRUM
BARBARIAN
BATTLE-AXE
BOLSHEVIK
BOVVER BOY
BULLDOZER
BULLY-ROOK
CHARLATAN
CHISELLER
CORNER-BOY
COURTLING
CRUCIFIER
CUDGELLER
DEBAUCHEE
DEFAULTER
DEPRESSOR
DESPERADO
DESPOILER
DETRACTOR
DOMINATOR
EGOMANIAC
EXPLOITER
EXTREMIST
FLAY-FLINT
FREE-LIVER
FRITTERER
FRUGALIST
GROVELLER
GUERRILLA
HARD-LINER
HUMBUGGER
HYPOCRITE
ILL-WISHER
INEBRIATE
INFORMANT
INSURGENT
INTRIGUER
INVEIGLER
JACK NASTY
JAYWALKER
LAND-SHARK
LAWMONGER
LAZY-BONES
LIBERTINE
LOAN-SHARK
LOOSE-FISH
LOUD-MOUTH
MASOCHIST

MERCENARY
MISCREANT
MISLEADER
MUCK-RAKER
MUTILATOR
NEGLECTER
NIGHT-HAWK
NIP-CHEESE
OPPRESSOR
PANDERESS
PASSENGER
PICK-THANK
PIG-SCONCE
PINCHFIST
PIPSQUEAK
POISON PEN
POODLE-DOG
PRÉCIEUSE
PROCURESS
PROFITEER
PROVOCANT
PUSSYFOOT
PYTHONESS
RANTIPOLE
REPRESSOR
REPROBATE
RIDICULER
ROISTERER
ROUGHNECK
SCALLYWAG
SCARIFIER
SCAVENGER
SCHNORRER
SCOUNDREL
SCROUNGER
SEA-LAWYER
SKINFLINT
SLABBERER
SNIVELLER
SORCERESS
SOUTENEUR
SPLENETIC
SPOILSMAN
SQUARE-TOE
SUBVERTER
SUNDOWNER
SURFEITER
SWAGGERER
SYCOPHANT
TARTARIAN
TEMPTRESS
TERMAGANT

TERRORIST
TOAD-EATER
TORMENTOR
TREGETOUR
TRICKSTER
TYRANNESS
VULGARIAN
WARMONGER
WOMANISER
XANTHIPPE
YELLOW-DOG

10

ADVENTURER
AVENGERESS
BACKSLIDER
BELL-WETHER
BIG BROTHER
BLACKGUARD
BLACK SHEEP
BLASPHEMER
BOOTLICKER
CHEAPSKATE
COCKALORUM
CONTACT MAN
CROSSPATCH
CURMUDGEON
DAGGLE-TAIL
DEFLOWERER
DEGENERATE
DELINQUENT
DENIGRATOR
DESECRATOR
DESTRUCTOR
DISPARAGER
DRAWCANSIR
ENCROACHER
ENDANGERER
EVIL-WORKER
FAST WORKER
FLAGELLANT
FLY-BY-NIGHT
FOOT-LICKER
FREELOADER
GOLD-DIGGER
GOODY-GOODY
GUNFIGHTER
GUNSLINGER
HEADHUNTER
HELLBENDER

HIGH-ROLLER
HILL-DIGGER
HOLY TERROR
HOUND'S-FOOT
HUMGRUFFIN
HUMILIATOR
IMPORTUNER
IMPRECATOR
INCANTATOR
INSINUATOR
INSTIGATOR
INTERLOPER
INTOLERANT
JACKANAPES
LAND-LOUPER
LED CAPTAIN
LIBIDINIST
LISTENER-IN
LOTUS-EATER
MALINGERER
MEDICASTER
MONEY-TAKER
MONOMANIAC
MOUNTEBANK
MUD-SLINGER
NARCISSIST
NE'ER-DO-WELL
NEWSMONGER
NIGHT-RIDER
NOTE-SHAVER
OBSTRUCTOR
PAEDOPHILE
PANHANDLER
PATRONISER
PEEPING TOM
PERSECUTOR
PHILISTINE
PINCHPENNY
PRACTISANT
PROFLIGATE
PROSTITUTE
RACK-RENTER
RAGAMUFFIN
RETRIBUTOR
RETROGRADE
RING-LEADER
SCAPEGRACE
SCRAPE-GOOD
SCREECH-OWL
SEDUCTRESS
SELF-SEEKER
SHANGHAIER

SMART-ALICK
SMELL-FEAST
SOBERSIDES
SPOIL-SPORT
SQUANDERER
SUBJUGATOR
SUBVERSIVE
SUPERGRASS
SUPPRESSOR
TALE-BEARER
TALE-TELLER
TANTALISER
TERRORISER
THREATENER
TICKET-TOUT
TIME-SERVER
TUFT-HUNTER
UNDERMINER
VICTIMISER
VILLAINESS
WET BLANKET
WIFE-BEATER

11

ADVENTURESS
APPLE-SQUIRE
BEACHCOMBER
BLACKBIRDER
BLOODSUCKER
BLOUSON NOIR
BRAGGADOCIO
BUSHWHACKER
CALUMNIATOR
CARD-SHARPER
CHUCKLE-HEAD
CLAIM-JUMPER
CONDOTTIERE
COPPER'S NARK
DETRACTRESS
DETRIMENTAL
DISMAL JIMMY
DRAGGLE-TAIL
EXASPERATOR
FLAGELLATOR
FLESH-MONGER
FOUR-FLUSHER
GATE-CRASHER
GAY DECEIVER
GORMANDISER

GUERRILLERO
GULLY-HUNTER
HARD DRINKER
HEDGE-PARSON
HUMGRUFFIAN
HYPERCRITIC
INFILTRATOR
INTEMPERANT
LAND-GRABBER
LIBERTICIDE
LICK-PLATTER
LICKSPITTLE
LINE-SHOOTER
MANIPULATOR
MOONLIGHTER
NAME-DROPPER
NECROMANCER
NIGHT-HUNTER
NIGHT-WALKER
NOSEY PARKER
OUT-AND-OUTER
OVERTHROWER
PANIC-MONGER
PEACE-MONGER
PETTIFOGGER
PHILANDERER
PLACE-MONGER
POODLE-FAKER
PROSTITUTOR
PUBLIC ENEMY
PUSSYFOOTER
QUACKSALVER
QUEUE-JUMPER
RAPSCALLION
SCAREMONGER
SCATTERGOOD
SCRAPE-PENNY
SEPTEMBRIST
SHARE-PUSHER
SLAVE-DRIVER
SLAVE-TRADER
SMARTYBOOTS
SMARTYPANTS
SONOFABITCH
SPENDTHRIFT
STOOL-PIGEON
STRAIT-LACER
UNDESIRABLE
VITUPERATOR
WEARY WILLIE
WHITE SLAVER
WHOREMONGER

12

BACKWOODSMAN
BLABBERMOUTH
BUCKLE-BEGGER
CARPETBAGGER
COLLABORATOR
CONVENTICLER
COPROPHAGIST
DEMI-MONDAINE
DISSIMULATOR
DOUBLE-DEALER
EAVESDROPPER
FRAME-BREAKER
GOOD-TIME GIRL
HEADSHRINKER
HEARTBREAKER
HEDGE-CREEPER
INCORRIGIBLE
INTERMEDDLER
INTRANSIGENT
JACK-IN-OFFICE
LEGACY-HUNTER
LICK-TRENCHER
LOUNGE-LIZARD
MONEY-GRABBER
MONEY-GRUBBER
NIGHT-BRAWLER
OBSESSIONIST
PAEDOPHILIAC
PINCHCOMMONS
PORNOGRAPHER
PREVARICATOR
PSEUDOLOGIST
RECALCITRANT
RODOMONTADER
SCARLET WOMAN
SCOPOPHILIAC
SECURITY RISK
SENSATIONIST
SEPTEMBRISER
SHORT-CHANGER
STUFFED SHIRT
SWASHBUCKLER
TRANSVESTITE
TROUBLEMAKER
TROUBLE-MIRTH
TRUCE-BREAKER
UGLY CUSTOMER

PEOPLE – UNDESIRABLES

13

ANTHROPOPHAGI
ATTITUDINISER
COPPER-CAPTAIN
CREEPING JESUS
DOUBLE-CROSSER
EXHIBITIONIST
FINE GENTLEMAN
FORTUNE-HUNTER
INDOCTRINATOR
JOB'S COMFORTER
MACHIAVELLIAN
MISCHIEF-MAKER
PAIN IN THE NECK
REVOLUTIONARY
SADO-MASOCHIST

SCANDAL-BEARER
SCANDAL-MONGER
SEMI-BARBARIAN
SPEED MERCHANT
STICK-IN-THE-MUD
STREET-FIGHTER
SWINGEBUCKLER
TERGIVERSATOR
THIMBLE-RIGGER
WHEELER-DEALER

14

BACK-SEAT DRIVER
BLACK MARKETEER
DOG IN THE MANGER

ENFANT TERRIBLE
GOOD-FOR-NOTHING
PANTOPRAGMATIC
PHILOSOPHASTER
SHILLY-SHALLIER
SNIPPER-SNAPPER
SOCCER HOOLIGAN
TATTERDEMALION

15

INSURRECTIONIST
SENSATION-MONGER
SLAVE-TRAFFICKER
SNAKE IN THE GRASS

PEOPLE – WORKERS

3	BARD	ICER	BOBBY	FRIER	NANNY	SMOOT
	BEAK	LYON	BONNE	GROOM	NAVVY	SOWER
BOY	BEAR	MAID	BOOTS	GUARD	NAZIR	SUPER
COP	BOGY	MATE	BUYER	GUIDE	NOTER	SUTOR
DEY	BOSS	MUTE	CABBY	HAKIM	NURSE	SWEEP
DOC	BULL	PAGE	CHIPS	HELOT	ODIST	TAWER
DON	BUSY	PEON	CLERK	HEWER	OILER	TAXER
DUN	CADI	POET	COACH	INKER	PASHA	TAXOR
LAD	CHAR	SERF	CODER	JUDGE	PAVER	THEOW
MAN	CHEF	SNIP	COPER	JURAT	PILOT	THETE
MAY	COOK	SNOB	COWAN	KNAVE	PLIER	TILER
PRO	DEAN	SYCE	CRIER	LAYER	POSER	TUNER
REP	DICK	TEMP	CURER	LINER	RAKER	TUTOR
SPY	DOGE	WARD	DAILY	LOCUM	RATER	TYLER
SUB	DYER	WHIP	DARZI	MACER	REEVE	UNCLE
TEC	FOUD		DEWAN	MADAM	RIMER	USHER
VET	GIRL		DHOBI	MAIRE	ROPER	VALET
	G-MAN	**5**	DIVER	MAKER	ROVER	VINER
	HACK		DRUID	MAMMY	SCOUT	WALLA
4	HAND	AD-MAN	EGGER	MASON	SCREW	WATCH
	HEAD	AGENT	ELCHI	MAYOR	SEPOY	WAXER
AMAH	HELP	AMBAN	ENVOY	MEDIC	SEWER	WAZIR
AYAH	HIND	AUMIL	EPHOR	MINER	SHOER	WENCH
BAAS	HOER	AVOUÉ	FILER	MODEL	SLAVE	WIPER
BABU	HUER	BAKER	FINER	MUDIR	SMITH	WIRER

6

AEDILE
AMTMAN
ARCHON
ARTIST
ATABEG
AU PAIR
AURIST
AUTEUR
AUTHOR
AVOYER
BAGMAN
BAILEE
BAILER
BAILIE
BANIAN
BANKER
BANYAN
BARBER
BARGEE
BARKER
BARMAN
BATMAN
BEADLE
BEAGLE
BEAMER
BEARER
BHISTI
BIGWIG
BINDER
BOFFIN
BOOKIE
BORDAR
BOWYER
BREWER
BROKER
BUFFER
BUMBLE
BUNNIA
BURLER
BURSAR
BUSBOY
BUSMAN
BUSTER
BUTLER
CABBIE
CABMAN
CANNER
CARMAN
CARTER
CARVER

CENSOR
CHASER
CODIST
COINER
COMMIS
COMBER
CONDER
CONNER
CONSUL
COOLIE
COOPER
COPPER
CORKER
COSTER
COWBOY
COWMAN
CRITIC
CUBIST
CULLER
CUPPER
CUSTOS
CUTLER
CUTTER
DATARY
DEALER
DEPUTY
DIGGER
DOCKER
DOCTOR
DOFFER
DRAPER
DRAWER
DRIVER
DROVER
DRUDGE
DUENNA
EARNER
EDITOR
ESCORT
ETCHER
EXTERN
FABLER
FACTOR
FARMER
FELLER
FISHER
FITTER
FLY-MAN
FOGGER
FOGMAN
FORMER
FOSSOR

FRAMER
FULLER
GANGER
GAOLER
GARÇON
GAUCHO
GAUGER
GELDER
GIGMAN
GIGOLO
GILDER
GINNER
GLAZER
GRAVER
GROCER
GROWER
GUTTER
GUV'NOR
HAIDUK
HAMMAL
HARLOT
HARMAN
HATTER
HAWKER
HEADER
HEALER
HEDGER
HELPER
HERALD
HODMAN
HOOPER
HOPPER
HORNER
HOSIER
HUSKER
ICEMAN
INTERN
IRONER
JAGGER
JAILER
JAILOR
JARVEY
JOBBER
JOINER
JURIST
KEELER
KEENER
KEEPER
KOTWAL
LACKEY
LAGGER
LAPPER

LASTER
LAWMAN
LAWYER
LEADER
LEGATE
LEGGER
LEGIST
LEG-MAN
LICTOR
LIMNER
LOADER
LOGGER
LOG-MAN
LOPPER
LUMPER
LYRIST
MAHOUT
MAPPER
MARKER
MAROON
MASTER
MATRON
MEDICO
MENDER
MENIAL
MERCER
MILKER
MILLER
MINDER
MINTER
MONGER
MOPPER
MUGGER
MULLER
MUNSHI
NAILER
NIPPER
NOTARY
NUNCIO
ODD-MAN
OIL-MAN
OSTLER
PACKER
PADDER
PASTER
PATROL
PATRON
PEDLAR
PEELER
PENMAN
PICKER
PIECER

PIEMAN
PINDER
PIN-MAN
PINNER
PITMAN
PLANER
PLATER
PORTER
POSTER
POT-BOY
POT-MAN
POTTER
PROVER
PURSER
PUTTER
RACKER
RAFTER
RAGMAN
RANGER
RATTER
READER
REAPER
RECTOR
REEDER
REGENT
RELIEF
RHETOR
RHYMER
RIGGER
ROOFER
ROZZER
RUNNER
SALTER
SARTOR
SATRAP
SAWYER
SBIRRO
SCALER
SCHOUT
SCRIBE
SCRIER
SEALER
SEAMER
SELLER
SERVER
SETTER
SHAMAN
SHAVER
SHROFF
SIRCAR
SISTER
SITTER

PEOPLE – WORKERS

SKIVVY
SLATER
SLAVEY
SLEUTH
SMOKER
SNARER
SORTER
SPICER
STOKER
STONER
STORER
SUTLER
SYNDIC
TAILOR
TAMPER
TANNER
TAPPER
TASKER
TASTER
TAXMAN
TEAMER
TEDDER
TELLER
TESTER
TILLER
TINKER
TINMAN
TINNER
TINTER
TITHER
TITLER
TOILER
TOLLER
TONSOR
TOPMAN
TOTTER
TOYMAN
TRACER
TRADER
TUBBER
TURNER
TWEENY
TWICER
TYPIST
USURER
VALUER
VANNER
VASSAL
VENDER
VENDOR
VERIST
VERSER

VIEWER
VIZIER
WAITER
WALLAH
WALLER
WARDEN
WARDER
WASHER
WEAVER
WELDER
WHALER
WORKER
WRIGHT
WRITER

7

ABIGAIL
ACTUARY
ADJOINT
ADVISER
ADVISOR
AGISTOR
ALCAIDE
ALCALDE
ALEWIFE
ALMONER
ALNAGER
AMILDAR
ANALYST
ARBITER
ARRIERO
ARTISAN
ARTISTE
ASSAYER
ASSIZER
ASSURER
ATTACHÉ
AUDITOR
BAILIFF
BARMAID
BELL-BOY
BELL-HOP
BELLMAN
BENCHER
BIG-SHOT
BLASTER
BOATMAN
BONDMAN
BOTCHER
BOTTLER
BOUNCER

BRAZIER
BREEDER
BUILDER
BURGESS
BURGHER
BUSGIRL
BUTCHER
BUTTONS
CALL-BOY
CAMBIST
CARRIER
CASEMAN
CASHIER
CATAPAN
CATERER
CAULKER
CHANGER
CHAPMAN
CHARLEY
CHECKER
CHEKIST
CHEMIST
CHOBDAR
CLEANER
CLICKER
CLIPPIE
CLOGGER
COALMAN
COBBLER
COLLIER
CO-PILOT
COPYIST
CORONER
COUÉIST
COUNSEL
COURIER
COWGIRL
COWHAND
COWHERD
COWPOKE
CRAMMER
CRISPIN
CROFTER
CROPPER
CURATOR
CURRIER
DADAIST
DAYSMAN
DENTIST
DIALIST
DIARIST
DILUTEE

DITCHER
DOBHASH
DOMINIE
DOORMAN
DRAG-MAN
DRAW-BOY
DRAYMAN
DREDGER
DRESSER
DRIFTER
DRUMMER
DUMAIST
DUSTMAN
DUUMVIR
DVORNIK
EBONIST
ELEGIST
ENACTOR
EPICIST
EQUERRY
EVICTOR
FAMULUS
FANCIER
FARRIER
FAUNIST
FAUVIST
FEOFFOR
FILACER
FIREMAN
FISH-FAG
FLORIST
FLUNKEY
FLUSHER
FOOTBOY
FOOTMAN
FOREMAN
FOUNDER
FRISEUR
FROGMAN
FUELLER
FUGUIST
FURRIER
GATE-MAN
GAULTER
GIRDLER
GLAZIER
GLEANER
GLOSSER
GRAFTER
GRAINER
GRANGER
GRASSER

GRAZIER
GREASER
GRINDER
GUMSHOE
HANDLER
HANGMAN
HARMOST
HAULIER
HELLIER
HEN-WIFE
HERBIST
HOBBLER
HOGHERD
HOGWARD
HOSEMAN
HOSTLER
HURDLER
IAMBIST
IMAGIST
INDEXER
INLAYER
INSURER
IVORIST
JANITOR
JEMADAR
JERQUER
JUNKMAN
JUSTICE
KEELMAN
KHEDIVA
KHEDIVE
KILLCOW
KNACKER
KNAPPER
KNEADER
KNITTER
KOFTGAR
LACE-MAN
LAUNDER
LINEMAN
LINK-MAN
LOCKMAN
LORIMER
LORINER
LUTHIER
MAILMAN
MALTMAN
MANAGER
MANURER
MARBLER
MARSHAL
MASSEUR

MATCHER
MEAL-MAN
MEAT-MAN
MÉTAYER
METRIST
MIDWIFE
MILKMAN
MINT-MAN
MODISTE
MONITOR
MOULDER
MOUNTIE
MOURNER
MOUSMEE
MUKHTAR
NEEDLER
NEWSBOY
NEWSMAN
NUT-HOOK
OCULIST
OFFICER
OMNIBUS
OPERANT
ORDERER
ORDERLY
OSTIARY
OVERMAN
PACKMAN
PADRONE
PAGEBOY
PAINTER
PALMIST
PARTNER
PATCHER
PAVIOUR
PEARLER
PEASANT
PEATMAN
PEDDLER
PICKLER
PIG-HERD
PIKEMAN
PIONEER
PIVOTER
PLANNER
PLANTER
PLUMBER
PLUMIST
PODESTÀ
POETESS
PORTMAN
POSTBOY

POSTMAN
PRAETOR
PREFECT
PREMIER
PRESSER
PRINTER
PROCTOR
PROVOST
PUDDLER
PUNCHER
PUTTIER
QUILTER
RABBLER
RAFTMAN
RAILMAN
RANCHER
REALTOR
REFEREE
REFINER
REMOVER
RESINER
REVISER
REVISOR
RHYMIST
RIDDLER
RIPPLER
RIVETER
ROADMAN
ROPER-IN
ROUGHER
ROUSTER
SADDLER
SAMPLER
SCANNER
SCRAPER
SCYTHER
SEA-COOK
SECURER
SENATOR
SERVANT
SETTLER
SHARKER
SHEARER
SHELLER
SHERIFF
SHIFTER
SHIPPER
SHOCKER
SHOP-BOY
SHOPMAN
SHOWMAN
SHUCKER

SHUNTER
SIMPLER
SKIMMER
SKINNER
SLIPPER
SMELTER
SNUFFER
SOUNDER
SPEAKER
SPECIAL
SPINNER
SPOOLER
SPOTTER
STAINER
STAMPER
STAPLER
STATIST
STEWARD
STICKER
STILLER
STOOKER
STYLIST
SUFFETE
SURGEON
SWABBER
SWEEPER
TACHIST
TANADAR
TAPSTER
TEACHER
TEXT-MAN
TIPSTER
TOLLMAN
TRACKER
TRAINEE
TRAINER
TRAPPER
TRAWLER
TRIBUNE
TRIMMER
TRUCKER
TRUSSER
TURNKEY
VAQUERO
VENERER
VICEROY
VINTNER
VOIVODE
WAGONER
WEIGHER
WIREMAN
WOODMAN

WOOLMAN
WORKMAN
WRECKER
YARDMAN
ZANJERO
ZAPTIEH

8

ADVOCATE
AERONAUT
ALDERMAN
ALGUAZIL
ALIENIST
ANIMATOR
ANNALIST
ANNEALER
APHORIST
APIARIST
AQUARIST
ARBORIST
ARCHAIST
ARMORIST
ARMOURER
ARRESTER
ARRESTOR
ASSESSOR
ATTORNEY
AVIARIST
BAGMAKER
BANDSTER
BANKSMAN
BARGEMAN
BARTERER
BAYADÈRE
BEARWARD
BEDMAKER
BELLETER
BIT-MAKER
BLACK ROD
BLAZONER
BLEACHER
BONDAGER
BONDMAID
BONDSMAN
BONIFACE
BOTANIST
BOURSIER
BOWMAKER
BOXMAKER
BREWSTER

BUCKAROO
BUMMAREE
BURGRAVE
BURINIST
CABIN-BOY
CALL-GIRL
CAMELEER
CATERESS
CELLARER
CERAMIST
CHAIRMAN
CHANDLER
CHARLADY
CHASSEUR
CHOKIDAR
CICERONE
CISELEUR
CLAQUEUR
CLAVIGER
CLERKESS
CLOTHIER
COACHMAN
CO-AUTHOR
CODIFIER
COIFFEUR
COLLATOR
COMPILER
COMPOSER
CONVENER
COOKMAID
COW-LEECH
CREMATOR
CROUPIER
CURSITOR
DAIRYMAN
DECEMVIR
DECK-HAND
DECURION
DEEMSTER
DELEGATE
DEPICTER
DESIGNER
DEY-WOMAN
DIPLOMAT
DIRECTOR
DOG-LEECH
DOMESTIC
DOUANIER
DRAGOMAN
DRAGSMAN
DRUGGIST
DRUIDESS

PEOPLE – WORKERS

EDITRESS
EDUCATOR
ELEGIAST
EMBALMER
EMBOSSER
EMISSARY
EMPLOYEE
EMPLOYER
ENGINEER
ENGRAVER
ENROLLER
ESSAYIST
EUROCRAT
EXAMINER
EXECUTOR
EXPLORER
EXPONENT
EXPORTER
FABULIST
FACTOTUM
FAMILIAR
FARM-HAND
FERRETER
FERRYMAN
FIGURIST
FINISHER
FISHWIFE
FLAT-FOOT
FLETCHER
FLOWERER
FLYMAKER
FOOTPAGE
FOOTPOST
FORESTER
FORGEMAN
FRESCOER
GANGSMAN
GARDENER
GATHERER
GENDARME
GEOMETER
GLASSMAN
GOADSMAN
GOADSTER
GOATHERD
GONGSTER
GOVERNOR
GREFFIER
GUARDIAN
GUNMAKER
GUNSMITH
HANDMAID

HANDYMAN
HAT-MAKER
HAYMAKER
HEADSMAN
HENCHMAN
HERDSMAN
HIRELING
HOISTMAN
HOME HELP
HORSE-BOY
HORSEMAN
HOTELIER
HOUSEBOY
HOUSEMAN
HOVELLER
HUCKSTER
HUISSIER
HUMORIST
IDYLLIST
IMPORTER
INDENTER
INTIMIST
INVENTOR
JACKAROO
JAMPANEE
JEWELLER
JIG-BORER
JUSTICER
KING'S-MAN
KIPPERER
KNIFE-BOY
LABOURER
LADY-HELP
LAND-GIRL
LANDLADY
LANDLORD
LAPIDARY
LARDERER
LAW-AGENT
LAW-GIVER
LAW-MAKER
LECTURER
LEGALIST
LETTERER
LIBRAIRE
LICENSEE
LICENSER
LINESMAN
LINGUIST
LOCKSMAN
LODESMAN
LOGICIAN

LUMBERER
LUMINIST
LUNARIAN
LYRICIST
MAGISTER
MALTSTER
MAMELUKE
MANCIPLE
MANDARIN
MANDATOR
MAN OF LAW
MAP-MAKER
MARKETER
MASSEUSE
MAXIMIST
MAYORESS
MEASURER
MECHANIC
MEDIATOR
MERCHANT
MILKMAID
MILL-GIRL
MILL-HAND
MILLINER
MINISTER
MISTRESS
MODELLER
MONODIST
MOTORMAN
MULETEER
MULTURER
MURALIST
NARRATOR
NAZARENE
NEAT-HERD
NEWSHAWK
NIELLIST
NIGHT-MAN
NOVELIST
OBSERVER
OCEANAUT
OFFICIAL
OOLOGIST
OPERATOR
OPIFICER
OPTICIAN
OUTRIDER
OVERSEER
OVERSMAN
PALATINE
PAPER-BOY
PARGETER

PARODIST
PATENTOR
PATTERER
PEN-MAKER
PENWOMAN
PERFUMER
PEWTERER
PIECENER
PIG-WOMAN
PIN-MAKER
PLACEMAN
PLATEMAN
PLOUGHER
POLEMIST
POLISHER
POLITICO
POT-MAKER
PRAEDIAL
PRESSMAN
PRODUCER
PROFILER
PROMOTER
PROMPTER
PROSAIST
PROVISOR
PSALMIST
PSYCHIST
PUBLICAN
PURVEYOR
QUAESTOR
QUARRIER
QUILLMAN
RAFTSMAN
RAGWOMAN
RANCHERO
RANCHMAN
RECEIVER
RECORDER
REDACTOR
REPORTER
RESETTER
RESIDENT
RESTORER
RETAILER
RETAINER
REVIEWER
REWRITER
RIVERMAN
ROADSMAN
RUG-MAKER
SALESMAN
SATIRIST

SAUCEMAN
SAW-BONES
SCAVAGER
SCENE-MAN
SCRAP-MAN
SCRUBBER
SCULLION
SCULPTOR
SCUTCHER
SEAMSTER
SEARCHER
SEEDSMAN
SEMPSTER
SERGEANT
SERVITOR
SHEARMAN
SHEPHERD
SHINGLER
SHIREMAN
SHOP-GIRL
SIMPLIST
SITTER-IN
SMOOTHER
SODA-JERK
SOLDERER
SOL-FAIST
SPACEMAN
SPEED-COP
SPURRIER
STALLMAN
STARCHER
STATUARY
STIPPLER
STITCHER
STOCKIST
STOCKMAN
STOREMAN
STRAPPER
STREAMER
STRIPPER
STUCCOER
STUNTMAN
SUBAHDAR
SUMMONER
SUPPLIER
SURFACER
SURVEYOR
SWANHERD
TALLYMAN
TALUKDAR
TAVERNER
TEAMSTER

TEMPERER
TEXTUARY
THATCHER
THEORIST
THRASHER
THRESHER
TIDESMAN
TIN-MINER
TINSMITH
TIPSTAFF
TOYMAKER
TOYWOMAN
TRACKMAN
TREADLER
TRENCHER
TRIADIST
TRIBUTER
TRIPEMAN
TRIUMVIR
TURNCOCK
TUTORESS
USHERESS
VALUATOR
VENDEUSE
VENEERER
VERDERER
VESTURER
VIGNERON
VINTAGER
VOLUMIST
VOYAGEUR
WAGGONER
WAITRESS
WARDRESS
WATCHMAN
WATERMAN
WATER-RAT
WHALEMAN
WHIFFLER
WIGMAKER
WINCHMAN
WINNOWER
WOODSMAN
WOODWARD
ZEMINDAR

9

ALE-CONNER
AMPUTATOR
ANALOGIST

ANATOMIST
ANNOTATOR
ANNOUNCER
ANTIQUARY
APPARITOR
APPLE-WIFE
APPRAISER
ARBITRESS
ARCHITECT
ARCHIVIST
ART DEALER
ART EDITOR
ARTIFICER
ART MASTER
ASSEMBLER
ASSISTANT
ASTRONAUT
ATTENDANT
AUDITRESS
AUTHORESS
AUXILIARY
BALLADIST
BAR-KEEPER
BARRISTER
BARROW-BOY
BARTENDER
BEEFEATER
BEEKEEPER
BEEMASTER
BEGLERBEG
BIOLOGIST
BODYGUARD
BOILERMAN
BONDSLAVE
BOOKMAKER
BOOTBLACK
BOOTMAKER
BOXKEEPER
BOXWALLAH
BRAKES-MAN
BRINJARRY
BUG-HUNTER
BURNISHER
BUS-DRIVER
BUSHELLER
BUSH PILOT
CAB-DRIVER
CAB-RUNNER
CALENDRER
CAMERAMAN
CANVASSER
CARETAKER

CARPENTER
CASE-MAKER
CASTELLAN
CATCHPOLE
CATTLEMAN
CELLARIST
CELLARMAN
CENTENIER
CENTUMVIR
CEREALIST
CERTIFIER
CHAPRASSI
CHARWOMAN
CHARTERER
CHAUFFEUR
CHIEF WHIP
CHINOVNIK
CLINICIAN
COAL-MINER
COD-FISHER
COIFFEUSE
COLLECTOR
COLOURIST
COLOURMAN
COLUMNIST
COMITATUS
COMMISSAR
COMITATUS
COMMISSAR
COMPANION
COMPRADOR
CONCIERGE
CONCOCTOR
CONDUCTOR
CONSTABLE
CO-PARTNER
CORRECTOR
CORSETIER
COSMONAUT
COST CLERK
COSTUMIER
COUTURIER
COWFEEDER
CRAFTSMAN
CUISINIER
CUPBEARER
CUSTODIAN
DACTYLIST
DAILY HELP
DAIRYMAID
DAK RUNNER
DECORATOR

DETECTIVE
DIALOGIST
DIE-SINKER
DIETICIAN
DIETITIAN
DIGNITARY
DIPTERIST
DIRECTRIX
DISPENSER
DISSECTOR
DISTILLER
DOGGERMAN
DRAMATIST
DRAMATURG
DRYSALTER
DRY-WALLER
DUNGEONER
DYNAMITER
ECOLOGIST
ECONOMIST
EMENDATOR
ENCOMIAST
ENGINE-MAN
ENGLISHER
ENGRAINER
EPITOMIST
ERRAND-BOY
ESCHEATOR
ESTIMATOR
EXAMINANT
EXCAVATOR
EXCHANGER
EXCISEMAN
EXECUTIVE
EXEGETIST
EX-LIBRIST
EYE DOCTOR
FABRICANT
FIELD HAND
FINANCIER
FISHERMAN
FISHWOMAN
FLAX-WENCH
FOREWOMAN
FOSSICKER
FREELANCE
FRESCOIST
FRUITERER
FULL-TIMER
FURBISHER
FURNISHER
GALVANIST

GARROTTER
GAS-FITTER
GEODESIST
GEOLOGIAN
GEOLOGIST
GLOSSATOR
GLUEMAKER
GOLD-MINER
GOLDSMITH
GONDOLIER
GOOSEHERD
GOVERNESS
GUTTER-MAN
HAIR-WAVER
HALF-TIMER
HAMMERMAN
HARPOONER
HARVESTER
HELIPILOT
HERBALIST
HERBARIAN
HERBORIST
HERRINGER
HIERODULE
HIRED HELP
HISTORIAN
HOG-RINGER
HOMEOPATH
HOP-PICKER
HOROLOGER
HOSTELLER
HOUSEMAID
HOUSEWIFE
HUNDREDER
HYGIENIST
HYPNOTIST
IMPEACHER
IMPOUNDER
INNKEEPER
INSCRIBER
INSPECTOR
INTENDANT
IRON-MINER
IRONSMITH
IRRIGATOR
JAGHIRDAR
JAILORESS
JANITRESS
JOB-MASTER
JOKESMITH
JUDICATOR
JUSTICIAR

PEOPLE – WORKERS

KENNEL-MAN
KITCHENER
KNOCKER-UP
LACEMAKER
LACQUERER
LADY'S-MAID
LAMPOONER
LAND-AGENT
LANDAMMAN
LANDDROST
LAND-REEVE
LAUNDERER
LAUNDRESS
LAW-WRITER
LEGENDARY
LEGENDIST
LIBRARIAN
LICHENIST
LIFEGUARD
LIFE-SAVER
LINOTYPER
LIVERYMAN
LOCK-MAKER
LOCKSMITH
LOG-ROLLER
LORD MAYOR
LUMBERMAN
MACERATOR
MACHINIST
MAGNETIST
MAJOR-DOMO
MAKE-UP MAN
MALE MODEL
MALE NURSE
MAN-FRIDAY
MANNEQUIN
MARKET-MAN
MECHANIST
MEDALLIST
MEDIATRIX
MEMOIRIST
MESSENGER
METALLIST
METEORIST
METRICIAN
METRICIST
METRIFIER
MIDDLEMAN
MIDINETTE
MILL-OWNER
MINE-OWNER
MNEMONIST

MODERATOR
MONITRESS
MORTICIAN
MOSAICIST
MUFFIN-MAN
MYOLOGIST
MYTHOPOET
NAVIGATOR
NEOLOGIAN
NEOLOGIST
NEOTERIST
NEWSAGENT
NEWSHOUND
NOMOTHETE
NURSEMAID
ODALISQUE
ODD-JOBBER
ODD-JOB MAN
OFFICE-BOY
OMBUDSMAN
ONCOSTMAN
OPERATIVE
ORGANISER
OROLOGIST
OSTEOPATH
OTOLOGIST
OUTFITTER
OUT-PORTER
PAINTRESS
PANELLIST
PANTRYMAN
PAPER-GIRL
PARACLETE
PARAMEDIC
PART-TIMER
PATROLLER
PATROLMAN
PAYMASTER
PAYSAGIST
PEDAGOGUE
PEN-PUSHER
PERFECTOR
PHONETIST
PHRASE-MAN
PHYSICIAN
PHYSICIST
PINKERTON
PIN-UP GIRL
PIPE-LAYER
PIT-SAWYER
PLASTERER
PLOUGHBOY

PLOUGHMAN
POETASTER
POINTSMAN
POLEMARCH
POLICEMAN
PONTONEER
PONTOONER
PORTERESS
PORTREEVE
POSTILION
POSTILLER
POSTWOMAN
POT-BOILER
POULTERER
PRACTISER
PRECEPTOR
PRELECTOR
PRESIDENT
PRINCIPAL
PROCESSER
PROCONSUL
PROFESSOR
PROFILIST
PROJECTOR
PRORECTOR
PROSECTOR
PROSODIST
PROTECTOR
PUBLICIST
PUBLISHER
PUNCTATOR
QUARRYMAN
RECORDIST
RECTIFIER
RECTORESS
REGISSEUR
REGISTRAR
REGULATOR
REPAIR-MAN
RETOUCHER
RHYMESTER
RINGMAKER
ROADMAKER
ROBE-MAKER
ROCKETEER
ROPE-MAKER
ROUNDSMAN
RUDDLEMAN
SAFE-MAKER
SAIL-MAKER
SCAVENGER
SCENARIST

SCHOLIAST
SCIENTIST
SCISSORER
SCRIBBLER
SCRIVENER
SCRUTATOR
SCYTHEMAN
SECOND MAN
SECRETARY
SENESCHAL
SEPTEMVIR
SERIALIST
SHAMPOOER
SHIP-OWNER
SHOEBLACK
SHOEMAKER
SHOPWOMAN
SICK-NURSE
SICKLEMAN
SIGNALMAN
SOB-SISTER
SOLICITOR
SOMMELIER
SONGSMITH
SONNETEER
SONNETIST
SOOTERKIN
SOUBRETTE
SOW-GELDER
SPADESMAN
SPAGYRIST
SPIDERMAN
SPOKESMAN
STABLE-BOY
STABLE-MAN
STAGE-HAND
STATESMAN
STATIONER
STAY-MAKER
STEERSMAN
STEVEDORE
STUD-GROOM
SUB-EDITOR
SUBSOILER
SUBVASSAL
SUBWARDEN
SUMMARIST
SURMASTER
SURROGATE
SWINEHERD
SWITCHMAN
SYNOPTIST

TABELLION
TABLE-MAID
TACTILIST
TAHSILDAR
TAILORESS
TATTOOIST
TAXONOMER
TEA-DEALER
TEASELLER
TEA-TASTER
TEMPORARY
TENEBRIST
TENT-MAKER
TEST-PILOT
THEOLOGER
THEOLOGUE
THEORISER
THERAPIST
THEURGIST
THUNDERER
TIC-TAC MAN
TIMBER-MAN
TOOL-MAKER
TOOLSMITH
TOPIARIST
TOP-SAWYER
TOWN-CLERK
TOWN-CRIER
TRADESMAN
TRAVELLER
TREASURER
TREPANNER
TRIBUTARY
TRIPEWIFE
TROWELLER
TUNESMITH
TUTWORKER
UFOLOGIST
UNDERCOOK
USHERETTE
VAN-DRIVER
VARNISHER
VASSALESS
VERBARIAN
VERSIFIER
VETTURINO
VICEREINE
VIGILANTE
VIGNETTER
VISAGISTE
VISITATOR
VOITURIER

VORTICIST
WALDGRAVE
WASHERMAN
WAXWORKER
WAY-WARDEN
WELL-BORER
WHERRYMAN
WINE-MAKER
WOOD-REEVE
WORKWOMAN
ZOO-KEEPER
ZOOLOGIST
ZOONOMIST
ZOOPERIST
ZOOTOMIST

10

ABSTRACTOR
ACCOUCHEUR
ACCOUNTANT
ADVERTISER
AEROLOGIST
AERONOMIST
AGROLOGIST
AGRONOMIST
AIR-HOSTESS
AIR-STEWARD
ALGEBRAIST
ALGOLOGIST
AMANUENSIS
AMBASSADOR
APOTHECARY
APPLE-WOMAN
APPRENTICE
ARBITRATOR
AREOPAGITE
ASTROLOGER
ASTRONOMER
ATMOLOGIST
AUBERGISTE
AUCTIONEER
AUDIT CLERK
AUSTRINGER
AVVOGADORE
AXIOLOGIST
BABY-FARMER
BABY-SITTER
BATOLOGIST
BEAUTICIAN
BELLHANGER

BELL-RINGER
BIBLIOPOLE
BILINGUIST
BILL-BROKER
BILLPOSTER
BIOCHEMIST
BIOGRAPHER
BLACKSMITH
BLADESMITH
BLOCKMAKER
BLUEBOTTLE
BONDSWOMAN
BONESETTER
BOOK-BINDER
BOOK-HOLDER
BOOKKEEPER
BOOKSELLER
BOOT-MENDER
BRICKLAYER
BRICKMAKER
BRUSHMAKER
BRYOLOGIST
BUM-BAILIFF
BUREAUCRAT
BUTTER-WIFE
CALOTYPIST
CAMERLENGO
CAREER GIRL
CARTOONIST
CARTWRIGHT
CASE-WORKER
CASH-KEEPER
CATALOGUER
CATEGORIST
CHAIR-MAKER
CHAIRWOMAN
CHANCELLOR
CHARGE-HAND
CHARIOTEER
CHAUFFEUSE
CHECK-CLERK
CHECK-TAKER
CHREMATIST
CHRONICLER
CHUCKER-OUT
CIRCUITEER
CITY EDITOR
CLAPPER-BOY
CLASSIFIER
CLOCKMAKER
CLOTH-MAKER
CLUBMASTER

COACHMAKER
COAL-FITTER
COAL-HEAVER
COALMASTER
COAL-PORTER
COASTGUARD
COLPORTEUR
COMBURGESS
COMMISSARY
COMPILER
COMPOSITOR
COMPRADORE
COMPUTATOR
CONCURRENT
CONSULTANT
CONTRACTOR
CONTROLLER
COPYHOLDER
COPYWRITER
CORDON BLEU
CORDWAINER
CORK-CUTTER
CORN-CUTTER
CORN-DEALER
CORN-FACTOR
CORN-MILLER
CORPORATOR
CORREGIDOR
CORSETIÈRE
COUNCILLOR
COUNCILMAN
COUNSELLOR
COUTURIÈRE
COWPUNCHER
CROP-DUSTER
CROWN-AGENT
CULTIVATOR
CYTOLOGIST
DECIMALIST
DEMOTICIST
DEPOSITARY
DEPUTY-HEAD
DESK-WORKER
DIASKEUAST
DINNER-LADY
DIRECTRESS
DISC-JOCKEY
DISCOUNTER
DISCOVERER
DISPATCHER
DISTRAINOR
DIURNALIST

DOCK-MASTER
DOG-FANCIER
DOORKEEPER
DRAMATURGE
DRESSMAKER
DRY-CLEANER
EMBLAZONER
ENAMELLIST
ENIGMATIST
EPHEMERIST
EPIGRAPHER
EPITAPHIST
EPITOMISER
ERGONOMIST
ERRAND-GIRL
ESTANCIERO
ETHOLOGIST
EXAMINATOR
EXPRESSMAN
EXPURGATOR
FABRICATOR
FACE WORKER
FELLMONGER
FICTIONIST
FILE-CUTTER
FILM-EDITOR
FIRE-MASTER
FISH-GUTTER
FISHMONGER
FLOWER-GIRL
FLUXIONIST
FOLKLORIST
FORECASTER
FRAME-MAKER
FREE-VERSER
FRUITERESS
FUND-RAISER
FUSTIANIST
GAME-DEALER
GAMEKEEPER
GAME-WARDEN
GARBAGE-MAN
GATE-KEEPER
GEAR-CUTTER
GENETICIST
GEOCHEMIST
GEOGRAPHER
GEOMETRIST
GIRL FRIDAY
GLACIALIST
GLOSSARIST
GOLD-BEATER

PEOPLE – WORKERS

GOLD-DIGGER
GOLD-WASHER
GRAMMARIAN
GRAMMATIST
GROUNDSMAN
GUBERNATOR
HABIT-MAKER
HACKNEYMAN
HALL PORTER
HANDMAIDEN
HARMAN-BECK
HARPOONEER
HARVESTMAN
HEADMASTER
HEAD PORTER
HEAD WAITER
HEADWORKER
HOROLOGIST
HORSE-LEECH
HORSE-SHOER
HORSE-TAMER
HOUSE-AGENT
HUSBANDMAN
IMPRESARIO
INOCULATOR
INQUISITOR
INSTRUCTOR
INVENTRESS
IRONMASTER
IRONMONGER
IRONWORKER
JOURNALIST
JOURNEYMAN
JUNK-DEALER
JUSTICIARY
KENNEL-MAID
KERB-TRADER
KERB-VENDOR
KHIDMUTGAR
KINESIPATH
KING-AT-ARMS
KING-OF-ARMS
LADY DOCTOR
LAMPOONIST
LAND-JOBBER
LAND-WAITER
LAND-WORKER
LANTERNIST
LAPIDARIST
LAUNDRY-MAN
LAW-OFFICER
LEGISLATOR

LIBRETTIST
LIGHTERMAN
LIME-BURNER
LINOTYPIST
LIQUIDATOR
LOBSTERMAN
LOCK-KEEPER
LORD OF SEAT
LUMBERJACK
LUMINARIST
MACE-BEARER
MACHINEMAN
MAGISTRATE
MANAGERESS
MANICURIST
MAN-SERVANT
MAP-MOUNTER
MARSHALLER
MASTER-HAND
MATCH-MAKER
MAYOLOGIST
MEAL-MONGER
MERCERISER
METAPHRAST
MILITARIST
MILLWRIGHT
MIND-READER
MINERALIST
MINE-WORKER
MINISTRESS
MINT-MASTER
MODERATRIX
MONEY-TAKER
MOUTHPIECE
MUSHROOMER
MUTESSARIF
MYSTERY-MAN
MYTHOLOGER
NATURALIST
NATUROPATH
NEGOTIATOR
NEWSCASTER
NEWS EDITOR
NEWSMONGER
NEWS-READER
NEWS-VENDOR
NEWS-WRITER
NIGHT NURSE
NOMOLOGIST
NOSOLOGIST
NURSERYMAN
OBITUARIST

OENOLOGIST
OFFICE-GIRL
OFFICIATOR
ONTOLOGIST
OPERETTIST
OPTOLOGIST
ORCHARDIST
ORCHARDMAN
ORNAMENTER
ORTHOPTIST
PAEDOTRIBE
PALFRENIER
PANDECTIST
PANEGYRIST
PANTRYMAID
PAPER-MAKER
PARADOCTOR
PARK-KEEPER
PARK-RANGER
PARNASSIAN
PARTY AGENT
PASQUILANT
PASTELLIST
PASTICHEUR
PASTRYCOOK
PAWNBROKER
PEARL-DIVER
PEARMONGER
PEAT-CASTER
PEDICURIST
PEDOLOGIST
PELTMONGER
PENOLOGIST
PERRUQUIER
PHARMACIST
PHILOLOGER
PHILOLOGUE
PIANO-TUNER
PIKE-KEEPER
PLATE-LAYER
PLAYWRIGHT
PLAY-WRITER
PLUMASSIER
PODIATRIST
POLEMICIST
POLITICIAN
POMOLOGIST
POSTILLION
POSTMASTER
PRACTICIAN
PRESCRIBER
PRESS-AGENT

PRINT-BUYER
PRIVATE EYE
PROCURATOR
PROGRAMMER
PROPAGATOR
PROPRAETOR
PROPROCTOR
PROSECUTOR
PROSPECTOR
PROSTITUTE
PROTECTRIX
PROVEDITOR
PSYCHIATER
PURSUIVANT
PYRAMIDIST
QUADRUMVIR
QUANTIFIER
QUIZMASTER
RAILROADER
RAILWAYMAN
RAPPORTEUR
RAT-CATCHER
READING-BOY
RÉPÉTITEUR
RESEARCHER
RHEOLOGIST
ROAD-MENDER
ROUGH-RIDER
ROUSTABOUT
SALES-CLERK
SALESWOMAN
SANITARIST
SCAFFOLDER
SCHEMATIST
SCHOLASTIC
SCHOOL-DAME
SCHOOL-MA'AM
SCRUB-RIDER
SCRUTINEER
SCULPTRESS
SEAL-FISHER
SEAMSTRESS
SEANNACHIE
SEMPSTRESS
SEROLOGIST
SERVANT-MAN
SERVING-MAN
SERVITRESS
SEXOLOGIST
SHALE-MINER
SHIP-BROKER
SHIPWRIGHT

SHIRE-REEVE
SHOPFITTER
SHOPKEEPER
SHOP-WALKER
SHRIMP-GIRL
SIGN-WRITER
SILK-GROWER
SILK-WEAVER
SINOLOGIST
SLOP-SELLER
SOAP-BOILER
SOUND-MIXER
SPACEWOMAN
SPASMODIST
SPECIALIST
SPINSTRESS
STAFF NURSE
STENCILLER
STENOTYPER
STEWARDESS
STOCKINGER
STOCK-TAKER
STONE-MASON
STREET-WARD
SUBPREFECT
SUPERCARGO
SUPERVISOR
SURFACEMAN
SURREALIST
SYNONYMIST
TALLY CLERK
TALLYWOMAN
TASKMASTER
TAXI-DANCER
TAXI-DRIVER
TAXONOMIST
TEA-BLENDER
TEA-PLANTER
TECHNICIAN
TECHNICIST
TELECASTER
TELPHERMAN
TEXTUALIST
THEOGONIST
THEOLOGIAN
THEOLOGIST
THIEF-TAKER
THRENODIST
TIDE-WAITER
TIMEKEEPER
TRACKLAYER
TRAM-DRIVER

TRANSLATOR
TRANSPOSER
TRAWLERMAN
TRECENTIST
TRIPEWOMAN
TROLLEY-MAN
TRUNK-MAKER
TYPE-CUTTER
TYPE-SETTER
TYPOLOGIST
UNDERAGENT
UNDER-CLERK
UNDERLAYER
UNDERTAKER
UNGUENTARY
UTILITY-MAN
VACCINATOR
VETERINARY
VICE-CONSUL
VICEGERENT
VICTUALLER
VIGNETTIST
VINOLOGIST
VIROLOGIST
VIVISECTOR
VOCABULIST
WAGE-EARNER
WAINWRIGHT
WARD SISTER
WATCHMAKER
WEATHER-MAN
WELL-SINKER
WHARFINGER
WHITESMITH
WHOLESALER
WINE-GROWER
WINE-TASTER
WINE-WAITER
WIRE-DRAWER
WIREWORKER
WOOD-CARVER
WOODCUTTER
WOODWORKER
WOOL-CARDER
WOOL-COMBER
WOOL-DRIVER
WOOL-GROWER
WOOL-PACKER
WOOL-SORTER
WOOL-TRADER
WOOL-WINDER
WOOL-WORKER

WORK-FELLOW
WORKING MAN
WORKMASTER
YARD-MASTER
ZINC-WORKER
ZOOGRAPHER
ZYMOLOGIST

11

ACAROLOGIST
ACCOUCHEUSE
ACOUSTICIAN
ADJUDICATOR
ALLOPATHIST
ANNUNCIATOR
ANTHOLOGIST
ANTIQUARIAN
APPARATCHIK
APPLE-GROWER
AQUAFORTIST
AQUARELLIST
ARTICULATOR
ART MISTRESS
ASSAY-MASTER
ASSEMBLYMAN
AUDIOLOGIST
AUDIO-TYPIST
AUSCULTATOR
BACKBENCHER
BANK CASHIER
BANK MANAGER
BARGEMASTER
BASKET-MAKER
BELL-FOUNDER
BETWEEN-MAID
BILLSTICKER
BIMETALLIST
BIRD-CATCHER
BIRD-FANCIER
BLOODLETTER
BOATBUILDER
BODY-BUILDER
BODY SERVANT
BOILERMAKER
BONDSERVANT
BOOT-CATCHER
BOUQUETIÈRE
BRANCH-PILOT
BREADWINNER
BURGOMASTER

BUSINESSMAN
BUTTER-WOMAN
CALENDARIST
CANDLEMAKER
CARABINIERE
CAR SALESMAN
CHAMBERLAIN
CHAMBERMAID
CHIFFONNIER
CHILDMINDER
CHIROPODIST
CHOIRMASTER
CHOROLOGIST
CIRCLE-RIDER
CLAIRVOYANT
CLOTH-WORKER
COAL-TRIMMER
COAL-WHIPPER
COAST-WAITER
COFFIN-MAKER
COMMENTATOR
COMPTROLLER
CONCILIATOR
CONDUCTRESS
CONGRESSMAN
CONSTRUCTOR
CONTRIBUTOR
CONVEYANCER
COOK-GENERAL
COPPERSMITH
COSMOLOGIST
COST-ANALYST
CRANE-DRIVER
CRIME-WRITER
CRIMINALIST
CROWN-LAWYER
CUB REPORTER
DAY-LABOURER
DELIVERY-MAN
DEMOGRAPHER
DETECTIVIST
DIPLOMATIST
DISPENSATOR
DISTRIBUTOR
DOUBLE-AGENT
DOXOGRAPHER
DRAUGHTSMAN
DRILL-MASTER
ELECTRICIAN
EMBLEMATIST
EMBROIDERER
ENTERPRISER

PEOPLE – WORKERS

EPIGRAPHIST
ESTATE AGENT
ETHNOLOGIST
ETYMOLOGIST
EXECUTIONER
FACSIMILIST
FACTORY HAND
FIELDWORKER
FILING-CLERK
FIRE-FIGHTER
FIRE-WATCHER
FLAX-DRESSER
FLESH-MONGER
FLOCK-MASTER
FLOORWALKER
FRUIT-PICKER
FUNCTIONARY
GALLEY-SLAVE
GAMES-MASTER
GEMMOLOGIST
GENEALOGIST
GHOST-WRITER
GLASS-BENDER
GLASS-BLOWER
GLASS-CUTTER
GONFALONIER
GOUVERNANTE
GRAVE-DIGGER
GREEK MASTER
GREENGROCER
GREEN-KEEPER
GYMNASIARCH
HABERDASHER
HAGIOLOGIST
HAIRDRESSER
HAIR-STYLIST
HANDICAPPER
HARDWAREMAN
HEDGE-WRITER
HEXAMETRIST
HIEROLOGIST
HIGH BAILIFF
HIGH SHERIFF
HIPPIATRIST
HIPPODAMIST
HISTOLOGIST
HOME-CROFTER
HOMESTEADER
HOPLOLOGIST
HOROGRAPHER
HOROSCOPIST
HORSE-DEALER

HORSE-DOCTOR
HOSPITALLER
HOTEL-KEEPER
HOUSE-FATHER
HOUSEKEEPER
HOUSEMASTER
HOUSE-MOTHER
HYDROLOGIST
HYMNOLOGIST
ICONOLOGIST
ILLUMINATOR
ILLUSTRATOR
INSPECTRESS
INSTITUTIST
INTERNUNCIO
INTERPRETER
INTERVIEWER
INVIGILATOR
IRON-FOUNDER
KITCHEN-MAID
LAMPLIGHTER
LANDSCAPIST
LAND-STEWARD
LATIN MASTER
LAUNDRY-MAID
LEDGER-CLERK
LIFEBOATMAN
LIMNOLOGIST
LINEN-DRAPER
LITHOLOGIST
LITHOTOMIST
LODGEKEEPER
LOGOGRAPHER
LOLLIPOP MAN
LORD PROVOST
LORRY-DRIVER
MADRIGALIST
MAGNETICIAN
MAIDSERVANT
MAIL-CARRIER
MAMMALOGIST
MAN-MILLINER
MANTUA-MAKER
MARKET-WOMAN
MASTER BAKER
MATHS MASTER
MECHANICIAN
MEDICINE MAN
MEMORIALIST
METAL-WORKER
METAPHORIST
MICROLOGIST

MICROTOMIST
MIMOGRAPHER
MINE-CAPTAIN
MINIATURIST
MOLE-CATCHER
MONEY-BROKER
MONEY-LENDER
MONOGRAPHER
MOONLIGHTER
MULE-SPINNER
MUNITIONEER
MUSIC-MASTER
MUSIC-SELLER
MYOGRAPHIST
MYTHOLOGIAN
MYTHOLOGIST
NECROLOGIST
NEEDLEWOMAN
NEPHOLOGIST
NEUROLOGIST
NIGHT PORTER
NIGHT SISTER
NIGHT-WORKER
NOMENCLATOR
NOMOGRAPHER
NOSOGRAPHER
ONION-SELLER
OPHIOLOGIST
OPHTHALMIST
OPTOMETRIST
ORNAMENTIST
OSTEOLOGIST
PAEDIATRIST
PAMPHLETEER
PANEL-BEATER
PANEL DOCTOR
PAPER-HANGER
PARAGRAPHER
PARISH CLERK
PARK-OFFICER
PARLOUR-MAID
PASTORALIST
PATHOLOGIST
PEARL-FISHER
PENNY-A-LINER
PESTOLOGIST
PETROLOGIST
PHENOLOGIST
PHILATELIST
PHILOLOGIAN
PHILOLOGIST
PHONETICIAN

PHONOLOGIST
PHONOTYPIST
PHYCOLOGIST
PHYSICIANER
PHYTOLOGIST
PHYTOTOMIST
PIECE-WORKER
PLEIN-AIRIST
PLUTOLOGIST
PLUTONOMIST
POINTILLIST
POLICE-JUDGE
POLICEWOMAN
PORK-BUTCHER
PORTRAITIST
POSTILLATOR
POUND-KEEPER
POUND-MASTER
PRECEPTRESS
PRIMITIVIST
PRINT-SELLER
PRISCIANIST
PROCLAIMANT
PROMULGATOR
PROOF-READER
PROPERTY-MAN
PROSECUTRIX
PROSE-WRITER
PROTOCOLIST
PROTONOTARY
PUNKA WALLAH
PURSE-BEARER
RADIOLOGIST
REFECTIONER
REFECTORIAN
REFERENDARY
RELIC-MONGER
REPUBLISHER
RHETORICIAN
RHINOLOGIST
ROAD-SWEEPER
SALESPERSON
SANDWICH-MAN
SCARABAEIST
SCRAP-DEALER
SCRIMSHONER
SECRET AGENT
SEMANTICIST
SERIGRAPHER
SERVANT-GIRL
SERVANT-LASS
SERVANT-MAID

SERVING-MAID
SHARE-BROKER
SHEEP-FARMER
SHEEP-MASTER
SHEPHERDESS
SHIP-BREAKER
SHIPBUILDER
SHOP-STEWARD
SIGN-PAINTER
SILK-THROWER
SILVERSMITH
SILVER-STICK
SMALLHOLDER
SOCIOLOGIST
SPACE-WRITER
SPOKESWOMAN
STADTHOLDER
STAGE-DRIVER
STALLMASTER
STEEL-WORKER
STEEPLEJACK
STENOTYPIST
STEREOTYPER
STIPENDIARY
STOCKBROKER
STOCK-FARMER
STOCK-FEEDER
STOCK-JOBBER
STONE-CUTTER
STOREKEEPER
STORY-TELLER
SUPREMATIST
SWEEP-WASHER
SWORD-BEARER
SYMPOSIARCH
TALENT SCOUT
TAX-GATHERER
TAXIDERMIST
TELEGRAPHER
TELEPHONIST
THEOLOGISER
THESMOTHETE
TICKET AGENT
TIN-STREAMER
TOAST-MASTER
TOBACCONIST
TOPOGRAPHER
TOUCH-TYPIST
TOWN-PLANNER
TRACK-WALKER
TRADESWOMAN
TRAIN-DRIVER

TRANSCRIBER
TRANSPORTER
TRAVEL AGENT
TRANSHIPPER
TRUCK-DRIVER
TRUCK-FARMER
TURNPIKE-MAN
TYPE-FOUNDER
TYPOGRAPHER
UNDERLOOKER
UNDER-SAWYER
UNDERWORKER
UNDERWRITER
UPHOLSTERER
UPHOLSTRESS
VESTRY-CLERK
VERSE-MONGER
VINE-DRESSER
VITRAILLIST
WAGON-WRIGHT
WAITING-MAID
WASHERWOMAN
WATCH-MENDER
WATER-DOCTOR
WAX-CHANDLER
WHALE-FISHER
WHEELWRIGHT
WHITEWASHER
WITCH-DOCTOR
WITCH-FINDER
WOOL-STAPLER
WRECK-MASTER
XYLOGRAPHER
ZOOGRAPHIST

12

ACTOR-MANAGER
AMBASSADRESS
AMBULANCEMAN
ANAESTHETIST
APICULTURIST
APPROPRIATOR
ARMOUR-BEARER
ARTIST'S MODEL
BALLADMONGER
BALLET MASTER
BALNEOLOGIST
BASKET-WEAVER
BELLOWS-MAKER
BIBLIOLOGIST

BIBLIOPEGIST
BIBLIOPOLIST
BIOMETRICIAN
BOOKING-CLERK
BOROUGH-REEVE
BOTTLE-WASHER
BOTTOM-SAWYER
BOUND-BAILIFF
BRASSFOUNDER
BRONCO-BUSTER
BUS-CONDUCTOR
BUTTY-COLLIER
CABINET-MAKER
CALLIGRAPHER
CAMP-FOLLOWER
CARDIOLOGIST
CARICATURIST
CARTOGRAPHER
CEROGRAPHIST
CHAPEL-MASTER
CHARTER-MAYOR
CHECK-WEIGHER
CHEESEMONGER
CHEIROLOGIST
CHIEF-CASHIER
CHIEF-JUSTICE
CHIMNEY-SWEEP
CHIROPRACTOR
CHOREOLOGIST
CHRONOLOGIST
CIRCUIT JUDGE
CIVIL SERVANT
CLERK OF WORKS
COACH-BUILDER
COLEOPTERIST
COMMISSIONER
CONCHOLOGIST
CONFECTIONER
CORN-CHANDLER
CORN-MERCHANT
COSMOGRAPHER
COSTERMONGER
CRANIOLOGIST
CROSSBENCHER
CRYPTOGAMIST
CRYPTOLOGIST
CRYSTAL-GAZER
DAME D'HONNEUR
DANCE HOSTESS
DEEP-SEA DIVER
DELTIOLOGIST
DEMONOLOGIST

PEOPLE – WORKERS

DEMONSTRATOR
DENDROLOGIST
DEONTOLOGIST
DIALECTICIAN
DISCOGRAPHER
DITHYRAMBIST
DOCK-LABOURER
DRAMA TEACHER
DRAMATURGIST
EDUCATIONIST
EGYPTOLOGIST
ELECTROTYPER
ELOCUTIONIST
EMBRYOLOGIST
ENGINE-DRIVER
ENGINE-FITTER
ENTOMOLOGIST
ENTREPRENEUR
ENZYMOLOGIST
ETHNOGRAPHER
EXPERIMENTER
FAMILY DOCTOR
FARM-LABOURER
FILM DIRECTOR
FILM PRODUCER
FISH-SALESMAN
FLINT-KNAPPER
FLYING DOCTOR
FOOTPLATEMAN
FRENCH MASTER
FRONT-BENCHER
FUTUROLOGIST
GALLOWS-MAKER
GARRET-MASTER
GEOMETRICIAN
GEOPHYSICIST
GERIATRICIAN
GERMAN MASTER
GLACIOLOGIST
GLOSSOLOGIST
GREASE-MONKEY
HAGIOGRAPHER
HARNESS-MAKER
HEAD-GARDENER
HEADMISTRESS
HEADSHRINKER
HEORTOLOGIST
HEPATOLOGIST
HERMENEUTIST
HIEROGRAMMAT
HIEROGRAPHER
HOMEOPATHIST

HORSE-BREAKER
HORSE-KNACKER
HORSE-TRAINER
HOTEL MANAGER
HOUSE-STEWARD
HOUSE SURGEON
HYDROGRAPHER
HYDROPATHIST
HYMNOGRAPHER
IAMBOGRAPHER
IATROCHEMIST
IMMUNOLOGIST
INCUNABULIST
INQUISITRESS
INSTRUCTRESS
INTERPLEADER
INVESTIGATOR
INVOICE CLERK
JERRY-BUILDER
JURISCONSULT
JURISPRUDENT
KING'S COUNSEL
KING'S PROCTOR
KITCHEN-KNAVE
KITCHEN-WENCH
KNIFE-GRINDER
LAND-SURVEYOR
LATH-SPLITTER
LATIN TEACHER
LAW-STATIONER
LEADER-WRITER
LEGAL ADVISER
LEGISLATRESS
LETTER-WRITER
LEXICOLOGIST
LINE-ENGRAVER
LITHOGRAPHER
LITHOTRITIST
LOGODAEDALUS
LOLLIPOP LADY
LONGSHOREMAN
LOSS ADJUSTER
MADAMOISELLE
MAID OF HONOUR
MAÎTRE D'HÔTEL
MAKE-UP ARTIST
MALACOLOGIST
MANUAL WORKER
MANUFACTURER
MARBLE-CUTTER
MATHS TEACHER
MEAT-SALESMAN

MERCANTILIST
MESSENGER-BOY
METALLURGIST
MICROGRAPHER
MICROGRAPHER
MICROSCOPIST
MINERALOGIST
MISCELLANIST
MONEY-CHANGER
MONOCHROMIST
MONOGRAPHIST
MONTHLY NURSE
MORPHOLOGIST
MUNITIONETTE
MUSICOLOGIST
MUSIC-TEACHER
MYTHOGRAPHER
NECROGRAPHER
NEPHROLOGIST
NEUROPATHIST
NEUROPTERIST
NEUROSURGEON
NEWSPAPER-MAN
NOTARY PUBLIC
OBSTETRICIAN
ODONTOLOGIST
OFFICE-BEARER
OFFICE-HOLDER
OFFICE JUNIOR
ONEIROCRITIC
ORCHESTRATOR
ORGAN-BUILDER
ORTHODONTIST
ORTHOGRAPHER
ORTHOPAEDIST
ORTHOPTERIST
OVARIOTOMIST
PALINDROMIST
PANTOGRAPHER
PAPER-MARBLER
PAPER-STAINER
PAPYROLOGIST
PARAGRAPHIST
PATTERN-MAKER
PEACE-OFFICER
PEARL-SHELLER
PETROGRAPHER
PHLEBOTOMIST
PHONOGRAPHER
PHOTOGRAPHER
PHRASE-MONGER
PHRENOLOGIST

PHYSIOLOGIST
PHYTOGRAPHER
PLOUGHWRIGHT
PLUMBER'S MATE
POET LAUREATE
POSTMISTRESS
POTAMOLOGIST
PRACTITIONER
PREHISTORIAN
PRESIDENTESS
PRESS OFFICER
PRISON WARDER
PROCESSIONER
PROFESSIONAL
PROPAGANDIST
PSEPHOLOGIST
PSYCHIATRIST
PSYCHOLOGIST
PUBLICITY MAN
PUBLIC ORATOR
PUPIL-TEACHER
PYROTECHNIST
QUARRYMASTER
RADIOGRAPHER
RECEPTIONIST
REMEMBRANCER
REPRESENTANT
RESTAURATEUR
RIDING-MASTER
ROAD-SURVEYOR
SALES MANAGER
SALOON-KEEPER
SCENE-PAINTER
SCENE-SHIFTER
SCHOOL-DOCTOR
SCHOOLMASTER
SCREEN-WRITER
SCRIPTWRITER
SCULLERY-MAID
SEED-MERCHANT
SEISMOLOGIST
SELENOLOGIST
SENIOR MASTER
SERVING-WENCH
SESSION-CLERK
SHARE-CROPPER
SHEEP-SHEARER
SHIP CHANDLER
SHIP'S HUSBAND
SHOEING-SMITH
SHOE-REPAIRER
SHOE-SHINE BOY

SILVER-BEATER
SLAUGHTERMAN
SLINK-BUTCHER
SOCIAL WORKER
SPECIAL AGENT
SPECKTIONEER
SPEECH-WRITER
SPOKESPERSON
SPONGE-FISHER
SPONGOLOGIST
SPORTSCASTER
SPORTS MASTER
SPORTS WRITER
STAGE-MANAGER
STATISTICIAN
STEEL ERECTOR
STENOGRAPHER
STOCK-BREEDER
STONE-BREAKER
STONE-DRESSER
STORIOLOGIST
STREET-KEEPER
STREET-TRADER
STREET-WALKER
SUBINSPECTOR
SUBLIBRARIAN
SUBTREASURER
SUGAR-REFINER
SUPERREALIST
SYSTEMATISER
TACHYGRAPHER
TASKMISTRESS
TAX-COLLECTOR
TAXING-MASTER
TECHNOLOGIST
TELEGRAPH BOY
TELEGRAPHIST
TENANT-FARMER
TERATOLOGIST
THEOREMATIST
THEORETICIAN
THERAPEUTIST
THIEF-CATCHER
THIRDBOROUGH
TICKET-PORTER
TICKET-WRITER
TITHE-PROCTOR
TOLL-GATHERER
TOURIST AGENT
TOUR OPERATOR
TOXICOLOGIST
TRANSPLANTER

TRICHOLOGIST
TRICK-CYCLIST
TRIGONOMETER
TYPOGRAPHIST
UNDERBUILDER
UNDERMANAGER
UNDERSHERIFF
UNDERWORKMAN
URBANOLOGIST
VETERINARIAN
VICE-CHAIRMAN
VICE-GOVERNOR
VOCABULARIAN
WAITING-WOMAN
WAREHOUSEMAN
WATER-BAILIFF
WINE-MERCHANT
WOOD-ENGRAVER
WORKING WOMAN
WORKMISTRESS
WORKS MANAGER
ZINCOGRAPHER

13

ADMINISTRATOR
AGRICULTURIST
AGROBIOLOGIST
AGROSTOLOGIST
ANTIQUE DEALER
ARACHNOLOGIST
ARCHAEOLOGIST
ARITHMETICIAN
ARTICLED CLERK
ASSYRIOLOGIST
ATTORNEY AT LAW
AUDIO-ENGINEER
BARBER-SURGEON
BIBLIOGRAPHER
BIOGEOGRAPHER
BIOLOGY MASTER
BOOK-CANVASSER
BUSINESSWOMAN
CALICO-PRINTER
CAMPANOLOGIST
CANDLE-LIGHTER
CARCINOLOGIST
CARDIOGRAPHER
CHALCOGRAPHER
CHLOROFORMIST
CHOREOGRAPHER

PEOPLE – WORKERS

CHRISTOLOGIST
CHRONOGRAPHER
CIVIL ENGINEER
CLEAR-STARCHER
CLIMATOLOGIST
COMMERCIALIST
CONGRESSWOMAN
COOK-HOUSEMAID
CORRESPONDENT
COTTON-SPINNER
CRANIOSCOPIST
CRIMINOLOGIST
CRYPTOGRAPHER
DANCING-MASTER
DEAN OF FACULTY
DEBT COLLECTOR
DENTAL SURGEON
DERMATOLOGIST
DIAGNOSTICIAN
DIAMOND-CUTTER
DISTRICT NURSE
DRAUGHTSWOMAN
DRAWING-MASTER
DRESS DESIGNER
DUBBING EDITOR
ELECTROTYPIST
ENGLISH MASTER
ENTREPRENEUSE
EPIGENETICIST
EPIGRAMMATIST
ESTATE MANAGER
EXPRESSIONIST
FELLOW-SERVANT
FENCING-MASTER
FEUILLETONIST
FORTUNE-TELLER
FREE COMPANION
FRENCH TEACHER
GAMES-MISTRESS
GERMAN TEACHER
GLOSSOGRAPHER
GLYPHOGRAPHER
GREEK MISTRESS
GROUND OFFICER
GYNAECOLOGIST
HAEMATOLOGIST
HAGIOGRAPHIST
HARBOUR-MASTER
HERESIOLOGIST
HERPETOLOGIST
HIEROGLYPHIST
HIGH CONSTABLE

HISTORY MASTER
HOUSEMISTRESS
ICHTHYOLOGIST
IMPRESSIONIST
INDUSTRIALIST
INSECTOLOGIST
INTERPRETRESS
JUDGE-ADVOCATE
KAPELLMEISTER
KINESIOLOGIST
KINESIPATHIST
KNIGHT-MARSHAL
LADY-IN-WAITING
LARYNGOLOGIST
LEPIDOPTERIST
LETTER-CARRIER
LETTER-FOUNDER
LEXICOGRAPHER
LICHENOLOGIST
LIGHTHOUSEMAN
LITERARY AGENT
LITHOGRAPHIST
LIVERY-SERVANT
LOLLIPOP WOMAN
LORD-IN-WAITING
LORD OF SESSION
LORD PRESIDENT
MACHINE-MINDER
MAID-OF-ALL-WORK
MALARIOLOGIST
MARTYROLOGIST
MASTER BUILDER
MATHEMATICIAN
MATHS MISTRESS
MELODRAMATIST
MESSENGER-GIRL
METEOROLOGIST
METOPOSCOPIST
MNEMOTECHNIST
MORPHOGRAPHER
MUSIC-MISTRESS
MYRMECOLOGIST
NEOGRAMMARIAN
NIGHT-WATCHMAN
OCEANOGRAPHER
OLD-CLOTHESMAN
OLFACTOLOGIST
ONEIROSCOPIST
ORCHESTRALIST
ORCHIDOLOGIST
ORNITHOLOGIST
ORTHOGRAPHIST

PAEDIATRICIAN
PALAEOGRAPHER
PALINGENESIST
PANGRAMMATIST
PANTHEOLOGIST
PEASANT-FARMER
PERIODICALIST
PHARMACEUTIST
PHONOGRAPHIST
PHRASEOLOGIST
PHYSICS MASTER
PHYSIOGNOMIST
PIGEON-FANCIER
POLICE OFFICER
POSTURE-MASTER
PREFABRICATOR
PRE-RAPHAELITE
PRIME MINISTER
PRINTER'S DEVIL
PRISON OFFICER
PROCESS-SERVER
PROJECTIONIST
PSYCHOANALYST
PSYCHOPATHIST
PTERIDOLOGIST
PUBLIC TRUSTEE
QUATERNIONIST
QUEEN'S COUNSEL
QUEEN'S PROCTOR
RAG-AND-BONE-MAN
RENT-COLLECTOR
RETINOSCOPIST
RODENT OFFICER
RUBBER-PLANTER
RUSSIAN MASTER
SANITATIONIST
SCHOOL-TEACHER
SCIENCE MASTER
SCRAP MERCHANT
SEISMOGRAPHER
SELENOGRAPHER
SERICULTURIST
SHOP-ASSISTANT
SINGING MASTER
SOVIETOLOGIST
SPANISH MASTER
SPECTROLOGIST
SPELAEOLOGIST
SPHAGNOLOGIST
SPORTS TEACHER
STAGE-COACHMAN
STATION-MASTER

STENOGRAPHIST
STEREOSCOPIST
STETHOSCOPIST
STILL-ROOM-MAID
STRATIGRAPHER
STREET-ORDERLY
STREET-SWEEPER
SUBCONTRACTOR
SUPPLY TEACHER
SURFACE WORKER
SYPHILOLOGIST
SYSTEMATICIAN
TACHYGRAPHIST
THERMOCHEMIST
TOLL COLLECTOR
TRAFFIC WARDEN
TRAM-CONDUCTOR
TRICHOPTERIST
VENEREOLOGIST
VICE-PRESIDENT
VICE-PRINCIPAL
VINICULTURIST
VITICULTURIST
VULCANOLOGIST
WELFARE WORKER
WHALING-MASTER
WINDOW-CLEANER
WINDOW-DRESSER
WOOLLEN-DRAPER
ZOOGEOGRAPHER

14

ADMINISTRATRIX
AERODYNAMICIST
ANTHROPOLOGIST
ASTROGEOLOGIST
ASTROPHYSICIST
AUDIOMETRICIAN
AUTOBIOGRAPHER
BACTERIOLOGIST
BALLET-MISTRESS
BILL-DISCOUNTER
BILLIARD-MARKER
BIOLOGY TEACHER
BUS-CONDUCTRESS
CASUAL LABOURER
CATHODOGRAPHER
CHALCOGRAPHIST
CHAMBER-COUNSEL
CHEIROGRAPHIST
CHIEF EXECUTIVE

CLAIMS ASSESSOR
CLASSICS MASTER
COMMISSIONAIRE
COST-ACCOUNTANT
CUSTOMS OFFICER
DESIGN ENGINEER
DISCOUNT-BROKER
DYSTELEOLOGIST
ECCLESIOLOGIST
ECONOMETRICIAN
EDUCATIONALIST
ELECTROCHEMIST
ENCYCLOPAEDIST
ENGLISH TEACHER
EPIDEMIOLOGIST
EXCHANGE-BROKER
FEMME DE CHAMBRE
FIFTH COLUMNIST
FLORICULTURIST
FOOD-CONTROLLER
FRENCH MISTRESS
FRENCH POLISHER
GENERAL MANAGER
GENERAL SERVANT
GENTLEMAN USHER
GERMAN MISTRESS
GROOM-IN-WAITING
GUTTER-MERCHANT
HANDICRAFTSMAN
HEPATICOLOGIST
HERESIOGRAPHER
HIGH-COURT JUDGE
HISTORY TEACHER
HORTICULTURIST
HOUSE-PHYSICIAN
HYDROTHERAPIST
KINDERGARTENER
KING'S MESSENGER
LANGUAGE MASTER
LARYNGOSCOPIST
LEADING COUNSEL
LEXICOGRAPHIST
LIAISON-OFFICER
LIPOGRAMMATIST
LITURGIOLOGIST
LORD LIEUTENANT
MAINTENANCE-MAN
MAÎTRE DE BALLET
MANUAL LABOURER
MARKET-GARDENER
MARRIAGE-BROKER
MERCHANT-TAILOR

METALLOGRAPHER
MISCELLANARIAN
MONEY-SCRIVENER
MUNITION-WORKER
MUSIC PUBLISHER
NEUROANATOMIST
PALAEOBOTANIST
PALAEOGRAPHIST
PARAGRAMMATIST
PARASITOLOGIST
PAVEMENT-ARTIST
PETTY CONSTABLE
PHARMACOLOGIST
PHARMACOPOLIST
PHYSICS TEACHER
PHYSIOGRAPHIST
PISCICULTURIST
PLASTIC SURGEON
PNEUMATOLOGIST
PROOF-CORRECTOR
PROPERTY-MASTER
PROTISTOLOGIST
PROTOZOOLOGIST
QUATTROCENTIST
QUESTION-MASTER
RECEPTION CLERK
REPRESENTATIVE
RHEUMATOLOGIST
RHYPAROGRAPHER
RUNNING FOOTMAN
RUSSIAN TEACHER
SCHOOLMISTRESS
SCIENCE TEACHER
SERGEANT-AT-ARMS
SHIP'S-CARPENTER
SPACE-TRAVELLER
SPANISH TEACHER
SPECTROSCOPIST
SPORTS MISTRESS
STATION-MANAGER
STEGANOGRAPHER
STORE DETECTIVE
STRATIGRAPHIST
SUPERINTENDENT
SYSTEMS ANALYST
TALLOW-CHANDLER
TIMBER MERCHANT
TOBACCO-PLANTER
TOWN COUNCILLOR
TRAFFIC-MANAGER
TRANSLITERATOR
TROUBLESHOOTER

PEOPLE – WORKERS

TURF ACCOUNTANT
UNDER-SECRETARY
UTTER BARRISTER
VALET DE CHAMBRE
VICE-CHANCELLOR
VISITOR GENERAL
VIVISECTIONIST
WATER-COLOURIST
WOODWORK MASTER
ZOOPATHOLOGIST

15

AGRICULTURALIST
AMBULANCE DRIVER
ANCILLARY WORKER
ARBORICULTURIST
ASSISTANT MASTER
ATHLETICS MASTER
ATTORNEY-GENERAL
AVERAGE ADJUSTER
BIOLOGY MISTRESS
BOW STREET RUNNER
CABINET MINISTER
CASTING DIRECTOR
CHARGÉ D'AFFAIRES
CHEMISTRY MASTER
CINEMATOGRAPHER
COMMISSION AGENT
COMPANY DIRECTOR
COMPANY PROMOTOR
CROSSING-SWEEPER

DANCING-MISTRESS
DIAMOND MERCHANT
DISTRICT VISITOR
DOMESTIC SERVANT
ENGLISH MISTRESS
FASHION-DESIGNER
FIELD NATURALIST
FORWARDING AGENT
FUNERAL DIRECTOR
GENTLEMAN FARMER
GEOCHRONOLOGIST
GEOGRAPHY MASTER
GEOMORPHOLOGIST
GOVERNOR-GENERAL
HACKNEY-COACHMAN
HEART SPECIALIST
HIEROGRAMMATIST
HISTORIOGRAPHER
HISTORY MISTRESS
HYDRODYNAMICIST
INSURANCE BROKER
JACK-OF-ALL-TRADES
JOBBING-GARDENER
JUDICIAL TRUSTEE
LOGICAL DESIGNER
LORD HIGH STEWARD
MASTER CARPENTER
MESSENGER-AT-ARMS
METALWORK MASTER
MINISTER OF STATE
MUSICAL DIRECTOR
NUMISMATOLOGIST
OPHTHALMOLOGIST

OSTREICULTURIST
PALAEONTOLOGIST
PALAEOZOOLOGIST
PAROEMIOGRAPHER
PHYSICS MISTRESS
PHYSIOTHERAPIST
PHYTOGEOGRAPHER
PICTURE-RESTORER
PLENIPOTENTIARY
POLICE CONSTABLE
POLICE INSPECTOR
PORTRAIT-PAINTER
PRIVY COUNCILLOR
PROGRAMME-SELLER
PSYCHOMETRICIAN
PSYCHOPHYSICIST
PSYCHOTHERAPIST
QUEEN'S MESSENGER
RAILWAY ENGINEER
RECEIVER-GENERAL
RESIDENT SURGEON
RUSSIAN MISTRESS
SCHOOL-INSPECTOR
SCIENCE MISTRESS
SPANISH MISTRESS
SPEECH THERAPIST
STEGANOGRAPHIST
STRETCHER-BEARER
THALASSOGRAPHER
TICKET-COLLECTOR
VICE-CHAMBERLAIN
WOODWORK TEACHER

PEOPLE – WORTHIES & ACADEMICS

3

DON
WIT

4

HERO
PROF
SAGE

5

ADEPT
BRAIN
DONOR
DOYEN
GIVER
HAKAM
KHOJA
RISHI
SAINT
SOLON
TITAN

6

DANIEL
EXPERT
FELLOW
GENIUS
KNIGHT
LEGEND
MARTYR
MASTER
MENTOR
NESTOR
ORACLE
PATRON
PILLAR
PUNDIT
ROLAND
SAVANT
TROJAN
WIZARD
WONDER
WORTHY

7

ACADEME
BASBLEU
BOOKMAN
CASUIST
CLERISY
DOYENNE
EGGHEAD
ENDOWER
ERUDITE
FOUNDER
HEROINE
MAHATMA
PRODIGY
RESCUER
RHEMIST
RIGHTER
SAVIOUR
SCHOLAR
SOLOMON
TRIBUNE
WITLING

8

ACADEMIC
BACHELOR
CHAMPION
EMERITUS
FOLK-HERO
GRADUATE
HEBRAIST
HIGHBROW
LATINIST
LITERATE
LITERATI
LUMINARY
MAECENAS
MANDARIN
POLYGLOT
POLYMATH
PRIZE-MAN
REFORMER
SAXONIST
SUPERMAN
THEOSOPH
VIRTUOSO
WELL-DOER

WRANGLER

9

AUTHORITY
BEL ESPRIT
CAMPEADOR
FOUNDRESS
HAGGADIST
LIBERATOR
LIFE-SAVER
LION-HEART
LITERATOR
PATRONESS
PROFESSOR
PROMACHUS
RUBRICIAN
SAMARITAN
SCHOOLMAN
SINOLOGUE
TALMUDIST
TARGUMIST
VERBALIST

10

BENEFACTOR
BLOOD DONOR
CLASSICIST
HONOURS-MAN
LICENTIATE
MASTERMIND
PEACEMAKER
POLYHISTOR
PROFICIENT
RUBRICIAN
SCHOLASTIC
THEOSOPHER

11

ACADEMICIAN
BRAINS TRUST
EMANCIPATOR
HOSPITALLER
LITTÉRATEUR
ORIENTALIST

SANSKRITIST
THAUMATURGE
THEOSOPHIST

12

ABOLITIONIST
BENEFACTRESS
BLUESTOCKING
INTELLECTUAL
MAN OF LETTERS
MASTER OF ARTS
PHILANTHROPE
POST-GRADUATE
PROFESSORESS
THAUMATURGUS

13

BACHELOR OF LAW
METAPHYSICIAN
NEOCLASSICIST
OCCIDENTALIST
POLYHISTORIAN
PROFESSORIATE
RHODES SCHOLAR

14

BACHELOR OF ARTS
INTELLIGENTSIA
PHILANTHROPIST
UNIVERSAL DONOR

15

BACHELOR OF MUSIC
EMANCIPATIONIST
KNIGHT OF THE ROAD
MASTER OF SCIENCE
REGIUS PROFESSOR
TOWER OF STRENGTH

PERSONAL – BELONGINGS

3

FAG
FAN
KEY
NET
PEN
WIG

4

CANE
COMB
GAMP
PASS
PIPE
QUIZ
SWAT
VISA

5

BRIAR
BRUSH
CIGAR
DIARY
DUMPY
JASEY
LINER
PARER
PURSE
RAZOR
ROMAL
ROUGE
SLANG
SLIDE
SNOOD
SPECS
STICK
STROP
STUMP
TOWEL
TRAPS
TRUNK
WATCH

6

ALBERT

BAG-WIG
BOBWIG
BROLLY
CHATTA
CHOWRY
COLMAR
CURLER
DUDEEN
FILLET
HANKIE
HUNTER
LOCKET
MIRROR
OCULAR
PEG-LEG
PENCIL
PERUKE
ROLLER
SACHET
SHAVER
SUDARY
TETTIX
TIE-WIG
TISSUE
TOUPEE
VALISE
WALLET

7

BUZZ-WIG
CHIBOUK
CHIGNON
COB-PIPE
COMPACT
CORK-LEG
CRACKER
CRIMPER
DEAF-AID
DENTURE
EAR-PICK
EAR-PLUG
EFFECTS
EYE-BATH
FLANNEL
FLY-SWAT
GINGHAM
GLASSES
GOGGLES
HAIR-NET
HAIRPIN

HAND-BAG
JUMELLE
KEY-RING
LANYARD
LEG-IRON
LIGHTER
LORGNON
LUGGAGE
MEMENTO
MONOCLE
PARASOL
PASS-KEY
PASS-OUT
PERIWIG
PIPE-KEY
SPENCER
STARERS
TOP-KNOT

8

BIFOCALS
CLAY-PIPE
CLIPPERS
CRUTCHES
DALMAHOY
DENTURES
EYEGLASS
EYE-LINER
EYE-PIECE
FLAPJACK
GIG-LAMPS
GLASS EYE
HAIR-GRIP
HANDBOOK
HIP-FLASK
HORN-RIMS
KEEPSAKE
KERCHIEF
LATCH-KEY
LIPSTICK
MARQUISE
MONTEITH
MOUCHOIR
NAIL-FILE
NOTEBOOK
NOTE-CASE
PASS-BOOK
PASSPORT
PEN-KNIFE
PINCE-NEZ

PIPE-CASE
POCHETTE
POMANDER
POSTICHE
ROULETTE
SCENT-BOX
SCISSORS
SHOE-HORN
SHOE-TREE
SIDE-COMB
SNUFF-BOX
SOUVENIR
SUDARIUM
SUIT-CASE
SUN-SHADE
TOILETRY
TWEEZERS
UMBRELLA
VALUABLE
WATCH-KEY
WIG-BLOCK

9

BARNACLES
CHEVELURE
CIGAR-CASE
CIGARETTE
CURL-PAPER
CUT-THROAT
DESK-DIARY
DONOR CARD
EN TOUT CAS
EYE-SHADOW
FACE-CLOTH
HAIR-BRUSH
HAIR-PIECE
HAIR-SLIDE
HAND-GLASS
JEWEL-CASE
LORGNETTE
MASTER-KEY
NAIL-BRUSH
PACEMAKER
PASS-CHECK
PICK-TOOTH
POWDER-BOX
PRESERVES
SEAT-STICK
SHOE-BRUSH
SNEEZE-BOX

TOOTHCOMB
TOOTH-PICK
TRAPPINGS
TRIFOCALS
VADE MECUM
VALUABLES
VANITY-BAG
VANITY-BOX
VIATICLES
WASH-CLOTH
WOODEN LEG

10

BELONGINGS
CHEQUE-BOOK
CREDIT CARD
DENTIFRICE
EAR-TRUMPET
EMERY-BOARD
EYE-GLASSES
FALSE TEETH
FOOT-WARMER
FULL-BOTTOM
HALF-HUNTER
HAND-MIRROR
HEARING AID
MEERSCHAUM
OPERA-GLASS
PERSONALIA
POCKET-BOOK
POCKET-COMB
POSSESSION
POUNCET-BOX
POWDER-PUFF
RATION-BOOK
RATION-CARD
RAZOR-BLADE
RAZOR-STROP
SHAVING-MUG
SPECTACLES
SUNGLASSES
TOILETRIES
TOILET-ROLL
TOOTHBRUSH
TOOTHPASTE
VANITY-CASE
WARMING-PAN
WATCH-CHAIN
WATCH-GUARD
WATCH-STRAP

WRIST-WATCH

11

ADDRESS-BOOK
BANKER'S CARD
CONTACT LENS
CORN-COB PIPE
CORNEAL LENS
CRISPING-PIN
CURLING-IRON
FACE-FLANNEL
FOUNTAIN-PEN
NOSE-NIPPERS
ORANGE-STICK
PENSION-BOOK
PIPE-CLEANER
POCKET-GLASS
POCKET-KNIFE
SAFETY-RAZOR
SCENT-BOTTLE
SCISSOR-CASE
SCRATCH-BACK
SKELETON KEY
SNOW-GOGGLES
TOBACCO-PIPE
TOILET-PAPER
TOOTH-POWDER
WALKING-CANE

12

CHURCHWARDEN

CIGAR-PIERCER
CRIMPING-IRON
CRISPING-IRON
CURLING-TONGS
DIGITAL WATCH
DRESSING-CASE
GLADSTONE BAG
HANDKERCHIEF
IDENTITY CARD
IDENTITY DISC
MOUSTACHE-CUP
NAIL-CLIPPERS
NAIL-SCISSORS
OVERNIGHT BAG
PASSE-PARTOUT
PENANG LAWYER
PORTE-MONNAIE
SHAVING-BRUSH
SHAVING-CREAM
SHAVING-STICK
TOBACCO-POUCH
TOILET-TISSUE
WALKING-STICK

13

BACK-SCRATCHER
BATTERY SHAVER
CIGARETTE-CASE
CONTACT LENSES
ELECTRIC RAZOR
EYEBROW-PENCIL
JOURNAL INTIME

LAISSEZ-PASSER
OVERNIGHT CASE
PARAPHERNALIA
POWDER COMPACT
QUIZZING-GLASS
SANITARY TOWEL
SHAVING-MIRROR
SHOOTING-STICK
SPECTACLE-CASE
STYPTIC PENCIL
WARDROBE TRUNK

14

ARTIFICIAL LIMB
CIGARETTE-PAPER
CUT-THROAT RAZOR
ELECTRIC SHAVER
FALSE EYELASHES
GLOVE-STRETCHER
HOT-WATER BOTTLE
SNOW-SPECTACLES
TOBACCO-STOPPER

15

CIGARETTE-HOLDER
FINE-TOOTHED COMB
LADIES' COMPANION
MAGNIFYING GLASS

PERSONAL – HAIRDRESSING & COSMETICS

3	MOP	4	FARD	PEAK	ROOT	WAVE	BRUSH
	NET		HAIR	PERM	SHAG		BUTCH
BOB	PIN	BANG	KOHL	PILE	TAIL		CAXON
BUN	TAG	CLIP	LASH	POLL	TALC	5	CRIMP
CUE	TIE	COMB	LOCK	POUF	TINT		CROWN
DYE	WIG	CROP	MUSK	PUFF	TRIM	BEARD	FRIZZ
MAT		CURL	PACK	ROLL	TUFT	BRAID	FRONT

PERSONAL – HAIRDRESSING & COSMETICS

HENNA
JASEY
LINER
PAINT
PATCH
PILUS
PLAIT
QUEUE
QUIFF
RAZOR
RINSE
ROUGE
RUSMA
SCENT
SHAVE
SHOCK
SINGE
SLIDE
SNOOD
STYLE
TRESS

6

BAG-WIG
BAY RUM
BINGLE
BOBWIG
BRUTUS
CHYPRE
CURLER
FACIAL
FILLET
FRINGE
GOATEE
HAIR-DO
LOTION
MAKE-UP
MARCEL
PAPPUS
PENCIL
PERUKE
POMADE
POUFFE
POWDER
PULVIL
RASURE
ROLLER
SHAVER
STRAND
TANGLE

TATTOO
TETTIX
THATCH
TIE-WIG
TOUPEE
WAVING

7

BEEHIVE
BLOW-DRY
BLUSHER
BRISTLE
BUZZ-WIG
CHARLIE
CHIGNON
COMBING
COMB-OUT
COMPACT
COWLICK
CRACKER
CREW CUT
CRIMPER
CUSHION
EARLOCK
ESSENCE
EYEBROW
EYELASH
FORETOP
FRIZZLE
FROUNCE
HAIRCUT
HAIR-DYE
HAIR-NET
HAIR-OIL
HAIRPIN
LACQUER
MASCARA
MUD-PACK
PAGE-BOY
PANCAKE
PARTING
PERFUME
PERIWIG
PIGTAIL
RINGLET
SHAMPOO
SHAVING
SHINGLE
SPENCER
STUBBLE

STYLING
TONSURE
TOP-KNOT
TRIPSIS
VANDYKE
WHISKER

8

AMANDINE
ATOMISER
BACK-HAIR
BANGTAIL
CLIPPERS
CLIPPING
COIFFURE
COLD PACK
COLD WAVE
COSMETIC
CURLICUE
DALMAHOY
EPILATOR
ETON CROP
EYE-LINER
FACE-LIFT
FACE-PACK
FIXATURE
FORELOCK
FRISETTE
HAIR-GRIP
HAIR-WAVE
HEADRING
IMPERIAL
KISS-CURL
LIPSTICK
LOVELOCK
MANICURE
PEROXIDE
POMANDER
PONY-TAIL
POSTICHE
RAT'S-TAIL
ROULETTE
SCENT-BOX
SCISSORS
SIDE-COMB
SIDELOCK
SPIT-CURL
TRIMMING
TWEEZERS
WAR PAINT

WHISKERS

9

BLUE RINSE
BURNT-CORK
CHEVELURE
COLD-CREAM
COSMETICS
CURL-PAPER
DEODORANT
EPILATION
EYE-SHADOW
FACE-CREAM
FAVOURITE
HAIR-BRUSH
HAIR-DRIER
HAIRINESS
HAIR-PIECE
HAIR-SLIDE
HAIR-STYLE
HAND-CREAM
MOUSTACHE
MUSTACHIO
PATCHOULI
PERFUMERY
POMPADOUR
POWDER-BOX
ROSE-WATER
SCALP-LOCK
SIDE-BURNS
SPIRIT-GUM
SUNTAN OIL
VAPORISER
WATER-WAVE

10

AFTER-SHAVE
BEAUTY SPOT
DEPILATION
DEPILATORY
FACE-POWDER
FALSE BEARD
FOUNDATION
FULL-BOTTOM
HAIR-POWDER
HAIR-WAVING
HEADPHONES
MAQUILLAGE

MARCEL WAVE
MILLEFLEUR
NAIL-POLISH
PEARL-WHITE
POCKET-COMB
POGONOTOMY
POUNCET-BOX
POWDER-PUFF
PRISON-CROP
RAZOR-BLADE
SHAGGINESS
SHAMPOOING
SIDE-BOARDS
SPADE-BEARD
WIDOW'S PEAK

11

BACK-COMBING
CONDITIONER
CURLING-IRON
FACE-LIFTING
GREASE-PAINT
HAIR-REMOVER
HIRSUTENESS
MACASSAR-OIL
NAIL-VARNISH
ORANGE-STICK

PEARL-POWDER
RUBEFACIENT
RUBEFACTION
SAFETY-RAZOR
SCENT-BOTTLE
SHAVING-SOAP
SIDE-WHISKER

12

BRILLIANTINE
COURT-PLASTER
CRIMPING-IRON
CRISPING-IRON
CURLING-TONGS
EAU DE COLOGNE
ELECTROLYSIS
HAIRDRESSING
HAIR-RESTORER
HEARTBREAKER
MOUSTACHE-CUP
NAIL-CLIPPERS
NAIL-SCISSORS
NEWGATE FRILL
SCALPING-TUFT
SHAVING-BRUSH
SHAVING-CREAM
SHAVING-STICK

SIDE-WHISKERS
SUNTAN LOTION
TALCUM-POWDER
VANDYKE BEARD

13

BATTERY SHAVER
EYEBROW-PENCIL
LAVENDER-WATER
NEWGATE FRINGE
PERMANENT WAVE
POWDER-COMPACT

14

CUT-THROAT RAZOR
ELECTRIC SHAVER
FALSE EYELASHES
VANISHING CREAM

15

FOUNDATION CREAM
WALRUS MOUSTACHE

PERSONAL – JEWELLERY & TRINKETS

3	**DROP**	**5**	CULET	**6**	DIADEM	OLIVET
	JADE		CURIO		DOODAD	PEBBLE
GEM	MACE	AGATE	FACET	ALBERT	EARBOB	POMPOM
ICE	ONYX	AMBER	JEWEL	AMULET	FIBULA	POPPET
JET	OPAL	BERYL	LAPIS	ANKLET	FINERY	PRETTY
ORB	OUCH	BEZEL	MOTIF	ARMLET	GARNET	PYROPE
PIN	PAVÉ	BIJOU	PASTE	BANGLE	GEWGAW	QUARTZ
	RING	BUGLE	PEARL	BAUBLE	HATPIN	RONDEL
	ROCK	BULLA	STONE	BROOCH	IOLITE	ROSARY
4	ROPE	CAMEO	TIARA	CHATON	JASPER	SCARAB
	RUBY	CHARM	TOPAZ	CHOKER	JIMJAM	SIGNET
BEAD	SARD	CLASP		COLLET	LEGLET	STRASS
BORT		CROWN		CORALS	LOCKET	TIE-PIN

PERSONAL – JEWELLERY & TRINKETS

TORQUE
WAMPUM
ZIRCON

7

ANNULET
ARMILLA
ASTERIA
AXINITE
BAROQUE
BIBELOT
CAT'S EYE
CORONET
CRYSTAL
DIAMOND
EARDROP
EARRING
EMERALD
EUCLASE
GEMMERY
GIRASOL
JACINTH
JARGOON
JEWELRY
MANILLA
NECKLET
OLIVINE
PARAGON
PENDANT
PERIDOT
REGALIA
RIVIÈRE
SARDIUS
SCEPTRE
SETTING
SLEEPER
SMARAGD
SPANGLE
TIE-TACK
TORSADE
TRINKET
YU-STONE

8

AIGRETTE

AMETHYST
BAGUETTE
BRACELET
BRELOQUE
CABOCHON
CARCANET
CARDIASE
CUFF-LINK
DIAGLYPH
DIAMANTÉ
FIRE-OPAL
FRIPPERY
GEMSTONE
GIMCRACK
HELIODOR
HYACINTH
INTAGLIO
MARQUISE
MELANITE
NECKLACE
NEGLIGEE
NOSE-RING
ORNAMENT
PEAR-DROP
SAPPHIRE
SARDONYX
SCARABEE
SCARF-PIN
SEMI-OPAL
SNAP-LINK
SPARKLER
SUNSTONE
TREASURE
TRUMPERY
WRISTLET

9

ALMANDINE
BALAS RUBY
BREASTPIN
BRIC-À-BRAC
BRILLIANT
CACHOLONG
CARBUNCLE
CYMOPHANE
GIRANDOLE
GUARD-RING

JEWELLERY
JOB'S TEARS
MARCASITE
MOONSTONE
NOBLE OPAL
RING-SMALL
ROSE-TOPAZ
RUBELLITE
SCARABOID
SEED-PEARL
SOLITAIRE
STAR-STONE
TRINKETRY
TURQUOISE
UVAROVITE
VALUABLES

10

ANDALUSITE
AQUAMARINE
BIJOUTERIE
BLOODSTONE
CHALCEDONY
CHANK-SHELL
CHÂTELAINE
CHRYSOLITE
CROWN-JEWEL
HYDROPHANE
KNICK-KNACK
LAVALLIÈRE
PHYLACTERY
RHINESTONE
SIGNET-RING
SPINEL RUBY
TOPAZOLITE
TOURMALINE
WATCH-CHAIN
WORRY-BEADS

11

ALEXANDRITE
CHALCEDONYX
CHRYSOBERYL
COLOPHONITE
DENDRACHATE

FERRONNIÈRE
KIDNEY-STONE
LAPIS LAZULI
ROSE-DIAMOND
SCARABAEOID
WEDDING-RING

12

BOHEMIAN RUBY
ETERNITY RING
MOURNING-RING
ORIENTAL RUBY
SCOTCH PEBBLE
STAR SAPPHIRE

13

BOHEMIAN TOPAZ
BONE-TURQUOISE
CINNAMON-STONE
CULTURED PEARL
ORIENTAL PEARL
ORIENTAL TOPAZ
PEARL NECKLACE
PRECIOUS STONE
STRING OF BEADS
WATER-SAPPHIRE

14

ASPARAGUS-STONE
ENGAGEMENT RING
SIMULATED PEARL
STRING OF PEARLS
URALIAN EMERALD

15

OCCIDENTAL TOPAZ
ORIENTAL EMERALD

PHOTOGRAPHY

3

CAT

4

FILM
HYPO
LENS
MASK
PACK
PYRO
REEL
SAXE
SHOT
SNAP
SPOT
TAKE
TINT

5

ALBUM
BLIMP
FLASH
FOCUS
INSET
KODAK
METOL
ORTHO
PANEL
PHOTO
PLATE
PRINT
PROOF
SHOOT
SLIDE
SPOOL
STILL
TRAIL

6

CAMERA
FILTER
QUINOL
RÉSEAU
RETAKE
SCREEN

STUDIO
TISSUE
TRIPOD
UNIPOD
VIEWER

7

BELLOWS
CLOSE-UP
CYANINE
ENPRINT
MONTAGE
OPALINE
PICTURE
REPRINT
RETOUCH
SHUTTER
TINTYPE
VIDICON

8

APERTURE
CALOTYPE
CASSETTE
DARK-ROOM
DISC FILM
DRY-PLATE
EMULSION
ENLARGER
EXPOSURE
FLASH-BAR
FLASH-GUN
FOCUSING
GELATINE
HALATION
HOLOGRAM
MOUNTANT
NEGATIVE
PARALLAX
PORTRAIT
POSITIVE
SNAPSHOT
SQUEEGEE
SUN-PRINT
VIGNETTE
WET-PLATE
ZOOM LENS

9

AIR-BUBBLE
AMPLIFIER
ANGIOGRAM
BLUEPRINT
BOX-CAMERA
CELLULOID
COLLODION
DEVELOPER
FERROTYPE
FLASH-BULB
FOCIMETER
HALF-PLATE
HELIOTYPE
HELIOTYPY
KALLITYPE
MAGNIFIER
MEZZOTINT
MICROFILM
MOSAIC MAP
PHOTOCELL
PHOTO-COPY
PHOTOGENE
PHOTOSTAT
PHOTOTYPE
PHOTOTYPY
ROTOGRAPH
SHEET FILM
SPOTLIGHT
SWING-BACK
TALBOTYPE
TELEMETER
TELEMETRY
WIRE-PHOTO
XENON LAMP

10

ABERRATION
ANASTIGMAT
APOCHROMAT
CHROMATYPE
CHROMOGRAM
CHROMOTYPE
CINE-CAMERA
COLOUR FILM
DEVELOPING
DISC CAMERA
FERRO-PRINT
FLASHLIGHT

HELIOGRAPH
HOLOGRAPHY
ICONOMETER
ICONOMETRY
ICONOSCOPE
LITHOGRAPH
MICROFICHE
MONOCHROME
MONOCHROMY
NEPHOGRAPH
PANTOSCOPE
PHOTOGLYPH
PHOTOGRAPH
PROCESSING
SILVER-BATH
STANNOTYPE
STICKY-BACK
STIGMATISM
SUN-PICTURE
VERTOSCOPE
VIEWFINDER
WHOLE-PLATE
XEROGRAPHY

11

ACHROMATISM
ANGIOGRAPHY
ASTIGMATISM
AUTOGRAVURE
BARYTA PAPER
COMPOSITION
DEVELOPMENT
DIAPOSITIVE
ENLARGEMENT
FISH-EYE LENS
HELIOCHROME
HELIOGRAPHY
INTENSIFIER
IRRADIATION
KINETOGRAPH
KINETOSCOPE
LITHOGRAPHY
PHOTOGLYPHY
PHOTOGRAPHY
PHOTO-RELIEF
PLATINOTYPE
RANGEFINDER
ROTOGRAVURE
STOPPING-OUT

PHOTOGRAPHY

12

BROMIDE PAPER
CANDID CAMERA
CHROMATOGRAM
COLOUR FILTER
COLOUR SCREEN
EVAPOROGRAPH
HELIOGRAVURE
HYDROQUINONE
MICROCOPYING
OVEREXPOSURE
PANORAMA HEAD
PAPER-WASHING
PHOTO-COPYING
PHOTO-ETCHING
PHOTOGRAVURE
PHOTO-PROCESS
QUARTER-PLATE
REPRODUCTION
RÖNTGENOGRAM
SHUTTER-SPEED
SOLARISATION
THERMOGRAPHY

TIME-EXPOSURE
TRANSPARENCY
WOODBURYTYPE

13

ANASTIGMATISM
APOCHROMATISM
CAMERA OBSCURA
CARBON PROCESS
DAGUERREOTYPE
DAGUERREOTYPY
FOCUSING CLOTH
IRIS DIAPHRAGM
MAGNIFICATION
PANCHROMATISM
TELEPHOTO LENS
UNDEREXPOSURE
WIDE-ANGLE LENS

14

ALL-ROUND CAMERA

CHROMATOGRAPHY
LANTHANUM GLASS
PHOTO-ENGRAVING
POLAROID CAMERA
PYROPHOTOGRAPH
RÖNTGENOGRAPHY
TELEPHOTOGRAPH

15

CINEMICROGRAPHY
ELECTRONIC FLASH
MICROPHOTOGRAPH
PANORAMIC CAMERA
PERIPHERY CAMERA
PHOTOGRAPH ALBUM
PHOTOLITHOGRAPH
PHOTOMICROGRAPH
PYROPHOTOGRAPHY
TELEPHOTOGRAPHY

PLANTS — FLOWERS & GENERAL PLANTS

3

BAY
COS
DAL
FOG
HOP
IVY
KAT
KOA
LOP
MAY
MEU
NEP
OAT
OCA
PEA
PIA
RUE
RYE
TEA
TEF
TIL
UDO
YAM

4

ALFA
ALGA
ALOE
ARUM
BALM
BAST
BEAN
BEAR
BEET
BENT
BIGG
CHAY
COCA
CORN
DILL
DISS
DOCK
DOOB
FERN
FLAG
FLAX
GALE
GRAM

GUAR
HEMP
IRIS
JUTE
KALE
KALI
KANS
KAVA
KELP
LEEK
LILY
LING
LOCO
MATÉ
MINT
MOSS
NABK
OATS
PINK
POKE
RAGI
RAMI
RAPE
REED
RHEA
RICE
ROSE
RUSA
RUSH
SAGE
SEGO
SOLA
SOMA
SOYA
SUNN
TANG
TARA
TARE
TARO
TULE
TUNA
TUTU
VINE
WELD
WHIN
WOAD

5

ABACA
AGAVE

ALGAE
ANISE
ARNUT
ASPIC
ASTER
BABUL
BAJRA
BASIL
BLITE
BRAKE
BRANK
BRIAR
BRIER
BROOM
BUAZE
BUGLE
CACTI
CALLA
CANNA
CHIVE
CHUFA
CLARY
CLOTE
CORAL
COUCH
CRESS
CUMIN
DAGGA
DAISY
DILDO
DOORN
DULSE
DURRA
DURUM
DWALE
EMMER
FRAIL
FURZE
GLAUX
GORSE
GOWAN
GRAMA
GUACO
GUMBO
HALFA
HAVER
HENNA
HOLLY
JOWAR
KUDZU
LAVER
LIANA

LILAC
LOTUS
LUPIN
MAIZE
MAQUI
MELIC
MOREL
MULGA
MYALL
MYRRH
NAVEW
NOPAL
ONION
ORACH
ORRIS
OSHAC
OXEYE
OXLIP
PANIC
PANSY
PEONY
PHLOX
POPPY
PULSE
QUICK
RAMIE
REATE
RIVET
SALAL
SAVIN
SEDGE
SENNA
SENVY
SPELT
SPINK
STARR
STOCK
SWEDE
TANSY
THYME
TIMBÓ
TORCH
TULIP
VETCH
VIOLA
WAHOO
WHEAT
WHISK
WRACK
YERBA
YUCCA
YULAN

6

ACACIA
AGARIC
AJOWAN
ALSIKE
AMADOU
ARCHIL
ARGHAN
AZALEA
BABLAH
BALSAM
BAMBOO
BARLEY
BATATA
BETONY
BLINKS
BORAGE
BRYONY
BURNET
BYSSUS
CACTUS
CAMASS
CARROT
CASHAW
CASSIA
CASUAL
CATNIP
CELERY
CICELY
CLOVER
COCKLE
COMBER
COROZO
COSTUS
COTTON
COWAGE
COW-PEA
CROCUS
CROTAL
CUMMIN
DAHLIA
DAPHNE
DARNEL
DESMID
DODDER
DRAGON
ENDIVE
ERYNGO
FENNEL
FESCUE
FIMBLE

FIORIN
FRIJOL
FRUTEX
GARLIC
GOLLAN
HENBIT
HYSSOP
IVY-TOD
JUJUBE
KIE-KIE
KISS-ME
KNAWEL
KOWHAI
LABLAB
LALANG
LAUREL
LAWYER
LENTIL
LOVAGE
LUNARY
MADDER
MAGUEY
MALLOW
MARRAM
MARROW
MATICO
MEDICK
MILLET
MIMOSA
MOUTAN
MUSCAT
MYRTLE
NETTLE
OLD MAN
OPULUS
ORCHID
ORPINE
OURALI
OURARI
PAIGLE
PEPPER
POTATO
PRIVET
PROTEA
QUINOA
QUITCH
RADISH
RAMSON
RATTAN
RETAMA
ROCKET
RUNNER

PLANTS – FLOWERS & GENERAL PLANTS

RUSCUS
SALLEE
SAVORY
SEA-FAN
SEA-PEN
SEMSEM
SENEGA
SESAME
SORGHO
SORREL
SPURGE
SQUASH
SQUILL
STACTE
SUN-DEW
TANGLE
TEASEL
THRIFT
TOMATO
TURNIP
TUTSAN
VIOLET
WILLOW
YARROW
YAUPON
ZINNIA

7

ACONITE
ALE-HOOF
ALFALFA
ALKANET
ALL-GOOD
ALLHEAL
ALLSEED
ANEMONE
BEGONIA
BENTHOS
BISTORT
BLAWORT
BOGBEAN
BOG-MOSS
BONESET
BRACKEN
BRAMBLE
BRINJAL
BUGBANE
BUGLOSS
BUGWORT
BULLACE

BULRUSH
BURDOCK
BUR-REED
BURWEED
CABBAGE
CALAMUS
CALTROP
CAMPANA
CAMPION
CANDOCK
CARAWAY
CARDOON
CARLINE
CATMINT
CAT'S-EAR
CAYENNE
CHAMISO
CHERVIL
CHESSEL
CHICORY
CLARKIA
CLOTBUR
COMFREY
COONTIE
COWBANE
COWHAGE
COWSLIP
CROTTLE
CUDWEED
DAY-LILY
DIONAEA
DITTANY
DOG-ROSE
DOGWOOD
ESPARTO
FELWORT
FIGWORT
FLYBANE
FLY-TRAP
FOX-TAIL
FREESIA
FROGBIT
FUCHSIA
GENISTA
GENTIAN
GILTCUP
GINGILI
GINSENG
GLADDON
GOA BEAN
GODETIA
GOLLAND

GUARANA
GUAYALE
GUNNERA
HAGWEED
HARICOT
HARMALA
HASSOCK
HAWKBIT
HEATHER
HEMLOCK
HENBANE
HOGWEED
HONESTY
HOP-VINE
ISOKONT
IVY-BUSH
JASMINE
JEW'S EAR
JONQUIL
JUNIPER
KINGCUP
LETTUCE
LOBELIA
LUCERNE
MADWORT
MATWEED
MAY-LILY
MAYWEED
MERCURY
MILFOIL
MUDWORT
MUGWORT
MULLEIN
MUSTARD
NIGELLA
OAK-FERN
OAK-LUMP
OARWEED
OREGANO
PALMIET
PANACEA
PAPYRUS
PAREIRA
PARELLA
PARSLEY
PARSNIP
PETUNIA
PICOTEE
PIG-LILY
PIGWEED
PILCORN
PINGUIN

POP-WEED
PUCCOON
QUICKEN
RAGWEED
RAGWORT
RAMPION
RED ALGA
RED-ROOT
RHATANY
RHODORA
RHUBARB
RIBWORT
ROSE-BAY
ROSELLE
SAFFRON
SAGUARO
SALFERN
SALSIFY
SANICLE
SAW-WORT
SEA-BEET
SEA-KALE
SEA-LILY
SEA-MOSS
SEA-PINK
SEA-REED
SEA-TANG
SEA-WARE
SEAWEED
SERINGA
SETWALL
SHALLON
SHALLOT
SKIRRET
SOLDIER
SORGHUM
SPIGNEL
SPINACH
SQUITCH
SYRINGA
TARWEED
TEA-ROSE
THISTLE
TOBACCO
TREFOIL
TRUFFLE
UVA-URSI
VANILLA
VERVAIN
WALL-RUE
WARATAH
WHANGEE

WILD-OAT
WITLOOF
WOURALI
ZEDOARY

8

ABSINTHE
ACANTHUS
AGAR-AGAR
AGRIMONY
ALUM-ROOT
AMARACUS
AMARANTH
AMBROSIA
AMELCORN
ANGELICA
ARGEMONY
ARUM LILY
ASPHODEL
AURICULA
BARBERRY
BAROMETZ
BEARBINE
BEAR'S-EAR
BEDSTRAW
BELLWORT
BIGNONIA
BILBERRY
BINDWEED
BIRD'S-EYE
BLUEBELL
BLUEWEED
BORECOLE
BOY'S LOVE
BROCCOLI
BUCKBEAN
BUDDLEIA
BULL-HOOF
BUPLEVER
BUSH-ROPE
CALAMINT
CAMELLIA
CAMOMILE
CANAIGRE
CANNABIS
CAPSICUM
CARL-HEMP
CATCHFLY
CAT'S-FOOT
CHARLOCK

276

CHAY-ROOT
CHICK-PEA
CLEAVERS
CLEMATIS
CLUB-MOSS
CLUB-RUSH
CORN-FLAG
COSTMARY
COWGRASS
COW-PLANT
COW-WHEAT
CROWFOOT
CRUCIFER
CUCUMBER
CUP-CORAL
CYCLAMEN
DAFFODIL
DEATH-CAP
DEATH-CUP
DEER-HAIR
DIANTHUS
DOGBERRY
DOG-DAISY
DOG-GRASS
DOG'S-BANE
DOG-WHEAT
DROP-WORT
DUCKWEED
DUMB-CANE
EARTHNUT
EARTH-PEA
EEL-GRASS
EEL-WRACK
EGG-PLANT
ESCAROLE
ESCHALOT
EUPHRASY
FERN-ALLY
FEVERFEW
FIREWEED
FLAX-BUSH
FLAX-LILY
FLEA-BANE
FLIX-WEED
FLUELLIN
FOALFOOT
FOXGLOVE
FUMITORY
GARDENIA
GAS-PLANT
GERANIUM
GLORY-PEA

GLOXINIA
GOAT'S-RUE
GOATWEED
GOUTWEED
GOUTWORT
GROMWELL
GULF-WEED
HAG-TAPER
HARD-HACK
HARDHEAD
HAREBELL
HARE'S-EAR
HAT-PLANT
HAWKWEED
HEARTPEA
HEMP-BUSH
HEMP-PALM
HENEQUEN
HIBISCUS
HORNWORT
HYACINTH
ICE-PLANT
ITCHWEED
JAPONICA
KAKA-BEAK
KAKA-BILL
KNAPWEED
KOHLRABI
LADY-FERN
LARKSPUR
LAVENDER
LENT-LILY
LICORICE
LIMA BEAN
LIVELONG
LOCO-WEED
LONG MOSS
LOPGRASS
LUNGWORT
MAGNOLIA
MALE-FERN
MANDRAKE
MANY-ROOT
MARIGOLD
MARJORAM
MARTAGON
MATFELON
MAT-GRASS
MAY-APPLE
MAY-BLOOM
MESQUITE
MEZEREON

MILK-WEED
MILKWORT
MOONSEED
MOONWORT
MOSS-ROSE
MOUSE-EAR
MULBERRY
MUSCATEL
MUSHROOM
MUSK-ROSE
NECKWEED
NENUPHAR
NEPENTHE
NIT-GRASS
NOISETTE
NONESUCH
NUT-GRASS
OAT-GRASS
OLEANDER
ORIGANUM
OX-TONGUE
PASPALUM
PATIENCE
PEA-PLANT
PIE-PLANT
PILEWORT
PILLWORT
PINKROOT
PIPEWORT
PLANTAIN
POKEWEED
POLYPODY
POND-LILY
PONDWEED
PRIMROSE
PUFF-BALL
PURSLANE
PUTCHOCK
RATSBANE
RIB-GRASS
ROCK-ROSE
ROCKWEED
ROSEMARY
ROSE-ROOT
ROT-GRASS
RYE-GRASS
SAINFOIN
SALT-BUSH
SALT-WORT
SAMPHIRE
SANDWORT
SARCODES

SARGASSO
SARRASIN
SCABIOUS
SCAMMONY
SEA-BERRY
SEA-BLITE
SEA-GRAPE
SEA-GRASS
SEA-HEATH
SEA-HOLLY
SEA-ONION
SEA-ORACH
SEA-SHRUB
SEA-WRACK
SELF-HEAL
SENGREEN
SEPT-FOIL
SHADBUSH
SHAMROCK
SILPHIUM
SKULLCAP
SLOE-BUSH
SMALLAGE
SNOWBALL
SNOWDROP
SOAP-ROOT
SOAPWORT
SOW-BREAD
SPEKBOOM
SPHAGNUM
STARWORT
STONE-RAG
STONE-RAW
SUN-DROPS
SUNN-HEMP
SWEET-BAY
SWEET-PEA
SWEET-SOP
TAMARISK
TARA-FERN
TARRAGON
TEA-PLANT
TOAD-FLAX
TOAD-RUSH
TREE-FERN
TREE-LILY
TREE-MOSS
TUBEROSE
TUCKAHOE
TURK'S CAP
TURMERIC
TURNSOLE

VALERIAN
WALL-MOSS
WALLWORT
WARTWEED
WARTWORT
WATER-YAM
WHIPCORD
WILD RICE
WILD ROSE
WISTARIA
WISTERIA
WOODBIND
WOODBINE
WOODRUFF
WOODRUSH
WOODSAGE
WORMWOOD
XANTHIUM
ZINGIBER

9

AARON'S ROD
ADDERWORT
AMARYLLID
AMARYLLIS
ARRACACHA
ARROW-HEAD
ARROW-ROOT
ARTICHOKE
ASCLEPIAD
ASPARAGUS
AUBRIETIA
BALDMONEY
BANEBERRY
BEAR-BERRY
BEAR'S-FOOT
BEECH-FERN
BEE-FLOWER
BEE-ORCHIS
BENT-GRASS
BIRD'S-FOOT
BIRTHWORT
BLOOD-ROOT
BLUE-GRASS
BLUE POPPY
BLUSH-ROSE
BOG-MYRTLE
BREADROOT
BROAD BEAN
BROMELIAD

277

PLANTS – FLOWERS & GENERAL PLANTS

BROOKLIME
BROOKWEED
BROOMRAPE
BUCKTHORN
BUCKWHEAT
BUTTERCUP
CALAVANCE
CALENDULA
CALLA LILY
CANDYTUFT
CAPER-BUSH
CARNATION
CATCHWEED
CELANDINE
CERASTIUM
CHICKLING
CHICKWEED
CHINA JUTE
CINERARIA
CLOVE-PINK
COCKLE-BUR
COCKSCOMB
COCKSFOOT
COLOCYNTH
COLTSFOOT
COLUMBINE
CONE WHEAT
CORALLINE
CORAL-ROOT
CORALWORT
CORIANDER
CORN-SALAD
CORD-GRASS
COURGETTE
CRANBERRY
CROSSWORT
CROW-BERRY
CULVER-KEY
CUP-LICHEN
CYNOSURUS
DANDELION
DAY-NETTLE
DELPHARIA
DESERT PEA
DEVIL'S BIT
DITTANDER
DOCK-CRESS
DOG-VIOLET
DOORN-BOOM
DOVE'S-FOOT
DRIFTWEED
DUCK'S-FOOT

DUCK'S-MEAT
DULCAMARA
DUTCH RUSH
DYER'S-WEED
EARTH-STAR
EDELWEISS
EGLANTINE
EPILOBIUM
EYEBRIGHT
FENUGREEK
FLAGEOLET
FLAME-LEAF
FLY-AGARIC
FLY-ORCHIS
FORSYTHIA
FRIAR'S CAP
GALINGALE
GAMA-GRASS
GERMANDER
GLADIOLUS
GLASSWORT
GOLDEN ROD
GOOSEFOOT
GORGONIAN
GRAPEVINE
GRASS-TREE
GREENWEED
GROUND-IVY
GROUNDSEL
GYPSYWORT
HAIR-GRASS
HARD-GRASS
HARE'S-FOOT
HEARTSEED
HEATH BELL
HELLEBORE
HERB-PARIS
HERB-PETER
HERD GRASS
HIGH-TAPER
HOLLY-FERN
HOLLYHOCK
HOLY GRASS
HOREHOUND
HORSEMINT
HORSETAIL
HOUSE-LEEK
HYALOMENA
HYDRANGEA
INDIAN FIG
IRISH MOSS
ISOKONTAN

JESSAMINE
JEWEL-WEED
JEWS' THORN
KNEE-HOLLY
KNOTGRASS
LARK'S-HEEL
LASERWORT
LEMON-WEED
LIQUORICE
LIVERWORT
LOCO-PLANT
LOUSEWORT
LYME-GRASS
MADREPORE
MAN-ORCHIS
MARE'S-TAIL
MARIHUANA
MARIJUANA
MARSHWORT
MAYFLOWER
MEADOW-RUE
MILK-VETCH
MISTLETOE
MONEYWORT
MONKSHOOD
MOSCHATEL
MOSS-PLANT
MOUSE-TAIL
MUSK-PLANT
NAKED LADY
NARCISSUS
NAVELWORT
NULLIPORE
PAPER-REED
PARROT-JAW
PATCHOULI
PEARLWORT
PELLITORY
PENNYWORT
PETTY WHIN
PIGEON-PEA
PIMPERNEL
PINEAPPLE
POINCIANA
POISON-IVY
POKEBERRY
PYRACANTH
PYRETHRUM
QUILLWORT
RED RATTLE
REED-GRASS
RHAPONTIC

RICE-GRASS
RIVERWEED
ROCAMBOLE
ROCK-BRAKE
ROCK-CRESS
ROSE-ELDER
ROSIN-WEED
ROYAL FERN
RUSA GRASS
RUSTY-BACK
SAFFLOWER
SAGE-BRUSH
SAND-GRASS
SASKATOON
SAXIFRAGE
SCALE-FERN
SCALE-MOSS
SEA-BOTTLE
SEA-GINGER
SEA-GIRDLE
SEA-LENTIL
SEA-ROCKET
SEA-TANGLE
SEED-CORAL
SHEEP'S BIT
SHORE-WEED
SILK-GRASS
SLINKWEED
SMARTWEED
SMOKE-BUSH
SNAKEROOT
SNAKEWEED
SNOWBERRY
SNOWFLAKE
SOFT-GRASS
SOUR-GOURD
SPEARMINT
SPEARWOOD
SPEARWORT
SPEEDWELL
SPICE-BUSH
SPIKENARD
SPIKE-RUSH
STAFF-TREE
STAR-GRASS
STAR-JELLY
STINKHORN
STONECROP
STONEWORT
STRAPWORT
STRING-PEA
SUGAR-BEET

SUGAR-CANE
SUNFLOWER
SUN-SPURGE
SWEETCORN
SWEET-FLAG
SWEET-GALE
SWORD-BEAN
TAPE-GRASS
THORN-BUSH
TIGER-LILY
TOAD-GRASS
TOADSTOOL
TOOTHWORT
TORCH-LILY
TORMENTIL
TRITICALE
TWAY-BLADE
VETCHLING
WAKE-ROBIN
WALL-CRESS
WART-CRESS
WATER-FLAG
WATER-LEAF
WATER-LILY
WATER-RICE
WATER-VINE
WAX-FLOWER
WIDOW-WAIL
WILD GRAPE
WIRE-GRASS
WOLF'S-BANE
WOLF'S-CLAW
WOLF'S-FOOT
WORM-GRASS
WOUNDWORT

10

ALEXANDERS
AMPELOPSIS
ARROW-GRASS
ASARABACCA
ASPIDISTRA
BARRENWORT
BASIL-THYME
BEARD-GRASS
BELLADONNA
BELL-FLOWER
BIRD-PEPPER
BISHOP'S CAP
BITTER-KING

BITTER-ROOT
BLACKTHORN
BLUEBOTTLE
BLUE-ROCKET
BRAIN CORAL
BROME-GRASS
BROWN ALGAE
BROWN JOLLY
BUFFALO-NUT
BUNCH-GRASS
BURNET ROSE
BUR-THISTLE
BUSY-LIZZIE
BUTTERDOCK
BUTTERWORT
BUTTON-BUSH
CALICO-BUSH
CANADA RICE
CANCER-ROOT
CANDELILLA
CARRAGHEEN
CHAMPIGNON
CHINA ASTER
CHINA GRASS
CHURNSTAFF
CINQUE-FOIL
CITRONELLA
CLUSTER-CUP
CORAL-BERRY
CORNCOCKLE
CORNFLOWER
COTTON-WEED
COUCH-GRASS
COW-CHERVIL
COW-PARSLEY
COW-PARSNIP
CRANE'S-BILL
CUCKOO-PINT
DAMASK ROSE
DELPHINIUM
DOG-PARSLEY
DOG'S-FENNEL
DOG'S-TONGUE
DRAGON-ROOT
DYER'S-BROOM
EARTH-SMOKE
ELECAMPANE
FALLEN STAR
FLEUR-DE-LIS
FLOAT-GRASS
FOUR-O-CLOCK
FRANGIPANI

FRENCH BEAN
FRIAR'S COWL
FROG'S MOUTH
FURROW-WEED
GIBBERELLA
GOAT'S-BEARD
GOAT'S-THORN
GOLDEN-SEAL
GOLDILOCKS
GOLD-THREAD
GOOSE-GRASS
GRASS-WRACK
GREASEWOOD
GREEN ALGAE
GUINEA-CORN
GYPSOPHILA
HAEMANTHUS
HAWKSBEARD
HEART'S-EASE
HELIANTHUS
HELIOTROPE
HEMP-NETTLE
HERB-BENNET
HERB-ROBERT
HOBBLE-B'JSH
HOP-TREFOIL
IMMORTELLE
INDIAN CORN
INDIAN PINK
INDIAN PIPE
INDIAN POKE
INDIAN RICE
INDIAN SHOT
JEW'S-MALLOW
JEW'S-MYRTLE
KAFFIR CORN
KIDNEY-BEAN
KING'S-SPEAR
KNAP-BOTTLE
LADY'S-SMOCK
LAURUSTINE
LEMON-GRASS
MAIDENHAIR
MAIDEN PINK
MAIDENWEED
MALE ORCHIS
MANNA-GRASS
MARGUERITE
MARSHLOCKS
MASTERWORT
MAY-BLOSSOM
MELIC-GRASS

MEXICAN TEA
MIGNONETTE
MIST-FLOWER
MOCK-ORANGE
MOCK-PRIVET
MONKEY-ROPE
MONTBRETIA
MOON-FLOWER
MOTHERWORT
MOTH-FLOWER
MUMMY-WHEAT
MUSK-MALLOW
NASTURTIUM
NIGHTSHADE
NIPPLEWORT
ORANGE-LILY
ORANGE-ROOT
OUVIRANDRA
OXEYE DAISY
PAINTED CUP
PARKLEAVES
PARROT-BEAK
PARROT-BILL
PENNYCRESS
PENNYROYAL
PEPPERMINT
PEPPERWORT
PERIWINKLE
PERSICARIA
PLUME-GRASS
POINSETTIA
POLYANTHUS
QUICK-GRASS
QUINSYWORT
RAGGED-LADY
RANUNCULUS
RED JASMINE
RED SEAWEED
REST-HARROW
RHINEBERRY
RIBBON-WEED
ROCK-VIOLET
ROSE-LAUREL
ROSE-MALLOW
ROSIN-PLANT
RUNNER-BEAN
SARRACENIA
SCORZONERA
SCOTCH ROSE
SEA-BURDOCK
SEA-FEATHER
SEA-LETTUCE

PLANTS – FLOWERS & GENERAL PLANTS

SEA-WHISTLE
SERRADILLA
SETTERWORT
SHAVE-GRASS
SHEEP-PLANT
SHIELD-FERN
SILVERWEED
SNAPDRAGON
SNEEZEWEED
SNEEZEWORT
SOW-THISTLE
SPEAR-GRASS
SPIDERWORT
SPIKE-GRASS
SPIRIT-LEAF
SPLEENWORT
SPONGEWOOD
SPRINGWORT
STAVESACRE
STITCHWORT
STONE-BREAK
STORK'S-BILL
STRAMONIUM
STRING-BEAN
SUDAN GRASS
SUGAR-GRASS
SUGAR-WRACK
SUPPLE JACK
SWEET-BRIAR
SWEET-BRIER
SWORD-GRASS
THALE-CRESS
THORN-APPLE
THROATWORT
TOUCH-ME-NOT
TOWEL-GOURD
TRAGACANTH
TREE-MALLOW
TREE-TOMATO
TROPAEOLUM
TUMBLEWEED
VELVET-LEAF
VENUS'S COMB
WALLFLOWER
WALL-PEPPER
WALL-ROCKET
WATER-CRESS
WATER-ELDER
WATER-LEMON
WATER-MAIZE
WATER-MELON
WATER-OUZEL

WATER-THYME
WELSH POPPY
WILD INDIGO
WILLOW-HERB
WILLOW-WEED
WIND-FLOWER
WOOD-SORREL
YEAST-PLANT
YELLOW-ROOT
YELLOW-WEED
YELLOW-WORT

11

AARON'S BEARD
ADAM'S NEEDLE
ANTIRRHINUM
BALLOON-VINE
BEAR'S-BREECH
BELLE-DE-NUIT
BELL-HEATHER
BETEL-PEPPER
BISCUIT-ROOT
BISHOP'S WEED
BITTER-CRESS
BITTERSWEET
BITTER-VETCH
BLADDERWORT
BLOOD-FLOWER
BOG-ASPHODEL
BOTTLE-BRUSH
BOTTLE-GOURD
BRAMBLE-BUSH
BRANKURSINE
BRISTLE-FERN
BUR-MARIGOLD
BURNING-BUSH
CABBAGE-ROSE
CALYCANTHUS
CAMEL'S THORN
CANARY-GRASS
CANDLE-BERRY
CAPER-SPURGE
CAULIFLOWER
CHANTERELLE
CHEDDAR PINK
CLOVER-GRASS
CONTRAYERVA
CONVALLARIA
CONVOLVULUS
COTTON-GRASS

COTTON-PLANT
DAME'S-VIOLET
DOG'S-MERCURY
DRAGON'S-HEAD
DUSTY-MILLER
DUTCH CLOVER
DYER'S-ROCKET
ELKHORN FERN
EVERLASTING
FALSE ACACIA
FEATHER-STAR
FIELD MADDER
FINGER-GRASS
FORGET-ME-NOT
FRENCH BERRY
GENTIANELLA
GIANT FENNEL
GILLYFLOWER
GLOBE-FLOWER
GOOSE-FLOWER
GREEN DRAGON
GUELDER ROSE
GUINEA-GRASS
HART'S-TONGUE
HEATHER BELL
HEDGE-HYSSOP
HELLEBORINE
HERB-OF-GRACE
HERB-TRINITY
HONEYSUCKLE
HOOK-CLIMBER
HORNED POPPY
HORSERADISH
HOUND'S-BERRY
HUCKLEBERRY
ICELAND MOSS
INDIAN BREAD
INDIAN CRESS
INDIGO PLANT
IPECACUANHA
ITHYPHALLUS
JACQUEMINOT
JAPAN LAUREL
JIMPSON-WEED
KIDNEY-VETCH
KIKUYU GRASS
LABRADOR TEA
LADY'S-FINGER
LADY'S-MANTLE
LATTICE-LEAF
LONDON PRIDE
LONG-PURPLES

LOOSESTRIFE
LOVE-IN-A-MIST
MADONNA-LILY
MANNA-LICHEN
MARSHMALLOW
MEADOW-GRASS
MEADOW-SWEET
MILK-THISTLE
MILLET-GRASS
MUSK-THISTLE
MUSTARD-TREE
NANCY-PRETTY
NEEDLE-FURZE
ORANGE-GRASS
PAINTED LADY
PAMPAS GRASS
PARMA VIOLET
PARSLEY FERN
PEARL-BARLEY
PEARL-MILLET
PENCIL-CEDAR
PEPPER-GRASS
PIGEON-BERRY
PLUM-BLOSSOM
PRICKLY-PEAR
PURGING FLAX
QUITCH-GRASS
RAGGED-ROBIN
RED-HOT POKER
RED VALERIAN
RESCUE-GRASS
RHODODAPHNE
RIBBON-GRASS
ROMAN NETTLE
ROMAN SORREL
ROSE-CAMPION
RUPTUREWORT
SALAD BURNET
SALLOW-THORN
SCARLET BEAN
SCURVY-GRASS
SEA-COLEWORT
SEA-FURBELOW
SEA-LAVENDER
SEA-MILKWORT
SEA-PURSLANE
SESAME GRASS
SLIME-FUNGUS
SLIPPERWORT
SNAIL-FLOWER
SPINACH BEET
SPINDLE-TREE

STAR-THISTLE
STEEPLE-BUSH
ST JOHN'S WORT
SULPHURWORT
SWALLOW-WORT
SWEET-CICELY
SWEET-POTATO
SWEET-ROCKET
SWEET-SULTAN
SWINE'S-CREST
SWITCH-PLANT
THOROUGHWAX
TIGER-FLOWER
TOMATO-PLANT
VERNAL GRASS
VIPER'S GRASS
WALL-MUSTARD
WATER-PEPPER
WATER-VIOLET
WHITE-BOTTLE
WHITLOW-WORT
WILD MUSTARD
WINDLESTRAW
WINTER-BERRY
WINTER-BLOOM
WINTER-CRESS
WINTERGREEN
WOOD-ANEMONE
WOOD-SANICLE
XERANTHEMUM

12

ADAM'S FLANNEL
ADDER'S TONGUE
AMERICAN ALOE
APPLE-BLOSSOM
BLACK MUSTARD
BLACK SALSIFY
BLADDER SENNA
BLADDER-WRACK
BOG PIMPERNEL
BOUGAINVILIA
BUFFALO-BERRY
BUFFALO-GRASS
CALICO-FLOWER
CAROLINA PINK
CENTURY PLANT
CHECKER-BERRY
CHERRY-PEPPER
CHRIST'S-THORN

COMMON SORREL
CORN-MARIGOLD
CUCKOO-FLOWER
CUSHION-PLANT
DARLINGTONIA
DEVIL-IN-A-BUSH
EASTER CACTUS
ECHINO-CACTUS
FALSE PAREIRA
FEATHER-GRASS
FENNEL-FLOWER
FLOWER OF JOVE
FOOL'S PARSLEY
FRENCH SORREL
FROG'S LETTUCE
GLOBE-THISTLE
GRAPPLE-PLANT
HEDGE-MUSTARD
HEDGE-PARSLEY
HEMEROCALLIS
HEMP-AGRIMONY
HOUND'S-TONGUE
ICELAND POPPY
INDIAN MILLET
INDIAN TURNIP
JACOBEAN LILY
JACOB'S LADDER
LADY'S-CUSHION
LADY'S-SLIPPER
LADY'S-THISTLE
LAMB'S-LETTUCE
LEOPARD'S-BANE
MANGEL-WORZEL
MARVEL OF PERU
MILL-MOUNTAIN
MONKEY-FLOWER
MONK'S-RHUBARB
MORNING GLORY
MOUNTAIN FLAX
MULBERRY-BUSH
NEW JERSEY TEA
NONE-SO-PRETTY
OLD MAN'S BEARD
ORCHARD-GRASS
PAINTED GRASS
PARSLEY-PIERT
PASQUE-FLOWER
PATIENCE-DOCK
PHEASANT'S-EYE
PICKEREL-WEED
PITCHER-PLANT
PLEURISY-ROOT

QUAKING-GRASS
REINDEER MOSS
RHODODENDRON
ROEBUCK-BERRY
ROSE OF SHARON
SALPIGLOSSIS
SARSAPARILLA
SCOTCH BARLEY
SCOTCH BONNET
SCYTHIAN LAMB
SEA-BUCKTHORN
SHEEP'S SORREL
SHEPHERD'S ROD
SHIRLEY POPPY
SKUNK-CABBAGE
SNOW-IN-SUMMER
SOLOMON'S-SEAL
SPANISH BROOM
SPANISH CRESS
SPANISH GRASS
SPANISH ONION
SPEAR-THISTLE
SPRING-BEAUTY
SPURGE-LAUREL
SPUR VALERIAN
SQUIRREL-TAIL
STAGHORN FERN
STAGHORN MOSS
STONE-BRAMBLE
ST PETER'S WORT
STRANGLE-WEED
SWEET-SORGHUM
SWEET-WILLIAM
TIMOTHY-GRASS
TOBACCO-PLANT
TORCH-THISTLE
TUSSOCK-GRASS
VENUS FLY TRAP
VIRGIN'S-BOWER
WANDERING JEW
WATER-HEMLOCK
WATER-MILFOIL
WATER-PARSNIP
WATER-SOLDIER
WHITE PAREIRA
WHORTLEBERRY
WOOD-HYACINTH
YELLOW-ROCKET
YELLOW-SULTAN
YORKSHIRE FOG

13

AFRICAN VIOLET
ALMOND-BLOSSOM
BARBADOS PRIDE
BLEEDING HEART
BOWSTRING-HEMP
BULRUSH MILLET
BUTCHER'S BROOM
BUTTERFLY-WEED
CANARY-CREEPER
CARRION-FLOWER
CAYENNE PEPPER
CHERRY-BLOSSOM
CHRISTMAS ROSE
CHRYSANTHEMUM
COTTON-THISTLE
CREEPING JENNY
CREOSOTE-PLANT
CROWN-IMPERIAL
DOG'S-TAIL-GRASS
DUTCHMAN'S PIPE
ELEPHANT GRASS
ELEPHANT'S-EARS
ELEPHANT'S-FOOT
FLANDERS POPPY
FLOWERING RUSH
GARLIC-MUSTARD
GOOD-KING-HENRY
GRAPE-HYACINTH
GREEK VALERIAN
HORSE MUSHROOM
INDIAN TOBACCO
JERUSALEM SAGE
JOINTED CACTUS
JUPITER'S BEARD
KANGAROO-APPLE
KANGAROO-GRASS
KANGAROO-THORN
LILY OF THE NILE
MANGOLD-WORZEL
MARSH-MARIGOLD
MARSH-SAMPHIRE
MAURITIUS HEMP
MEADOW-SAFFRON
MOURNING-BRIDE
NOLI ME TANGERE
ORANGE-BLOSSOM
PASSION-FLOWER
PEACOCK-FLOWER
PELICAN-FLOWER
PINEAPPLE-WEED

RASPBERRY-BUSH
ROE-BLACKBERRY
ROSE-BAY LAUREL
ROSE OF JERICHO
SAVANNA-FLOWER
SCARLET RUNNER
SCORPION-GRASS
SCOTCH-THISTLE
SHEPHERD'S CLUB
SPANISH DAGGER
SPIKE-LAVENDER
SWINE'S SUCCORY
TORTOISE-PLANT
TRAVELLER'S-JOY
TRUMPET-FLOWER
VIPER'S BUGLOSS
VIRGINIA STOCK
WATER-CHESTNUT
WATER-DROPWORT
WATER-HYACINTH
WATER-PLANTAIN
WATER-PURSLANE
WATER-STARWORT
WILD LIQUORICE
WITCHES'-BUTTER
WOOD-GERMANDER

14

ALDER-BUCKTHORN
ARTILLERY-PLANT
BASTARD SAFFRON
BELLADONNA LILY
BLACKBERRY-BUSH
BLACK HOREHOUND
BRUSSELS SPROUT
CANTERBURY BELL
CAPE GOOSEBERRY
CARDINAL-FLOWER
CHINCHERINCHEE
CHRISTMAS DAISY
DEVIL'S SNUFF-BOX
DOG'S-TOOTH-GRASS
DOGTOOTH-VIOLET
DYER'S-GREENWEED
FLORENTINE IRIS
FRENCH MARIGOLD
GOLD-OF-PLEASURE
GOOSEBERRY-BUSH
JACK-BY-THE-HEDGE
LOVE-IN-IDLENESS

MAIDENHAIR FERN
MOCCASIN-FLOWER
MOUNTAIN LAUREL
MOUNTAIN SORREL
NEW ZEALAND FLAX
ORGAN-PIPE CORAL
PARTRIDGE-BERRY
PORCUPINE-GRASS
PRINCE'S FEATHER
PROVINCIAL-ROSE
SANDWORT-SPURRY
SCOTCH ATTORNEY
SCOTCH BLUEBELL
SEA-GILLIFLOWER
SHEEP'S SCABIOUS
SHEPHERD'S CRESS
SHEPHERD'S GLASS
SHEPHERD'S PURSE
SPANISH BAYONET
SPANISH NEEDLES
ST AGNES'S FLOWER
STARCH-HYACINTH
STAR-OF-THE-EARTH
STAR-OF-THE-NIGHT
STINGING-NETTLE
TELEGRAPH-PLANT
TREACLE-MUSTARD
WATER-PIMPERNEL
WITCHES'-THIMBLE
WOOD-NIGHTSHADE
YELLOW-CENTAURY

15

AFRICAN MARIGOLD
BLACK NIGHTSHADE
BURNET SAXIFRAGE
BUTTERFLY-FLOWER
BUTTERFLY-ORCHIS
CHRISTMAS CACTUS
DYER'S-YELLOWWEED
EVENING-PRIMROSE
GOLDEN SAXIFRAGE
GRASSCLOTH PLANT
HERB-CHRISTOPHER
HOTTENTOT'S BREAD
INDIAN LIQUORICE
JACK-IN-THE-PULPIT
LILY OF THE VALLEY
MEADOW-SAXIFRAGE
MICHAELMAS-DAISY

SCARLET GERANIUM
SHEPHERD'S MYRTLE
SHEPHERD'S NEEDLE
STAR-OF-BETHLEHEM
ST BARBARA'S CRESS

STRAWBERRY SHRUB
STURT'S DESERT PEA
TASMANIAN MYRTLE
VIRGINIA CREEPER
WALL-GILLYFLOWER

WOODY NIGHTSHADE
YELLOW-EYED GRASS
YELLOW PIMPERNEL

PLANTS – TREES & WOOD

3

ASH
BAY
BOX
ELM
FIG
FIR
GUM
ITA
JAK
LOG
NIM
OAK
SAL
ULE
YEW

4

AKEE
ALOE
ARAR
ATAP
BAEL
BALM
BITO
COCO
DALI
DEAL
DHAK
DIKA
DITA
EBON
HOLM
ILEX

JACK
LANA
LIME
LIND
NIPA
OMBÚ
PALM
PEAR
PINE
PIPI
POLE
POON
RATA
SHEA
SORB
TEAK
TEIL
TOON
TREE
UPAS
WOOD
YANG

5

ABELE
AGILA
ALDER
ALGUM
ALMUG
ARBOR
ARGAN
ASPEN
ASSAI
BALSA
BEECH

BIRCH
BOREE
BUNYA
BUSSU
CACAO
CAROB
CEDAR
CHOCK
EBONY
ELDER
GUAVA
HAZEL
JAMBU
JARUL
KARRI
KAURI
KOKRA
KOKUM
LARCH
LILAC
LOTUS
MAHWA
MANGO
MAPLE
MAZER
MVULE
MYALL
NGAIO
OLIVE
OSIER
PALAS
PALAY
PAPAW
PIÑON
PIPAL
PLANE
PLANK

QUINA
ROBLE
ROWAN
SAPAN
SUMAC
TUART
WITCH
WITHY
YACCA
ZANTE

6

ACAJOU
ALERCE
ANGICO
ANTIAR
ARBUTE
AROLLA
BANANA
BANYAN
BAOBAB
BILIAN
BOG-OAK
BONSAI
BO TREE
BRAZIL
BURITI
CASHEW
CASSIA
CERRIS
CHENAR
CITRUS
COHUNE
CORDON
CORNEL

DEODAR
DURIAN
EMBLIC
FUSTET
FUSTIC
GINKGO
GOMUTI
GOPHER
GRU-GRU
GURJUN
ILLIPE
JARRAH
JUPATI
KAMALA
KARAKA
KARITE
KITTUL
LAUREL
LEBBEK
LIGNUM
LINDEN
LITCHI
LOGGAT
LONGAN
LOQUAT
LUMBER
MACOYA
MALLEE
MANUKA
MASTIC
MEDLAR
MIRITI
OBECHE
PADAUK
PAPAYA
PAWPAW
POPLAR

RAFFIA
RED-BUD
RED-GUM
SALLOW
SANDAL
SANTAL
SAPELE
SAPPAN
SAXAUL
SISSOO
SOUARI
SPRUCE
SUMACH
TAMANU
TIMBER
TITOKI
TUPELO
WALNUT
WILLOW

7

AILANTO
AMBATCH
APRICOT
BABASSU
BARWOOD
BAY TREE
BEBEERU
BILIMBI
BOX-TREE
BOXWOOD
BUBINGA
BUCK-EYE
BUNTING
CAM-WOOD

PLANTS – TREES & WOOD

CANELLA
CHAMPAK
COCONUT
CONIFER
COQUITO
CORK-OAK
COW-TREE
CYPRESS
DOGWOOD
DURAMEN
DURMAST
DYE-WOOD
FAN PALM
FIG-TREE
FIR-TREE
FIR-WOOD
GEEBUNG
GENIPAP
GUM TREE
HEMLOCK
HICKORY
HOG-PLUM
HOLM-OAK
HOOP-ASH
HORN-NUT
LENTISK
LIVE-OAK
LOGWOOD
LUMBANG
MADROÑO
MANJACK
MARGOSA
MORICHE
NUT-PINE
NUT-TREE
OAKLING
OAK-TREE
OAK-WOOD
OIL-PALM
PALMYRA
PAXIUBA
PIMENTO
PLATANE
PLYWOOD
POLLARD
PUPUNHA
QUASSIA
REDWOOD
SAKSAUL
SANDERS
SAOUARI
SAPLING

SEQUOIA
SERINGA
SERVICE
SHITTIM
SOUR-SOP
SUNDARI
TALIPOT
TANGHIN
TROOLIE
WALLABA
WAX-PALM
WAX-TREE
WITCHEN
WYCH-ELM
YEW-TREE

8

AGALLOCH
ALBURNUM
BASSWOOD
BEAN TREE
BEEF-WOOD
BENTWOOD
BLACKBOY
CARNAUBA
CHESTNUT
CINCHONA
CINNAMON
COCO-PALM
COCOPLUM
COCO-WOOD
COOLABAH
CORK-TREE
CORKWOOD
CRAB-TREE
CRAB-WOOD
DATE-PALM
DATE-TREE
DOUM-PALM
EUCALYPT
FUMED OAK
HAGBERRY
HARDBEAM
HARDWOOD
HAWTHORN
HOLLY-OAK
HORNBEAM
HUON-PINE
IRON-BARK
IRONWOOD

JACK-PINE
JACK-TREE
JELUTONG
JOINT-FIR
KALUMPIT
KINGWOOD
LABURNUM
LACEBARK
LIMA-WOOD
LIME-TREE
LIME-WOOD
LOBLOLLY
MACAHUBA
MAHOGANY
MANGROVE
MANNA-ASH
MEAL-TREE
MILK-TREE
MILKWOOD
MULBERRY
OITICICA
OLEASTER
OVENWOOD
PALMETTO
PALM-TREE
PEAR-TREE
PICHURIM
PINASTER
PINE-TREE
PINE-WOOD
PIPE-TREE
PITH-TREE
PLUM-TREE
POON-WOOD
PYENGADU
QUANDONG
RAIN-TREE
RAMBUTAN
RED CEDAR
ROSE-TREE
ROSEWOOD
SACK-TREE
SAGO-PALM
SCOTS FIR
SEBESTEN
SHADDOCK
SHAG-BARK
SHEA-TREE
SLOE-TREE
SOAP-BARK
SOAP-TREE
SOFTWOOD

SUGAR-GUM
SWAMP OAK
SYCAMORE
TAMARACK
TAMARIND
TEIL TREE
TUNG-TREE
UPAS-TREE
WALL-TREE
WHITE ASH
WINE-PALM
WITCH-ELM

9

AILANTHUS
ALGARROBA
ALOES-WOOD
APPLE-TREE
BALSAM FIR
BERG-CEDAR
BLACKWOOD
BLOODWOOD
BODHI TREE
BREAD TREE
BULLY-TREE
CARAMBOLA
CHILE PINE
CHINKAPIN
CIGAR-TREE
CLOVE-TREE
COCUS-WOOD
CORAL-TREE
COURBARIL
COVIN-TREE
CURRY-LEAF
DECIDUOUS
DRIFT-WOOD
EAGLEWOOD
EVERGREEN
FOREST-OAK
FRUIT-TREE
GAUZE-TREE
GRAPE-TREE
GREENWOOD
GROUND ASH
GROUND OAK
HACKBERRY
HEARTWOOD
INDIAN FIG
IVORY-PALM

IVORY-TREE
JACARANDA
JUDAS-TREE
KAURI-PINE
KERMES OAK
KURRAJONG
LANCE-WOOD
LEMON-TREE
LILAC TREE
MACAW-PALM
MACAW-TREE
MATCHWOOD
NASEBERRY
NUX VOMICA
PEACH-PALM
PEACH-TREE
PEACH-WOOD
PECAN-TREE
PERSIMMON
PITCHPINE
PITCH-TREE
PLANE-TREE
POISON-OAK
PONTIANAC
QUEBRACHO
ROSE-APPLE
ROWAN-TREE
ROYAL PALM
SAPODILLA
SASSAFRAS
SATINWOOD
SCALY-BARK
SCOTCH ELM
SCOTS PINE
SCREW-PINE
SHADE-TREE
SHELLBARK
SILVER-FIR
SMOKE-TREE
SNAKEWOOD
SOAPBERRY
SOUR-GOURD
SPRUCE-FIR
STAR-ANISE
STINK-WOOD
STONE-PINE
SUGAR-PALM
SUGAR-PINE
SWEETWOOD
TACAMAHAC
TEREBINTH
TIGER-WOOD

TODDY-PALM
TOUCHWOOD
TULIP-TREE
TULIP-WOOD
TURKEY OAK
WAGENBOOM
WAX-MYRTLE
WHITEBEAM
WHITE TEAK
WHITEWOOD
WILD MANGO
WILD OLIVE
WINEBERRY
ZANTE-WOOD
ZEBRA-WOOD

10

AFRORMOSIA
ALMOND-TREE
BEAVER-TREE
BEAVER-WOOD
BIRD-CHERRY
BITTERWOOD
BLACK-BULLY
BOTTLE-TREE
BRAZIL-WOOD
BUNYA-BUNYA
BUTTER-TREE
BUTTON-BALL
BUTTON-WOOD
CALAMANDER
CALICO-TREE
CALICO-WOOD
CANARY-WOOD
CANDLE-TREE
CANDLE-WOOD
CEMBRA PINE
CHASTE TREE
CHERRY-TREE
CITRON TREE
CITRON WOOD
COFFEE-TREE
CORNEL-TREE
COROMANDEL
COTTON-TREE
COTTON-WOOD
DOUGLAS FIR
DRAGON-TREE
EUCALYPTUS
FIDDLEWOOD

FOREST TREE
GOAT-SALLOW
GOAT-WILLOW
GREENHEART
HACKMATACK
KAFFIR-BOOM
LETTER-WOOD
LINDEN TREE
LOCUST-TREE
MANCHINEEL
MANGABEIRE
MANGOSTEEN
MANNA LARCH
MISSEL-TREE
NETTLE-TREE
NORWAY PINE
ORANGE-TREE
ORANGE-WOOD
PADDLE-WOOD
PAGODA TREE
PALISANDER
PAPER-BIRCH
PARANÁ PINE
PRICKLY-ASH
PURPLE WOOD
QUERCITRON
QUICKTHORN
RED SANDERS
RUBBER TREE
SANDALWOOD
SAND-CHERRY
SAPPAN-WOOD
SILVER-BELL
SILVER-TREE
SNEEZEWOOD
SUGAR-MAPLE
TALLOW-TREE
TIMBER-TREE
WEEPING-ASH
WEEPING-ELM
WHITETHORN
WILD-CHERRY
WITCH-ALDER
WITCH-HAZEL
WOODEN PEAR
YELLOW-WOOD
YLANG-YLANG

11

AFRICAN TEAK

AGNUS CASTUS
AMBOINA PINE
AMBOINA-WOOD
BASTARD TEAK
BLACK WALNUT
CABBAGE PALM
CABBAGE-TREE
CHAULMOOGRA
CLUSTER-PINE
COCONUT PALM
COPPER-BEECH
CRYPTOMERIA
DAWN CYPRESS
DAWN REDWOOD
DWARFED TREE
FEATHER-PALM
HONEY-LOCUST
LACQUER-TREE
LEOPARD-WOOD
LIGNUM VITAE
LOBLOLLY-BAY
MACERANDUBA
MAMMEE APPLE
MAMMOTH-TREE
MONKEY-BEARD
MOUNTAIN-ASH
MOUNTAIN-TEA
MULBERRY-FIG
OSAGE ORANGE
PALMYRA-WOOD
POISON-SUMAC
POMEGRANATE
PURPLE HEART
PUSSY WILLOW
RHODIUM-WOOD
SANDERSWOOD
SAUSAGE-TREE
SERVICE-TREE
SHAWNEE-WOOD
SHITTAH TREE
SILVER BIRCH
SITKA SPRUCE
SLIPPERY ELM
STRINGY-BARK
SWEET ORANGE
SWEET-WILLOW
TRUMPET-TREE
TRUMPET-WOOD
UMBRELLA-FIR
VARNISH-TREE
WEEPING-TREE
WHITE POPLAR

PLANTS – TREES & WOOD

WILD-SERVICE

12

ANGELICA-TREE
BALSAM POPLAR
BENJAMIN-TREE
CALABASH TREE
CHERRY-LAUREL
CHESTNUT-TREE
CHIQUICHIQUI
CUCUMBER-TREE
GROUND-CHERRY
HERCULES' CLUB
JAMAICA CEDAR
JAMAICA EBONY
LOBLOLLY-PINE
LOBLOLLY-TREE
MAMMEE-SAPOTA
MASSARANDUBA
MONKEY-PUZZLE
NORWAY SPRUCE
SEASIDE-GRAPE
SNOWDROP-TREE
SOUTHERNWOOD
SWAMP CYPRESS

TREE OF HEAVEN
UMBRELLA-TREE
WEEPING-BIRCH
WINTER-CHERRY

13

CALIATURE-WOOD
CAMPEACHY-WOOD
CAMPHOR LAUREL
CHRISTMAS TREE
COMPASS-TIMBER
CORNELIAN-TREE
CRANBERRY-TREE
HORSE-CHESTNUT
JAPANESE CEDAR
MARMALADE TREE
PAPER-MULBERRY
PARTRIDGE-WOOD
PORCUPINE-WOOD
QUEENSLAND-NUT
RED SANDALWOOD
SANDARACH TREE
SAVANNA-WATTLE
TOOTHACHE-TREE
WAYFARING-TREE

WEEPING-WILLOW

14

ALLIGATOR APPLE
CANNONBALL-TREE
CASTANOSPERMUM
CEDAR OF LEBANON
CHITTAGONG WOOD
EUCALYPTUS TREE
FLAMBOYANT-TREE
GRANADILLA TREE
JAPANESE MEDLAR
LOMBARDY POPLAR
MAIDENHAIR-TREE
STRAWBERRY-TREE
TRAVELLER'S-TREE
TURPENTINE-TREE

15

EMBLIC MYROBALAN
HORSERADISH TREE
TREMBLING POPLAR
WHITE SANDALWOOD

PRINTING & STATIONERY

3

GUM
INK
KEY
MAG
MAP
NIB
OUT
PAD
PEN
PIE
POT
RAG
RUN
TAG
WAX
WEB

4

BACK
BAND
BILL
BIRO
BODY
BOLT
BOOK
BULL
BUMF
CAPS
CARD
CASE
CHIT
COPY
CYAN
DEMY
EDIT
FACE
FILE
FILM
FLAP
FONT
FORM
GLUE
GRID
HEAD
HEFT
ITEM
J-PEN
KERN

LEAD
LEAF
LINE
LIST
LOGO
MARK
MEMO
MONK
NEWS
NOTE
OVER
PACK
PAGE
PICA
PICK
PLUG
POST
POTT
PULL
PULP
REAM
ROLL
RUBY
RULE
SIDE
SLIP
SLUG
SORT
STAR
STET
TAKE
TAPE
TEXT
TICK
TINT
TOME
TURN
TYPE
TYPO
YAPP

5

ALBUM
ANNAL
ATLAS
BIBLE
BLANK
BLOCK
BLURB
BOARD

BRACE
CANON
CARET
CHART
CHASE
CODEX
COMIC
COVER
CROWN
DAILY
DEVIL
DIARY
DONAT
DRAFT
DUMMY
ÉLITE
EXTRA
FLONG
FOLIO
FOREL
FORME
FOUNT
FRIAR
FUDGE
GLOSS
GUARD
GUIDE
INDEX
INKER
INSET
ISSUE
JÉSUS
JOINT
LABEL
LINEN
LITHO
NOVEL
PAPER
PASTE
PATCH
PEARL
PLATE
POINT
PRESS
PRINT
PROEM
PROOF
PUNCH
QUILL
QUIRE
RALPH
RECTO

ROMAN
RONDE
ROUGH
ROYAL
RULER
SCOOP
SCRIP
SERIF
SHEET
SIGLA
SLICK
SPACE
SPINE
STATE
STICK
STONE
STORY
STRAP
STRIP
STYLE
STYLO
SWASH
TABLE
TIE-UP
TITLE
TRACT
TUTOR
TWINE
VERSO
WAFER
WEDGE
WIDOW
XEROX
ZINCO

6

ANNUAL
BALAAM
BINDER
BORDER
BRAYER
BYLINE
CAHIER
CANCEL
CARTON
CAXTON
CHROMO
CICERO
COCK-UP
COLUMN

COUPON
CRAYON
DABBER
DAGGER
DECKLE
DIESIS
DIGEST
DOSSIL
ECTYPE
ERASER
ERRATA
EXPOSÉ
FLIMSY
FOLDER
FORMAT
GALLEY
GOBBET
GRADUS
GUTTER
HERBAL
INCAVO
INDENT
INK-POT
INSERT
ITALIC
JACKET
JOTTER
LAYOUT
LEADER
LEDGER
LEGEND
LETTER
MACKLE
MACULE
MAKE-UP
MANILA
MANUAL
MARGIN
MATTER
METHOD
MINION
MISSAL
MOCK-UP
MODERN
MORGUE
NOTICE
NUMBER
OBELUS
OCTAVO
OFFSET
OZALID
PAGING

PARAPH
PASTER
PENCIL
PEN-NIB
PLANER
PLATEN
POSTIL
POUNCE
PRIMER
QUARTO
READER
RECORD
REFILL
REGLET
REHASH
REPORT
RETURN
REVIEW
RIBBON
ROUNCE
RUBBER
RUBRIC
SCREEN
SCRIPT
SCROLL
SERIAL
SERIES
SOURCE
SPACER
SPREAD
STAPLE
STRING
STYLUS
TABLET
TABULA
TERMLY
TICKET
TWICER
TYMPAN
TYPING
UNCIAL
UPMAKE
VELLUM
VERSAL
VOLUME
WEEKLY

7

ADDENDA
ALMANAC

PRINTING & STATIONERY

ALVEARY
ANTIQUE
APOSTIL
ARTICLE
ART-WORK
AUTONYM
BACKLOG
BALLOON
BINDING
BLOOMER
BLOTTER
BOOKLET
BRACKET
BRAILLE
BREVIER
BULLARY
CALAMUS
CAPITAL
CAPTION
CARTOON
CHAPTER
CUSHION
CUTTING
DELENDA
DIAMOND
DIURNAL
D-NOTICE
DOG'S-EAR
DOSSIER
DYE-LINE
EDITING
EDITION
ELZEVIR
EMPEROR
ENGLISH
ERRATUM
EXAMPLE
EXTRACT
FANFARE
FEATURE
FICTION
FLYLEAF
FRAKTUR
FRISKET
FUNNIES
GALLOWS
GAZETTE
GOLD INK
GRADUAL
GRAMMAR
GRAVURE
GROLIER

GUMMING
GUTTERS
HANDOUT
HEADING
HELL-BOX
IMPRINT
INK-FEED
INKHORN
INSIDES
ITALICS
JOBBING
JOTTING
JOURNAL
LAW-BOOK
LAW-CALF
LAW-LIST
LEAFLET
LEXICON
LITERAL
LOG-BOOK
MAP-BOOK
MASKING
MEASURE
MEMOIRS
MISCOPY
MONTHLY
NOTE-PAD
OLD FACE
OMNIBUS
OPENING
ORARIUM
OVERLAY
OVERRUN
PACKING
PAPYRUS
PARAGON
PASTE-UP
PEELING
PEN-CASE
PILCROW
POTHOOK
PREFACE
PRELIMS
PRINTER
PROCESS
PROFILE
QUADRAT
RAG-BOOK
RED-BOOK
REISSUE
RELEASE
REPRINT

REVERSO
REWRITE
ROYALTY
SHERIAT
SHOCKER
SNIPPET
SOLIDUS
SPECIAL
STAPLER
STICKER
SUBBING
TABLOID
TERNION
TRIBBLE
TRIGLOT
TRINDLE
TRIGRAM
TWELVES
TYPE-BAR
WEBBING
WRAPPER
WRITE-UP
WRITING

8

ADDENDUM
ADHESIVE
APOGRAPH
APPENDIX
ARMORIAL
ART PAPER
ASCENDER
ASTERISK
AUTOTYPE
BACK PAGE
BESTIARY
BI-WEEKLY
BLEEDING
BOLD FACE
BOOK CLUB
BOOK-MARK
BRACKETS
BREVIARY
BREVIATE
BROCHURE
CALENDAR
CAP-PAPER
CASEBOOK
CAUSERIE
CHAPBOOK

CHINA INK
CLIPPING
CLUB-LINE
COLOPHON
CONTENTS
COPYBOOK
DATELINE
DEADLINE
ELEPHANT
END-PAPER
ENVELOPE
EPIGRAPH
EXEMPLAR
EX-LIBRIS
EXPOSURE
FACETIAE
FAIR COPY
FASCICLE
FILE COPY
FOOLSCAP
FOOTNOTE
FORE-EDGE
FOREWORD
FOUNTAIN
FUDGE-BOX
GARAMOND
GIFT-BOOK
GLASSINE
GLOSSARY
HACK-WORK
HAIRLINE
HALF-TONE
HANDBILL
HANDBOOK
HARDBACK
HEADBAND
HEADLINE
HEADNOTE
HEADWORD
HERD-BOOK
HORNBOOK
IDEOGRAM
IMPERIAL
INKSTAND
INTAGLIO
JESTBOOK
JIFFY-BAG
KEYBOARD
LEGENDRY
LIGATURE
LINOTYPE
LOGOGRAM

LOGOTYPE
LONGHAND
MAGAZINE
MANIFOLD
MAQUETTE
MISPRINT
MONOGRAM
MONOTYPE
MOON-TYPE
MUSIC-PEN
NEWSROOM
NOCTUARY
NOTANDUM
NOTEBOOK
OBITUARY
OFFPRINT
OLD STYLE
OUTSIDES
PAMPHLET
PARALLEL
PECULIAR
PEN-WIPER
PLAGIARY
POSTCARD
PREAMBLE
PRE-PRINT
PRINTING
PRINT-RUN
QUILL-NIB
QUILL-PEN
REGISTER
REMARQUE
REVIEWAL
ROAD-BOOK
SCHOLION
SEMI-BULL
SEPARATE
SIDE-NOTE
SIXPENNY
SNIPPING
SONGBOOK
SPACE-BAR
STEEL-PEN
STEEVING
STICKFUL
STREAMER
STUD-BOOK
SUBTITLE
SYNGRAPH
SYNONYMY
TALL COPY
TETRAPLA

TEXT-BOOK
THRILLER
TRACTATE
TRANSFER
TREE-CALF
TURNOVER
TYPE-BODY
TYPE-FACE
UNDERLAY
UPMAKING
VARIORUM
VIGNETTE
WAX-PAPER
WIRE-LINE
WOOD-PULP
WORDBOOK
WRAPPAGE
WRAPPING
YEAR-BOOK

9

AMPERSAND
ANTHOLOGY
ANTICHLOR
AUTOGRAPH
BACK COVER
BALAAM-BOX
BALL-POINT
BI-MONTHLY
BIOGRAPHY
BLACK LIST
BLOCK-BOOK
BLOCK TYPE
BLUEPRINT
BOND PAPER
BOOKPLATE
BOOK-TOKEN
BOOK TRADE
BOURGEOIS
BRILLIANT
BORADSIDE
CALLIGRAM
CARDBOARD
CARTOGRAM
CARTRIDGE
CARTULARY
CATALOGUE
CHARACTER
CHEMITYPE
CHEMITYPY

CHRONICLE
CLARENDON
CO-EDITION
COLLATION
COLLOTYPE
COPY-PAPER
COPYRIGHT
CROSSWORD
CROW-QUILL
CUNEIFORM
CYANOTYPE
DANDY-ROLL
DESCENDER
DESK-DIARY
DIME NOVEL
DIRECTORY
DUODECIMO
DUPLICATE
DUST-COVER
EDITORIAL
ENGRAVING
EXCLUSIVE
FACSIMILE
FOLIATION
FORMULARY
FRONT PAGE
FURNITURE
GATHERING
GAZETTEER
GHOST-WORD
GIFT-TOKEN
GUARD-BOOK
GUIDE-BOOK
HAIR-SPACE
HALF-ROYAL
HALF-TITLE
HAND-PAPER
HAND-PRESS
HEADPIECE
HEADSTICK
HELVETICA
HIERATICA
HIEROGRAM
HORS TEXTE
IDEOGRAPH
IDIOGRAPH
INDENTION
INDIAN INK
INK-BOTTLE
INK-ERASER
INK-HOLDER
INK PENCIL

INSERTION
INTERLEAF
ITINERARY
KEELIVINE
LACE-PAPER
LAID PAPER
LEGENDARY
LETTERING
LIVRAISON
LOWER CASE
MACROCOPY
MAJUSCULE
MAKE-READY
MEMORIALS
MICROCARD
MILL-BOARD
MINUSCULE
MUSIC-DEMY
NEWSPAPER
NEWSPRINT
NEWS-SHEET
NEWS-VALUE
NONPAREIL
NOTEPAPER
NOVELETTE
ONION-SKIN
ORDER-BOOK
OVERPRINT
PACK-TWINE
PAGE-PROOF
PAPERBACK
PAPER-CLIP
PAPER-FILE
PAPER-PULP
PAPETERIE
PARAGRAPH
PARCHMENT
PEN-AND-INK
PENHOLDER
PERFECTOR
PHONOTYPE
PHONOTYPY
PHOTOCOPY
PHOTOSTAT
PHOTOTYPE
PHOTOTYPY
PICTOGRAM
PICTORIAL
POINT-SIZE
PRESS-BOOK
PRESS-MARK
PRESS-WORK

PROGRAMME
QUARTERLY
QUOTATION
RECENSION
REDACTION
REFERENCE
REMAINDER
REPORTAGE
REPORTING
RICE-PAPER
ROXBURGHE
ROYALTIES
SCARE-HEAD
SCARE-LINE
SCRAP-BOOK
SECRETARY
SELLOTAPE
SEPARATUM
SHELF-LIFE
SHELF-MARK
SHORTHAND
SIGNATURE
SMALL CAPS
SMALL PICA
SPACE-BAND
SPICILEGE
STENOTYPE
STENOTYPY
STITCHING
STOP-PRESS
STORY-BOOK
STRAP-LINE
STYLE-BOOK
SYMPOSIUM
SYNDICATE
TABLE-BOOK
TABLE-WORK
TABULATOR
TAILPIECE
TETRAGRAM
THESAURUS
THUMB-TACK
TINT-BLOCK
TITLE-LEAF
TITLE-PAGE
TRI-WEEKLY
UPPER CASE
VADE MECUM
WASTE-BOOK
WATER-LINE
WATERMARK
WEB-OFFSET

PRINTING & STATIONERY

WOODBLOCK

10

ANNOTATION
ASSEMBLING
AUTOGRAPHY
BACK NUMBER
BESTSELLER
BIBLIOLOGY
BIBLIOPEGY
BIBLIOPOLY
BOWDLERISM
BROADSHEET
BROWN PAPER
CARBON COPY
CARICATURE
CENTRE-FOLD
CHRONOGRAM
CHURCH-TEXT
COLLECTION
COLPORTAGE
COMMENTARY
COMPENDIUM
COPYING-INK
CORRIGENDA
CRÊPE PAPER
CUL-DE-LAMPE
CYCLOSTYLE
DAILY PAPER
DECKLE-EDGE
DEDICATION
DICTIONARY
DIORTHOSIS
DISCLAIMER
DRAWING-PEN
DRAWING-PIN
DUST-JACKET
EDITORSHIP
EMENDATION
FEUILLETON
FILE-LEADER
FRONT COVER
GRAND JÉSUS
GRANGERISM
HALF-YEARLY
HECTOGRAPH
HIEROGLYPH
HOUSE-STYLE
IDEOGRAPHY
IMPOSITION

IMPRESSION
IMPRIMATUR
INCUNABULA
INDIA PAPER
JELLYGRAPH
JOURNALESE
JOURNALISM
LEADERETTE
LEADER PAGE
LEAD-PENCIL
LEAF-MARGIN
LETTER-BOOK
LETTER-CARD
LETTER-CLIP
LETTER-FILE
LETTERHEAD
LEXIGRAPHY
LIPOGRAPHY
LITERATURE
LITHOGRAPH
LONG PRIMER
MACULATURE
MANUSCRIPT
MARGINALIA
MARKING-INK
MASS MEDIUM
MEMORANDUM
MINUTE-BOOK
MUSIC-PAPER
NEWSLETTER
OCTODECIMO
OLD ENGLISH
OVERMATTER
PACKET-NOTE
PAGINATION
PALAEOTYPE
PALIMPSEST
PASIGRAPHY
PASTEBOARD
PENCIL-CASE
PENCIL-LEAD
PEN-FEATHER
PERIODICAL
PHRASE-BOOK
PICTOGRAPH
PLAGIARISM
PLATE-PROOF
POWER-PRESS
PRESS-PROOF
PROMPTUARY
PROOF-SHEET
PUBLISHING

PYROGRAPHY
READERSHIP
REVIEW-COPY
SATIN-PAPER
SCHOOL-BOOK
SCOTCH TAPE
SEALING WAX
SECOND-MARK
SELF-BINDER
SELF-FILLER
SEMI-WEEKLY
SEPARATION
SEPARATRIX
SKETCH-BOOK
SOURCE-BOOK
SPHENOGRAM
SPORTS PAGE
SPOT-COLOUR
SPRINKLING
STATIONERY
STENOGRAPH
STEREOTYPE
STEREOTYPY
STYLOGRAPH
SUB-EDITING
SUB-HEADING
SUPPLEMENT
TACHYGRAPH
THUMB-INDEX
TITLE-SHEET
TRADE-PAPER
TRIPLICATE
TYPE-CUTTER
TYPE-HOLDER
TYPE-SCRIPT
TYPE-SETTER
TYPEWRITER
TYPOGRAPHY
VOCABULARY
WOODEN TYPE
WRITING-INK
XEROGRAPHY
YELLOWBACK
ZINCOGRAPH

11

ADVANCE COPY
AGONY COLUMN
AIDE-MÉMOIRE
ANTIQUARIAN

AUTOGRAVURE
AVANT-PROPOS
BASKERVILLE
BASTARD TYPE
BIBLIOTHECA
BLACK LETTER
BLOCK LETTER
BLOTTING-PAD
BOOKBINDING
BULLDOG-CLIP
CALLING CARD
CARBON PAPER
CHEIROGRAPH
CHRONOGRAPH
CIRCULATION
CLOG-ALMANAC
COMPILATION
CONCORDANCE
COOKERY-BOOK
COPPERPLATE
CROWN OCTAVO
CYCLOPAEDIA
DITTOGRAPHY
DUPLICATION
ELECTROTINT
ELECTROTYPE
ELECTROTYPY
EMERALD TYPE
EXPURGATION
FORTUNE-BOOK
FOUNTAIN-PEN
GALLEY-PROOF
GLYPHOGRAPH
GRAMMALOGUE
GREAT PRIMER
GUTTER PRESS
HALF-BINDING
HALF-MEASURE
HAPLOGRAPHY
ILLUSTRATED
IMPERIAL CAP
INDIA-RUBBER
INKING-TABLE
INSCRIPTION
INTERLINING
LETTER-BOARD
LETTERPRESS
LETTER-STAMP
LINE-DRAWING
LITHOGRAPHY
MAGNETIC INK
MARBLE-PAPER

MASKING TAPE
NEEDLE-PAPER
OMNIBUS WORK
ONOMASTICON
ORTHOGRAPHY
PAPER-CUTTER
PAPER-FEEDER
PAPER-FOLDER
PAPER-MAKING
PAPER-WEIGHT
PARENTHESES
PARENTHESIS
PHRASEOGRAM
PICTOGRAPHY
PICTURE-BOOK
PLATE-MAKING
PRINTER'S INK
PRINTING-INK
PUBLICATION
PYROGRAVURE
READING-BOOK
REITERATION
RUBBER-STAMP
RUNNING-HEAD
SADDLE-STITCH
SAFETY-PAPER
SECTION-MARK
SEMI-MONTHLY
SEXTODECIMO
SILLY SEASON
SILVER-PAPER
SLATE-PENCIL
SMALL QUARTO
SOLID MATTER
STATUTE-BOOK
STENOCHROME
STENOCHROMY
STENOGRAPHY
STICKY-LABEL
STOPPING-OUT
STYLOGRAPHY
SYNDICATION
SYNONYMICON
TACHIGRAPHY
THIRTY-TWO-MO
THREAD-PAPER
TISSUE-PAPER
TYPE-SETTING
TYPEWRITING
TYPOGRAPHIA
WEDDING-CARD
WRITING-BOOK

YELLOW PAGES
YELLOW PRESS
ZINCOGRAPHY

12

ADHESIVE TAPE
ADVANCE PROOF
BALL-POINT PEN
BASTARD TITLE
BIBLIOGRAPHY
BIRTHDAY-BOOK
BIRTHDAY-CARD
BLOCK CAPITAL
BLOCK LETTERS
BRACHYGRAPHY
BUSINESS CARD
CHEIROGRAPHY
CHINESE PAPER
CHRESTOMATHY
CONTEMPORARY
CONTRIBUTION
COUNTERPROOF
CROSS-HEADING
DISTRIBUTION
DOUBLE-DAGGER
DOUBLE OBELUS
DRAWING-PAPER
ECTYPOGRAPHY
ENCHEIRIDION
ETYMOLOGICON
EXERCISE-BOOK
EXTRA-SPECIAL
FASHION-PLATE
FEATURES PAGE
FOURTH ESTATE
FRONTISPIECE
GLOSSOGRAPHY
GLYPHOGRAPHY
GOSSIP COLUMN
HIEROGLYPHIC
ILLUMINATION
ILLUSTRATION
INDELIBLE INK
INKING-ROLLER
INTERCHAPTER
INTRODUCTION
INVISIBLE INK
LETTER-WEIGHT
LETTER-WRITER
LEXICOGRAPHY

MACHINE-RULER
MANILA-FOLDER
MARGINAL NOTE
MULTIPLICATE
PACKING-PAPER
PASSE-PARTOUT
PATENT INSIDE
PHOTOCOPYING
PHOTOGRAVURE
PHOTOSETTING
PHRASEOGRAPH
POSTILLATION
PRESS CUTTING
PRESS RELEASE
PRINTER'S MARK
PROCESS-BLOCK
PROOF-READING
RUNNING TITLE
SCANDAL SHEET
SCARE-HEADING
SHOULDER-NOTE
SMALL CAPITAL
SPELLING-BOOK
STEREOTYPING
STRIP CARTOON
SUBLINEATION
SULPHITE PULP
SWASH LETTERS
THERMOGRAPHY
TIRONIAN SIGN
TORCHON PAPER
TRACING-PAPER
TRANSFER-BOOK
TRANSPARENCY
TRIPLICATION
TWENTY-FOUR-MO
TYPE-CYLINDER
TYPE-FOUNDING
VISITING-BOOK
VISITORS' BOOK

13

AUTOBIOGRAPHY
BLOCK CAPITALS
BLOTTING-PAPER
CARBON PROCESS
CHRISTMAS CARD
CONDENSED TYPE
COPYING-PENCIL
CROCODILE CLIP

PRINTING & STATIONERY

DRAWING-PENCIL
ELEPHANT FOLIO
ENCYCLOPAEDIA
GREETINGS CARD
HEIGHT TO PAPER
INTERPOLATION
JAPANESE PAPER
JUSTIFICATION
LOMBARD SCRIPT
MANIFOLD-PAPER
MIDDLE ARTICLE
PAPER-FASTENER
PATENT OUTSIDE
PENNY-DREADFUL
PHARMACOPOEIA
PLATE-PRINTING
PLOTTING-PAPER
PRELIMINARIES
PRINTING-PAPER
PRINTING-PRESS
QUADRUPLICATE
QUESTIONNAIRE
QUINTUPLICATE
READING MATTER
READY RECKONER
REFERENCE BOOK
REFERENCE-MARK
REPUBLICATION
SALE-CATALOGUE
SCRIBBLING-PAD
SECRETARY TYPE
SERIALISATION
SPIRAL BINDING
STANHOPE PRESS

STAR-CATALOGUE
STOP-PRESS NEWS
SUB-EDITORSHIP
SUBJECT MATTER
SYMBOLOGRAPHY
TRANSFER-PAPER
VALENTINE CARD
WRAPPING PAPER

14

ACKNOWLEDGMENT
AUTOTYPOGRAPHY
BANNER HEADLINE
CABINET-EDITION
CARTRIDGE-PAPER
CLASSIFICATION
COMPOSING STICK
CROSS-REFERENCE
FOLDING MACHINE
GLOSSY MAGAZINE
IMPERIAL OCTAVO
INTERLINEATION
INVITATION CARD
LATE-NIGHT FINAL
LITTLE MAGAZINE
NATURE-PRINTING
NEWSWORTHINESS
OFFSET PRINTING
OMNIBUS EDITION
PARCHMENT PAPER
PAROEMIOGRAPHY
PERFECT BINDING

PERSONAL COLUMN
PHOTOTELEGRAPH
PSEUDEPIGRAPHY
REVISED VERSION
SCREEN PRINTING
SCRIBBLING-BOOK
SENSATIONALISM
SHELF-CATALOGUE
SPECIAL EDITION
SUBJECT HEADING
SUPERSCRIPTION
SYMPATHETIC INK
WINDOW-ENVELOPE
XYLOTYPOGRAPHY

15

ACKNOWLEDGEMENT
CROSSWORD PUZZLE
DOUBLE-SIDED TAPE
INDELIBLE PENCIL
LOOSE-LEAF BINDER
NAUTICAL ALMANAC
PENCIL-SHARPENER
PICTURE-POSTCARD
PROOF-CORRECTING
PROOF-CORRECTION
QUADRUPLICATION
QUINTUPLICATION
RUNNING HEADLINE
SHILLING SHOCKER
VIRGIN PARCHMENT

292

PSYCHOLOGY

3

EGO

4

BIAS
ESSE
MIND
NOT-I
SELF
TRIP
WILL
WISH

5

ANGST
ANIMA
HORME
IMAGO
LIMEN
MANIA

6

ANIMUS
ANOMIE
CENSOR
DÉJÀ VU
EGOISM
ENGRAM
EONISM
FETISH
HANG-UP
LIBIDO
MAKE-UP
NON-EGO
PHOBIA
PSYCHE
REASON
SADISM
STRESS
TRANCE
TRAUMA

7

ANAGOGE

ANOESIS
ANXIETY
AUFGABE
COMPLEX
CONATUS
COUÉISM
EGOTISM
EGO-TRIP
EMPATHY
ESSENCE
FANTASY
INSIGHT
MANDALA
NOOLOGY
PERSONA
PHOBISM
TENSION
THERAPY

8

ALTER EGO
ANALYSIS
CATHEXIS
CONATION
DELUSION
DEMENTIA
EGOMANIA
FIXATION
FROTTAGE
HEDONICS
HYPNOSIS
HYSTERIA
IDÉE FIXE
INSTINCT
NEUROSIS
NOMOLOGY
PARANOIA
PERSEITY
PSYCHICS
PSYCHOID
SUPER-EGO
SYNDROME
ZOOPHILY
ZOOSCOPY

9

AUTOPHOBY
BREAKDOWN

CATATONIA
CATHARSIS
COGNITION
DEATH WISH
DEVIATION
DIANETICS
ESEMPLASY
FETISHISM
HYPOMANIA
HYSTERICS
HYPNOTISM
INTUITION
LIFE-FORCE
MAGNETISM
MASOCHISM
MECHANISM
MENTAL AGE
MENTICIDE
MONOMANIA
NEOPHOBIA
OBSESSION
PARAMETER
PSYCHOSIS
PYROMANIA
SPLIT MIND
THEOMANIA
TYPOMANIA
UNDERSELF
WORD SALAD
XENOMANIA
ZELOTYPIA
ZOOPHILIA
ZOOPHOBIA

10

ACROPHOBIA
AEROPHOBIA
ANIMA MUNDI
ANSCHAUUNG
CANOPHOBIA
CHILD-STUDY
CONSCIENCE
ERGOPHOBIA
IMPRESSION
INHIBITION
MONOPHOBIA
MUSOPHOBIA
MYSOPHOBIA
MYTHOMANIA
NOSOPHOBIA

NOSTOMANIA
NOSTOPATHY
OBJECT-SOUL
PANOPHOBIA
PARAGNOSIS
PARAMNESIA
PARAPHILIA
PROJECTION
PSYCHIATRY
PSYCHOGONY
PSYCHOLOGY
REGRESSION
REPRESSION
SITOPHOBIA
SOCIOPATHY
SOPHOMANIA
THEOPHOBIA
TOXIPHOBIA
UNDERSENSE
XENOPHOBIA
ZOANTHROPY

11

AGORAPHOBIA
ASSOCIATION
ASTRAPHOBIA
BATHOPHOBIA
BISOCIATION
CHRONOMANIA
CYCLOTHYMIA
DEMONOMANIA
DERANGEMENT
DROMOPHOBIA
HABITUATION
HYDROPHOBIA
HYPNOPAEDIA
HYPSOPHOBIA
INFERIORITY
INK-BLOT TEST
INTEGRATION
KLEPTOMANIA
MEGALOMANIA
MELANCHOLIA
NECROPHOBIA
NEUROTICISM
NYCTOPHOBIA
OCHLOPHOBIA
OVER-ANXIETY
PANTOPHOBIA
PATHOPHOBIA

PSYCHOLOGY

PERSONALITY
PHOBOPHOBIA
PHONOPHOBIA
PHOTOPHOBIA
PSYCHODRAMA
PSYCHOPATHY
SCOPOPHOBIA
SUBLIMATION
TAPHEPHOBIA

12

AESTHESIOGEN
APPERCEPTION
BEHAVIOURISM
COMPENSATION
CONSENTIENCE
DISSOCIATION
ESSENTIALITY
EXTROVERSION
FREUDIAN SLIP
GROUP THERAPY
HERD-INSTINCT
HORMIC THEORY
HYPNOGENESIS
HYPNOTHERAPY
HYPOCHONDRIA
HYSTEROMANIA
INTROVERSION
LIBIDINOSITY
NARCOPHERAPY
PARAPSYCHISM
PSEUDOCYESIS
PSYCHOGRAPHY
SCHIZOTHYMIA
TOXICOPHOBIA

TRANSFERENCE
VISCEROTONIA
ZOOMAGNETISM

13

AILOUROPHOBIA
ARACHNOPHOBIA
AUTOCHTHONISM
CONSCIOUSNESS
EXHIBITIONISM
GROUP DYNAMICS
HALLUCINATION
HYPNO-ANALYSIS
INTROSPECTION
JEKYLL AND HYDE
NARCO-ANALYSIS
NARCOHYPNOSIS
PARAPSYCHOSIS
PERSEVERATION
PSYCHASTHENIA
PSYCHOGENESIS
PSYCHOMETRICS
PSYCHOTHERAPY
REPRESENTAMEN
RORSCHACH TEST
SADO-MASOCHISM
SCHIZOPHRENIA
SUBJECT-OBJECT
SYPHILOPHOBIA
THANATOPHOBIA
ZOOPSYCHOLOGY

14

AUTO-SUGGESTION

BATTERY OF TESTS
CLAUSTROPHOBIA
DISASSOCIATION
ELECTRA COMPLEX
IDENTIFICATION
LUCID INTERVALS
NARCO-CATHARSIS
NARCOSYNTHESIS
OEDIPUS COMPLEX
PARAPSYCHOLOGY
PHAEDRA COMPLEX
PSYCHOANALYSIS
PSYCHODYNAMICS
PSYCHONEUROSIS
PSYCHOSOMATICS
PUERPERAL MANIA
THE UNCONSCIOUS
WISH FULFILMENT

15

ANIMAL MAGNETISM
AVERSION THERAPY
CHEMOPSYCHIATRY
DEMENTIA PRAECOX
DUAL PERSONALITY
ESCAPE MECHANISM
FREE ASSOCIATION
HYPNOGOGIC IMAGE
MASS OBSERVATION
NEUROPSYCHIATRY
ORTHOPSYCHIATRY
PSYCHOPATHOLOGY
THE SUBCONSCIOUS

RELIGION & THE CHURCH

3

ARK
AVE
LAW
PAX
PEW
PIE
PYX
SEE
SIN
USE
VOW

4

AMBO
AMEN
ANKH
APSE
BEMA
CULT
DAIS
FAST
FOLD
FONT
HADJ
HALO
HELL
HOST
HYMN
ICON
IDOL
JOSS
KIRK
MASS
NAVE
PALL
POME
PUJA
RITE
ROOD
ROTA
RULE
SEAT
SECT
SEXT
SIGN
SOUL
TEXT
THUS

TOMB

5

AISLE
ALTAR
AMBRY
ANNAT
BANNS
BEADS
BIBLE
CANON
CELLA
CHANT
CHOIR
CLASS
CREDO
CREED
CROSS
CRUET
CRYPT
CURIA
DOGMA
DOSEH
DULIA
FAITH
FLOCK
GLEBE
GLORY
GRACE
GRAIL
IHRAM
IMAGE
JESSE
JEHAD
JIHAD
KORAN
LABIS
LAUDS
LOGIA
MANNA
MECCA
MINAR
MISSA
NONES
ORANT
ORDER
PATEN
PIETÀ
PIETY
PLATE

PSALM
PURIM
QUEST
RELIC
SHEMA
SLYPE
SPIRE
STALL
STOUP
SUNNA
SYNOD
TABLE
TENET
TITHE
TITLE
TRACT
VAULT
VIGIL
WAFER

6

ABBACY
ADYTUM
ANTHEM
AUMBRY
BELFRY
BELIEF
CENSER
CHAPEL
CHORAL
CHRISM
CHURCH
CORBAN
CURSUS
DHARMA
DORSEL
DORSER
DOSSAL
DOSSEL
DOSSER
FLÈCHE
GLORIA
GOSPEL
GRADIN
HADITH
HEAVEN
HOMAGE
HOMILY
HOUSEL
HYMNAL

HYSSOP
INDULT
JATAKA
KIBLAH
LATRIA
LAVABO
LESSON
LITANY
LIVING
MANTRA
MATINS
MAUNDY
MEMORY
MIHRAB
MIMBAR
MISSAL
NIPTER
NOMISM
NOVENA
OFFICE
ONYCHA
ORACLE
ORDERS
ORISON
PAPACY
PARDON
PARISH
PARVIS
PATERA
PATINA
PITAKA
POPERY
PRAISE
PRAYER
PROPER
PULPIT
REFORM
REGULA
RITUAL
ROCHET
ROSARY
RUBRIC
SATORI
SCHISM
SCREEN
SERMON
SHRIFT
SHRINE
SPIRIT
SQUINT
SUTTEE
SYMBOL

TABULA
T-CROSS
TERAPH
VESTRY
VIRGIN
XENIUM

7

ABTHANE
ANGELUS
ARMOIRE
ASPERGE
AUREOLE
BAPTISM
BENISON
CANONRY
CANTATE
CHALICE
CHANCEL
CHANTRY
CHAPLET
CHAPTER
CHORALE
CHRISOM
COLLECT
COUNCIL
CREEPIE
CROSIER
CRUSADE
DARSHAN
DEANERY
DEODATE
DIOCESE
DIPTYCH
DIURNAL
DRY MASS
EPISTLE
FASTING
FISTULA
FONTLET
FRONTAL
FUNERAL
GODHEAD
GODSHIP
GRADINE
GRADINO
GRADUAL
GREMIAL
HASSOCK
HOLY WAR

HOSANNA
HYMNERY
HYMNODY
ICHTHYS
IMPIETY
INCENSE
INTROIT
JUBILEE
KADDISH
KERYGMA
KHUTBAH
KIRKING
KNEELER
LECTERN
LECTION
LICHWAY
LITURGY
LOW MASS
LUNETTE
LYCHNIC
MADONNA
MANDALA
MENORAH
MINARET
MIRACLE
MISHNAH
MISSION
MONKERY
MYSTERY
NAGMAAL
NARTHEX
NIRVANA
NOCTURN
NOTITIA
ORARIUM
ORATORY
ORDINAL
ORTHROS
PASSION
PENANCE
PEW-RENT
PISCINA
PLACEBO
POOR-BOX
POPEDOM
PRAYERS
PREBEND
PREFACE
PRELACY
PSALTER
RECTORY
REQUIEM

295

RELIGION & THE CHURCH

REREDOS
RESPOND
RETABLE
RETREAT
REVIVAL
SABAISM
SABBATH
SANCTUM
SANCTUS
SANKHYA
SEDILIA
SERVICE
SESSION
SISTRUM
SITTING
SRADDHA
STEEPLE
STIPEND
SYNAPTE
SYNAXIS
TAMBOUR
TEMENOS
THE WORD
TRIBUNE
TRIDUUM
TRINITY
UNCTION
VESPERS
WEDDING
WORSHIP

8

ABLUTION
ADVOWSON
AFFUSION
AGNUS DEI
AGRAPHON
ANTIPHON
APOSTASY
ASPERGES
AUDIENCE
AVE MARIA
BARRATRY
BEAD-ROLL
BENEFICE
BENITIER
BLESSING
BREVIARY
CANON LAW
CANTICLE

CATHEDRA
CATHISMA
CEREMONY
CHAPELRY
CIBORIUM
CLOISTER
COMPLINE
CONCLAVE
CORPORAL
COVENANT
CREATION
CREDENCE
CRESCENT
CRUCIFIX
DEACONRY
DEANSHIP
DECRETAL
DEVOTION
DIVINITY
DOCTRINE
DOXOLOGY
ELEMENTS
EMBOLISM
EVENSONG
EXEGESIS
EXERCISE
EXORCISM
FERETORY
FILIOQUE
FRACTION
FUNCTION
GLORIOLE
HIERURGY
HIGH MASS
HOLINESS
HOLY-ROOD
HYMN-BOOK
IDOLATRY
ISODICON
JUBILATE
KIRKYARD
LICH-GATE
LYCH-GATE
MACARISM
MARABOUT
MARRIAGE
MASS-BELL
MASS-BOOK
MENOLOGY
MINISTRY
MISERERE
NATIVITY

NAVICULA
NUPTIALS
OBLATION
OFFERING
ORDERING
OVERSOUL
PANHAGIA
PARADISE
PARCLOSE
PAROUSIA
PARTICLE
PASTILLE
PASTORAL
PAX-BOARD
PERICOPE
PETITION
PEW-CHAIR
PLATFORM
PLENARTY
POPEHOOD
POPESHIP
PREDELLA
PRIE-DIEU
PRIORATE
PSALMODY
PULPITRY
PULPITUM
RELIGION
RESCRIPT
RESPONSE
ROGATION
ROOD-BEAM
ROOD-LOFT
SACRISTY
SAINTDOM
SAINTISM
SANCTION
SANCTITY
SANGRAAL
SEAT-RENT
SEMINARY
SINECURE
STIGMATA
SUFFRAGE
TAU-CROSS
TE IGITUR
TENEBRAE
THEODICY
THEOLOGY
THURIBLE
TRANSEPT
TRIODION

TRIPTYCH
TRIUNITY
TYPOLOGY
VERNICLE
VERSICLE
VESTIARY
VIATICUM
VOIDANCE

9

ADI GRANTH
ALTAR-TOMB
ANOINTING
APSIDIOLE
ATONEMENT
BALDACHIN
BEATITUDE
BELL-TOWER
BISHOPRIC
BLASPHEMY
CAMPANILE
CANTHARIS
CANTILENA
CARTULARY
CATECHISM
CHURCHING
CLERICATE
CLERICITY
COLLEGIUM
COMMUNION
CONCORDAT
CONFITEOR
CRAB'S-EYES
CREDENDUM
DAMNATION
DECALOGUE
DECRETALS
DOGMATICS
DONA NOBIS
EIRENICON
ELEVATION
ENCOLPION
EPICLESIS
EUCHARIST
EUCHOLOGY
EXPIATION
FALDSTOOL
FEAST-RITE
FESTILOGY
FLABELLUM

FONT-STONE
GODLINESS
HAGIARCHY
HEADSTONE
HIGH ALTAR
HOLY GRAIL
HOLY WATER
IMMERSION
INCENSORY
INTERDICT
INTROITUS
INUNCTION
ISAGOGICS
JOSS-STICK
KNEE-DRILL
LAMB OF GOD
LAUDATION
LITURGICS
LOW CHURCH
MARTYRDOM
MERCY-SEAT
MONACHISM
MONOLATRY
MYSTAGOGY
MYSTERIES
NEW CHURCH
NEXT WORLD
NOVITIATE
OBEDIENCE
OBEISANCE
OFFERINGS
OFFERTORY
ORDINANCE
ORNAMENTS
ORTHODOXY
OSTENSORY
PANEGYRIC
PASTORATE
PATRIMONY
PATRONAGE
PENITENCE
PERDITION
PLAINSONG
PLURALISM
PLURALITY
PRAYER-MAT
PRAYER-RUG
PREACHING
PRELATION
PRIORSHIP
PROOF-TEXT
PROSEUCHE

PROTHESIS
PROVISION
PSALM-BOOK
PSALM-TUNE
PURGATION
PURGATORY
RABBINATE
RECLUSION
RECLUSORY
RECTORATE
REFECTORY
RHIPIDION
ROOD-TOWER
ROSE-CROSS
SACRAMENT
SACRARIUM
SACRIFICE
SAINTHOOD
SALVATION
SANCTUARY
SCRIPTURE
SEPULCHRE
SOLEMNITY
SOLEMN VOW
SPIRATION
SPIRITUAL
SPRINKLER
STABILITY
STASIDION
STICHERON
THEOCRACY
THEOMACHY
THEOPATHY
THEOPHANY
THEOSOPHY
TOMBSTONE
TRANSENNA
TRICERION
TRISAGION
VICARIATE

10

ABSOLUTION
ALLOCUTION
ALTAR-CLOTH
ALTARPIECE
ALTAR-RAILS
ALTAR-STEPS
ALTAR-STONE
ANOINTMENT

ANTECHAPEL
APOSTOLATE
APOTHEOSIS
AQUAMANILE
ASCRIPTION
BAPTISTERY
BAR MITZVAH
BELL-TURRET
BENEDICITE
BENEDICTUS
BIBLE-CLASS
CANTERBURY
CASSOLETTE
CHOIR-STALL
CHURCH-RATE
CHURCHYARD
CLERESTORY
COMMIXTURE
CONFESSION
CONSISTORY
CONVERSION
CONVICTION
DEACONSHIP
DEVOUTNESS
DIACONICON
DRY SERVICE
ECPHONESIS
ENCYCLICAL
EPISCOPACY
EPISCOPATE
EVANGELIAR
EXALTATION
EYE-SERVICE
FENESTELLA
FREE CHURCH
FRITH-STOOL
FULL ORDERS
GOSPEL SIDE
GRAVESTONE
GREEK CROSS
HAGIOSCOPE
HALLELUJAH
HIEROCRACY
HIEROLATRY
HIGH CHURCH
HOLY OFFICE
HOLY ORDERS
HOUSELLING
HOUSE OF GOD
HYPERDULIA
HYPOSTASIS
ICONOCLASM

ICONOLATRY
IMMOLATION
IMPANATION
IMPOSITION
INCUMBENCY
INDULGENCE
INITIATION
INTERSTICE
INTINCTION
INVITATION
INVOCATION
IRRELIGION
LADY-CHAPEL
LATIN CROSS
LAY BAPTISM
LECTIONARY
LITANY-DESK
LITHOLATRY
LORD'S TABLE
LUSTRATION
LYCHNAPSIA
MAGNIFICAT
MARIOLATRY
MILLENNIUM
MISERICORD
MONSTRANCE
OBSERVANCE
OFFICE-BOOK
ORDINATION
ORTHOPRAXY
PAPAL CROSS
PASTORSHIP
PEACE OF GOD
PHYLACTERY
PILGRIMAGE
PONEROLOGY
PONTIFICAL
PRAYER-BEAD
PRAYER-BOOK
PREACHMENT
PREFERMENT
PRESBYTERY
PRIESTHOOD
PROCESSION
PROFESSION
PROPHETISM
PROVIDENCE
RECTORSHIP
REDEMPTION
REPENTANCE
REQUIESCAT
RESPONSORY

RETROCHOIR
REVELATION
ROOD-SCREEN
ROUEN CROSS
SANCTIMONY
SANCTITUDE
SCHISM-SHOP
SETTLEMENT
SEXTONSHIP
SINFULNESS
SISTERHOOD
SOLEMN MASS
STIGMATISM
SUBDEANERY
SUBSELLIUM
SUPERALTAR
SYNAXARION
SYNTHRONUS
TABERNACLE
TERSANCTUS
THEOLOGATE
UNDERWORLD
VENERATION
VERGERSHIP
VESPER-BELL
VESTRY-ROOM
WATCH-NIGHT

11

ALTAR-SCREEN
ANTEPENDIUM
ARCHDIOCESE
ASPERGILLUM
ASPERSORIUM
BENEDICTION
BROAD CHURCH
CAMP-MEETING
CATECHETICS
CELTIC CROSS
CHALICE-VEIL
CHOIR SCREEN
CHRISMATORY
CHRISTENDOM
CHRISTENING
CHURCH-COURT
COMMANDMENT
COMMINATION
CONVENTICLE
CONVOCATION
CROWN LIVING

RELIGION & THE CHURCH

DEIFICATION
DEPRECATION
DESECRATION
EPISTLE-SIDE
EUCHOLOGION
EVANGELIARY
GENUFLEXION
GLOSSOLALIA
GRAVEN IMAGE
GREEK CHURCH
HAGIOGRAPHY
HIEROGRAPHY
HUNTING-MASS
ICONOSTASIS
IMPENITENCE
INCARNATION
INCENSE-BOAT
INQUISITION
INSTITUTION
IRREVERENCE
JESSE WINDOW
KIRK SESSION
KISS OF PEACE
LATIN CHURCH
LITANY-STOOL
LORD'S PRAYER
LORD'S SUPPER
LYCHNOSCOPE
MINISTERIUM
MINOR ORDERS
MONASTICISM
MUSCATORIUM
NORMAN CROSS
NUPTIAL MASS
OBSECRATION
ORGAN-SCREEN
ORIGINAL SIN
ORTHOPRAXIS
PANEGYRICON
PARABAPTISM
PASSING-BELL
PATERNOSTER
PERSECUTION
PONTIFICATE
PRAYER-WHEEL
PREACHINESS
PRELATESHIP
PREPARATION
PRIESTCRAFT
PRIMATESHIP
PROCURATION
PROSELYTISM

RECANTATION
REFORMATION
RELIGIOSITY
REPROBATION
RESERVATION
RITUAL CHOIR
ROMAN CHURCH
ROOD-STEEPLE
RUBRICATION
RULE OF FAITH
RUSH-BEARING
SACRING BELL
SAINTLINESS
SAVING GRACE
SCHISM-HOUSE
SERVICE-BOOK
SHORT SHRIFT
SINLESSNESS
SIN-OFFERING
STAR OF DAVID
SUBDEACONRY
SUBLIMATION
SUBPANATION
THAUMATURGY
THEOPNEUSTY
UNIFICATION
UNORTHODOXY

12

ABBEY-COUNTER
ANNUNCIATION
ALTAR FRONTAL
ARCHDEACONRY
BAPTISMAL VOW
CALVARY CROSS
CANONISATION
CAPITAL CROSS
CHAPLAINSHIP
CHOIR-SERVICE
CHRISTOLATRY
CHRISTOPHANY
CHURCH-PARADE
CLAUSTRATION
COLLEGIALITY
CONFESSIONAL
CONFIRMATION
CONGREGATION
CONSECRATION
CONSOCIATION

DEAMBULATORY
DENOMINATION
DISCIPLESHIP
DISPENSATION
ECCLESIOLOGY
EXSUFFLATION
FIELD MEETING
FUNERAL RITES
GENERAL SYNOD
HAMARTIOLOGY
HEART-SERVICE
IMAGE-WORSHIP
INSTALLATION
INSUFFLATION
INTERCESSION
INTERDICTION
KYRIE ELEISON
LAY COMMUNION
LESSER LITANY
LITTLE OFFICE
LITURGIOLOGY
MEAT-OFFERING
MINISTRATION
MOTHER CHURCH
NEW TESTAMENT
NUNC DIMITTIS
OLD TESTAMENT
OPISTHOMODOS
ORGAN-GALLERY
PAEDOBAPTISM
PATRISTICISM
PENITENT FORM
PENITENTIARY
PILGRIM'S SIGN
POSTILLATION
PRESBYTERATE
PRIESTLINESS
PROCESSIONAL
PROMISED LAND
PURIFICATION
REAL PRESENCE
RECONVERSION
RESPONSORIAL
RESURRECTION
SACRAMENTARY
SUPERFRONTAL
SUPPLICATION
SYMBOLOLATRY
THANKSGIVING
THAUMATOGENY
THE HEREAFTER
VISITORS' BOOK

13

ARCHBISHOPRIC
ARCHDEACONATE
BAPTISM OF FIRE
BEATIFICATION
BIDDING PRAYER
BURIAL SERVICE
CAPUCHIN CROSS
CHURCH SERVICE
CLOISTER-GARTH
COMMUNICATION
COMPREHENSION
CONFESSORSHIP
CREDENCE TABLE
DILAPIDATIONS
EASTERN CHURCH
ECCLESIOLATRY
ENCLOSED ORDER
EVANGELISTARY
FLOWER-SERVICE
GLORIFICATION
HOUSE OF PRAYER
IMPROPRIATION
INCENSE-BURNER
INFALLIBILITY
LECTISTERNIUM
MISSA SOLEMNIS
MODERATORSHIP
MORNING-PRAYER
NONCONFORMITY
PASCHAL CANDLE
PASTORAL STAFF
PEACE-OFFERING
PECTORAL CROSS
PRAYER-MEETING
PRECONISATION
PRECENTORSHIP
PRESBYTERSHIP
SACROSANCTITY

SANCTUARY-LAMP
SOLEMNISATION
STATE-RELIGION
SUBDEACONSHIP
SUFFRAGANSHIP
TEMPORALITIES
THE ASSUMPTION
THURIFICATION
VISIBLE CHURCH
WAY OF THE CROSS
WESTERN CHURCH
WESTERN SCHISM

14

BEATIFIC VISION
CANONICAL HOURS
CHURCH ASSEMBLY
CHURCH MILITANT
COMMUNION TABLE
DECONSECRATION
EVANGELISATION
EXCLAUSTRATION
EXTREME UNCTION
FIELD PREACHING
GREGORIAN CHANT
HIGH PRIESTHOOD
HOUSE OF WORSHIP
INTERCOMMUNION
JERUSALEM CROSS
NATIONAL CHURCH
ORTHODOX CHURCH
PARISH REGISTER
PASTORAL CHARGE
PASTORAL LETTER
PLACE OF WORSHIP
PONTIFICAL MASS
PREACHING-CROSS

PREDESTINATION
PROTEVANGELIUM
RECONSECRATION
REFORMED CHURCH
REVIVAL MEETING
SACRAMENT-HOUSE
SANCTIFICATION
SCEUOPHYLACIUM
SCHOOL-DIVINITY
SELF-IMMOLATION
SERPENT-WORSHIP
SIGN OF THE CROSS
ST ANDREW'S CROSS
ST GEORGE'S CROSS
STIGMATISATION
SYNOPTIC GOSPEL
THE CRUCIFIXION
TRIDENTINE MASS

15

ARCHIEPISCOPATE
ARTICLES OF FAITH
BYZANTINE CHURCH
CIRCUMINCESSION
COVENANT OF GRACE
ECCLESIASTICISM
EXCOMMUNICATION
GENERAL EPISTLES
HARVEST FESTIVAL
METROPOLITANATE
NATURAL RELIGION
NATURAL THEOLOGY
PASTORAL ADDRESS
ST ANTHONY'S CROSS
ST PATRICK'S CROSS
TRANSFIGURATION

SCIENCE – ARCHAEOLOGY

3

DIG
HUT
PIT

4

ABRI
CAMP
CAVE
DYKE
DYSS
KILN
KIVA
OVEN
RATH
RUNE
SESE
TELL
TOMB

5

BROCH
CAIRN
GRAVE
HENGE
HOARD
MOUND
MUMMY
QUOIT
RELIC
SHARD
STELE

6

BARROW
BOSING
CASTRO
CIRCLE
CURSUS
DATING
DOLMEN
DROMOS
EOLITH
FOSSIL
ICE AGE

KURGAN
MENHIR
MIDDEN
NAVETA
SERIES
SYRINX

7

ANTIQUE
BONE-BED
CHULLPA
CUP-MARK
DEMOTIC
DIGGING
IRON AGE
NEOLITH
PAPYRUS
TALAYOT
TRILITH
TUMULUS
ZOOLITH

8

AMMONITE
ARTEFACT
ARTIFACT
BONE-CAVE
CALAMITE
CROMLECH
GRATTOIR
HIERATIC
HILL-FORT
MEGALITH
OSTRAKON
POTSHERD
STONE AGE
TROCHITE
TYPOLOGY
URNFIELD

9

ALIGNMENT
ANTIQUITY
BARBOTINE
BONE-BLACK
BRACTEATE

BRADISISM
BRONZE AGE
CARTOUCHE
COPPER AGE
GONIATITE
HOAR-STONE
HUT-CIRCLE
JEW'S-STONE
MICROLITH
MUMMY-CASE
PALAFITTE
PARCHMENT
PICTOGRAM
SERIATION
SERPULITE
TERRAMARA
TRILITHON
TRILOBITE

10

ASSEMBLAGE
BELL BARROW
CARINATION
CARTONNAGE
CHRONOLOGY
COURT CAIRN
CUP-AND-RING
DISC BARROW
EGYPTOLOGY
EXCAVATION
HIEROGLYPH
PALAEOLITH
PETROGLYPH
PICTOGRAPH
POND BARROW
PREHISTORY
SHADOW-MARK
WHEEL-HOUSE

11

ARCHAEOLOGY
ASSYRIOLOGY
BONE-BRECCIA
CHAMBER TOMB
CONTOUR-FORT
CYPRO-MINOAN
HIEROGLYPHS
HORNED CAIRN
ICHTHYOLITE

PERISTALITH
RADIOCARBON
REINDEER AGE
SARCOPHAGUS
STONE CIRCLE
TENTACULITE
VARVE DATING

12

CARBON DATING
CYLINDER-SEAL
FLUORINE TEST
GALLERY GRAVE
LAKE-DWELLING
MOABITE STONE
OPISTHOGRAPH
ORNITHICNITE
PALAEOGRAPHY
PASSAGE GRAVE
PROTOHISTORY
ROSETTA STONE
STRATIGRAPHY

13

ACCULTURATION
FOSSILISATION
GEOCHRONOLOGY
GLACIAL PERIOD
HIEROGLYPHICS
KITCHEN-MIDDEN
OPISTHOGRAPHY
PALAEONTOLOGY
STANDING-STONE

14

ANCHOR ORNAMENT
ANCIENT HISTORY
COLLECTIVE TOMB
OBSIDIAN DATING
PICTURE-WRITING
POLLEN-ANALYSIS

15

ANCIENT MONUMENT
DRUIDICAL CIRCLE
ICHTHYODORULITE
OCCUPATION LEVEL

SCIENCE – ASTRONOMY

3

MAP
ORB
SKY
SUN

4

COMA
CUSP
DISC
EAST
HALO
MARE
MARS
MOON
NODE
NOVA
PATH
POLE
RING
STAR
VOID
WEST

5

APSIS
COMET
CYCLE
DIGIT
EARTH
EPACT
EPOCH
GLOBE
GLORY
LUNAR
NADIR
NORTH
ORBIT
PHASE
PLAGE
PLUTO
PULSE
SAROS
SOUTH
SPACE
TRINE
UMBRA

VENUS
WORLD

6

ALBIDO
APOGEE
BOLIDE
CIRCLE
COLURE
CORONA
COSMOS
CRATER
DOUBLE
FACULA
GALAXY
MACULA
METEOR
NEBULA
OCTANT
ORIENT
ORRERY
PARSEC
PERIOD
PHASIS
PLANET
PULSAR
QUASAR
SATURN
SECTOR
SPHERE
SUN-DOG
SYSTEM
SYZYGY
URANUS
VERTEX
WANING
WAXING
ZENITH
ZODIAC

7

ANOMALY
APPULSE
AUREOLE
AZIMUTH
ECLIPSE
ELEMENT
EQUATOR

EQUINOX
GRAVITY
HEAVENS
HORNING
JUPITER
MERCURY
MOCK SUN
NEPTUNE
NEW MOON
NUCLEUS
PERIGEE
PRIMARY
QUARTER
RADIANT
STARLET
STAR-MAP
SUN-DISC
SUNSPOT
TRANSIT

8

AEROLITE
APHELION
ASTEROID
CRESCENT
ECLIPTIC
EMERSION
EVECTION
FIREBALL
FULL MOON
HALF-MOON
LATITUDE
LUMINARY
LUNATION
MERIDIAN
MOCK MOON
NORTHING
NUTATION
OCCIDENT
PENUMBRA
RED DWARF
RED GIANT
SAECULUM
SOLSTICE
SOUTHING
STAR-DUST
STARSPOT
TERRELLA
TWINKLER
UNIVERSE

9

ASTRONOMY
BLACK HOLE
CHEVELURE
EPHEMERIS
EXOSPHERE
FIRMAMENT
FIXED STAR
FLOCCULUS
HELIOLOGY
HOUR-ANGLE
IMMERSION
LIGHT TIME
LIGHT YEAR
LONGITUDE
LUNAR YEAR
MACROCOSM
MAGNITUDE
METEORITE
METEOROID
MID-HEAVEN
MOONSCAPE
PARHELION
PLANETOID
PLENILUNE
RADIO STAR
REFRACTOR
RICE-GRAIN
SATELLITE
SOLAR TIME
SOLAR WIND
SOLAR YEAR
STAR-DRIFT
SUPERNOVA
TELESCOPE
TWINKLING
URANOLOGY
VARIATION
WHITE HOLE

10

ABERRATION
ALMACANTAR
AREOGRAPHY
BINARY STAR
BIQUINTILE
EARTH-SHINE
ELONGATION
HOUR-CIRCLE

INSOLATION
LUNAR CYCLE
METAGALAXY
NEBULOSITY
OPPOSITION
OUTER SPACE
PARASELENE
PERIHELION
PRECESSION
PULSATANCE
QUADRATURE
SELENOLOGY
SERIAL TIME
SIDEROSTAT
SOLAR FLARE
STARGAZING
TERMINATOR
URANOMETRY
WHITE DWARF

11

BAILY'S BEADS
COSMOSPHERE
CULMINATION
DECLINATION
FALLING STAR
GIBBOUS MOON
GRAVITATION
HARVEST MOON
HUNTER'S MOON
KEPLER'S LAWS
LUNAR THEORY
MINOR PLANET
NEUTRON STAR
OBSERVATORY
OCCULTATION
PHOTOSPHERE
PLANISPHERE
SELENOGRAPH
SOLAR SYSTEM
URANOGRAPHY

12

AEROSIDERITE
APPARENT TIME
ASTROPHYSICS
BINARY SYSTEM
CHROMOSPHERE

SCIENCE – ASTRONOMY

CRESCENT MOON
HEAVENLY BODY
METEOR CRATER
MULTIPLE STAR
PARANTHELION
PERTURBATION
PLANETESIMAL
PRIMUM MOBILE
PROPER MOTION
SELENOGRAPHY
SHOOTING-STAR
SIDEREAL TIME
SIDEREAL YEAR
TOTAL ECLIPSE

EPHEMERIS TIME
INTERLUNATION
MEAN SOLAR TIME
METEOR STREAMS
PRIMARY PLANET
RETROGRESSION
STAR-CATALOGUE
ZODIACAL LIGHT

RADIO-TELESCOPE
RETROGRADATION
REVERSING LAYER
RIGHT ASCENSION
SUPERIOR PLANET
VERTICAL CIRCLE
ZENITH DISTANCE

13

BIG BANG THEORY
COMPANION STAR
CONFIGURATION
CONSTELLATION

14

ANACOUSTIC ZONE
ANNULAR ECLIPSE
EQUATION OF TIME
HELIACAL RISING
INFERIOR PLANET
ISLAND UNIVERSE
METEORIC SHOWER
METEORIC STONES
PARTIAL ECLIPSE
RADIO-ASTRONOMY

15

ANOMALISTIC YEAR
ARMILLARY SPHERE
CHANDLER'S WOBBLE
HELIACAL SETTING
MERIDIAN PASSAGE
PTOLEMAIC SYSTEM
SOLAR MICROSCOPE
SOLAR PROMINENCE
ULTRAVIOLET STAR

SCIENCE – BIOLOGY

3

DNA
EGG
GUM
OVA
PUS
RNA
SEX
WAX

4

BILE
BLOW
CELL
COMB

DUNG
FLUX
GALL
GENE
GERM
GLIT
GORE
HOST
LIFE
MALE
MILK
OVUM
PACK
SEED
SOMA
TEAR
UREA
YOLK
ZOON

5

ATOKE
AUXIN
AZYGY
BLOOD
CHYLE
CLINE
CLONE
CODON
CRUOR
CYTON
GALEA
GENUS
GLEET
GONAD
GRUME
HELOT
ICHOR

IDANT
ISSUE
JUICE
LININ
LIPID
LOCUS
LYMPH
LYSIN
LYSIS
MNEME
MUCIN
MUCUS
MUTON
PLASM
RHEUM
SCALE
SEBUM
SEMEN
SERUM

SKEIN
SPERM
SPORE
STAGE
STOOL
STYLE
SUDOR
SUGAR
SWEAT
TAXIS
TAXON
TREAD
URINE
VIRUS
WATER
ZOOID

6

AEROBE
ALEXIN
ALLELE
AMOEBA
ANLAGE
AREOLA
ATOCIA
BIOGEN
BIOTIN
BIVIUM
BUNDLE
CILIUM
CYTODE
DIAXON
EARWAX
EMBRYO
ENZYME

FAECES
FEMALE
FIBRIN
FLATUS
FOETUS
GAMETE
GENDER
GENOME
HUMOUR
HYBRID
LACUNA
LIGULA
LIVING
LOCHIA
LYSINE
MATTER
MEDIUM
MENSES
MERISM
MONOSY
MUTANT
MYELIN
MYOGEN
MYOSIN
OOCYTE
OOGAMY
OOGENY
OSSEIN
PEPSIN
PERIOD
PHLEGM
PLASMA
SALIVA
SANIES
SEPTUM
SMEGMA
SOMITE
SPUTUM
STEROL
STROMA
SUCCUS
TISSUE
TOPHUS
URACIL
VIBRIO
ZYGOTE

7

ADENINE
ALBUMEN

AMPULLA
ANNULUS
ATAVISM
AUXESIS
BIGENER
BIOGENY
BIOLOGY
BIOPSIS
CERUMEN
CHALONE
CHIMERA
DENDRON
ECDYSIS
EMBOLUS
ENERGID
EXOGAMY
EXCRETA
GEMMULE
GUMMING
HORMONE
HYDATID
HYDROID
INSULIN
ISOGAMY
ISOGENY
KERATIN
LACINIA
LACTEAL
LAMELLA
LINKAGE
LITHITE
MEIOSIS
MICELLA
MICELLE
MICROBE
MITOSIS
MONOSIS
MUCIGEN
MUTAGEN
NUCLEIN
NUCLEUS
OOSPORE
OPSONIN
PANGENE
PEPTIDE
PHAEISM
PITUITA
PLASMIN
PLASTID
PROCESS
PROTEIN
PTYALIN

PUTAMEN
SACCULE
SALTANT
SAPROBE
SARCODE
SEX-CELL
SPECIES
SPINDLE
SPIREME
SPORULE
SYMBION
SYNGAMY
SYNOVIA
SYSTOLE
TACTISM
THYMINE
TROPISM
TRYPSIN
VACUOLE
VALENCY
VARIETY
VESTIGE
VITREUM
VOLUTIN
ZOOGAMY
ZOOGENY
ZOOGONY
ZOOPERY
ZOOTOMY
ZYGOSIS
ZYMOGEN

8

AMITOSIS
ANAEROBE
ANAPHASE
ANTIBODY
APOMIXIS
AUTACOID
AUTOGAMY
AUTOGENY
AUTOSOME
BACILLUS
BACTERIA
BATHMISM
BIOBLAST
BIOPHORE
BIOPLASM
BIOPLAST
BLASTOID

BLASTULA
CHONDRIN
CHONDRUS
CLEAVAGE
COAGULUM
COLLAGEN
CREATINE
CYTOLOGY
CYTOSINE
ECCRISIS
ECLOSION
ECTODERM
ECTOSARC
ECTOZOON
EFFECTOR
EGGSHELL
ENDOSARC
EPIPHYTE
EXHALANT
FEED-BACK
FUNCTION
GANGLION
GASTRULA
GENETICS
GENITURE
GENOTYPE
GEOTAXIS
GERM-CELL
GLYCOGEN
GUMMOSIS
GYNANDRY
HEAMATIN
HAPLOIDY
HEREDITY
HOMEOSIS
HOMOGENY
HOMOLOGY
HOMOTYPE
HOMOTYPY
INTERSEX
ISOMORPH
JOINT-OIL
LECITHIN
MECONIUM
MELANISM
MENARCHE
MEROGENY
MONOGENY
MONOGONY
MUTATION
MYOBLAST
NIDATION

NOMOGENY
NUCELLUS
NUCLEOLE
ONTOGENY
OOGONIUM
OOPHORON
OOSPHERE
ORGANISM
OXYTOCIN
PANMIXIA
PARASITE
PHOTOGEN
PLANKTON
PLATELET
POLARITY
POLYSOMY
PROPHASE
RH-FACTOR
RIBOSOME
RUDIMENT
SACCULUS
SECRETIN
SYMBIONT
SYNAPSIS
SYNDESIS
SYNTONIN
TEAR-DROP
TELEGONY
THYROXIN
TYROSINE
URIC ACID
UROCHORD
UROSTYLE
VENATION
VIRILISM
VITELLUS
XANTHINE
ZOOBLAST
ZOOECIUM
ZOOGLOEA
ZOOSPERM
ZOOSPORE
ZOOTHOME

9

ACTIVATOR
ADRENALIN
AEROPHYTE
AEROTAXIS
ALLOPLASM

303

SCIENCE – BIOLOGY

AMINO-ACID
ANABIOSIS
APOPHYSIS
AUTOLYSIS
AUTOTROPH
BACTERIUM
BIOSPHERE
CELLULITE
CHEMOSTAT
CHROMATIN
CLAVATION
COENOBIUM
COLOSTRUM
COMMENSAL
CONNATION
CONNATURE
CORPUSCLE
CYTOLISIS
CYTOPLASM
CYTOTOXIN
DIGESTION
DISCHARGE
ECTOBLAST
ECTOPLASM
ENDOLYMPH
ENDOMIXIS
ENDOPLASM
EVOLUTION
EXCREMENT
EXCRETION
EXUDATION
FATTY ACID
FERTILITY
FLAGELLUM
FOOD CHAIN
GERM-LAYER
GERM-PLASM
GESTATION
GREGORINE
HALOPHILY
HELIOZOAN
HETEROSIS
HEXAPLOID
HISTAMINE
HISTIDINE
HISTOGENY
HISTOLOGY
HYBRIDISM
HYBRIDITY
HYDROSOMA
IDIOPLASM
LEUCOCYTE

LIFE-CYCLE
LUCIFERIN
MACROCYTE
MENDELISM
MENOPAUSE
METAPHASE
METAPLASM
MICROCYTE
MICROSOME
MORPHOSIS
MUTUALISM
NUCLEOLUS
OCTAPLOID
OESTROGEN
OOGENESIS
ORGANISER
OSTEOGENY
OVULATION
PATHOGENY
PERILYMPH
PHAGOCYTE
PHENOTYPE
PHOTOPHIL
PITUITRIN
POLYMORPH
PROGESTIN
PROPERDIN
PROTOZOAN
PROTOZOON
PSEUDOPOD
RACIATION
RECREMENT
REVERSION
RHEOTAXIS
SALTATION
SECRETION
SECUNDINE
SEPTATION
SEXUALITY
SPERMATID
SPERM-CELL
SPIRILLUM
STERILITY
SYMBIOSIS
SYNCYTIUM
TELOPHASE
TERATOGEN
THELYTOKY
UNIVALENT
VARIATION
VESTIGIUM
VITELLINE

VOLTINISM
ZOOCYTIUM
ZOOGAMETE

10

ACAROPHILY
ACTIVATION
AEROBIOSIS
AFTERBIRTH
AGGLUTININ
AMPHIMIXIS
ANTIBIOSIS
ATTRACTANT
AUTOMATISM
BIOGENESIS
BIOPOIESIS
BLASTOCYST
BLASTODERM
BLASTOMERE
BLASTOPORE
BLOOD GROUP
BLOOD-PLATE
CATABOLISM
CENTROSOME
CHROMIDIUM
CHROMOSOME
CONCEPTION
CONSORTISM
CREATININE
CYTOCHROME
DERIVATION
DIAPEDESIS
DIMORPHISM
DYNAMOGENY
EMBRYOGENY
ENCYSTMENT
ENDOSMOSIS
EPIGENESIS
EPIPHYTISM
FIBRINOGEN
GONOCOCCUS
GYNANDRISM
HAEMATOSIS
HAEMOCONIA
HAEMOLYSIS
HAUSTELLUM
HELIOTAXIS
HETEROGAMY
HETEROGENY
HETEROGONY

HETEROKONT
HETEROLOGY
HETEROTAXY
HISTIOLOGY
HISTOBLAST
HISTOLYSIS
HOMOPLASMY
HYALOPLASM
HYDROTAXIS
HYDROTHECA
IMPRINTING
INCUBATION
INFUSORIAN
INTERPHASE
KARYOPLASM
KATABOLISM
LEUCOPLAST
LEPTOSPIRA
LYMPHOCYTE
LYSENKOISM
MACROBIOTA
MACROSPORE
METABOLISM
METASTASIS
MICROBIOTA
MICROSPORE
MONOHYBRID
MORPHOGENY
MORPHOLOGY
MOTHER-CELL
MYCOPLASMA
NEUROPLASM
NEUROTOXIN
OCTAPLOIDY
ORGANOGENY
OSTEOBLAST
OSTEOCLAST
PANCREATIN
PANGENESIS
PARABIOSIS
PARAMECIUM
PENTAPLOID
PERIDINIAN
PHOTONASTY
PHOTOPHILY
PHOTOTAXIS
PLASMODESM
PLASMODIUM
PLASMOGAMY
PLASMOSOMA
PLASMOSOME
PLASTOGAMY

POLYPLOIDY
PRECIPITIN
PROCRYPSIS
PROTOPLASM
PROTOPLAST
RH-NEGATIVE
RH-POSITIVE
SEMINALITY
SEMINATION
SPECIATION
SYNGENESIS
TERATOGENY
TRYPTOPHAN
ZOOTHECIUM

11

ABIOGENESIS
ABSTRICTION
AEROBIOLOGY
AGROBIOLOGY
ALLELOMORPH
APLANOSPORE
ARRHENOTOKY
ASSOCIATION
BIOCOENOSIS
BLOODSTREAM
CHOLESTEROL
CICATRICULA
CINE-BIOLOGY
CLOSTRIDIUM
CONJUGATION
CONNASCENCE
COPROSTEROL
CYTOGENESIS
DEOXYRIBOSE
DETERMINANT
DISJUNCTION
DISMUTATION
DOUBLE HELIX
ECCRINOLOGY
ENCYSTATION
EPINEPHRINE
ERYTHROCYTE
EUBACTERIUM
FISSIPARISM
FISSIPARITY
GAMETANGIUM
GAMOGENESIS
GAMOTROPISM
GEMMULATION

GENERIC NAME
GENETIC CODE
GNOTOBIOSIS
GOLGI BODIES
HAEMOCYANIN
HAEMOGLOBIN
HETEROECISM
HETEROTAXIS
HETEROTROPH
HOMOGENEITY
HOMOGENESIS
ISOMORPHISM
LACINIATION
LIFE-HISTORY
MACROGAMETE
MELANOPHORE
MEROGENESIS
METAGENESIS
MICHURINISM
MICROCOCCUS
MICROGAMETE
MONOGENESIS
NUMMULATION
ODONTOBLAST
ONTOGENESIS
OSTEOCLASIS
PENTAPLOIDY
PEPTISATION
PERIGENESIS
PERISTALSIS
PHAGOCYTISM
PLANOGAMETE
POIKILOCYTE
POLYPEPTIDE
PROCREATION
PROGESTOGEN
PROTEOLYSIS
RHEOTROPISM
SACCULATION
SEGREGATION
SOMATOPLASM
SPIROCHAETE
SUPPURATION
SYSSARCOSIS
TETRAPLOIDY
THERMOTAXIS
TRIMORPHISM
TRYPANOSOME
VACUOLATION
VASOPRESSIN
VIVISECTION
WEISMANNISM

XENOGENESIS
ZOOGONIDIUM
ZOOSPERMIUM

12

AEROPLANKTON
AGAMOGENESIS
AGGLUTINOGEN
ANAEROBIOSIS
APLANOGAMETE
AUTO-IMMUNITY
BIOMECHANICS
BIOSYNTHESIS
BLASTOSPHERE
CHONDRIOSOME
COCCIDIOSTAT
COMMENSALISM
CRASSAMENTUM
CYTOGENETICS
DIPLOGENESIS
ELECTROTONUS
FIBRINOLYSIN
GASTRIC JUICE
GNOTOBIOLOGY
HAEMATOBLAST
HAEMATOLYSIS
HEMIPARASITE
HETEROCHRONY
HETEROMORPHY
HETEROPLASIA
HETEROPLASTY
HETEROTROPHY
HETEROZYGOTE
HISTOGENESIS
HOMOMORPHISM
HYDROTROPISM
INOSCULATION
INSEMINATION
KARYOKINESIS
MENSTRUATION
MICROBIOLOGY
MITOCHONDRIA
MODIFICATION
MORPHALLAXIS
MORPHOGRAPHY
NEUROBIOLOGY
ORGANOGRAPHY
ORTHOGENESIS
OSSIFICATION
OSTEOGENESIS

SCIENCE – BIOLOGY

OSTEOPOROSIS
PALINGENESIA
PALINGENESIS
PATHOGENESIS
PERSPIRATION
PHENYLALANIN
PLEIOTROPISM
PLEOMORPHISM
POLYEMBRYONY
POLYMORPHISM
PREFORMATION
PROGESTERONE
PSEUDOPODIUM
RADIOBIOLOGY
RED CORPUSCLE
REPRODUCTION
RESTING-SPORE
RHESUS FACTOR
SCISSIPARITY
SOMATOPLEURE
SPERMATOCYTE
SPERMATOGENY
SPERMATOZOID
SPERMATOZOON
STROPHANTHIN
TESTOSTERONE
TRANSDUCTION
VIRILESCENCE
WALLACE'S LINE
ZOOCHEMISTRY

13

AGGLUTINATION
AMNIOTIC FLUID
APOGEOTROPISM
AQUEOUS HUMOUR
BACTERIOPHAGE
BLASTOGENESIS

CHROMATOPHORE
CIRCUMFLUENCE
COENAESTHESIS
COLON BACILLUS
COMMA BACILLUS
CONNATURALITY
DISSIMILATION
DYNAMOGENESIS
EXPECTORATION
FRAGMENTATION
GAMETOGENESIS
HERMAPHRODITE
HETEROGENESIS
HOMOMORPHOSIS
METAMORPHOSIS
MICRO-ORGANISM
MORPHOGENESIS
NITROBACTERIA
NUCLEO-PROTEIN
ORGANOGENESIS
PROLIFERATION
PROPIONIC ACID
SCHIZOGENESIS
SCLEROPROTEIN
SEX-CHROMOSOME
SEX-INTERGRADE
SPERMATOBLAST
SPERMATOPHORE
STREPTOCOCCUS
SYNOVIAL FLUID
THERMOGENESIS
THIGMOTROPISM
TRANSLOCATION
TRANSPIRATION
VACUOLISATION

14

BIOELECTRICITY

DINOFLAGELLATE
ELECTROBIOLOGY
ERYTHROPOIESIS
HAEMATOGENESIS
HETEROMORPHISM
HISTOCHEMISTRY
HOLOMETABOLISM
INTERSEXUALITY
KERATINISATION
LEUCOCYTOLYSIS
OXYHAEMOGLOBIN
REJUVENESCENCE
SANGUIFICATION
SPERMATOGONIUM
STAPHYLOCOCCUS
SUPERFOETATION
SUPEROVULATION
THROMBO-PLASTIN
TRICHOBACTERIA
ULTRASTRUCTURE
UTEROGESTATION
VITREOUS HUMOUR
WHITE CORPUSCLE

15

ANTHROPOGENESIS
BIOLOGICAL CLOCK
BIOLUMINESCENCE
CHONDRIFICATION
CIRCUMVALLATION
HERMAPHRODITISM
MACROSPORANGIUM
MICRODISSECTION
MICROSPORANGIUM
MICROSPOROPHYLL
PARTHENOGENESIS
RIBONUCLEIC ACID
SPERMATOGENESIS

SCIENCE – BOTANY – BOTANICAL CLASSIFICATION

3

POA
ZEA

4

ACER
ALOE
ARUM
BIXA
GEUM
ILEX
MEUM
MUSA
OLEA
RAPA
RHUS
ROSA
RUTA
SIDA
SIUM
THEA
ULEX

5

ABIES
ABRUS
AGAVE
ALGAE
ANONA
ARECA
BRIZA
BUTEA
CANNA
CAREX
CARYA
CHARA
ERICA
GLAUX
HOSTA
LARIX
LEDUM
LEMNA
LOTUS
MALVA
MELIA
MORUS
MUCOR

MUSCI
NAIAS
ORYZA
PANAX
PHLOX
PICEA
PINUS
PIPER
PYRUS
RHEUM
RIBES
RUBIA
RUBUS
RUMEN
SABAL
SALIX
SEDUM
STIPA
TAXUS
THUJA
TILIA
TSUGA
TUBER
TYPHA
ULMUS
URENA
USNEA
VINCA
VIOLA
VITEX
VITIS
XYRIS
YUCCA
ZAMIA

6

ABROMA
ACACIA
ACORUS
ALHAGI
ALISMA
AMOMUM
ARABIS
ARALIA
AUCUBA
AZALEA
BETULA
CARAPA
CARICA
CASSIA

CEDRUS
CELTIS
CEREUS
CICUTA
CISTUS
CLUSIA
CNICUS
COSMOS
COSTUS
CROTON
DAPHNE
DATURA
DERRIS
ELAEIS
ELODEA
EMPUSA
GNETUM
HEDERA
HYPNUM
IBERIS
ISATIS
KALMIA
LAURUS
LUCUMA
MIMOSA
MYRICA
MYRTUS
NERIUM
NOSTOC
NUPHAR
ORCHIS
OXALIS
PEZIZA
PHLEUM
PROTEA
PTERIS
PUNICA
PYROLA
RAPHIA
RESEDA
RICCIA
RUSCUS
SAGINA
SALVIA
SAPIUM
SAPOTA
SCILLA
SESELI
SILENE
SMILAX
STYRAX
SYLVIA

TULIPA
URTICA
VISCUM
ZINNIA

7

ALTHAEA
ALYSSUM
ARACEAE
ARACHIS
ARBUTUS
BANKSIA
BEGONIA
BOLETUS
BURSERA
CALLUNA
CATALPA
CEDRELA
CLARKIA
CORYLUS
CORYPHA
CURCUMA
CYATHEA
CYPERUS
CYTISUS
DEUTZIA
DIGYNIA
DIOECIA
DIONAEA
DROSERA
EPACRIS
EPHEDRA
ERODIUM
EUGENIA
FILICES
FREESIA
FUCHSIA
FUMARIA
GENISTA
GERBERA
GODETIA
HORDEUM
IPOMOEA
ISOËTES
JUGLANS
LACTUCA
LANTANA
LOBELIA
LOGANIA
LYCHNIS

LYTHRUM
MANIHOT
MARANTA
MELILOT
MIMULUS
MONILIA
MORINGA
MUSALES
NEMESIA
NIGELLA
NOPALEA
OPUNTIA
OSMUNDA
PANICUM
PAPAVER
PHALLUS
POPULUS
PRIMULA
PYTHIUM
QUERCUS
RHAMNUS
RICINUS
ROBINIA
RUELLIA
SALSOLA
SCANDIX
SCIRPUS
SENECIO
SEQUOIA
SKIMMIA
SOLANUM
SONCHUS
SORGHUM
SPIRAEA
STATICE
SYRINGA
TAGETES
TAMARIX
TRITOMA
VERBENA
XYLOPIA
ZIZANIA
ZOSTERA

8

ABUTILON
ACCENTOR
ACHILLEA
ADIANTUM
AESCULUS

SCIENCE – BOTANY – BOTANICAL CLASSIFICATION

AGARICUS
AILANTUS
APOCYNUM
ASPIDIUM
ATRIPLEX
BARBAREA
BERBERIS
BIXACEAE
BRASSICA
BROMELIA
BUDDLEIA
CALADIUM
CAMELLIA
CAPPARIS
CAPSICUM
CARYOCAR
CASTANEA
CECROPIA
CETERACH
CINCHONA
DACTYLIS
DIANDRIA
DIANTHUS
DICENTRA
DIPSACUS
DOLICHOS
ERIGERON
ERYSIMUM
ERYSIPHE
EUONYMUS
FRAXINUS
FUCACEAE
FUNTUMIA
FURCRAEA
GARCINIA
GARDENIA
GENTIANA
GERANIUM
GESNERIA
GLAUCIUM
GLOXINIA
GNETALES
GUAIACUM
HESPERIS
HIBISCUS
HIPPURIS
ILLICIUM
KRAMERIA
LABIATAE
LAPORTEA
LATHYRUS
LECANORA

LEUCOJUM
MAGNOLIA
MARATTIA
MARSILEA
MAURITIA
MEDICAGO
MERULIUS
MONOECIA
MOROCEAE
MUSACEAE
MYOSOTIS
NAVICULA
NYMPHAEA
OLEACEAE
ONCIDIUM
ORIGANUM
PANDANUS
PHORMIUM
PHYSALIS
PLANTAGO
PLATANUS
PLUMBAGO
POLYGALA
PORPHYRA
PRUNELLA
PSILOTUM
PUCCINIA
RAPHANUS
RHIZOPUS
RHYTISMA
ROCCELLA
ROSACEAE
RUTACEAE
SALVINIA
SANICULA
SANTALUM
SAPINDUS
SAXICOLA
SCABIOSA
SCHIZAEA
SILPHIUM
SIMARUBA
SPERGULA
SPHAGNUM
SPIGELIA
SPINIFEX
STAPELIA
TAXACEAE
TAXODIUM
THEACEAE
TRIGYNIA
TRILLIUM

TRITICUM
TRITONIA
ULMACEAE
ULOTHRIX
USTILAGO
VELLOZIA
VERATRUM
VERONICA
VIBURNUM
VICTORIA
VITACEAE
WISTARIA
WISTERIA
ZIZYPHUS

9

ADOXACEAE
ALEURITES
AMARYLLIS
AMYGDALUS
ANACHARIS
ANDROMEDA
ANONACEAE
ANTHURIUM
AQUILEGIA
ARAUCARIA
ARTEMISIA
ASCLEPIAS
ASPARAGUS
ASPLENIUM
ASTRANTIA
AUBRIETIA
BRYOPHYTA
CALENDULA
CAMPANULA
CANAVALIA
CARDAMINE
CASUARINA
CEANOTHUS
CHARACEAE
CICHORIUM
CINERARIA
CISTACEAE
COLCHICUM
COLOCASIA
COMBRETUM
COMMELINA
CONIFERAE
CORYDALIS
COTYLEDON

CRATAEGUS
CUPRESSUS
DECAGYNIA
DECANDRIA
DESMODIUM
DICKSONIA
DICOTYLAE
DIDYNAMIA
DIGITALIS
DIOSCOREA
ELAEAGNUS
EPIPACTIS
EQUISTEUM
ERICACEAE
ERYTHRINA
EUMYCETES
EUPHORBIA
FORSYTHIA
FRANKENIA
GNETACEAE
GOSSYPIUM
GRAMINEAE
HALORAGIS
HAMAMELIS
HEPATICAE
HEXAGYNIA
HEXANDRIA
HYDRANGEA
HYPERICUM
ISOKONTAE
JUNIPERUS
KNIPHOFIA
LAURACEAE
LEMNACEAE
MALPYGHIA
MALVACEAE
MELASTOMA
MELIACEAE
MIRABILIS
MONANDRIA
MONOGYNIA
MONOTROPA
MORCHELLA
MUCORALES
MYRISTICA
MYRTACEAE
NARCISSUS
NELUMBIUM
NEMOPHILA
NEPENTHES
NICOTIANA
OCTANDRIA

OCTOGYNIA
OENOTHERA
ORCHIDEAE
OROBANCHE
PAULOWNIA
PERNETTYA
PHILLYREA
PSALLIOTA
POINCIANA
POLYGAMIA
POLYGONUM
POLYGYNIA
POLYPORUS
PORTULACA
PTERIDIUM
RAFFLESIA
RAUWOLFIA
RUBIACEAE
RUDBECKIA
SACCHARUM
SAPONARIA
SAXIFRAGA
SINNINGIA
SPIROGYRA
SPONDYLUS
STAPHYLEA
STELLARIA
STERCULIA
SYMPHYTUM
TARAXACUM
THEOBROMA
TILIACEAE
TRIANDRIA
TRIFOLIUM
TYPHACEAE
UREDINEAE
VACCINIUM
VERBASCUM
VIOLACEAE
XYRIDALES

10

ALISMACEAE
ANACARDIUM
ARALIACEAE
ARTOCARPUS
ASPIDISTRA
BETULACEAE
CARICACEAE
CHAROPHYTA

CHIONODOXA
CLUSIACEAE
COMMIPHORA
COMPOSITAE
CROTOLARIA
CYPERACEAE
DELPHINIUM
DENDROBIUM
DIADELPHIA
DIPLOTAXIS
DRACONTIUM
ENNEANDRIA
ERIOCAULON
ERIOPHORUM
ESCALLONIA
EUCALYPTUS
FILICINEAE
FLINDERSIA
FONTINALIS
GAULTHERIA
GIBBERELLA
GINKGOALES
HELIANTHUS
HELLEBORUS
HEPTAGYNIA
HEPTANDRIA
HYOSCYAMUS
ICOSANDRIA
ILLECEBRUM
ISOETACEAE
LYCOPODIUM
LYTHRACEAE
MARCGRAVIA
MARCHANTIA
MECONOPSIS
MIMOSACEAE
MUCORINEAE
MYRICACEAE
NAIADACEAE
NASTURTIUM
NOTHOFAGUS
PARONYCHIA
PASSIFLORA
PENNISETUM
PENTAGYNIA
PENTANDRIA
PENTSTEMON
PHYTOLACCA
PILLULARIA
PILOCARPUS
PIMPINELLA
PINGUICULA

PIPERACEAE
PODOCARPUS
PODOSTEMON
POLEMONIUM
POLIANTHES
POLYANDRIA
POLYPODIUM
PONTEDERIA
POTENTILLA
PROTEACEAE
PROTOPHYTA
PULMONARIA
PULSATILLA
PUNICACEAE
PYROLACEAE
RANUNCULUS
RHAMNACEAE
RHIZOPHORA
RHODYMENIA
RHOEADALES
RHYNIACEAE
SAGITTARIA
SALICACEAE
SALICORNIA
SAPOTACEAE
SARRACENIA
SIGILLARIA
SOLANACEAE
SPARGANIUM
STRATIOTES
STRELITZIA
SYMPETALAE
SYNGENESIA
TERMINALIA
TETRAGYNIA
TETRANDRIA
THALICTRUM
TILLANDSIA
TUBERACEAE
UREDINALES
URTICACEAE
XYRIDACEAE

11

ACANTHACEAE
ACTINOMYCES
AMELANCHIER
ANTIRRHINUM
APOCYNACEAE
BEGONIACEAE

BURSERACEAE
CAESALPINIA
CALCEOLARIA
CALLISTEMON
CALLITRICHE
CALYCANTHUS
CANELLACEAE
CHENOPODIUM
CONVALLARIA
CONVOLVULUS
COTONEASTER
CRYPTOGAMIA
CRYPTOMERIA
CUPULIFERAE
CYATHEACEAE
CYPRIPEDIUM
DIPSACACEAE
DODECAGYNIA
DODECANDRIA
DRACUNCULUS
DROSERACEAE
EQUISETINAE
ERIODENDRON
FOTHERGILLA
FUMARIACEAE
GERANIACEAE
HYDNOCARPUS
HYDROCHARIS
ITHYPHALLUS
LASERPICIUM
LOBELIACEAE
LOGANIACEAE
LYCOPODINAE
MARANTACEAE
MENISPERMUM
MONADELPHIA
MORINGACEAE
MYXOPHYCEAE
ORCHIDACEAE
OSMUNDACEAE
OXALIDACEAE
PANDANACEAE
PEDALIACEAE
PEDICULARIS
PELARGONIUM
PLATANACEAE
PODOPHYLLUM
POLYGONATUM
POLYTRICHUM
POTAMOGETON
PRIMULACEAE
PROTOCOCCUS

PSEUDOMONAS
PSILOPHYTON
PSILOTACEAE
RIBESIACEAE
SAINTPAULIA
SALVINACEAE
SANGUINARIA
SANGUISORBA
SANSEVIERIA
SANTALACEAE
SAPINDACEAE
SAPROLEGNIA
SARCOCYSTIS
SCHIZANTHUS
SELAGINELLA
SPERGULARIA
SPHAGNACEAE
STEPHANOTIS
STYRACACEAE
THALLOPHYTA
UTRICULARIA
VALLISNERIA
VERBENACEAE
WELWITSCHIA
XANTHOXYLUM
XERANTHEMUM

12

ALSTROEMERIA
ANGIOSPERMAE
ARISTOLOCHIA
BERTHOLLETIA
BORAGINACEAE
BROMELIACEAE
CALYCIFLORAE
COMBRETACEAE
CYANOPHYCEAE
DISCOMYCETES
ELAEAGNACEAE
ENTEROMORPHA
EPACRIDACEAE
EQUISETACEAE
FRINGILLIDAE
GENTIANACEAE
GESNERIACEAE
HAEMATOXYLON
HELIANTHEMUM
HELIOTROPIUM
HETEROCONTAE
HYPERICACEAE

SCIENCE – BOTANY – BOTANICAL CLASSIFICATION

LIGULIFLORAE
LIRIODENDRON
LITHOSPERMUM
LORANTHACEAE
LYCOPODIALES
LYCOPODINEAE
MAGNOLIACEAE
MARATTIACEAE
MARSILEACEAE
NEPENTHACEAE
NYMPHAEACEAE
OPHIOGLOSSUM
ORNITHOGALUM
PAPAVERACEAE
PHAEOPHYCEAE
PHILODENDRON
PHYCOMYCETES
POLYADELPHIA
POLYGALACEAE
POLYGONACEAE
PTERIDOPHYTA
RHODODENDRON
RHODOPHYCEAE
SCHIZAEACEAE
SCROPHULARIA
SIMARUBACEAE
STROPHANTHUS
TAMARICACEAE
TETRADYNAMIA
TRADESCANTIA
TUBULIFLORAE
ULOTRICHALES
UMBELLIFERAE
USTILAGINEAE
VACCINIACEAE
VACCINIOIDAE
VELLOZIACEAE
WASHINGTONIA
WELLINGTONIA
ZANTEDESCHIA

13

ANACARDIACEAE
AQUIFOLIACEAE

ARCHEGONIATAE
BERBERIDACEAE
CAMPANULACEAE
CAPPARIDACEAE
CASUARINACEAE
CHRYSANTHEMUM
COMMELIANCEAE
CUCURBITACEAE
CYCLANTHACEAE
DENDROCALAMUS
DICOTYLEDONES
DIPTEROCARPUS
ENCEPHALARTOS
ERIOCAULACEAE
ESCHSCHOLTZIA
EUPHORBIACEAE
HYMENOMYCETES
ILLECEBRACEAE
LEPIDODENDRON
LYCOPODIACEAE
MALPIGHIACEAE
MELASTOMACEAE
MYRISTICACEAE
NYCTAGINACEAE
ODONTOGLOSSUM
OROBANCHACEAE
PAPILIONACEAE
PHYLLOSTACHYS
PODOSTEMACEAE
POLEMONIACEAE
POLYPODIACEAE
PORTULACACEAE
PROTOCOCCALES
PSILOPHYTALES
PYRENOMYCETES
RAFFLESIACEAE
RANUNCULACEAE
SACCHAROMYCES
SAXIFRAGACEAE
SCOLOPENDRIUM
SPARGANIACEAE
SPERMATOPHYTA
STAPHYLEACEAE
STERCULIACEAE
THALAMIFLORAE
THYMELAEACEAE

TROPAEOLACEAE
USTILAGINALES
VALERIANACEAE
ZINGIBERACEAE

14

AMARYLLIDACEAE
ASCLEPIADACEAE
BOUGAINVILLAEA
CALYCANTHACEAE
CAPRIFOLIACEAE
CHENOPODIACEAE
CONVOLVULACEAE
GASTEROMYCETES
HALORAGIDACEAE
HAMAMELIDACEAE
HYDROPTERIDEAE
MARCGRAVIACEAE
MARCHANTIACEAE
MENISPERMACEAE
MONOCHLAMYDEAE
PASSIFLORACEAE
PHYTOLACCACEAE
PLANTAGINACEAE
PLUMBAGINACEAE
PONTEDERIACEAE
RHIZOPHORACEAE
SARRACENIACEAE
SIGILLARIACEAE
USTILAGINACEAE
ZYGOPHYLLACEAE

15

ARCHICHLAMYDEAE
CAESALPINIACEAE
CALLITRICHACEAE
JUNGERMANNIALES
MONOCOTYLEDONES
OPHIOGLOSSACEAE
SELAGINELLACEAE

SCIENCE — BOTANY — BOTANICAL TERMS

3

AWN
BEN
BUD
EAR
JAG
KEX
KEY
NUT
OIL
PAN
PIP
PIT
POD
RAG
RIB
ROD
SAP
TAN

4

ARIL
AXIL
AXIS
BARK
BAST
BEAN
BIND
BINE
BLET
BOLE
BOLL
BULB
BUNT
BURR
BUSH
BUTT
CANE
CELL
CLAW
COMA
CONE
CORE
CORK
CORM
CULM
CYME
DISC
DUCT

EDDO
FERN
FOOD
FOOT
GALL
GERM
GILL
GOUT
HAFT
HAIR
HEAD
HERB
HULL
HUSK
IRID
KEEL
KNAG
KNEE
KNOP
KNOT
KNUR
LEAF
LIFE
LIMB
LOAF
LOBE
MINT
NIBS
NODE
NOSE
PEEL
PIPI
PITH
POME
PULP
RIND
RING
ROOT
RUNT
RUSH
RUST
SCAR
SEED
SERE
SETA
SKIN
SLIP
SMUT
SOMA
SPUR
STEM
STUD

TAPA
TREE
TUBE
TUFT
TWIG
UMBO
VEIL
VEIN
WEED
WILT
WOOD

5

ARROW
ASCUS
AUXIN
AVENS
BACCA
BEARD
BERRY
BETEL
BLADE
BLOOM
BOUGH
BRACT
BRAND
CALYX
CAPER
CRENA
CROWN
CUTIN
CYCAD
ERGOT
FLESH
FLORA
FLOSS
FROND
FRUIT
FUNGI
GEMMA
GENUS
GLANS
GLUME
GNARL
GRAFT
GRASS
GUILD
HAULM
HEART
HEATH
HILUM

HONEY
HUMUS
HYPHA
JUICE
KNARL
KNOSP
KNURR
LASER
LATEX
LAYER
LIBER
LOBUS
LOOFA
LUFFA
LUMEN
MOULD
NERVE
OVULE
PALEA
PALET
PETAL
PINNA
PIÑON
PLANT
PULSE
PUSSY
QUICK
QUINA
RAMUS
RAPHE
REGMA
RIGOR
SCALE
SCAPE
SCION
SCRUB
SEPAL
SERUM
SHELL
SHOOT
SHRUB
SHUCK
SILVA
SIRIH
SLEEP
SNARL
SORUS
SPAWN
SPEAR
SPICE
SPIKE
SPINE

SPIRE
SPORE
SPORT
SPRAY
SPRIG
STAGE
STALK
STELE
STICK
STING
STIPE
STOCK
STOMA
STONE
STOOL
STRAW
STUMP
STYLE
SUBER
TESTA
THECA
THORN
TORUS
TRACE
TRUNK
TRUSS
TUBER
TWINE
UMBEL
UREDO
VALVE
VAREC
VELUM
VINEW
VITTA
VOLVA
WHORL
WITHE
WITHY
XENIA
XYLEM

6

ALPINE
ANNUAL
ANTHER
AREOLE
ARISTA
ASH-KEY
ASTELY

BIG-BUD
BLIGHT
BLOTCH
BOG-OAK
BOTANY
BRANCH
BUCKET
BULBIL
CACOON
CALCAR
CALLUS
CANKER
CARINA
CARINO
CARPEL
CATKIN
CAUDEX
CAULIS
CEREAL
CILIUM
CIRRUS
CLIMAX
COCCUS
COLUMN
CORNUS
CORONA
CORTEX
CORYMB
CUPULE
CUSCUS
CYBELE
DRUPEL
ELATER
EMBRYO
EXARCH
EXOGEN
EXTINE
FAMILY
FARINA
FAUCES
FIBRIL
FLORET
FLOWER
FOLIUM
FUNGUS
GERMEN
GERMIN
GIRDER
GROWTH
HYBRID
INTINE
KERNEL

311

SCIENCE – BOTANY – BOTANICAL TERMS

LABIUM
LAMINA
LEADER
LEGUME
LICHEN
LIGNIN
LIGULE
LOBING
LOBULE
LOOFAH
MIDRIB
MILDEW
MORULA
MOSAIC
NEB-NEB
NEEDLE
NEUTER
NODULE
NUCULE
NUTLET
OAK-NUT
OCHREA
OEDEMA
OFFSET
OIDIUM
PALATE
PAPPUS
PEA-POD
PELORY
PHLOEM
PHYLUM
PILEUS
PISTIL
POLLEN
PRUINA
PTYXIS
PYRENE
RACEME
RACHIS
RAPHIS
RATOON
RATTLE
RED ROT
REPLUM
RICKER
RICTUS
RUNNER
SAMARA
SCAPUS
SHEATH
SINKER
SOBOLE

SPADIX
SPATHE
SPONGE
SPROUT
SQUASH
STAMEN
STIGMA
STIPEL
STOLON
STRIGA
STROMA
STRUMA
SUCKER
SWITCH
TABULA
TEGMEN
THYRSE
TILLER
TUFFET
TUNGUS
TURGOR
TURION
TWINER
TYLOTE
UNGUIS
VAGINA
VENTER
VESSEL
VILLUS
VISCIN
XYLOMA
ZYGOTE

7

ACANTHA
ACROGEN
AIR-CELL
ALTERNE
AMENTUM
APETALY
APHYLLY
APOGAMY
ARAROBA
ARMILLA
AURICLE
BIVALVE
BLOOMER
BLOSSOM
BLUE-ROT
BOSTRYX
CALYCLE

CAMBIUM
CAPSULE
CASCARA
CAULOME
CHALAZA
CLADODE
CLASPER
CLIMBER
CLUSTER
CORN-COB
COROLLA
CREEPER
CUP-GALL
CUTICLE
DENIZEN
DIANDRY
DRIP-TIP
EPACRID
EPICARP
EPIGYNY
ETAERIO
EXOCARP
FERNERY
FERRUGO
FIG-LEAF
FIR-CONE
FOLIAGE
FOLIOLE
FUNICLE
GALL-NUT
HADROME
HERBAGE
HOPBINE
LABIATE
LACINIA
LEAFAGE
LEAF-BUD
LEAFLET
LEPTOME
LINSEED
LOBELET
LOBULUS
LOCULUS
LUPULIN
LYCOPOD
MARYBUD
MYCETES
NECTARY
NERVULE
NERVURE
NUT-GALL
OAK-GALL

OAK-MAST
OLITORY
OOPHYTE
OOSPORE
PANICLE
PAPILLA
PATELLA
PEDICEL
PELORIA
PETIOLE
PHELLEM
PINNULE
PITCHER
PLEROME
PLUMULE
POT-HERB
PRICKLE
PRIMINE
PUTAMEN
RADICAL
RADICLE
RAMULUS
RHIZINE
RHIZOID
RHIZOME
RINGLET
ROOT-CAP
ROOTLET
ROSE-BUD
SAND-BOX
SAPWOOD
SARCOMA
SARMENT
SEA-BEAN
SEGMENT
SILICLE
SILIQUA
SILIQUE
SOROSIS
SPECIES
SPINULE
SPORULE
SPURREY
STINGER
STIPULE
SYMBION
TAPROOT
TAPETUM
TAR-SPOT
TENDRIL
THALLUS
THYRSUS

TIL-SEED
TRACHEA
TRAILER
TREETOP
TREFOIL
TROOLIE
TRUMPET
TUSSOCK
UTRICLE
VALVULE
VARIETY
VELAMEN
VERDURE
VESTURE
VETIVER
WILDING
XANTHIN
XYLOGEN
YELLOWS
ZYMOGEN

8

ACORN-CUP
AECIDIUM
AIR-PLANT
AIR-SPACE
ALBURNUM
ALLOGAMY
ALLIANCE
ANTHESIS
APOSPORY
ASCIDIUM
AUTOCARP
BASIDIUM
BEDEGUAR
BIENNIAL
BLASTEMA
BLOWBALL
BRACTLET
BROWSING
BRYOLOGY
BUD-SCALE
BURNT-EAR
CALISAYA
CALYCULE
CALYPTRA
CARUNCLE
CAT'S-TAIL
CAUDICLE
CAULICLE

CHORISIS
CICINNUS
CINCHONA
COHESION
COLONIST
CONIDIUM
CYATHIUM
DIHYBRID
DIMERISM
DIOECISM
DIVIDIVI
DOCK-LEAF
DOMATIUM
DOMINANT
DRUPELET
DUMOSITY
ECTODERM
ECTOGENY
ENDOCARP
ENDODERM
ENDOGAMY
ENDOGENY
ENTODERM
ENVELOPE
EPIBLAST
EPICALYX
EPICOTYL
EPINASTY
EPIPHYTE
EPISPERM
EPISPORE
EUTROPHY
EXOSPORE
FERN-SEED
FIBRILLA
FILAMENT
FLAX-SEED
FLORIGEN
FLOSCULE
FLOWERER
FLOWERET
FOLLICLE
FRONDAGE
FRUITAGE
FRUIT-BUD
FRUITING
FRUSTULE
GEMMA-CUP
GEOCARPY
GEOPHYTE
GEOTAXIS
GERM-CELL

GLUMELLA
GNETALES
GONIDIUM
GREENERY
HAPTERON
HEART-ROT
HELIOSIS
HISTOGEN
HOLDFAST
HOMOGAMY
HONEY-DEW
HYMENIUM
HYPOCIST
HYPOGYNY
INDUSIUM
INDUVIAE
ISOSPORY
ISOTROPY
KEY-FRUIT
LABELLUM
LEAF-BASE
LEAF-CURL
LEAF-FALL
LEAF-ROLL
LEAF-SCAR
LENTICEL
LINTSEED
LOBATION
LODICULA
LODICULE
LOMENTUM
MAD-APPLE
MATURITY
MERICARP
MERISTEM
MESOCARP
MONANDRY
MUCILAGE
MYCELIUM
NERVELET
NUTATION
NUTSHELL
OAK-APPLE
OFFSHOOT
OOGONIUM
PEABERRY
PEDUNCLE
PELORISM
PERIANTH
PERIBLEM
PERICARP
PERIDERM

PERIDIUM
PERIGONE
PERIGYNY
PETALODY
PHYLLARY
PHYLLODE
PHYLLODY
PHYLLOME
PHYTOSIS
PICHURIM
PINE-CONE
PLACENTA
PLANTLET
PLANTULE
POLARITY
POLYGAMY
POLYMERY
POROGAMY
PROPHYLL
PROP-ROOT
PULVINUS
PYRENOID
PYXIDIUM
QUICKSET
RACEMISM
RACHILLA
RADICULE
RAMENTUM
RAPE-SEED
RATOONER
REED-MACE
REGROWTH
RIPENESS
ROOT-HAIR
ROOT-KNOT
ROSE-LEAF
SAPROPEL
SCARRING
SCLEREID
SEED-COAT
SEED-LEAF
SEED-LOBE
SEPALODY
SILICULA
SILICULE
SKELETON
SOAP-BARK
SOREDIUM
SPIKELET
STAG-HEAD
STANDARD
STEREOME

STERIGMA
STICK-LAC
STIMULUS
STROMBUS
SURCULUS
SYCONIUM
SYMBIONT
SYNANTHY
SYNERGID
TACAHOUT
TEGUMENT
THALAMUS
TOMENTUM
TRACHEID
TRANSECT
TRICHOME
UPGROWTH
VAGINULA
VAGINULE
VALVELET
VERDANCY
VERJUICE
VERTICIL
VEXILLUM
VINE-GALL
VIRIDITY
VIVIPARY
WHEAT-EAR
WORM-SEED
XENOGAMY
XYLOCARP
ZONATION
ZOOCHORE

9

ABJECTION
ACROSPIRE
AIR-CAVITY
ALLOCARPY
ANDROGYNY
ANTHOCARP
ANTICLINE
ASCOSPORE
BEANSTALK
BITTER-PIT
BLACK SPOT
BRACTEOLE
BRANCHERY
BRANCHLET
BRYOPHYTE

CANAL-CELL
CAPITULUM
CARPOLOGY
CARYOPSIS
CATAPHYLL
CHLOROSIS
CICATRICE
CINCINNUS
COCCOLITH
COCOA-BEAN
COENOSARC
COLUMELLA
COMPOSITE
CORNSTALK
COTYLEDON
CREMOCARP
CRENATURE
CROWN-BARK
CROWN-GALL
CYSTOCARP
DIAPHYSIS
DICHASIUM
DICHOGAMY
DICLINISM
DREPANIUM
EAR-COCKLE
ECTOBLAST
ECTOPHYTE
ELATERIUM
EMBRYO-SAC
EMERGENCE
ENDOBLAST
ENDOPHYTE
ENDOSPERM
ENDOSPORE
ENTOBLAST
ENTOPHYTE
EPIDERMIS
EPIPHYSIS
EVERGREEN
EXODERMIS
EXOSMOSIS
FAIRY-RING
FIRE-BLAST
FLAGELLUM
FLOWERAGE
FLOWER-BUD
FOLIATION
FOOTSTALK
FORMATION
GEMMATION
GERM-LAYER

GLOMERULE
GOA POWDER
GONOPHORE
GRAPESEED
GUARD-CELL
GUTTATION
GYNAECEUM
GYNOPHORE
HALOPHYTE
HEARTWOOD
HERBARIUM
HERCOGAMY
HETEROSIS
HEXAPLOID
HISPIDITY
HYBRIDISM
HYBRIDITY
HYDATHODE
HYLOPHYTE
HYPOCOTYL
HYPONASTY
INVOLUCEL
INVOLUCRE
LEAF-GREEN
LEAF-STALK
LEAF-TRACE
LICHENISM
MEGASPORE
MESOBLAST
MESOPHYLL
MESOPHYTE
MICROPYLE
MONKEY-POT
MONOECISM
MOSAICISM
MOSS-PLANT
NERVATION
NERVATURE
NEURATION
NUX VOMICA
OESTROGEN
ORRIS-ROOT
OUTGROWTH
PALMATION
PAPILLULE
PERENNIAL
PERICYCLE
PERISPERM
PETIOLULE
PHAENOGAM
PHELLOGEN
PHOTOPHIL

PHYTOGENY
PHYTOLOGY
PHYTOTOMY
PIXIE-RING
PLANTLING
PLUM-STONE
POISON-NUT
POLLEN-SAC
POLLINIUM
POLYPOSIS
POPPY-HEAD
POPPY-SEED
POTATO-ROT
PROEMBRYO
PROTANDRY
PROTOGYNY
PROTONEMA
PSEUDAXIS
PULVINULE
PYCNIDIUM
PYRETHRUM
REMONTANT
RHIZOCARP
RHIZOCAUL
RING-SHAKE
ROCK-PLANT
ROOTSTOCK
ROSE-PETAL
ROSTELLUM
SABADILLA
SAGE-APPLE
SANTONICA
SARCOCARP
SARCOLOGY
SARMENTUM
SCALE-LEAF
SCLEROSIS
SCUTELLUM
SECUNDINE
SEED-PLANT
SEED-STALK
SIEVE-TUBE
SNOW-PLANT
SPINDLING
SPORE-CASE
SPORIDESM
SPORIDIUM
SPOROCARP
SPOROCYST
SPOROGENY
STAMINODE
STAMINODY

STATOCYST
STATOLITH
STIGMARIA
STONE-CELL
STROBILUS
SUBSTRATE
SUCCULENT
SUSPENSOR
SWORD-BEAN
SYMBIOSIS
SYMPODIUM
SYNANGIUM
TABASHEER
TEGMENTUM
TERRICOLE
TETRARCHY
TONKA-BEAN
TREE-TRUNK
TRI-HYBRID
TULIP-ROOT
TURNIP-TOP
UMBELLULE
UNDERWOOD
UREDINIUM
UTRICULUS
VALLECULA
VEGETABLE
VERNATION
VISCIDITY
WATER-CORE
WATER-FERN
WATER-WEED
WINTER-BUD
WITCH-MEAL
XENOGRAFT
XEROCHASY
XEROMORPH
XEROPHILY
XEROPHYTE
ZYGOPHYTE
ZYGOSPERM
ZYGOSPORE

10

ABJUNCTION
ABSCISSION
ACOTYLEDON
AERENCHYMA
ANDROECIUM
ANDROPHORE

ANEMOPHILY
ANGIOSPERM
ANISOTROPY
ANTHOPHORE
APOSTROPHE
APOTHECIUM
APPOSITION
BABLAH PODS
BACTERIOID
BEECH-DROPS
CARPOPHORE
CARPOSPORE
CASCARILLA
CASSIA-BARK
CAULIFLORY
CHASMOGAMY
COFFEE-BEAN
COLEORHIZA
CONSORTIUM
CORMOPHYTE
COSTUS-ROOT
COTTON-BOLL
COTTONSEED
CRYPTOGAMY
DAMPING-OFF
DEHISCENCE
DENDROLOGY
DERMATOGEN
DIATROPISM
DISC-FLORET
DISC-FLOWER
DISJUNCTOR
ENDODERMIS
ENDOPLEURA
EPIGENESIS
EPIPHYTISM
ETIOLATION
FASCIATION
FIRE-BLIGHT
FLOWER-BELL
FLOWER-HEAD
GEMINATION
GEOTROPISM
GRAPESTONE
GYMNOSPERM
HAUSTORIUM
HELIOPHYTE
HELIOTROPY
HETEROGAMY
HETEROGENY
HETEROGONY
HETEROLOGY

HOMOZYGOTE
HONEY-GUIDE
HYBRIDISER
HYDROCHORE
HYDROPHILY
HYDROPHYTE
HYGROCHASY
HYGROPHYTE
HYPANTHIUM
HYPOPHYSIS
HYPSOPHYLL
INNOVATION
INTEGUMENT
INVOLUCRUM
ISOTROPISM
KLENDUSITY
LACERATION
LEAF-MOSAIC
LEAF-SHEATH
LITHOPHYTE
LOCULAMENT
LYCOPODIUM
MANNA-CROUP
MATURATION
MICROPHYTE
MILLET-SEED
MONOHYBRID
MONOPODIUM
MYCORRHIZA
MYXOMYCETE
NANISATION
NIGER-SEEDS
NYCTINASTY
OMBROPHILE
OMBROPHOBE
ORDEAL-BEAN
ORTHOTROPY
OSTEOCOLLA
OSTEOPHYTE
OVERGROWTH
PALM-KERNEL
PALYNOLOGY
PARAPHYSIS
PARASTICHY
PARENCHYMA
PEACH-BLOOM
PEACH-STONE
PERCEPTION
PERIGONIUM
PHAENOTYPE
PHANEROGAM
PHELLODERM

PHOTOLYSIS
PHOTOPHILY
PHOTOTROPE
PHOTOTROPY
PHYLLOTAXY
PILEORHIZA
PILLAR-ROOT
PINE-KERNEL
PINE-NEEDLE
PISTILLODE
PLUS STRAIN
POLLEN-TUBE
POPULATION
PORE FUNGUS
PROPHALLUS
PROTOPHYTE
PSAMMOPHIL
PSEUDOBULB
PSEUDOCARP
PUBESCENCE
PYCNOSPORE
PYRENOCARP
QUATREFOIL
QUERCITRON
RACEMATION
RECEPTACLE
RHIZOMORPH
RHIZOPHORE
ROOT-SHEATH
ROOT-SYSTEM
SAPROPHYTE
SARCOLEMMA
SCHIZOCARP
SCLERODERM
SCLEROTIUM
SEED-VESSEL
SEMINALITY
SEMINATION
SHADE-PLANT
SIEVE-PLATE
SILK-COTTON
SILVER-LEAF
SIPHONOGAM
SILVERSKIN
SLING-FRUIT
SPERMATIUM
SPLINTWOOD
SPORANGIUM
SPOROPHORE
SPOROPHYLL
SPOROPHYTE
SPOROZOITE

SPRINGWOOD
STICHIDIUM
STIGMARIAN
STINK-BRAND
STROPHIOLE
SWARM-SPORE
SYNANDRIUM
TETRASPORE
TRICHOGYNE
TROPOPHYTE
TUBEROSITY
UMBELLIFER
UMBONATION
UNDERBOUGH
UNDERBRUSH
UNDERSCRUB
UNDERSHRUB
UREDOSORUS
UREDOSPORE
VEGETATION
VINE-MILDEW
VITAL STAIN
VIVIPARISM
VIVIPARITY
WATER-BLOOM
WATER-PLANT
WATTLE-BARK
ZYGOMORPHY
ZYGOMYCETE

11

AEROTROPISM
ANNUAL RINGS
ANTHERIDIUM
ANTHEROZOID
APPLE-BLIGHT
ARCHEGONIUM
ARTHROSPORE
BACTERIOSIS
BIFURCATION
BORDERED PIT
CALABAR-BEAN
CALYPTROGEN
CARPOGONIUM
CHALAZOGAMY
CHERRY-STONE
CHLOROPHYLL
CHROMOPLAST
CITRUS FRUIT
CLEISTOGAMY

COENENCHYMA
COLLENCHYMA
CONVOLUTION
CORK-CAMBIUM
CRYSTALLOID
CYPRESS-KNEE
DEFOLIATION
DICOTYLEDON
DIPTEROCARP
DISCOMYCETE
DISSEMINULE
DISSEPIMENT
ECBLASTESIS
ENGRAFTMENT
ENTOMOPHILY
EXFOLIATION
FLORESCENCE
FLOWER-STALK
FOLIAGE LEAF
GAMETOPHYTE
GEITONOGAMY
GERMINATION
GONIMOBLAST
GRAFT HYBRID
GROUND COVER
GYNOSTEMIUM
HARDY ANNUAL
HESPERIDIUM
HETEROGRAFT
HETEROSPORY
HETEROSTYLY
HOLOPHYTISM
HOMOZYGOSIS
HYDROPHYTON
HYDROPONICS
INITIAL CELL
INOCULATION
INTERGROWTH
JAMAICA BARK
JESUITS' BARK
KAFFIR BREAD
LACINIATION
LEAF-CLIMBER
LEAF-CUSHION
MANNA-GROATS
MINUS STRAIN
MONOCHASIUM
MYXOMYCETES
NERVURATION
NIGHT-FLOWER
ORTHOSTICHY
PALM-CABBAGE

PERITHECIUM
PETALOMANIA
PHOTOPERIOD
PHYLLOCLADE
PHYLLOMANIA
PHYLLOTAXIS
PHYTOGRAPHY
PHYTOSTEROL
PNEUMATHODE
POLLEN-COUNT
POLLEN-GRAIN
POLLINATION
PREMATURITY
PROLETARIAN
PROMYCELIUM
PROPAGATION
PROSENCHYMA
PROTERANDRY
PROTEROGYNY
PROTHALLIUM
PSAMMOPHYTE
PUDDING-PIPE
PULLULATION
RECTIPETALY
RETINACULUM
ROOT-CLIMBER
SCLEROCAULY
SCLEROPHYLL
SEISMONASTY
SIGILLATION
SILVER-GRAIN
SPORANGIOLE
SPOROGONIUM
SPORULATION
STAMINODIUM
STARCH-GRAIN
STYLOPODIUM
SYNANTHESIS
THALLOPHYTE
THERMONASTY
THISTLE-DOWN
TROPHOTAXIS
UNDERGROWTH
VARIEGATION
VASCULARITY
VERSATILITY
VINE-DISEASE
WATER-FLOWER
WHEAT-MILDEW
WITCHES'-MEAT
XANTHOPHYLL
ZYGOMYCETES

12

AMPELOGRAPHY
ANTICLINORUM
ARBORESCENCE
BACTERIOSTAT
BASIDIOSPORE
BUTTRESS-ROOT
CALYCANTHEMY
CARIBBEE BARK
CHEMOTROPISM
COMPASS-PLANT
COMPOUND LEAF
CONIDIOPHORE
CONIDIOSPORE
CONSOCIATION
CUSPARIA BARK
DORSAL SUTURE
DORSIFLEXION
EFFIGURATION
EGG-APPARATUS
EMARGINATION
ENANTIOSTYLY
ENGRAFTATION
ETHEREAL OILS
FIBRILLATION
FINGER-AND-TOE
FRONDESCENCE
GLAUCESCENCE
GROWING-POINT
GYNODIOECISM
HAPTOTROPISM
HELICOID CYME
HELIOTROPISM
HETERAUXESIS
HETEROBLASTY
HETEROMORPHY
HETEROPHYLLY
HETEROTHALLY
HETEROZYGOTE
HIBERNACULUM
HOMOTHALLISM
INDEHISCENCE
MEDULLARY RAY
MORPHALLAXIS
MYCODOMATIUM
NATURAL ORDER
NYCTITROPISM
ORGANOGRAPHY
ORTHOTROPISM
PALAEOBOTANY
PEACH-YELLOWS

PERICHAETIUM
PHOTOTROPISM
PHREATOPHYTE
PHYTOBENTHOS
PHYTOGENESIS
PICHURIM BEAN
PLEIOCHASIUM
PREFLORATION
PREFOLIATION
PTERIDOPHYTE
RACEMISATION
RAMIFICATION
RECEPTACULUM
RESTING-SPORE
RESUPINATION
ROOT-PARASITE
ROOT-PRESSURE
ROOT-TUBERCLE
SAPROPHYTISM
SCLERENCHYMA
SCLEROPHYLLY
SCUTELLATION
SNUFFBOX BEAN
SOLARISATION
SPHACELATION
SPORANGIOLUM
SPOROGENESIS
TRANSUDATION
TRIFURCATION
TRIPARTITION
TROPHALLAXIS
TROPHIC LEVEL
TROPHOBIOSIS
TUBEROUS ROOT
TWINING PLANT
VOLATILE OILS
WITCHES'-BROOM
ZOOPHYTOLOGY
ZYGOMORPHISM

13

AMPHIGASTRIUM
CHLAMYDOSPORE
CLIMBING PLANT
COFFEE-DISEASE
COMPOUND UMBEL
CONTABESCENCE
DIAGEOTROPISM
DIAPHOTOTROPY
EFFLORESCENCE

ESSENTIAL OILS
GENETIC SPIRAL
GYNOMONOECISM
HERMAPHRODITE
HETEROSTYLISM
INFLORESCENCE
JEQUIRITY BEAN
MICRONUTRIENT
MONOCOTYLEDON
MOSAIC DISEASE
MULTIPLE FRUIT
NATURAL SYSTEM
NITROGEN CYCLE
PARTHENOCARPY
PHYTOPLANKTON
PLAGIOTROPISM
PNEUMATOPHORE
POTATO DISEASE
PROLIFERATION
PROLIFICATION
PYCNIDIOSPORE
PYCNOCONIDIUM
QUAKER-BUTTONS
RECTIPETALITY
SCORPIOID CYME
SPERMATOPHYTE
THERMOTROPISM
TRANSLOCATION

TRANSPIRATION
TROPHOTROPISM
VASCULAR PLANT
ZOOSPORANGIUM
ZYGOTIC NUMBER

14

AMERICAN BLIGHT
ANTIPODAL CELLS
APHELIOTROPISM
BACTERIOSTASIS
CIRCUMNUTATION
DEXTROROTATION
ELECTROCULTURE
EUTROPHICATION
FRUCTIFICATION
HELIOSCIOPHYTE
HETEROMORPHISM
HETEROTHALLISM
LEPIDODENDROID
LINNAEAN SYSTEM
MEGASPORANGIUM
MEGASPOROPHYLL
MULTIPLICATION
NATURAL HISTORY
PALISADE TISSUE

PHOTOPERIODISM
PHOTOSYNTHESIS
PLANT FORMATION
ROSETTE DISEASE
SENSITIVE PLANT
SERAL COMMUNITY
SPORANGIOPHORE
SPORANGIOSPORE
STRAWBERRY-LEAF
VASCULAR BUNDLE
VERTICILLASTER

15

COLLECTIVE FRUIT
DIAHELIOTROPISM
DORSIVENTRALITY
DUTCH ELM DISEASE
ESSENTIAL ORGANS
MEDULLARY SHEATH
PALAEOPHYTOLOGY
PLANT SUCCESSION
QUADRIPARTITION
SELF-POLLINATION
ST IGNATIUS'S BEAN
TETRASPORANGIUM

SCIENCE – CHEMISTRY – ALLOYS

4

GILT

5

ALLOY
BRASS
INVAR
METAL
POTIN
STEEL
TERNE
WOOTZ

6

ALBATA
BILLON
BRONZE
LATTEN
OCCAMY
OREIDE
ORMOLU
OROIDE
PEWTER
SOLDER
TOMBAC
VELLON

7

AMALGAM
GILDING
PAKTONG
SIMILOR
TEA-LEAD
TUTANIA
TUTENAG

8

CAST-IRON
ELECTRON

EUTECTIC
GUNMETAL
MANGANIN
NICHROME
ORICHALC
POT-METAL
PROMETAL

9

BASE METAL
BELL-METAL
BUSH-METAL
CAST-STEEL

DURALUMIN
DUTCH GOLD
EUTECTOID
HARD-METAL
LEAF-METAL
MAGNALIUM
MILD STEEL
PINCHBECK
PLATINOID
TYPE-METAL
WHITE GOLD
WHITE IRON

SCIENCE – CHEMISTRY – ALLOYS

10

CONSTANTAN
DUTCH METAL
FERRO-ALLOY
IRIDOSMINE
MISCHMETAL
MONEL METAL
MOSAIC GOLD
MUNTZ METAL
NICROSILAL
OSMIRIDIUM
ROLLED GOLD
SILVER-GILT
SUPERALLOY
TERNE METAL
TERNEPLATE
WHITE BRASS
WHITE METAL

CHROME-STEEL
CUPRO-NICKEL
FERRO-NICKEL
NICKEL-STEEL
POROUS ALLOY
WHITE COPPER
WROUGHT-IRON
YELLOW-METAL

12

BRITISH PLATE
DURALUMINIUM
FUSIBLE METAL
GERMAN SILVER
NICKEL-SILVER
PRINCE'S METAL
SPIEGELEISEN

FERRO-CHROMIUM
SPECULUM METAL

14

ALPHA-BETA BRASS
BLISTERED-STEEL
BRITANNIA METAL
FERRO-MANGANESE
HIGH-SPEED STEEL
PHOSPHOR-BRONZE
STAINLESS STEEL

15

ALUMINIUM BRONZE
CORINTHIAN BRASS
FERRO-MOLYBDENUM
MANGANESE BRONZE

11

CANNON-METAL

13

BABBITT'S METAL

SCIENCE – CHEMISTRY – CHEMICAL SUBSTANCES

3

AIR
FAT
GAS
OIL
TAR
TNT

COKE
DERV
LIME
SALT
SNOW
SOAP
SODA
URAO
UREA
ZEIN

AMIDE
AMINE
BORAX
BUTYL
CERIA
CONIA
ESTER
ETHAL
ETHER
ETHYL
FREON
FURAL
FURAN
FUROL
GESSO
GLASS
GUTTA
HEPAR

INDOL
LIVER
LYSIN
METHS
NITRE
OLEIN
ORCIN
OXIDE
PHENE
PURIN
SMOKE
STEAM
SUGAR
TRONA
URATE
VINYL
WATER
XYLOL

XYLYL

6

ACETAL
ACETYL
AIR-GAS
ALDOSE
ALKALI
AMATOL
AMYLUM
ARSINE
AURATE
BARYTA
BENZAL
BENZIL
BENZOL

BENZYL
BIOTIN
BORANE
BORATE
BORIDE
BUTANE
BUTENE
CASEIN
CERUSE
CETANE
CHITIN
CHROME
CINEOL
CITRIN
CONINE
CRESOL
CURARE
CYTASE

4

ACID
ALUM
AMYL
ARYL
BASE
COAL

5

ALGIN
ALKYD
ALKYL
ALLYL

318

DECANE	PEPSIN	BAUXITE	INDICAN	STIBINE
DIOXIN	PETROL	BAY SALT	INSULIN	STYRENE
DRY ICE	PHENOL	BENZENE	INULASE	SUDERIN
DUALIN	PHENYL	BENZINE	JALAPIN	SUCROSE
ELUANT	PICENE	BENZOLE	KERATIN	SYLVINE
ELUATE	POTASH	BENZOYL	LACTASE	TANNATE
ENZYME	PROPYL	BITUMEN	LACTATE	TURPENE
ETHANE	PURINE	BORAZON	LACTOSE	THYMINE
ETHENE	PYRENE	BROMATE	LEGUMIN	TOLUENE
ETHYNE	QUINOL	BROMIDE	LIGROIN	TORULIN
FIBRIN	RETENE	BRUCINE	LYDDITE	TRYPSIN
FORMOL	RIBOSE	CACODYL	MALTASE	URICASE
GALENA	SPIRIT	CALICHE	MALTOSE	VISCOSE
GAS-TAR	STARCH	CALOMEL	MANNITE	VITAMIN
GLUTEN	STEROL	CAPRATE	MANNOSE	VITRIOL
GLYCIN	TANNIN	CARBIDE	MECONIN	WOOD-TAR
GLYCOL	TARTAR	CAUSTIC	METAMER	XYLENOL
GUANIN	THEINE	CHLORAL	METHANE	XYLODIN
HAEMIN	THORON	CHOLINE	MUCIGEN	ZEOLITE
HALIDE	THULIA	CITRATE	NAPHTHA	
HALOID	THYMOL	COLLOID	NEURINE	
HARMIN	TONITE	CONIINE	NITRATE	**8**
HEXANE	TOLUOL	CORDITE	NITRIDE	
HEXENE	URACIL	CUPRITE	NITRILE	ACROLEIN
HEXOSE	VERDET	CYANATE	NITRITE	AESCULIN
HOLMIA	XYLENE	CYANIDE	OLEFINE	ALDEHYDE
INDENE	XYLOSE	DIABASE	ORCINOL	ALEURONE
INDOLE	YTTRIA	DIOXIDE	OSMIATE	ALGINATE
INULIN	ZYMASE	DULCITE	OUABAIN	ALIZARIN
IODATE		DULCOSE	OXALATE	ALKALOID
IODIDE		ELASTIN	OXIDASE	ALLERGEN
LEUCIN	**7**	EMULSIN	OXONIUM	AMANDINE
LIPAZE		EREPSIN	PECTOSE	AMMONIUM
LITHIA	ACETATE	ETHANOL	PENTANE	ANDROGEN
LITMUS	ACETONE	ETHIOPS	PENTENE	ARSENATE
LYSINE	ACRIDIN	EUGENOL	PENTOSE	ARSENIDE
MALATE	ADENINE	EXTRACT	PEPTIDE	ARSENITE
METHYL	ADERMIN	FERRATE	PEPTONE	ATROPINE
MINIUM	ALCOHOL	FORMATE	PHALLIN	BENZOATE
MUCATE	ALUMINA	GALLATE	PHENATE	BERYLLIA
MYOGEN	ALUNITE	GAS-LIME	PICRATE	BUTYLENE
MYOSIN	AMALGAM	GLAIRIN	PLASMIN	BUTYRATE
NIACIN	AMMONAL	GLIADIN	PLASTIC	CAFFEINE
NITRYL	AMMONIA	GLUCINA	PROPANE	CALOMINE
NONANE	AMYLASE	GLUCOSE	PROTEIN	CAMPHANE
OCTANE	AMYLENE	GLYCINE	QUININE	CAMPHINE
OIL-GAS	ANEURIN	GLYCOSE	QUINONE	CARBONYL
OLEATE	ANTIGEN	HALOGEN	RED LEAD	CARBOXYL
OLEFIN	ARSENIC	HEPTANE	SALICIN	CATALASE
OSMATE	ASPHALT	HORDEIN	SAPONIN	CATECHOL
PAPAIN	ASTATKI	HYDRATE	SKATOLE	CHARCOAL
PECTIN	BARILLA	HYDRIDE	STEARIN	CHLORATE

SCIENCE — CHEMISTRY — CHEMICAL SUBSTANCES

CHLORIDE
CHLORITE
CHROMATE
COENZYME
COLLAGEN
COPPERAS
COUMARIN
CREATINE
CURARINE
CYANOGEN
CYTISINE
DATURINE
DEXTROSE
DIASTASE
DIMETHYL
DIPHENYL
DULCITOL
DYNAMITE
EPSOMITE
ETHYLENE
EUTECTIC
FIREDAMP
FIXED AIR
FLUORIDE
FORMALIN
FRUCTOSE
FURFURAL
FURFURAN
FURFUROL
GASOLENE
GASOLINE
GAS-WATER
GERANIOL
GLOBULIN
GLYCERIN
GLYCEROL
GLYCERYL
GLYCOGEN
HAEMATIN
HARMALIN
HEXYLENE
HYDROXYL
INOSITOL
IODOFORM
ISOPRENE
KEROSENE
KEROSINE
LEVULOSE
LECITHIN
LICHENIN
LITHARGE
LOBELINE

LYSOZYME
MAGNESIA
MANNITOL
MARGARIN
MARSH-GAS
MASSICOT
MECONATE
MELINITE
MESCALIN
METHANOL
MONOXIDE
NAPHTHOL
NICOTINE
NUCLEASE
PALMITIN
PARAFFIN
PEARL-ASH
PENTOSAN
PEROXIDE
PHOSGENE
PHOTOGEN
PHTHALIN
PIPERINE
PLUMBATE
PLUMBITE
PROLAMIN
PROTEASE
PTOMAINE
PYRIDINE
PYROXYLE
RESINATE
RESORCIN
ROBURITE
ROCK-ALUM
SECRETIN
SELENATE
SELENIDE
SELENITE
SILICANE
SILICATE
SILICIDE
SILICONE
SINOPITE
SODA-LIME
SODAMIDE
SOLANINE
STANNATE
STANNITE
STEARATE
STRONTIA
SUBERATE
SULPHATE

SULPHIDE
SULPHITE
SULPHONE
SYNTONIN
TARTRATE
THEBAINE
THERMITE
THIAMINE
THROMBIN
THYROXIN
TITANATE
TRIPTANE
TYROSINE
URETHANE
URIC ACID
VANADATE
VANILLIN
VERATRIN
VERDITER
VITELLIN
WATER-GAS
WOOD-COAL
XANTHATE
XANTHENE
XANTHINE
ZIRCONIA

9

ACETAMIDE
ACETYLENE
ADRENALIN
AFTER-DAMP
ALUMINATE
ALUM-STONE
AMINO-ACID
AMYGDALIN
ANHYDRIDE
AQUA REGIA
ARABINOSE
AURIC ACID
AUSTENITE
BASIC SALT
BEBEERINE
BENZIDINE
BENZOLINE
BERBERINE
BLUESTONE
BORIC ACID
BROMOFORM
BUTADIENE

CARBAMIDE
CARBONATE
CELESTINE
CELLULOSE
CHOKEDAMP
CHROMATIN
COLCOTHAR
COLUMBATE
COMPOUND E
CORTISONE
CYANAMIDE
CYCLAMATE
DIESEL-OIL
DIGITALIN
FATTY ACID
FINE METAL
FOLIC ACID
GALACTOSE
GAS-CARBON
GAS-LIQUOR
GELIGNITE
GELSEMINE
GLASS-SOAP
GLUCOSIDE
GLYCERIDE
GLYCERINE
GLYCOCOLL
GUNPOWDER
HISTAMINE
HISTIDINE
HYDRAZIDE
HYDRAZINE
HYDROXIDE
INDIGO RED
INDIRUBIN
INVERTASE
IODIC ACID
LAEVULOSE
LIMEWATER
LUCIFERIN
MANGANATE
MANGANITE
MENADIONE
MERCAPTAN
METHYLATE
MOLYBDATE
OESTROGEN
OLEIC ACID
OSMIC ACID
OZOKERITE
PALMITATE
PANTHENOL

PENTYLENE
PERIODATE
PETROLEUM
PHENOLATE
PHOSPHATE
PHOSPHIDE
PHOSPHINE
PHOSPHITE
PHOTOGENE
PHTHALATE
PHTHALEIN
PITUITRIN
POMPHOLYX
PROENZYME
PROGESTIN
PROLAMINE
PROPERDIN
PROPYLENE
PROTOXIDE
PRUSSIATE
PULVERINE
PYRIDOXIN
PYROXYLIN
QUICKLIME
QUINOLINE
RAFFINOSE
RHODANATE
RHOEADINE
SACCHARIN
SALTPETRE
SUCCINATE
SYNAPTASE
TANTALATE
TELLURATE
TELLURIDE
TELLURITE
TUNGSTATE
UREA RESIN
VERDIGRIS
YOHIMBINE
ZINC OXIDE

10

ACETIC ACID
ADIPIC ACID
ALBUMINATE
ANTHRACENE
ANTHRACITE
ANTIMONATE
ANTIMONIDE

ANTIMONITE
AQUA FORTIS
ASPARAGINE
AZOBENZENE
BAKING SODA
BALLISTITE
BENZPYRENE
BICHROMATE
BISULPHATE
BROMIC ACID
CALCIFEROL
CARCINOGEN
CARRIER GAS
CHLOROFORM
CHOLIC ACID
CHROME-ALUM
CINCHONINE
CITRIC ACID
CORYDALINE
CREATININE
CYANIC ACID
DICHROMATE
DISULPHATE
DISULPHIDE
DITHIONATE
DOUBLE SALT
EPSOM SALTS
ERGOSTEROL
ETHYLAMINE
ETHYL ETHER
EUCALYPTOL
EUCHLORINE
FIBRINOGEN
FORMIC ACID
GALLIC ACID
HEAVY WATER
LACTIC ACID
LAURIC ACID
LEAD-GLANCE
LUCIFERASE
MALEIC ACID
MARINE ACID
MERCAPTIDE
NATURAL GAS
NITRIC ACID
PAPAVERINE
PECTIC ACID
PHALLOIDIN
PHOSPHORET
PICRIC ACID
PICROTOXIN
PIPERIDINE

POLYMERIDE
PRECIPITIN
PUTRESCINE
PYROGALLOL
PYROXYLINE
QUICK-WATER
QUINIC ACID
RESORCINOL
RIBOFLAVIN
SACCHARATE
SACCHARIDE
SACCHARINE
SALICYLATE
SORBIC ACID
STRYCHNINE
TANNIC ACID
THIOPENTAL
TOCOPHEROL
TRYPTOPHAN
VINYLIDENE
VINYL RESIN
WOOD-SPIRIT

11

ACRYLIC ACID
AMYL NITRATE
AXEROPHTHOL
BARBITURATE
BENZOIC ACID
BICARBONATE
BLUE VITRIOL
BUTYRIC ACID
CAUSTIC LIME
CAUSTIC SODA
CHLORIC ACID
CHLOROPRENE
CHOLESTEROL
CHROMIC ACID
COPROSTEROL
DEOXYRIBOSE
EPINEPHRINE
FLUORESCEIN
GIANT-POWDER
HAEMOCYANIN
HAEMOGLOBIN
HORN MERCURY
HYDROCARBON
HYDROGEN ION
HYOSCYAMINE
LACTOFLAVIN

LAUGHING GAS
MALONIC ACID
MESONIC ACID
METALDEHYDE
METHYLAMINE
NAPHTHALENE
NITRIC OXIDE
NITROUS ACID
NUCLEIC ACID
OLEFIANT GAS
ORTHOBORATE
OXONIUM SALT
PARALDEHYDE
PERCHLORATE
PHENOL RESIN
PHOSPHONIUM
PHYTOSTEROL
PILOCARPINE
PIPERIC ACID
PLUMBIC ACID
POLYPEPTIDE
POTASH-WATER
PRODUCER GAS
PROGESTOGEN
PROPYLAMINE
PRUSSIC ACID
PSILOMELANE
PTEROIC ACID
SAL AMMONIAC
SAL PRUNELLA
SAL VOLATILE
SCOPOLAMINE
SEBACIC ACID
SELENIC ACID
SILICIC ACID
SMITHSONITE
STANNIC ACID
STEARIC ACID
STROPANTHIN
SUBERIC ACID
THEOBROMINE
THIOCYANATE
THIOPENTONE
TITANIC ACID
TRITHIONATE
VALERIC ACID
WOOD-NAPHTHA
WOOD-VINEGAR
XANTHIC ACID

12

ACETALDEHYDE
AGGLUTINOGEN
ASCORBIC ACID
ASPARAGINASE
ASPARTIC ACID
BAKING-POWDER
BENZALDEHYDE
BLUE WATER-GAS
CARBOHYDRATE
CARBOLIC ACID
CARBONIC ACID
CETYL ALCOHOL
CHLOROUS ACID
CUPRAMMONIUM
CYCLOPROPANE
DIETHYLAMINE
DISACCHARIDE
ETHANOLAMINE
ETHYL ALCOHOL
FERRICYANIDE
FERROCYANIDE
FIBRINOLYSIN
FLUOROCARBON
FORMALDEHYDE
FULLER'S EARTH
FULMINIC ACID
GLUTAMIC ACID
GREEN VITRIOL
HAEMATOXYLIN
HYPOCHLORITE
HYPOSULPHATE
HYPOSULPHITE
JAVELLE WATER
LINOLEIC ACID
METASILICATE
MOLYBDIC ACID
MYRISTIC ACID
NICOTINAMIDE
NITRO-ANILINE
NITROBENZENE
NITROTOLUENE
NITROUS OXIDE
OIL OF VITRIOL
PALMITIC ACID
PARACYANOGEN
PEBBLE-POWDER
PERIODIC ACID
PERMANGANATE
PHENYLALANIN
PHTHALIC ACID

PROGESTERONE
PYROTARTRATE
RIBONUCLEASE
ROCHELLE-SALT
SAL ALEMBROTH
SALT OF SORREL
SALT OF TARTAR
SEMI-WATER-GAS
SODIUM AMYTAL
SPIRIT OF SALT
STROPHANTHIN
SUCCINIC ACID
TANTALIC ACID
TARTARIC ACID
TELLURIC ACID
TESTOSTERONE
THEOPHYLLINE
TRIMETHYLENE
TUNGSTIC ACID
VINYL ACETATE
VINYL PLASTIC
WHITE ARSENIC
WHITE VITRIOL

HYDROXYLAMINE
HYPOPHOSPHITE
LAURYL ALCOHOL
METAPHOSPHATE
NAPHTHYLAMINE
NICOTINIC ACID
ORTHOSILICATE
PHOSPHORYLASE
PHYLLOQUINONE
PLATINUM BLACK
POLYCARBONATE
PROPIONIC ACID
PYROPHOSPHATE
SACCHARIC ACID
SALICYLIC ACID
SALT OF VITRIOL
SCHEELE'S GREEN
SEMICARBAZIDE
SEMICARBAZONE
SULPHURIC ACID
TELLUROUS ACID
TRIETHYLAMINE
TRISACCHARIDE
TURNBULL'S BLUE
VINYL CHLORIDE

MONOSACCHARIDE
NITROCELLULOSE
NITROGLYCERINE
ORTHOBORIC ACID
OXYHAEMOGLOBIN
PAROROSANILINE
PERCHLORIC ACID
PHOSPHORIC ACID
POLYSACCHARIDE
PYROGALLIC ACID
RICENOLEIC ACID
SALT OF WORMWOOD
SULPHUR DIOXIDE
SULPHUROUS ACID
TETRAETHYL LEAD
THIOCYANIC ACID
TRIMETHYLAMINE
TRINITROPHENOL
TRIPHENYLAMINE
TRITHIONIC ACID
TURPETH MINERAL

15

AMINO-ACETIC ACID
DULCIFIED SPIRIT
ELIXIR OF VITRIOL
GIBBERELLIC ACID
HYGROSCOPIC SALT
MALEIC HYDRAZIDE
MICROCOSMIC SALT
NITRIC ANHYDRIDE
NORWAY SALTPETRE
PERMANGANIC ACID
PHENOLPHTHALEIN
PHOSPHOROUS ACID
PRISMATIC POWDER
RIBONUCLEIC ACID
TRINITROBENZENE
TRINITROTOLUENE

13

ACRYLONITRILE
ALKALINE EARTH
CARBON DIOXIDE
CAUSTIC POTASH
CEVITAMIC ACID
CHLORINE WATER
CREAM OF TARTAR
DIMETHYLAMINE
DITHIONIC ACID
FERRICYANOGEN
FERROCYANOGEN
GLAUBER'S SALTS
HYDROCHLORIDE
HYDROSULPHIDE
HYDROSULPHITE

14

ANOMALOUS WATER
CARBON MONOXIDE
CAUSTIC AMMONIA
CHILE SALTPETRE
CHLORAL HYDRATE
CYANOCOBALAMIN
DINITROBENZENE
ETHYLENE GLYCOL
FERROPRUSSIATE
FURFURALDEHYDE
HYDROXONIUM ION
MARGARITIC ACID
METHYL CHLORIDE

SCIENCE — CHEMISTRY — CHEMICAL TERMS

3

FAT
ION
LAW
WAX

4

ACID
ATOM
BATH
BELL
DUAD
DYAD
ETNA
KIPP
MOLE
TEST
WORM

5

AGENT
ANION
ANODE
CHAIN
CHELA
CLAMP
CYCLE
HEXAD
METAL
MONAD
PHASE
STAND
STILL
TITRE
TOXIN
TRIAD

6

ACTION
ALKALI
ARGAND
BEAKER
BUFFER
CALCAR
CATION

CRASIS
ELIXIR
ELUTOR
ENERGY
ENZYME
FILTER
FUNNEL
GAS-JAR
GAS-JET
HEPTAD
ISOMER
MORTAR
PENTAD
PERIOD
PESTLE
PHASIS
POISON
POWDER
RETORT
SIPHON
SOLUTE
SPIRIT
TEMPER
TETRAD
TRACER
TRIPOD

7

ACIDITY
ALCHEMY
ALCOHOL
ALEMBIC
ATHANOR
AUREITY
BALANCE
BATTERY
BELL-JAR
BITUMEN
BURETTE
CATHODE
CO-AGENT
DILUENT
ELEMENT
ELUTION
EMULSOR
ESSENCE
EUTEXIA
EUTROPY
FORMULA
HORMONE

ISOBARE
ISOTOPE
ISOTOPY
LATTICE
LINKAGE
MATRASS
MIXTURE
MONOMER
OSMOSIS
PELICAN
PIPETTE
PLASTIC
POLYMER
PRODUCT
PROTEIN
RADICAL
RADICLE
REACTOR
REAGENT
SALT-PAN
SOLVATE
SOLVENT
STEROID
VALENCE
VALENCY
VITAMIN
ZYMOSIS
ZYMURGY

8

ACID TEST
ACTINISM
ALKAHEST
ANALYSIS
BATSWING
CATALYST
CHEMICAL
CHEMURGY
COMPOUND
CRUCIBLE
CUCURBIT
DIALYSER
DIALYSIS
DILUTION
DOCIMASY
EMULSION
ENTHALPY
EQUATION
FIXATION
FUEL-CELL

GELATION
INFUSION
ISOMORPH
MICRURGY
MOLALITY
MOLARITY
MOLECULE
NON-METAL
OXIDISER
OZONISER
PRODUCER
PROMOTER
REACTANT
REACTION
REAGENCY
RECEIVER
SALINITY
SATURATE
SCRUBBER
SOAP-TEST
SOLUTION
SOLVENCY
SYNTEXIS
TAUTOMER
TEST-TUBE
TOXICANT
VOLATILE

9

ALLOTROPE
ALLOTROPY
ANABOLISM
APPARATUS
ATMOLYSIS
AZEOTROPE
BAIN-MARIE
BIVALENCE
BIVALENCY
CATALYSIS
CHEMISTRY
CONDENSER
CO-POLYMER
CORROSION
COVALENCY
CYANIDING
DESICCANT
DILATANCY
EXPLOSIVE
FULMINANT
HYDRATION

HYDROLYTE
INDICATOR
INHIBITOR
INTERFACE
IODOPHILE
ISOLATION
ISOMERISM
LEYDEN JAR
LIQUEFIER
MAGISTERY
MOTHER-LYE
NITRATION
NITRIDING
OXIDATION
OZONATION
PERCOLATE
PERFUSION
PRINCIPLE
PYROLYSIS
RAFFINATE
REDUCTANT
RESOLVENT
RESONANCE
RINGSTAND
SATURATOR
SEPARATOR
SOLVATION
STABILITY
SUBLIMATE
SUBSTANCE
SYNERGISM
SYNERGIST
TACTICITY
TEMPERING
TEST-PAPER
TITRATION
WATER-BATH
WIRE-GAUZE
ZYMOLYSIS

10

ALKALINITY
CALEFACTOR
CAUSTICITY
CHEMONASTY
CHEMOTAXIS
COMBUSTION
COMMIXTURE
CONDENSATE
COVER GLASS

323

SCIENCE — CHEMISTRY — CHEMICAL TERMS

DENATURANT
DEOXIDISER
DESICCATOR
DEWAR FLASK
DIMORPHISM
DISSOLVENT
DOUBLE SALT
ELUTRIATOR
EMULSIFIER
EQUIVALENT
ESCHAROTIC
EUDIOMETER
EVAPORATOR
EXPERIMENT
EXTRACTANT
FILTRATION
HEAVY METAL
HOMEOMORPH
HYDROLYSIS
INGREDIENT
INTERPHASE
INTERSTICE
MASS NUMBER
MESOMERISM
METAMERISM
NITRO-GROUP
PERCOLATOR
PHOTOLYSIS
PHOTOTROPE
PHOTOTROPY
PNEUMATICS
POLYMERISM
PSEUDO-ACID
PYROPHORUS
PYROTECHNY
REGENERACY
RESOLUTION
SATURATION
SEPARATION
SOLUBILITY
STABILISER
STABLENESS
SUBACIDITY
SURFACTANT
SUSPENSION
SUSPENSOID
TRANSMUTER
TRITURATOR
TRIVALENCE
TRIVALENCY
TURBULATOR
TURBULENCE

UNIVALENCE
UNIVALENCY
WASH-BOTTLE

11

ACCUMULATOR
ACTINIC RAYS
ANTI-VITAMIN
ASSOCIATION
AZOCOMPOUND
CALCINATION
CALEFACTION
CHLORIMETRY
CONCENTRATE
DEFLAGRATOR
DEHYDRATION
DENITRATION
DESICCATION
DRYING AGENT
ELECTROLYTE
EQUILIBRIUM
EQUIVALENCE
EQUIVALENCY
EREMACAUSIS
EVAPORATION
FILTER-PAPER
FREE-RADICAL
FUME-CHAMBER
HYDROCARBON
INTERACTION
ION-EXCHANGE
LITMUS PAPER
MAGISTERIUM
METHYLATION
MICRONEEDLE
MORPHOTROPY
MOTHER-WATER
NEUTRALISER
NITROSATION
OXYGENATION
PERCOLATION
PERIODIC LAW
PRECIPITANT
PRECIPITATE
RAIN-CHAMBER
REGENERATOR
RUPERT'S DROP
STACTOMETER
STARCH-PAPER
SULPHURATOR

TAUTOMERISM
TRIMORPHISM
TRITURATION

12

ATOMIC NUMBER
BIOCHEMISTRY
BOILING POINT
BUNSEN-BURNER
BURNING POINT
CHLORINATION
CONCENTRATOR
CONDENSATION
CONSTITUTION
DEFLAGRATION
DISSOCIATION
ELECTROLYSIS
ENANTIOTROPY
FERMENTATION
FILTER-FUNNEL
FLUORINATION
FUME-CUPBOARD
GEOCHEMISTRY
GRAM-MOLECULE
INSOLUBILITY
INTERMEDIATE
INTERSTITIAL
LABELLED ATOM
LAW OF OCTAVES
LIQUEFACTION
METASOMATISM
MICROPIPETTE
MOLECULARITY
MONO-COMPOUND
MOTHER-LIQUOR
MULTIVALENCE
MULTIVALENCY
NITROSO-GROUP
PEROXIDATION
PHOTOTROPISM
POLARISATION
PRECIPITANCE
PRECIPITANCY
PRECIPITATOR
REGENERATION
RING-COMPOUND
SALIFICATION
SPECTROSCOPY
STABILISATOR
STEREOISOMER

SUBERISATION
SULPHURATION
VISCOUS WATER
VITRIOLATION
WATER-BATTERY
WETTING AGENT
WOULFE-BOTTLE

13

AUTOCATALYSIS
CALCIFICATION
CONFIGURATION
DELIQUESCENCE
EFFERVESCENCE
EXOTHERMICITY
FREEZING POINT
HIGH EXPLOSIVE
HOMEOMORPHISM
HYDROGENATION
HYDROCRACKING
LAEVOROTATION
MACROMOLECULE
METASTABILITY
MICROANALYSIS
NITRIFICATION
NUCLEO-PROTEIN
PERIODIC TABLE
PETROCHEMICAL
PRECIPITATION
QUADRIVALENCE
QUANTIVALENCE

REDUCING AGENT
REDUCING FLAME
REFRIGERATORY
SACCHARIMETRY
SHADOW-CASTING
STABILISATION
STOICHIOMETRY
TRACER ELEMENT
TRANSMUTATION
TURMERIC PAPER
WASHING-BOTTLE
WATER-SOFTNESS

14

AUTO-INTOXICANT
CHLORITISATION
CHROMATOGRAPHY
CYCLIC COMPOUND
DESULPHURATION
DEXTRO-ROTATION
ELECTROVALENCY
ESTERIFICATION
GRAM-EQUIVALENT
GRAPHIC FORMULA
HEAVY CHEMICALS
HISTOCHEMISTRY
IATROCHEMISTRY
ISOTOPIC NUMBER
KIPP'S APPARATUS
MICROCHEMISTRY
NON-ELECTROLYTE

NORMAL SOLUTION
OXIDISING AGENT
PHOTOCHEMISTRY
PIEZOCHEMISTRY
POLYMERISATION
PSEUDO-SOLUTION
QUINQUEVALENCE
RADIOCHEMISTRY
REVIVIFICATION
SAPONIFICATION
SILICIFICATION
STORAGE BATTERY
VITRIOLISATION

15

BOMB CALORIMETER
CITRIC ACID CYCLE
CO-ORDINATE BONDS
DEVITRIFICATION
ENANTIOMORPHISM
EVAPORATING DISH
FREEZING MIXTURE
IMMUNO-CHEMISTRY
LIEBIG CONDENSER
MOLECULAR WEIGHT
NITRO-DERIVATIVE
PNEUMATIC TROUGH
SATURATION POINT
STEREOCHEMISTRY
STEREOISOMERISM
SUPERSATURATION

SCIENCE – CHEMISTRY – ELEMENTS

3

TIN

4

GOLD
IRON

LEAD
NEON
ZINC

5

ARGON
AZOTE
AZOTH

BORON
OZONE
RADON
XENON

6

BARIUM

CARBON
CERIUM
COBALT
COPPER
CURIUM
DIPLON
ERBIUM
HELIUM
INDIUM

IODINE
IONIUM
KALIUM
NICKEL
OSMIUM
OXYGEN
RADIUM
SILVER
SODIUM

7

ACTINON
ARSENIC
BISMUTH
BROMINE
CADMIUM
CAESIUM
CALCIUM

SCIENCE – CHEMISTRY – ELEMENTS

ELEMENT
FERMIUM
GALLIUM
HAFNIUM
HALOGEN
HOLMIUM
IRIDIUM
ISOTOPE
KRYPTON
LITHIUM
MERCURY
NATRIUM
NIOBIUM
PROTIUM
RHENIUM
RHODIUM
SILICON
STIBIUM
SULPHUR
TERBIUM
THORIUM
THULIUM
TRITIUM
URANIUM
WOLFRAM
YTTRIUM

CHLORINE
CHROMIUM
DIPLOGEN
EUROPIUM
FLUORINE
FRANCIUM
GLUCINUM
HYDROGEN
LUTECIUM
LUTETIUM
NITROGEN
NOBELIUM
PLATINUM
POLONIUM
RUBIDIUM
SAMARIUM
SCANDIUM
SELENIUM
TANTALUM
THALLIUM
TITANIUM
TUNGSTEN
VANADIUM

GERMANIUM
LANTHANUM
MAGNESIUM
MANGANESE
NEODYMIUM
NEPTUNIUM
PALLADIUM
PLUTONIUM
POTASSIUM
RARE EARTH
RUTHENIUM
STRONTIUM
TELLURIUM
YTTERBIUM
ZIRCONIUM

EINSTEINIUM
HYDRARGYRUM
MENDELEVIUM
QUICKSILVER
RADIOCARBON

12

PRASEODYMIUM
PROTACTINIUM
RADIO-ELEMENT
RADIO-ISOTOPE
RADIO-THORIUM

10

DYSPROSIUM
GADOLINIUM
LANTHANIDE
LAURENTIUM
MOLYBDENUM
PHOSPHORUS
PROMETHIUM
TECHNETIUM

13

HEAVY HYDROGEN
PROTOACTINIUM
RADIO-ACTINIUM

14

RADIO-STRONTIUM

9

ALUMINIUM
AMERICIUM
BERKELIUM
BERYLLIUM
BRIMSTONE
DEUTERIUM
EMANATION

11

ALKALI METAL
CALIFORNIUM
CARBON BLACK

15

RADIUM EMANATION

8

ACTINIDE
ACTINIUM
ANTIMONY
ASTATINE

SCIENCE – GEOLOGY

3

ASH
DIP
EON
ERA
ICE
JET
ORE

PLY
PUY
WAD

4

AEON
BIND

BLAE
BOLE
CALP
CAUK
CLAY
COAL
CONE
CRAG
DOME

DYKE
GRIT
GÜNZ
HADE
JADE
JURA
KAME
LAVA
LIAS

LOAM
LODE
MALM
MARL
MICA
ONYX
OPAL
PLUG
RISS

ROCK
RUBY
SAND
SIAL
SILL
SIMA
SINK
SLAG
SOIL

SOLE
SPAR
TALC
TILL
TUFA
TUFF
VEIN
WÜRM
ZONE

5

AGATE
AMBER
ANTRE
ARGIL
ARRIS
ASSAY
BASIN
BERYL
BORAX
BRASH
CHALK
CHERT
CLOAM
CRUST
DRIFT
DRUSE
EARTH
ELVAN
EMERY
EPOCH
ESKER
FAKES
FAULT
FLINT
FLUOR
GAULT
GEODE
GLASS
HORST
JOINT
KAROO
LAHAR
LAYER
LEDGE
LOESS
LOGAN
MACLE
MAGMA
NAPPE
PRASE
SCREE
SÉRAC
SHALE
SHIFT
SILEX
SLATE
STAGE
STOCK
STONE
TALUS

THROW
TOPAZ
TRASS
TRIAS
UMBER
VARVE
WACKE

6

ACMITE
ALBITE
ARKOSE
AUGITE
BANKET
BASALT
BLENDE
BOG-ORE
BUNTER
CERITE
CHESIL
CLUNCH
COULÉE
DACITE
DÉBRIS
DUNITE
EOCENE
FLASER
FLYSCH
FOSSIL
GABBRO
GALENA
GANGUE
GARNET
GLANCE
GNEISS
GOSSAN
GYPSUM
HALITE
HAÜYNE
HOODOO
HUMITE
ICE AGE
INLIER
IOLITE
JASPER
KAOLIN
KERMES
KEUPER
KUNKUR
MANTLE

MARBLE
MINDEL
MORION
MOULIN
MUNDIC
NATRON
NEEDLE
NORITE
NOSEAN
OOLITE
OPHITE
PEBBLE
PELITE
PILLAR
PLASMA
POCKET
PUMICE
PYROPE
QUARTZ
RIPRAP
RUTILE
SARSEN
SCHIST
SCHORL
SERIES
SHIELD
SILICA
SINTER
SPHENE
SPINEL
STRATA
STRIKE
SYSTEM
TALCUM
TINCAL
WINDOW
ZIRCON

7

ANATASE
APATITE
AQUIFER
AXINITE
AZURITE
BARYTES
BEDROCK
BIOTITE
BOG-IRON
BORNITE
BOULDER

BRECCIA
BRUCITE
CALCITE
CALDERA
CAPTURE
CAT'S-EYE
CHIMNEY
CHONDRE
CITRINE
COAL-BED
CRINITE
CRYSTAL
CYANITE
DEBACLE
DESMINE
DIAMOND
DIORITE
DIRT-BED
DRUMLIN
ELUVIUM
EMERALD
EPIDOTE
ERINITE
EROSION
EUCLASE
EUCRITE
EUSTACY
EXUVIAE
FAHLERZ
FAHLORE
FELSITE
FERRITE
FOLDING
GAHNITE
GEOGENY
GEOGONY
GEOLOGY
GLIMMER
GOTHITE
GRANITE
GREISEN
GUMMITE
HORIZON
HORNITO
HYALITE
ICE-FALL
ICE-SPAR
IRON ORE
IRON-PAN
ISOBASE
JACINTH
JADEITE

KAINITE
KERNITE
KYANITE
LAPILLI
LEUCITE
LIGNITE
MELLITE
MINERAL
MINETTE
MIOCENE
MOFETTE
MOLASSE
MORAINE
NACRITE
NEOGENE
OLIGIST
OLIVINE
OUTCROP
OUTLIER
OVERLAP
PEA-IRON
PENNINE
PERIDOT
PERLITE
PERMIAN
PICRITE
POTHOLE
PYCNITE
PYRITES
REALGAR
RED CLAY
RED CRAG
REMANIÉ
RHAETIC
SALBAND
SARSDEN
SCAGLIA
SEA-SAND
SECTION
SHINGLE
SINKAGE
SLITHER
SPILITE
STRATUM
SUBSOIL
SWALLET
SYENITE
SYLVITE
TEKTITE
THORITE
THULITE
TILLITE

TRIPOLI
URALITE
URANITE
VARIOLE
VEINING
VERGLAS
VOLCANO
WOOD-TIN
ZARNICH
ZEUXITE
ZINCITE
ZOISITE
ZORGITE

8

ADULARIA
AEGIRINE
AIGUILLE
ALLUVIUM
AMBERITE
AMETHYST
AMYGDULE
ANALCIME
ANDESINE
ANDESITE
ANKERITE
ARCHAEAN
ASBESTOS
AUTUNITE
BACULITE
BASANITE
BLUE JOHN
BORACITE
BRONZITE
BROOKITE
CALCSPAR
CALC-TUFF
CAMBRIAN
CERUSITE
CHONDRUS
CHROMITE
CIMINITE
CIMOLITE
CINNABAR
CLAY-MARL
CLEAVAGE
CLEVEITE
COALBALL
CORALLUM
CORAL RAG
CORUND'JM

327

SCIENCE – GEOLOGY

CREVASSE
CROCOITE
CROPPING
CRYOLITE
DATOLITE
DENDRITE
DETRITUS
DEVONIAN
DIALLAGE
DIASPORE
DILUVIUM
DIOPSIDE
DIOPTASE
DIP-SLOPE
DISTHENE
DOLERITE
DOLOMITE
ECLOGITE
ELVANITE
ENHYDROS
ESSONITE
EUTAXITE
EUXENITE
FAHLBAND
FAYALITE
FELDSPAR
FLUORITE
FUCHSITE
FUMAROLE
GALENITE
GANISTER
GEOGNOSY
GRAPHITE
HEPATITE
HORNFELS
HURONIAN
ICE-FRONT
IDOCRASE
ILMENITE
IODYRITE
IRON CLAY
IRON SAND
ISOMORPH
ISOSTASY
JURASSIC
KALINITE
LANDSLIP
LATERITE
LAZULITE
LAZURITE
LENTICLE
LEWISITE

LIMONITE
LIPARITE
MEASURES
MEIONITE
MELANITE
MELILITE
MENEVIAN
MESOLITE
MIMETITE
MONAZITE
MUDSTONE
MYLONITE
NEPHRITE
NOSELITE
OBSIDIAN
OIL-SHALE
ONYCHITE
ORPIMENT
OVERSTEP
OVERWASH
PEA-STONE
PEPERINO
PERTHITE
PETUNTZE
PHENGITE
PHYLLITE
PICOTITE
PINAKOID
PIPEWORK
PISOLITE
PLIOCENE
PLUMBAGO
POROSITY
PORPHYRY
POTSTONE
PREHNITE
PSAMMITE
PSEPHITE
PYROXENE
RAIN-WASH
REGOLITH
RETINITE
RHYOLITE
RILLMARK
RING-DYKE
ROCK-FALL
ROCK-SALT
ROCK-WOOD
ROESTONE
ROT-STONE
RUBELLAN
SAECULUM

SAGANITE
SALT-CAKE
SAND-FLAG
SAND-PIPE
SANIDINE
SAPONITE
SAPPHIRE
SASSOLIN
SAXONITE
SCHILLER
SELENITE
SERICITE
SIDERITE
SILURIAN
SMALTITE
SODALITE
SPHENOID
STALAGMA
STANNITE
STEATITE
STIBNITE
STILBITE
SUBSTAGE
SUCCINUM
SUN-CRACK
SUNSTONE
SYNCLINE
TENORITE
TEPHRITE
TERTIARY
TIGER-EYE
TINSTONE
TITANITE
TONALITE
TRACHYTE
TRIASSIC
TRICHITE
TRILLING
TROILITE
UINTAITE
VESUVIAN
VIRIDITE
WAY-BOARD
WURTZITE
XENOLITH
XENOTIME
ZARATITE

9

ALABASTER

ALBERTITE
ALMANDINE
ALUM-SHALE
ALUM-SLATE
AMORPHISM
AMPHIBOLE
ANGLESITE
ANHYDRITE
ANORTHITE
ANTICLINE
APOPHYSIS
ARAGONITE
ARGENTITE
ARGILLITE
ATACAMITE
AVALANCHE
BATHOLITE
BATHOLITH
BATHONIAN
BELEMNITE
BLACKBAND
BLACKJACK
BRICK-CLAY
BROWN COAL
BROWNSPAR
BUHRSTONE
BYTOWNITE
CAEN-STONE
CAINOZOIC
CAIRNGORM
CARBUNCLE
CARNOTITE
CATACLASM
CATACLYSM
CAT-SILVER
CAVE-EARTH
CELESTINE
CEMENTITE
CEYLONITE
CHABAZITE
CHALYBITE
CHERALITE
CHERNOZEM
CHINA CLAY
CHONDRITE
CHONDRULE
CIPOLLINO
CLAY-SLATE
COAL-BRASS
COBALTITE
COCCOLITE
COFFINITE

COLUMBITE
COPROLITE
CORALLIAN
CORALLITE
CORAL-ROCK
CORN-BRASH
CORNELIAN
CORNSTONE
COVELLITE
DALRADIAN
DETRITION
DIALOGITE
DIATOMITE
DICHROISM
DICHROITE
DOWN-THROW
DROP-STONE
EARTHFLAX
ELAEOLITE
ENCRINITE
ENDOMORPH
ENHYDRITE
ENSTATITE
EPIDOSITE
ERYTHRITE
EUDIALYTE
FIBROLITE
FIRESTONE
FLUORSPAR
FOLIATION
FOOL'S GOLD
FORMATION
FULGURITE
GEOSPHERE
GEYSERITE
GLOBULITE
GMELINITE
GOSLARITE
GRANITITE
GRANULITE
GREENSAND
GREYWACKE
GROSSULAR
HAEMATITE
HARMOTOME
HEAVY SPAR
HEDYPHANE
HEMIHEDRY
HEMITROPE
HERCYNITE
HESSONITE
HIDDENITE

HIPPURITE	OTTRELITE	SHELL-MARL	**10**
HOMOTAXIS	OXFORDIAN	SHELL-SAND	
HORNSTONE	PAPER-COAL	SOLFATARA	ALABANDINE
ICE-ACTION	PARAMETER	SPHAERITE	ANDALUSITE
INJECTION	PARAMORPH	SPILOSITE	AQUAMARINE
INSELBERG	PARGASITE	SPODUMENE	ARGYRODITE
INTRUSION	PEARL-SPAR	STEP-FAULT	ASSAY-PIECE
IRONSTONE	PECTOLITE	STONE-COAL	AUSTRALITE
KAOLINITE	PEGMATITE	SUBSTRATE	AVENTURINE
KERMESITE	PENCIL-ORE	SUCCINITE	BARYSPHERE
KIDNEY-ORE	PENEPLAIN	SYLVANITE	BASAL PLANE
KIESERITE	PENNINITE	SYLVINITE	BITTER-SPAR
LACCOLITE	PERICLASE	SYNCLINAL	BLACK CHALK
LACCOLITH	PERICLINE	TACHYLITE	BLACK EARTH
LANDSLIDE	PERIMORPH	TANTALITE	BLOODSTONE
LARDALITE	PETROLOGY	TECTONICS	BLUE GROUND
LARVIKITE	PHACOLITE	TELLURITE	BOTTOM-LAND
LIMESTONE	PHACOLITH	TEPHROITE	BRACHYDOME
LITHOLOGY	PHENACITE	THERALITE	BRADYSEISM
LOADSTONE	PHONOLITE	TINGUAITE	BROWNSTONE
LODESTONE	PIPESTONE	TOADSTONE	CALC-SINTER
MACRODOME	PLEONASTE	TORBANITE	CAMPTONITE
MAGNESITE	PLUTONISM	TREMOLITE	CARNALLITE
MAGNETITE	POLIANITE	TRIDYMITE	CHALCEDONY
MALACHITE	POWELLITE	TURQUOISE	CHALKSTONE
MARCASITE	PREROSION	UINTAHITE	CHESSYLITE
MARGARITE	PROPYLITE	URANINITE	CHINA STONE
MARIALITE	PROTOGINE	UVAROVITE	CHRYSOLITE
MARLSTONE	PROUSTITE	VARIOLITE	CHRYSOTILE
MELAPHYRE	PYRENEITE	VARISCITE	CLINKSTONE
MICA-SLATE	QUARTZITE	VEINSTONE	COMPACTION
MICROLITE	RAIN-PRINT	VENTIFACT	CONCRETION
MILLERITE	RHODOLITE	VIVIANITE	CONFORMITY
MISPICKEL	RHODONITE	VULCANISM	COQUIMBITY
MIZZONITE	RIVER-SAND	VULCANITE	CORDIERITE
MONOCLINE	ROCK-BASIN	VULPINITE	CRETACEOUS
MONZONITE	ROCK-GUANO	WATER-PORE	CROCOISITE
MOONSTONE	RUBELLITE	WAVELLITE	CROSS-STONE
MOSS-AGATE	RUBICELLE	WERNERITE	CRYOCONITE
MUGEARITE	RUIN AGATE	WHET-SLATE	CYLINDRITE
MUSCOVITE	SANDARACH	WHINSTONE	DENUDATION
NATROLITE	SANDSTONE	WILLEMITE	DOPPLERITE
NEEDLE-TIN	SASSOLITE	WITHERITE	DREIKANTER
NEOCOMIAN	SATIN-SPAR	WULFENITE	DYSCRASITE
NEPHELINE	SCAPOLITE	XENOCRYST	EAGLE-STONE
NEPHELITE	SCHEELITE	ZECHSTEIN	EPIDIORITE
NICCOLITE	SCHLIEREN	ZINC-BLOOM	ERUBESCITE
NITRATINE	SCOLECITE	ZINKENITE	FAIRY-STONE
NUMMULITE	SCORODITE		FLINTSTONE
OLIGOCENE	SENNONIAN		FLOAT-STONE
OLIVENITE	SEPIOLITE		GADOLINITE
OMPHACITE	SEPTARIUM		GARNET-ROCK

SCIENCE – GEOLOGY

GARNIERITE
GLAUBERITE
GLAUCONITE
GONIOMETRY
GRANOPHYRE
GRAPTOLITE
GREEN EARTH
GREENSTONE
GREY-WETHER
GROUNDMASS
HALLOYSITE
HELIOTROPE
HEMIHEDRON
HEULANDITE
HONEY-STONE
HORNBLENDE
HORN SILVER
HYALOPHANE
IRON-GLANCE
JAMESONITE
KENTISH RAG
KERSANTITE
KIESELGUHR
KIMBERLITE
LAURDALITE
LAURVIKITE
LEAD-GLANCE
LEPIDOLITE
LHERZOLITE
LIMBURGITE
LITHOMARGE
LITHOPHYSA
LIVING ROCK
LOGAN-STONE
LONDON CLAY
MACROPRISM
MANTLE ROCK
MARMAROSIS
MEERSCHAUM
MELACONITE
METASTASIS
MICA-SCHIST
MICROCLINE
MOCHA STONE
MORPHOLOGY
NATIVE ROCK
NOVACULITE
ODONTOLITE
OLIGOCLASE
ONYX-MARBLE
ORDOVICIAN
OROGENESIS

ORTHOCLASE
ORTHOPHYRE
ORTHOPRISM
OVERTHRUST
OXFORD CLAY
PALAEOGENE
PALAGONITE
PANDERMITE
PARAGONITE
PARIS GREEN
PEACOCK-ORE
PEARL-STONE
PERIDOTITE
PHENOCRYST
PHLOGOPITE
PITCHSTONE
POLYHALITE
PURBECKIAN
PYROLUSITE
PYROMERIDE
PYROXENITE
PYRRHOTINE
PYRRHOTITE
QUARTZ-ROCK
QUATERNARY
REDRUTHITE
REGELATION
RESORPTION
RETINALITE
REVOLUTION
RHINESTONE
RIEBECKITE
RIPIDOLITE
RIPPLE-MARK
RIVER-DRIFT
ROCK-BOTTOM
ROCK-BUTTER
ROCK-FLOWER
ROSE-QUARTZ
RUBY-SILVER
RUBY-SPINEL
RUIN MARBLE
SAMARSKITE
SAPPHIRINE
SATIN-STONE
SAUSSURITE
SCHALSTEIN
SCHORL-ROCK
SELBORNIAN
SERPENTINE
SIDEROLITE
SMARAGDITE

SNAKESTONE
SOMBRERITE
SPERRYLITE
SPHALERITE
SPHERULITE
STALACTITE
STALAGMITE
STAUROLITE
STEPHANITE
STINKSTONE
SUBSTRATUM
SWINESTONE
TALC-SCHIST
TENNANTITE
TERRA-ROSSA
TESCHENITE
THAUMASITE
TOPAZOLITE
TORBERNITE
TOUCHSTONE
TOURMALINE
TRAVERTINE
TROCTOLITE
TROUTSTONE
TRUNCATION
TURKEY HONE
UNDERLAYER
VANADINITE
VENICE TALC
VITREOSITY
WATER-LEVEL
WATER-TABLE
WHEWELLITE
ZINC-BLENDE
ZONAL INDEX

11

ALEXANDRITE
AMAZON-STONE
AMPHIBOLITE
ANNABERGITE
APOPHYLLITE
BADDELEYITE
BONE-BRECCIA
BOULDER-CLAY
BRACHYPRISM
CARBORUNDUM
CASSITERITE
CERARGYRITE
CHALCEDONYX

CHIASTOLITE
CHRYSOBERYL
CHRYSOCOLLA
CHRYSOPRASE
CLINOCHLORE
COBALT BLOOM
CORNISH CLAY
COUNTRY-ROCK
CRAG-AND-TAIL
CROCIDOLITE
CRYSTALLINE
CRYSTALLITE
DENDRACHATE
DISLOCATION
EARTH-PILLAR
EJECTAMENTA
EPISTILBITE
FELSPATHOID
FRANKLINITE
GEANTICLINE
GEOSYNCLINE
GREENOCKITE
HÄLLEFLINTA
HEMIHEDRISY
HYALOMELANE
HYPERSTHENE
ICELAND SPAR
IGNEOUS ROCK
IRON PYRITES
ISOMORPHISM
ITACOLUMITE
KERATOPHYRE
KIMERIDGIAN
LABRADORITE
LAMPROPHYRE
LAPIS LAZULI
LITHOSPHERE
LUXULYANITE
LYDIAN STONE
MASTER-JOINT
MELANTERITE
METEOROLITE
MINERALISER
MOLYBDENITE
MONCHIQUITE
MUSCHELKALK
NEPHELINITE
NICKEL-BLOOM
NICKEL-OCHRE
OCTAHEDRITE
OLIVINE-ROCK
OPHICALCITE

PASSAGE BEDS
PENCIL-STONE
PENTLANDITE
PERISTERITE
PETROGRAPHY
PHILLIPSITE
PITCHBLENDE
PLAGIOCLASE
PLEISTOCENE
PLEOCHROISM
POLYCHROISM
PORTLANDIAN
PRE-CAMBRIAN
PROTEROZOIC
PSEUDOMORPH
PUMICE-STONE
RAISED BEACH
REPLACEMENT
ROCK-CRYSTAL
ROTTENSTONE
SAMIAN EARTH
SAPROPELITE
SARCOPHAGUS
SARSEN-STONE
SCHISTOSITY
SILLIMANITE
SINGING SAND
SLICKENSIDE
SMOKY QUARTZ
SPATHIC IRON
SPESSARTITE
STRIKE-FAULT
SURTURBRAND
SWALLOW-HOLE
THRUST-PLANE
TITANIC IRON
TORRIDONIAN
TROUGH-FAULT
TURKEY STONE
TURTLE-STONE
VESUVIANITE
WEEPING-ROCK
YTTRO-CERITE

12

AEOLIAN ROCKS
ARFVEDSONITE
BABINGTONITE
BOLOGNA STONE
CENTROSPHERE

CHALCOPYRITE
CHROME-SPINEL
COAL MEASURES
COBALT GLANCE
COLOGNE-EARTH
CONFIRMATION
CONNATE WATER
COPPER-GLANCE
COPPER-NICKEL
CROSS-BEDDING
DIASTROPHISM
DOGTOOTH-SPAR
ERRATIC BLOCK
FALSE BEDDING
FELDSPATHOID
FOREST MARBLE
FULLER'S EARTH
GEOCHEMISTRY
GRANODIORITE
GROSSULARITE
HEMIMORPHITE
HYDROPHOLITE
HYDROZINCITE
INTERBEDDING
LATERISATION
LEMNIAN EARTH
LEPIDOMELANE
METAMORPHISM
METEORIC IRON
MINERAL PITCH
MONTICELLITE
MORPHOGRAPHY
MOUNTAIN BLUE
MOUNTAIN-SOAP
NAILHEAD-SPAR
PALINGENESIS
PARAMORPHISM
PERCHED BLOCK
PETRIFACTION
PHOTO-GEOLOGY
PLASTER-STONE
PORCELLANITE
POST-TERTIARY
PUDDING-STONE
PURBECK STONE
PYRARGARGITE
PYROMORPHITE
PYROPHYLLITE
QUARTZ-SCHIST
SCHILLER-SPAR
SILVER-GLANCE
SKUTTERUDITE

SOLIFLUCTION
SPEAR PYRITES
SPECULAR IRON
SPEISS-COBALT
STRATIGRAPHY
STRONTIANITE
SUPERSTRATUM
SYNADELPHITE
SYNCLINORIUM
SYNTAGMATITE
TETRAHEDRITE
UNCONFORMITY
UNDERSTRATUM
VOLCANIC ROCK
VOLCANIC SAND
WHITE PYRITES
WOLLASTONITE

13

AGGLOMERATION
ANTHOPHYLLITE
ARSENO-PYRITES
ASTHENOSPHERE
AUTOCHTHONISM
BARBADOS EARTH
BONE-TURQUOISE
CHLORARGYRITY
CHLORITIC MARL
CLAY-IRONSTONE
CLINOPINACOID
CORALLINE CRAG
DISCONFORMITY
EARTH-MOVEMENT
EMERALD-COPPER
EPEIROGENESIS
GEOCHRONOLOGY
GROUND MORAINE
HORSEFLESH ORE
HYPERSTHENITE
ISODIMORPHISM
LEUCITOHEDRON
LIGHTNING-TUBE
MACROPINAKOID
MANGANESE SPAR
MILLSTONE-GRIT
NATURAL MAGNET
ORTHOPINAKOID
PEACOCK-COPPER
PETRIFICATION
PNEUMATOLYSIS

SCIENCE – GEOLOGY

POLYSYNTHESIS
PORCELAIN-CLAY
PORTLAND STONE
PURBECK MARBLE
RHODOCHROSITE
SARACEN'S-STONE
SCALENOHEDRON
SEDENTARY SOIL
SEDIMENTATION
SLATY CLEAVAGE
SPECULAR STONE
URALITISATION
VOLCANIC GLASS

14

BRACHYDIAGONAL
BRACHYPINAKOID
CHLORITE-SCHIST
CONFORMABILITY
CONGLOMERATION

CURRENT-BEDDING
DERBYSHIRE SPAR
GRAPHIC GRANITE
GREYWACKE-SLATE
KNOTENSCHIEFER
KUPFERSCHIEFER
MICROPEGMATITE
MOUNTAIN-MARROW
MYLONITISATION
OTTRELITE-SLATE
PALAGONITE-TUFF
POLYSYNTHETISM
PSEUDOSYMMETRY
QUARTZ-PORPHYRY
RHOMBENPORPHYR
SAPPHIRE-QUARTZ
SERICITISATION
SERPENTINE-ROCK
SHELL-LIMESTONE
SPHAEROCRYSTAL
STRATIFICATION
TERRA SIGILLATA
URALIAN EMERALD

YTTRO-COLOMBITE
YTTRO-TANTALITE

15

CORALLINE OOLITE
GOOSEBERRY-STONE
HEXAGONAL SYSTEM
INFUSORIAL EARTH
LANDSCAPE-MARBLE
MAGNETIC PYRITES
MOUNTAIN-LEATHER
NEPHELINE-BASALT
OCCIDENTAL TOPAZ
OLD RED SANDSTONE
PILLOW STRUCTURE
RHOMBENPORPHYRY
SCHILLERISATION
SEDIMENTARY ROCK
SPHAEROSIDERITE
STILPNOSIDERITE

SCIENCE – MATHEMATICS – MATHS TERMS

3

ARC
COS
COT
LOG
MAT
NET
RAY
SET
SUM
TAN
TOT

4

APEX
AREA

AXIS
BASE
BIAS
CONE
COSH
COTH
CUBE
CUSP
DASH
DUAD
DUAL
DYAD
EDGE
FACE
JOIN
LINE
LINK
LOCI
LUNE

MEAN
MODE
NODE
OVAL
PLUS
POLE
QUAD
RANK
RATE
RING
ROOT
SIDE
SIGN
SINE
SINH
STAR
SURD
TANH
TERM

TERN
TORE
TREE
TRIG
TURN
UNIT

5

ACUTE
ANGLE
ARRAY
AXIOM
AXOID
CHORD
CONIC
COSEC
COTAN
COUNT

CURVE
DECAD
DEPTH
DIGIT
FIELD
FOCUS
GRADE
GRAPH
GROUP
HELIX
HEXAD
IDEAL
IMAGE
INDEX
JOINT
LEMMA
LEVEL
LIMIT
LOCUS

LOGIC
MATHS
MINUS
NAPPE
OCTAD
ORDER
OVOID
PLANE
POINT
POWER
PRIME
PRISM
PROOF
RADII
RADIX
RANGE
RATIO
RHOMB
RHUMB

RIDER
SCALE
SHAPE
SHEAR
SLANT
SLOPE
SOLID
SPIRE
TABLE
TALLY
TORUS
TOTAL
TRIAD
UNITY
VALUE
WHOLE
WIDTH

6

ABACUS
ADDEND
AMOUNT
BINARY
CENTRE
CIPHER
CIRCLE
COLUMN
CONICS
CONOID
CONVEX
CORNER
COSECH
COSINE
CRUTCH
CUBAGE
CUBING
CUBOID
DEGREE
DENARY
DOMAIN
ENNEAD
FACTOR
FAMILY
FIGURE
FLUENT
FOREST
GNOMON
GUNTER
HEIGHT
HEPTAD
LENGTH
LITUUS
LOGLOG
LUNULA
LUNULE
MATRIX
MEDIAN
MOMENT
NORMAL
NUMBER
OBLONG
OBTUSE
OCTANT
ORIGIN
PENCIL
PENTAD
PERIOD
PORISM
RADIAL

RADIAN
RADIUS
SECANT
SECTOR
SENARY
SERIES
SPHERE
SPIRAL
SPIRIC
SQUARE
SUBSET
SUFFIX
SYMBOL
TENSOR
TETRAD
TRIGON
UNGULA
VECTOR
VERTEX
VOLUME
VOLUTE

7

ALGEBRA
ALIQUOT
ANALOGY
ANNULUS
ANTILOG
APOTHEM
ASTROID
AVERAGE
BALANCE
BREADTH
CISSOID
CONCAVE
CONTACT
CYCLOID
DECAGON
DECIMAL
DENSITY
DIAGRAM
DIAMOND
DIVISOR
ELLIPSE
EVOLUTE
EXAMPLE
FLEXURE
FLUXION
FORMULA
FRUSTUM

HEXAGON
INDICES
INTEGER
INVERSE
ISOTYPE
LATTICE
LIMAÇON
LINKAGE
LOZENGE
MAPPING
MAXIMUM
METRICS
MINIMUM
MINUEND
MODULUS
NETWORK
NONAGON
NUMERAL
OBLIQUE
OCTAGON
ODDNESS
OPERAND
PER CENT
POLYGON
POTENCY
PROBLEM
PRODUCT
PYRAMID
QUANTIC
QUARTIC
RADIANT
RADICAL
RHOMBUS
ROSETTE
SAGITTA
SCALING
SECTION
SEGMENT
SIMPLEX
SOROBAN
SPINODE
SQUARER
SUMMAND
SUMMING
SURFACE
TABLING
TANGENT
TANGRAM
TERNARY
THEOREM
TOTIENT
VARIATE

VERSINE

8

ABSCISSA
ADDITION
ALGORISM
ALIQUANT
ANALYSIS
ARGUMENT
BAR-GRAPH
BINOMIAL
BISECTOR
BRACKETS
CALCULUS
CAPACITY
CARDIOID
CATENARY
CATHETUS
CENTRODE
CENTROID
CONCHOID
CONSTANT
CONVERSE
COSECANT
COUNTING
CRESCENT
CUBATURE
CUBE ROOT
CYLINDER
DIAGONAL
DIAMETER
DIANODAL
DIHEDRON
DILATION
DISTANCE
DIVIDEND
DIVISION
DYNAMICS
EMPTY SET
ENNEAGON
ENVELOPE
EPICYCLE
EQUALITY
EQUATION
EVENNESS
EXPONENT
EXTERIOR
FINITUDE
FLUXIONS
FRACTION

FUNCTION
GENERANT
GEOMETRY
GRADIENT
GRAPHICS
HEPTAGON
HEXAGRAM
HOMALOID
INCENTRE
INFINITY
INTEGRAL
INTERIOR
INVOLUTE
LOGISTIC
MANIFOLD
MANTISSA
MATRICES
MENISCUS
MERIDIAN
MONOMIAL
MULTIPLE
NEGATIVE
NOMOGRAM
NOTATION
OPERATOR
OPPOSITE
ORDINATE
PARABOLA
PARALLEL
PENTAGON
PIE CHART
PIE GRAPH
PLUS SIGN
POINT-SET
POSITION
POSITIVE
PRACTICE
PRISMOID
QUADRANT
QUADRATE
QUANTITY
QUARTILE
QUOTIENT
RATIONAL
RELATION
REPETEND
RHOMBOID
ROTATION
ROULETTE
SEMI-AXIS
SEMI-LUNE
SEMI-RING

SENTENCE
SEQUENCE
SINUSOID
SOLUTION
SPHERICS
SPHEROID
SPHERULE
SQUARING
SUBTENSE
SUM TOTAL
SYMMETRY
TANGENCY
TETRAGON
TOPOLOGY
TOTATIVE
TRACTRIX
TRIANGLE
TROCHOID
VARIABLE
VARIANCE
VERTICAL
VINCULUM

9

AGGREGATE
ALGORITHM
ALIGNMENT
AMPLITUDE
ASYMPTOTE
BIPYRAMID
BISECTION
CHAIN-RULE
CHILIAGON
CONGRUITY
COROLLARY
COTANGENT
CURVATURE
DATUM-LINE
DEDUCTION
DIMENSION
DIRECTRIX
DODECAGON
ECCENTRIC
ELEVATION
ELLIPSOID
EVOLUTION
EXPANSION
FACTORIAL
FLOW CHART
HAVERSINE

HEMICYCLE
HISTOGRAM
HODOGRAPH
HYPERBOLA
INCIDENCE
INCREMENT
INTEGRAND
INTERCEPT
INTERFACE
INTERNODE
INTERSECT
INVARIANT
INVERSION
LIE GROUPS
LINEALITY
LINEARITY
LOGARITHM
LOXODROME
MAGIC CUBE
MAJOR AXIS
MINOR AXIS
MINUS SIGN
NOMOGRAPH
NUMBERING
NUMERATOR
PARAMETER
PENTAGRAM
PENTANGLE
PERIMETER
PERIMETRY
POSTULATE
PROJECTOR
QUADRATIC
QUOTITION
RABATMENT
RABATTING
RADIALITY
RECKONING
RECTANGLE
REDUCTION
RE-ENTRANT
REMAINDER
RESULTANT
SEMI-ANGLE
SET THEORY
SIGMATION
STATISTIC
STERADIAN
SUBNORMAL
SUMMATION
TETRAGRAM
TRAPEZIUM

TRAPEZOID
TRINOMIAL
TRISECTOR

10

ACUTE ANGLE
ALINEATION
ALLIGATION
ANCHOR-RING
ANTECEDENT
ARITHMETIC
CALCULATOR
COMPLEMENT
CO-ORDINATE
CROSS-RATIO
DECAHEDRON
DERIVATIVE
DIACAUSTIC
DIFFERENCE
DISPERSION
EIGENVALUE
EPICYCLOID
EQUALS SIGN
EQUIVALENT
EVALUATION
EXPRESSION
GENERATRIX
GOLDEN MEAN
GRAND TOTAL
HEMIHEDRON
HEMISPHERE
HENDECAGON
HEXAHEDRON
HOLOHEDRON
HORIZONTAL
HYPOTENUSE
HYPOTHESIS
INEQUALITY
INEQUATION
INVOLUTION
IRRATIONAL
LEMNISCATE
LIE ALGEBRA
MULTIPLIER
NUMERATION
OCTAHEDRON
PARABOLOID
PERCENTAGE
PERCENTILE
PERVERSION

PLANIMETRY
POLYHEDRON
POLYNOMIAL
PROJECTION
PROPORTION
QUADRANGLE
QUADRATRIX
QUADRATURE
QUADRICONE
QUATERNARY
QUATERNION
QUATERNITY
REAL NUMBER
RECIPROCAL
RE-ENTRANCE
RE-ENTRANCY
REGULARITY
REGRESSION
REVOLUTION
RIGHT ANGLE
SEMI-CIRCLE
SEXAGENARY
SIMILARITY
SQUARE ROOT
STATISTICS
SUBDIVIDER
SUBTANGENT
SUBTRAHEND
SUPPLEMENT
TABULATION
TRILATERAL
TRISECTION
TRISECTRIX
TRUNCATION
TRUTH TABLE

11

AGGREGATION
ASSES' BRIDGE
BINARY SCALE
BIQUADRATIC
CALCULATION
COEFFICIENT
COMBINATION
COMMON CHORD
COMPUTATION
CONCURRENCE
CONVERGENCE
CONVERGENCY
CONVOLUTION

DENOMINATOR
DETERMINANT
DEVELOPMENT
ELLIPTICITY
ENNEAHEDRON
ENUMERATION
EPITROCHOID
FACTORISING
GREAT CIRCLE
HARMONOGRAM
HELICOGRAPH
HOLOHEDRISM
HYPERBOLOID
HYPOCYCLOID
ICOSAHEDRON
INDEX NUMBER
INDIVISIBLE
INFINITE SET
INTEGRATION
INTERRADIUS
KLEIN BOTTLE
LATUS RECTUM
MAGIC CIRCLE
MAGIC SPHERE
MAGIC SQUARE
MATHEMATICS
MENSURATION
METRICATION
MÖBIUS STRIP
NAPIER'S RODS
OBTUSE ANGLE
ORTHOCENTRE
PERMUTATION
POINT-SOURCE
PRIME NUMBER
PROBABILITY
PROGRESSION
PROPOSITION
QUADRIC CONE
QUATERNIONS
RADICAL AXIS
RECIPROCANT
REFLEX ANGLE
RULE OF THREE
SEMI-ELLIPSE
SEXAGESIAMAL
SMALL CIRCLE
SUBDIVISION
SUBMULTIPLE
SUBTRACTION
SUPERFICIES
TAUTOCHRONE

TETRAHEDRON
TRANSLATION
TRANSVERSAL
VENN DIAGRAM
WHOLE NUMBER

12

ACCELERATION
ANTIPARALLEL
CENTRAL CONIC
CHILIAHEDRON
CIRCUMCENTRE
CONIC SECTION
DECIMAL PLACE
DECIMAL POINT
DIFFERENTIAL
DISCRIMINANT
DIVISIBILITY
DIVISION SIGN
DODECAHEDRON
ECCENTRICITY
EQUIDISTANCE
EQUIMULTIPLE
GEODESIC LINE
GUNTER'S SCALE
HARMONIC MEAN
HEMISPHEROID
HYPOTROCHOID
INTERSECTION
INVERSE RATIO
ISOPERIMETER
ISOPERIMETRY
LONG-DIVISION
MISRECKONING
MULTIPLICAND
NAPIER'S BONES
NEGATIVE SIGN
NUMBER SYSTEM
NUMBER THEORY
NUMERABILITY
OPEN SENTENCE
POSITIVE SIGN
PROPORTIONAL
PYRITOHEDRON
QUADRINOMIAL
RADIUS VECTOR
RANDOM NUMBER
REGULAR SOLID
RELATIONSHIP
RHOMBOHEDRON

SEMI-CYLINDER
SEMI-DIAMETER
SLIDING SCALE
STRAIGHT LINE
SUBSTITUTION
TESSELLATION
TOTALISATION
TRANSVERSION
TRIGONOMETRY
TURNING-POINT
UNITY ELEMENT
UNIVERSAL SET

13

ANGULAR MOTION
ANTILOGARITHM
APPROXIMATION
CIRCUMFERENCE
COMMON MEASURE
COMPLEX NUMBER
COMPOUND RATIO
CONCENTRICITY
CONFIGURATION
CONNUMERATION
ELLIPTIC SPACE
EXTERIOR ANGLE
FACTORISATION
GEOMETRIC MEAN
GOBANG NUMERAL
GOLDEN SECTION
HARMONIC RANGE
IMAGINARY LINE
INFINITESIMAL
INTERIOR ANGLE
INTERPOLATION
MAGIC CYLINDER
MULTIPLICATOR
NATURAL NUMBER
NEGATIVE ANGLE
NEIGHBOURHOOD
ORDINAL NUMBER
PARALLEL LINES
PARALLELOGRAM
PERFECT NUMBER
PERPENDICULAR
PLANE GEOMETRY
PLATONIC SOLID
POLAR EQUATION
POLYNOMIALISM
POSITIVE ANGLE

SCIENCE — MATHEMATICS — MATHS TERMS

PROBABLE ERROR
QUADRATIC MEAN
QUADRILATERAL
QUADRISECTION
RIEMAN SURFACE
SEMI-PERIMETER
SHORT-DIVISION
SOLID GEOMETRY
STANDARD ERROR
STRAIGHT ANGLE
SUPERADDITION
TANGENTIALITY
TAUTOCHRONISM
TRAPEZOHEDRON
TRIANGULARITY
TRIANGULATION
VERTICAL ANGLE

14

AFFINE GEOMETRY
ALIGNMENT CHART
ARABIC NUMERALS
ARITHMETIC MEAN
BOOLEAN ALGEBRA
CARDINAL NUMBER
CHARACTERISTIC

COMMON FRACTION
COMMON MULTIPLE
CURVILINEARITY
DECIMALISATION
DIFFERENTIATOR
DIRECTOR CIRCLE
DUPLICATE RATIO
EQUIANGULARITY
HARMONIC PENCIL
HORIZONTAL LINE
IMAGINARY POINT
INDIVISIBILITY
INNUMERABILITY
LOXODROMIC LINE
MISCALCULATION
MISCOMPUTATION
MULTIPLICATION
OBLATE SPHEROID
PARALLELEPIPED
PERCENTILE RANK
PROPER FRACTION
RADIAL SYMMETRY
RATIONAL NUMBER
RECTILINEARITY
RIEMAN INTEGRAL
SIMPLIFICATION
TRANSFORMATION
TRANSVERSALITY
TRISOCTAHEDRON

VULGAR FRACTION

15

BINARY OPERATION
BINOMIAL THEOREM
BIQUADRATIC ROOT
BRACHISTOCHRONE
CIRCUMSCRIPTION
DECIMAL FRACTION
DECIMAL NOTATION
DIFFERENTIATION
FIBONACCI SERIES
FIGURATE NUMBERS
FIRST PRINCIPLES
GOLDEN RECTANGLE
IDENTITY ELEMENT
LOGARITHMIC SIGN
LOGICAL ELEMENTS
LOXODROMIC CURVE
POLAR CO-ORDINATE
PROLATE SPHEROID
PURE MATHEMATICS
RIEMANNIAN SPACE
SEMI-LATUS RECTUM
TRIANGULAR PRISM
UNKNOWN QUANTITY

SCIENCE — MATHEMATICS — NUMBERS & FRACTIONS

3

NIL
ONE
SIX
TEN
TWO

4

FIVE
FOUR

HALF
NINE
ZERO

5

DOZEN
EIGHT
FIFTH
FIFTY
FORTY
GROSS

NINTH
SCORE
SEVEN
SIXTH
SIXTY
TENTH
THIRD
THREE

6

CIPHER

EIGHTH
EIGHTY
ELEVEN
FOURTH
GOOGOL
MYRIAD
NINETY
NOUGHT
THIRTY
TWELVE
TWENTY

7

BILLION
CHILIAD
FIFTEEN
HUNDRED
MILLION
NOTHING
QUARTER
SEVENTH
SEVENTY
SIXTEEN
TWELFTH

UMPTEEN

8

EIGHTEEN
ELEVENTH
FIFTIETH
FIFTY-ONE
FIFTY-SIX
FIFTY-TWO
FORTIETH
FORTY-ONE

FORTY-SIX
FORTY-TWO
FOURTEEN
MILLIARD
NINETEEN
SIXTIETH
SIXTY-ONE
SIXTY-SIX
SIXTY-TWO
THIRTEEN
THOUSAND
TRILLION

9

BILLIONTH
DECILLION
EIGHTIETH
EIGHTY-ONE
EIGHTY-SIX
EIGHTY-TWO
FIFTEENTH
FIFTY-FIVE
FIFTY-FOUR
FIFTY-NINE
FORTY-FIVE
FORTY-FOUR
FORTY-NINE
FOURSCORE
HALF-DOZEN
HUNDREDTH
MILLIONTH
NINETIETH
NINETY-ONE
NINETY-SIX
NINETY-TWO
NONILLION
OCTILLION
SEVENTEEN
SIXTEENTH
SIXTY-FIVE
SIXTY-FOUR
SIXTY-NINE
THIRTIETH
THIRTY-ONE
THIRTY-SIX
THIRTY-TWO

TWENTIETH
TWENTY-ONE
TWENTY-SIX
TWENTY-TWO
TWO THIRDS

10

CENTILLION
EIGHTEENTH
EIGHTY-FIVE
EIGHTY-FOUR
EIGHTY-NINE
FIFTY-EIGHT
FIFTY-SEVEN
FIFTY-THREE
FORTY-EIGHT
FORTY-SEVEN
FORTY-THREE
FOURTEENTH
NINETEENTH
NINETY-FIVE
NINETY-FOUR
NINETY-NINE
ONE HUNDRED
SEPTILLION
SEVENTIETH
SEVENTY-ONE
SEVENTY-SIX
SEVENTY-TWO
SEXTILLION
SIX HUNDRED
SIXTY-EIGHT
SIXTY-SEVEN
SIXTY-THREE
THIRTEENTH
THIRTY-FIVE
THIRTY-FOUR
THIRTY-NINE
THOUSANDTH
THREESCORE
TRILLIONTH
TWENTY-FIVE
TWENTY-FOUR
TWENTY-NINE
TWO HUNDRED

11

BAKER'S DOZEN
DEVIL'S DOZEN
EIGHTY-EIGHT
EIGHTY-SEVEN
EIGHTY-THREE
FIVE HUNDRED
FOUR HUNDRED
LONG HUNDRED
NINE HUNDRED
NINETY-EIGHT
NINETY-SEVEN
NINETY-THREE
QUADRILLION
QUINTILLION
SEVENTEENTH
SEVENTY-FIVE
SEVENTY-FOUR
SEVENTY-NINE
TEN THOUSAND
THIRTY-EIGHT
THIRTY-SEVEN
THIRTY-THREE
TWENTY-EIGHT
TWENTY-SEVEN
TWENTY-THREE

12

EIGHT HUNDRED
SEVEN HUNDRED
SEVENTY-EIGHT
SEVENTY-SEVEN
SEVENTY-THREE
THREE HUNDRED

13

THREE QUARTERS

15

HUNDRED THOUSAND

SCIENCE – METEOROLOGY

3

AIR
COL
DEW
EYE
FOG
HOT
ICE
LOW
SKY
SUN

4

BANK
BISE
BLOW
BORA
BORE
CALM
CELL
COLD
CONE
DAMP
FALL
FLAW
FÖHN
FRET
GALE
GUST
HAAR
HAIL
HAZE
HEAT
HIGH
HOAR
IRIS
LULL
MELT
MIST
PELT
PUFF
PUNA
RAIN
RIME
ROKE
SCAT
SCUD
SMOG
SNAP

SNOW
SPAT
SPIT
THAW
TIDE
VANE
WIND

5

BLAST
BLORE
BRUME
BURAN
CHILI
CHILL
CLOUD
DEVIL
DRIFT
EAGRE
ETHER
EURUS
FLOOD
FRONT
FROST
LAPSE
NOSER
NOTUS
QUAKE
RAINS
SEISM
SLANT
SLEET
SLUSH
SONDE
SPATE
SPOUT
STONE
STORM
VIRGA
ZONDA

6

AURORA
AUSTER
BAGUIO
BOREAS
BREATH
BREEZE

BUSTER
CIRRUS
DELUGE
DEW-BOW
DOCTOR
FLURRY
FOG-BOW
FOG-DOG
FREEZE
HABOOB
ICICLE
ISOBAR
ISOHEL
LEVANT
MAY-DEW
METEOR
MIZZLE
NIMBUS
PELTER
SAMIEL
SEA-FOG
SEICHE
SEREIN
SHOWER
SIMOOM
SOLANO
SQUALL
SUNBOW
TEBBAD
TRADES
TREMOR
TROUGH
VORTEX
WELKIN
ZEPHYR

7

AQUILON
AUREOLE
BACKING
BACKSET
BLUSTER
BROILER
CAT'S-PAW
CHINOOK
CLIMATE
CUMULUS
CYCLONE
DEW-DROP
DEW-FALL

DOG-VANE
DRAUGHT
DRIZZLE
DROUGHT
FOG-BANK
GREGALE
ICINESS
ISOGRAM
ISOHYET
KHAMSIN
MELTING
MISTRAL
MONSOON
MOONBOW
NORTHER
PAMPERO
PELTING
RAINBOW
RED SNOW
ROASTER
SCUDDER
SEA-FRET
SEA-HAAR
SEA-MIST
SEA-TURN
SEA-WIND
SHAITAN
SIROCCO
SIZZLER
SNIFTER
SNORTER
SOUTHER
SPATTER
STRATUS
SUMATRA
TEMPEST
THAWING
THERMAL
THUNDER
TIDE-RIP
TORNADO
TSUNAMI
TYPHOON
VEERING
WEATHER

8

ABLATION
AEROLOGY
AERONOMY

ARGESTES
BLIZZARD
CLOUDLET
COLD SNAP
DEWPOINT
DOWNFALL
DOWNPOUR
EAST WIND
ELEMENTS
FIREBALL
FLOODING
FOG-SMOKE
FOREWIND
FREEZE-UP
FROSTING
GRADIENT
HEAD WIND
HEAT WAVE
HUMIDITY
ISOBRONT
ISOCHASM
ISOCHEIM
ISOCRYME
ISOPLETH
ISOTHERE
ISOTHERM
KUROSHIO
LANDWIND
LEVANTER
LIBECCIO
LIGHT AIR
MARIGRAM
MICROBAR
MILLIBAR
MOISTURE
NEAP TIDE
NUBECULA
RAINDROP
RAINFALL
SCORCHER
SCUDDING
SEAQUAKE
SEA-STORM
SEISMISM
SIDE-WIND
SNIFFLER
SNOW-COLD
SNOWFALL
SPLATTER
SUNBURST
SUNSHINE
VARIABLE

WATER-DOG
WHITE-OUT
WILDFIRE
WINDROSE
WOOL-PACK

9

ADVECTION
AEROGRAPH
AEROMANCY
AFTERGLOW
ANEMOGRAM
ANEMOLOGY
ANTHELION
ANTITRADE
BAROMETER
BAROMETRY
BAROSCOPE
BLOOD-RAIN
BOURASQUE
CLOUD-BANK
COLD FRONT
CROSS-WIND
DUST-DEVIL
DUST-STORM
EPICENTRE
FRESH GALE
GOAT'S-HAIR
HAILSTONE
HAIL-STORM
HARMATTAN
HOAR-FROST
HURRICANE
HYETOLOGY
HYGRODEIK
ISALLOBAR
ISOTHERAL
LAND-FLOOD
LAPSE RATE
LIGHTNING
LINE-STORM
MAELSTROM
MARIGRAPH
MELT-WATER
MESSENGER
NIGHT-TIDE
NOR'-EASTER
NORTH WIND
NOR'-WESTER
OCCLUSION

OMBROLOGY
PEA-SOUPER
PYROMETRY
RAIN-CLOUD
RAIN-GAUGE
RAINSTORM
RAIN-WATER
SAND-BLAST
SAND-DEVIL
SAND-SPOUT
SANDSTORM
SEA-BREEZE
SNOW-BREAK
SNOWDRIFT
SNOWFLAKE
SNOWSTORM
SOU'-WESTER
STORM-WIND
TEPHIGRAM
TIDAL WAVE
UP-DRAUGHT
WARM FRONT
WHIRLPOOL
WHIRLWIND
WHOLE GALE
WIND-CHART
WIND-GAUGE

10

AEROGRAPHY
ANEMOMETER
ANEMOMETRY
ATMOSPHERE
BLACK FROST
CAPE DOCTOR
CLOUDBURST
CLOUDINESS
CONVECTION
DEPRESSION
EARTHQUAKE
EXHALATION
FLOODWATER
FROST-SMOKE
HYETOGRAPH
HYETOMETER
HYGROGRAPH
HYGROMETER
HYGROMETRY
HYGROSCOPE
INCLEMENCY

INUNDATION
IONOSPHERE
ISOSEISMAL
ISOTHERMAL
LAND-BREEZE
LINE-SQUALL
MARES' TAILS
MICROSEISM
NIGHT-CLOUD
NUCLEATION
RADIO SONDE
RAIN-SHADOW
RIPSNORTER
SCOTCH MIST
SEISMOGRAM
SNOW-WREATH
SPRING TIDE
STORM-TRACK
STORM-WATER
STRONG GALE
SULTRINESS
THERMOGRAM
THUNDERING
TRADE WINDS
TRAMONTANA
TURBULENCE
VISIBILITY
WATER-FLOOD
WATERQUAKE
WATER-SMOKE
WATER-SPOUT
WEATHER-EYE
WEATHER-MAP
WINTRINESS
YELLOW SNOW

11

ANTICYCLONE
BANNER CLOUD
EARTH-TREMOR
GROUND FROST
GROUND SWELL
HUMECTATION
HYDROMETEOR
HYETOGRAPHY
LIGHT BREEZE
LOW PRESSURE
MACKEREL SKY
METEOROLOGY
NORTH-EASTER

NORTH-WESTER
PLUVIOMETER
PRECIPITATE
PSYCHOMETRY
QUARTER-WIND
SOUTH-EASTER
SOUTH-WESTER
STORM-CENTRE
TEMPERATURE
THERMOGRAPH
THERMOMETER
THERMOMETRY
THUNDERBOLT
THUNDER-CLAP
THUNDER-DART
THUNDER-PEAL
TOURBILLION
TROPOSPHERE
WEATHERCOCK
WEATHER-SIGN
WHITE SQUALL

12

CIRRO-CUMULUS
CIRRO-STRATUS
CONDENSATION
CUMULO-CIRRUS
CUMULO-NIMBUS
GENTLE BREEZE
HIGH PRESSURE
INDIAN SUMMER
JAPAN CURRENT
MICROCLIMATE
MODERATE GALE
PERIODIC WIND
RICHTER SCALE
STRATOSPHERE
STRONG BREEZE
THERMOGRAPHY
THUNDER-CLOUD
THUNDER-PLUMP
THUNDER-STORM
WEATHER-GLASS

13

BALL LIGHTNING
BEAUFORT SCALE
ELECTRIC STORM

SCIENCE – METEOROLOGY

FORK LIGHTNING
LAG OF THE TIDES
MAGNETIC STORM
OCCLUDED FRONT
PRECIPITATION
STRATO-CUMULUS
THUNDER-SHOWER
WEATHER REPORT
WEATHER-SYMBOL

14

AURORA BOREALIS
CHAIN LIGHTNING
HYGROSCOPICITY
MACKEREL-BREEZE
MODERATE BREEZE
NORTHERN LIGHTS
SHEET LIGHTNING
SOUTHERN LIGHTS
WEATHER-STATION

15

AURORA AUSTRALIS
CENTIGRADE SCALE
FAHRENHEIT SCALE
HYETOMETROGRAPH
SATURATION POINT
SUBSTRATOSPHERE
WEATHER FORECAST
WEATHER NOTATION

SCIENCE – PHYSICS

3

ARC
CAN
GAS
ION
KEY
LAW
PEC
RAY
SOL

4

ATOM
CELL
CHIP
COIL
CORE
FLUX
FUSE
GATE
GRID
HEAD
HEAT
HOLE
LEAD
LEAK
LENS

LOAD
MAKE
MASS
MUON
NODE
PILE
PION
POLE
RING
SPIN
TUBE
WAVE
WIRE
WORK
ZETA

5

ANION
ANODE
BOSON
CHARM
CREEP
CYCLE
DECAY
DIODE
EARTH
FIELD
FLUID

FOCUS
FORCE
GLASS
IMAGE
LASER
LEVER
LIGHT
MASER
MESON
MONAD
MOTOR
ORBIT
OUTER
PITCH
PLATE
POWER
PRISM
QUARK
RELAY
SHADE
SHIFT
SHORT
SOLID
SOUND
SPARK
SPEED
STAGE
SURGE
VALVE
X-RAYS

6

AIR-GAP
APOZEM
BARYON
BUS-BAR
CATION
CHARGE
COUPLE
CRATER
CUT-OFF
DIPOLE
DOPING
DUPLET
DYNAMO
ENERGY
FILTER
FUSION
HADRON
IMPACT
JACKET
LEPTON
LIQUID
MAGNET
MATTER
MIRROR
MODULE
MOMENT
MOTION
OPTICS

PEBBLE
PERIOD
PHONON
PHOTON
PICK-UP
PLASMA
POISON
PROTON
RECOIL
REFLEX
SHADOW
SHOWER
SPACER
STATIC
STROBE
SWITCH
TAPPER
TARGET
TOGGLE
TOROID
TORQUE
TRIODE
TRITON
VACUUM
VAPOUR
VOLUME
VORTEX
WEIGHT
WIRING

7

BALANCE
BATTERY
BLANKET
BREEDER
CATHODE
CAUSTIC
CHARGER
CIRCUIT
COHERER
CONDUIT
CONTACT
CRYOGEN
CURRENT
DENSITY
DIOPTER
DRY CELL
DYNAMIC
ELEMENT
ENTROPY
EXCITON
FALL-OUT
FERMION
FISSION
FULCRUM
GRATING
GRAVITY
HYPERON
IMPETUS

IMPULSE
INERTIA
ISOCHOR
ISOTONE
ISOTRON
LATENCY
LINKAGE
MACHINE
MODULUS
MU-MESON
MUONIUM
NETWORK
NEUTRAL
NEUTRON
NUCLEAR
NUCLEON
NUCLEUS
NUCLIDE
OHM'S LAW
OSMOSIS
PEDESIS
PENTODE
PHOTICS
PHYSICS
PI-MESON
POSITON
PRIMARY
QUANTUM
REACTOR
RED HEAT
RETICLE
SCATTER
SEGMENT
SETTING
SOLVENT
SORBENT
STATICS
SUBATOM
SUCTION
SURGING
TACHYON
TENSION
TETRODE
TORSION

8

ABSORBER
ACCEPTOR
AERATION
ANTINODE

ANTIPOLE
ARMATURE
BETA RAYS
BETATRON
BEVATRON
COHESION
CRYOGENY
CRYOSTAT
CRYOTRON
DETECTOR
DEUTERON
DILATION
DOUGHNUT
DRY STEAM
DYNAMICS
ELECTRIC
ELECTRON
EMISSION
EMULSOID
ENTHALPY
ENVELOPE
ERGOGRAM
EXCITANT
FILAMENT
FIXATION
FLIPFLOP
FLUIDICS
FLUIDITY
FRICTION
FUEL-CELL
GELATION
GRAVITON
HALF-LIFE
HARMONIC
IGNITRON
INDUCTOR
KINETICS
KLYSTRON
LEVERAGE
MAGNETON
MENISCUS
MESOTRON
MOBILITY
MODIFIER
MOLECULE
MOMENTUM
NEGATRON
NEUTRINO
OVERLOAD
PARALLAX
PARTICLE
PENDULUM

POLARITY
POROSITY
POSITRON
PRESSURE
REACTION
RED SHIFT
RESISTOR
RHEOTOME
SOLATION
SOLENOID
SOLIDITY
SONORITY
SPARK-GAP
SPECTRUM
SYMMETRY
TERMINAL
THERMION
TRACKING
TRIVALVE
VARACTOR
VELOCITY
VOLTAISM
WAVEBAND
WAVEFORM

9

ACOUSTICS
ADSORBENT
AEROMETRY
ALPHA RAYS
AMPHOLYTE
AMPLIFIER
ANTIMESON
APPARATUS
ATOMICITY
AVALANCHE
BAR-MAGNET
BOYLE'S LAW
CALANDRIA
CANAL-RAYS
CAPACITOR
CONDENSER
CONDUCTOR
CONTACTOR
COSMOTRON
CYCLOTRON
DECOHERER
DIFFUSION
DIOPTRICS
DISCHARGE

EIGEN-TONE
ELASTANCE
ELECTRODE
EXPANSION
EXPLOSION
FLOTATION
FREQUENCY
GAMMA RAYS
GENERATOR
IMPEDANCE
IMPLOSION
INCIDENCE
INDUCTION
INSULANCE
INSULATOR
INVENTORY
IRISATION
LASER BEAM
LEYDEN JAR
LIBRATION
LIQUIDITY
MAGNETICS
MAGNETISM
MAGNETRON
MAGNIFIER
MECHANICS
MICROCHIP
MODERATOR
MULTIPLET
NEUTRETTO
OBJECTIVE
OPTIC AXIS
PARAMETER
PERMEANCE
PHOTOCELL
POROSCOPY
POTENTIAL
RADIATION
RADIO WAVE
REACTANCE
REAL IMAGE
RECTIFIER
REFLEXION
REFRACTOR
RESONANCE
RESULTANT
RHEOTROPE
SEMIFLUID
SHOCK WAVE
SIDE-CHAIN
SOLAR CELL
SOUND-WAVE

SCIENCE – PHYSICS

SPARK-COIL
SUBLIMATE
SUBMICRON
SUPERHEAT
SWITCHING
TELESCOPY
THYRATRON
THYRISTOR
VIBRATION
VISCOSITY
WATER-LENS
WAVEFRONT
WAVEGUIDE
WAVESHAPE
WHITE HEAT

10

ABSORPTION
ACTIVATION
ADMITTANCE
ADSORPTION
AEOLOTROPY
AGONIC LINE
ALTERNATOR
ANTILEPTON
ANTIMATTER
ANTIPROTON
ARAEOMETRY
ATHERMANCY
ATMOSPHERE
ATOMIC PILE
BLACK LIGHT
CALORIFIER
CAVITATION
CHRONOTRON
COMMUTATOR
CONDUCTION
CONVECTION
CONVEX LENS
COSMIC RAYS
CRYOGENICS
DIELECTRIC
DILATATION
DISCHARGER
DISJUNCTOR
DISPERSION
DISPERSOID
DISSOLVENT
EARTH-PLATE
ELASTICITY

ELECTROMER
EMISSIVITY
EVAPORATOR
EXTINCTION
FLASH-POINT
FUSIBILITY
GEOPHYSICS
HYDRAULICS
HYDROMETRY
HYGROMETRY
HYSTERESIS
INDUCTANCE
INSULATION
INVARIANCE
IONISATION
IONOSPHERE
LATENT HEAT
MASS DEFECT
MASS NUMBER
METACENTRE
MODERATION
MODULATION
MULTIPLIER
MUONIC ATOM
NUCLEATION
NUCLEONICS
OMEGA-MESON
OSCILLATOR
OUTGASSING
OZONE LAYER
PERMEATION
PHOTOMETRY
PRECESSION
REFLECTION
REFRACTION
RELATIVITY
RELUCTANCE
RESISTANCE
REVOLUTION
SCATTERING
SKIN EFFECT
SPALLATION
STREAMLINE
SUBATOMICS
SUBTRACTOR
SUPERSONIC
SUPERSOUND
SUPPRESSOR
TAGGED ATOM
THERMISTOR
THERMOPILE
THIXOTROPY

TRAJECTORY
TRANSDUCER
TRANSISTOR
TRINISCOPE
TROCHOTRON
TROPOPAUSE
ULTRASOUND
UNDULATION
VACUUM-TUBE
VAPOROSITY
VISCOMETRY
WATER-POWER
WAVELENGTH
WAVE-MOTION
WHITE LIGHT
ZWITTERION

11

ACCELERATOR
ANTICATHODE
ANTINEUTRON
ASTIGMATISM
ATOMIC POWER
ATOMISATION
ATTENUATION
AUGER EFFECT
CALORIMETER
CALORIMETRY
CAPACITANCE
CAPILLARITY
CARNOT CYCLE
CATHODE RAYS
CHARLES'S LAW
COAXIAL PAIR
COEFFICIENT
COMPOSITION
COMPRESSION
CONCAVE LENS
CONDUCTANCE
CONGELATION
CONTRACTION
CRYOPHYSICS
DESALINATOR
DIACOUSTICS
DIATHERMACY
DIFFRACTION
DISSYMMETRY
ELECTRIC EYE
ELECTRICITY
ENTRAINMENT

EQUILIBRIUM
EVAPORATION
FAST BREEDER
FIBRE OPTICS
FIRING POINT
FLUCTUATION
FOCAL LENGTH
FUSING POINT
GRAVITATION
GROUND STATE
HYPERCHARGE
ILLIQUATION
INDUCTIVITY
ION-EXCHANGE
INTERRUPTER
IRIDESCENCE
IRIDISATION
IRRADIATION
LAMINAR FLOW
LECHER WIRES
LIQUESCENCE
LIQUESCENCY
LIVE CIRCUIT
LOADING COIL
LOW PRESSURE
MIRROR-IMAGE
MOTIVE POWER
NICOL'S PRISM
OBJECT-GLASS
OPEN CIRCUIT
OSCILLATION
OSCILLOGRAM
OZONOSPHERE
PEBBLE-STONE
PENETRATION
PLANAR DIODE
PLASMOLYSIS
POLAR FORCES
POLARIMETRY
POSITRONIUM
PRIMARY CELL
PRIMARY COIL
REFLECTANCE
REFLEX LIGHT
REFRIGERANT
REPLENISHER
RESISTIVITY
RING-WINDING
RÖNTGEN RAYS
SENSITIVITY
SILICON CHIP
SOLAR ENERGY

SOUND-SHADOW
SPECTRALITY
SPECTROGRAM
SPECTROLOGY
STEREOMETRY
STRANGENESS
SUBLIMATION
SUBSTITUENT
SUPERFUSION
SUPERHEATER
SWITCHBOARD
SYNCHROTRON
TEMPERATURE
THERMIONICS
THERMOLYSIS
TRANSDUCTOR
TRANSFORMER
TRIPLE POINT
TROPOSPHERE
ULTRASONICS
VENTURI TUBE
VISCOUS FLOW
VOLTAIC PILE

12

ABSOLUTE ZERO
ACCELERATION
ANTIPARTICLE
ASTROPHYSICS
ATOMIC ENERGY
ATOMIC NUMBER
ATOMIC THEORY
ATOMIC WEIGHT
AVOGADRO'S LAW
BARYON NUMBER
BETA PARTICLE
BOILING POINT
BURNING-GLASS
CALORESCENCE
CATAPHORESIS
CENTRE OF MASS
CHAIN REACTOR
CLOUD-CHAMBER
COACERVATION
COAXIAL CABLE
COMPENSATION
CONDUCTIVITY
COUNTER-FORCE
CROSS-SECTION
DESALINATION

DIAMAGNETISM
DISPLACEMENT
EBULLIOSCOPY
ELASTIC LIMIT
ELECTROLYSIS
ELECTROMOTOR
ELECTRON PAIR
ELECTRON TUBE
FARADISATION
FLUIDISATION
FLUORESCENCE
FREEZE-DRYING
GALVANOMETRY
GEOMAGNETISM
HIGH PRESSURE
HYDROSTATICS
INFILTRATION
INSOLUBILITY
INTERFERENCE
IONOPHORESIS
KALEIDOPHONE
LABELLED ATOM
LAWS OF MOTION
LOW-FREQUENCY
MAGNETIC FLUX
MARIOTTE'S LAW
MELTING POINT
MICROCIRCUIT
MICROPHYSICS
MOLECULARITY
NEGATIVE POLE
NON-CONDUCTOR
NUCLEAR POWER
NUCLEAR WASTE
OBJECT-FINDER
OPTICAL MASER
OSCILLOGRAPH
PERFECT FLUID
PERMITTIVITY
PHOTOFISSION
POLARISATION
POSITIVE POLE
POSITIVE RAYS
REACTIVATION
RÉAUMUR SCALE
RECALESCENCE
RING-ARMATURE
SELENIUM CELL
SHORT-CIRCUIT
SOLAR BATTERY
SPACE-LATTICE
SPECIFIC HEAT

SPECTROGRAPH
SPECTROMETRY
SPECTROSCOPE
SPECTROSCOPY
STANDING WAVE
STRATOSPHERE
STRIPPED ATOM
SUBSTITUTION
THERMO-COUPLE
TOGGLE-SWITCH
UNIFIED FIELD
UNIFIED SCALE
VAPORISATION
VIRTUAL IMAGE
VISCOSIMETRY
VORTEX THEORY
ZEEMAN EFFECT

13

ALPHA PARTICLE
APPLETON LAYER
AUGER ELECTRON
BUBBLE-CHAMBER
BURNING-MIRROR
CENTRAL FORCES
CHAIN REACTION
CRITICAL ANGLE
DIRECT CURRENT
DISCHARGE TUBE
DOPPLER EFFECT
EFFERVESCENCE
ELECTRIC FIELD
ELECTRIC MOTOR
ELECTROMAGNET
ELECTROMERISM
ELECTRON SHELL
ELECTROPHORUS
EVEN-ODD NUCLEI
FREEZING POINT
GAY-LUSSAC'S LAW
GYROMAGNETISM
HERTZIAN WAVES
HIGH-FREQUENCY
HYDRODYNAMICS
HYDROKINETICS
IMMERSION LENS
INCLINED PLANE
INDUCTION COIL
IONTOPHORESIS
KINETIC ENERGY

SCIENCE – PHYSICS

LAEVOROTATION
MAGNET FORMING
MAGNETIC FIELD
MAGNETISATION
MAGNETOSPHERE
MAGNIFICATION
MIRROR MACHINE
MUSHROOM CLOUD
NUCLEAR ENERGY
NUCLEAR FUSION
PARAMAGNETISM
PHASE-CONTRAST
PHOTO-ELECTRON
PHOTO-EMISSION
PHOTOPHORESIS
QUANTUM NUMBER
QUANTUM THEORY
RADIOACTIVITY
RECTIFICATION
REMOTE CONTROL
RESISTANCE-BOX
SCINTILLATION
SECONDARY CELL
SECONDARY COIL
SELF-INDUCTION
SEMICONDUCTOR
SIGMA PARTICLE
STALAGMOMETRY
SUPERFLUIDITY
TUMBLER-SWITCH
WAVE MECHANICS
YOUNG'S MODULUS
ZÖLLNER'S LINES

14

BREEDER REACTOR
BREMSSTRAHLUNG

CIRCUIT-BREAKER
CROSSBAR SWITCH
DEPOLARISATION
DISPERSED PHASE
EIGEN-FREQUENCY
ELECTROSTATICS
EMISSION THEORY
EVEN-EVEN NUCLEI
FERROMAGNETISM
HARMONIC MOTION
HEAVISIDE LAYER
HYDROMECHANICS
INDUCED CURRENT
INDUCTION MOTOR
LAMBDA PARTICLE
LYOPHILISATION
MAGNETIC BOTTLE
MAGNETIC CURVES
MICROCOMPONENT
MIRROR NUCLIDES
NEGATIVE PROTON
NUCLEAR FISSION
NUCLEAR PHYSICS
NUCLEAR REACTOR
OVERCORRECTION
PARALLEL MOTION
PIEZOMAGNETISM
PRIMARY BATTERY
PRINCIPAL FOCUS
PRINTED CIRCUIT
RESISTANCE-COIL
SELF-ABSORPTION
SELF-INDUCTANCE
SUPERCONDUCTOR
SUPERINDUCTION
SUPPRESSOR GRID
SURFACE TENSION
THERMIONIC TUBE
THERMODYNANICS
WREATH-FILAMENT

15

AXIS OF INCIDENCE
BOMB-CALORIMETER
BRACHISTOCHRONE
CENTRE OF GRAVITY
CENTRE OF INERTIA
COMPLEMENTARITY
COMPRESSIBILITY
DELAYED NEUTRONS
DEMAGNETISATION
ELECTRIC BATTERY
ELECTRIC CURRENT
ELECTRIFICATION
ELECTRODYNAMICS
ELECTROKINETICS
ELECTROPHORESIS
FERTILE MATERIAL
FISSION SPECTRUM
HORSE-SHOE MAGNET
INDIRECT CURRENT
MAGNETIC BATTERY
METASTABLE STATE
MOLECULAR WEIGHT
PARTIAL PRESSURE
PERMANENT MAGNET
PERPETUAL MOTION
PHASE-DIFFERENCE
PLANCK'S CONSTANT
POTENTIAL ENERGY
PYRO-ELECTRICITY
REFRACTIVE INDEX
RELATIVE DENSITY
SOLID-STATE LIGHT
SONOROUS FIGURES
SPECIFIC GRAVITY
STAGNATION POINT
STRANGE PARTICLE
THERMIONIC VALVE
ULTRAVIOLET RAYS
UPPER ATMOSPHERE
WATER-EQUIVALENT

SCIENCE – ZOOLOGY – ANIMAL ANATOMY

3

ARM
DAG
DIB
DUG
EAR
EYE
FIN
FUR
GUT
HAM
HAW
JAW
KIP
LEG
MAW
NEB
NIB
OAR
PAD
PAW
PEN
POD
RAY
ROE
SAC
TOE
WEB

4

ANUS
AXIS
BACK
BARB
BEAK
BILL
BODY
BONE
BURR
CERE
CLAW
COMB
COXA
CRAW
CROP
DOWN
FANG
FELL
FLAG

FOOT
FROG
GILL
GULA
GUTS
HAIR
HAND
HEAD
HEEL
HIDE
HOCK
HOOD
HOOF
HORN
HUMP
JOWL
KNEE
LIMB
LOIN
LOMA
LORE
LUNG
MAIL
MANE
MASK
MILT
NAIL
NECK
NOSE
PALM
PALP
PELT
POLE
RASP
READ
RING
RUFF
RUMP
SAIL
SCUT
SIDE
SKIN
SOUL
SPUR
SWIM
TAIL
TINE
TUSK
UMBO
VEIN
VELL
VENT

WALL
WING
WOOL
WORM

5

BEARD
BELLY
BERRY
BRAIN
BRUSH
BURSA
CHELA
CHEST
CNIDA
CONCH
COSTA
CREST
CROUP
CROWN
CRYPT
CTENA
ELBOW
FLANK
FLESH
FLEWS
FLUKE
GORGE
HEART
HINGE
JOINT
LIVER
LYTTA
MANUS
MEDIA
MOUTH
NACRE
NERVE
NODUS
NOTUM
OFFER
ORBIT
ORGAN
PEARL
PENNA
PINNA
PLATE
PLEON
PLUCK
PLUME

PODEX
PORTA
POUCH
PRONG
PYGAL
QUILL
RAMUS
REMEX
ROYAL
RUMEN
SCALE
SCAPE
SCOPA
SCRAG
SHAFT
SHANK
SHARD
SHELL
SNOUT
SOUND
SPECK
SPICA
SPINE
SPIRE
SPOUT
STING
TALON
TEWEL
TIBIA
TOOTH
TORUS
TRAIN
TRUNK
TUNIC
UDDER
UNCUS
URITE
VALVE
VELUM
VERMIS
WAIST

6

ANTLER
ANTILA
BALEEN
BARBET
BARREL
BONNET
BYSSUS

CALCAR
CARNAL
CLOACA
CLUTCH
COCOON
COTYLE
CROCHE
CRUMEN
CULMEN
DACTYL
DEWLAP
EXOPOD
FARDEL
FASCIA
FEELER
FINGER
FIN-RAY
FLEECE
FORFEX
GANOIN
GIRDLE
GULLET
HACKLE
HALLUX
HAUNCH
INK-BAG
INK-SAC
INSTEP
KIDNEY
LABIUM
LAMINA
LIGHTS
LORICA
MANTLE
MANUAL
MEDIAN
MEMBER
MENTUM
MEROME
MUFFLE
NIPPER
OMASUM
ONYCHA
OSCULE
OVISAC
PADDLE
PALAMA
PAUNCH
PAXWAX
PECTEN
PELAGE
PELVIS

PILEUM
PINCER
PINION
PODITE
PODIUM
POUNCE
PROLEG
RADIUS
RADULA
RECTUM
RIBBON
RICTUS
ROTULA
SADDLE
SCOLEX
SCUTUM
SEA-PEN
SEPIUM
SHEATH
SINGLE
SIPHON
SLOUGH
SPONGE
SQUAMA
SQUAME
STEMMA
STIFLE
STROMA
STROMB
STYLET
SYRINX
TARSUS
TEGMEN
TEGULA
TELSON
TERGUM
THORAX
THROAT
TIPPET
TOMIUM
TONGUE
TROPHI
UMBLES
UNGUIS
UNGULA
UROPOD
VENULE
VERMIS
VESSEL
VISCUS
WATTLE
WINKER

SCIENCE – ZOOLOGY – ANIMAL ANATOMY

7

ALFORJA
ANTENNA
BARBULE
BLADDER
BLUBBER
BOBTAIL
CALIPEE
CAMBREL
CAPSULE
CHALAZA
CLYPEUS
CORONET
COUNTER
CRUPPER
DART-SAC
DEW-CLAW
EGG-CASE
ELYTRUM
ENTERON
EYE-SPOT
FALCULA
FEATHER
FETLOCK
FIMBRIA
FLIPPER
FLOCCUS
FOOT-JAW
FORELEG
FOX-TAIL
FURCULA
GAMBREL
GIBLETS
GIZZARD
GLADIUS
HACKLES
HIND-LEG
HOG-MANE
INNARDS
INSIDES
ISOMERE
JAW-FOOT
LARMIER
LIMACEL
LOCULUS
MARABOU
MAXILLA
MUSK-BAG
MUSK-COD
MUSK-POD
MUSK-SAC

NERVURE
NOSTRIL
NOTAEUM
OCELLUS
OMENTUM
OSCULUM
PALLIUM
PASTERN
PEDICEL
PEDICLE
PEREION
PETIOLE
PHALANX
PINNULE
PLEOPOD
PLEURON
PLUMAGE
PLUMULA
PLUMULE
PRIMARY
PTERYLA
RECTRIX
RHABDUS
RHABDOM
ROSTRUM
SEA-BEAN
SEGMENT
SENSORY
SEPIOST
SPICULE
SPONGIN
SPURIAE
STERNUM
STOMACH
STRIGIL
TEAR-PIT
TECTRIX
TEREBRA
TERGITE
TERTIAL
TORULUS
TRIVIUM
TROCHUS
TROTTER
UNCINUS
UROMERE
UROSOME
VENTRAL
VISCERA
WEBBING
WEB-FOOT
WHISKER

WINGLET
WITHERS
YOLK-SAC
ZOONITE

8

ABOMASUM
AQUEDUCT
BACKBONE
BALANCER
BLOW-HOLE
BRANCHIA
BROW-TINE
CALIPASH
CARAPACE
COCKSPUR
DEER-HORN
EGG-PURSE
EGG-TOOTH
ENTRAILS
EPIPLOON
FALSE LEG
FISH-BONE
FISH-SKIN
FOLLICLE
FOREFOOT
FOX-BRUSH
GNATHITE
GRALLOCH
HALTERES
HIND-FOOT
HIND-WING
HONEY-BAG
INDUSIUM
LUNG-BOOK
MANDIBLE
MEMBRANE
MEROSOME
METAMERE
NARICORN
NOSE-LEAF
OIL-GLAND
OMMATEUM
ONYCHIUS
OVARIOLE
OVERHAIR
PATAGIUM
PECTORAL
PEDIPALP
PERISARC

PHALANGE
PLASTRON
PLUMELET
POPE'S EYE
PRONOTUM
PUPA-CASE
PUPARIUM
PYGIDIUM
RECEPTOR
RETINULA
ROSE-COMB
RUMP-POST
SCAPULAR
SCENT-BAG
SEA-PURSE
SEA-SHELL
SHOULDER
SIPHONET
SKELETON
SPICULUM
SPIRACLE
SQUAMULA
SQUAMULE
STAG-HORN
STANDARD
STERNITE
STROBILA
STROBILE
SUBCOSTA
SURROYAL
TENTACLE
TERTIARY
THROPPLE
TROCHLEA
TUBE-FOOT
TYMPANUM
UMBRELLA
UNDERFUR
URCEOLUS
UROSTEGE
VELARIUM
VERTEBRA
VIBRISSA
WATER-BAG
WING-CASE
WISH-BONE
XENOPHYA

9

ALLANTOIS

ANTENNULE
APPENDAGE
BAY-ANTLER
CASTOREUM
CHELICERA
CLAM-SHELL
CLITELLUM
COCK'S-COMB
COLUMELLA
CORBICULA
COTYLEDON
CRAMP-BONE
CREMASTER
CREBELLUM
DRUMSTICK
EPIDERMIS
EPIPHRAGM
EPIPHYSIS
EXOPODITE
FARDEL-BAG
FILOPLUME
GASTRAEUM
GILL COVER
GONOPHORE
HALF-SHELL
HYPOBLAST
INGLUVIES
INSERTION
KING'S-HOOD
LOVE-ARROW
MANUBRIUM
MANYPLIES
MARSUPIUM
MAXILLULA
MESOGLOEA
MICROPYLE
MILK-GLAND
MUSK-GLAND
MUSK-POUCH
PEDAL-BONE
PELVIC FIN
PEREIOPOD
PERIPLAST
PERIPROCT
PERISTOME
PERRADIUS
PINEAL EYE
PREPOLLEX
PRESCUTUM
PROBOSCIS
PROMUSCIS
PROPODEON

PROTHORAX
PTERYGIAL
PTERYGIUM
PULVILLUS
PYGOSTYLE
RENNET-BAG
RETICULUM
RING-CANAL
ROSTELLUM
SECTORIAL
SPUTELLUM
SEMIPLUME
SENSORIUM
SHANK-BONE
SILK-GLAND
SIPHUNCLE
SOFT-SHELL
SPINNERET
SPIRASTER
SQUAMELLA
SUBMENTUM
SWIMMERET
TENTORIUM
TUSK-SHELL
UMBILICUS
UNDERWING
UROPYGIUM
WATER-CELL
WHALEBONE
YOLK-STALK
ZYGANTRUM

10

AMBULACRUM
ARTHROMERE
BROOD-POUCH
BROW-ANTLER
CALCAR AVIS
CARNASSIAL
CHANK-SHELL
CHEEK-POUCH
CNIDOBLAST
COFFIN-BONE
CORNICULUM
CRAB-STONES
CUTTLE-BONE
EGG-CAPSULE
ENDOPODITE
FOURCHETTE

HYPOPHYSIS
MAXILLIPED
MESOTHORAX
METACARPUS
METATHORAX
NECTOCALYX
NEMATOCYST
NEPHRIDIUM
NETTLE-CELL
NIDAMENTUM
OLIVE-SHELL
OMMATIDIUM
OSMETERIUM
OVIPOSITOR
PARAGLOSSA
PARAPODIUM
PARENCHYMA
PEARL-SHELL
PIN-FEATHER
POISON-FANG
POWDER-DOWN
PREEN GLAND
PROGLOTTIS
PROSTOMIUM
PSALTERIUM
RAZOR-SHELL
RHABDOLITH
RHINOTHECA
RHODOPHANE
SCENT-GLAND
SCENT-ORGAN
SCENT-SCALE
SCLERODERM
SNAIL-SHELL
SPINNERULE
SPIRACULUM
SPLINT-BONE
STIFLE-BONE
STONE-CANAL
SUSPENSORY
TENDERLING
TENTACULUM
THREAD-CELL
TREY-ANTLER
TROCHANTER
UNDERBELLY
UROSTEGITE
VENTRAL FIN
VIBRACULUM
VITELLICLE
WING-SHEATH
ZYGOSPHENE

11

BASTARD-WING
BLOOD-VESSEL
COCKLESHELL
COPPLE-CROWN
CROWN-ANTLER
DISSEPIMENT
EPIPLASTRON
GASTRIC MILL
HYOPLASTRON
MADREPORITE
ODONTOPHORE
OMMATOPHORE
OYSTER-SHELL
PECTORAL FIN
PLOUGHSHARE
POISON-GLAND
POLLEN-BRUSH
PULMOBRANCH
RETINACULUM
RHYNCHOCOEL
SECOND JOINT
SEPIOSTARE
SILKWORM-GUT
SPERMATHECA
SPHAERIDIUM
STIFLE-JOINT
STRIDULATOR
SUBUMBRELLA
SWALLOW-TAIL
SWIM-BLADDER
TAIL-FEATHER
TURTLE-SHELL
WHITLEATHER
WISHING-BONE

12

CHITTERLINGS
ENTOPLASTRON
GREAT OMENTUM
HINDQUARTERS
HYPOPLASTRON
LIVE-FEATHERS
MARRIAGE-BONE
MERRYTHOUGHT
PEDICELLARIA
PERIOSTRACUM
POLLEN-BASKET
QUILL-FEATHER

SCIENCE — ZOOLOGY — ANIMAL ANATOMY

RHAMPHOTHECA
SADDLE-HACKLE
SCALLOP-SHELL
SUBOPERCULUM
SUSPENSORIUM
SWIMMING-BELL

ELECTRIC ORGAN
FLIGHT-FEATHER
MERMAID'S-PURSE
MOTHER-OF-PEARL
PTERYGOID BONE
SADDLE-FEATHER
SCLERODERMITE
SICKLE-FEATHER
TORTOISE-SHELL
VIBRACULARIUM
XIPHIPLASTRAL
XIPHIPLASTRON

14

CHONDROCRANIUM
ECLIPSE PLUMAGE
OSTRICH-FEATHER
XIPHIHUMERALIS

13

CEPHALOTHORAX
COSTAL NERVURE

15

CARPOMETACARPUS
INTERAMBULACRUM
TARSOMETATARSUS

SCIENCE — ZOOLOGY — ANIMAL DISEASES

3

GID
HAW
PIP
POX
ROT

4

CURB
GALL
GAPE
GOUT
ROUP
SANG
SCAB
WIND

5

BLOAT
BRAXY
FARCY
GRAPE
HOOVE

HUSKS
MANGE
SCOUR
SURRA
VIVES
WORMS

6

ANBURY
CANKER
COWPOX
GARGET
GREASE
HEAVES
NAGANA
PLAGUE
RABIES
SPAVIN
SPLINT
STURDY
SWEENY
THRUSH
WARBLE

7

ANTHRAX

DOURINE
EQUINIA
FOOTROT
FUR-BALL
HARD PAD
HOOFROT
MOONEYE
MURRAIN
OSSELET
OTOLITH
PÉBRINE
PINK-EYE
PURPLES
QUITTER
RAT-TAIL
ROARING
RUBBERS
SITFAST
TWITTER
YELLOWS

8

BLACKLEG
BURSITIS
CAPELLET
CRATCHES

CREPANCE
DUST-BALL
ENZOOTIC
FARCY-BUD
FILANDER
FOWL-PEST
GLANDERS
LIVER-ROT
OX-WARBLE
RED-WATER
RINGBONE
SCALY-LEG
SEEDY-TOE
SHEEP-POX
SHEEP-ROT
STAGGERS
SWAY-BACK
SWINE-POX
VACCINIA
WILDFIRE
WIND-GALL
WIRE-HEEL
WOOD-EVIL
WOOL-BALL

9

BOG-SPAVIN

DISTEMPER
FLUKE-WORM
FOUL-BROOD
MILK-FEVER
SAND-CRACK
SCRATCHES
SHEEP-SCAB
SIDE-BONES
SPEEDY CUT
STRANGLES
TICK FEVER

10

BLACKWATER
BLUE TONGUE
BONE-SPAVIN
BUMBLE-FOOT
FOWL-PLAGUE
HOG-CHOLERA
LIMBER-NECK
LIVER-FLUKE
LOUPING-ILL
MALLENDERS
MONILIASIS
MUSCARDINE
ORNITHOSIS

QUARTER-ILL
RINDERPEST
SALLENDERS
SPRING-HALT
SWINE-FEVER
TEXAS FEVER
TULARAENIA

QUARTER-EVIL
WOODY-TONGUE

LEPTOSPIROSIS
PARROT DISEASE
SALMON-DISEASE
TOXOPLASMOSIS

12

BLACK-QUARTER
CATTLE-PLAGUE
PEARL DISEASE
SPLENIC FEVER

14

EAST COAST FEVER
SLEEPY-STAGGERS
TRICHOMONIASIS

11

BLOOD-SPAVIN
BRUCELLOSIS
COCCIDIOSIS
GREASE-HEELS
MAD STAGGERS
MYXOMATOSIS
PSITTACOSIS

13

GRASS STAGGERS
GROUSE-DISEASE
HELMINTHIASIS

15

PLEURO-PNEUMONIA

SCIENCE — ZOOLOGY – ZOOLOGICAL CLASSIFICATION

3	**5**	MUREX	**6**	MERGUS	SCARUS
BOA	AGAMA	MUSCA	ANABAS	MEROPS	SUIDAE
MUS	ANURA	OLIVA	ANCONA	MILVUS	TAENIA
MYA	ARDEA	PERCA	AQUILA	MORPHO	TEREDO
	CANIS	PHOCA	ARANEA	MULLUS	TERMES
4	CEBUS	PICUS	CARANX	NEREIS	THECLA
	CIMEX	PINNA	CORVUS	NERITA	THRIPS
ANAS	CULEX	PULEX	CYNIPS	NESTOR	TIPULA
AVES	DORAS	RATEL	CYPRIS	NOCTUA	TRITON
CLIO	DORIS	SALMO	DAFILA	OSTREA	TRYGON
CRAX	EQUUS	SALPA	DIODON	PECORA	TUPAIA
EMYS	FELIS	SCOPS	DIPNOI	PECTEN	TURDUS
HOMO	FUSUS	SIREN	EPEIRA	PERDIX	VIPERA
JYNX	GADUS	SIREX	GALAGO	PERNIS	VOLUTA
NAIA	GOURA	SITTA	GEOMYS	PHASMA	VOLVOX
NAJA	HELIX	SOLEN	GLIRES	PHOLAS	VULPES
ORCA	HYRAX	SOREX	GOBIUS	PIERIS	
ORYX	INDRI	TALPA	IGUANA	PISCES	
PAVO	LARUS	TINEA	INDRIS	PODURA	**7**
PICA	LIMAX	TURBO	LABRUS	PROGNE	
RANA	MIDAS	URSUS	LEIPOA	PSYCHE	ACARIDA
RUSA	MIMUS	VENUS	LOLIGO	QUELEA	ACARINA
UNIO	MONAS	VESPA	LYCOSA	RALLUS	ALCIDAE
XEMA	MUGIL	VIREO	MANTIS	SARGUS	APTERYX
				SAURIA	AVICULA

349

SCIENCE — ZOOLOGY — ZOOLOGICAL CLASSIFICATION

BALANUS
BRYOZOA
BUBALIS
BUPHAGA
CALANUS
CANIDAE
CARABUS
CEBIDAE
CETACEA
COLOBUS
COLUBER
COLUMBA
COTINGA
DASYPUS
DIPTERA
ECHIDNA
EQUIDAE
EUGLENA
FELIDAE
FELINAE
FILARIA
FLUSTRA
GADIDAE
GLAUCUS
KALLIMA
LACERTA
LARIDAE
LIMNAEA
LIMULUS
LINGULA
LYCAENA
MESOZOA
METAZOA
MODIOLA
MOMOTUS
MONODON
MORMOPS
MURAENA
MURIDAE
MUSTELA
MYCETES
MYTILUS
NASALIS
OCTOPUS
ODONATA
OEDEMIA
ONISCUS
OPHIDIA
OPHIURA
OSCINES
PANDION
PAPILIO

PARAZOA
PATELLA
PEGASUS
POLYZOA
PROTEUS
PSOPHIA
PURPURA
PYRALIS
RANIDAE
RATITAE
REGULUS
SABELLA
SCIAENA
SCIURUS
SCOMBER
SCORPIO
SILURUS
SIRENIA
SOLPUGA
SPATULA
SQUILLA
STRIGES
STURNUS
STYLOPS
SYRPHUS
TABANUS
TANAGRA
TARSIUS
TEREBRA
TESTUDO
TORPEDO
TORTRIX
TOTANUS
TROCHUS
URODELA
VANESSA
VARANUS
VITRINA
VIVERRA
XENOPUS
XENURUS
XIPHIAS
ZIPHIUS
ZONURUS
ZYGAENA

8

AGAMIDAE
AMPHIBIA
ANABLEPS

ANGUILLA
ANOPLURA
ANTHOZOA
ANTILOPE
ARANEIDA
ARANIDAE
ARVICOLA
ATHERINA
AURICULA
CAECILIA
CAMPODEA
CENTETES
CHELONIA
CHORDATA
CORVIDAE
CORVINAE
COTURNIX
CRICETUS
CYPRINUS
DASYURUS
DECAPODA
DINORNIS
DYTISCUS
EDENTATA
EPHEMERA
EUTHERIA
GOBIIDAE
GORGONIA
HALIOTIS
HATTEIRA
HELIOZOA
HEXAPODA
HOLOSTEI
HYDROMYS
HYDROZOA
ISOPTERA
LABRIDAE
LIMACEAE
MASTODON
METABOLA
MODIOLUS
MOLLUSCA
MONACHUS
MUSCIDAE
NEMATODA
NERITINA
NOCTILIO
NOTORNIS
OCHOTONA
OCTOPODA
PASSERES
PERCIDAE

PETRONIA
PHAETHON
PHOCAENA
PHOCIDAE
PHYSALIA
PIERIDAE
PODARGUS
PODOGONA
PORIFERA
PRIMATES
PROTISTA
PROTOZOA
PUFFINUS
PYROSOMA
RALLIDAE
RANGIFER
RAPTORES
REPTILIA
RODENTIA
ROTIFERA
SATURNIA
SAURURAE
SAXICAVA
SCALARIA
SCARIDAE
SCOLOPAX
SCOLYTUS
SCOPELUS
SERRANUS
SPARIDAE
SPIRIFER
SPOROZOA
SQUAMATA
STRIGOPS
STROMBUS
STRUTHIO
SUCTORIA
SYMPHYLA
TALPIDAE
TANTALUS
TARSIPES
TENEBRIO
TINEIDAE
TUNICATA
TYLOPODA
UNGULATA
VESPIDAE
XANTHURA
ZALOPHUS
ZOANTHUS
ZOOPHAGA

9

ACIPENSER
ACTINOZOA
ALCYONIUM
AMETABOLA
AMPHIPODA
ANOPHELES
ARACHNIDA
BACULITES
BATRACHIA
BILHARZIA
BRACHYURA
BUPRESTIS
CARABIDAE
CARNIVORA
CERATODUS
CHAETODON
CHILOPODA
CICHLIDAE
CICINDELA
CIMICIDAE
COELOMATA
COREGONUS
CRUSTACEA
CULICIDAE
CYNIPIDAE
DENTALIUM
DIDELPHIA
DIDELPHYS
DIPODOMYS
DORIDIDAE
EPEIRIDAE
FRANCOLIN
GEOMYIDAE
HELICIDAE
HEMIPTERA
HERBIVORA
HERPESTES
HIPPARION
HOMINIDAE
HOMOPTERA
IGUANIDAE
INFUSORIA
LEUCISCUS
LOPHORTYX
LUMBRICUS
LYCOSIDAE
MECOPTERA
MELLIVORA
MEROPIDAE
MYCETOZOA

MYRIAPODA
NEOPILINA
NERITIDAE
NOCTUIDAE
NOTODONTA
NOTONECTA
NOTOTREMA
OCYDROMUS
OPHIURIDA
ORIOLIDAE
OSTRACION
OSTRACODA
PEDICULUS
PEDIPALPI
PENNATULA
PERIPATUS
PHASMIDAE
PLANORBIS
PORPHYRIO
PROCONSUL
PSITTACUS
PTEROPODA
PULICIDAE
PULMONATA
PYRALIDAE
RHIZOPODA
RHYNCHOTA
RICINULEI
SALIENTIA
SARCOPTES
SARCODINA
SATYRIDAE
SAUROPODA
SCIARIDAE
SCIURIDAE
SCORPAENA
SCYPHOZOA
SILURIDAE
SOLIFUGAE
SORICIDAE
SPATANGUS
SPHENODON
STEGOMYIA
STRINGOPS
STURNIDAE
SYLVIIDAE
SYLVIINAE
SYRPHIDAE
TABANIDAE
TARANTULA
TELEOSTEI
THYSANURA

TIPULIDAE
TOTANINAE
TRACHEATA
TRACHINUS
TREMATODA
TRILOBITA
TROCHIDAE
TROCHILUS
TUBULARIA
TUPAIIDAE
UNIONIDAE
UROCHORDA
VARANIDAE
VIPERIDAE
XENARTHRA
XIPHIIDAE
XIPHOSURA
XYLOPHAGA
ZAPODIDAE
ZIPHIIDAE
ZONURIDAE

10

AMBYLSTOMA
AMPHINEURA
ANGUILLULA
APTERYGOTA
ARTHROPODA
ARTICULATA
AVICULARIA
BATHYERGUS
CARANGIDAE
CECIDOMYIA
CHARADRIUS
CHIRONOMUS
CIRRIPEDIA
COLEOPTERA
COLLEMBOLA
COLUBRIDAE
COTINGIDAE
CTENOPHORA
CYPRINIDAE
DASYURIDAE
DENDROPHIS
DIDUNCULUS
DINOSAURIA
DIPLODOCUS
DISCOPHORA
DOLICHOTIS
DROSOPHILA

ETHEOSTOMA
EURYPTERUS
EUTHYNEURA
FLAGELLATA
FRATERCULA
GALVULIDAE
GASTROPODA
HEMICHORDA
HETEROCERA
HETEROPODA
INSESSORES
LACERTILIA
LEISHMANIA
LEMUROIDEA
LIMNAEIDAE
LINGULELLA
LITHISTIDA
LITHODOMUS
LYCAENIDAE
MALLOPHAGA
METATHERIA
MONAXONIDA
MURAENIDAE
MUSTELIDAE
MUSTELINAE
NEMATOIDEA
NEMERTINEA
NEUROPTERA
ONYCHOPORA
ORTHOPTERA
PEDICULATI
PELECYPODA
PELMATOZOA
PERIDINIUM
PERITRICHA
PHYLLOPODA
PHYLLOXERA
PINNIPEDIA
PLECOPTERA
PLUMULARIA
POLYCHAETA
POLYPTERUS
PSOCOPTERA
PTERYGOTUS
PYROPHORUS
QUADRUMANA
RADIOLARIA
RHIPIPTERA
RICKETTSIA
RUMINANTIA
SALMONIDAE
SARCOPHAGA

SAUROPSIDA
SCAPHOPODA
SCARABAEUS
SCHIZOPODA
SCIAENIDAE
SCITAMINAE
SCOLYTIDAE
SCOMBRESOX
SCOMBRIDAE
SCOPELIDAE
SERRANIDAE
SERRASALMO
SERTULARIA
SPHENISCUS
SPHINGIDAE
TANAGRIDAE
TARDIGRADA
TELEOSTOMI
TRACHEARIA
TRICHIURUS
TROGONIDAE
TURRITELLA
TYRANNIDAE
VERTEBRATA
VIREONIDAE
VIVERRIDAE
VIVERRINAE
VORTICELLA
ZOANTHARIA
ZOANTHIDAE
ZYGAENIDAE

11

AMPHISBAENA
APHANIPTERA
ATHERINIDAE
BALENOPTERA
BRACHIOPODA
BUPRESTIDAE
CENTROPOMUS
CHILOGNATHA
COTYLOPHORA
DASYPODIDAE
DELPHINIDAE
DIABRANCHIA
EPHEMERIDAE
GASTEROPODA
GEOMETRIDAE
GLOBIGERINA
GRYLLOTALPA

HESPERIIDAE
HETEROPTERA
HOMO SAPIENS
HYDROPHIDAE
HYMENOPTERA
INSECTIVORA
LEPIDOPTERA
LEPIDOSTEUS
LOLIGINIDAE
LOPHOPHORUS
LUMBRICIDAE
MARSUPIALIA
MONODELPHIA
MONOTREMATA
NOTOTHERIUM
NYMPHALIDAE
OLIGOCHAETA
OPHIUROIDEA
PEDIPALPIDA
PENTACRINUS
PINNOTHERES
PLACENTALIA
PLAGIOSTOMI
PROBOSCIDEA
PROCELLARIA
PROCYONIDAE
PROTOTHERIA
PYCNOGONIDA
RHAMPHASTOS
RHOPALOCERA
SCHISTOSOMA
SCOLOPENDRA
SPIROCHAETA
STOMATOPODA
STRUTHIONES
SUBUNGULATA
TELEOSAURUS
TEREBRATULA
THYROSTRACA
TORTRICIDAE
TRACHINIDAE
TRICHINELLA
TRICHOMONAS
TRICHOPTERA
TROCHILIDAE
TROGLODYTES
TRYPANOSOMA
TURBELLARIA
TYROGLYPHUS
URANOSCOPUS
ZONOTRICHIA

12

BALAENOPTERA
BRANCHIOPODA
BRONTOSAURUS
CHARACINIDAE
CHARADRIIDAE
CHIRONOMIDAE
CICINDELIDAE
COELENTERATA
CYCLOSTOMATA
DIDELPHYIDAE
DISCOMEDUSAE
ENTOMOSTRACA
HEMICHORDATA
HETEROSOMATA
HISTIOPHORUS
HYDROMEDUSAE
ICHTHYOPSIDA
LYMANTRIIDAE
MASTIGOPHORA
MOLLUSCOIDEA
MYRMECOPHAGA
NEMATOMORPHA
NOTODONTIDAE
NOTONECTIDAE
ODONTOPHORUS
ONCORHYNCHUS
PACHYDERMATA
PAPILIONIDAE
PARADISEIDAE
PERODICTICUS
PLEURONECTES
RHIPIDOPTERA
RHIZOCEPHALA
RHYNCHONELLA
RHYNCHOPHORA
SCARABAEIDAE
SCIUROPTERUS
SCOLOPACIDAE
SCORPAENIDAE
SCORPIONIDEA
SIPHONAPTERA
SIPHONOPHERA
SIPUNCULACEA
SPATANGOIDAE
SPERMOPHILUS
STEGANOPODES
STREPSIPTERA
STREPTONEURO
STRIGIFORMES
SYNGNATHIDAE

THERIODONTIA
THERIOMORPHA
THYSANOPTERA
TORPEDINIDAE
TRACHYPTERUS
TRICHIURIDAE
TRICHOPHYTON
ZEUGLODONTIA

13

AVICULARIIDAE
BALANOGLOSSUS
CERCOPITHECUS
DIPROTODONTIA
DOLICHOSAURUS
ENTEROPNEUSTA
EPHEMEROPTERA
ICHTHYOSAURIA
LASIOCAMPIDAE
PASSERIFORMES
PLAGIOSTOMATA
RICKETTSIALES
SAUROPTERYGIA
SCOLECIFORMIA
SCYPHOMEDUSAE
SEMNOPITHECUS
SIPUNCULOIDEA
STAPHYLINIDAE
STEGOCEPHALIA
TENEBRIONIDAE
TESTICARDINES
TETRABRANCHIA

14

ARCHAEORNITHES
CHAETODONTIDAE
CROSSOPTERYGII
ELASMOBRANCHII
GNATHOBDELLIDA
HEXACTINELLIDA
MALACOPTERYGII
MONOPLACOPHORA
NEUROPTEROIDEA
NUDIBRANCHIATA
ORNITHODELPHIA
OSTEOGLOSSIDAE
PERIOPHTHALMUS

PERISSODACTYLA
PLEURONECTIDAE
POLYPLACOPHORA
PROTOTRACHEATA
RHINOCEROTIDAE
SCOMBRESOCIDAE
TRACHYPTERIDAE
TROCHELMINTHES
ZYGOBRANCHIATA

HYDROCORALLINAE
MARSIPOBRANCHII
MEGACHEIROPTERA
MICROCHIROPTERA
NEMATHELMINTHES
OPISTHOBRANCHIA
ORNITHORHYNCHUS

PLATYHELMINTHES
POLYPROTODONTIA
RHYNCHOBDELLIDA
RHYNCHOCEPHALIA
SPHENISCIFORMES
TECTIBRANCHIATA
TETRABRANCHIATA
TETRACTINELLIDA

SCIENCE — ZOOLOGY – ZOOLOGICAL TERMS

3

DEN
EGG
FRY
NID
NIT
ROE
RUT
WEB

4

BIRD
DREY
FISH
FORM
GRUB
HIVE
HOLE
HOLT
LAIR
MILT
NEST
PREY
PUPA
SALT
SETT
SPAT
TENT
ZOEA

5

AERIE
BIPED
EARTH
EYRIE
FAUNA
GENUS
HATCH
IMAGO
LARVA
LODGE
MINER
MOULT
NIDUS
ORDER
ORNIS
REDIA
RIGOR
SPAWN
VENOM

6

ALBINO
ANIMAL
BURROW
COBWEB
COCOON
COLONY
FAMILY

GRAINE
IMPLEX
INSECT
ISOPOD
LAYING
LITTER
MAGGOT
MAMMAL
NEUTER
OWLERY
PHYLUM
QUARRY
RAPTOR
RODENT
SIMIAN
TUNNEL
WARREN

7

ANT-HILL
BIVALVE
DASYPOD
DASYURE
DECAPOD
DENIZEN
EELFARE
EPIZOAN
EPIZOON
FLYBLOW
FOXHOLE

HERONRY
HEXAPOD
HOMINID
MIGRANT
MOUSERY
NEOTENY
OCTOPOD
OESTRUS
PERCHER
PLANULA
POLYPOD
PRIMATE
RATTERY
REPTILE
ROOKERY
RUTTING
SOLIPED
SPECIES
TELEOST
TYLOPOD
VELIGER
ZOARIUM
ZOOTYPE

8

ALBINISM
AMPHIPOD
ANTS' NEST
AVIFAUNA
BIRD'S-EGG

CETACEAN
CREATURE
DIDACTYL
ECTOZOAN
ECTOZOON
EDENTATE
ENDOZOON
ENTOZOON
FROGGERY
HIVE-NEST
HOMINOID
HUMANOID
LEMURIAN
LEMURINE
LEMUROID
MAMMIFER
METAZOON
MONOTYPE
MOULTING
MULTIPED
MYRIAPOD
NAUPLIUS
NOTOGAEA
OMNIVORE
OPHIDIAN
ORGANISM
PALMIPED
PARASITE
PELAGIAN
PINNIPED
POLYGAMY
POLYGENY

POLYZOAN
POLYZOON
POND-LIFE
PREDATOR
PTILOSIS
PUPATION
RESIDENT
RHIZOPOD
RUMINANT
SECODONT
SIRENIAN
SPAWNING
SUBCLASS
SUBGENUS
SUBIMAGO
SUBORDER
SWARMING
SYMPHILE
SYMPHILY
TETRAPOD
TUNICATE
UNGULATE
UNIVALVE
VESPIARY
VOLATILE
WORM-HOLE
ZOOTOXIN

9

AMPHIBIAN
ARCTOGAEA
BIRD'S-NEST
CAECILIAN
CARNIVORE
CHAETOPOD
CHELONIAN
CHRYSALID
CHRYSALIS
COELOMATE
DIPLOZOON
ECHIDNINE
EUTHERIAN
FISSIPEDE
FORMICARY
FROG-SPAWN
GASTROPOD
GLASS-CRAB
HERBIVORE
HETEROPOD
HISPIDITY

HOMEOMERY
HYDROZOON
IMPLEXION
LATITANCY
LOPHODONT
MAMMALIAN
MARSUPIAL
MIGRATION
MONOCEROS
MONOTREME
MOUSE-HOLE
NOTOCHORD
OVIPARITY
PACHYDERM
PALMATION
PALMIPEDE
PHALANGER
PHYLLOPOD
PLACODERM
POLYMASTY
PREDATION
PULMONATE
QUADRUPED
SCAPHOPOD
SCAVENGER
SCHIZOPOD
SELACHIAN
SHELLFISH
SUBFAMILY
SYNOECETE
TERMITARY
TERRICOLE
TREMATODE
WASPS' NEST
XYLOPHAGE
ZOOPHAGAN
ZOOTROPHY

10

BIPINNARIA
BRACHIOPOD
CEPHALOPOD
CONY-BURROW
CRUSTACEAN
CYCLOIDEAN
DIPHYODONT
GASTEROPOD
GNOTOBIOTE
HOMOBLASTY
HOMOCHROMY

INDUMENTUM
INFUSORIAN
INVOLUTION
MACROBIOTE
METAMERISM
METAPLASIA
METAPLASIS
NEONTOLOGY
NIDULATION
OCELLATION
ODONTOCETE
OPHIOMORPH
PARASITISM
PARASITOID
PENGUINERY
PHOLIDOSIS
PISCIFAUNA
POLYCHAETE
POLYMASTIA
PSEUDIMAGO
PTERYLOSIS
QUADRUMANE
RABBIT-HOLE
SAND-SAUCER
SCARABAEID
SQUAMATION
SQUAMOSITY
STEGANOPOD
STOMATOPOD
SUBSPECIES
SUPERORDER
SYMPHILISM
TARDIGRADE
TELEOSTEAN
TELEOSTOME
VERTEBRATE
VISCACHERA
VISITATION
ZYGOBRANCH

11

AESTIVATION
BRANCHIOPOD
DIGITIGRADE
DIPROTODONT
ECTOGENESIS
FORMICARIUM
HIBERNATION
HYDROMEDUSA
ICHTHYOPSID

INSECTIVORE
LATERIGRADE
LEPTODACTYL
LOPHOBRANCH
METACHROSIS
ORNITHOGAEA
OVIPOSITION
PENTADACTYL
PLAGIOSTOME
POLYDACTYLY
POLYGENESIS
POLYMASTISM
REMIGRATION
SCHISTOSOME
SCYPHISTOMA
SEAL-ROOKERY
SERTULARIAN
SNAKE-POISON
STRIDULATOR
SUBUNGULATE
TECTIBRANCH
TERMITARIUM
TETRADACTYL
ZOANTHARIAN
ZOOPLANKTON

12

AMPHIBIOLOGY
COELENTERATE
ECHINOCOCCUS
ECTOPARASITE
ELASMOBRANCH
ENDOPARASITE
ENTEROPNEUST
HERERODACTYL
HIBERNACULUM
HYPERDACTYLY
INVERTEBRATE
MONOPHYODONT
MULTUNGULATE
MYRMECOPHILY
NESTING-PLACE
OESTRUS CYCLE
PAEDOGENESIS
RABBIT-WARREN
RETROMINGENT
SEMIPARASITE
SINISTRALITY
STROBILATION
SYNDACTYLISM

TESTACEOLOGY
TETRADACTYLY
ZALAMBDODONT

13

ACARIDOMATIUM
ENTOMOSTRACAN
GYNANDROMORPH
LAMELLIBRANCH
LEPTOCEPHALUS
MALACOSTRACAN
MARSIPOBRANCH
METAMORPHOSIS
NATURAL SYSTEM

OPISTHOBRANCH
PALAEOZOOLOGY
PERENNIBRANCH
PERFECT INSECT
PERISSODACTYL
POIKILOTHERMY
POLYDACTYLISM
POLYPROTODONT
RETROMINGENCY
SEMIPALMATION
WATER-BREATHER
ZYGODACTYLISM

14

DIZYGOTIC TWINS

FRATERNAL TWINS
GYNANDROMORPHY
INTERMIGRATION
NATURAL HISTORY
STROBILISATION
SYNAPOSEMATISM
ZYGOBRANCHIATE

15

COLONIAL ANIMALS
HETEROCERCALITY
ORNITHODELPHIAN
TECTIBRANCHIATE

SOUNDS

3

BAA
BAY
BOO
BUM
CAW
COO
CRY
DIN
HEM
HUE
HUM
LAP
LOW
MEW
MOO
PAT
POP
RAP
ROW
SOB
TAP
YAP
YIP
ZIP

4

BANG
BARK
BAWL
BIRR
BONG
BOOM
BRAY
BUMP
BURP
BURR
BUZZ
CALL
CHUG
CLAM
CLAP
CLOP
CROW
DING
DONG
ECHO
FIZZ
FLOP
GASP

HA-HA
HE-HE
HISS
HONK
HOOT
HOWL
HUFF
KEEN
MOAN
NOTE
PEAL
PEEP
PHEW
PING
PINK
PIPE
PLAP
PLOP
PUFF
PURR
RÂLE
RASP
RING
RISP
ROAR
ROLL
RUFF
SIGH
SLAM
SNAP
SNIP
TACK
TANG
THUD
TICK
TING
TINK
TOLL
TOOT
WAIL
WAUL
WHEW
WOOF
YELL
YELP
YOOP
YOWL
ZOOM

5

BELCH

BLARE
BLAST
BLEAT
BLEEP
BROOL
CHEEP
CHEER
CHIME
CHINK
CHIRL
CHIRM
CHIRP
CHUCK
CHURR
CLACK
CLANG
CLANK
CLASH
CLICK
CLINK
CLONK
CLOOP
CLUCK
CLUNK
COUGH
CRACK
CRASH
CREAK
CROAK
DRONE
FLUMP
GRIND
GROAN
GROWL
GRUNT
HURRA
HUZZA
KLANG
KNELL
KNOCK
LAUGH
MIAOW
MIAUL
NEIGH
NOISE
PLASH
PLUMP
PLUNK
QUACK
SHOUT
SKIRL
SLURP

SMACK
SNARL
SNIFF
SNORE
SNORT
SOUND
SWASH
SWISH
TEHEE
THUMP
TRILL
TROAT
TWANG
TWEET
WHANG
WHINE
WHIRR
WHIZZ
WHOOP

6

BAAING
BABBLE
BAYING
BELLOW
BOOING
BOWWOW
BURBLE
CACKLE
CAWING
COOING
CRUNCH
CRYING
GIGGLE
GUFFAW
GURGLE
HALLOO
HAW-HAW
HEE-HAW
HICCUP
HOORAY
HURRAH
HURRAY
JANGLE
JINGLE
JUDDER
LOWING
MOOING
MURMUR
OUTCRY

PATTER
PIPING
PITTER
POPPLE
PULING
QUAVER
RACKET
RATTAN
RATTLE
RE-ECHO
REPORT
RIPPLE
ROW-DOW
RUFFLE
RUMBLE
RUSTLE
SCREAK
SCREAM
SCROOP
SHRIEK
SHRILL
SIZZLE
SNEEZE
SNIVEL
SQUALL
SQUAWK
SQUEAK
SQUEAL
SQUISH
TCHICK
THWACK
TINKLE
TITTER
UPROAR
WARBLE
WAR CRY
WHEEZE
WHINNY

7

BANGING
BARKING
BAWLING
BLARING
BLUSTER
BOOMING
BRATTLE
BRAYING
BUMMING
BURPING

356

BURRING
BUZZING
CALLING
CATCALL
CHIMING
CHIRRUP
CHORTLE
CHUCKLE
CLAMOUR
CLARION
CLATTER
CRACKLE
CROWING
DINGING
DRONING
ECHOING
EUPHONY
FIZZING
GASPING
HEMMING
HISSING
HONKING
HOOTING
HOWLING
HUFFING
HUMMING
KEENING
LAPPING
LOONING
MOANING
OVATION
PEALING
PINGING
PINKING
PITAPAT
POPPING
PUFFING
PURRING
RAPPING
RASPING
RAT-A-TAT
RINGING
RISPING
ROARING
ROOTING
SCRATCH
SCREECH
SCRITCH
SCRUNCH
SIGHING
SINGING
SNICKER

SNIFFLE
SNIGGER
SNORING
SNUFFLE
SOBBING
SPUTTER
SQUELCH
STRIDOR
TANTARA
TAPPING
THUNDER
TICKING
TOLLING
TOOTING
TRUMPET
TWITTER
WAILING
WAULING
WHIMPER
WHISPER
WHISTLE
YAPPING
YELLING
YELPING
YOWLING

8

APPLAUSE
BABBLING
BELCHING
BLASTING
BLEATING
BLEEPING
BUBBLING
BURBLING
CACKLING
CALL-NOTE
CHEEPING
CHEERING
CHIRLING
CHIRPING
CHUGGING
CHURRING
CLACKING
CLANGING
CLANGOUR
CLANKING
CLAPPING
CLASHING
CLICKING

CLINKING
CLIP-CLOP
CLOPPING
CLUCKING
CLUNKING
COUGHING
CRACKING
CRASHING
CREAKING
CROAKING
DING-DONG
FLOPPING
FLUMPING
FOOTFALL
GAGGLING
GIGGLING
GRINDING
GROANING
GROWLING
GRUNTING
GURGLING
HICCOUGH
HIRRIENT
JANGLING
JINGLING
KNOCKING
LAUGHING
LAUGHTER
MIAOWING
MUMBLING
NEIGHING
QUACKING
RATAPLAN
RATTLING
ROW-DE-DOW
ROWDYDOW
RUMBLING
RUSTLING
SHOUTING
SIZZLING
SKIRLING
SLAMMING
SLURPING
SNAPPING
SNARLING
SNEEZING
SNIFFING
SNIPPING
SNIP-SNAP
SNORTING
SPLUTTER
SUSURRUS

THUDDING
THUMPING
TICK-TICK
TICK-TOCK
TINKLING
TRILLING
TWEETING
WARBLING
WAR-WHOOP
WHEEZING
WHIRRING
WHIZZING
WHOOPING

9

BATTLE-CRY
BELLOWING
BEWAILING
CACOPHONY
CATERWAUL
CHORTLING
CHUCKLING
CRACKLING
CRUNCHING
GUFFAWING
HALLOOING
HAMMERING
HEE-HAWING
HICCUPING
HUE AND CRY
JUDDERING
LATRATION
MURMURING
PARROT-CRY
RASPBERRY
REBOATION
RESONANCE
SCREAMING
SHRIEKING
SHRILLING
SNIFFLING
SNUFFLING
SONIC BANG
SONIC BOOM
SQUALLING
SQUAWKING
SQUEAKING
SQUEALING
TANTARARA
TARANTARA

SOUNDS

TCHICKING
THRUMMING
THWACKING
TING-A-LING
TITTERING
ULULATION
WHINNYING
WHISTLING
YODELLING

SNIGGERING
SNIVELLING
SPUTTERING
SQUELCHING
THUNDERING
TRUMPETING
TWEET-TWEET
TWITTERING
WHIMPERING
WHISPERING

12

CACHINNATION
CATERWAULING
CLIP-CLOPPING
CONCLAMATION
JINGLE-JANGLE
PECTORILOQUY
PITTER-PATTER
REPERCUSSION
STRIDULATION
TU-WHIT TU-WHOO

10

BELLY-LAUGH
BLUSTERING
BRONX CHEER
CATCALLING
CLAMOURING
CLATTERING
CLICK-CLACK
CLISH-CLASH
CURMURRING
HORSE-LAUGH
MATING CALL
RUB-A-DUB-DUB
SCRATCHING
SCREECHING
SCRUNCHING
SNICKERING

11

ACCLAMATION
BORBORYGMUS
CREPITATION
HICCOUGHING
LAMENTATION
MURMURATION
SPLUTTERING
SUSURRATION
TARATANTARA
THUNDER-CLAP
THUNDER-PEAL
VOCIFERANCE
WATER-HAMMER
WOLF-WHISTLE

13

CLICK-CLACKING
DECREPITATION
REVERBERATION

14

CLITTER-CLATTER
COCK-A-DOODLE-DOO

SPORT — GAMES & SPORTS EQUIPMENT

3

BAG
BAR
BAT
BOW
BOX
CAT
CUE
DIE
FLY
GUN
KIT
MAN
MAT
NET
OAR
PAD
PEG
PIN
ROD
SKI
TAW
TEE
TIP

4

BAIL
BAIT
BALL
BARB
BEAM
BOWL
BUCK
CARD
CHIP
CLUB
CUSH
DART
DICE
DISC
DISK
ÉPÉE
FLAG
FOIL
HOOK
HOOP
IRON
JACK
JUMP

KAIL
KING
LINE
LUGE
LURE
MALL
NETS
OCHE
PAWN
PILL
POLE
POOL
POST
PUCK
RACK
REST
ROOK
ROPE
SHOE
SHOT
SLED
SPOT
TILE
WHIP
WOOD

5

ALLEY
ARROW
BAFFY
BANDY
BLADE
BOARD
BONCE
BONES
CABER
CAMAN
CHALK
CHUCK
CLEEK
DECOY
FLOAT
FRAME
HORSE
JERID
JETON
JOKER
KITTY
MERIL
PIECE

PITON
PLATE
PRESS
QUEEN
QUOIT
RIFLE
RINGS
ROVER
SABRE
SCUBA
SCULL
SKATE
SPOON
STACK
STICK
STOOL
STUMP
SWEEP
SWORD
TRAIN
WEDGE

6

BISHOP
BOB-FLY
BULGER
BULLET
CASTLE
CHEESE
DISCUS
DOMINO
DRIVER
DRY SKI
DUBBIN
ÉTRIER
FLY ROD
HURDLE
ICE-AXE
JETTON
KNIGHT
LOFTER
LOGGAT
MALIBU
MALLET
MARBLE
MARKER
MASHIE
NICKER
PADDLE
PEEVER

PIOLET
POCKET
PUTTER
QUIVER
RACKET
RAPIER
RINGER
ROCKER
SKI-BOB
SKI-TOW
SLEDGE
SLEIGH
SPIDER
SQUAIL
STICKS
TACKLE
TARGET
TENPIN
WICKET

7

ARM-BAND
BAR-BELL
BEAN-BAG
BRASSIE
COUNTER
CRAMPET
CRAMPON
CUE-BALL
CUSHION
DICE-BOX
FLIPPER
FLY LINE
GAME-BAG
GOLF-BAG
HARNESS
JAVELIN
LEATHER
LEG-BAIL
MINI-SKI
NET-CORD
NETTING
NIBLICK
NINEPIN
OFF-BAIL
RACQUET
SHIN-PAD
SHUTTLE
SKI-LIFT
SKI-POLE

SKITTLE
SNORKEL
TRAPEZE
UPRIGHT
WHISTLE

8

AQUALUNG
BIRDCALL
CAT-STICK
CHESSMAN
CROSSBAR
DUMB-BELL
FOOTBALL
GOALPOST
GOLF-BALL
GOLF-CLUB
LEG-GUARD
OBSTACLE
PEG-BOARD
PLASTRON
PUNT-POLE
SAND-IRON
SCENT-BAG
SKI-STICK
SQUAILER
TOBOGGAN
WALL-BARS
WATER-SKI

9

APPARATUS
AQUABOARD
AQUAPLANE
BLACK FLAG
BOBSLEIGH
BOWSTRING
BULL-BOARD
CADDIE CAR
DART-BOARD
DEVELOPER
FACE-GUARD
JACK-STRAW
KARABINER
POGO-STICK
POOL-TABLE
PUNCH-BALL
QUAIL-PIPE

359

SAND-WEDGE
SCHNORKEL
SCORE-BOOK
SCORE-CARD
SPILLIKIN
STANCHION
STOP-WATCH
STRETCHER
SURF-BOARD
SWEAT-BAND
TAROT-CARD
TELEGRAPH
THUMB-RING
TRAP-STICK

10

ACE OF CLUBS
BANDERILLA
BATTLEDORE
CHESSBOARD
CHESSPIECE
CLAY-PIGEON
CORNER-FLAG
CRICKET-BAG
CRICKET-BAT
FISHING-ROD
FOWLING-NET
GREENCLOTH
HOCKEY-BALL
INDIAN CLUB
OBJECT-BALL
ROPE-LADDER
RUGGER-BALL
SCORE-BOARD
SCORE-SHEET
SIX OF CLUBS
SKATE-BOARD
SQUASH-BALL
TENNIS-BALL
TEN OF CLUBS
TIDDLYWINK
TRAMPOLINE
TWO OF CLUBS
WATER-WINGS

11

ACE OF HEARTS
ACE OF SPADES

BASEBALL-BAT
BODY-BUILDER
BOXING-GLOVE
CRICKET-BALL
DIVING-BOARD
DRAUGHTSMAN
FIGURE-SKATE
FIVE OF CLUBS
FOUR OF CLUBS
FRENCH CHALK
GAMING-TABLE
HOCKEY-STICK
HUNTING-CROP
JACK OF CLUBS
KING OF CLUBS
MALIBU BOARD
NINE OF CLUBS
PLAYING-CARD
RACKET-PRESS
ROLLER-SKATE
SHINTY-STICK
SHUTTLECOCK
SIGHT-SCREEN
SIX OF HEARTS
SIX OF SPADES
SKITTLE-BALL
SNOOKER-BALL
SPRINGBOARD
TEN OF HEARTS
TEN OF SPADES
TWO OF HEARTS
TWO OF SPADES
WINNING-POST

12

BILLIARD-BALL
CHECKER-BOARD
CUE-EXTENSION
CURLING-STONE
DRAUGHTBOARD
EIGHT OF CLUBS
ELECTRIC HARE
FIVE OF HEARTS
FIVE OF SPADES
FOUR OF HEARTS
FOUR OF SPADES
GIANT'S-STRIDE
JACK OF HEARTS
JACK OF SPADES
KING OF HEARTS

KING OF SPADES
MEDICINE-BALL
NINE OF HEARTS
NINE OF SPADES
PARALLEL BARS
PUTTING-CLEEK
PUTTING-STONE
QUEEN OF CLUBS
SEVEN OF CLUBS
SKIPPING-ROPE
SQUASH-RACKET
SURFING-BOARD
TENNIS-RACKET
THREE OF CLUBS

13

ACE OF DIAMONDS
BILLIARD-CLOTH
BILLIARD-TABLE
CHECKERED FLAG
CRIBBAGE-BOARD
EIGHT OF HEARTS
EIGHT OF SPADES
FINISHING-POST
FISHING TACKLE
ISOMETRIC BARS
MASHIE-NIBLICK
QUEEN OF HEARTS
QUEEN OF SPADES
ROULETTE-WHEEL
SEVEN OF HEARTS
SEVEN OF SPADES
SIX OF DIAMONDS
STARTING BLOCK
TEN OF DIAMONDS
THREE OF HEARTS
THREE OF SPADES
TWO OF DIAMONDS
VAULTING-HORSE

14

ASYMMETRIC BARS
CHEST-EXPANDERS
COCONUT MATTING
FIVE OF DIAMONDS
FOUR OF DIAMONDS
JACK OF DIAMONDS
KING OF DIAMONDS

NINE OF DIAMONDS
SOLITAIRE-BOARD
STARTING PISTOL
TABLE-TENNIS BAT
WHEEL OF FORTUNE

BADMINTON RACKET
EIGHT OF DIAMONDS
QUEEN OF DIAMONDS

SEVEN OF DIAMONDS
TABLE-TENNIS BALL
THREE OF DIAMONDS

SPORT – GAMES & SPORTS TERMS

3	RUB	CLUE	JINK	PITS	TURF	CARTE
	RUN	COUP	JUMP	PLAY	TURN	CATCH
ACE	SET	CRIB	KAYO	PLOY	VASE	CHASE
BAG	SHY	DEAL	KICK	POLE	VOID	CHECK
BET	SIX	DECK	KILL	POOL	VOLE	CHEVY
BID	TEE	DIVE	KING	PORT	WALK	CLOUT
BOX	TIE	DRAG	KISS	POSE	WALL	CLUBS
BYE	TIP	DRAW	LEAD	POST	WARD	COURT
CUP	TON	DUCK	LEAP	PULL	WIDE	COVER
CUT	TOP	DUMP	LEFT	PUNT	WING	CRABS
DIP	TRY	ECHO	LIDO	PUSH	WORK	CRAWL
END	VAN	FACE	LIFE	PUTT		CROSS
FIX	WIN	FALL	LIFT	RACE		DERBY
GIN		FILE	LIKE	RANK	5	DEUCE
GYM		FIST	LINE	RING		DITCH
HIT	4	FOIL	LOCK	RUCK	ALLEY	DIVOT
HOG		FORM	LOFT	RUFF	ANGLE	DOLLY
HUG	ANTE	FOUL	LOOP	SAVE	APPUI	DRAIL
JAB	BALL	FOUR	LOSS	SHOT	ARENA	DRIVE
LAP	BANK	GAME	LOVE	SIDE	AWARD	DUMMY
LAW	BARB	GATE	MAIN	SKIP	BADGE	EAGLE
LBW	BASE	GOAL	MAKE	SLAM	BAKER	ENTRY
LEG	BIAS	GRUB	MARK	SLIP	BASTO	EVENS
LET	BITE	HACK	MATE	SLOG	BAULK	EVENT
LIE	BLOT	HALF	MEET	SPIN	BLANK	EXTRA
LOB	BOOK	HAND	MILE	SPOT	BLAST	FAULT
LOT	BOUT	HEAT	MISS	STOP	BLIND	FEINT
NAP	BOWL	HEEL	MOVE	STUN	BLOCK	FIELD
NIL	BULL	HOLD	NICK	SUIT	BLUFF	FIGHT
NOB	BUMP	HOLE	NOCK	SWIM	BOGEY	FINAL
ODD	BUTT	HOME	ODDS	TAPE	BOTTE	FIRST
OFF	CALL	HOOK	OVER	TEST	BOWER	FLUFF
PAM	CAST	HUFF	PACE	TOSS	BREAK	FLUKE
PAR	CERT	HUNK	PACK	TOTE	BULLY	FLUSH
PIP	CHIP	HUNT	PAIR	TRAP	CAPOT	FRAME
PIT	CHOP	JACK	PASS	TREY	CAROM	GAPER
POT	CLUB	JERK	PERM	TRIP	CARRY	GLIDE

361

SPORT – GAMES & SPORTS TERMS

GO-OFF	ROUGH	BAILER	JIGGER	SOCKET	CONTEST
GREEN	ROUND	BASKET	KISSER	SPADES	COUNTER
GUARD	ROVER	BATTUE	LEAGUE	SPRINT	DECIDER
GULLY	SCENT	BEAMER	LEG-BYE	SQUARE	DEFENCE
HEART	SCORE	BIRDIE	LENGTH	STAKES	DIAMOND
HOMER	SCREW	BISQUE	LET-OFF	STANCE	DISCARD
HOUSE	SCRUM	BORROW	LONG-ON	STRIKE	DOCTORS
INNER	SCULL	BOTTOM	LOSING	STROKE	DOGGING
IN-OFF	SERVE	BOUNCE	MAGPIE	STUMPS	DOG-RACE
JENNY	SIXER	BRIDGE	MAIDEN	STYMIE	DOUBLES
KITTY	SIXTE	BUMPER	MARINA	SWERVE	DRIBBLE
KNAVE	SKIER	BUNKER	MID-OFF	SWITCH	DRIVING
LIGHT	SLICE	CANNON	MISCUE	TACKLE	ENGLISH
LINKS	SLIPS	CARTON	MISÈRE	TACTIC	FAIRWAY
LOOSE	SMASH	CHERRY	MISHIT	TENACE	FEATHER
LUNGE	SNEAK	CHUKKA	NELSON	THWART	FINE LEG
LURCH	SNICK	CLINCH	NO-BALL	TICKLE	FINESSE
MASSÉ	SPADE	COMBAT	NO-SIDE	TIERCE	FIXTURE
MATCH	SPARE	CORNER	OARAGE	TIMING	FLOORER
MID-ON	SPOOR	COURSE	ONSIDE	TOSS-UP	FLUTTER
NODDY	SPORT	CREASE	PARADE	TREBLE	FLY-KICK
OMBRE	SPURT	CUP-TIE	PARLEY	TROPHY	FORFEIT
OUTER	STAKE	DEDANS	PERIOD	TRY-OUT	FORMULA
PARRY	STALK	DEFEAT	PICK-UP	UPSHOT	FOX-HUNT
PETER	STAND	DICING	PLUNGE	VENERY	GOLFING
PIQUE	START	DOG-LEG	POLING	VOLLEY	GOULASH
PISTE	STEAL	DOUBLE	POT-LID	WARM-UP	GRUBBER
PITCH	STOCK	DUPLET	RACING	WEIGHT	HALF-ONE
PLACE	SWEEP	ÉCURIE	RECORD	WICKET	HAND-OFF
PLANT	SWING	ENIGMA	REMISE	YANKEE	HIGHMAN
PLATE	TARRY	FIGURE	REPLAY	YORKER	HIP-LOCK
POINT	TALON	FINISH	RESULT		HOME-RUN
POOLS	THIRD	FIZZER	RETURN		ICE-HILL
PRESS	THROW	FLÈCHE	REVOKE		ICE-RINK
PRIAL	TITLE	FOOZLE	RIDDLE	**7**	INCURVE
PRICE	TOUCH	FULHAM	RINGER		INFIELD
PRIME	TRACK	GAMBIT	ROLL-UP	AMBS-ACE	INNINGS
PRIZE	TRIAL	GAMBLE	ROQUET	ANAGRAM	INSWING
PUNTO	TRICK	GAMMON	RUBBER	AUCTION	JACKPOT
PURSE	TRUMP	GLANCE	RUN-OFF	AVERAGE	JAMBONE
QUART	TWOER	GOBBLE	RUN-OUT	BATHING	JUMP-OFF
QUEEN	VAULT	GOOGLY	SAFETY	BATTING	KICK-OFF
QUINT	VENUE	GOURDS	SANCHO	BEATING	KNOCK-ON
RACES	VOLTE	GROUND	SCHUSS	BENEFIT	KNOCK-UP
RAILS	WAGER	HAZARD	SECOND	BOUNCER	LAST LAP
RAKER	WIDOW	HEADER	SERIES	BOWLING	LATE CUT
RALLY		HEARTS	SHIKAR	BOWSHOT	LAYBACK
RANGE		HONOUR	SIGNAL	BRICOLE	LEG-SIDE
REACH	**6**	ICE-RUN	SINGLE	CENTURY	LINE-OUT
REBID		IMPOST	SITTER	CHICANE	LONG HOP
RELAY	APPEAL	INJURY	SLALOM	CHOCTAW	LONG-LEG
ROUGE	ATTACK	INWICK	SNATCH	CIRCUIT	LONG-OFF
				CODILLE	

362

LONG TEN	SWINGER	CUP-MATCH	JAMBOREE	SEQUENCE
MANILLE	TACTICS	DEAD HEAT	KNOCKOUT	SHOOTING
MAXIMUM	TERRACE	DECK-GAME	LEFT HOOK	SHORT LEG
MEETING	THE DEEP	DELIVERY	LEFT WING	SHOT-PUTT
MISDEAL	THE FLAT	DEUCE-ACE	LEG-BREAK	SIDE-SLIP
MONTANT	THROW-IN	DIAMONDS	LEG-GUARD	SKIPPING
NET-PLAY	TOE-HOLD	DICE-PLAY	LEG-SWEEP	SKI-SLOPE
NO-TRUMP	TOP-SPIN	DISTANCE	LONG JUMP	SPADILLE
NURSERY	TOURNEY	DIVISION	LONG ODDS	SPARRING
OFFSIDE	TRUDGEN	DRAG-HUNT	LONG SHOT	SPEEDWAY
OPENING	TUFTING	DRAG RACE	LONG-SLIP	SQUEEZER
OVERBID	TWISTER	DRAG-SHOT	LONG-STOP	STAG-HUNT
PADDOCK	TWOSOME	DRESSAGE	LOVE-GAME	STALKING
PATBALL	UPSWING	DROP-GOAL	MARRIAGE	STOCCADO
PEGGING	VANTAGE	DROP-KICK	MATADORE	STOPPING
PENALTY	VICTORY	DROP-SHOT	MIDFIELD	STRADDLE
PICTURE	WEIGH-IN	EXERCISE	MISMATCH	STRAIGHT
PISCINA	WINNING	FACE-CARD	NAPOLEON	STRIKING
PIT-STOP	WORK-OUT	FAIR PLAY	NOBLE ART	STUMPING
PLAYING	WRESTLE	FIELDING	NO-TRUMPS	STUN-SHOT
PLAY-OFF	WRONG 'UN	FLAT-RACE	OFF-BREAK	SWERVING
POTTING		FOLLOW-ON	OFF-DRIVE	TAC-AU-TAC
PRE-EMPT		FOOT-RACE	OLYMPIAD	TEAM-WORK
PURSUIT		FOOTWORK	OLYMPICS	TELEMARK
PUTTING	**8**	FORECAST	OUTFIELD	THE COUNT
PYRAMID		FOREHAND	OUTSIDER	THE FANCY
QUARTER	APRÈS-SKI	FOUL-PLAY	OUTSWING	THIRD MAN
RACE-CUP	AQUACADE	FOURSOME	OVERHAND	THROWING
RECOVER	AQUATICS	FREE BALL	OVER RATE	TICK-TACK
RE-ENTRY	AVERAGES	FREE KICK	OVER-RUFF	TRAINING
REGATTA	BACKFALL	FREE SHOT	OVERSPIN	TRANSFER
REPIQUE	BACKHAND	FULL HAND	PAVILION	TRAVERSE
REVERSO	BACK-PASS	FULL TIME	PINOCHLE	UMPIRAGE
RIPOSTE	BACK-SPIN	FULL TOSS	PLACE-BET	UMPIRING
RIVALRY	BALL-GAME	GLASS JAW	POSITION	UPPER CUT
ROUNDER	BASE-LINE	GOAL AREA	PRACTICE	VAULTING
RUBICON	BIATHLON	GOAL-KICK	PUGILISM	VENATION
RUNNING	BOAT-RACE	GOAL-LINE	PUSH-OVER	VERONICA
SCORING	BONSPIEL	GRIDIRON	PUSH-SHOT	WALK-AWAY
SCRATCH	BOUNDARY	GROUNDER	QUATORZE	WALK-OVER
SECONDE	BULL-RING	GYMKHANA	RACE-CARD	WEIGH-OUT
SERVICE	BULL'S-EYE	HALF-COCK	RACE-PATH	WORD-PLAY
SESSION	BULLY-OFF	HALF-TIME	REDOUBLE	ZUGZWANG
SHUFFLE	CAROUSEL	HAND BALL	RINGSIDE	
SINGLES	CHEATING	HANDICAP	ROCK-WORK	
SKI-JUMP	CHINAMAN	HAT TRICK	SACK-RACE	**9**
SQUEEZE	CHIP-SHOT	HAYMAKER	SAND-TRAP	
STADIUM	CLINCHER	HEAD-LOCK	SCISSORS	ABUNDANCE
STAMINA	CLUB-FACE	HIGH JUMP	SCRAMBLE	ADVANTAGE
STRETCH	COAT-CARD	HOG-SCORE	SCREWING	BACKSIGHT
SWABBER	COMMONEY	HOME BASE	SCULLING	BACK-SWING
SWERVER	CONTRACT	HURDLING	SEPTLEVA	BAULK-LINE
	CUP-FINAL			

363

SPORT — GAMES & SPORTS TERMS

BELLY-FLOP
BLEACHERS
BROAD JUMP
BULLFIGHT
BUTTERFLY
CARAMBOLE
CHALLENGE
CHECKMATE
CONUNDRUM
COURT-CARD
CROWN-HEAD
DECATHLON
DEEP FIELD
DIRT-TRACK
DISMISSAL
DOUBLETON
DRABBLING
DRIBBLING
ELDER HAND
EN TOUT CAS
EQUALISER
EVEN MONEY
EXTRA TIME
FALSE CARD
FAVOURITE
FINESSING
FIRST BASE
FIRST SLIP
FIXED ODDS
FOOL'S MATE
FOOTFAULT
FOUR-FLUSH
FREE-STYLE
FULL HOUSE
FULL PITCH
GATE-MONEY
GLASS CHIN
GOLD MEDAL
GOLF-LINKS
GRAND PRIX
GRAND SLAM
GYMNASIUM
GYMNASTIC
HANDSTAND
HORSE RACE
INSWINGER
JACK-KNIFE
LEG-BEFORE
LEG-GLANCE
LEG-THEORY
LOB VOLLEY
LOGOGRIPH

LONG-FIELD
LONG WHIST
MAJOR SUIT
MATCH PLAY
MEDAL PLAY
MIDSTREAM
MIDWICKET
MINIATURE
MINOR SUIT
MISTIGRIS
MOURNIVAL
NINE HOLES
NO-TRUMPER
OBJECTION
OVERTHROW
OVERTRICK
PAIR-ROYAL
PLACE-KICK
POLE-VAULT
PRIZE-RING
PROGRAMME
PROMOTION
RACEGOING
RACE-TRACK
RAIN-CHECK
RELAY-RACE
REPÊCHAGE
RESCUE BID
RESHUFFLE
RETRACTOR
RIGHT HOOK
RIGHT WING
ROCK-CLIMB
SCREW-SHOT
SCRIMMAGE
SCRUMMAGE
SELECTION
SEMI-FINAL
SHORT ODDS
SHORT-SLIP
SINGLETON
SMALL SLAM
SPRINTING
SQUARE LEG
STALEMATE
SWORDPLAY
TERRACING
TEST MATCH
THIRD BASE
THIRD SLIP
THREESOME
THROW-AWAY

TORCH-RACE
TOTALISER
TOUCH-BACK
TOUCH-DOWN
TOUCH-LINE
TOXOPHILY
TRAMLINES
TRUMP-CARD
VELODROME
WATER-JUMP
WHITEWASH
WRIST-SHOT

10

AQUABATICS
ATTENDANCE
BACKSTROKE
BARRACKING
BLOOD SPORT
BOOBY-PRIZE
BOXING-RING
BRIDGERAMA
BRIDLE-HAND
CENTRE SPOT
CINDER-PATH
COMMENTARY
CONVENTION
COVER POINT
CROWN-GREEN
CYCLE-TRACK
DAILY DOZEN
DISCOBOLUS
ELIMINATOR
EQUITATION
ESKIMO ROLL
EXTRA COVER
FIANCHETTO
FIELD EVENT
FIELD SPORT
FIVES COURT
FLANCONADE
FLAT-RACING
FLYING MARE
FORMULA ONE
FORMULA TWO
FOURCHETTE
FULL-NELSON
GAMBIT PAWN
GAME OF GOLF
GLOVE-FIGHT

GOLF-COURSE
GRANDSTAND
HALF-NELSON
HALF-VOLLEY
HAMMERLOCK
HOME-THRUST
HURDLE-RACE
IMBROCCATA
INFIGHTING
INJURY TIME
INSIDE EDGE
INSIDE LANE
ISOMETRICS
KARATE CHOP
LOADED DICE
LOSING GAME
MAIDEN OVER
MARTINGALE
MASTER-CARD
MATCH-POINT
NATATORIUM
ORTHODROMY
OUTSWINGER
PALINDROME
PENTATHLON
PILE-DRIVER
POST-MORTEM
POT-HUNTING
PRE-EMPTION
PRIZE-FIGHT
PRIZE-MONEY
PSYCHIC BID
PUSH-STROKE
QUERSPRUNG
QUICK-TRICK
QUINT MAJOR
QUINT MINOR
RACECOURSE
RECREATION
REFEREEING
RELEGATION
RETRIEVING
ROPING-DOWN
ROYAL FLUSH
RUGBY MATCH
RUGBY PITCH
SAFETY PLAY
SAFETY SHOT
SECOND BASE
SECOND SLIP
SHUT-OUT BID
SIDE-STROKE

SILLY MID-ON
SILLY POINT
SOMERSAULT
SPOT-STROKE
STAKE MONEY
STOP VOLLEY
STROKE PLAY
SUBMISSION
SUSPENSION
SWEEPSTAKE
SWERVE-SHOT
TAKE-OUT BID
TARGET AREA
TEAM SPIRIT
TETRATHLON
THE COUNTRY
TIME-THRUST
TITLE-FIGHT
TOURNAMENT
TRACK EVENT
TRAVERSING
TRICK-TRACK
TRIPLE JUMP
UNDERTRICK
WATER SPORT
WELTER-RACE
WHIPPETING
WHIST-DRIVE
YARBOROUGH

11

ACCUMULATOR
ATHLETICISM
BEETLE-DRIVE
BRIDGE-DRIVE
BRONZE MEDAL
BUMPING RACE
CHRISTIANIA
CINDER-TRACK
CLASSIC RACE
CLOSE SEASON
COMPETITION
COUNTY MATCH
CURLING-POND
DAISY-CUTTER
DECLARATION
DEVIL'S BONES
DEVIL'S BOOKS
DOUBLE FAULT
EURHYTHMICS

FAST BOWLING
FLYING START
FOSBURY FLOP
GAMBIT-PIECE
GOLDEN SCOOP
HOCKEY MATCH
HOCKEY-PITCH
HOME-STRETCH
INSIDE TRACK
LAP OF HONOUR
LEAGUE MATCH
NET-PRACTICE
OBSTRUCTION
OUTSIDE EDGE
OUTSIDE LANE
OVERBIDDING
PENALTY AREA
PENALTY GOAL
PENALTY KICK
PENALTY LINE
PENALTY SPOT
PHOTO-FINISH
PICTURE-CARD
POOLS COUPON
PUNTO DRITTO
PURPLE PATCH
RABBIT-PUNCH
RACE-MEETING
RACKET-COURT
RETURN MATCH
ROUND OF GOLF
SEAM BOWLING
SELLING RACE
SERVICE-LINE
SILLY MID-OFF
SILVER MEDAL
SKATING RINK
SLOW BOWLING
SPIN BOWLING
SPREAD-EAGLE
SQUASH-COURT
STRAIGHT TIP
SUDDEN DEATH
SWALLOW-DIVE
TENNIS-COURT
TENNIS-MATCH
TEST CRICKET
TOTALISATOR
TRACK RECORD
TRIPLE EVENT
WESTERN ROLL
WHITECHAPEL

WOODEN SPOON
WORLD RECORD

12

ANCHOR CANNON
APPROACH SHOT
BASEBALL GAME
BOWLING-ALLEY
BOWLING-GREEN
BREAST-STROKE
CENTRE-CIRCLE
CHAMPIONSHIP
CLAIMING RACE
CRASH-BARRIER
CRICKET MATCH
CRICKET PITCH
CROSS-BUTTOCK
CROSS-RUFFING
CRUSH-BARRIER
DEBT OF HONOUR
GAMESMANSHIP
GROUND-STROKE
HITCH AND KICK
HOME-STRAIGHT
HORSEMANSHIP
INFRINGEMENT
LAMPADEDROMY
LOSING HAZARD
MAIDEN STAKES
MARATHON RACE
MIXED BATHING
MIXED DOUBLES
NETBALL MATCH
NURSERY SLOPE
OBSTACLE RACE
OLYMPIC GAMES
ONE-FOR-HIS-NOB
ORTHODROMICS
PLAYING-FIELD
POINT-TO-POINT
POLE POSITION
POSTPONEMENT
PRIZE-WINNING
PUNTO REVERSO
PUTTING-GREEN
QUARTER-FINAL
RACKET-GROUND
RETURN CREASE
RIGHT-AND-LEFT
RINGSIDE SEAT

SPORT – GAMES & SPORTS TERMS

RUNNING FLUSH
RUNNING TRACK
SACRIFICE BID
SACRIFICE HIT
SELLING PLATE
SERVICE-COURT
SHADOW-BOXING
SHAMATEURISM
SKITTLE-ALLEY
SPEED SKATING
SPORTS CENTRE
STARTING GATE
STARTING POST
STAYING-POWER
STEEPLECHASE
STICKY WICKET
STONEWALLING
STRANGLEHOLD
SUBSTITUTION
SWIMMING GALA
SWIMMING POOL
TEEING-GROUND
UNDERBIDDING
WATERMANSHIP
WELTER-STAKES
WINTER SPORTS

13

BACK-PEDALLING
BOWLING-CREASE
COUNTER-ATTACK
COUNTY CRICKET
DOUBLE FIGURES

DOUBLE OR QUITS
EIGHTEEN HOLES
EQUESTRIANISM
EXPLOSION SHOT
FIGURE OF EIGHT
FIGURE-SKATING
FINISHING LINE
FINISHING POST
FOLLOW-THROUGH
FOOTBALL MATCH
FOOTBALL PITCH
FOOTBALL POOLS
HUNDRED METRES
INTERNATIONAL
MISÈRE OUVERTE
MIXED FOURSOME
MOMENT OF TRUTH
NURSERY CANNON
ONE-DAY CRICKET
PITCH INVASION
POPPING-CREASE
PRE-EMPTIVE BID
QUALIFICATION
ROYAL MARRIAGE
SHOOTING-RANGE
SPHERISTERION
SMOTHERED MATE
SPORTSMANSHIP
SPORTS STADIUM
STARTING PRICE
STARTING STALL
STRAIGHT FLUSH
SWIMMING BATHS
SWORDSMANSHIP
TONGUE-TWISTER

VULNERABILITY
WRESTLING-RING

14

BADMINTON COURT
CAULIFLOWER EAR
CORRIDA DE TOROS
FIGHTING CHANCE
FOOTBALL GROUND
HOP, STEP AND JUMP
LEAGUE FOOTBALL
NINETEENTH HOLE
QUART AND TIERCE
SHEEPDOG TRIALS
SPORTING CHANCE
THOUSAND METRES
TWO-FOR-HIS-HEELS
WEIGHT TRAINING

15

BODY-LINE BOWLING
BUTTERFLY STROKE
CONSOLATION RACE
EGG-AND-SPOON RACE
FOOTBALL STADIUM
KNIGHT'S PROGRESS
PROFESSIONALISM
SHOOTING GALLERY
THREE-LEGGED RACE

SPORT – INDOOR GAMES & SPORTS

3

DIB
GIN
HEX
LOO
MAW
NAP
NIM
PAM
PIT

4

BRAG
CRIB
DIBS
DICE
FARO
FISH
GRAB
I-SPY
JUDO
LUDO
MAIN
MORA
POOL
PUTT
QUIZ
RUFF
SKAT
SLAM
SNAP
SOLO
SUMO
SWAB
VINT

5

BANDY
BINGO
BOOBY
CARDS
CHEAT
CHESS
CRAPS
DARTS
FIVES
GLEEK

GOOSE
HALMA
HOUSE
JACKS
KAILS
KENDO
LOTTO
LURCH
MONTE
NODDY
OMBRE
OUIJA
PAIRS
POKER
PRIME
REBUS
RUMMY
SHOOT
SPOOF
TAROT
TIP-IT
TRUMP
WHIST

6

AIKIDO
BANKER
BASSET
BEETLE
BO-PEEP
BOSTON
BOXING
BRIDGE
CHEMMY
CLUMPS
CRAMBO
DIVING
DOMINO
DONKEY
ECARTÉ
EUCHRE
FAN-TAN
GOBANG
HAZARD
KARATE
KUNG FU
MERILS
MORRIS
MURDER
PELOTA

PIQUET
PUZZLE
QUINZE
RAFFLE
SAVATE
SEVENS
SQUASH

7

AUCTION
BEZIQUE
BOWLING
CANASTA
CASSINO
CHICAGO
CONKERS
COON-CAN
DIABOLO
FENCING
IN-AND-IN
JACKPOT
JAI ALAI
JO-JOTTE
JU-JITSU
LEXICON
LOTTERY
MAH-JONG
MARBLES
MUGGINS
OLD MAID
PACHISI
PASSAGE
PINBALL
PLAFOND
PONTOON
PRIMERO
RACKETS
REVERSI
SKATING
SNOOKER
SQUAILS
TENPINS
TOMBOLA
WAR-GAME

8

ACROSTIC
AEROBICS

ALL-FIVES
ALL-FOURS
BACCARAT
CARD-GAME
CHARADES
CHECKERS
CONTRACT
CRIBBAGE
DOMINOES
DRAUGHTS
FIVEPINS
FORFEITS
GIN RUMMY
HAND-BALL
JINGLING
KLONDIKE
KORFBALL
LUCKY-DIP
MAH-JONGG
NAPOLEON
NATATION
NINEPINS
PATIENCE
PEEKABOO
PING-PONG
PINOCHLE
PIN-TABLE
POPE JOAN
PURPOSES
PUSH-BALL
PYRAMIDS
REVERSIS
ROULETTE
SCRABBLE
SHOW-DOWN
SKITTLES
SWABBERS
SWIMMING
TEETOTUM
VERQUERE

9

BADMINTON
BAGATELLE
BILLIARDS
BLACKJACK
BOARD-GAME
CROSSWORD
CUT-THROAT
DIB-STONES

FIVE-A-SIDE
HONEYPOTS
ICE-HOCKEY
JINGO-RING
LANTERLOO
LONG WHIST
MATRIMONY
MISTIGRIS
NEWMARKET
NINEHOLES
PARTY-GAME
POKER DICE
QUADRILLE
ROUND GAME
SOLITAIRE
SOLO WHIST
SPOIL-FIVE
SQUAILING
STUD POKER
TABLE-GAME
TREDRILLE
VINGT-ET-UN
WRESTLING

10

BACKGAMMON
BASKETBALL
BLACK MARIA
BOUILLOTTE
CANNON-GAME
CAT'S CRADLE
CRISS-CROSS
CUP-AND-BALL
DUMB CRAMBO
DUMMY WHIST
FLAP-DRAGON
GYMNASTICS
HANDY-DANDY
HOT-COCKLES
ICE-SKATING
JACK-STRAWS
KITTLE-PINS
KRIEGSPIEL
LANSQUENET
PANCRATIUM
PHILOPOENA
PREFERENCE
PUT-AND-TAKE
REAL TENNIS

SPORT — INDOOR GAMES & SPORTS

SHORT WHIST
SHUFFLE-CAP
SNAPDRAGON
SPILLIKINS
VOLLEY-BALL

11

BATTLEDORES
BLIND HOOKEY
BUMBLE-PUPPY
CATCH-THE-TEN
CHASE-THE-ACE
CHEMIN DE FER
FOX AND GEESE
HIDE-AND-SEEK
INDOOR BOWLS
PARLOUR GAME
POST AND PAIR
ROUGE-ET-NOIR
SANCHO-PEDRO
SHOWJUMPING
SHUTTLECOCK
SPECULATION
SPELLING-BEE
TABLE-SOCCER
TABLE-TENNIS
TIDDLYWINKS

12

ARM-WRESTLING
BAR BILLIARDS
BLOW-FOOTBALL
CONSEQUENCES
HOUSEY-HOUSEY
INDOOR TENNIS
JIGSAW PUZZLE
KNUCKLE-BONES
NINE-CARD BRAG
PARTNER WHIST
TRAMPOLINING

13

AMERICAN BOWLS
AUCTION BRIDGE
BLINDMAN'S-BUFF
CALLISTHENICS
CROSS PURPOSES
HAPPY FAMILIES
KISS-IN-THE-RING
KNOCKOUT WHIST
MUSICAL CHAIRS
POSTMAN'S KNOCK
PRIZE-FIGHTING
ROLLER-SKATING
SLOT-CAR RACING
SQUASH RACKETS

TABLE-SKITTLES
TENPIN BOWLING
THREE-CARD BRAG
WEIGHT-LIFTING

14

ALL-IN WRESTLING
CONTRACT BRIDGE
CROWN AND ANCHOR
FOLLOW-MY-LEADER
HUNT-THE-SLIPPER
HUNT-THE-THIMBLE
NINE MEN'S MORRIS
NINEPIN BOWLING
SHOVE-HALFPENNY
SNIP-SNAP-SNORUM
THREE-CARD MONTE

15

CATCH-AS-CATCH-CAN
CHINESE CHECKERS
CROSSWORD PUZZLE
DUPLICATE BRIDGE
INDOOR ATHLETICS
PUSS IN THE CORNER

SPORT — OUTDOOR GAMES & SPORTS

3

HOB
TAG
TAW
TIG

4

BASE
BULL

5

BANDY
BOWLS

DOGS
GOLF
I-SPY
MALL
POLO
TICK

ROQUE
RUGBY
SKEET
TOUCH

6

BOULES
DIVING
FOOTER
FOXING

HIKING
HOCKEY
HURLEY
KIT-CAT
LUGING
QUOITS
RACING
RIDING
ROVING
RUGGER
SHINTY
SKIING

SOCCER
TENNIS
TIP-CAT

7

ANGLING
ARCHERY
BALLING
BIRDING
BOATING

BUNTING
CONKERS
CRICKET
CROQUET
CURLING
CYCLING
DUCKING
FISHING
FOWLING
GLIDING
HUNTING
HURLING

JOGGING
KARTING
LOGGATS
MARBLES
NETBALL
PALLONE
PATBALL
PEEVERS
PUTTING
RING-TAW
RUNNING
SAILING
SKATING
SURFING
TAILING
TILTING
WALKING

8

BASEBALL
CANOEING
CLIMBING
COURSING
EVENTING
FOOTBALL
HANDBALL
HURDLING
JOUSTING
LACROSSE
LANGLAUF
LEAP-FROG
PALL-MALL
PÉTANQUE
RALLYING
RAMBLING
ROLY-POLY
ROUNDERS
SCULLING
SHOOTING
SKIPPING
SLEDDING
SLEDGING
SOFTBALL
SPEEDWAY
SWIMMING
TRAP-BALL
TROTTING
TUG-OF-WAR
WALL-GAME
YACHTING

9

ABSEILING
ATHLETICS
AUTOCROSS
AUTOPOINT
BADMINTON
BANDY-BALL
BICYCLING
CAMANACHD
CHERRY-PIT
CLOCK-GOLF
DOG-RACING
DRY SKIING
GO-KARTING
HOP-SCOTCH
MOTOCROSS
PICKABACK
PIGGYBACK
POTHOLING
SKIJORING
SKI-KITING
SKY-DIVING
SLEIGHING
STOOLBALL
THE EIGHTS
WATER POLO

10

BALLOONING
BATFOWLING
BIRD-SKIING
BOAT-RACING
COCKALORUM
CYCLOCROSS
DECK-QUOITS
DECK-TENNIS
DRAG-RACING
FLY-FISHING
FOOT-RACING
FOX-HUNTING
FREE-DIVING
ICE-HILLING
ICE-SKATING
KITE-FLYING
LAWN TENNIS
PAPER-CHASE
PONY-RACING
SAIL-FLYING
SCRAMBLING

SEA-BATHING
SEA-FISHING
SEVEN-A-SIDE
SKI-BOBBING
SKI-JUMPING
SKIN-DIVING
SKI-RUNNING
SKY-JUMPING
SURF-RIDING
TAUROMACHY
VOLLEY-BALL
WHIPPETING

11

BACKPACKING
BARLEY-BRAKE
BUMBLE-PUPPY
CLOSE-TENNIS
DUCK-HUNTING
HANG-GLIDING
HIDE-AND-SEEK
HORSE RACING
ICE-YACHTING
PARACHUTING
PARAGLIDING
PIGEON-HOLES
PIG-STICKING
ROAD-BOWLING
ROYAL TENNIS
SCUBA-DIVING
SHOVEL-BOARD
SHOWJUMPING
SPAN-COUNTER
STAG-HUNTING
SURF-BATHING
TENT-PEGGING
TOBOGGANING
TUFT-HUNTING
WATER-SKIING
WILDFOWLING
WIND-SURFING

12

BOBSLEIGHING
BULLFIGHTING
CROSS-COUNTRY
DEERSTALKING
HURDLE-RACING

KNUR AND SPELL
LAND-YACHTING
MOTORCYCLING
ORIENTEERING
PARASCENDING
PIGEON-FLYING
PITCH AND TOSS
PONY-TREKKING
ROCK-CLIMBING
SAND-YACHTING
SINGLE WICKET
SPEEDBOATING
SURF-BOARDING
TREASURE HUNT
TROUT-FISHING

13

CHUCKIE-STONES
COARSE FISHING
FRENCH CRICKET
HARE-AND-HOUNDS
HARNESS RACING
HOUND-TRAILING
PRISONER'S BASE
ROLLER-SKATING
ROUGH-SHOOTING
RUGBY FOOTBALL
SALMON-FISHING

14

DOWNHILL SKIING
DUCKS AND DRAKES
FOLLOW-MY-LEADER
GAELIC FOOTBALL
MOUNTAINEERING
PIG IN THE MIDDLE
STEEPLECHASING
STOCK-CAR RACING

15

AUSTRALIAN RULES
CROWN-GREEN BOWLS
GREYHOUND RACING
KING-OF-THE-CASTLE
POWERBOAT-RACING

STUDIES

3

ART
LAW

4

LORE

5

LOGIC
MUSIC
STUDY

6

BOTANY
CIVICS
OOLOGY
OPTICS
SONICS

7

ANATOMY
BIOLOGY
BIONICS
ECOLOGY
GEOLOGY
HAPTICS
HISTORY
METRICS
MYOLOGY
NAUTICS
OROLOGY
OTOLOGY
OVOLOGY
PHONICS
PHOTICS
PHYSICS
SCIENCE
STATICS
UFOLOGY
UROLOGY
VITRICS
ZOOLOGY
ZOONOMY

ZOOTAXY

8

AEROLOGY
AGROLOGY
ALGOLOGY
AREOLOGY
ATMOLOGY
AUTOLOGY
AXIOLOGY
BAROLOGY
BATOLOGY
BIOMETRY
BRYOLOGY
CETOLOGY
CYTOLOGY
DEMOLOGY
DYNAMICS
ETHOLOGY
EUGENICS
FLUIDICS
FOLKLORE
GENETICS
HEDONICS
HOROLOGY
KINESICS
KINETICS
MAYOLOGY
MEDICINE
MYCOLOGY
NOMOLOGY
NOSOLOGY
OENOLOGY
ONCOLOGY
ONTOLOGY
OPTOLOGY
PEDOLOGY
PELOLOGY
PENOLOGY
POLITICS
POSOLOGY
PYROLOGY
RHEOLOGY
ROBOTICS
ROCKETRY
RUNOLOGY
SEROLOGY
SEXOLOGY
SINOLOGY
SITOLOGY

TAXOLOGY
TAXONOMY
TECHNICS
THEOLOGY
TIDOLOGY
TOCOLOGY
TOPOLOGY
TYPOLOGY
VINOLOGY
VIROLOGY
XYLOLOGY
ZOOPATHY
ZYMOLOGY

9

ACOUSTICS
AGRIOLOGY
ASTROLOGY
ASTRONOMY
ATHEOLOGY
AUDIOLOGY
BIONOMICS
CALIOLOGY
CARPOLOGY
CARTOLOGY
CHEMISTRY
CHOROLOGY
COSMOLOGY
CRYOSCOPY
DESMOLOGY
DIDACTICS
DIETETICS
DOSIOLOGY
DYSGENICS
ECONOMICS
ETHNOLOGY
ETYMOLOGY
EUTHENICS
EXEGETICS
FORENSICS
FUNGOLOGY
GEMMOLOGY
GENEALOGY
GEOGRAPHY
GEOPONICS
HELCOLOGY
HELIOLOGY
HIEROLOGY
HIPPOLOGY
HISTOLOGY

HOPLOLOGY
HYDROLOGY
HYGIENICS
HYGROLOGY
HYMNOLOGY
HYPNOLOGY
IATROLOGY
ICHNOLOGY
ICONOLOGY
LIMNOLOGY
LITHOLOGY
LOGISTICS
MAGNETICS
MAGNETISM
MAIEUTICS
MAMMALOGY
MASTOLOGY
METROLOGY
MICROLOGY
MNEMONICS
MUSCOLOGY
MYOGRAPHY
MYTHOLOGY
NEPHOLOGY
NEUROLOGY
NOSTOLOGY
OMBROLOGY
OPHIOLOGY
OSTEOLOGY
PATHOLOGY
PATROLOGY
PESTOLOGY
PETROLOGY
PHENOLOGY
PHILATELY
PHILOLOGY
PHONEMICS
PHONETICS
PHONOLOGY
PHYCOLOGY
PHYTOLOGY
PLUTOLOGY
PLUTONOMY
PTEROLOGY
QUINOLOGY
RADIOLOGY
RHINOLOGY
RHYTHMICS
SARCOLOGY
SCATOLOGY
SEMANTICS
SIGNIFICS

SOCIOLOGY
SYMBOLICS
SYMBOLOGY
SYNECTICS
TECTOLOGY
TECTONICS
TETRALOGY
THEROLOGY
TRIBOLOGY
URANOLOGY
URINOLOGY
ZOIATRICS
ZOOGRAPHY
ZOOTECHNY

10

ARISTOLOGY
ARTHROLOGY
AUTECOLOGY
AUTONOMICS
AXIOMATICS
BALLISTICS
BATHYMETRY
BIBLIOLOGY
BIOECOLOGY
BIOMETRICS
BIOPHYSICS
CACOGENICS
CARDIOLOGY
CATOPTRICS
CEROGRAPHY
CHEIROLOGY
CHOREOLOGY
CHROMATICS
CHRONOLOGY
COMETOLOGY
CONCHOLOGY
CRANIOLOGY
CRYPTOLOGY
DELTIOLOGY
DEMOGRAPHY
DEMONOLOGY
DENDROLOGY
DEONTOLOGY
DOXOGRAPHY
EDAPHOLOGY
EGYPTOLOGY
EMBRYOLOGY
EMMENOLOGY
ENERGETICS

ENTEROLOGY
ENTOMOLOGY
ENZYMOLOGY
EPIZOOTICS
ERGONOMICS
ESCAPOLOGY
FLORISTICS
FUTUROLOGY
GASTROLOGY
GEOPHYSICS
GEOSTATICS
GLACIOLOGY
GLOSSOLOGY
GRAPHEMICS
GRAPHOLOGY
HEORTOLOGY
HEPATOLOGY
HERNIOLOGY
HISTIOLOGY
HYDRAULICS
IMMUNOLOGY
KINEMATICS
LEXICOLOGY
LINGUISTRY
MALACOLOGY
METALLURGY
MIASMOLOGY
MINERALOGY
MORPHEMICS
MORPHOLOGY
MUSICOLOGY
MYCETOLOGY
NEONTOLOGY
NEPHROLOGY
NOMOGRAPHY
NUCLEONICS
NUMEROLOGY
OCEANOLOGY
ODONTOLOGY
ONEIROLOGY
ONOMASTICS
ORGANOLOGY
PALAEOLOGY
PALYNOLOGY
PAPYROLOGY
PATRISTICS
PHILOSOPHY
PHLEBOLOGY
PHRENOLOGY
PHYSIOLOGY
PLASMOLOGY
PNEUMATICS

POTAMOLOGY
PSEPHOLOGY
PSYCHOLOGY
PYRETOLOGY
PYRITOLOGY
SATANOLOGY
SEISMOLOGY
SELENOLOGY
SEMEIOLOGY
SEMEIOTICS
SILPHOLOGY
SOCIOMETRY
SOMATOLOGY
SPECIOLOGY
SPERMOLOGY
SPLENOLOGY
SPONGOLOGY
STORIOLOGY
STYLISTICS
SUBATOMICS
TECHNOLOGY
TERATOLOGY
THERMOLOGY
THERMOTICS
TIMBROLOGY
TOXICOLOGY
TRICHOLOGY
TROPHOLOGY
URBANOLOGY
VERMEOLOGY

11

AERONAUTICS
AGROBIOLOGY
AGROSTOLOGY
ARACHNOLOGY
ARCHAEOLOGY
ASSYRIOLOGY
BIODYNAMICS
CAMPANOLOGY
CARCINOLOGY
CATAPHONICS
CHONDROLOGY
CHRISTOLOGY
CLIMATOLOGY
COSMOGRAPHY
CRIMINOLOGY
CYBERNETICS
DACTYLOLOGY
DERMATOLOGY

DISCOGRAPHY
DOGMATOLOGY
ELECTROLOGY
ELECTRONICS
ENDEMIOLOGY
EPIGENETICS
ETHNOGRAPHY
ETRUSCOLOGY
GALVANOLOGY
GEODYNAMICS
GERONTOLOGY
GIGANTOLOGY
GYNAECOLOGY
HAEMATOLOGY
HERESIOLOGY
HERPETOLOGY
HYDROGRAPHY
HYDROPONICS
HYMNOGRAPHY
HYPERSONICS
HYSTEROLOGY
ICHTHYOLOGY
INSECTOLOGY
KINESIOLOGY
LARYNGOLOGY
LICHENOLOGY
LINGUISTICS
MALARIOLOGY
MARTYROLOGY
MATHEMATICS
METAPHYSICS
METEORITICS
METEOROLOGY
METHODOLOGY
METOPOSCOPY
MICROGRAPHY
MYRMECOLOGY
NATURE STUDY
OLFACTOLOGY
ORNITHOLOGY
PANTHEOLOGY
PLANKTOLOGY
PSYCHOMETRY
PTERIDOLOGY
PURE SCIENCE
SEMASIOLOGY
SKELETOLOGY
SOIL SCIENCE
SPECTROLOGY
SPELAEOLOGY
SPHAGNOLOGY
SPHYGMOLOGY

STEREOPTICS
STOMATOLOGY
SUPERSONICS
SYNOECOLOGY
SYPHILOLOGY
SYSTEMATICS
THANATOLOGY
THERMIONICS
THREPSOLOGY
ULTRASONICS
VENEREOLOGY
VOLCANOLOGY
ZOOTECHNICS

12

AMPHIBIOLOGY
ANTHROPOGENY
ANTHROPOLOGY
ANTHROPOTOMY
ASTROGEOLOGY
ASTROPHYSICS
BACTERIOLOGY
BIBLIOGRAPHY
BIOGEOGRAPHY
BIOMECHANICS
CATACOUSTICS
CATALLACTICS
CERAMOGRAPHY
CHRONOGRAPHY
COSMONAUTICS
CYTOGENETICS
DACTYLIOLOGY
DIALECTOLOGY
DYSTELEOLOGY
ECCLESIOLOGY
ECONOMETRICS
ELECTROMETRY
EPIDEMIOLOGY
EPISTEMOLOGY
GEOMAGNETISM
GEOTECTONICS
GNOTOBIOLOGY
GNOTOBIOTICS
HEPATICOLOGY
HERMENEUTICS
HISTORIOLOGY
LITURGIOLOGY
MACROBIOTICS
METAPSYCHICS
MICROBIOLOGY

STUDIES

OCEANOGRAPHY
PALAEOBOTANY
PARADOXOLOGY
PARASITOLOGY
PAROEMIOLOGY
PHARMACOLOGY
PHOTOGEOLOGY
PHYSIOGRAPHY
PNEUMATOLOGY
PROTISTOLOGY
PROTOZOOLOGY
PYROTECHNICS
RHEUMATOLOGY
RÖNTGENOLOGY
SEISMOGRAPHY
SELENOGRAPHY
SPECTROSCOPY
SPERMATOLOGY
SPHRAGISTICS
STATISTOLOGY
STROMATOLOGY
SYNDESMOLOGY
TESTACEOLOGY
THERMATOLOGY
ZOOGEOGRAPHY
ZOOPATHOLOGY
ZOOPHYTOLOGY
ZYMOTECHNICS

13

CATHODOGRAPHY
CHREMATISTICS
CHRONOBIOLOGY
CLIMATOGRAPHY
CRUSTACEOLOGY
DACTYLOGRAPHY

DIPLOMATOLOGY
ELECTROGRAPHY
GEOCHRONOLOGY
HELMINTHOLOGY
MAGNETO-OPTICS
METALLOGRAPHY
MNEMOTECHNICS
NUMISMATOLOGY
OPHTHALMOLOGY
PALAEONTOLOGY
PALAEOZOOLOGY
PHARMACEUTICS
PHENOMENOLOGY
PHONOCAMPTICS
PSYCHOMETRICS
PSYCHOPHYSICS
SOCIAL SCIENCE
SOIL MECHANICS
SPLANCHNOLOGY
STEGANOGRAPHY
SYNCHRONOLOGY
SYSTEMATOLOGY
THREMMATOLOGY
WAVE MECHANICS
ZOOPSYCHOLOGY

14

ANTHROPOGRAPHY
APPLIED SCIENCE
BIOSYSTEMATICS
DACTYLIOGRAPHY
ELECTROSTATICS
HISTORIOGRAPHY
METAMORPHOLOGY
MICROCOSMOLOGY
NATURAL SCIENCE

NEUROPATHOLOGY
NUCLEAR PHYSICS
ORTHOPTEROLOGY
PALAEETHNOLOGY
PALAEOPEDOLOGY
PHYTOGEOGRAPHY
PHYTOPATHOLOGY
PSYCHONOSOLOGY
PSYCHOSOMATICS
SYMPTOMATOLOGY
THALASSOGRAPHY
THERMODYNAMICS

15

ANAESTHESIOLOGY
ANTHROPOBIOLOGY
BIOASTRONAUTICS
BUSINESS STUDIES
CRYSTALLOGRAPHY
DERMATOGLYPHICS
DOMESTIC SCIENCE
ELECTROTECHNICS
ELECTROTHERMICS
ETHNOMUSICOLOGY
META-LINGUISTICS
MORPHOPHONEMICS
PALAEOLIMNOLOGY
PALAEOMAGNETISM
PALAEOPHYTOLOGY
PANTOPRAGMATICS
PHYSICAL SCIENCE
PSYCHOPATHOLOGY
PURE MATHEMATICS
THERMOCHEMISTRY
ULTRAMICROSCOPY

TIME, DATES & EVENTS

3

AGE
DAY
EON
ERA
EVE
MAY
NOW
RAG

4

AEON
AGES
DATE
DAWN
DUSK
FALL
FAST
FÊTE
GALA
HOUR
IDES
JULY
JUNE
LENT
MASS
MOON
MORN
NOËL
NOON
OBIT
PAST
SPAN
STAY
TERM
TICK
TIDE
TIME
WAKE
WEEK
XMAS
YEAR
YULE

5

APRIL
BREAK

CYCLE
EPOCH
EVENT
FASTI
FEAST
FLASH
GAUDY
GLOOM
JIFFY
KALPA
LAPSE
LEAVE
MARCH
MONTH
NIGHT
NONES
NOWEL
PAUSE
PURIM
REIGN
REVEL
SAROS
SHIFT
SPELL
SUN-UP
TODAY
TRICE
WATCH
WHILE

6

ADVENT
AUGUST
AUTUMN
BOX-DAY
CURFEW
DECADE
DIWALI
EASTER
FESTAL
FIESTA
FRIDAY
FUTURE
HAYSEL
HEYDAY
ISODIA
JUDICA
LAMMAS
LAW-DAY
MAY DAY

MIDDAY
MINUTE
MOMENT
MONDAY
MORROW
OCTAVE
OFF-DAY
PAY-DAY
PENTAD
PERIOD
SEASON
SECOND
SPRING
SUMMER
SUNDAY
SUNSET
VESPER
WINTER
YOM TOB

7

BEDTIME
BELTANE
CALENDS
CENTURY
CHILIAD
DAWNING
DAYTIME
DOG-DAYS
EQUINOX
EVENING
FAIR-DAY
FAST-DAY
FÊTE DAY
FISH-DAY
FLAG-DAY
HALF-DAY
HIGH DAY
HOCK-DAY
HOLIDAY
HOLY DAY
INSTANT
INTERIM
IRON AGE
JANUARY
JAZZ AGE
JUBILEE
LADY DAY
LAETARE
LEAP-DAY

LEMURIA
LUSTRUM
MAY-TIME
MID-LENT
MIDNOON
MIDWEEK
MOONSET
MORNING
NAME-DAY
NOONDAY
NUNDINE
OCTOBER
PALILIA
POST-DAY
PRESENT
QUARTER
RAMADAN
RENT-DAY
REST-DAY
SABBATH
SESSION
SETTING
SOJOURN
SUNDOWN
SUNRISE
TEA-TIME
TERM-DAY
TIME-LAG
TONIGHT
TRIDUUM
TUESDAY
WARTIME
WEEKDAY
WEEKEND
WHITSUN
WORK-DAY

8

ANTEDATE
ARBOR DAY
BIRTHDAY
CARNIVAL
CIVIL DAY
COCKCROW
COURT-DAY
DAFT DAYS
DARK AGES
DAYBREAK
DEADLINE
DECEMBER

DEMI-JOUR
DOG-WATCH
DOOMSDAY
DURATION
EMBER-DAY
EPIPHANY
ETERNITY
EVENFALL
EVENTIDE
FEAST-DAY
FEBRUARY
FESTIVAL
FÊTE-DIEU
FIELD DAY
FIRST-DAY
FORENOON
FULL-TIME
FUTURITY
GAUDY-DAY
GLOAMING
HALF-TERM
HALF-TIME
HALF-YEAR
HEBDOMAD
HIGH NOON
HIGH TIME
HOGMANAY
HOLY WEEK
INTERVAL
JAMBOREE
JUBILATE
JUNCTURE
LEAP-YEAR
LORD'S DAY
LUPERCAL
MEAL-TIME
MEANTIME
MEAN TIME
MERIDIAN
MIDNIGHT
MOONRISE
NOONTIDE
NOVEMBER
NOWADAYS
OCCASION
OVERTIME
OWL-LIGHT
PANEGYRY
PASSOVER
PLAYTIME
POPPY DAY
POST-TIME

TIME, DATES & EVENTS

POUND-DAY
RIGHT NOW
RUSH HOUR
SATURDAY
SEMESTER
SENNIGHT
SOLAR DAY
SOLSTICE
SPACE AGE
STONE AGE
TEA-BREAK
TERM-TIME
THURSDAY
TOMORROW
TWILIGHT
VACATION
WHIT-WEEK
YULETIDE
ZERO HOUR

LEAN YEARS
LEGAL YEAR
LIGHT YEAR
LOCAL TIME
LOW SUNDAY
LUNAR YEAR
LUNCH-HOUR
LUNCH-TIME
MARDI GRAS
MARKET-DAY
MARTINMAS
MID-SEASON
MIDSUMMER
MIDWINTER
MILLENARY
NIGHTFALL
NIGHT-TIDE
NIGHT-TIME
ONE O'CLOCK
PARASCEVE
PEACETIME
PENTECOST
QUASIMODO
SAINT'S DAY
SALAD DAYS
SCHOOL-DAY
SECOND-DAY
SEPTEMBER
SEPTENARY
SILVER AGE
SIX O'CLOCK
SOLAR TIME
SOLAR YEAR
SPACE-TIME
SPEECH DAY
SPORTS DAY
THARGELIA
TICKET-DAY
TIME-LAPSE
TIME OF DAY
TRIMESTER
TWO O'CLOCK
VULGAR ERA
WAKES WEEK
WEDNESDAY
YESTERDAY
YESTEREVE
YOM KIPPUR
YOM TERUAH

9

AFTERNOON
ANNO MUNDI
ANTIQUITY
BATH-NIGHT
BOXING DAY
BRONZE AGE
CANDLEMAS
CENTENARY
CHRISTMAS
CHURCH-ALE
CIVIL TIME
CIVIL YEAR
COPPER AGE
DECENNARY
EASTER DAY
EMBER DAYS
EMBER WEEK
EMPIRE DAY
FEISEANNA
FORTNIGHT
GOLDEN AGE
HALF-LIGHT
HALLOWE'EN
HAPPENING
HEREAFTER
HEROIC AGE
INTERLUDE
LABOUR DAY

10

ALL-HALLOWS
AMBARVALIA
ANNO DOMINI
ATOMIC TIME
AUTUMN TERM
BARNABY DAY
BIRTHNIGHT
BISSEXTILE
CENTENNIAL
CHILDERMAS
CORONATION
CREPUSCULE
DINNER-HOUR
DINNER-TIME
DREAMWHILE
DRESSED DAY
EASTER TERM
EASTERTIDE
EASTERTIME
EISTEDDFOD
FATHER'S DAY
FENCE MONTH
FIELD NIGHT
FISCAL YEAR
FIVE O'CLOCK
FOUR O'CLOCK
GANDER-MOON
GAUDY-NIGHT
GENERATION
GOOD FRIDAY
GUEST-NIGHT
HALLOWMASS
HEBREW YEAR
HEXAËMERON
HILARY TERM
JOUR DE FÊTE
JULIAN YEAR
LAMMAS-TIDE
LUNAR CYCLE
LUNAR MONTH
MEAL MONDAY
MICHAELMAS
MILLENNIUM
MOTHER'S DAY
MUMPING-DAY
NANOSECOND
NINE O'CLOCK
OCCURRENCE
OLDEN TIMES
PALM SUNDAY

PANCAKE DAY
PEAK-PERIOD
PERPETUITY
PRESSED-DAY
QUARTER-DAY
QUIRINALIA
RECORD TIME
SABBATH DAY
SATURNALIA
SCHOOLDAYS
SCHOOL-TIDE
SCHOOL-TIME
SEPTENNATE
SEPTENNIUM
SEVENTH-DAY
SEXAGESIMA
SHROVETIDE
SMALL HOURS
SOLAR MONTH
SOTHIC YEAR
SPRINGTIDE
SPRINGTIME
ST JOHN'S DAY
SUMMER TERM
SUMMERTIDE
SUMMERTIME
SUPPER-TIME
TERMINALIA
THEBAN YEAR
THE FORTIES
THE FIFTIES
THE SIXTIES
TWELFTH-DAY
VULCANALIA
WANDER-YEAR
WASHING-DAY
WATCH-NIGHT
WEDDING-DAY
WHIT MONDAY
WHITSUN-ALE
WHIT SUNDAY
WINTERTIME
WORKING-DAY
YESTERYEAR

11

ALL FOOLS' DAY
ALL SOULS' DAY
ANNIVERSARY
ANTHESTERIA

BANK HOLIDAY
BICENTENARY
BIMILLENARY
BLACK FRIDAY
BLACK MONDAY
CLOSE SEASON
CLOSING TIME
CONTANGO DAY
DECOLLATION
DISCOUNT DAY
EIGHT O'CLOCK
ELDERS' HOURS
FEAST OF LOTS
FEEDING TIME
FIVE-DAY WEEK
GANDER-MONTH
HALCYON DAYS
HALF-HOLIDAY
HARVEST-HOME
HARVEST-TIME
HOLIDAY-TIME
HOLYROOD DAY
HUNTING-TIDE
INTERREGNUM
JUBILEE YEAR
JUDGMENT DAY
LONG WEEKEND
MEMORIAL DAY
MICROSECOND
MORNING-TIDE
NATURAL YEAR
NEW YEAR'S DAY
NEW YEAR'S EVE
OAK-APPLE DAY
OPENING TIME
PANATHENAEA
PASSION-TIDE
PASSION-WEEK
PREPARATION
QUADRENNIAL
QUADRENNIUM
SEMI-JUBILEE
SETTLING DAY
SEVEN O'CLOCK
SIDEREAL DAY
SOTHIC CYCLE
SPLIT SECOND
ST AGNES'S EVE
ST DAVID'S DAY
THE EIGHTIES
THE NINETIES
THE THIRTIES

THE TWENTIES
TRANSFER DAY
TRINITY TERM
TWELFTH-TIDE
TWELVEMONTH
VINTAGE YEAR
VISITING-DAY
WHITSUNTIDE
WHITSUN-WEEK
WORKING-WEEK

12

ALL SAINTS' DAY
ARMISTICE DAY
ASCENSION DAY
ASH WEDNESDAY
ATOMIC SECOND
BICENTENNIAL
BIMILLENNIUM
CALENDAR YEAR
CARNIVAL WEEK
CHRISTIAN ERA
CHRISTMAS DAY
CHRISTMAS EVE
DONKEY'S YEARS
EASTER SUNDAY
ELEVEN O'CLOCK
FEAST OF ASSES
FEAST OF FOOLS
HOLY THURSDAY
INNOCENTS' DAY
LATENT PERIOD
LESSER BAIRAM
MIDSUMMER DAY
MOVABLE FEAST
NYCHTHEMERON
OPENING HOURS
PERPETUATION
PLOUGH MONDAY
QUADRAGESIMA
QUADRIENNIUM
QUINQUENNIAD
QUINQUENNIAL
QUINQUENNIUM
RED-LETTER DAY
ROGATION DAYS
ROGATION WEEK
SEPTUAGESIMA
SEXCENTENARY
SIDEREAL YEAR

SOTHIC PERIOD
STANDARD TIME
ST ANDREW'S DAY
STELLAR MONTH
ST GEORGE'S DAY
SYNODIC MONTH
THE SEVENTIES
THESMOPHORIA
TRICENTENARY
TROPICAL YEAR
TWELFTH NIGHT
TWELVE O'CLOCK

13

ALL HALLOWS' DAY
ALL-HALLOWTIDE
APRIL FOOLS' DAY
ASCENSIONTIDE
BREAKFAST-TIME
CALENDAR MONTH
CANICULAR YEAR
CHRISTMASTIDE
CHRISTMAS-TIME
COMMEMORATION
CORPUS CHRISTI
DECORATION DAY
FINANCIAL YEAR
GLACIAL PERIOD
GOLDEN JUBILEE
GOLDEN WEDDING
GREATER BAIRAM
HANDSEL MONDAY
HOLIDAY SEASON
LUNISOLAR YEAR
OCTOCENTENARY
PASSION SUNDAY
PERIODIC MONTH
PUBLIC HOLIDAY
QUADRINGENARY
QUINCENTENARY
QUINGENTENARY
QUINQUAGESIMA
SHROVE TUESDAY
SIDEREAL MONTH
SILVER JUBILEE
SILVER WEDDING
ST CRISPIN'S DAY
ST PATRICK'S DAY
ST SWITHIN'S DAY
TERCENTENNIAL

TIME, DATES & EVENTS

TRINITY SUNDAY
TROPICAL MONTH
VERNAL EQUINOX
VISITING HOURS

14

CANONICAL HOURS
DAY OF ATONEMENT
DIAMOND JUBILEE
DIAMOND WEDDING
EMBOLISMIC YEAR
GEOLOGICAL TIME

MAUNDY THURSDAY
MICHAELMAS TERM
PANCAKE TUESDAY
ROGATION SUNDAY
SABBATICAL YEAR
SUMMER SOLSTICE
WALPURGIS NIGHT
WINTER SOLSTICE

15

ANNUNCIATION DAY

ANOMALISTIC YEAR
AUTUMNAL EQUINOX
BARTHOLOMEW-TIDE
EARLY-CLOSING DAY
EQUINOCTIAL YEAR
EXPECTATION WEEK
HARVEST FESTIVAL
MOTHERING SUNDAY
QUATERCENTENARY
REFECTION SUNDAY
ST VALENTINE'S DAY
THANKSGIVING DAY
UNIVERSAL SECOND

TOOLS & EQUIPMENT

3

AWL
AXE
BIT
BOB
DIE
DOG
GAD
GIN
GUM
GUN
HOD
HOE
JIG
KEY
KIT
LOY
MAT
NUT
PEG
PIN
RAM
SAW
SAX
SET
TAP
TAR
TUP
VAN

IRON
JACK
LAST
LEAD
LOOT
MACE
MAIN
MALL
MAUL
NAIL
PALE
PALM
PEEL
PICK
PLUG
PROD
RAKE
RASP
RISP
ROLL
ROSE
RULE
SHIM
SIZE
SLEY
SLOT
SNAP
SPUD
STAY
STUD
TACK
TANG
TOOL
TRAP
VICE

4

ADZE
BOLT
BRAD
BURR
CARD
CELT
CLIP
FILE
FLEX
FORK
GEAR
GLUE
GRIP
HAFT
HASP
HAWK
HOOK
HOSE

CHUCK
CLAMP
CLASP
CLEAT
CLOUT
CORER
DOLLY
DOWEL
DRILL
EMERY
FLOAT
GAVEL
GOOSE
GOUGE
GROUT
HELVE
HINGE
JAPAN
JEMMY
KNIFE
LEVER
LINER
MADGE
MAKER
METHS
MISER
OCHRE
PAINT
PANGA
PAPER
PASTE
PINCH
PLANE
POINT
POKER
PRUNT
PUNCH
PUNTY
PUTTY
RAKER
RIVET
RULER
SCOOP
SCREW
SHAFT
SHANK
SHARE
SHAVE
SIEVE
SIZER
SLANE
SNARE

5

ANVIL
AUGER
BESOM
BETTY
BIPOD
BLADE
BORER
BRACE
BRAND
BRUSH
BULLY
BURIN
CABLE

SNATH
SNIPS
SPADE
SPICK
SPIKE
SPOON
SPRIG
STAKE
STAMP
STEEL
STEPS
STROP
STYLE
SWAGE
TEMSE
TONGS
TURPS
U-BOLT
WEDGE
WREST

6

BANKER
BED-KEY
BEETLE
BIDENT
BODKIN
BOW-SAW
BROACH
BURTON
CHASER
CHISEL
COTTER
CRADLE
CURSOR
DIBBER
DIBBLE
ENAMEL
FORFEX
FRAISE
GADGET
GARNET
GIMLET
GRATER
GRAVER
GURLET
HAMMER
HANDLE
HOPDOG
JIGSAW

JOGGLE
JUMPER
LADDER
LASTER
MALLET
MARKER
MASTIC
MONKEY
MORTAR
MULLER
NEEDLE
PADDLE
PALLET
PEAVEY
PECKER
PESTLE
PICKER
PIT-SAW
PLIERS
PLOUGH
POMMEL
PONTIL
PRIMER
PULLEY
PUTLOG
RABBLE
RAMMER
REAMER
RIBBON
RICKER
RIDDLE
RIPPER
RIPPLE
RIP-SAW
ROCKER
ROLLER
SANDER
SAW-SET
SCALER
SCREEN
SCRIBE
SCUTCH
SCYTHE
SEARCE
SHEARS
SHOVEL
SICKLE
SIFTER
SIZING
SKEWER
SLATER
SLEDGE

SPACER
SQUARE
STADDA
STAPLE
STYLET
STYLUS
TACKLE
TAMPER
TEDDER
TINGLE
TRACER
TREPAN
TROWEL
WASHER
WIMBLE
WRENCH

7

AIR-PUMP
BACKSAW
BAND-SAW
BATTERY
BOASTER
BOLSTER
BRADAWL
BUCK-SAW
BUZZ-SAW
CADRANS
CHOPPER
CLEAVER
CLINKER
CLIPPER
CLOBBER
CORN-VAN
CROW-BAR
CUPHEAD
FAT-LUTE
FLESHER
FRET-SAW
GANG-SAW
GIN-TRAP
GRAINER
GRAPNEL
GRAPPLE
GRIPPER
GRUBBER
HACK-LOG
HACK-SAW
HANDSAW
HATCHET

377

TOOLS & EQUIPMENT

HAYFORK
HOBNAIL
HOOK-PIN
JIM-CROW
JOINTER
LACQUER
MANDREL
MATTOCK
MORDANT
NAIL-GUN
NIPPERS
OUSTITI
PICKAXE
PIERCER
PINCERS
PLANTER
PLUNGER
POINTEL
POINTER
POLE-AXE
PRICKER
PRIMING
PUNCHER
QUANNET
RACLOIR
RAGBOLT
RAT-TRAP
RIFFLER
RIP-HOOK
RUFFLER
SCAUPER
SCOOPER
SCORPER
SCRAPER
SCRIBER
SCUFFLE
SCUMMER
SEAM-SET
SHACKLE
SHOE-PEG
SKIMMER
SLEEKER
SLICKER
SOLVENT
SPANNER
SPARGER
SPRAYER
SPRINGE
STAPLER
SWINGLE
TAP-BOLT
THINNER

TIN-TACK
TRAMMEL
TRENAIL
TRIMMER
T-SQUARE
UPRIGHT
UTENSIL
VARNISH
WHIP-SAW
WHITTLE
WIDENER

8

ABRADANT
ABRASIVE
ADHESIVE
AIGUILLE
AIR-BRUSH
ALLEN KEY
AUGER-BIT
AXE-STONE
BICK-IRON
BILLHOOK
BLOWLAMP
BOLT-HEAD
BOOTLAST
BOOT-TREE
CHAIN-SAW
CLIP-HOOK
CORUNDUM
CREOSOTE
CROWN-SAW
DOORNAIL
DOWEL-PIN
DOWEL-ROD
EDGE TOOL
EMULSION
FALL-TRAP
FIRE-HOOK
FIRE-HOSE
FIRE-PLUG
FLAX-COMB
FOOT-PUMP
FRAME-SAW
GAVELOCK
GROUTING
HANDBILL
HAND-VICE
HARDENER
HAY KNIFE

HOLDFAST
LAP-STONE
LAZY-JACK
LIMEWASH
MEAT-HOOK
MOLE-GRIP
MUCK-RAKE
OILSTONE
PANEL-PIN
PANEL-SAW
PEN-KNIFE
PICKLOCK
PINCHERS
POWER-SAW
PRONG-HOE
PUNCHEON
RAG-WHEEL
RING-BOLT
ROT-STONE
ROULETTE
RUBSTONE
SASH-TOOL
SAW-BLADE
SAW-FRAME
SAW-HORSE
SCISSORS
SCUFFLER
SCUTCHER
SET-SCREW
SHOEHORN
SHOE-NAIL
SHOE-TREE
SLATE-AXE
SMOOTHER
SNUFFERS
SPARABLE
SPRAY-GUN
SPRINGLE
STAY-BOLT
STIFF-BIT
STILETTO
STIPPLER
STONE-AXE
STRICKLE
STRIPPER
STUB-NAIL
STUD-BOLT
SURFACER
SWEEP-SAW
TAR-BRUSH
TENON-SAW
TEREBENE

TINT-TOOL
TOMMY-BAR
TWEEZERS
VIBRATOR
WINDLASS
WIRE WOOL

9

APPARATUS
APPLIANCE
BATH STONE
BUFF-STICK
BUFF-WHEEL
BURNISHER
BUTTER-PAT
CALLIPERS
CANNON BIT
CAN-OPENER
CEMENT GUN
CENTRE-BIT
CLEARCOLE
CLOUT-NAIL
COMPASSES
COPING-SAW
CORK-BORER
CORK-SCREW
COTTER-PIN
DISTEMPER
DRIFT-BOLT
DUTCH RUSH
EDGED TOOL
EQUIPMENT
FILLISTER
FORCE-PUMP
GOOSE-NECK
GLASS WOOL
GREASE-GUN
GRITSTONE
HAND-SCREW
HANDSPIKE
HEDGEBILL
HOLING-AXE
HONE-STONE
HORSE NAIL
IMPLEMENT
JACK-KNIFE
JACK-PLANE
LAZY-TONGS
LEAD-PAINT
MALE SCREW

MOLE-SPADE
MOON-KNIFE
MOUSE-TRAP
NUT-WRENCH
OUTSIDERS
PEAT-SPADE
PITCHFORK
PLANISHER
RABBET-SAW
REED-KNIFE
RICKSTICK
ROCK-DRILL
SANDPAPER
SCARIFIER
SCREWBOLT
SCREW-NAIL
SCROLL-SAW
SECATEURS
SEED-DRILL
SETSQUARE
SHARPENER
SLEEVE-NUT
SPIKE-NAIL
STEEL WOOL
STRETCHER
SUBSOILER
SUPERGLUE
TEE-SQUARE
THRUST-HOE
TIN-OPENER
TURF-SPADE
TURN-SCREW
UNDERCOAT
WHETSTONE
WHITEWASH
WIRE-BRUSH
WOOD-HORSE
WOOD-SCREW

10

CHURN-DRILL
CLAW-HAMMER
COLD CHISEL
COMPASS-SAW
CORKING-PIN
CREAM-SLICE
CUTTLE-BONE
EDULCORANT

EMERY-CLOTH
EMERY-PAPER
EMERY-WHEEL
EPOXY RESIN
FLOAT-STONE
FORE-HAMMER
GLASS-CLOTH
GLASS-PAPER
GLOSS PAINT
GRINDSTONE
GUILLOTINE
HOLING-PICK
INSTRUMENT
LACQUERING
LOGGERHEAD
MARINE GLUE
MASONRY-BIT
PAINT-BRUSH
PAPER-KNIFE
PERFORATOR
PEWTER-MILL
PIPE-WRENCH
PROTRACTOR
PUTTY-KNIFE
REAMING-BIT
RIPPING-SAW
ROAD-ROLLER
ROPE-LADDER
ROUGH-STUFF
SCOTCH HAND
SHACKLE-PIN
SHEEP'S-FOOT
SPOKESHAVE
STEP-LADDER
TENTER-HOOK
TURF-CUTTER
TURNBUCKLE
TURNING-SAW
TURPENTINE
TYPE-HOLDER
WATER-GLASS
WOOL-SHEARS

11

ABOUT-SLEDGE
BASTARD FILE
BOTTLE-BRUSH
BREAST-DRILL

BURLING-IRON
BUSHWHACKER
BUTTER-PRINT
CARBORUNDUM
CIRCULAR SAW
CROSSCUT SAW
EMERY-POWDER
FEELER-GUAGE
FEMALE SCREW
FLOORING SAW
FRENCH CHALK
GLASS-CUTTER
HEDGING BILL
HELVE-HAMMER
JACOB'S-STAFF
OVERGRAINER
OYSTER-KNIFE
OYSTER-TONGS
PAINT-ROLLER
PAPER-CUTTER
PINKING-IRON
PLOUGHSHARE
POCKET-KNIFE
PRUNING-BILL
PRUNING-HOOK
PUTTY-POWDER
RABBET-PLANE
REAPING-HOOK
ROAD-SCRAPER
ROCKING-TOOL
ROTTENSTONE
SAND-THROWER
SCREWDRIVER
SCREW-WRENCH
SCYTHE-STONE
SEARING-IRON
SHACKLE-BOLT
SHEATH-KNIFE
SPARROW-BILL
STONE-HAMMER
STOVE-ENAMEL
STRAW-CUTTER
STUBBLE-RAKE
SULPHURATOR
SWINGLE-HAND
SWING-PLOUGH
THROUGH-BOLT
TICKET-PUNCH
TURFING-IRON
WEEDING-FORK
WHITE SPIRIT
WOODRUFF KEY

TOOLS & EQUIPMENT

12

AVERRUNCATOR
BRANDING-IRON
BREASTPLOUGH
BUTTERFLY-NUT
CAULKING-IRON
COMPASS-PLANE
CRADLE-SCYTHE
CRIMPING-IRON
CRISPING-IRON
CURLING-TONGS
DIAMOND DRILL
DRAWING-KNIFE
ENDLESS SCREW
HEDGE-TRIMMER
JAPAN LACQUER
JAPAN VARNISH
JOINTING RULE
LEATHER-KNIFE
MONKEY-WRENCH
POTTER'S WHEEL
PRUNING-KNIFE
PUDDLING-IRON
SCARIFICATOR
SCISSOR-BLADE
SCRATCH-BRUSH
SELF-TAP SCREW

SLEDGE-HAMMER
SNARLING-IRON
SNARLING-TOOL
SPANISH CHALK
TORQUE-WRENCH
TRENCH-PLOUGH
WEEDING-TONGS

13

CHOPPING-BLOCK
DENTIST'S DRILL
ELECTRIC DRILL
EMULSION PAINT
ETCHING NEEDLE
EXPLOSIVE BOLT
EXTENSION LEAD
GRAPPLING-IRON
LUMINOUS PAINT
NETTING-NEEDLE
PACKING-NEEDLE
PAINT-STRIPPER
PINKING-SHEARS
POMPIER-LADDER
PRUNING-SHEARS
SCALING-LADDER
SECTION-CUTTER

SERVING-MALLET
SOLDERING BOLT
SOLDERING IRON
WEEDING-CHISEL
YORKSHIRE GRIT

14

BALL-PEIN HAMMER
BLOCK AND TACKLE
BUTTERFLY-SCREW
EXPLOSIVE RIVET
INSULATION TAPE
PERPETUAL SCREW
POLISHING-PASTE
SMOOTHING PLANE
STRETCHING-IRON
WEEDING-FORCEPS

15

ENTRENCHING TOOL
PESTLE AND MORTAR
POLISHING-POWDER
WHEEL-NUT SPANNER

TOYS & FIREWORKS

3
CAP
PEG
TAW
TOP
TOY

4
BALL
BIKE
DART
DOLL
FORT
HOOP
KITE
YO-YO

5.
ALLEY
BRICK
CORAL
DEVIL
DOLLY
DRAKE
GERBE
KNACK
SLIDE
SQUIB
SWING
TEDDY
TRICK

6
AMORCE
BANGER
BAUBLE
BONBON
CAP-GUN
DRAGON
FIZGIG
GEWGAW
JIGSAW
MARBLE
MOPPET
PEG-TOP

POP-GUN
PUPPET
PUZZLE
RATTLE
ROCKER
ROCKET
SEESAW
STILTS
SUCKER

7
BALLOON
BICYCLE
BOX-KITE
CRACKER
DIABOLO
FRISBEE
NOVELTY
OCARINA
PLONKER
PLUNKER
RAG-BABY
RAG-DOLL
RHOMBOS
SCOOTER
SERPENT
TANGRAM
TUMBLER
TURNDUN
VOLCANO
WAX-DOLL

8
CATAPULT
CORN-BABY
FIREWORK
FLIP-FLOP
GOLLIWOG
GOLLYWOG
HULA-HOOP
NOAH'S ARK
PEDAL-CAR
PIN-WHEEL
SKIPJACK
SLAP-BANG
SPARKLER
SQUEAKER

TEETOTUM
TRAIN SET
TRICYCLE

9
BANDALORE
CARTWHEEL
COCKHORSE
CORN-DOLLY
DOLL'S-PRAM
DUTCH DOLL
GIRANDOLE
GYROSCOPE
PARISH TOP
PIGGY-BANK
PLAYTHING
POGO STICK
SKY-ROCKET
TEDDY-BEAR
THROW-DOWN
THUNDERER
WHIRLIGIG
WHIZZ-BANG

10
BENGAL FIRE
BULL-ROARER
DOLL'S-HOUSE
DRAKESTONE
FAIRY-CYCLE
FANTOCCINI
HOBBY-HORSE
HUMMING-TOP
INDIAN FIRE
KEWPIE DOLL
MARIONETTE
MUSICAL BOX
MYRIOSCOPE
PANTOGRAPH
PEASHOOTER
RUBIK'S CUBE
SKATEBOARD
SPIROGRAPH
TIN SOLDIER
TOY THEATRE
WENDY HOUSE

11
BABY-BOUNCER
FIRE-CRACKER
GLOVE-PUPPET
JUMPING-BEAN
JUMPING-JACK
PYROTECHNIC
ROLLER-SKATE
ROMAN CANDLE
SCRATCH-BACK
SPINNING-TOP
TEETER-BOARD
THAUMATROPE
TOURBILLION
WATER-PISTOL
WHIPPING-TOP

12
EXECUTIVE TOY
JACK-IN-THE-BOX
JIGSAW PUZZLE
KALEIDOSCOPE
MODEL RAILWAY
PADDLING POOL
PRAXINOSCOPE
ROCKING-HORSE
SKIPPING-ROPE
TEETHING-RING

13
BUILDING-BLOCK
BUILDING-BRICK

14
CARTESIAN DIVER
CATHERINE-WHEEL
CHINESE CRACKER
CLOCKWORK-TRAIN

15
PHARAOH'S SERPENT
WATERLOO CRACKER

TRANSPORT – AIR & SPACE TRANSPORT

3
JET
LEM
UFO

4
KITE
MOTH

5
AVION
BLIMP
CAMEL
CRATE
DRONE
HOVER
PLANE
SCOUT
TAUBE

6
AIR-BUS
AIR-CAR
BOMBER
CANARD
FAN-JET
GLIDER
PUSHER
RAIDER

ROCKET
TANKER

7
AEROBUS
AIRSHIP
AVIETTE
BALLOON
BIPLANE
CAPSULE
CHOPPER
FIGHTER
HELIBUS
JETFOIL
JUMP-JET
PARASOL
SPUTNIK
TRACTOR
TRAINER

8
AERODYNE
AEROSTAT
AIRCRAFT
AIRLINER
AIRPLANE
AUTOGYRO
GYRODYNE
HOVER-BUS
HOVER-CAR
INTRUDER
JET-PLANE
JUMBO JET
SEAPLANE
TRIPLANE
ZEPPELIN

9
AEROPLANE
AEROTRAIN
AMPHIBIAN
DELTA-WING
DIRIGIBLE
EGG-BEATER
GYROPLANE
HYDROFOIL
LAND-PLANE
MONOPLANE
PARACHUTE
ROTAPLANE
SAILPLANE
SATELLITE
SPACESHIP
SWING-WING
TWO-SEATER

10
AIR-BALLOON
DIVE-BOMBER
FLOAT PLANE
FLYING BOAT
FLYING WING
GYROCOPTER
HANG-GLIDER
HELICOPTER
HOVERCRAFT
HOVER-TRAIN
JET FIGHTER
MICROLIGHT
MULTIPLANE
PARAGLIDER
ROTOR-PLANE
SPACECRAFT
SPACE PROBE
STEP-ROCKET
WATER-PLANE
WHIRLYBIRD

11
FIRE-BALLOON
INTERCEPTOR
KITE-BALLOON
MONTGOLFIER
ORNITHOPTER
ROCKET-PLANE
SPACE ROCKET
TOWING-PLANE

12
AIR-AMBULANCE
AIR-FREIGHTER
FLYING SAUCER
NIGHT-FIGHTER
SINGLE-SEATER
SPACE CAPSULE
SPACE SHUTTLE
TROOP-CARRIER

13
CONVERTIPLANE
FLYING MACHINE
HOT-AIR BALLOON
STRATOCRUISER

14
AEROHYDROPLANE
FLYING BEDSTEAD
HYDRO-AEROPLANE
PASSENGER PLANE

TRANSPORT – LAND TRANSPORT

3

BOB
BUS
CAB
CAR
CAT
FLY
GIG
VAN

4

AUTO
BIGA
BIKE
CART
DRAG
DRAY
DUCK
EKKA
HEAP
JEEP
KAGO
KART
LOCO
LUGE
POST
PRAM
SKIS
SLED
SOLO
TANK
TAXI
TRAM
TRAP
WAIN

5

ARABA
BANDY
BRAKE
BUGGY
COACH
COUPÉ
CRATE
CROCK
CYCLE
CYCLO

DILLY
FLOAT
HOBBY
LOCAL
LORRY
MOPED
MOTOR
NODDY
PULKA
RACER
SCOUT
SEDAN
STAGE
SULKY
T-CART
TONGA
TRAIN
TRUCK
WAGON

6

BANGER
BARROW
BERLIN
BOWSER
CALASH
CAMION
CAMPER
CHAISE
DENNET
DIESEL
DOOLIE
ENGINE
FIACRE
GHARRI
GO-KART
HANSOM
HEARSE
HERDIC
HOT ROD
JALOPY
JAMPAN
JINGLE
JITNEY
KIT-CAR
LANDAU
LITTER
MAHMAL
OX-CART
PICK-UP

PUFFER
REMISE
SALOON
SLEDGE
SLEIGH
SURREY
TANDEM
TANKER
TELEGA
TIPPER
TOURER
TRICAR
TROIKA
WAGGON
WEASEL
WHISKY

7

AMTRACK
AUTOBUS
AUTOCAR
BICYCLE
BOBSLED
BRITZKA
CACOLET
CAISSON
CARAVAN
CARIOLE
CAROCHE
CHARIOT
CRAWLER
DOG-CART
DROSHKY
EXPRESS
FLIVVER
FORECAR
FOURGON
GROWLER
GYROCAR
HACKERY
HACKNEY
HANDCAR
HIRE-CAR
KAJAWAH
KIBITKA
MAIL-VAN
MINI-BUS
MINI-CAB
MINI-CAR
OMNIBUS

PEDICAB
PEDRAIL
PHAETON
PILL-BOX
RICKSHA
SCOOTER
SHANDRY
SIDECAR
SPECIAL
STEAMER
TALLY-HO
TARTANA
TAX-CART
TAXI-CAB
TILBURY
TIP-CART
TRACTOR
TRAILER
TRAM-CAR
TRAVOIS
TRISHAW
TROLLEY
TUMBREL
TUMBRIL
UP-TRAIN
VEHICLE
VETTURA
VIS-À-VIS
VOITURE
VOLANTE
WHIPPET
WRECKER

8

AMPHICAR
BAROUCHE
BASSINET
BROUGHAM
BUCK-CART
CABLE-CAR
CAPE CART
CARRIAGE
CARRY-ALL
CLARENCE
CURRICLE
CYCLE-CAR
DRAGSTER
DUST-CART
HAND-CART
HOCK-CART

HORSE-BOX
HORSECAR
IRISH CAR
JUMP-SEAT
LAND-SHIP
MAIL-CART
MOTOR-BUS
MOTOR-CAR
ORDINARY
OWL-TRAIN
PANDA CAR
PUSH-BIKE
PUSH-CART
QUADRIGA
RICKSHAW
ROADSTER
ROCKAWAY
RUNABOUT
SCOUT CAR
SQUAD CAR
STAFF CAR
STANHOPE
STEAM-CAR
STOCK-CAR
TOBOGGAN
TRICYCLE
UNICYCLE
VICTORIA
WAY-TRAIN

9

AMBULANCE
AMPHIBIAN
APPLE-CART
AUTOCYCLE
BANDWAGON
BATH-CHAIR
BOAT-TRAIN
BOBSLEIGH
BUBBLE-CAR
BUCKWAGON
BULLDOZER
CABRIOLET
CHARABANC
DANDY-CART
DILIGENCE
DORMOBILE
DOWN-TRAIN
ESTATE CAR
EXCAVATOR

TRANSPORT – LAND TRANSPORT

HALF-TRACK
HANSOM CAB
HATCHBACK
INSIDE-CAR
IRON HORSE
LANDAULET
LAND-ROVER
LAND-YACHT
LIMOUSINE
LOW-LOADER
MAIL-COACH
MAIL-TRAIN
MILK-FLOAT
MOON-BUGGY
MOTORBIKE
PALANQUIN
PATROL CAR
PIPSQUEAK
POLICE CAR
PRISON-VAN
PUSH-CHAIR
PUSH-CYCLE
RACING-CAR
SALOON CAR
SAND-YACHT
SPORTS CAR
STREET-CAR
STRETCHER
TARANTASS
TIM-WHISKY
TUBE-TRAIN
TUMBLE-CAR
TWO-SEATER
TWO-STROKE
WAGONETTE
WATER-CART

FIRE-ENGINE
FOUR-IN-HAND
FOUR-SEATER
GOODS-TRAIN
HACKNEY-CAB
HAND-BARROW
INVALID CAR
JINRICKSHA
JUGGERNAUT
KNOCKABOUT
LOCOMOBILE
LOCOMOTIVE
MAMMY-WAGON
MOTOR-COACH
MOTORCYCLE
MOTOR-LORRY
NIGHT TRAIN
OUTSIDE-CAR
PEDAL-CYCLE
POST-CHAISE
QUADRUPLET
REMOVAL VAN
SEDAN-CHAIR
SHANDRYDAN
SNOWMOBILE
SNOW-PLOUGH
SPRING-CART
STAGE-COACH
STAGE-WAGON
STATE COACH
TIP-UP LORRY
TIP-UP TRUCK
TOURING-CAR
TRAMWAY-CAR
TROLLEY-BUS
TROLLEY-CAR
TUMBLE-CART
TWO-WHEELER
VELOCIPEDE
VETERAN CAR
VINTAGE CAR
WATER-WAGON
WHEEL-CHAIR

CATERPILLAR
CATTLE-TRUCK
COMBINATION
DELIVERY-VAN
ELECTRIC CAR
FOUR-WHEELER
GUN-CARRIAGE
JAUNTING-CAR
JINRICKSHAW
LANDAULETTE
LIGHTWEIGHT
MONORAIL CAR
PATROL WAGON
PICK-UP TRUCK
PILOT-ENGINE
SLEDGE-CHAIR
STEAM-ROLLER
THREE-IN-HAND
TRANSPORTER
WHEELBARROW

12

BABY CARRIAGE
BAGGAGE-WAGON
COACH-AND-FOUR
COACH-AND-PAIR
COVERED WAGON
DOUBLE-DECKER
EXPRESS TRAIN
FREIGHTLINER
FREIGHT-TRAIN
FURNITURE VAN
HACKNEY-COACH
HORSE AND CART
INVALID CHAIR
MOTOR-BICYCLE
MOTOR-SCOOTER
MOTOR-TRACTOR
OMNIBUS TRAIN
PANTECHNICON
PERAMBULATOR
PONY-CARRIAGE
RAILWAY TRAIN
SINGLE-DECKER
SINGLE-SEATER
SPACE VEHICLE
STATION-WAGON
THREE-WHEELER
THROUGH-TRAIN

10

AUTOMOBILE
BLACK MARIA
BLOOD-WAGON
BONESHAKER
CATAFALQUE
CHAISE-CART
CHAPEL CART
CHUCK-WAGON
CONVEYANCE
DANDY-HORSE
FAIRY-CYCLE

11

ARMOURED CAR
BREWER'S DRAY
BULLOCK-CART
CARAVANETTE

13

ARMOURED TRAIN
CORRIDOR-TRAIN
DEMOCRAT WAGON
DÉSOBLIGEANTE
DROPHEAD-COUPÉ
FORK-LIFT TRUCK
GOVERNESS CART
HORSE AND BUGGY
MOURNING-COACH
PENNY-FARTHING
SAFETY BICYCLE

SHOOTING-BRAKE
STEAM-CARRIAGE
STOPPING-TRAIN
WHEEL-CARRIAGE

14

CAR-TRANSPORTER
CONTAINER LORRY
FIELD AMBULANCE
LIMITED EXPRESS
PASSENGER TRAIN

SPRING-CARRIAGE
TRACTION-ENGINE

15

CARRIAGE AND PAIR
HACKNEY-CARRIAGE
PRAIRIE-SCHOONER
SHOPPING-TROLLEY
STRADDLE CARRIER
WHITECHAPEL CART

TRANSPORT – TRANSPORT TERMS

3

BAY
GAP
LEG
LIE
LYE
MAP
REV
ROW
RUN
TAR
TOW
WAY

4

BANK
BEND
CONE
DOCK
DRAG
EXIT
FARE
FLAT
FORD
FORK
FROG

GATE
HALT
HAUL
HILL
HOOT
KERB
LANE
LINE
LINK
LOAD
LOCK
MALL
MEWS
MUSH
PATH
PAWN
PIKE
RAIL
RANK
RIDE
ROAD
SAIL
SKID
SPIN
STEP
STOP
TILT
TOLL
TOOT

TOUR
TREK
TRIP
TUBE
TURN
VISA
WALK

5

ALLÉE
ALLEY
A-ROAD
B-ROAD
BYWAY
CANAL
CARGO
CHAIR
CLOSE
CORSO
CRASH
DEPOT
DRIFT
DRIVE
ENTRY
FOSSE
FRONT
GAUGE

GROVE
GULLY
JAUNT
LAY-BY
METAL
MÉTRO
PITCH
PLACE
PRANG
RAISE
RELAY
ROUTE
SHUNT
SPEED
SPURT
STAGE
TRACE
TRACK
TRAIL
TRAIN
TREAD
U-TURN
VISIT

6

ACCESS
ARCADE

AVENUE
BEACON
BOREEN
BRIDGE
BY-LANE
BYPASS
BYPATH
BYROAD
CAFILA
CAMBER
CARFAX
COBBLE
COGGLE
CONVOY
CORNER
COURSE
CRUISE
CUT-OFF
DETOUR
DROGUE
FILTER
FLIGHT
FLYING
GANTRY
GARAGE
HANGAR
HOGGIN
INTAKE
ISLAND

KAFILA
LADING
LINK-UP
LOCK-UP
MARKER
METALS
MIDWAY
OCTANE
OCTROI
OUTING
PAVING
PICK-UP
PILE-UP
POINTS
PULL-IN
PULL-UP
REFUGE
REPAIR
RETURN
ROTARY
RUELLE
RUNWAY
SEAWAY
SEASON
SIDING
SIGNAL
SINGLE
SKI-TOW
SKYWAY

TRANSPORT – TRANSPORT TERMS

SQUARE
STREET
SUBWAY
SWERVE
SWITCH
TARMAC
THRUST
TICKET
TIMING
TOWAGE
TOWING
TRAVEL
TUNNEL
UP-LINE
VOYAGE
Y-TRACK

7

AIR-RAIL
ALAMEDA
ASPHALT
BALLAST
BANKING
BERCEAU
BLOW-OUT
BOLLARD
BOOKING
BOOSTER
BRAKING
BUILD-UP
BUS-FARE
BUS-LANE
BUS-PASS
BUS-STOP
CAB-RANK
CARAVAN
CAR HIRE
CAR-LOAD
CAR PARK
CARPORT
CARTWAY
CAT'S-EYE
CAT-WALK
CUTTING
DECLINE
DRIVE-IN
DRIVING
DRY-DOCK
FAIRWAY
FLYOVER

FOOTWAY
FRAUGHT
FREEWAY
FREIGHT
GALLERY
GANGWAY
GATEWAY
HAULAGE
HIGHWAY
INCLINE
JOURNEY
JOY-RIDE
LOADING
LOG-BOOK
LOW GEAR
L-PLATES
MACADAM
MILEAGE
MIXTURE
MOT TEST
NETWORK
NEUTRAL
NO ENTRY
OFFSIDE
OPENING
PACKWAY
PARKING
PARKWAY
PASSAGE
PATHWAY
PAVIOUR
PINKING
PITCHER
PORTAGE
POTHOLE
PRANG-UP
RAILWAY
REVERSE
ROAD-BED
ROAD-END
ROAD-MAP
ROAD-TAX
ROADWAY
ROPEWAY
SAILING
SEA-LANE
SEA-ROAD
SERVICE
SKID PAD
SKID PAN
SKI-LIFT
SLEEPER

SLIDDER
SLIPPER
SMASH-UP
SNARL-UP
SPECIAL
STAGING
STATION
STOP-OFF
STRETCH
TELPHER
TERRACE
TEST RUN
TOP GEAR
TOURING
TOW-PATH
TRAFFIC
TRAMWAY
TRANSIT
TURNING
TURN-OFF
TURN-OUT
VIADUCT
WALKWAY
WAY-BILL
WAYFARE
WAYMARK
WAY-POST
WAYSIDE
WIRE-WAY

8

ALLEYWAY
AUTOBAHN
AUTOCADE
BACKFIRE
BLACKTOP
BLAST-OFF
BROADWAY
BUNCHING
BUS DEPOT
BUS TOKEN
CABLE-CAR
CABLEWAY
CAB-STAND
CARTLOAD
CART-ROAD
CAUSEWAY
CLEARWAY
COACH-WAY
CORNICHE

CRESCENT
CROSSING
CROSS-TIE
CROSSWAY
CRUISING
CUL-DE-SAC
DECK-LOAD
DIRT-ROAD
DOWN-LINE
DRIFT-WAY
DRIVEWAY
EDGE RAIL
FAST LANE
FERRIAGE
FLAT TYRE
FLY-UNDER
FOOTPATH
GARAGING
GRADIENT
HALT-SIGN
HAND-POST
HARDCORE
HIGHROAD
HORSEWAY
IGNITION
JUNCTION
KNOCKING
LANDFALL
LAUNCHER
LIVE-RAIL
LIVE-WIRE
LOOP-LINE
MADE ROAD
MAIN LINE
MAIN ROAD
MANIFEST
MILLIARY
MONORAIL
MOTORAIL
MOTORING
MOTORWAY
NEARSIDE
OPEN ROAD
OVERHAUL
OVERLOAD
OVERPASS
PASSPORT
PAVEMENT
PITCHING
PLATFORM
POST-ROAD
PROSPECT

PUNCTURE
QUADRANT
RACK-RAIL
RAILHEAD
RAILROAD
RED LIGHT
RIDGEWAY
RING-ROAD
ROADSIDE
ROAD-SIGN
ROAD-TEST
RUSH HOUR
SCHEDULE
SEA-FRONT
SHORT CUT
SHOULDER
SHUNTING
SIDE-LINE
SIDE-PATH
SIDE-ROAD
SIDE-SLIP
SIDEWALK
SIGNPOST
SKIDDING
SKID-MARK
SLIP ROAD
SLOW LANE
SPEEDING
SPEEDWAY
STARTING
STEERAGE
STOP-OVER
STOPPING
SWERVING
TAILBACK
TAIL-SKID
TAXI-RANK
TERMINAL
TERMINUS
TOLL-GATE
TRACKAGE
TRACKWAY
TRACTION
TRAM-LINE
TRAM-ROAD
TRANSFER
TRAVERSE
TRIAL RUN
TRUCKAGE
TRUCKING
TURNPIKE
WAGONAGE

WASH-AWAY
WATERWAY
WHARFING
WRITE-OFF

9

ANTIKNOCK
AUTOROUTE
BELL-PUNCH
BLACK SPOT
BLIND ROAD
BOULEVARD
BREAKDOWN
BUS TICKET
BY-PASSAGE
CHAIRLIFT
CHURCHWAY
CLEARANCE
COACH-ROAD
COLLISION
CONCOURSE
CRASH-DIVE
CROSSFALL
CROSSOVER
CROSSROAD
CROSS-SILL
CROSSWAYS
DECK-CARGO
DIRECTION
DIVERSION
DROVE-ROAD
ESPLANADE
EXCURSION
FISH-PLATE
FISHYBACK
FLAGSTONE
FLARE-PATH
GUIDE-POST
GUIDE-RAIL
HIGH CROSS
ITINERARY
JEW'S PITCH
JOY-RIDING
KERBSTONE
KICK-START
METALLING
MILESTONE
MONOCOQUE
MOTORCADE
MULE-TRAIN

OVERSTEER
PACK-TRAIN
POINT-DUTY
PORTERAGE
PROMENADE
REVERSING
ROAD-ATLAS
ROAD-BLOCK
ROAD-CRAFT
ROAD-METAL
ROAD-SENSE
ROAD-WORKS
SERVICING
SIDE-TRACK
SIGNAL-BOX
SLIP ANGLE
SPEED-TRAP
SPOT CHECK
STREETWAY
SURFACING
SWITCHING
TIMETABLE
T-JUNCTION
TRACK ROAD
TRANSPORT
TRIAL TRIP
TRIPTYQUE
TRUNK-LINE
TRUNK-ROAD
TURN-ROUND
TURNTABLE
UNDERPASS
WAGON-LOAD
WALKABOUT
WAYFARING
WHEEL-SPIN
WHITE LINE

CABIN CLASS
CAMINO REAL
CENTRE RAIL
COACH-STAND
CONNECTION
CONTRAFLOW
CROSSROADS
DERAILMENT
EMBANKMENT
EXCESS FARE
EXPRESSWAY
FINGERPOST
FIRST CLASS
FOOTBRIDGE
GRAVEL-WALK
GREEN LIGHT
HIGH STREET
HOME SIGNAL
JAYWALKING
LOCOMOTION
OVERTAKING
PARKING LOT
PASSAGEWAY
POLICE-TRAP
PROPULSION
RIGHT OF WAY
ROAD-BRIDGE
ROUNDABOUT
SEA-PASSAGE
SIDE-STREET
SIGNALLING
SLIPSTREAM
SPEED LIMIT
SUBSIDENCE
SWITCHBACK
TELPHERAGE
TELPHERWAY
THROUGHWAY
TOLL-BRIDGE
TRADE ROUTE
TRAFFIC JAM
TRAM TICKET
TRAVELLING
TRAVERSING
UNDERSTEER
UNMADE ROAD
WAGON-TRAIN
WATERFRONT
WAY-FREIGHT
WAY-STATION
WAY-TRAFFIC
YELLOW LINE

10

ACCESS ROAD
AMBER LIGHT
ANTIFREEZE
AUTOSTRADA
BLIND-ALLEY
BOTTLE-NECK
BRIDLE-PATH
BRIDLE-ROAD
BROAD GAUGE
BUS-STATION

11

BLIND CORNER
BLOCK SYSTEM
BOX JUNCTION
BUILT-UP AREA
CARBURATION
CARRIAGEWAY
COBBLESTONE
COMPRESSION
CRÉMAILLÈRE
DECK-PASSAGE
DESTINATION
DETRAINMENT
DISC PARKING
DRIVING TEST
DUAL CONTROL
EMBARKATION
ENTRAINMENT
GIVE-WAY SIGN
HAIRPIN-BEND
HIGHWAY CODE
HITCH-HIKING
INTERCHANGE
KNOCK-RATING
MARSHALLING
MYSTERY TOUR
NARROW GUAGE
NO-ENTRY SIGN
OVERHAULING
OVERHEATING
OVERLOADING
PACKAGE TOUR
PAVING-STONE
PISSASPHALT
PRE-IGNITION
QUARTER ROAD
RACK-RAILWAY
REQUEST STOP
RESERVATION
SECOND CLASS
SERVICE ROAD
SIDE-CUTTING
SPACE-TRAVEL
TÉLÉFÉRIQUE
TELPHER-LINE
THROUGH ROAD
TRAIN TICKET
TRANSPORTAL
UNDERGROUND
WATER-SPLASH
WHISTLE-STOP

TRANSPORT – TRANSPORT TERMS

12

ACCELERATION
APPROACH ROAD
ARTERIAL ROAD
CABLE-RAILWAY
CABLE-TRAMWAY
COACH-STATION
CORDUROY ROAD
DECELERATION
FREEWHEELING
HARD SHOULDER
INTERSECTION
INTERTRAFFIC
LAUNCHING-PAD
LIGHT RAILWAY
LOCOMOTIVITY
LORRY-HOPPING
MAIDEN VOYAGE
MINI-MOTORWAY
MOTORWAY SIGN
OCTANE NUMBER
ONE-WAY SYSTEM
ONE-WAY TICKET
PARKING METER
PARKING PLACE
PASSAGE-MONEY
PERMANENT WAY
PLEASURE TRIP
REGISTRATION
RETURN TICKET
ROAD JUNCTION
ROLLING STOCK
SEASON TICKET
STREAMLINING
SUPERHIGHWAY
THOROUGHFARE

TOURIST CLASS
TRAFFIC-LIGHT
TRANSFERENCE
TURNPIKE-ROAD
UNDERSEALING

13

AERIAL RAILWAY
AFFREIGHTMENT
ATTITUDE ANGLE
BELISHA BEACON
CARRIAGE-DRIVE
DISTANT-SIGNAL
EMERGENCY STOP
INSPECTION-PIT
LEFT-HAND DRIVE
LEVEL-CROSSING
MOTOR-TRACTION
PARKING TICKET
PEREGRINATION
ROAD-METALLING
RULE OF THE ROAD
SCENIC RAILWAY
STAGECOACHING
STOPPING-PLACE
STREET-RAILWAY
THROUGH-TICKET
TRAFFIC CIRCLE
TRAFFIC ISLAND
TRAFFIC-LIGHTS
TRAFFIC-SIGNAL
TURNING CIRCLE
UNADOPTED ROAD
ZEBRA CROSSING

14

ACCIDENT MARKER
CATENARY SYSTEM
DRIVING LICENCE
GREEN CROSS CODE
LIGHTING-UP TIME
MACADAMISATION
MINI-ROUNDABOUT
PLEASURE CRUISE
RAILWAY STATION
RIGHT-HAND DRIVE
SHUTTLE SERVICE
STEPPING-STONES
THREE-POINT TURN
THROUGH-TRAFFIC
TRANSFER TICKET
TRANSPORTATION

15

DECARBONISATION
DUAL CARRIAGEWAY
ELECTRIFICATION
INTERCONNECTION
JUMPING-OFF PLACE
MARSHALLING YARD
MOUNTAIN RAILWAY
PELICAN CROSSING
RAILWAY-CROSSING
SPACE-TRAVELLING
WHISTLE-STOP TOUR

TRANSPORT – VEHICLE PARTS

3		4					
	FIN		BOOT	DASH	GRID	JACK
	HUB		BUCK	DOME	HEAD	PADS
CAB	PAD	AXLE	BULB	DOOR	HOOD	PART
CAR	RIM	BELL	COIL	GATE	HORN	PAWL
FAN	VAN	BODY	COWL	GEAR	HULL	PLUG

PUMP
ROOF
SEAT
SUMP
TANK
TRIM
TYRE
WING

5

BEZEL
BOGIE
BRAKE
CABIN
CHAIN
CHOKE
COACH
COUPÉ
DINER
FACIA
FORKS
FRAME
MOTOR
PEDAL
RELAY
ROTOR
SIREN
SPARE
SPOKE
SQUAB
THILL
TRUNK
VALVE
VISOR
WAGON
WHEEL
WIPER

6

BAFFLE
BASKET
BIG END
BONNET
BOXCAR
BUFFER
BUMPER
CHAINS
CHUMMY

CLUTCH
COTTER
DAMPER
DE-ICER
DICKEY
DIPPER
DYNAMO
ENGINE
FELLOE
FENDER
GASKET
GRILLE
HEATER
HOOTER
HUB-CAP
KLAXON
PILLAR
PINION
PISTON
POINTS
ROCKER
RUMBLE
SADDLE
SMOKER
SPEEDO
TAPPET
TENDER
TOW-BAR
WINDOW
WINKER

7

AMMETER
ASH-TRAY
AUTOVAC
AXLE-BOX
BATTERY
BEARING
CABOOSE
CALIPER
CHASSIS
COASTER
COCKPIT
CONSOLE
DISC-PAD
DRAW-BAR
EXHAUST
FAN-BELT
FIREBOX
FLASHER

FOG-LAMP
FUTCHEL
GEAR-BOX
KING-PIN
MAGNETO
MAIL-CAR
MUD-FLAP
MUFFLER
OIL-PIPE
OIL-PUMP
PANNIER
PILLION
PULLMAN
PUSH-ROD
RAILBUS
RAIL-CAR
RAT-TRAP
REMOULD
RETREAD
SHUNTER
SIDECAR
SLEEPER
STARTER
TANK-CAR
TOE-CLIP
TONNEAU
TOP GEAR
TOWLINE
TOW-ROPE
VALANCE
WHISTLE
WING-NUT

8

AIR-BRAKE
ARMATURE
BACKBAND
BODYWORK
BRAKE-PAD
BRAKE-VAN
BOX-WAGON
BULKHEAD
CAMSHAFT
CANT-RAIL
CARRIAGE
CORRIDOR
COUPLING
CRASH-PAD
CROSSBAR
DE-MISTER

DIP-STICK
DOOR-LOCK
DRAFT-BAR
DRAW-GEAR
FLYWHEEL
FOOT-PUMP
FUEL-PIPE
FUEL-PUMP
FUEL-TANK
GEAR-CASE
HEADLAMP
HEADREST
HORSE BOX
HUB-BRAKE
IGNITION
IMPELLER
IMPERIAL
INFLATOR
LAY-SHAFT
MANIFOLD
MUD-GUARD
RADIATOR
REAR-DOOR
REAR-LAMP
REAR-WING
ROOF-RACK
ROTOR ARM
SEAT-BELT
SILENCER
SIDE-LAMP
SMALL END
SMOKE-BOX
SOLENOID
SPOTLAMP
SPROCKET
SUB-FRAME
SUN-VISOR
TAIL-GATE
THROTTLE
TRACK ROD
WAGON-BED
WAGON-BOX
WAGON-LIT
WHEEL-NUT
WIPER-ARM

9

AIR-FILTER
BACK-BOARD
BACK WHEEL

BALL-JOINT
BODY-SHELL
BRAKE-DRUM
BRAKE-SHOE
BUCKBOARD
BUFFET CAR
CARTWHEEL
COACHWORK
CONDENSER
COTTER-PIN
COUCHETTE
CRANK-CASE
DASHBOARD
DEFROSTER
DINING-CAR
DIP-SWITCH
DISC-BRAKE
DRAG-CHAIN
DRIVE-GEAR
FILLER-CAP
FIRST GEAR
FOOTBOARD
FOOTBRAKE
FOOTPLATE
FORE-WHEEL
FREE-WHEEL
FREIGHTER
FRONT-DOOR
FRONT-WING
FUEL GAUGE
GEAR-LEVER
GEAR-SHIFT
GEAR-STICK
GENERATOR
GUARD'S-VAN
HANDBRAKE
HEADLIGHT
HIND-WHEEL
INDICATOR
INNER-TUBE
LOCK-CHAIN
LOCOMOTIVE
MAIL-COACH
MAIN-SHAFT
NON-SMOKER
OIL-FILTER
OVERDRIVE
PALACE-CAR
PISTON-ROD
PROP-SHAFT
PUG-ENGINE
RAIL-MOTOR

TRANSPORT – VEHICLE PARTS

REAR-LIGHT
REAR WHEEL
REFLECTOR
RESONATOR
SADDLE-BAG
SADDLE-PIN
SALOON-CAR
SIDEBOARD
SIDELIGHT
SLIP-COACH
SPARE PART
SPARK-PLUG
SPOTLIGHT
STOP-LIGHT
TAIL-BOARD
TAIL-LIGHT
TANK-WAGON
THIRD GEAR
UNDERSEAL
WAGON-LOCK
WATER-PUMP
WHEEL-ARCH

10

ALTERNATOR
BAGGAGE-CAR
BARROW-TRAM
BONNET-LOCK
BOTTOM GEAR
BRAKE-BLOCK
BRAKE-PEDAL
BRAKE-WHEEL
BUCKET SEAT
COACH-WHEEL
CONTROL BOX
COWCATCHER
CRANKSHAFT
CROWN-WHEEL
DÉRAILLEUR
DOOR-HANDLE
DRIVE-SHAFT
DRIVE-WHEEL
DRIVING-BOX
FIXED WHEEL
FOURTH GEAR
FREIGHT-CAR
FRONT WHEEL
FUEL-FILTER
GOODS WAGON

GRIDDLE-CAR
HANDLEBARS
HEADER TANK
INLET VALVE
KNIFEBOARD
LOCOMOTIVE
LUGGAGE-VAN
MINI-BUFFET
PARLOUR-CAR
PETROL TANK
PISTON-RING
PONY-ENGINE
PULLMAN CAR
RADIAL TYRE
REAR-WINDOW
ROAD-SPRING
RUMBLE-SEAT
SAFETY-BELT
SCREENWASH
SECOND GEAR
SIDE-WINDOW
SPARE WHEEL
SUSPENSION
TACHOGRAPH
TACHOMETER
TANK-ENGINE
THERMOSTAT
WINDSCREEN
WINDSHIELD
WING-MIRROR
WIPER-BLADE

11

ACCELERATOR
ANTI-ROLL BAR
BALLOON TYRE
CARBURETTOR
CHECK-STRING
CLUTCH-PEDAL
COMPARTMENT
COUPLING-BOX
CUSHION TYRE
DISTRIBUTOR
EXHAUST-PIPE
FLASHER UNIT
GOODS-ENGINE
IGNITION KEY
LIGHT ENGINE
LUGGAGE-RACK

MONKEY-BOARD
NUMBER-PLATE
PARCEL SHELF
PILLION SEAT
RADIATOR-CAP
RAILROAD CAR
REVERSE GEAR
SELF-STARTER
SLEEPING-CAR
SPEEDOMETER
SPLASH-BOARD
STEERING-BOX
TIMING CHAIN
TRAFFICATOR
VACUUM-BRAKE

12

CROSS-PLY TYRE
CYLINDER HEAD
DIESEL ENGINE
DIFFERENTIAL
DORMITORY CAR
EXHAUST VALVE
FORECARRIAGE
FUEL INJECTOR
IGNITION COIL
LOADING GAUGE
MAIL-CARRIAGE
PETROL ENGINE
QUARTER-LIGHT
RADIATOR HOSE
REPAIR OUTFIT
ROTARY ENGINE
RUNNING-BOARD
SADDLE-PILLAR
SADDLE-SPRING
SEAT-ADJUSTER
SLIP-CARRIAGE
SPARKING-PLUG
STARTER-MOTOR
STEAM-WHISTLE
SUNSHINE ROOF
SUPERCHARGER
THROTTLE-PIPE
TROLLEY-WHEEL
TUBELESS TYRE
TWO-SPEED GEAR
WINDOW-WINDER

13

BRAKE-CYLINDER
CONNECTING-ROD
CONTACT POINTS
CYLINDER BLOCK
EXPANSION TANK
PNEUMATIC TYRE
RADIAL-PLY TYRE
RESTAURANT CAR
SHOCK-ABSORBER
SLEEPING-COACH
SPROCKET-WHEEL
STEERING-WHEEL
THROTTLE-LEVER
THROTTLE-VALVE

UNDERCARRIAGE

14

CLUTCH-CYLINDER
DEAD MAN'S HANDLE
DISTRIBUTOR-CAP
ENGINE MOUNTING
IGNITION SWITCH
INDUCTION VALVE
INTERIOR MIRROR
LUGGAGE-CARRIER
OBSERVATION CAR
PROPELLER SHAFT

REAR-VIEW MIRROR
SALOON-CARRIAGE
STARTING HANDLE
STEERING-COLUMN
THREE-SPEED GEAR
UNIVERSAL JOINT

15

INSTRUMENT PANEL
RAILWAY CARRIAGE
SMOKING CARRIAGE
SYNCHROMESH GEAR
WINDSCREEN-WIPER

TRANSPORT – WATER TRANSPORT

3

ARK
CAT
COG
COT
GIG
HOY
RAM
SUB
TUB
TUG

4

BARK
BOAT
BRIG
BUSS
DHOW
DORY
DUCK
FLAG
FOUR
GRAB

HULK
JUNK
KEEL
KOFF
PAIR
PINK
PRAM
PRAU
PROA
PUNT
RAFT
SAIC
SAIL
SCOW
SHIP
SNOW
YAWL

5

BALSA
BARCA
BARGE
BUTTY
CANOE

CASCO
COBLE
COPER
CRAFT
CRARE
DANDY
DRAKE
E-BOAT
EIGHT
FERRY
FLEET
FLOTA
FUNNY
KAYAK
KETCH
LAKER
LINER
OILER
PINKY
PRAAM
PRAHU
Q-BOAT
RAZEE
SCOUT
SCULL
SHELL

SKIFF
SLOOP
SMACK
SNORT
TRAMP
U-BOAT
UMIAK
WHIFF
WRECK
XEBEC
YACHT

6

ARGOSY
ARMADA
BARQUE
BATEAU
BAWLEY
BIREME
CAIQUE
CARVEL
CASTLE
COOPER
CRAYER

CUTTER
DINGHY
DOGGER
DROMON
DUGOUT
GALLEY
GAY-YOU
HOOKER
HOPPER
JIGGER
LAUNCH
LORCHA
LUGGER
MASULA
PACKET
PEDALO
PIRATE
PUFFER
PULWAR
PUTELI
RANDAN
RIGGER
SAIQUE
SAILER
SAMPAN
SANDAL

SANPAN
SCHUIT
SETTEE
SLAVER
TANKER
TARTAN
TENDER
TRADER
VESSEL
WAFTER
WHALER
WHERRY

7

BIRLINN
BUM-BOAT
CARAVEL
CARRACK
CARRIER
CAT-BOAT
CLIPPER
COASTER
COLLIER
CORACLE
CORSAIR

TRANSPORT – WATER TRANSPORT

CRUISER
CURRACH
DREDGER
DRIFTER
DROGHER
DROMOND
FELUCCA
FLIVVER
FLYBOAT
FOUR-OAR
FRIGATE
GABBART
GALLEON
GALLIOT
GEORDIE
GONDOLA
GUNBOAT
HABITAT
ICE-BOAT
KIT-BOAT
LIGHTER
MAIL-GIG
MINI-SUB
MISTICO
MONITOR
MUD-BOAT
MUD-SCOW
PAIR-OAR
PATAMAR
PEARLER
PIG-BOAT
PINNACE
PIRAGUA
PIROGUE
POLACCA
POLACRE
PONTOON
ROW-BOAT
SCOOTER
SCULLER
SEA-BOAT
SHALLOP
SPONGER
SPOUTER
STEAMER
TARTANE
TOW-BOAT
TRACKER
TRAMPER
TRAWLER
TRIREME
TUG-BOAT

VEDETTE
WARSHIP
WRECKER

8

AMPHICAR
BILANDER
BILLY-BOY
BUDGEROW
CAR-FERRY
COALSHIP
COCKBOAT
COROCORE
CORVETTE
EIGHT-OAR
FALTBOAT
FIREBOAT
FIRESHIP
FLAGSHIP
FLATBOAT
FLOTILLA
GALLEASS
GALLIASS
GALLIVAT
HOVELLER
HUSH-BOAT
ICE-YACHT
INDIAMAN
IRONCLAD
KEELBOAT
LIFEBOAT
LOG-CANOE
LONGBOAT
LONGSHIP
MACKINAW
MAIL-BOAT
MAN-OF-WAR
MASOOLAH
MONOHULL
MONTARIA
ROW-BARGE
SAIL-BOAT
SCHOONER
SHOW-BOAT
SMUGGLER
STEAM-TUG
SURF-BOAT
TILT-BOAT
TRIMARAN
WATER-BUS

WELL-BOAT
WOOD-SKIN

9

AMPHIBIAN
BLOCK-SHIP
BOMB-KETCH
BUCENTAUR
CABIN SHIP
CABLE SHIP
CANAL-BOAT
CARGO-BOAT
CATAMARAN
COMMODORE
DAHABIYAH
DEPOT SHIP
DESTROYER
FERRY-BOAT
FIREFLOAT
FIRST-RATE
FREIGHTER
FRIGATOON
FUNNY-BOAT
GUARD-SHIP
HATCH BOAT
HERRINGER
HOLLANDER
HORSE BOAT
HOUSE-BOAT
HYDROFOIL
HYDROVANE
JOLLYBOAT
LAPSTREAK
LIGHTSHIP
MINE-LAYER
MONOXYLON
MOTOR-BOAT
MOTOR-SHIP
NORWEGIAN
OIL-BURNER
OIL-TANKER
OUTRIGGER
PETER-BOAT
PILOT-BOAT
POWER-BOAT
PRIVATEER
RANDAN GIG
RIVER-BOAT
ROTOR-SHIP
SCULL-BOAT

SEINE-BOAT
SHELL-BOAT
SHORE-BOAT
SLAVE-SHIP
SPEEDBOAT
SPEEDSTER
STEAMBOAT
STEAM-SHIP
STORE-SHIP
SUBMARINE
SURF-CANOE
TANKA-BOAT
TRACK-BOAT
TROOPSHIP
TWO-DECKER
TWO-MASTER
WAGER-BOAT
WAIST-BOAT
WELL-SMACK
WHALE-BACK
WHALE-BOAT

10

ADVICE-BOAT
ARMOUR-CLAD
BANANA-BOAT
BARKENTINE
BATHYSCOPE
BATTLESHIP
BOMB-VESSEL
BRIGANTINE
CHAIN-FERRY
COFFIN-SHIP
DIVING-BELL
FOUR-MASTER
FREE-TRADER
HOVERCRAFT
HYDROPLANE
ICE-BREAKER
KNOCKABOUT
MESOSCAPHE
MONKEY-BOAT
MOTHER-SHIP
MOTOR-YACHT
NARROW-BOAT
NUCLEAR SUB
OCEAN LINER
PACKET-BOAT
PACKET-SHIP
PADDLE-BOAT

PATROL-BOAT
PIRATE SHIP
PRISON-SHIP
QUADRIREME
REPAIR-SHIP
RESCUE-BOAT
RIVER-CRAFT
ROWING-BOAT
SCHOOL-SHIP
SLOOP-OF-WAR
SMALL CRAFT
STEAM-YACHT
SUPPLY SHIP
SURVEY SHIP
TEA-CLIPPER
TRACK-SCOUT
TRAIN-FERRY
TRIACONTER
TURRET-SHIP
VIKING SHIP
WATER-CRAFT
WINDJAMMER

11

ASSAULT BOAT
BARQUENTINE
BATHYSCAPHE
BATHYSPHERE
BENTHOSCOPE
BERTHON-BOAT
BLACKBIRDER
BULK CARRIER
CAPITAL SHIP
CARLEY FLOAT
COCKLESHELL
DREADNOUGHT
FACTORY-SHIP
FISHING-BOAT
HERRING-BUSS
LANDING-SHIP
LIBERTY-BOAT
MERCHANTMAN

MINE-SWEEPER
MOTOR-LAUNCH
MOTOR-VESSEL
MYSTERY SHIP
NAVAL VESSEL
PASSAGE-BOAT
PENTECONTER
PRIZE VESSEL
QUINQUEREME
SAILING-BOAT
SAILING-SHIP
SALMON-COBLE
STEAM-LAUNCH
STEAM-PACKET
STEAM-VESSEL
SUBMERSIBLE
SUPERTANKER
THREE-DECKER
THREE-MASTER
TORPEDO-BOAT
TRADING SHIP
VEDETTE-BOAT
WEATHER-SHIP

12

CABIN CRUISER
DISPATCH-BOAT
DOUBLE-DECKER
EAST-INDIAMAN
FISHING SMACK
FORE-AND-AFTER
HEAVY CRUISER
HOSPITAL SHIP
LANDING-CRAFT
LIGHT CRUISER
MERCHANT SHIP
PLEASURE-BOAT
POLICE LAUNCH
RUBBER DINGHY
SCREW-STEAMER
SINGLE-DECKER
SQUARE-RIGGER

STERN-WHEELER
SURFACE-CRAFT
TRAINING SHIP
TRAMP STEAMER
TROOP-CARRIER

13

BATTLE-CRUISER
COASTAL VESSEL
CONTAINER SHIP
ESCORT CARRIER
FLOATING LIGHT
PADDLE-STEAMER
PASSENGER-SHIP
RECEIVING-SHIP
REVENUE-CUTTER
SAILING VESSEL
SHIP-OF-THE-LINE
SURFACE VESSEL
TRADING VESSEL
TRANSPORT SHIP
WATER CARRIAGE

14

BLOCKADE-RUNNER
OCEAN-GREYHOUND
TURBINE-STEAMER

15

AIRCRAFT-CARRIER
ARMOURED CRUISER
CABLE-LAYING SHIP
LOGISTICS VESSEL
SEAPLANE-CARRIER
VICTUALLING-SHIP

WEAPONRY

3

ARM
ASH
AXE
BAT
BOW
DAG
DOG
DOP
DUD
GAT
GUN
PAN
POP
RAM
ROD
WAD
YEW

4

AMMO
ARMS
BALL
BEAD
BILL
BOLT
BOMB
BORE
BREN
BUTT
CANE
CLUB
COCK
COLT
COSH
DART
DIRK
DUMP
ÉPÉE
FIRE
FLAK
FOIL
FORK
FROG
FUSE
FUZE
HAIR
HILT
KICK

KRIS
LOCK
MACE
MERE
MINE
MIRV
PIKE
PILE
PILL
REST
SEAR
SHOT
SILO
SLUG
STEN
SWAB
TIER
UMBO
WHIP

5

A-BOMB
AEGIS
ARROW
BATON
BEARD
BILBO
BIRCH
BLADE
BLANK
BLAST
BOLUS
BRAND
CHAPE
ESTOC
FLAIL
FORTE
FUSEE
FUSIL
GRAPE
GUARD
H-BOMB
KNIFE
KNOUT
KUKRI
KYLIE
LANCE
LASSO
LUGER
MAXIM

METAL
MORNE
MOUSE
ONION
OTTER
PANGA
PELTA
PIECE
PILUM
PROOF
QUOIN
RIFLE
ROUND
SABRE
SALVO
SCUTE
SHAFT
SHARP
SHEAF
SHELL
SIGHT
SKEAN
SKENE
SLING
SNAKE
SNIPE
SPEAR
SQUIB
SQUID
STICK
STOCK
SWORD
TARGE
TRAIL
V-BOMB
VOUGE
WADDY

6

ACK-ACK
AIR-GUN
ALPEEN
ANLACE
ARCHIE
BARKER
BARREL
BEATER
BODKIN
BOFORS
BREECH

BUDGET
BULLET
CANNON
CESTUS
CHARGE
CORVUS
CUDGEL
CUPOLA
CUT-OFF
DAGGER
DOPPER
DUMDUM
ENGINE
ESPADA
FIRING
GINGAL
HAMMER
HANDLE
HANJAR
JEZAIL
JINGAL
KILLER
LABRYS
LARIAT
LIMBER
MARTEL
MAUSER
MORTAR
MUSKET
MUZZLE
NAPALM
ONAGER
PARANG
PELLET
PELTER
PETARD
PISTOL
POMMEL
POMPOM
POP-GUN
POT-GUN
POWDER
PRIMER
QUAKER
QUIVER
RAMROD
RAPIER
RECOIL
ROCKET
SCUTUM
SHEATH
SHIELD

SIX-GUN
SPONGE
SUMPIT
SWIVEL
TARGET
TOLEDO
TOMBOC
TRACER
TULWAR
VOLLEY
VOULGE
WEAPON
WEBLEY

7

ARMOURY
ARSENAL
ASSEGAI
BATTERY
BAYONET
BAZOOKA
BLOWGUN
BOMBARD
BREN GUN
BUCKLER
BUNDOOK
CALIBRE
CALTROP
CARBINE
CARCASE
CHAMBER
CHASSIS
COEHORN
CURTANA
CUTLASS
DOGBOLT
DOG-HEAD
DRAGOON
DUDGEON
EJECTOR
FEATHER
FIRE-ARM
FIRE-POT
FLEURET
FOUGADE
G-AGENTS
GRENADE
GUNFIRE
GUNNAGE
GUNSHOT

HACKBUT
HALBERD
HAND-GUN
HARPOON
HATCHET
HOLSTER
IGNITER
JAVELIN
LOADING
LONGBOW
LONG TOM
MACHETE
MARTINI
MISFIRE
MISSILE
MUZZLER
PAYLOAD
PELICAN
PERRIER
PETRARY
POLARIS
POLE-AXE
PONIARD
POT-SHOT
PRIMING
PUMP-GUN
PUNT-GUN
QUARREL
QUILLON
RELEASE
RIFLING
SHOOTER
SHOTGUN
SIDEARM
SIGHTER
STEN GUN
STICKER
SWINGLE
SWIPPLE
TAMPION
TEAR-GAS
TEREBRA
TESTUDO
TIME-GUN
TOC-EMMA
TOMPION
TORPEDO
TOW-IRON
TRIDENT
TRIGGER
TUMBLER
TWIBILL

V-AGENTS
WARHEAD
WAR-WOLF
WHINGER
WINDAGE
WIND-GUN

8

AEROBOMB
AERODART
AMUSETTE
ARBALEST
ARMAMENT
ARQUEBUS
ATOM BOMB
BALLISTA
BASILISK
BED-STAFF
BISCAYAN
BLOWPIPE
BLUDGEON
BRICKBAT
BUCKSHOT
BUZZ BOMB
CANISTER
CARRIAGE
CASCABEL
CASE-SHOT
CATAPULT
CLAYMORE
CONGREVE
CROSSBOW
CULVERIN
DRUMFIRE
DUCK-SHOT
DUST-SHOT
FALCHION
FIELD GUN
FIREBALL
FIRE-LOCK
FOUGASSE
FULL-COCK
GAS-SHELL
GAVELOCK
GUNFLINT
GUNSIGHT
GUNSTICK
GUNSTOCK
HAILSHOT
HALF-COCK

HALF-PIKE
HIELAMAN
HOWITZER
LAND MINE
LANGRAGE
LEWIS GUN
LEWISITE
LINSTOCK
MAGAZINE
MANGONEL
MAXIM-GUN
MOULINET
MUNITION
MUSKETRY
NAIL-BOMB
NERVE GAS
OERLIKON
OMPHALOS
ORDNANCE
PALSTAFF
PARAVANE
PARTISAN
PEA-RIFLE
PEDERERO
PETRONEL
PIKE-HEAD
PISTOLET
PLATFORM
PORT-FIRE
PROLONGE
REPEATER
REVOLVER
RICOCHET
RONDACHE
SAUCISSE
SCABBARD
SCHLÄGER
SCIMITAR
SCORPION
SHRAPNEL
SIEGE-GUN
SILENCER
SKEAN-DHU
SKENE-DHU
SLOW FUSE
SNAPSHOT
SPONTOON
STERLING
STILETTO
STINK-POT
STONE AXE
STONE BOW

SWAN-SHOT
THRESHEL
TIME-BOMB
TIME-FUSE
TOMAHAWK
TOMMY-GUN
TRIP-WIRE
VESICANT
WEAPONRY
YATAGHAN

9

ARMAMENTS
ARROWHEAD
ARTILLERY
BACK-SIGHT
BACKSWORD
BANDOLEER
BATTLE-AXE
BIG BERTHA
BLACKJACK
BOAR-SPEAR
BOFORS GUN
BOMBSHELL
BOOBY-TRAP
BOOMERANG
BROADSIDE
BROWN BESS
BROWN BILL
CAMOUFLET
CANNELURE
CARRONADE
CARTOUCHE
CARTRIDGE
CHAIN-SHOT
CHASSEPOT
CHOKEBORE
COLD STEEL
CROW'S FOOT
DAMASCENE
DEMI-LANCE
DEPTH-BOMB
DERRINGER
DETERRENT
DETONATOR
DISCHARGE
DOODLE-BUG
ESCOPETTE
EXPLOSION
EXPLOSIVE

WEAPONRY

FIRE-ARROW
FIRING-PIN
FLINTLOCK
FORESIGHT
FOUR-BY-TWO
GRAPESHOT
GREEK FIRE
GUN-BARREL
GUNCOTTON
GUNPOWDER
GUN-TURRET
HANDSTAFF
HARQUEBUS
LIGHT-BALL
LINTSTOCK
LIVE ROUND
LIVE SHELL
MATCHLOCK
MILLS BOMB
MINUTEMAN
MITRAILLE
MUNITIONS
MUSKETOON
NEEDLE-GUN
PEEP-SIGHT
PIKESTAFF
PINEAPPLE
PIPSQUEAK
POISON GAS
PSYCHOGAS
QUEEN'S ARM
REINFORCE
RIFLE-SHOT
SAFETY-PIN
SARBACANE
SCHIAVONE
SIGHT-HOLE
SLINGSHOT
SLOW MATCH
SMALL ARMS
SMOKE-BALL
SMOKE-BOMB
SNAPHANCE
SONIC MINE
SPEARHEAD
SPRING-GUN
STAR-SHELL
STINK-BALL
STINK-BOMB
STONESHOT
SWIVEL-GUN
SWORD-BELT

SWORD-CANE
TEAR-SHELL
TEAR-SMOKE
TORMENTUM
TOUCH-HOLE
TREBUCHET
TRUNCHEON
TURRET-GUN
WHEEL-LOCK
WHIZZ-BANG
ZUMBOORUK

10

AMMUNITION
BLACK MARIA
BOWIE KNIFE
BROADSWORD
CANDLE-BOMB
CANNONBALL
CANNON-SHOT
CLASP-KNIFE
COBALT BOMB
COURT-SWORD
CROSS GUARD
DETONATION
DISCHARGER
ÉPROUVETTE
FIELDPIECE
FLICK-KNIFE
FLYING BOMB
FRONT-SIGHT
FUSION BOMB
GATLING-GUN
HAIR-SPRING
HARPOON-GUN
HEAVY METAL
INCENDIARY
KNOBKERRIE
KNUCKLE-BOW
LEE-ENFIELD
LETTER-BOMB
MACHINE-GUN
MARKER-BOMB
MISERICORD
MORRIS-TUBE
MUSKET-REST
MUSKET-SHOT
MUSTARD GAS
MUZZLE-RING
NAPALM BOMB

NIGHT-STICK
NULLA-NULLA
PEACEMAKER
PISTOL-SHOT
POWDER-HORN
POWDER-MILL
POWDER-ROOM
PROJECTILE
PROPELLANT
QUICK-MATCH
RIOT-SHIELD
SAFETY-BOLT
SAFETY FUSE
SAFETY LOCK
SCATTER-GUN
SELF-COCKER
SERPENTINE
SHILLELAGH
SHORT-SWORD
SIEGE-PIECE
SIX-SHOOTER
SKENE-OCCLE
SLINGSTONE
SMALL-SWORD
SMOOTH-BORE
SPEAR-SHAFT
SWORD-BLADE
SWORD-GUARD
SWORD-STICK
THROW-STICK
TOGGLE-IRON
TRIP-HAMMER
WINCHESTER

11

ANTI-TANK GUN
ARROW POISON
BLOCKBUSTER
BLUNDERBUSS
BOW AND ARROW
CALIBRATION
CAPTIVE BOLT
CORNICE-RING
COUP DE POING
DEPTH-CHARGE
EMPLACEMENT
FINGERGUARD
FISH-TORPEDO
FISSION BOMB
FOUR-POUNDER

GARAND RIFLE
GUN CARRIAGE
GUN PLATFORM
HAIR-TRIGGER
HALF-POUNDER
HAND-GRENADE
HORSE PISTOL
JACOB'S-STAFF
LOCHABER AXE
MAGAZINE-GUN
MEGATON BOMB
MINE-THROWER
MORGENSTERN
MORNING-STAR
MORSING-HORN
NEUTRON BOMB
NUCLEAR BOMB
PLASTIC BOMB
POWDER-FLASK
PRIMING-IRON
PRIMING-WIRE
PROOF-CHARGE
PULL-THROUGH
RANGEFINDER
SAFETY-CATCH
SINGLESTICK
SNICKERSNEE
STERN-CHASER
SWALLOW-TAIL
THOMPSON GUN
TORPEDO-TUBE
TRACER SHELL
WATER-CANNON

12

BATTERING-RAM
BIRDING-PIECE
BOARDING-PIKE
BREECH-LOADER
CANISTER-SHOT
DEMI-CULVERIN

DOUBLE CHARGE
EXPRESS RIFLE
FLAME-THROWER
FOWLING-PIECE
HUNTING-KNIFE
HUNTING-SWORD
HYDROGEN BOMB
JEDDART STAFF
MAGNETIC MINE
MARTINI-HENRY
MITRAILLEUSE
MUZZLE-LOADER
POCKET-PISTOL
QUARTER-STAFF
RIFLE-GRENADE
ROCKET-MORTAR
SHOOTING-IRON
SIGHTING-SHOT
SPEAR-THROWER
SWORD-BAYONET
SWORD-BREAKER
THREE-POUNDER
TRACER BULLET
TRENCH-MORTAR

13

AERIAL TORPEDO
BALL-CARTRIDGE
BUTTERFLY BOMB
CARTRIDGE-BELT
CAT-O'-NINE-TAILS
DAMASCUS BLADE
FLAMMENWERFER
GAUNTLET-GUARD
GREY-GOOSE WING
GUIDED MISSILE
HIGH EXPLOSIVE
KNUCKLEDUSTER
LIFE-PRESERVER
LIVE CARTRIDGE
MAGAZINE-RIFLE

NUCLEAR WEAPON
PERCUSSION CAP
POISONED ARROW
PRIMING POWDER
PROXIMITY FUSE
SCALPING-KNIFE
SCOURING-STICK
SUBMACHINE-GUN
THROWING-STICK

14

AMMUNITION-BELT
BLANK CARTRIDGE
CLOTH-YARD SHAFT
COUNTER-BATTERY
GREY-GOOSE QUILL
GREY-GOOSE SHAFT
INCENDIARY BOMB
NUCLEAR MISSILE
NUCLEAR WARHEAD
PERCUSSION-FUSE
PERCUSSION-LOCK
POWDER-MAGAZINE
PSYCHOCHEMICAL
SAWN-OFF SHOTGUN
SIEGE ARTILLERY
SMALL-BORE RIFLE

15

ANTI-AIRCRAFT GUN
INFERNAL MACHINE
LACHRYMATORY GAS
MOLOTOV COCKTAIL
SHOULDER-HOLSTER
SOFT-NOSED BULLET
TELESCOPIC SIGHT
WINCHESTER RIFLE

WEIGHTS & MEASURES

3

AMP
ARE
BAR
BEL
BIT
CAB
COR
CUT
ELL
END
ERG
FAT
HIN
KIN
LAY
LEA
LEY
LUX
MHO
MIL
NIP
NIT
OHM
OKE
PIN
RAD
REM
REP
ROD
TON
TUN
WEY

4

ACRE
BARN
BATH
BOLL
BOLT
BUTT
BYTE
CASK
CORD
COSS
CRAN
DRAM
DYNE
EPHA

FEET
FOOT
GILL
GRAM
HAND
HASP
HIDE
HOUR
INCH
KILO
KNOT
LAST
LINE
LINK
MARK
MILE
MINA
MUID
NAIL
OMER
PALM
PECK
PHON
PHOT
PINT
PIPE
POLE
POOD
REAM
ROOD
ROTL
SACK
SEER
SIZE
SLUG
SONE
SPAN
TAEL
TOLA
TORR
TROY
UNIT
VARA
VARE
VOLT
WARP
WATT
YARD

5

ANGLE

ANKER
ARDEB
BIGHA
BUNCH
CABLE
CANDY
CARAT
CATTY
CHAIN
CLOVE
COOMB
COUNT
CRITH
CUBIT
CURIE
CUSEC
CYCLE
DEBYE
DEPTH
DIGIT
FARAD
FERMI
GAUGE
GAUSS
GERAH
GIRTH
GLASS
GRAIN
GRIST
HENRY
HERTZ
HOMER
JOULE
KANEH
LIANG
LIGNE
LIPPY
LITRE
LIVRE
LUMEN
MAUND
MEASE
METRE
MINIM
NEPER
OUNCE
PERCH
PICUL
PINCH
POINT
POISE
POUND

PUGIL
QUART
QUIRE
STERE
STILB
STOKE
STONE
TESLA
THERM
TOISE
TONNE
TRUSS
VERST
WEBER
WIDTH
YOJAN

6

AMOUNT
AMPERE
ARPENT
ARROBA
ARSHIN
BARREL
BUNDLE
BUSHEL
CANDLE
CENTAL
CHOPIN
CUPFUL
DEGREE
DENIER
DIRHEM
DRACHM
FATHOM
FIRKIN
FIRLOT
FOTHER
GALLON
GRAMME
HATFUL
HEIGHT
JIGGER
JUGFUL
KANTAR
KELVIN
KILERG
LEAGUE
LENGTH
MAGNUM

MEGOHM
MICRON
MINUTE
MODIUS
MORGEN
NEWTON
NOGGIN
PARSEC
PASCAL
PHOTON
RADIAN
SAZHEN
SECOND
SHEKEL
SI UNIT
SQUARE
STOKES
TALENT
TIERCE
WEIGHT

7

ACREAGE
BRACCIO
BREADTH
CALIBRE
CALORIE
CANDELA
CENTNER
CHALDER
COULOMB
DECIARE
DECIBEL
DIOPTER
FARADAY
FOOTAGE
FURLONG
GILBERT
HANDFUL
HECTARE
KILOBAR
KILOTON
LAMBERT
LEAGUER
LONG TON
MAXWELL
MEASURE
MEGATON
MICROHM
MILEAGE

OERSTED
PAILFUL
POUNDAL
QUARTER
QUINTAL
RÉAUMUR
RÖNTGEN
SCRUPLE
SEA-MILE
SIEMENS
SI UNITS
STADIUM
TAEL BAR
TONNAGE
VIRGATE
VOLTAGE
WATTAGE
YARDAGE

8

AMPERAGE
ANGSTRÖM
CAPACITY
CENTIARE
CHALDRON
CUBIC TON
DECAGRAM
DECIGRAM
DISTANCE
GLASSFUL
HALF-INCH
HALF-MILE
HALF-PINT
HEAT UNIT
HOGSHEAD
JEROBOAM
KILOGRAM
KILOWATT
LADLEFUL
LAMP-HOUR
LISPOUND
MEGAVOLT
MEGAWATT
MICROBAR
MICROLUX
MILLIARE
MILLIBAR
MUTCHKIN
NANOGRAM
PARASANG

PLATEFUL
POUNDAGE
PUNCHEON
QUANTITY
QUARTERN
REHOBOAM
SCHOONER
SEMUNCIA
SHORT TON
SPOONFUL
WATT-HOUR
YARDLAND

9

BOARD-FOOT
BUCKETFUL
CENTIGRAM
CLOTH-YARD
CUBIC FOOT
CUBIC INCH
CUBIC YARD
DECALITRE
DECAMETRE
DECASTERE
DECILITRE
DECIMETRE
DECISTERE
FOOT-POUND
FREQUENCY
HALF-OUNCE
HALF-POUND
HECTOGRAM
HOP-POCKET
KETTLEFUL
KILDERKIN
KILOCYCLE
KILOHERTZ
KILOLITRE
KILOMETRE
LIGHT-YEAR
LUMINANCE
MEGACYCLE
MEGAFARAD
MEGAHERTZ
METRIC TON
MICROGRAM
MICROWATT
MILLIGRAM
NANOMETRE
NIPPERKIN

SCANTLING
SHIPPOUND
STERADIAN
TRAIN MILE
WHEELBASE

10

BARLEYCORN
BARREL-BULK
CENTIGRADE
CENTILITRE
CENTIMETRE
CENTISTERE
CUBIC METRE
DECAGRAMME
DECIGRAMME
DESSIATINE
DRY MEASURE
FAHRENHEIT
FLUID OUNCE
HECTOLITRE
HECTOMETRE
HECTOSTERE
HOPPUS FOOT
HORSEPOWER
KILOGRAMME
MEGANEWTON
MICROFARAD
MICROHENRY
MILLILITRE
MILLIMETRE
MINER'S INCH
NANOSECOND
RUTHERFORD
SQUARE FOOT
SQUARE INCH
SQUARE MILE
SQUARE YARD
TRON WEIGHT
TROY WEIGHT
YARD OF LAND

11

AVOIRDUPOIS
CABLE-LENGTH
CANDLE-POWER
CENTIGRAMME
HECTOGRAMME

WEIGHTS & MEASURES

ILLUMINANCE
KILOCALORIE
LAND MEASURE
LONG-MEASURE
MEASUREMENT
MEGAWATT DAY
MICROAMPERE
MICROSECOND
MILLIAMPERE
MILLIGRAMME
PENNYWEIGHT
SQUARE METRE
TEASPOONFUL
THERMAL UNIT
WINE MEASURE

CUBIC MEASURE
ELECTRON-VOLT
HAIR'S-BREADTH
HAND'S-BREADTH
HALF-QUARTERN
KILOWATT HOUR
METRIC SYSTEM
NAUTICAL MILE
PRINTER'S REAM
WATER-MEASURE

12

CABLE'S-LENGTH
CRANIAL INDEX

13

CUBIC CAPACITY
DECIMAL SYSTEM
HUNDREDWEIGHT
LINEAR MEASURE
LIQUID MEASURE
SQUARE MEASURE
TABLE-SPOONFUL

14

ANGULAR MEASURE
CUBIC DECIMETRE
CYCLE PER SECOND
FINGER'S-BREADTH
IMPERIAL WEIGHT

15

CUBIC CENTIMETRE
DESSERT-SPOONFUL
IMPERIAL MEASURE
MICROMILLIMETRE
SQUARE DECIMETRE
STANDARD MEASURE

INDEX

All main subjects in bold